AutoCAD 2006

AutoCAD 2006

One Step at a Time

One Step at a Time

Part II

Timothy Sean Sykes

Forager Publications
Spring, Texas
ForagerPub.com

ISBN 0-9765888-5-4

Forager Publications

2043 Cherry Laurel

Spring, TX 77386

www.foragerpub.com

AUTHOR'S NOTES

Where to Find the Required Files (and Review Questions) for Using This Text:

All of the files required to complete the lessons in this text can be downloaded free of charge from this site:

http://www.uneedcad.com/2006/Files/

Select on the file called *PartII.zip* and save it to your computer. (Windows XP will open a zipped file. If you need a zip utility, however, I suggest the free WinZip download at: http://www.winzip.com/. The evaluation version will do to get your files. You'll have to follow WinZip procedures to unzip the files.)

Once you've downloaded the zip file, follow these instructions to unzip it with Windows XP.

1. Double-click on the file. Windows XP will display a window with the Step folder listed.
2. Right click on the Step folder and select **Copy** from the menu that appears.
3. Using Windows Explorer, navigate to the C-drive.
4. Select **Paste** from the Edit pull down menu.

To get the review questions, go to the website indicated at the end of each lesson. A PDF file will open in your Internet browser. These files are fully printable, or you can save them to your disk if you wish. The last page of each file contains the answers to the questions in that file.

Contacting the Author/Publisher:

Although we tried awfully hard to avoid errors, typos, and the occasional boo boos, I admit to complete fallibility. Should you find it necessary to let me know of my blunders, or to ask just about anything about the text – or even to make suggestions as to how to better the next edition, please feel free to contact me at: *comments@foragerpub.com*. I can't promise a fast response (although I'm usually pretty good about answering my email), but I can promise to read (almost) everything that comes my way.

Frequently Asked Questions (and responses to less-frequently-asked but more annoying questions):

I went to the web site but got a Page cannot be found *error. What gives?*

This is the most common complaint I get. The fix is simple: make sure you capitalize the "Files" in the address. The web is case-sensitive.

Part II? Where's Part I?

Look for *Part I* (ISBN 0-9765888-0-3) at your local bookstore, at Amazon.com (or one of the web-based booksellers), or at forager.com. (See the next question for more details.)

Why two books to cover the basic material?

No, we're not trying to "pad" our income. We use a new technology to bring the material to our readers – it's called POD (Print on Demand). Using POD, we can avoid printing thousands of books that require warehouse space. Unfortunately, the technology limits the number of pages per book to 740. Although we squeezed the '06 books unmercifully, we just couldn't get them down to that number.

EBooks are also limited. In their case, it isn't the number of pages, however. LSI (the POD company that handles both our print and electronic books) limits us by file size. Although they've been very good at working with me, there's only so much I can ask of them.

Contents

Chapter 24: Drawing Sheet Sets

Chapter 25: Externally Referenced Drawings

Chapter 26: Other Application Files and AutoCAD

Chapter 27: Databases and AutoCAD

Appendices

Section IV
Razzle Dazzle

Lesson 17

Following this lesson, you will:

- ✓ *Know how to use tables in your drawing*
- ✓ *Know how to use fields in your drawing*
- ✓ *Know how to use these commands:*
  - ***Table***
  - ***Tablestyle***
  - ***DwgProps***
  - ***Field***

Tables and Fields

What we humans have worked for since the dawn of time has been a way to avoid work! (And oh, how hard we've worked to succeed at this most admirable goal!)

That's where things like tables and fields come in handy. Tables organize our world (nothing says lazy like pristine organizational skills, which of course, free up time to stare at the skyline or drift aimlessly in the pool); fields fill in those nicely organized blanks for us.

This section of our text will cover some razzle-dazzle tools. These are the tools that pushed CAD systems ahead of the drawing board as the preferred tool in design work. We'll begin with some text tools in this lesson; then, in subsequent lessons, we'll learn to create hatching, blocks of objects, and blocks of information.

So, stop yawning, and let's begin.

17.1 Tables

It's amazing just how much work can be avoided by the innovative use of rows and columns (just consider how the appendices at the end of this text help you avoid wasting time trying to find solutions to some basic CAD problems)! Of course, the collective name for rows and columns is *table*. Tables have saved time and effort in virtually every industry on earth (just ask any accountant).

AutoCAD makes tables available for legends, materials lists, revision blocks, spreadsheets, and just about any other use you might require. We'll look at creating a top-down table (a legend) and then at creating a bottom-up table (a revision block). More importantly, we'll look at the ease with which you can modify a list for your own uses.

17.1.1 Creating a Table

To keep it simple, AutoCAD provides a dialog box (Figure 17.001) for creating tables. Let's take a look at it.

- The first frame – **Table Style Settings** – allows you to change the style you'll use to create your table. The default (**Standard**) is shown. If you'd like to change to another existing style, use the down arrow next to the **Table Style name** control box. If you need to create a new style, you can use the **Table Style dialog** button next to the control box, or you can enter the ***Tablestyle*** command at the command prompt. We'll look more at table style creation later in this lesson.
- The **Insertion Behavior** frame contains two options:
    - A bullet next to **Specify insertion point** means that AutoCAD will prompt you for a location for your table.
    - A bullet next to the other option, **Specify window**, tells AutoCAD to prompt you for a windowed area for the table (much as it does for an MText insertion).
- The **Column and Row Settings** frame allows you to set up the number of columns and rows in your table. You'll also specify the width and height of your columns and rows here.

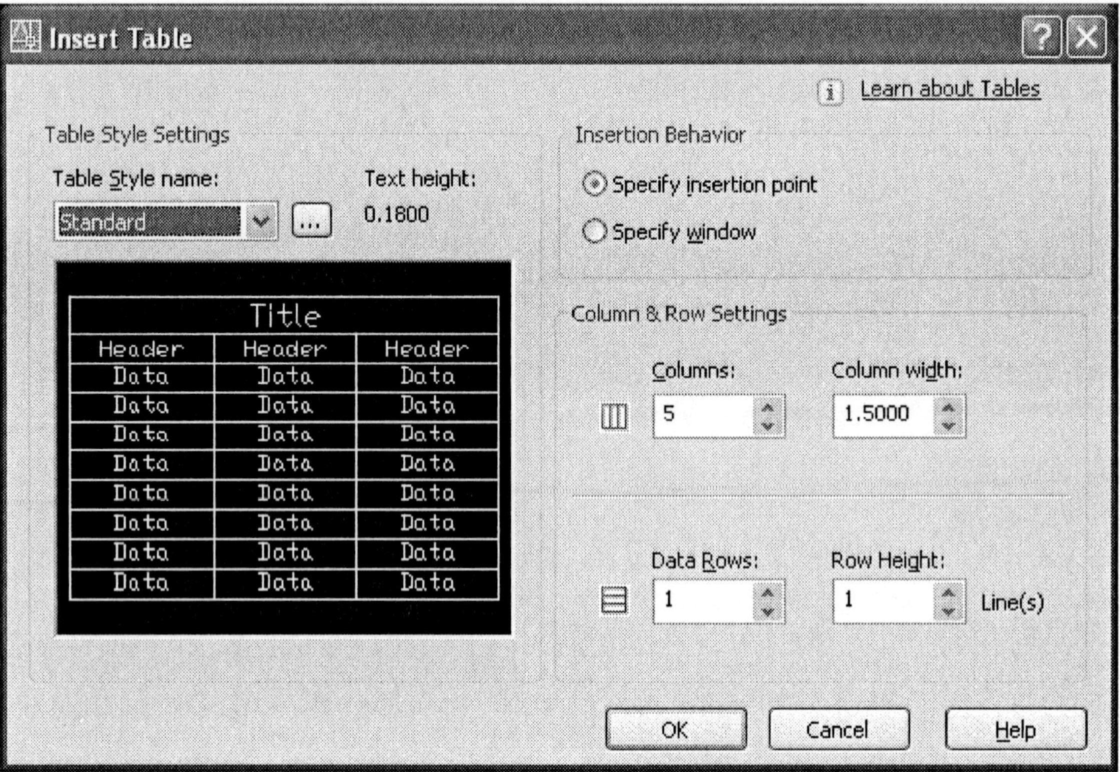

Figure 17.001

Does that sound simple enough? Let's try one.

The ***Table*** command is also available in the Draw pull-down menu.

Do This: 17.1.1.1	Creating a Table

I. Open the *Floor Plan Data Sheet* drawing in the C:\Steps\Lesson17 folder. The drawing looks like Figure 17.002.

II. Follow these steps.

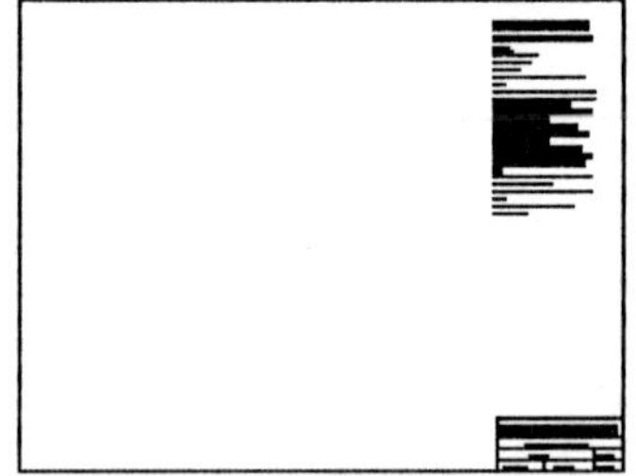

Figure 17.002

TOOLS	COMMAND SEQUENCE	STEPS
Table Button	**Command: *table***	1. Enter the ***Table*** command. Alternately, you can pick the **Table** button on the Draw toolbar. AutoCAD presents the Insert Table dialog box (Figure 17.001).

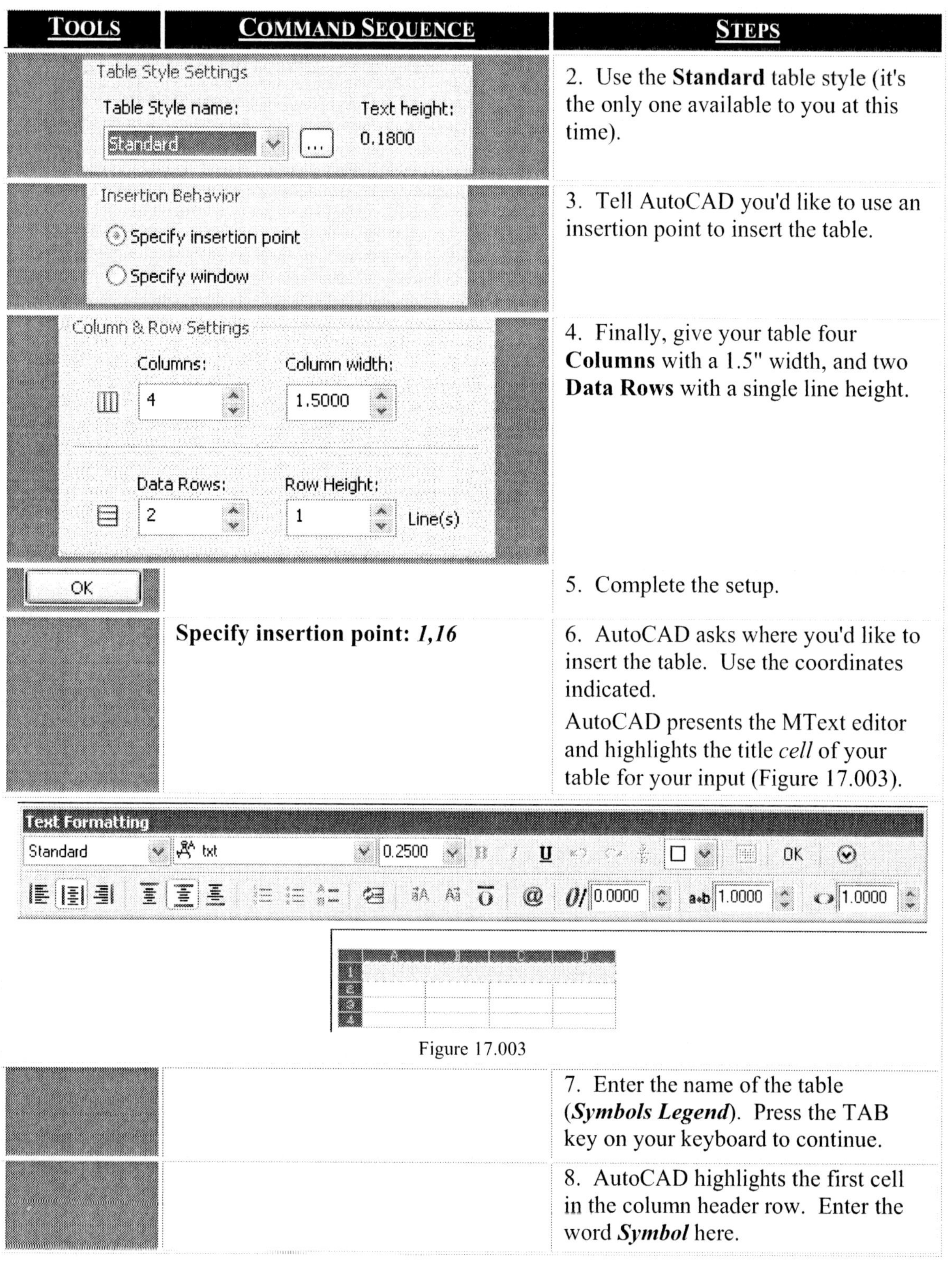

TOOLS	**COMMAND SEQUENCE**	**STEPS**
		2. Use the **Standard** table style (it's the only one available to you at this time).
		3. Tell AutoCAD you'd like to use an insertion point to insert the table.
		4. Finally, give your table four **Columns** with a 1.5" width, and two **Data Rows** with a single line height.
OK		5. Complete the setup.
	Specify insertion point: *1,16*	6. AutoCAD asks where you'd like to insert the table. Use the coordinates indicated. AutoCAD presents the MText editor and highlights the title *cell* of your table for your input (Figure 17.003).
	Figure 17.003	
		7. Enter the name of the table (***Symbols Legend***). Press the TAB key on your keyboard to continue.
		8. AutoCAD highlights the first cell in the column header row. Enter the word ***Symbol*** here.

TOOLS	COMMAND SEQUENCE	STEPS
		9. Using the **Tab** key to move to the next cells, complete the column header row as indicated in Figure 17.004. (Pick the **OK** button on the MText toolbar to complete the procedure.)

Symbols Legend			
Symbol	Descripti on	Symbol	Descripti on

Figure 17.004

TOOLS	COMMAND SEQUENCE	STEPS
	Command: ***qsave***	10. Save the drawing but don't exit.

17.1.2 Editing a Table's Properties

The first thing you probably noticed about the table you just inserted was that the *Column Heads* didn't fit in the cell provided for them. In fact, both description columns are far too narrow for much of a description. Additionally, you might have noticed that the text in the table doesn't match the text we've used in the Floor Plan drawings through our last several lessons.

We'll use the Properties palette a bit, but AutoCAD makes use of cursor menus for easier editing of a table's properties (as well as values).

Let's see what we can do with our table before we start entering values.

Do This: 17.1.2.1 Editing a Table's Properties

I. Be sure you're still in the *Floor Plan Data Sheet* drawing in the C:\Steps\Lesson17 folder. If not, please open it now.

II. Follow these steps.

TOOLS	COMMAND SEQUENCE	STEPS
	Command:	1. First, let's change the text style in the title and header cells. Pick once in the title cell. Notice that it highlights and that grips display.
Shift		2. Now hold down the SHIFT key and select a cell in the header row. Notice that both rows are highlighted and display grips (Figure 17.005).

TOOLS	COMMAND SEQUENCE	STEPS

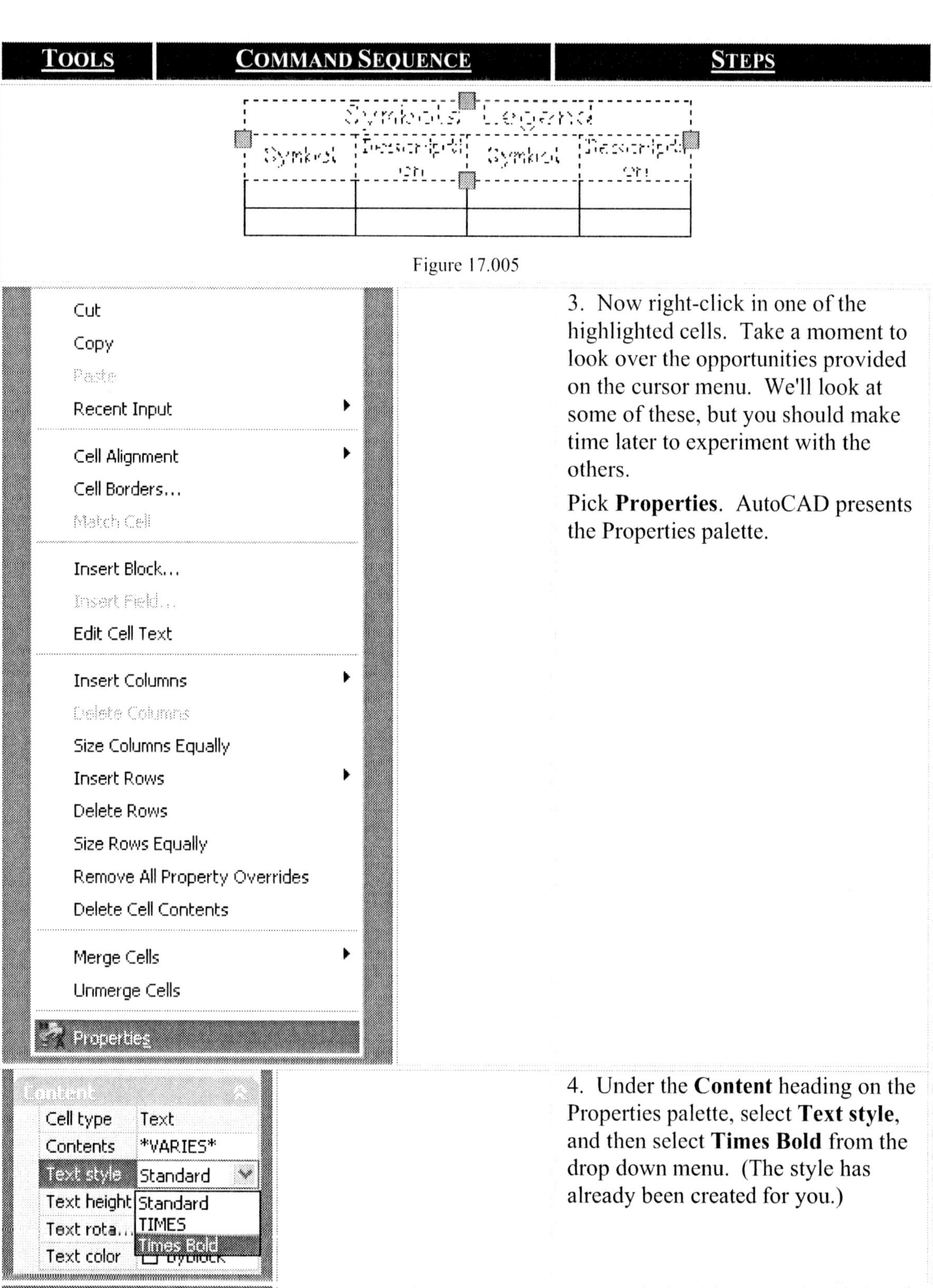

Figure 17.005

3. Now right-click in one of the highlighted cells. Take a moment to look over the opportunities provided on the cursor menu. We'll look at some of these, but you should make time later to experiment with the others.

Pick **Properties**. AutoCAD presents the Properties palette.

4. Under the **Content** heading on the Properties palette, select **Text style**, and then select **Times Bold** from the drop down menu. (The style has already been created for you.)

5. Close the Properties palette and clear the grips. Your table looks like Figure 17.006.

TOOLS	COMMAND SEQUENCE	STEPS

Symbols Legend			
Symbol	Description	Symbol	Description

Figure 17.006

TOOLS	COMMAND SEQUENCE	STEPS
		6. We'll also need more rows than we originally set up. Pick inside any of the cells on the bottom row. It'll highlight.
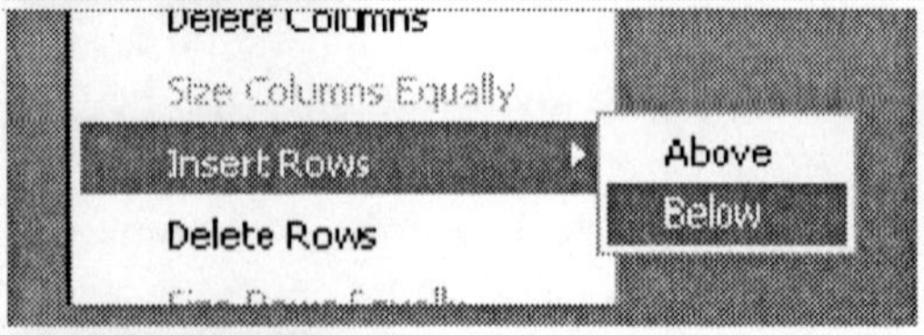 Delete Columns / Size Columns Equally / Insert Rows / Delete Rows — Above / Below		7. Right-click inside the highlighted cell and select **Insert Rows … Below** on the cursor menu. Repeat this step until you have six empty rows. Then clear the grips.
	Command:	8. Now we'll make the **Description** columns wider. Pick on any of the table's lines. Notice that the entire table highlights and displays grips.
 Ctrl		9. Refer to Figure 17.007. Pick on the line grip between the first **Symbol** and **Description** columns and move it to the left. Resize the other columns as well. Clear the grips. Your drawing looks like Figure 17.007.

Symbols Legend			
Symbol	Description	Symbol	Description

Figure 17.007

TOOLS	COMMAND SEQUENCE	STEPS
	Command:	10. Let's change one last property. Repeat Steps 1 and 2; but this time, select the bottom row in Step 2 (the entire table appears highlighted).
		11. Right-click in one of the cells and select Properties from the cursor menu.

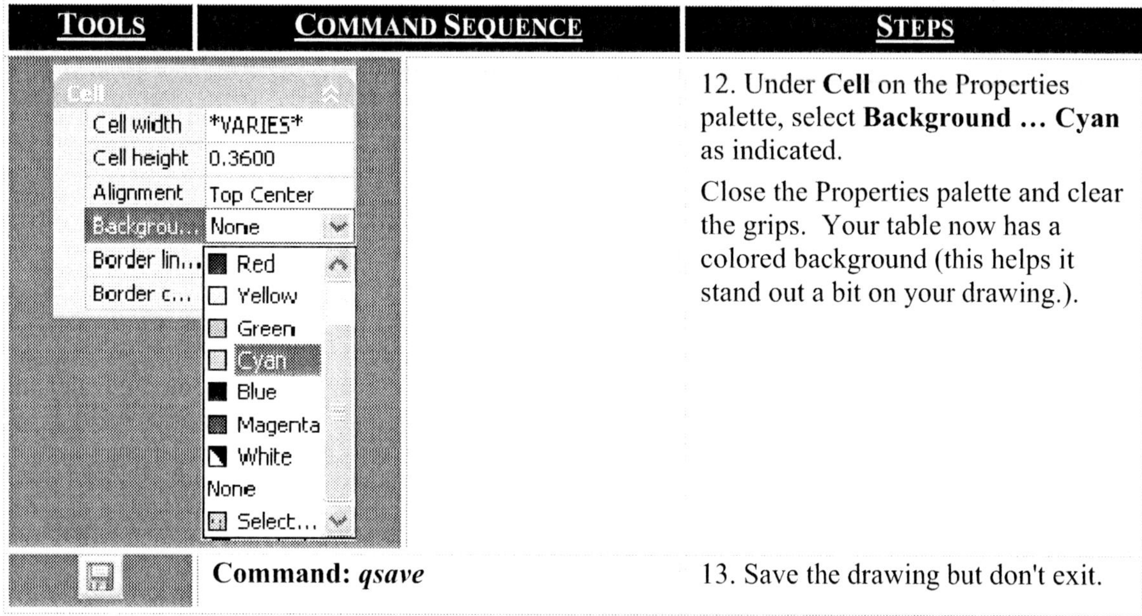

Tools	Command Sequence	Steps
Cell width *VARIES*; Cell height 0.3600; Alignment Top Center; Backgrou... None; Border lin...; Border c...; Red; Yellow; Green; Cyan; Blue; Magenta; White; None; Select...		12. Under **Cell** on the Properties palette, select **Background … Cyan** as indicated. Close the Properties palette and clear the grips. Your table now has a colored background (this helps it stand out a bit on your drawing.).
	Command: ***qsave***	13. Save the drawing but don't exit.

17.1.3 Adding Values to Table Cells

Now that you've set up your table, you'll need to add some values to the cells (otherwise, the table would be pretty … but useless). Luckily, adding values is the easy part! In fact, it's just a matter of inserting MText.

Do This: 17.1.3.1 Inserting Table Values

I. Be sure you're still in the *Floor Plan Data Sheet* drawing in the C:\Steps\Lesson17 folder. If not, please open it now.

In this exercise, you'll get a preview of those wondrous timesavers called *blocks*. We'll look at blocks in much greater detail in Lessons 19 and 20, but enjoy the preview for now.

II. Follow these steps.

Tools	Command Sequence	Steps
		1. We'll start right off with a block insertion. Pick inside the first empty cell in the first **Symbols** column. It highlights.
Insert Block... Insert Field... Insert Formula		2. Right-click in the highlighted cell and pick **Insert Block** on the cursor menu. AutoCAD presents the Insert a Block in a Table Cell dialog box shown in Step 3.

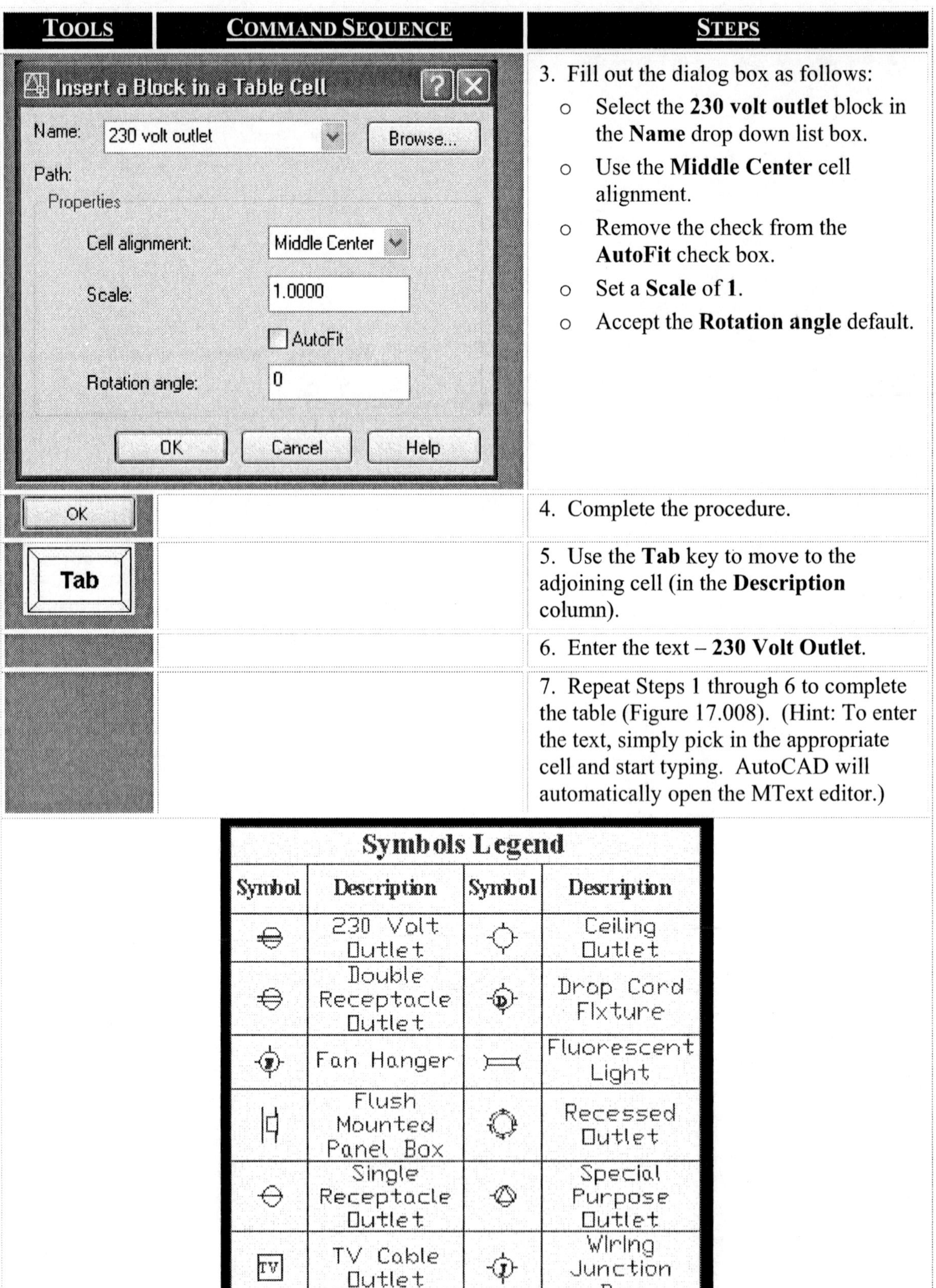

TOOLS	COMMAND SEQUENCE	STEPS
Insert a Block in a Table Cell dialog box		3. Fill out the dialog box as follows: o Select the **230 volt outlet** block in the **Name** drop down list box. o Use the **Middle Center** cell alignment. o Remove the check from the **AutoFit** check box. o Set a **Scale** of **1**. o Accept the **Rotation angle** default.
OK		4. Complete the procedure.
Tab		5. Use the **Tab** key to move to the adjoining cell (in the **Description** column).
		6. Enter the text – **230 Volt Outlet**.
		7. Repeat Steps 1 through 6 to complete the table (Figure 17.008). (Hint: To enter the text, simply pick in the appropriate cell and start typing. AutoCAD will automatically open the MText editor.)

Symbols Legend			
Symbol	**Description**	**Symbol**	**Description**
	230 Volt Outlet		Ceiling Outlet
	Double Receptacle Outlet		Drop Cord Fixture
	Fan Hanger		Fluorescent Light
	Flush Mounted Panel Box		Recessed Outlet
	Single Receptacle Outlet		Special Purpose Outlet
TV	TV Cable Outlet		Wiring Junction Box

Figure 17.008

TOOLS	COMMAND SEQUENCE	STEPS
		8. Finally, use the tools you found in the last exercise to convert the text to the **Times** style and change its justification to **Middle Center**. Your table looks like Figure 17.009.

Symbols Legend			
Symbol	Description	Symbol	Description
	230 Volt Outlet		Ceiling Outlet
	Double Receptacle Outlet		Drop Cord Fixture
	Fan Hanger		Fluorescent Light
	Flush Mounted Panel Box		Recessed Outlet
	Single Receptacle Outlet		Special Purpose Outlet
TV	TV Cable Outlet		Wiring Junction Box

Figure 17.009

TOOLS	COMMAND SEQUENCE	STEPS
	Command: ***qsave***	9. Save the drawing but don't exit.

Did you notice how AutoCAD automatically adjusted the height of the rows to accommodate what you inserted? Did you see the text automatically wrap within the cells? If you've ever had to create a table manually (with the ***Line*** command), you'll really appreciate these automated actions!

But there is more to tables than what you've seen. What about using a table for a revision block (one that grows from bottom to top)? Or how about setting up as defaults some of the things you had to do manually (text styles, justifications, etc.)?

Let's look next at table *styles*.

17.1.4 Customizing Tables

Since you've already mastered dimension styles, you'll probably find table styles fairly easy to set up; they look as though the same programmers designed them.

The ***Tablestyle*** command calls the Table Style dialog box (Figure 17.010). As you can see, the dialog box closely resembles the Dimension Style dialog box.

- The **Styles** list box indicates the names of styles available in this drawing. Luckily, however, AutoCAD doesn't inflict "children" styles here as it does with dimension styles, so your job is already easier!
- As with other tools, the **List** box below the **Styles** box serves as a filter for what goes in to the **Styles** box (**All styles** or **Styles in use**).

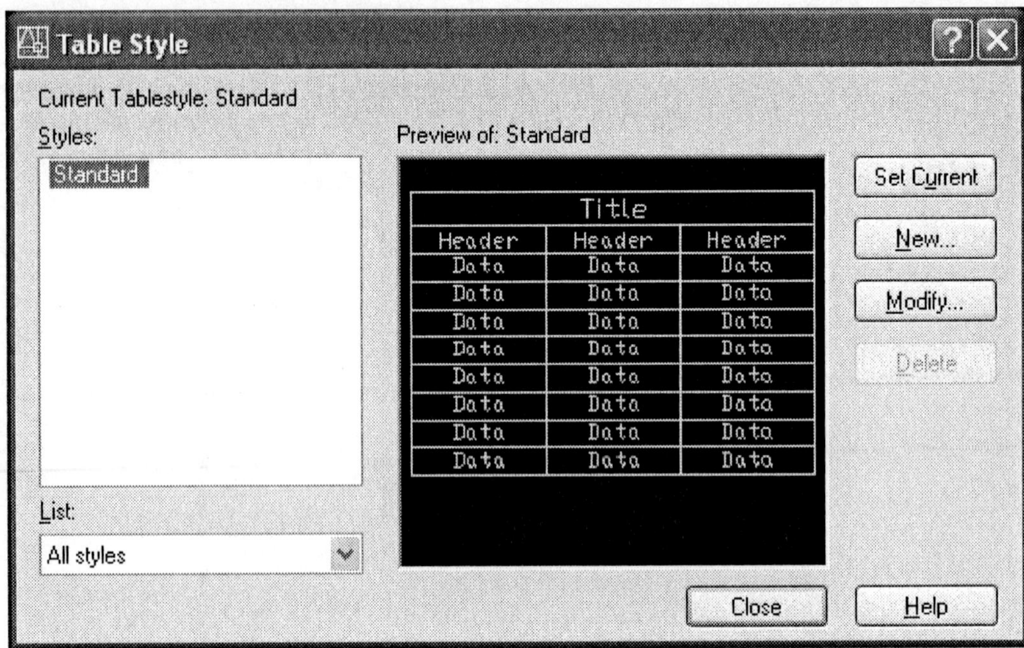

Figure 17.010

- The **Preview** box, of course, shows a preview of the selected style.
- A total of six buttons dwell on the dialog box. These are fairly self-explanatory:
  - **Set Current** sets the selected style as the one that AutoCAD will use when inserting a new table.
  - Use the **New** button to create a new table style. It calls the Create New Style dialog box (Figure 17.011). Use this familiar tool to name your new style, and then to access the New Table Style dialog box where you'll actually set up the style. (We'll see these in our next exercise.)

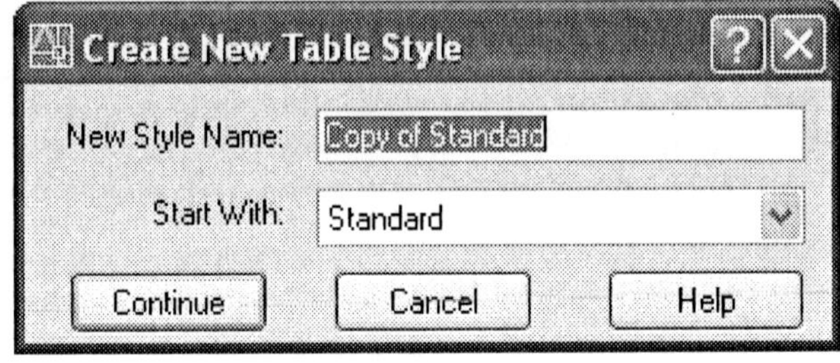

Figure 17.011

  - **Modify** allows you to alter settings for the selected style. You'll use the same dialog box as with the New Style procedure.
  - **Delete**, of course, allows you to delete the selected style. Note that you can't remove a style that's in use.
  - **Close** closes the dialog box.
  - **Help** calls AutoCAD's help window with information on the Table Style dialog box.

Let's set up table style to use in creating a revision block.

Do This: 17.1.4.1	Defining a Table Style

I. Be sure you're still in the *Floor Plan Data Sheet* drawing in the C:\Steps\Lesson17 folder. If not, please open it now.

II. Follow these steps.

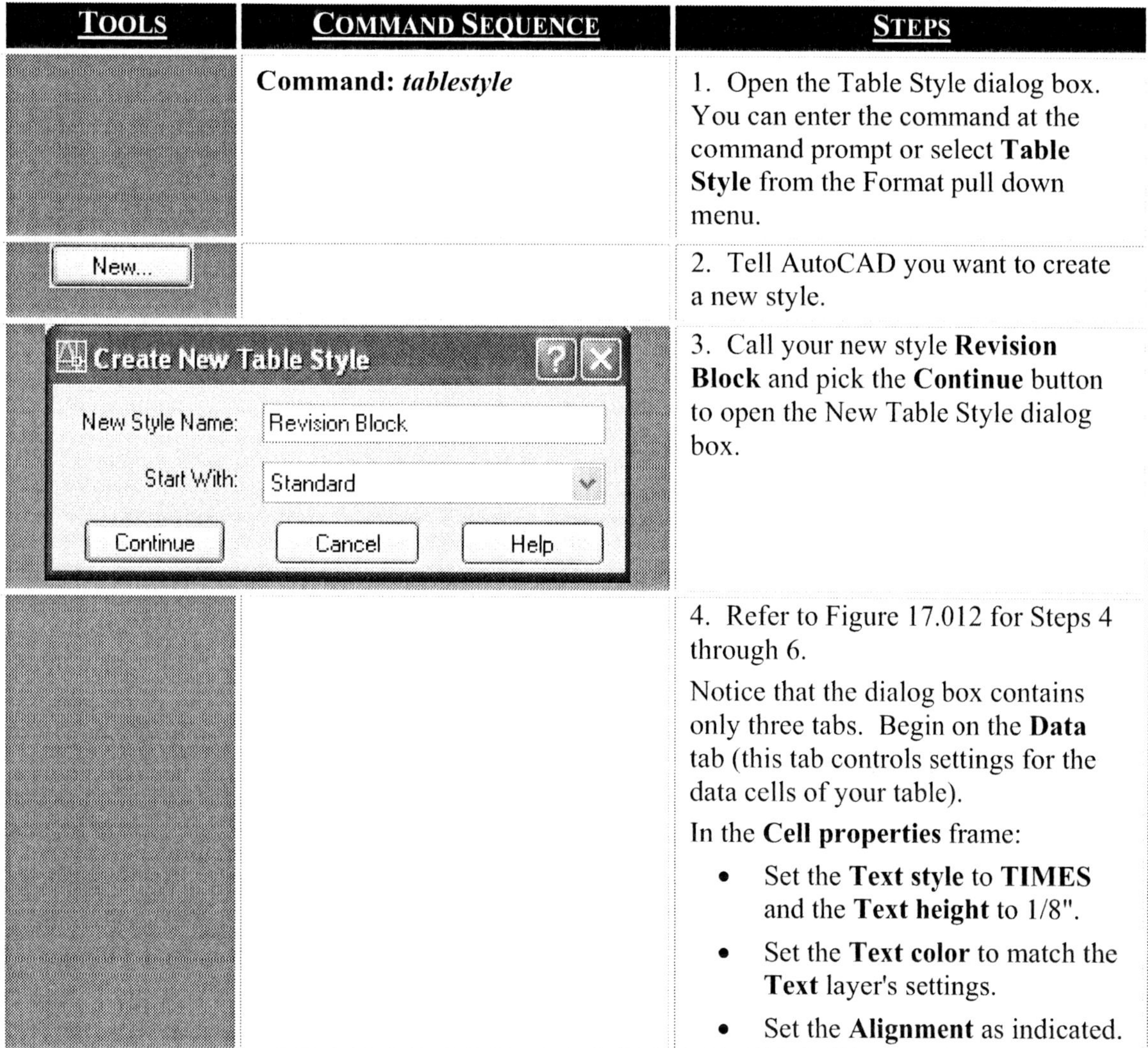

TOOLS	COMMAND SEQUENCE	STEPS
	Command: *tablestyle*	1. Open the Table Style dialog box. You can enter the command at the command prompt or select **Table Style** from the Format pull down menu.
New...		2. Tell AutoCAD you want to create a new style.
Create New Table Style New Style Name: Revision Block Start With: Standard Continue Cancel Help		3. Call your new style **Revision Block** and pick the **Continue** button to open the New Table Style dialog box.
		4. Refer to Figure 17.012 for Steps 4 through 6. Notice that the dialog box contains only three tabs. Begin on the **Data** tab (this tab controls settings for the data cells of your table). In the **Cell properties** frame: • Set the **Text style** to **TIMES** and the **Text height** to 1/8". • Set the **Text color** to match the **Text** layer's settings. • Set the **Alignment** as indicated.

TOOLS	**COMMAND SEQUENCE**	**STEPS**

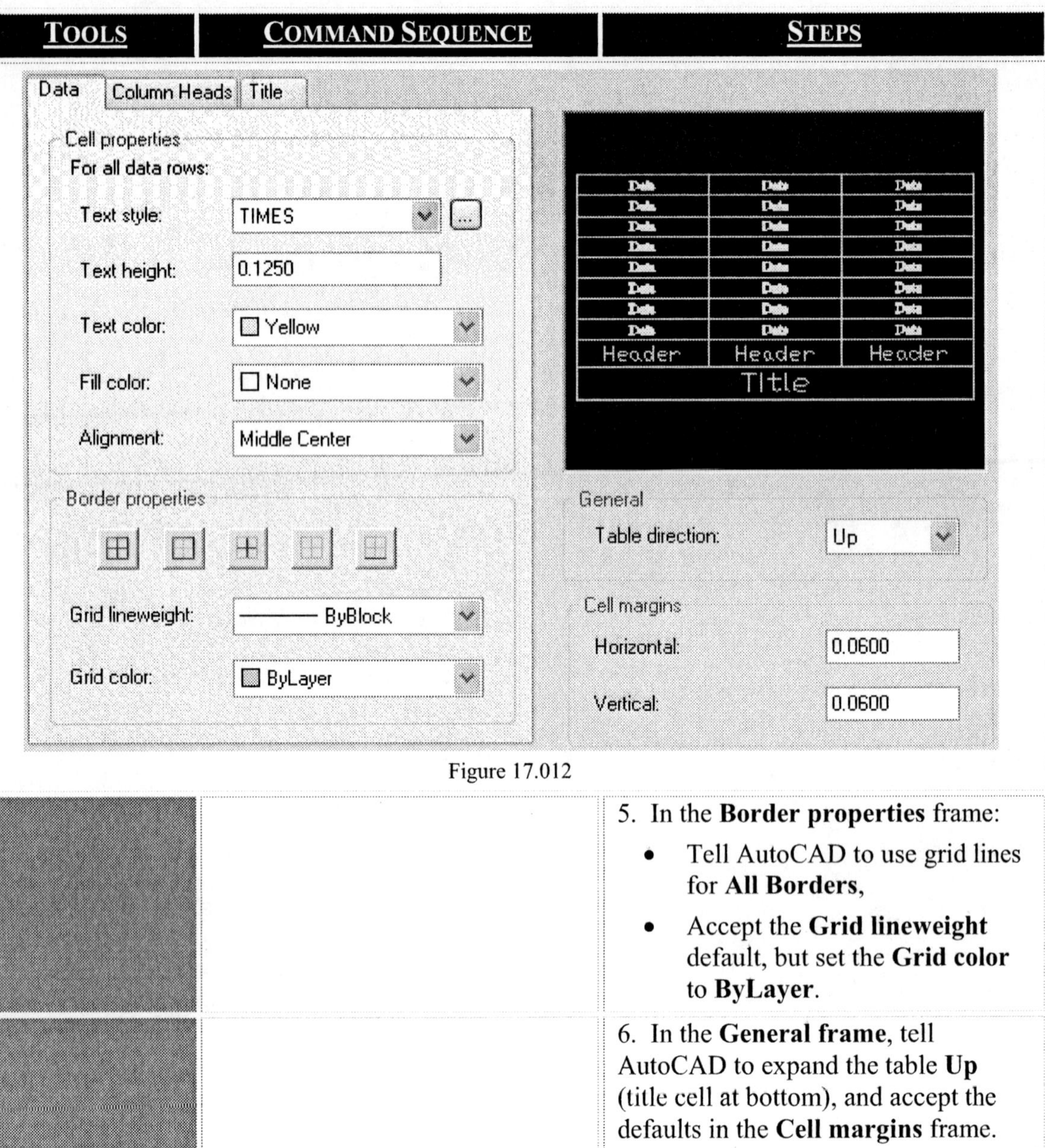

Figure 17.012

TOOLS	COMMAND SEQUENCE	STEPS
		5. In the **Border properties** frame: • Tell AutoCAD to use grid lines for **All Borders**, • Accept the **Grid lineweight** default, but set the **Grid color** to **ByLayer**.
		6. In the **General frame**, tell AutoCAD to expand the table **Up** (title cell at bottom), and accept the defaults in the **Cell margins** frame.
Column Heads		7. Pick the **Column Heads** tab to continue.

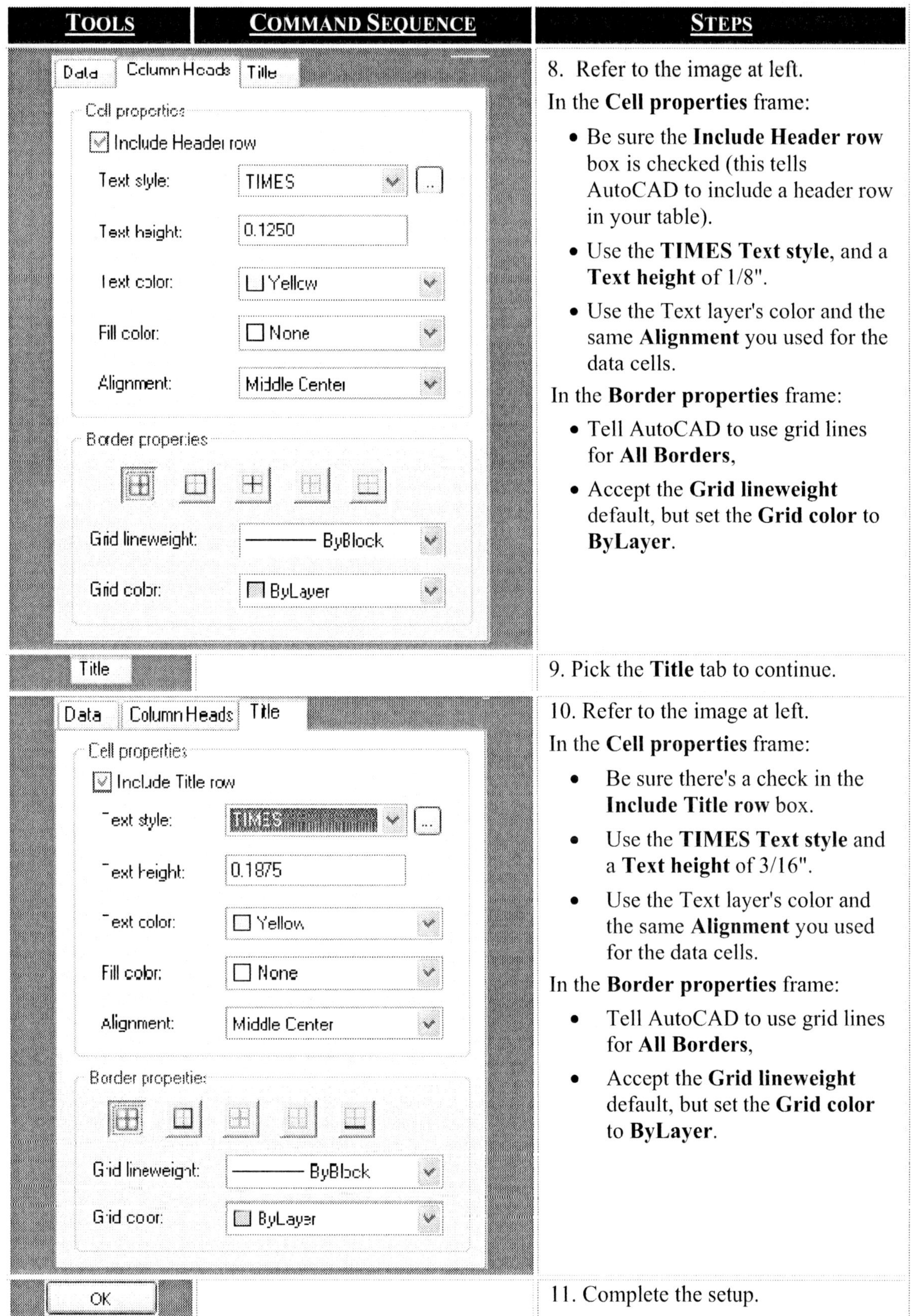

TOOLS	COMMAND SEQUENCE	STEPS
		8. Refer to the image at left. In the **Cell properties** frame: • Be sure the **Include Header row** box is checked (this tells AutoCAD to include a header row in your table). • Use the **TIMES Text style**, and a **Text height** of 1/8". • Use the Text layer's color and the same **Alignment** you used for the data cells. In the **Border properties** frame: • Tell AutoCAD to use grid lines for **All Borders**, • Accept the **Grid lineweight** default, but set the **Grid color** to **ByLayer**.
Title		9. Pick the **Title** tab to continue.
		10. Refer to the image at left. In the **Cell properties** frame: • Be sure there's a check in the **Include Title row** box. • Use the **TIMES Text style** and a **Text height** of 3/16". • Use the Text layer's color and the same **Alignment** you used for the data cells. In the **Border properties** frame: • Tell AutoCAD to use grid lines for **All Borders**, • Accept the **Grid lineweight** default, but set the **Grid color** to **ByLayer**.
OK		11. Complete the setup.

TOOLS	COMMAND SEQUENCE	STEPS
Close		12. Notice that the **Styles** list box in the Table Style dialog box now contains your new table style. Complete the procedure.
	Command: *qsave*	13. Save the drawing but don't exit.

Now let's take a look at our new style in action.

Do This: 17.1.4.2	Using Your New Table Style

I. Be sure you're still in the *Floor Plan Data Sheet* drawing in the C:\Steps\Lesson17 folder. If not, please open it now.

II. Zoom in just to the left of the title block.

III. Set the **BORDER** layer current.

IV. Follow these steps.

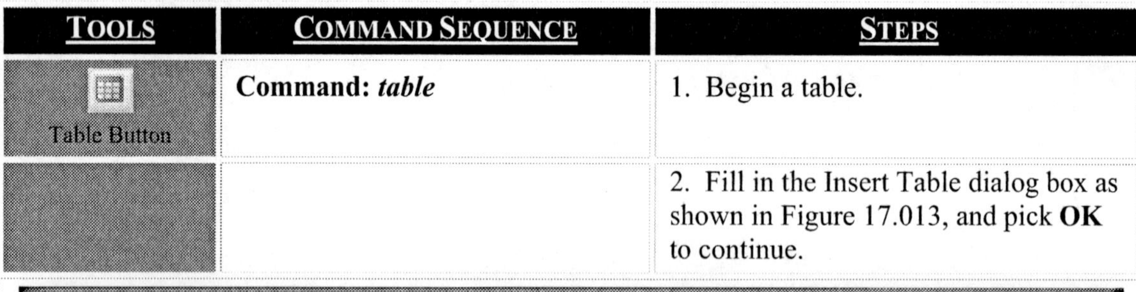

TOOLS	COMMAND SEQUENCE	STEPS
Table Button	**Command: *table***	1. Begin a table.
		2. Fill in the Insert Table dialog box as shown in Figure 17.013, and pick **OK** to continue.

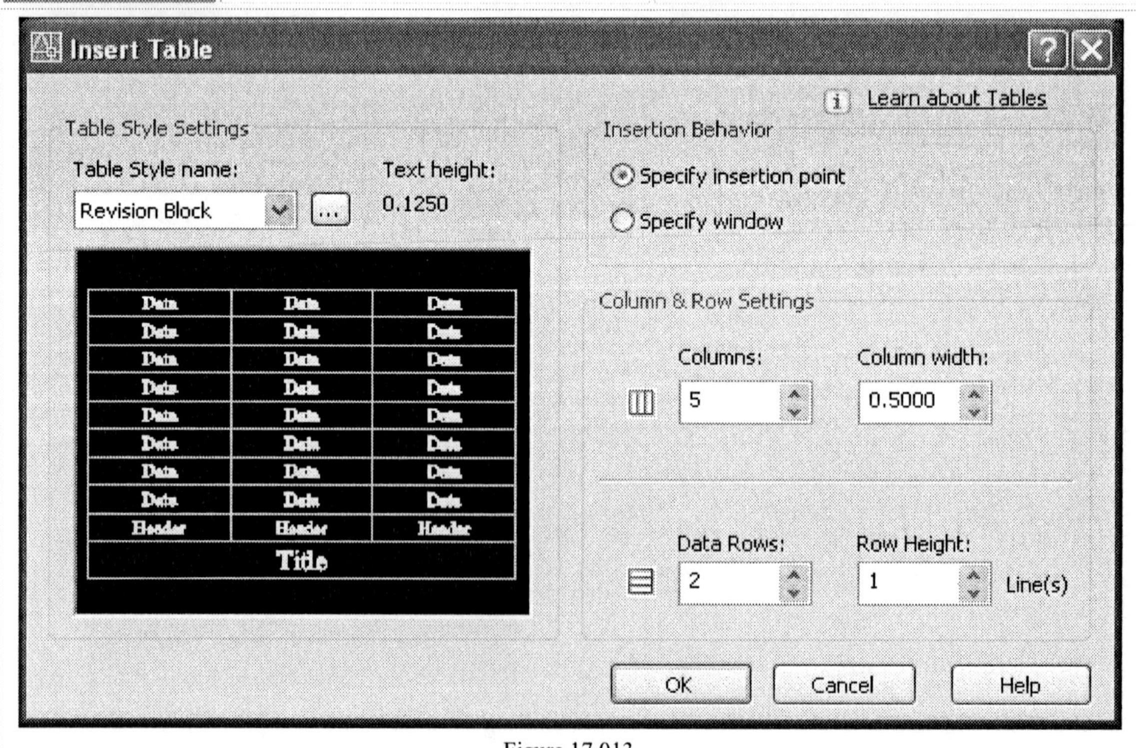

Figure 17.013

TOOLS	COMMAND SEQUENCE	STEPS
	Specify insertion point:	3. Insert the table next to the title block and fill in the **Title** and **Header** rows as shown in Figure 17.014.

Rev	Date	By	Desc ripti on	App
Revision				

Figure 17.014

TOOLS	COMMAND SEQUENCE	STEPS
		4. Pick anywhere on the revision block, select the grip between **App** and **Description** and stretch it about an inch to the right. (Polar snap will help this procedure.)
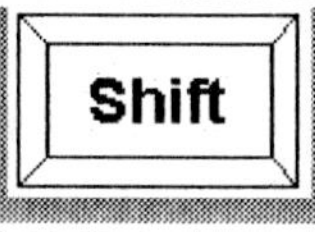 Shift		5. Pick in the **Rev** cell, hold down the SHIFT key, and pick in the **App** cell. AutoCAD highlights the row.
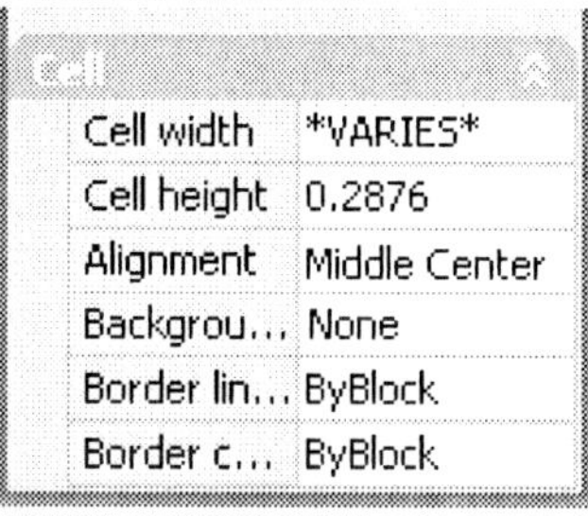 Cell Cell width *VARIES* Cell height 0.2876 Alignment Middle Center Backgrou... None Border lin... ByBlock Border c... ByBlock		6. Using the Properties palette, change the height of the row to **.2876"** (the height of the data rows). (Close the Properties palette and clear the grips.)
	**Command:** ***m***	7. Reposition the revision block next to the title block. The revision block now looks like Figure 17.015.

Rev	Date	By	Description	App
Revision				

Figure 17.015

TOOLS	COMMAND SEQUENCE	STEPS
		8. Fill in everything except the **Date** block with your own information (Figure 17.016).

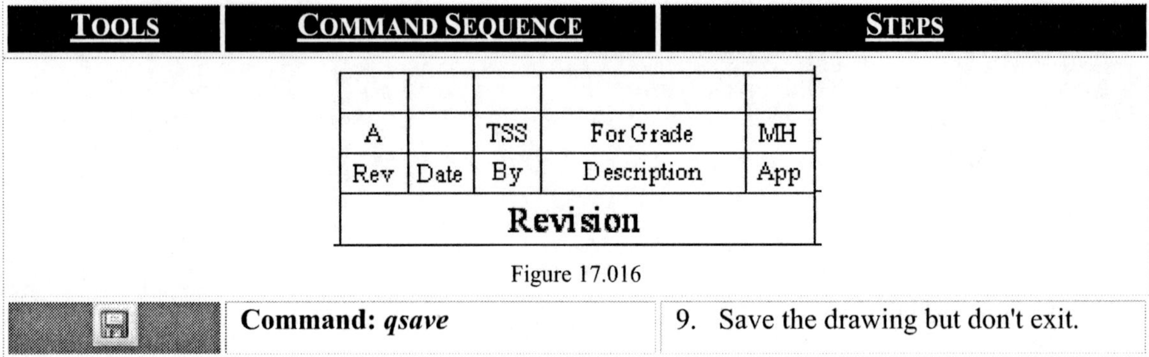

Tools	Command Sequence	Steps

A		TSS	For Grade	MH
Rev	Date	By	Description	App
Revision				

Figure 17.016

Tools	Command Sequence	Steps
	Command: ***qsave***	9. Save the drawing but don't exit.

Okay, tables were pretty easy (all things considered). They may take a bit of work to set things up, but once that's done, the rest is child's play. Try to remember as you do the setup, that you won't see the real benefit to tables until you discover later that you need to change something or (Heaven forbid!) move the entire table!

Our next tool requires less setup, and it can be even more of a timesaver!

17.2 The Wonders of Automation – Fields

Fields (placeholders for text) require very little setup, but they relieve the operator of some of the more mundane chores of life – automatically filling in some of the common requirements of virtually all documents (author, date, etc.). In the case of the draftsperson, they can help with the revision block we just created as well as the title block, and even provide a modifiable plot stamp for your drawings. But the usefulness of fields in a drawing go beyond the basic documentation benefits. You can also use fields to keep track of such things as length, area, and even elevation of an object!

First, we'll look at the source of some of the information AutoCAD will use to fill in the fields you'll create. Then we'll create some fields.

17.2.1 Drawing Properties

AutoCAD automatically sets up many of the things you'll want to use for field values – dates, object information, and so forth. But you'll have to set up some of the other things – drawing name, author name, and so forth. Luckily, AutoCAD limits your input to a single dialog box (with four fairly simple tabs). See the [Drawing Name] Properties dialog box in Figure 17.017. (Access the dialog box with the ***DwgProps*** command.)

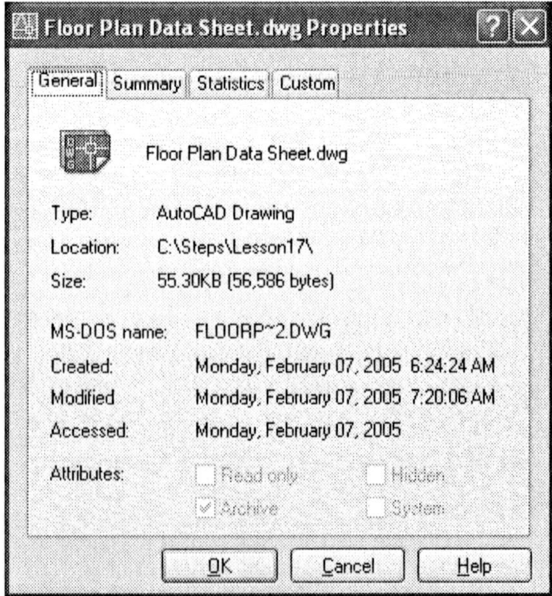

Figure 17.017

- The **General** tab provides information – file attributes, recent modification dates, and so forth. You can't change any of this information here, but some of it can prove useful in tracking things you may need to know (such as file size).

- The **Summary** tab (Figure 17.018) is your workhorse. You'll need to fill in this information. Remember, if you don't fill it in, it won't be available to you; so use your best judgment as to what to include.

  Most of the blanks are self-explanatory. But this information might help:

  - Use the **Keywords** box to include words that might be useful when searching a group of drawings for this one.
  - Use the **Comments** box to add any useful comments you'd like to make.
  - The **Hyperlink base** can be a folder or website – anywhere that drawings including or related to this one might be located.
- Like the **General** tab, you won't be able to alter the information provided on the **Statistics** tab (Figure 17.019). This one, however, has some really useful information that an operator can use to keep track of his time on a specific drawing, or when the drawing was edited last. (There's no defense before an irate employer like computer-generated facts!)
- The last tab – **Custom** (Figure 17.020) – provides an opportunity for including some of your own information.

You'll be able to see the benefits of this tool once you've set it up and we examine fields in more detail. Let's set up our drawing's properties.

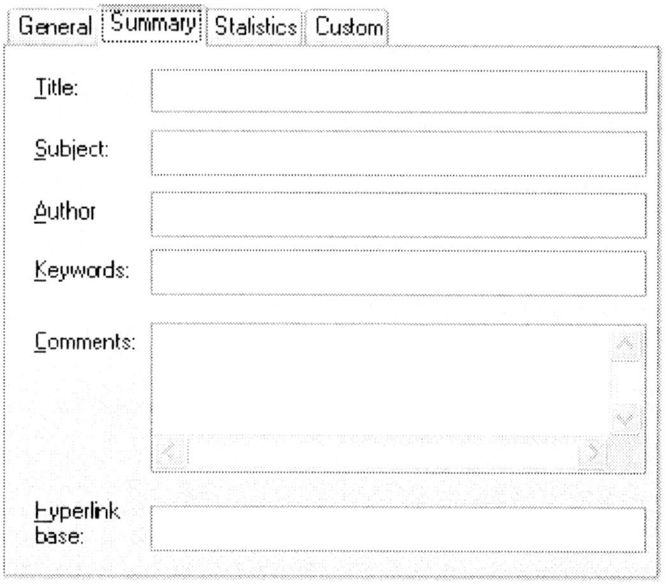

General | Summary | Statistics | Custom

Title:

Subject:

Author

Keywords:

Comments:

Hyperlink base:

Figure 17.018

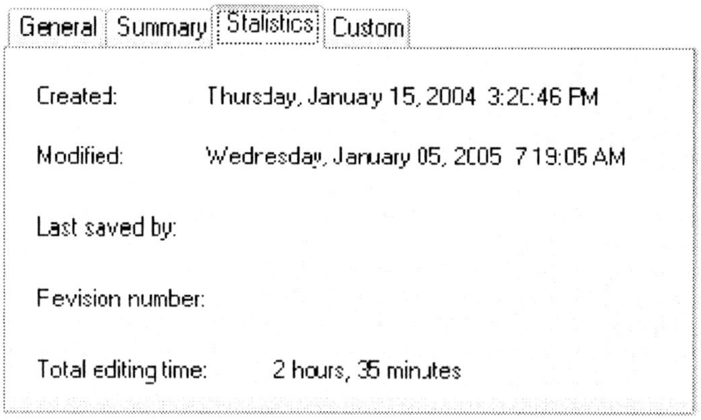

General | Summary | Statistics | Custom

Created: Thursday, January 15, 2004 3:20:46 PM

Modified: Wednesday, January 05, 2005 7:19:05 AM

Last saved by:

Revision number:

Total editing time: 2 hours, 35 minutes

Figure 17.019

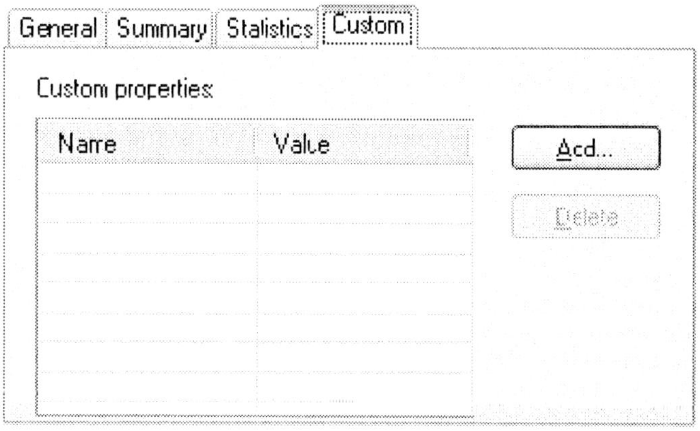

General | Summary | Statistics | Custom

Custom properties:

Name	Value

Add...

Delete

Figure 17.020

You can find an additional benefit of the properties dialog box shown here by right clicking on the file in Windows Explorer. Select **Properties** from the cursor menu, and Windows will show you the information you've provided without having to open the file!

Do This: 17.2.1.1	Setting Up Drawing Properties

I. Be sure you're still in the *Floor Plan Data Sheet* drawing in the C:\Steps\Lesson17 folder. If not, please open it now.

II. Follow these steps.

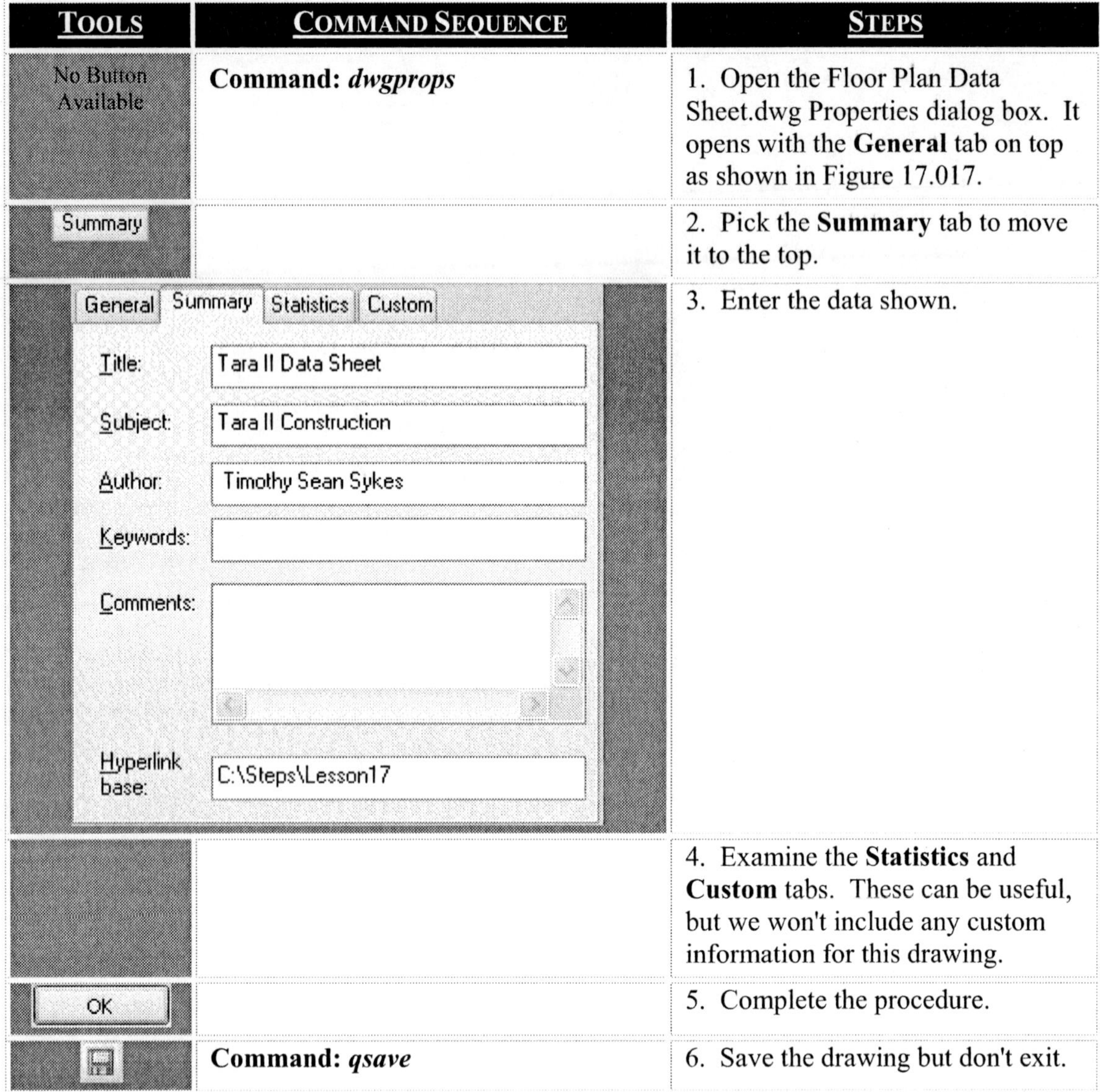

TOOLS	COMMAND SEQUENCE	STEPS
No Button Available	**Command:** ***dwgprops***	1. Open the Floor Plan Data Sheet.dwg Properties dialog box. It opens with the **General** tab on top as shown in Figure 17.017.
Summary		2. Pick the **Summary** tab to move it to the top.
		3. Enter the data shown.
		4. Examine the **Statistics** and **Custom** tabs. These can be useful, but we won't include any custom information for this drawing.
OK		5. Complete the procedure.
	Command: ***qsave***	6. Save the drawing but don't exit.

Nothing to it, right?

Now let's take a look at why we set up this dialog box. Let's look at fields.

17.2.2 Inserting Fields

You'll find two ways to insert a field – insertion via MText editor and simple insertion. (We'll use both in our next exercise.) Both methods involve the Field dialog box (Figure 17.021).

The dialog box, despite its simple appearance, allows for a great number of possibilities.

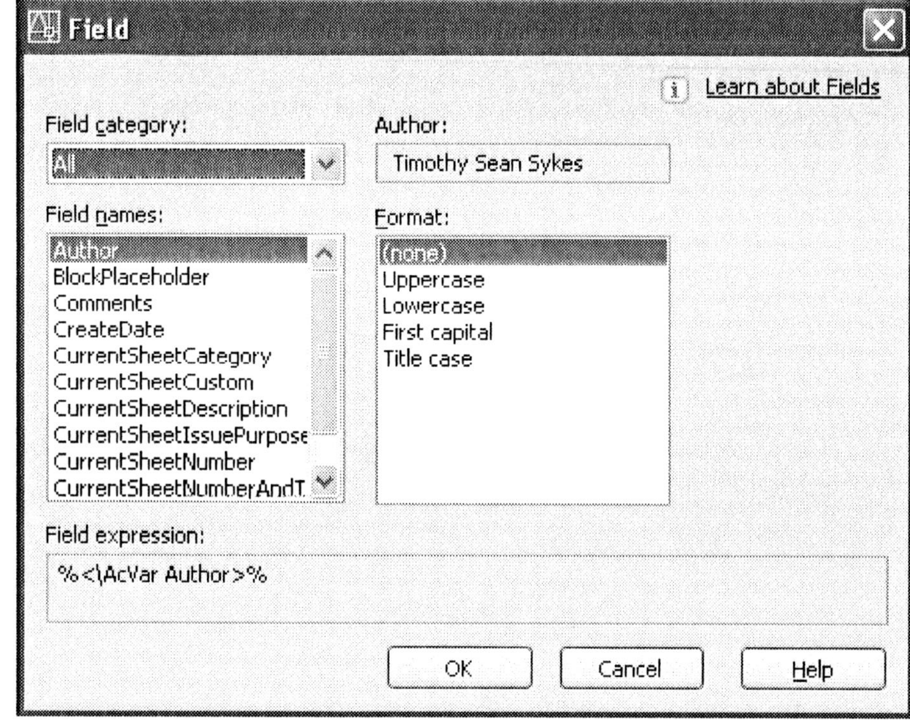

Figure 17.021

- The **Field category** drop down box provides a list of the various categories available for your field. If you aren't sure which category to use, leave the **All** default, which will provide a list of all the available field names in the list box below.
- The **Field names** list box provides a list of fields available in the selected category.
- The **Field value** box (shown here as **Author**) lets you know the current value of the selected field. This box changes with the selection of different fields in the **Field names** list box. It will show dashes if no value has been assigned to the selected field or pound symbols (#) if the field is invalid.
- The **Format** box allows you to select from a list of available formats for your field. Formats change with the selection of different fields.
- To the right of the **Field value** and **Format** boxes, you'll see a large empty space. AutoCAD will fill this space with hints or additional options as your selection requires.
- The **Field expression** box just above the buttons is informational only. It shows the coding required to create the selected field. Unless you're a programmer, you can ignore this area.

AutoCAD provides the usual buttons at the bottom of the dialog box, but I'd like to point out the **Help** button just to make sure you know it's there. This very intuitive dialog box may require some support as you get used to it.

Let's insert some fields.

Do This: 17.2.2.1	**Inserting Fields**

I. Be sure you're still in the *Floor Plan Data Sheet* drawing in the C:\Steps\Lesson17 folder. If not, please open it now.

II. Set the **TEXT** layer and the **TIMES** text style current.

III. Set the **TextSize** system variable to 1/8".

IV. If you're not already zoomed in around the title/revision blocks, please do so now.

V. Increase the size of the **Date** column by ¼" to the right (refer to Exercise 17.1.4.2 if you need help). Reposition the revision table as needed.

VI. Follow these steps.

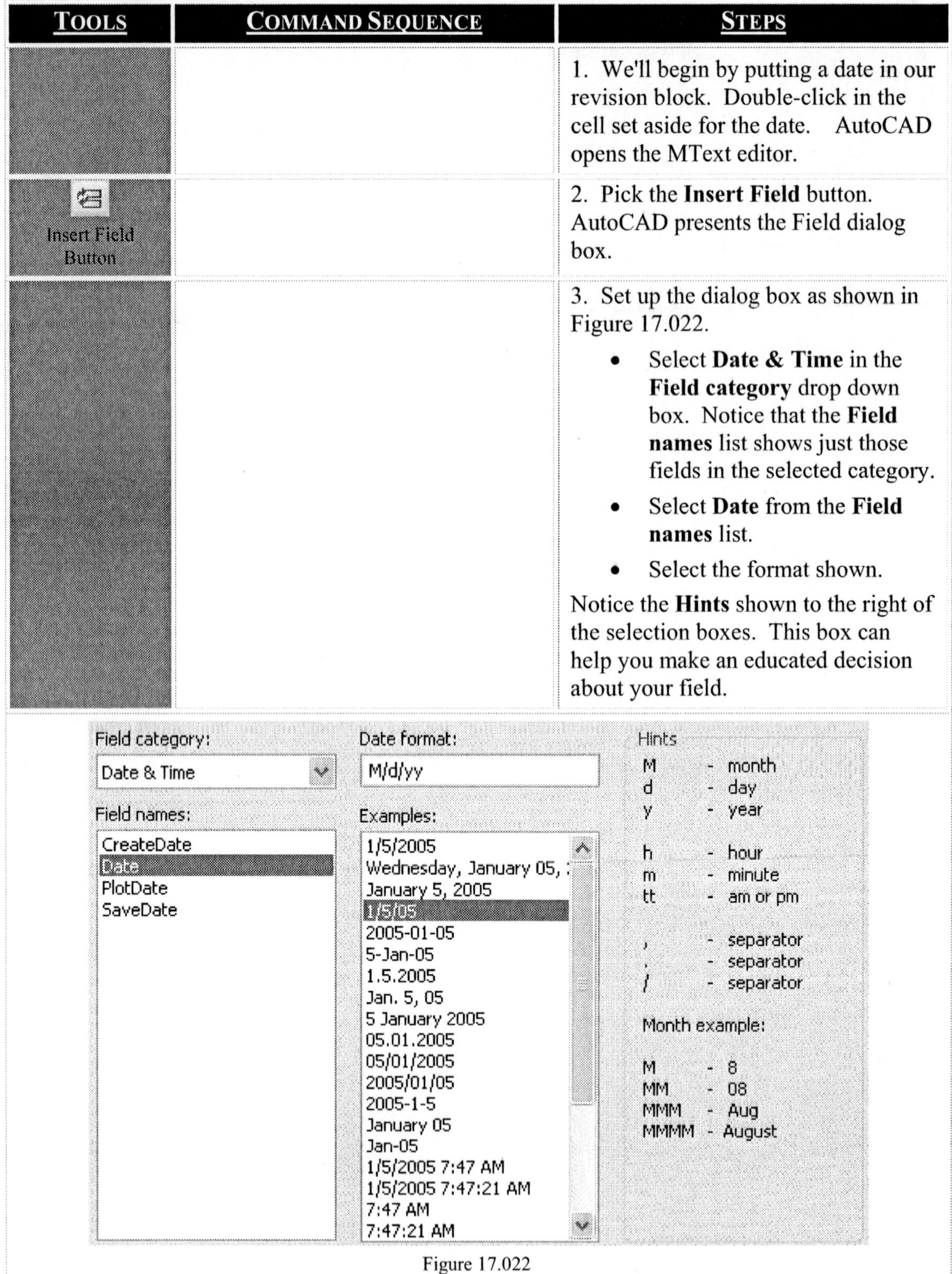

TOOLS	COMMAND SEQUENCE	STEPS
		1. We'll begin by putting a date in our revision block. Double-click in the cell set aside for the date. AutoCAD opens the MText editor.
Insert Field Button		2. Pick the **Insert Field** button. AutoCAD presents the Field dialog box.
		3. Set up the dialog box as shown in Figure 17.022. • Select **Date & Time** in the **Field category** drop down box. Notice that the **Field names** list shows just those fields in the selected category. • Select **Date** from the **Field names** list. • Select the format shown. Notice the **Hints** shown to the right of the selection boxes. This box can help you make an educated decision about your field.

Figure 17.022

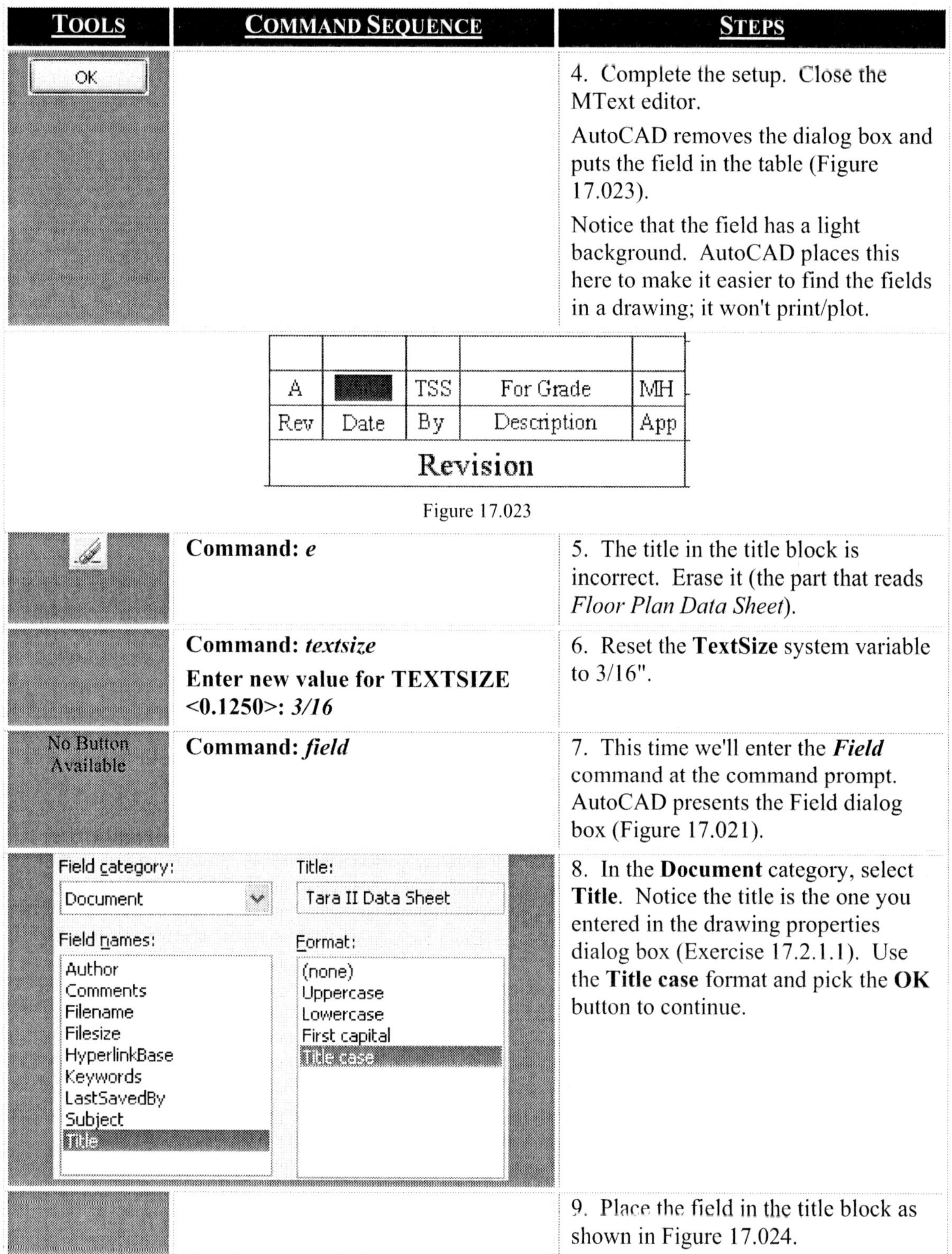

TOOLS	COMMAND SEQUENCE	STEPS
OK		4. Complete the setup. Close the MText editor. AutoCAD removes the dialog box and puts the field in the table (Figure 17.023). Notice that the field has a light background. AutoCAD places this here to make it easier to find the fields in a drawing; it won't print/plot.
	 Figure 17.023	
	Command: ***e***	5. The title in the title block is incorrect. Erase it (the part that reads *Floor Plan Data Sheet*).
	Command: ***textsize*** **Enter new value for TEXTSIZE <0.1250>:** ***3/16***	6. Reset the **TextSize** system variable to 3/16".
No Button Available	**Command:** ***field***	7. This time we'll enter the ***Field*** command at the command prompt. AutoCAD presents the Field dialog box (Figure 17.021).
		8. In the **Document** category, select **Title**. Notice the title is the one you entered in the drawing properties dialog box (Exercise 17.2.1.1). Use the **Title case** format and pick the **OK** button to continue.
		9. Place the field in the title block as shown in Figure 17.024.

Tools	Command Sequence	Steps

Figure 17.024

Tools	Command Sequence	Steps
	Command: *saveas*	10. Save the drawing as *Tara II Data Sheet* in the C:\Steps\Lesson17 folder.
	Command: *p*	11. Now let's look at something really cool. Adjust your view to see the text in the upper right corner of the drawing.
		12. Double-click on the text to open the MText editor.
		13. Place your cursor below the last note. (Refer to Figure 17.025, Step 22, for a look at where we're going.)
		14. Enter the text: ***This data sheet references the following drawings:***
		15. Pick the **Insert Field** button.
Field category: Linked; Text to display:; Field names: Hyperlink; Hyperlink...		16. On the Fields dialog box, select **Hyperlink** from the **Linked** category. Pick the **Hyperlink** button to select the drawing to which you'd like to link.
File...		17. AutoCAD presents an Insert Hyperlink text box (more on this when we talk about Web publishing in Lesson 21). For now, pick the **File** button.
		18. AutoCAD presents a standard Select File dialog box. Navigate to the C:\Steps\Lesson17 folder and double-click on the *Floor Plan 17.dwg* file.
OK		19. AutoCAD returns to the Insert Hyperlink text box. Pick the **OK** button to return to the Field text box.

TOOLS	COMMAND SEQUENCE	STEPS
Text to display: Floor Plan 17.dwg		20. In the **Text to display** box, remove the period and the backslash as shown.
		21. Complete the procedure and close the MText editor. Notice the new text.
	Command: ***qsave***	22. Save the drawing.
		22. Move your cursor over the field you just placed in the notes. Notice that AutoCAD tells you how to use the hyperlink (Figure 17.025).
Floor Plan 17.dwg CTRL + click to follow link Figure 17.025		
		23. Follow AutoCAD's instructions (hold down the CTRL key and click to follow the link). AutoCAD opens the referenced drawing! (Pretty cool, huh?)
	Command: ***closeall***	25. Close all open drawings.

17.2.3 Calculating Fields

You've really just scratched the surface of what you can do with tables. AutoCAD has incorporated some of the more useful elements of spreadsheets into their tables, too. If you've ever used MS Excel or any other spreadsheet program, you might see the potential!

We're going to use fields in an AutoCAD table to calculate the square footage of each of the rooms of our Tara II floor plan. Then we'll total the square footage … and even calculate the average square footage per room!

Let's get started right away.

Do This: 17.2.3.1 Calculating with Fields

I. Open the *Floor Plan 17* drawing in the C:\Steps\Lesson17 folder. This is the same floor plan we've been using except that I've added a Square Footage table in the lower left corner.

II. Zoom in around the Square Footage table.

III. Follow these steps.

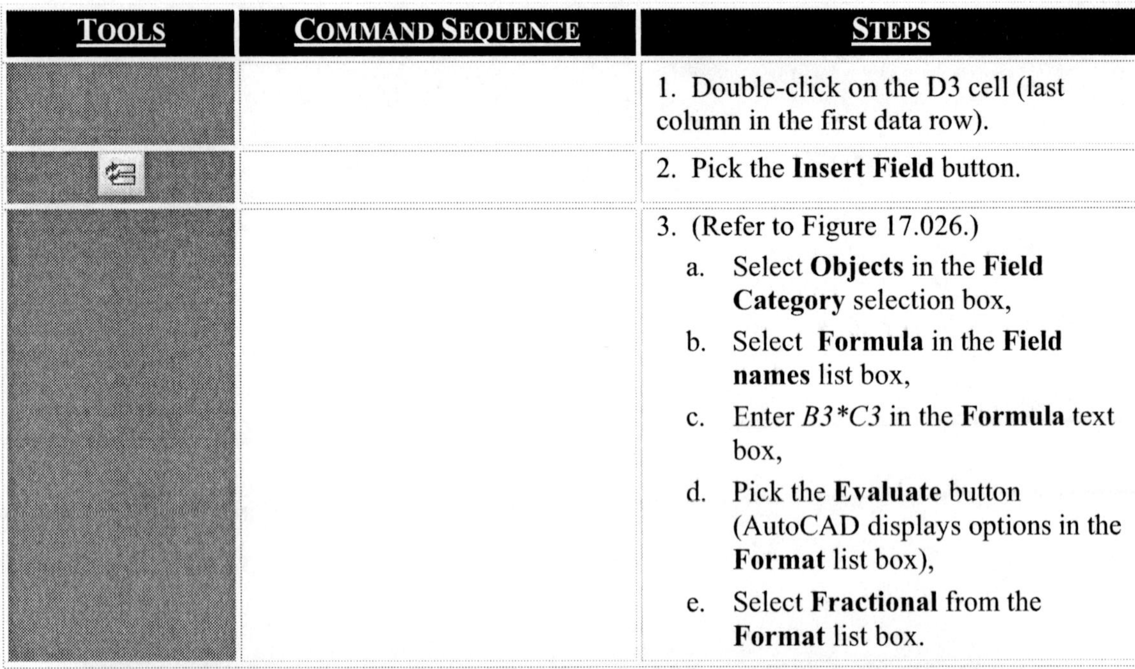

TOOLS	COMMAND SEQUENCE	STEPS
		1. Double-click on the D3 cell (last column in the first data row).
		2. Pick the **Insert Field** button.
		3. (Refer to Figure 17.026.) a. Select **Objects** in the **Field Category** selection box, b. Select **Formula** in the **Field names** list box, c. Enter *B3*C3* in the **Formula** text box, d. Pick the **Evaluate** button (AutoCAD displays options in the **Format** list box), e. Select **Fractional** from the **Format** list box.

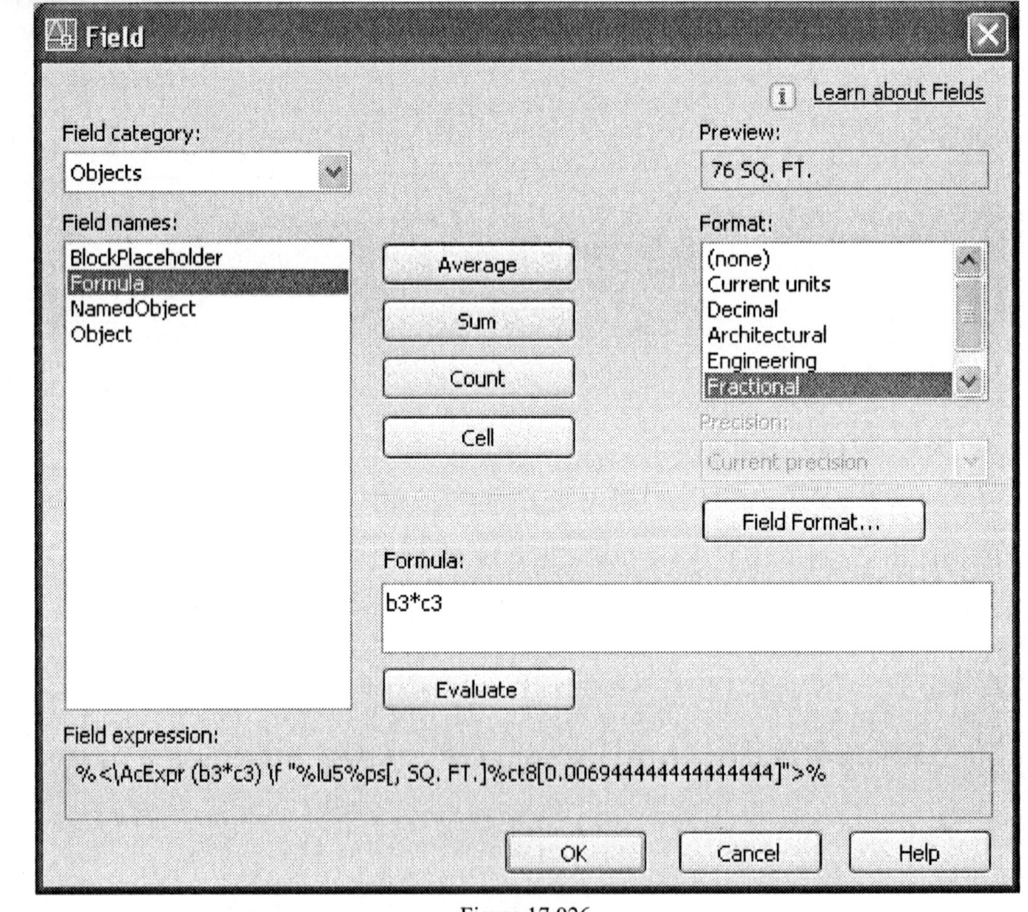

Figure 17.026

Tools	Command Sequence	Steps
OK		4. Pick the **OK** button to complete the procedure. Notice that AutoCAD places the product of the values of cells B3 and C3 into cell D3. (Or put more simply, AutoCAD multiples 8 by 9.5 and puts the answer in the location you selected in Step 1.)
		5. Use the down arrow key to move to cell D4.
		6. Repeat Steps 2 and 3 for this cell as well as cells D5 through D14.
		7. Now highlight cell D15 (down arrow into it or double-click on it if you've closed the MText editor). Here we'll sum the square feet column.
		8. Pick the **Insert Field** button.
Sum		9. This time, we'll let AutoCAD do the work. Pick the **Sum** button.
	Select first corner of table cell range: **Select second corner of table cell range:**	10. AutoCAD returns to the graphics screen and asks you to place a window around the **table cell range** you wish to total. Put the window around the cells you've been using (D3 through D14).
OK		11. AutoCAD returns to the Field dialog box. Select the **Fractional** format you've been using, and then pick the **OK** button to complete this procedure.
		12. Finally, we'll give our client an average figure for the rooms in our house. Use the down arrow to move to cell D16.
		13. Pick the **Insert Field** button.
Average		14. Again, we'll let AutoCAD do the work. Pick the **Average** button and select the same cells (D3 through D14).
OK		15. AutoCAD again returns to the Field dialog box. Again, use the **Fractional** format, and pick the **OK** button to complete this procedure.

TOOLS	COMMAND SEQUENCE	STEPS
OK		16. We've finished our calculations! Pick the **OK** button to close the MText editor. Your table looks like Figure 17.027. (Adjust your column width if necessary.)

Square Footage			
Room	Length	Width	Sq. Ft.
Closet - Mstr	8'	9.5'	[illegible]
Closet #1	10'	3'	[illegible]
Closet #2	5.5'	5'	[illegible]
Closet #3	5.5'	5'	[illegible]
Bath - Mstr	8'	9.5'	[illegible]
Bath - Com.	10'	5'	[illegible]
BR - Mstr.	16'	16.5'	[illegible]
Br #1	11.5'	10.5'	[illegible]
Br #2	11.5'	12.5'	[illegible]
Br #3	13.5'	9'	[illegible]
Kitchen	11.5'	19.5'	[illegible]
LR	21'	30.5'	[illegible]
Total			[illegible]
Rm. Avg.			[illegible]

Figure 17.027

TOOLS	COMMAND SEQUENCE	STEPS
	**Command:** ***qsave***	17. Save the drawing.

Cool, huh? Want to see something even cooler? Change the value in one of the **Length** or **Width** cells. AutoCAD will automatically adjust not only the value in the **Sq. Ft.** column, but the **Total** and **Rm. Avg.** values as well!

17.3 Extra Steps

Take a look at the **New Features Workshop** (under the **Help** pull down menu).

Specifically, follow the picks – **Create … Drafting tools … Create Fields**. Go through the exercise to see another way fields can be useful (here you'll automatically calculate and insert the area of a polygon). You'll also see how to update a field.

Remember to take advantage of AutoCAD's various training tools when you have a few extra minutes between lessons or projects at the job site; the effort will prove occasionally beneficial (but never harmful)!

17.4 What Have We Learned?

Items covered in this lesson include:

- *Field tools:*
    - ***Field***
    - ***DwgProps***
- *Table tools:*
    - ***Table***
    - ***Tablestyle***

AutoCAD makes dozens of combinations of fields and tables available to you. Hopefully, this lesson has whetted your appetite for knowledge and you'll spend some time exploring these new and innovative tools.

Try some of the exercises in Section 17.5, and then relax for a minute before tackling the lesson on hatching. It isn't difficult material, but it's always best to start a new lesson with a fresh mind.

17.5 Exercises

1. Add drawing properties and a revision block to the Piping Plan you've been working on. If you're not up to date on it, use *Piping Plan 17* in the C:\Steps\Lesson17 folder. (Refer to Figure 17.028.)
    1.1. Try setting up a new field (Scale) on the **Custom** tab of the [drawing] Properties dialog box. Give it a value of 3/8"=1'-0". Insert it as a field in the title block as shown.
    1.2. When you set up the new table style for the revision block, remember to take the drawing scale factor into account when you assign text sizes. (Hint: I gave you the scale for this drawing in the previous step.)
    1.3. Save the drawing.

0	1/5/05	TSS	For Construction	BB
No	Date	By	Description	App
Revision				

North Harris College Houston, Texas		
Sample Piping Plan		
Tim Sykes		PLN-002
July 4, 1776	3/8"=1'-0"	Sht. 1 of 1

Figure 17.028

2. Add a revision block to the *pid* drawing in the C:\Steps\Lesson17 folder (refer to Figure 17.029).

North Harris College
Houston, Texas

Fractionator Unit
Piping & Instrument Diagram
-- Sample --

0		TSS	For Construction	BB
Rev	Date	By	Description	App
Revision				

SIZE	FSCN NO.	DWG NO.	REV
D	N/A	100-D-1001	0

SCALE NTS SHEET 1 of 1

Figure 17.029

3. Add a reference block (Figure 17.030) to the same *pid* drawing you used in Exercise 2 above. The *PID Data Sheet* is in the C:\Steps\Lesson17 folder. The field should be a hyperlink to the data sheet.

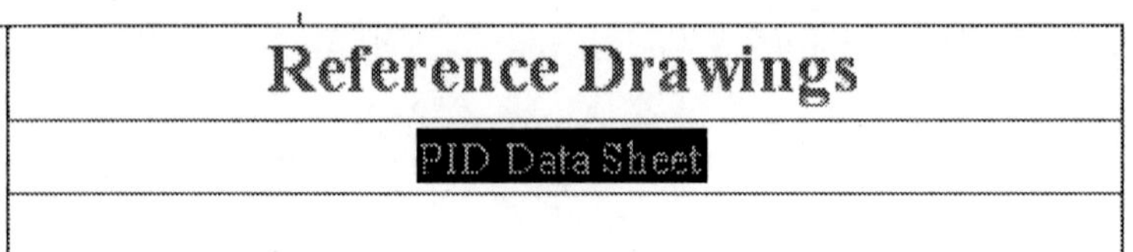

Figure 17.030

4. On the PID Data Sheet (in the C:\Steps\Lesson17 folder):
   4.1. Create the legend shown in Figure 17.031. (The appropriate blocks are already a part of the drawing.)
   4.2. Create the reference block shown in Figure 17.032.

Symbols Legend

Symbol	Description	Symbol	Description
	Check Valve		Drain Valve
	Control Valve		Gate Valve
	Globe Valve		

Figure 17.031

Reference Drawings

Piping and Instrument Diagram

Figure 17.032

17.6	For Web-Based Review Questions, visit: http://www.uneedcad.com/2006/Files/06R17.pdf

Ex. #4
#3

Lesson

Following this lesson, you will:

- ✓ *Know how to add Hatching and Section Lines to your AutoCAD drawing through:*
  - o *The **Hatch** dialog box*
  - o *Tool Palettes*
  - o *The ADC*
- ✓ *Know how to edit hatch patterns using the **Hatchedit** command*

Hatching and Filling

Remember all those templates I mentioned in Lesson 5 – the ones I needed to draw ellipses? Remember how much simpler (and more accurate) it was to draw ellipses with AutoCAD?

Here's another drawing tool that puts those pieces of plastic to shame. No longer will the drafter need to spend hours drawing each line or symbol to show section lines, a brick façade, concrete, and so forth. With AutoCAD's hatch commands, you can fill a large area with lines or symbols in a matter or seconds!

18.1 Hatching and Filling

There are actually two ways to draw hatch patterns. (Section lines and fills are created as styles of hatch pattern. Therefore, I'll refer to all as hatch patterns.) There's a dialog box approach and a simple drag-n-drop approach that utilizes the tool palettes. We'll begin with the Hatch and Gradient dialog box (Figure 18.001).

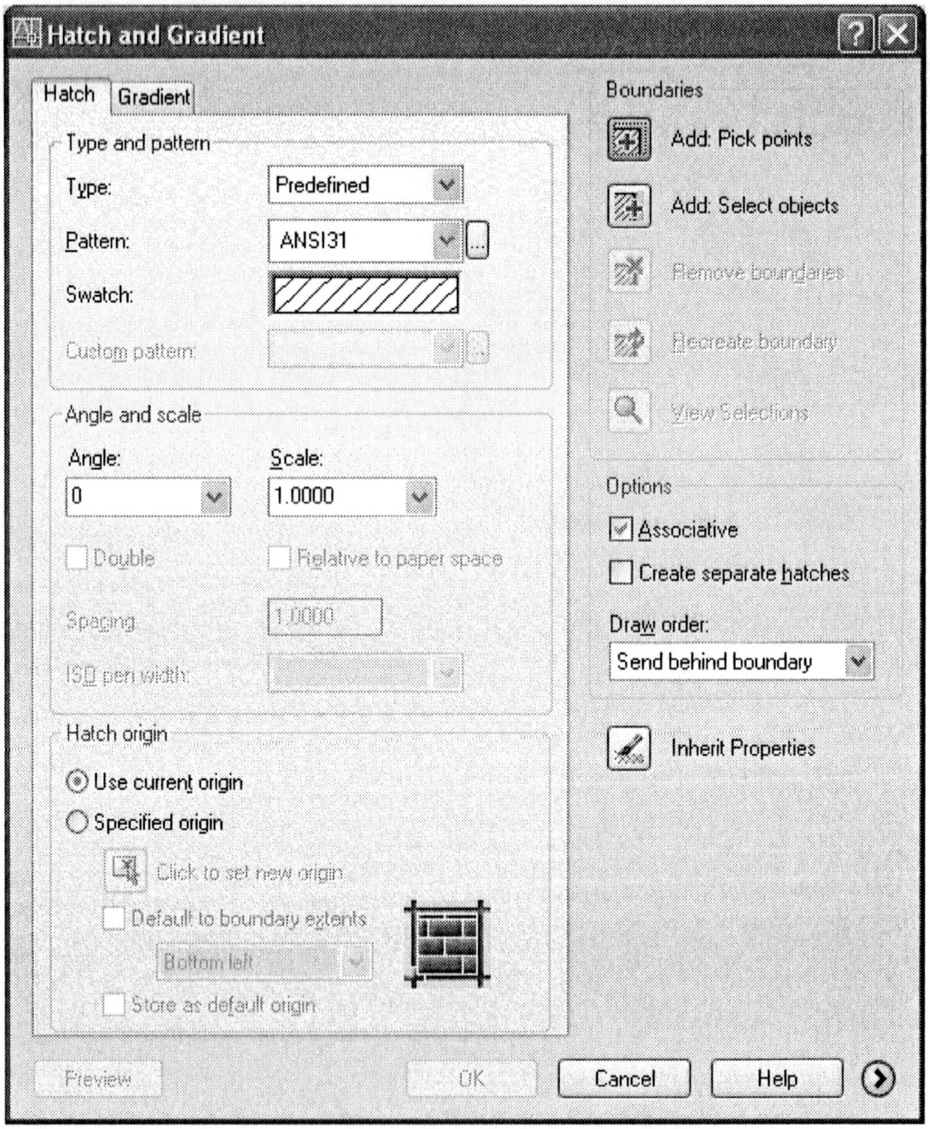

Figure 18.001

The first tab you see (**Hatch**) allows you to set up the **Type**, **Pattern**, **Scale**, **Angle**, and **Origin** of your desired hatching.

The second tab – **Gradient** (Figure 18.002) – allows you to create some interesting gradient fills – similar to the solid option but with more clout.

Additionally, you'll find a series of five buttons in the **Boundaries** frame. These allow you to identify where the hatch pattern will go.

Below the **Boundaries** frame, an **Options** frame helps you define how your hatch pattern or fill will behave.

- An **Associative** hatch pattern, like associative dimensions, dynamically updates when the defining boundaries change.
- A check next to **Create separate hatches** allows you to hatch several things at once, while maintaining the independence of each pattern when it comes to editing.
- **Draw order** lets you define where your pattern will lie – in **front** of or **behind** the boundaries. (This usually won't matter, but AutoCAD allows for the exception to most rules.)

Finally, you'll find an **Inherit Properties** button. Use this to duplicate an existing hatch definition.

Let's look at the tabs.

- The Hatch and Gradient dialog box defaults to the **Hatch** tab.
  - o The **Type and pattern** frame contains four different tools you can use to select a hatch pattern: the **Type** control box (which filters your selections), a **Pattern** control box (which lists the patterns available), a **Swatch** box (which you can pick to access a visual listing of available patterns), and a **Custom pattern** control box (which will list any custom patterns loaded into AutoCAD by the CAD guru on your job).
    - ▪ The **Type** control box allows you to select a **Predefined** pattern, a **User defined** pattern, or a **Custom** pattern.
      - ∴ **Predefined** patterns accompany AutoCAD. You'll see a sample of the selected pattern in the **Swatch** box or by picking the button next to the **Pattern** control box.
      - ∴ The **User defined** option allows you to set the **Angle** and **Spacing** of hatch lines in the **Angle and scale** frame. Use these tools to define your own hatch pattern. The **User defined** option also makes the **Double** check box available (also in the **Angle and scale** frame). A check here will cause AutoCAD to duplicate your hatch pattern within the same boundaries *but at 90° to the first pattern.*
      - ∴ Selecting **Custom** in the **Type** control box makes the **Custom pattern** control box available. A custom pattern is also predefined, but the definition is stored in a file other than the *Acad.pat* (the file where AutoCAD keeps hatch pattern definitions by default). The CAD guru will provide custom patterns if needed. If you select the **Custom** option in the **Pattern** control box, you must enter the name of the desired pattern in the **Custom Pattern** control box.
    - ▪ The **Pattern** control box allow you to scroll through the patterns one at a time; or you can pick the button to the right of the control box to display the Hatch Pattern Palette, which displays visual representations of several patterns at a time. (This is the same palette displayed when you pick in the **Swatch** box.)
  - o The **Angle and scale** frame contains tools for defining (or customizing) the pattern you've selected in the **Type and pattern** frame.
    - ▪ The **Angle** control box defaults to zero. This doesn't mean that the lines of the hatch pattern will be horizontal. It means that AutoCAD will draw the lines of the selected hatch pattern as they appear in the pattern's definition. Changing the angle here will cause AutoCAD to rotate the pattern (which may have defined the lines at an angle already) by the angle specified.

- Use the **Scale** control box to set the scale of your pattern. I suggest you start with the drawing scale factor for your drawing. You can adjust it later using the ***Hatchedit*** command.
- AutoCAD makes **Spacing** available only when you're creating a user defined hatch pattern. Use it to tell AutoCAD how far apart to place the lines.
- Ignore the **Relative to paper space** check box for now. We'll discuss paper space in Lessons 22 and 23.
- The **ISO pen width** option becomes available only when you've selected an ISO pattern. This control box allows you to select the width of the ISO lines.

  - You won't find the **Hatch** origin frame in earlier releases of AutoCAD, but its tools have been needed for quite some time.

    Normally, the hatch origin defaults to the 0,0 coordinates. Theoretically, bricks, grating, etc. will begin there even if you only see the portion of the hatch within the boundaries you've designated. This can result in partial bricks (or grating, etc.) along the bottom of the "wall" you're bricking. I doubt that a mason will cut bricks in half to start a new row just to make a building look like your hatching, so AutoCAD decided to allow you to start with a whole brick – by allowing you to redefine the hatch origin.

    - A check next to **Use current origin** (the default), will lay out hatching based on the 0,0 coordinate of your drawing. This works fine for most hatching.
    - You can set a new origin for your hatching by picking the **Click to set new origin** button. But this is the hard way (unless you want to put the origin in an odd place).
    - For fancier hatching (like bricks, grating, etc.), put your check next to **Default to boundary extents**. When you do, AutoCAD makes the boundary extents control box available to you (just below the **boundary extents** option). Here you can opt to locate your hatch origin in relation to the boundary (**Bottom left**, **Bottom right**, **Top left**, **Top right**, or **Center**).
    - Finally, you can put a check next to **Store as default origin** if you wish to use these settings by default.

- The other tab – **Gradient** (Figure 18.002) – allows you to apply a color or colors with graduated intensity; that is, you can create colors that get more or less intense from one part of the colored area to another.

  - You can select between a **One color** or a **Two color** gradient with the radio buttons at the top of the tab.

    If you opt for one, AutoCAD presents a color selection box

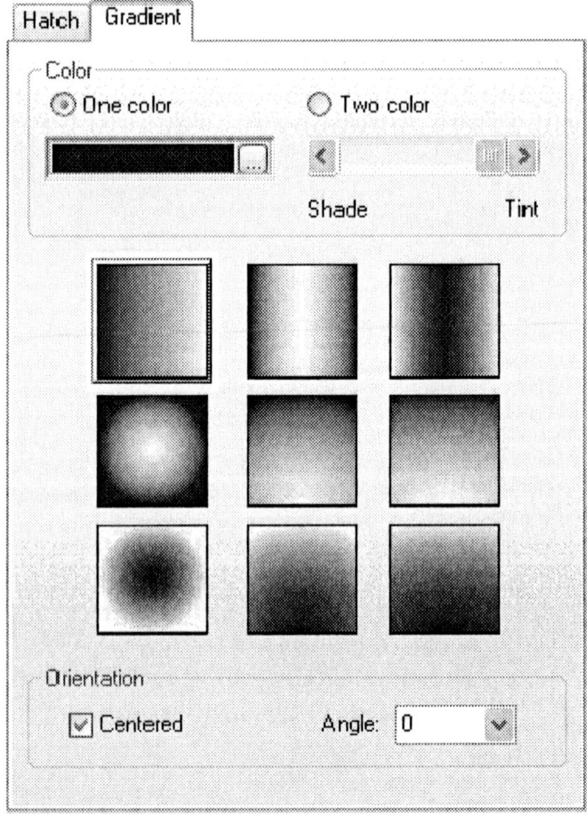

Figure 18.002

(below the radio buttons) and a **Shade/Tint** slider bar to help you control the intensity of the color.

If you opt for two colors, AutoCAD replaces the **Shade/Tint** slider bar with a second color selection box to allow you to select the second color.

- In the lower half of the tab, AutoCAD presents nine selections for how you'd like your gradient to behave. Select the one you prefer.
- Below the gradient selections, you'll find the **Orientation** frame.
  - The **Centered** check box controls how the graduations behave – remove the check and the intensity grows from mild in the upper left corner (appearing something like a light source) to more intense as you move away from the upper left corner.
  - The **Angle** selection box, of course, controls the angle of the gradients.

Once you've made your selections on the tabs, you must tell AutoCAD what to hatch using one of the buttons on the right side of the dialog box. Here, you'll find two frames, a button, and a quiet arrow button to assist you.

Figure 18.003

- Define the edges of your hatching with tools in the **Boundaries** frame (Figure 18.003).
  - When you use the **Add: Pick points** button, AutoCAD returns to the graphics screen and prompts:

    Pick internal point or [Select objects/remove Boundaries]:

    Pick anywhere within the boundaries (where you want to place your hatching). Be sure the area is closed; AutoCAD will *not* hatch an open area unless the gap tolerance has been properly set (more on that in a few minutes)! Alternately, you can enter an ***S*** and select an object to use as a boundary, or a ***B*** to remove boundaries from your selection set. (Remember to hit enter to complete the selection set.)
  - Use the **Add: Select objects** button to go straight to the **Select objects** option.
  - Use the **Remove boundaries** button to go straight to the **remove Boundaries** option.
  - You'll use **Recreate boundary** when you redefine existing hatching.
  - **View selections** returns you to the graphics screen and highlights the boundaries you've selected to use to create a new hatching.
- Below the **Boundaries** frame lies the **Options** frame (Figure 18.004).
  - **Associative** hatching means that hatch patterns will update automatically when the boundaries change (much as associate dimensions do).

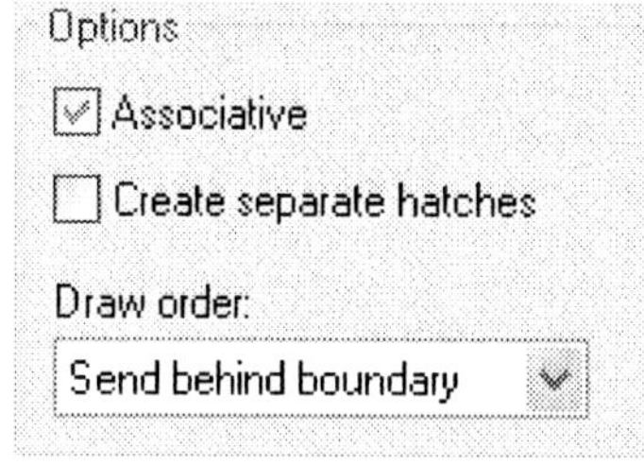

Figure 18.004

> You can convert a hatch pattern (associative or nonassociative) into its constituent lines using the ***Explode*** command. You cannot convert the other way, however, so do this with caution.

  - Normally, if you hatch within several boundaries at once, AutoCAD treats the different hatches as a single object. (That is, if you erase one, they all go.) Place a check next to **Create separate hatches** to avoid problems that this might present.

- Use the **Draw order** control box to place the hatching in relation to the boundaries. We'll discuss more on draw order in Lesson 26.

- Don't over look the solitary button – **Inherit Properties** – resting below the frames on the right side of the Hatch and Gradient dialog box. This handy tool makes it possible to duplicate any existing hatching in your drawing – even if you don't know how it was set up! Pick the button; AutoCAD will return to the graphics screen and prompt you to **Select hatch object**. Pick the one you wish to duplicate and voila! AutoCAD automatically adjusts the settings in the Hatch and Gradient dialog box to duplicate it! (Way cool!)
- You'll find another solitary button in the bottom left corner of the dialog box – **Preview**. This button allows you to see the hatched object before completing the command. This way, you can make any necessary adjustments before applying the hatching.

Think you're finished? Not quite yet! Notice that insignificant arrow button next to Help (at the bottom of the dialog box). Pick it now. Gadzooks! More options (Figure 18.005)!

- Islands are boundaries within boundaries. By default, AutoCAD recognizes islands and uses an island hopping approach to hatching. That is, hatch – skip – hatch. It does, however, allow other approaches in the **Islands** frame.
  - Leave the check next to **Island detection** for AutoCAD to recognize islands. Remove it, and AutoCAD will ignore any islands and hatch within the outer boundary. (Note: AutoCAD treats text as an island and will not hatch over it unless told to do so with the **Ignore** option.)
  - Use the three radio buttons below the check box (and the graphic representations) to determine how you wish AutoCAD to respond when it finds islands.

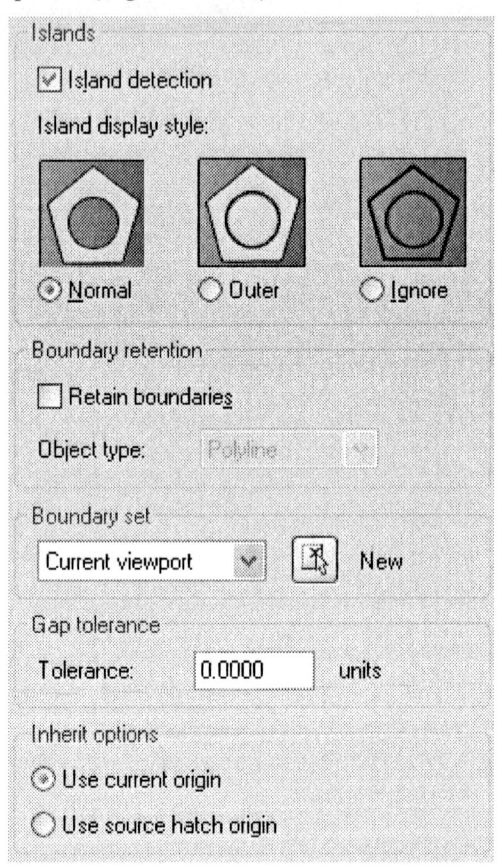

Figure 18.005

- Tools in the **Boundary retention** and **Boundary set** frames work together. Let me explain.

  You'll notice that, in larger drawings, it may take AutoCAD a while to locate boundaries when using the **Pick points** method. This is because AutoCAD must search the drawing database for information on all visible objects. Using the **New** button in the **Boundary set** frame can really hasten this process. When picked, AutoCAD will prompt you to **Select objects** on the screen, and then return to the Hatch and Gradient dialog box. AutoCAD will then restrict its search to the objects selected. You can make the new boundary set from the **Current viewport** or from an **Existing set** by selecting your choice from the control box in the **Boundary set** frame.

  When defining a new boundary set, you should use a window or crossing window; other methods will work, but these are faster in a large drawing. In the **Boundary retention** frame, you can tell AutoCAD to retain the defined area as a **Polyline** or a **Region** (an object similar to a 2-dimensional solid). Simply place a check in the **Retain boundaries** check box and then make your selection in the **Object type** control box.

Tools available in the Boundary retention and Boundary set frames can make a tremendous difference in the amount of time required for AutoCAD to hatch objects in larger drawings. However, you must decide if it's necessary to use these tools by considering how long you're willing to wait for the hatching and how long AutoCAD is taking to do the job.

- **Gap tolerance** can prevent temper tantrums! (I know, designers don't have tempers, right?) When trying to hatch an open grouping of objects, AutoCAD has always run into problems (okay, it wouldn't work). But set this to a number greater than 0. If the ends/edges of the objects fall within that tolerance, AutoCAD will hatch it without grief.
- The final frame (whew!) to consider in creating hatches – **Inherit options** – gives you the opportunity to adjust the hatch origin when you inherit hatch properties.

Are you thoroughly confused? Let's try an exercise.

Do This: 18.1.1	**Hatching with a Dialog Box**

I. Open the *demo-hatch.dwg* file the C:\Steps\Lesson18 folder. The drawing looks like Figure 18.006.

II. Follow these steps.

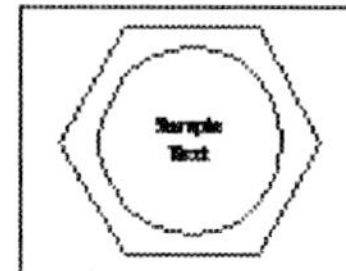

Figure 18.006

TOOLS	COMMAND SEQUENCE	STEPS
Hatch Button	**Command:** ***h***	1. Open the Hatch and Gradient dialog by entering the ***Hatch*** command – type ***hatch*** or ***h*** at the command prompt. Alternately, you can pick **Hatch** button on the Draw toolbar.
Pattern: ANSI31		2. On the **Hatch** tab, **Type and pattern** frame, pick the **Pattern** button. The Hatch Pattern Palette dialog box appears (Figure 18.007). Here you can select a pattern in one of two ways: • double-click on it; • click on the desired pattern and then pick the **OK** button. Pick the tabs and use the scroll bar to see other patterns.

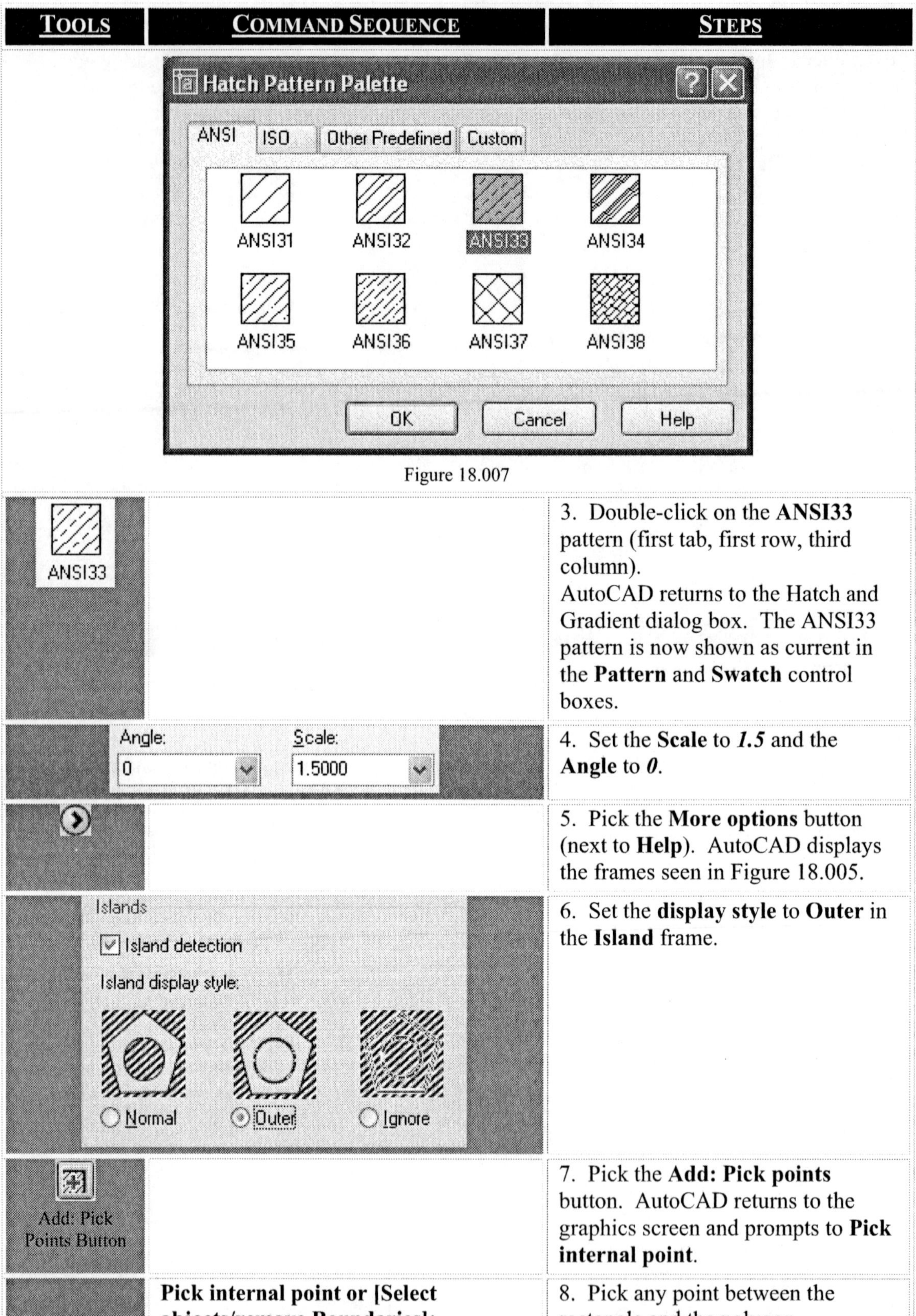

TOOLS	COMMAND SEQUENCE	STEPS
	Figure 18.007	
ANSI33		3. Double-click on the **ANSI33** pattern (first tab, first row, third column). AutoCAD returns to the Hatch and Gradient dialog box. The ANSI33 pattern is now shown as current in the **Pattern** and **Swatch** control boxes.
Angle: 0 Scale: 1.5000		4. Set the **Scale** to ***1.5*** and the **Angle** to ***0***.
		5. Pick the **More options** button (next to **Help**). AutoCAD displays the frames seen in Figure 18.005.
Islands Island detection Island display style: Normal Outer Ignore		6. Set the **display style** to **Outer** in the **Island** frame.
Add: Pick Points Button		7. Pick the **Add: Pick points** button. AutoCAD returns to the graphics screen and prompts to **Pick internal point**.
	Pick internal point or [Select objects/remove Boundaries]:	8. Pick any point between the rectangle and the polygon.

TOOLS	COMMAND SEQUENCE	STEPS
	Selecting everything... **Selecting everything visible...** **Analyzing the selected data...** **Analyzing internal islands...** **Pick internal point or [Select objects/remove Boundaries]:**	9. AutoCAD tells you what it's doing, and then repeats the prompt. Right click to display the cursor menu.
Enter Undo Last Select/Pick/Draw Clear All ✔ Pick Internal Point Select Objects Remove Boundaries Hatch Origin ▸ Normal Island Detection ✔ Outer Island Detection Ignore Island Detection Preview		10. We could return to the Boundary Hatch dialog box and pick the **Preview** button to see the hatching before applying it. But let's use the **Preview** option on the cursor menu. Your drawing looks like Figure 18.008.

Sample Text

Figure 18.008

TOOLS	COMMAND SEQUENCE	STEPS
	<Previewing the hatch> **Pick or press Esc to return to dialog or <Right-click to accept hatch>:**	11. Pick anywhere to return to the dialog box.
OK		12. Complete the command. AutoCAD returns to the graphics screen and the command prompt. Your drawing looks like Figure 18.009.

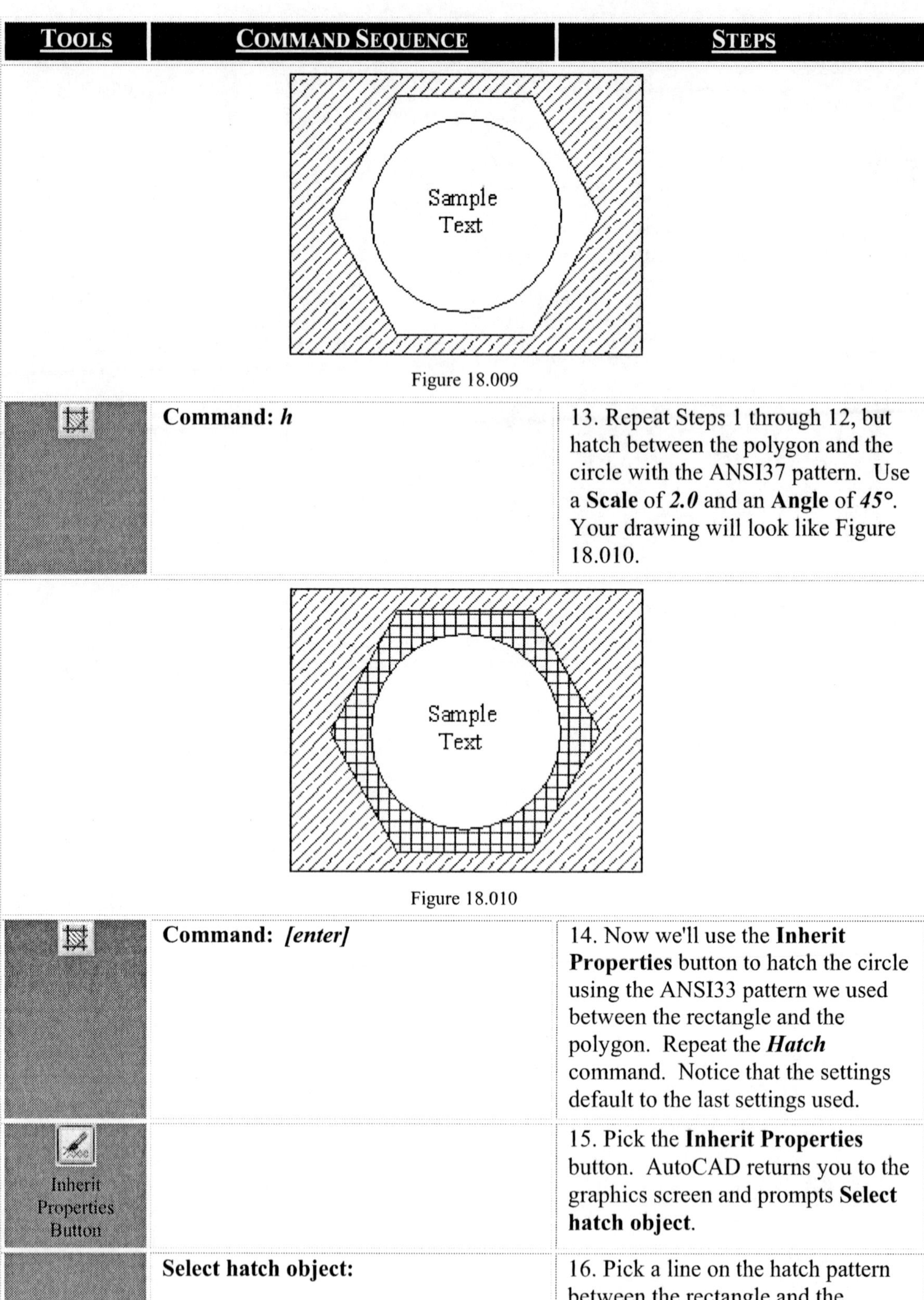

Figure 18.009

Figure 18.010

TOOLS	COMMAND SEQUENCE	STEPS
	Figure 18.009	
	Command: ***h***	13. Repeat Steps 1 through 12, but hatch between the polygon and the circle with the ANSI37 pattern. Use a **Scale** of ***2.0*** and an **Angle** of ***45°***. Your drawing will look like Figure 18.010.
	Figure 18.010	
	Command: ***[enter]***	14. Now we'll use the **Inherit Properties** button to hatch the circle using the ANSI33 pattern we used between the rectangle and the polygon. Repeat the ***Hatch*** command. Notice that the settings default to the last settings used.
Inherit Properties Button		15. Pick the **Inherit Properties** button. AutoCAD returns you to the graphics screen and prompts **Select hatch object**.
	Select hatch object:	16. Pick a line on the hatch pattern between the rectangle and the polygon.

TOOLS	COMMAND SEQUENCE	STEPS
	Inherited Properties: Name <ANSI33,_O>, Scale <1.5000>, Angle <0> **Pick internal point or [Select objects/remove Boundaries]:**	17. Pick a point inside the circle.
	Selecting everything... **Selecting everything visible...** **Analyzing the selected data...** **Analyzing internal islands...** **Pick internal point or [Select objects/remove Boundaries]:** ***[enter]***	18. Hit ***enter***. AutoCAD returns to the Boundary Hatch dialog box. Notice that the settings have changed to match those used when you created the first hatching.
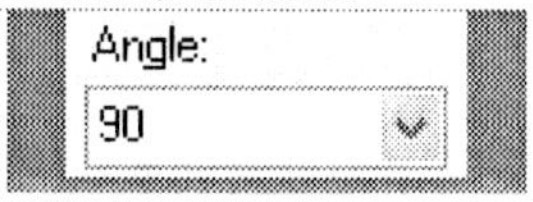 Angle: 90		19. Change the **Angle** setting to ***90°***.
 View Selections Button		20. Pick the **View Selections** button. AutoCAD returns to the graphics screen and highlights the boundaries you selected in the previous step.
	<Hit enter or right-click to return to the dialog>	21. Hit ***enter*** (or right-click) to return to the dialog box.
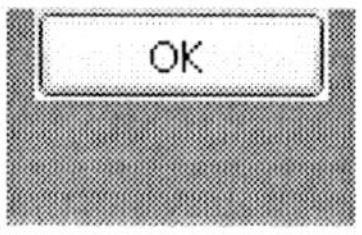 OK		22. **Preview** the hatching if you wish, then **OK** it. Your drawing looks like Figure 18.011.
	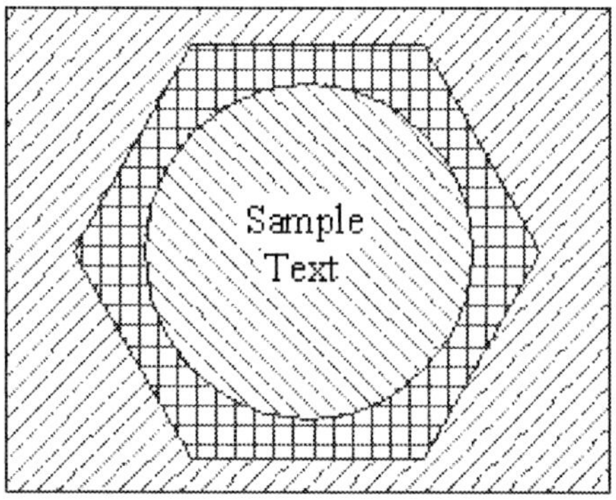 Sample Text Figure 18.011	
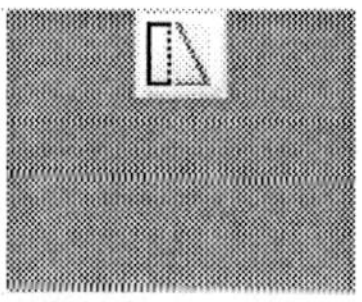	**Command:** ***s***	22. Now for a real treat, try stretching the rectangle or the polygon. Note the effects of *Associative* hatching!
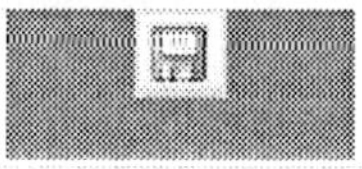	**Command:** ***qsave***	23. Undo the ***Stretch*** command and save the drawing.

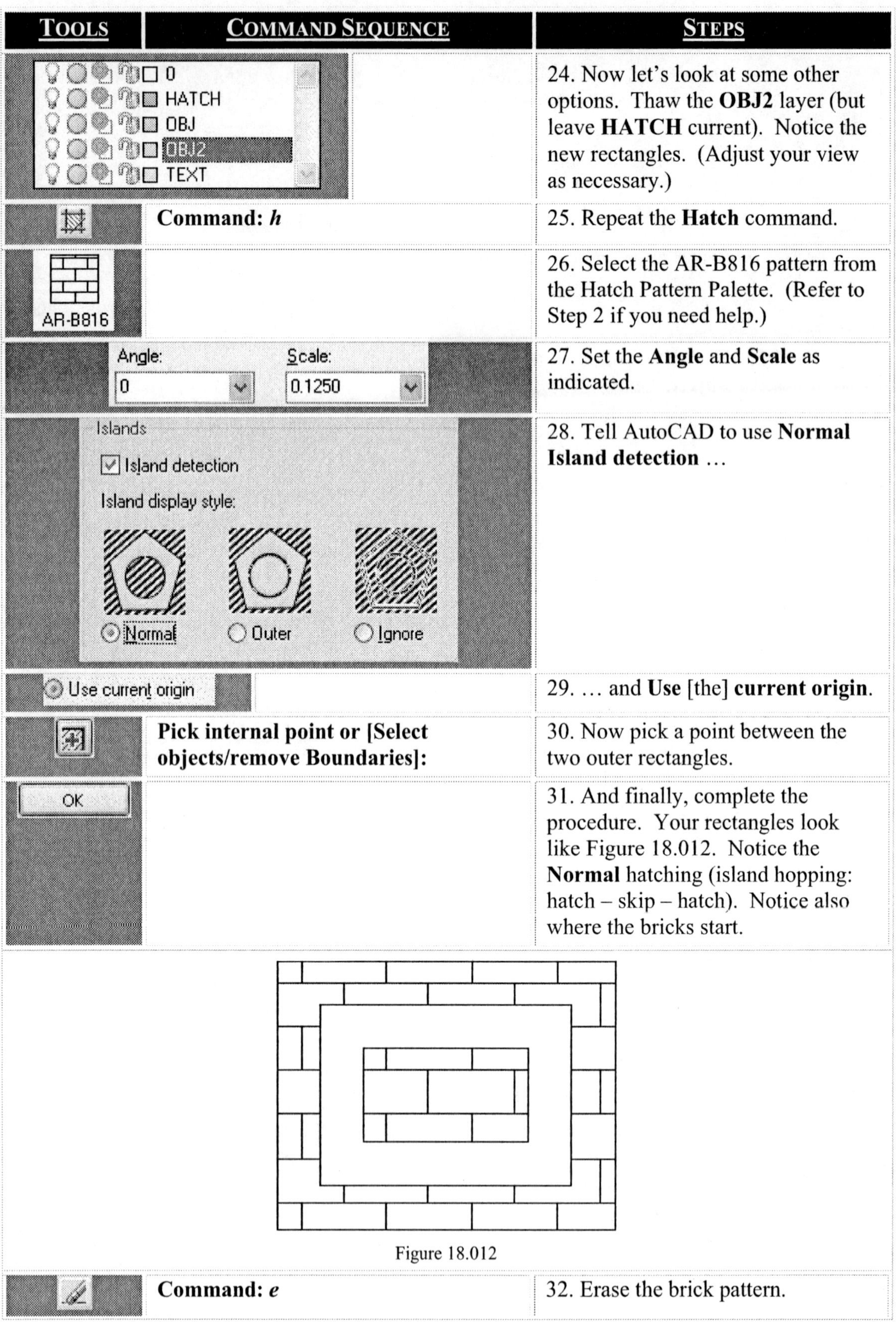

Tools	Command Sequence	Steps
0, HATCH, OBJ, OBJ2, TEXT		24. Now let's look at some other options. Thaw the **OBJ2** layer (but leave **HATCH** current). Notice the new rectangles. (Adjust your view as necessary.)
	Command: ***h***	25. Repeat the **Hatch** command.
AR-B816		26. Select the AR-B816 pattern from the Hatch Pattern Palette. (Refer to Step 2 if you need help.)
Angle: 0 Scale: 0.1250		27. Set the **Angle** and **Scale** as indicated.
Islands; Island detection; Island display style: Normal, Outer, Ignore		28. Tell AutoCAD to use **Normal Island detection** …
Use current origin		29. … and **Use** [the] **current origin**.
	Pick internal point or [Select objects/remove Boundaries]:	30. Now pick a point between the two outer rectangles.
OK		31. And finally, complete the procedure. Your rectangles look like Figure 18.012. Notice the **Normal** hatching (island hopping: hatch – skip – hatch). Notice also where the bricks start.

Figure 18.012

Tools	Command Sequence	Steps
	Command: ***e***	32. Erase the brick pattern.

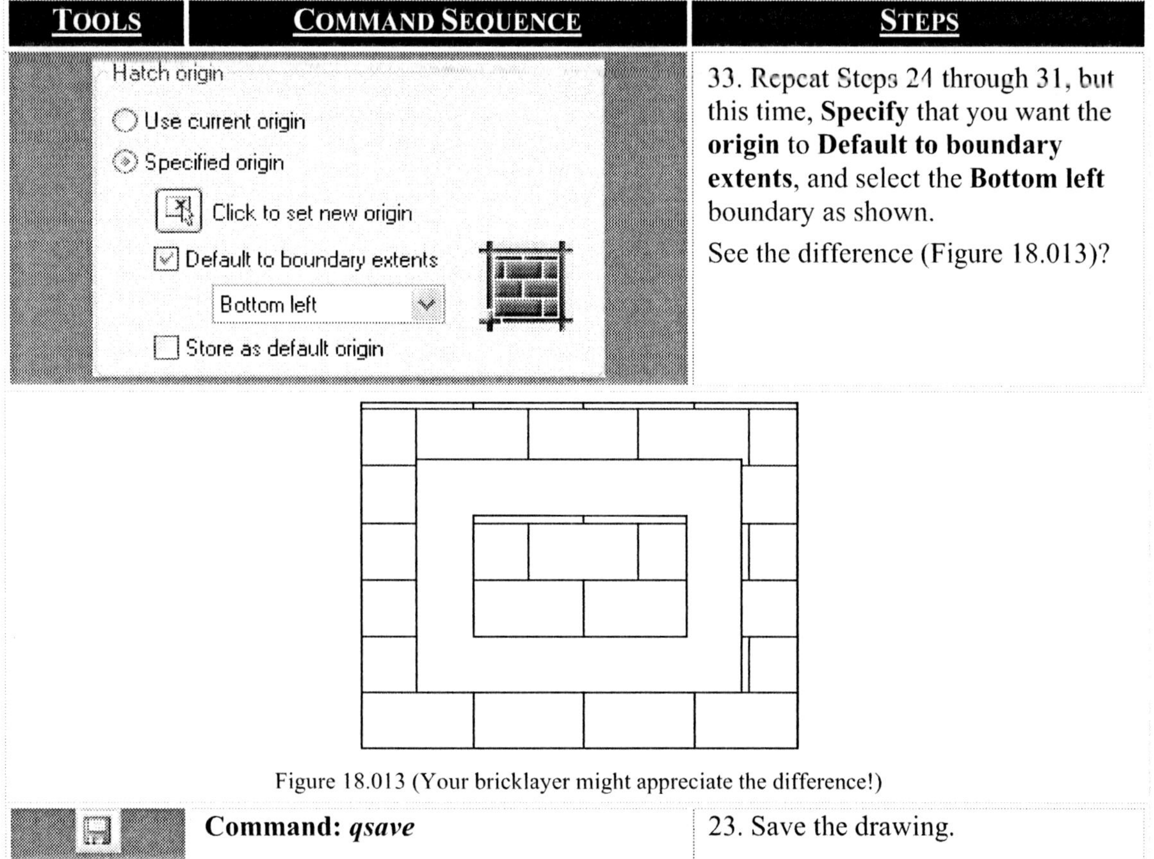

Tools	Command Sequence	Steps
	Hatch origin Use current origin Specified origin Click to set new origin Default to boundary extents Bottom left Store as default origin	33. Repeat Steps 24 through 31, but this time, **Specify** that you want the **origin** to **Default to boundary extents**, and select the **Bottom left** boundary as shown. See the difference (Figure 18.013)?
	Figure 18.013 (Your bricklayer might appreciate the difference!)	
	Command: *qsave*	23. Save the drawing.

Those familiar with the *One Step at a Time* series might recognize that I've removed instructions for the command line approach to the ***Hatch*** command. Some will welcome the removal; others may not. There are few things that can be done on the command line that you can't do better with the dialog box, but those who know how to use it will miss the direct hatch option (available only on the command line). For those of you interested in this tool, I'll post the appropriate sections of the '05 text on the web (www.uneedcad.com/2006/Files).

18.2 Editing Hatched Areas

We have a couple other ways to apply hatching, but before we look at them, let's take a quick look at editing the pattern once you've applied it. (This may seem a bit out of order, but it'll help in later explanations.)

Remember how the ***DDEdit*** command, when used on MText, returned you to the Multiline Text Editor? Once there, editing the text was as easy – and followed the same rules and procedures – as creating the text. The ***Hatchedit*** command works the same way on hatching. Simply enter the command and select the hatch pattern to be edited. AutoCAD returns you to the Hatch and Gradient dialog box (but calls it the Hatchedit dialog box). Then you can proceed as though you were creating the hatching for the first time.

Let's try it.

> ***HE*** will also access the ***Hatchedit*** command. Alternately, you can pick **Hatch** on the Modify pull-down menu (*Modify – Object – Hatch*), pick the **Hatch** button on the Modify II toolbar, or select the hatching to be edited and then select **Hatch Edit** from the cursor menu. Still too complicated? You can also double-click on the hatching you want to edit!

Do This: 18.2.1	Hatch Editing

I. Be sure you're still in the *demo-hatch.dwg* file in the C:\Steps\Lesson18 folder. If not, please open it now.

II. Follow these steps.

TOOLS	COMMAND SEQUENCE	STEPS
Edit Hatch Button	**Command: *he***	1. Enter the ***Hatchedit*** command.
		2. Select the hatching inside the circle. AutoCAD presents the Hatch Edit dialog box (Figure 18.014). Notice that the settings reflect those used to create the pattern.

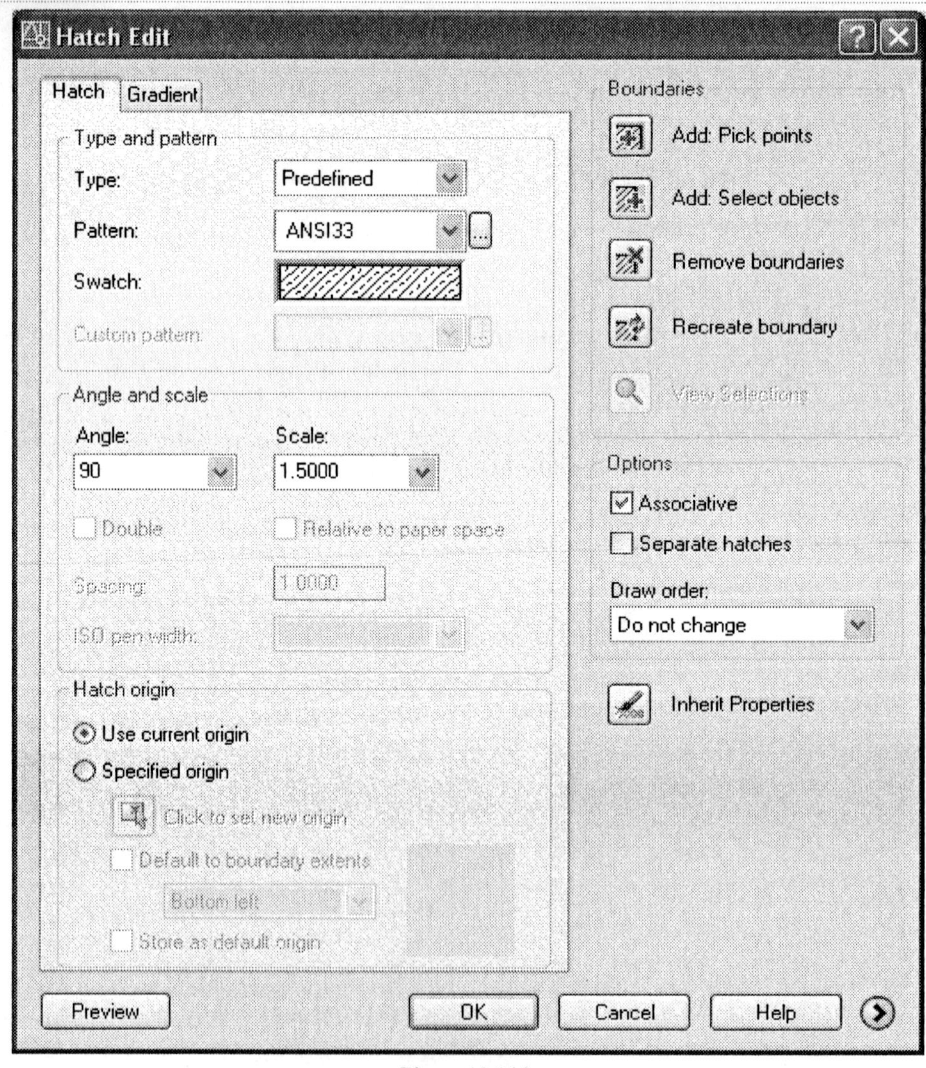

Figure 18.014

Tools	Command Sequence	Steps
Gradient		3. Pick the **Gradient** tab.
		4. Select the lower left gradient fill pattern.
OK		5. Pick the **OK** button. AutoCAD returns to the graphics screen and the drawing now looks like Figure 18.015.

Sample Text

Figure 18.015

	Command: ***qsave***	6. Save and close the drawing.

18.3 Drag-and-Drop Hatching – Using the ADC and Tool Palettes to Hatch

18.3.1 Using the ADC to Hatch

You've seen how to drag-and-drop layers into a drawing using the AutoCAD Design Center (Lesson 6). Although the procedure is slightly different, the same principle applies to drag-and-drop hatching. The difference in the procedures results from having different sources from which you mine desired objects. You mine layers from existing drawings or templates; you mine hatch patterns from a pattern file (a file with a .pat extension).

What exactly does drag-and-drop mean and how do I do it?

Drag-and-drop means to pick something up (with your mouse), carry it somewhere, and drop it into place.

The term *drag-and-drop* is actually quite illustrative of the procedure. To pick up the object to be dragged, place your cursor over it. Pick (generally with the left mouse button, but in AutoCAD hatching procedures, you'll use the right mouse button more often than the left) and *hold the button down.* Move the cursor to the target area (you'll notice that you're dragging the object you picked up) and release the button. That's really all there is to drag-and-drop. If you've used the left mouse button for your drag-and-drop procedure, the object will be placed without further ado. If you've used the right mouse button, AutoCAD will ask you what to do by presenting a cursor menu like that shown in Figure 18.016.

You also have more options when mining hatch patterns via the ADC as indicated in the right-click cursor menu (Figure 18.016). Let's consider these.

- The **Apply Hatch** option behaves as if you had performed the drag-and-drop with the left mouse button (see the previous insert).
- **Apply and Edit Hatch** applies the hatch pattern as if you'd used the **Add: Pick points** button in the Hatch and Gradient dialog box. It then immediately opens the Hatch Edit dialog box where you can adjust the settings as you did in our last exercise.

Apply Hatch
Apply and Edit Hatch...
Apply Hatch to Multiple Objects
BHATCH...
Cancel

Figure 18.016

- **Apply Hatch to Multiple Objects** allows you to place the hatch pattern as if you'd used the **Add: Pick points** button – picking as many different locations as you like – except that each location will contain individual hatch patterns (not a single pattern in multiple areas). Hit the ESC key on your keyboard to complete this procedure.
- The **BHatch** option calls the Hatch and Gradient dialog box with the selected pattern shown in the **Pattern** control box. This allows you to insert the hatch with whatever settings you wish.

> The last option doesn't appear on the cursor menu. You can drag-and-drop using the left mouse button just as drag-and-drop procedures work in most other applications. When you do this, AutoCAD hatches with the selected pattern as if you had used the **Add: Pick Points** button in the Boundary Hatch dialog box, using the last scale and angle settings entered in the dialog box or on the command line.

Let's see how some of these options work in an exercise.

Do This: 18.3.1.1	**Drag-and-Drop Hatching with the ADC**

I. Open the *d&d-hatch.dwg* file the C:\Steps\Lesson18 folder. It looks like Figure 18.017.

II. Open the AutoCAD Design Center.

III. Follow these steps.

Figure 18.017

TOOLS	COMMAND SEQUENCE	STEPS
		1. (Refer to Figure 18.018). Scroll to the *\AutoCAD 2006\UserDataCache\Support\acad.pat* file as indicated. This file contains the default hatch patterns that ship with AutoCAD. Notice the list on the right.

TOOLS	COMMAND SEQUENCE	STEPS

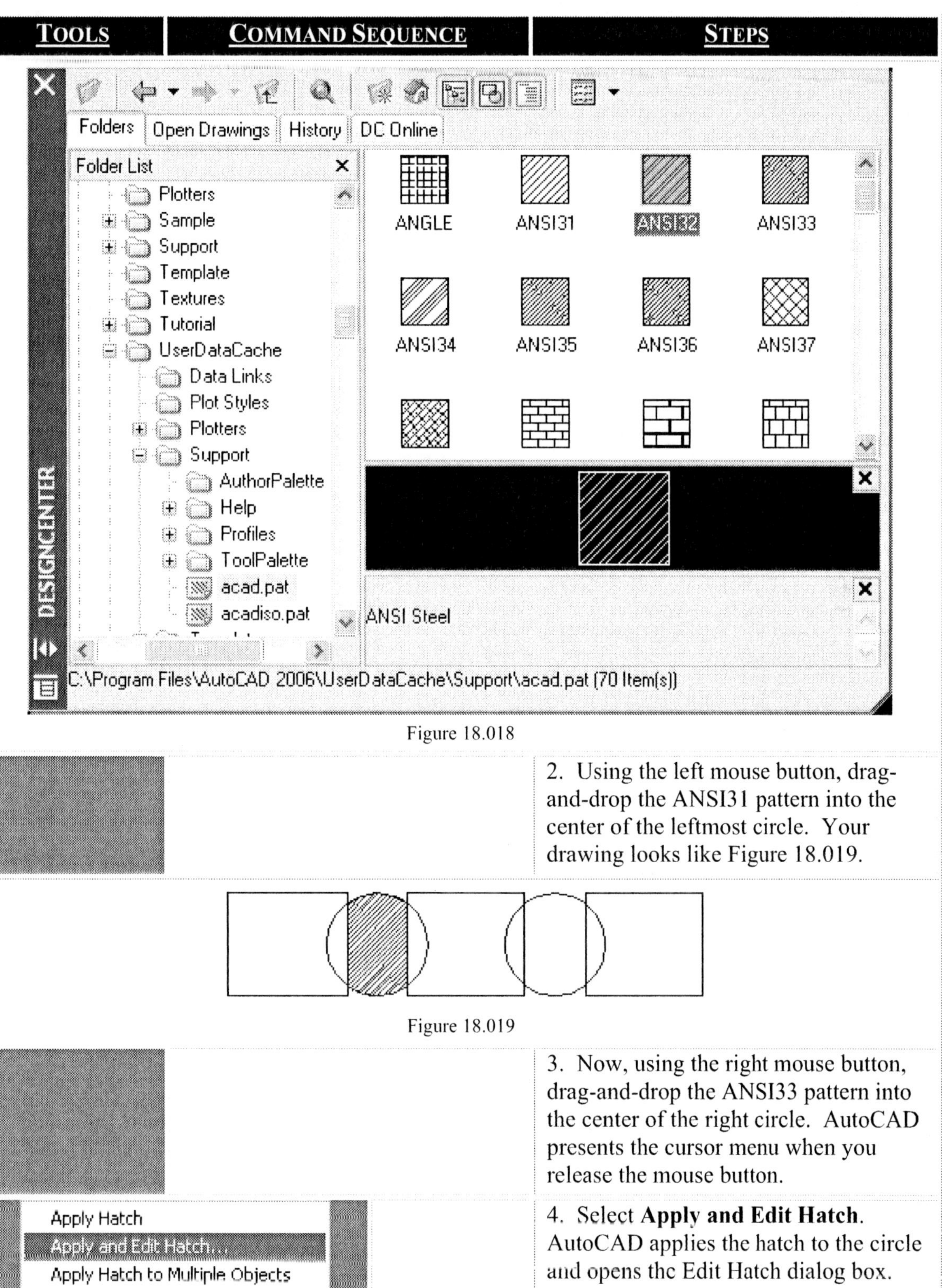

Figure 18.018

2. Using the left mouse button, drag-and-drop the ANSI31 pattern into the center of the leftmost circle. Your drawing looks like Figure 18.019.

Figure 18.019

3. Now, using the right mouse button, drag-and-drop the ANSI33 pattern into the center of the right circle. AutoCAD presents the cursor menu when you release the mouse button.

4. Select **Apply and Edit Hatch**. AutoCAD applies the hatch to the circle and opens the Edit Hatch dialog box.

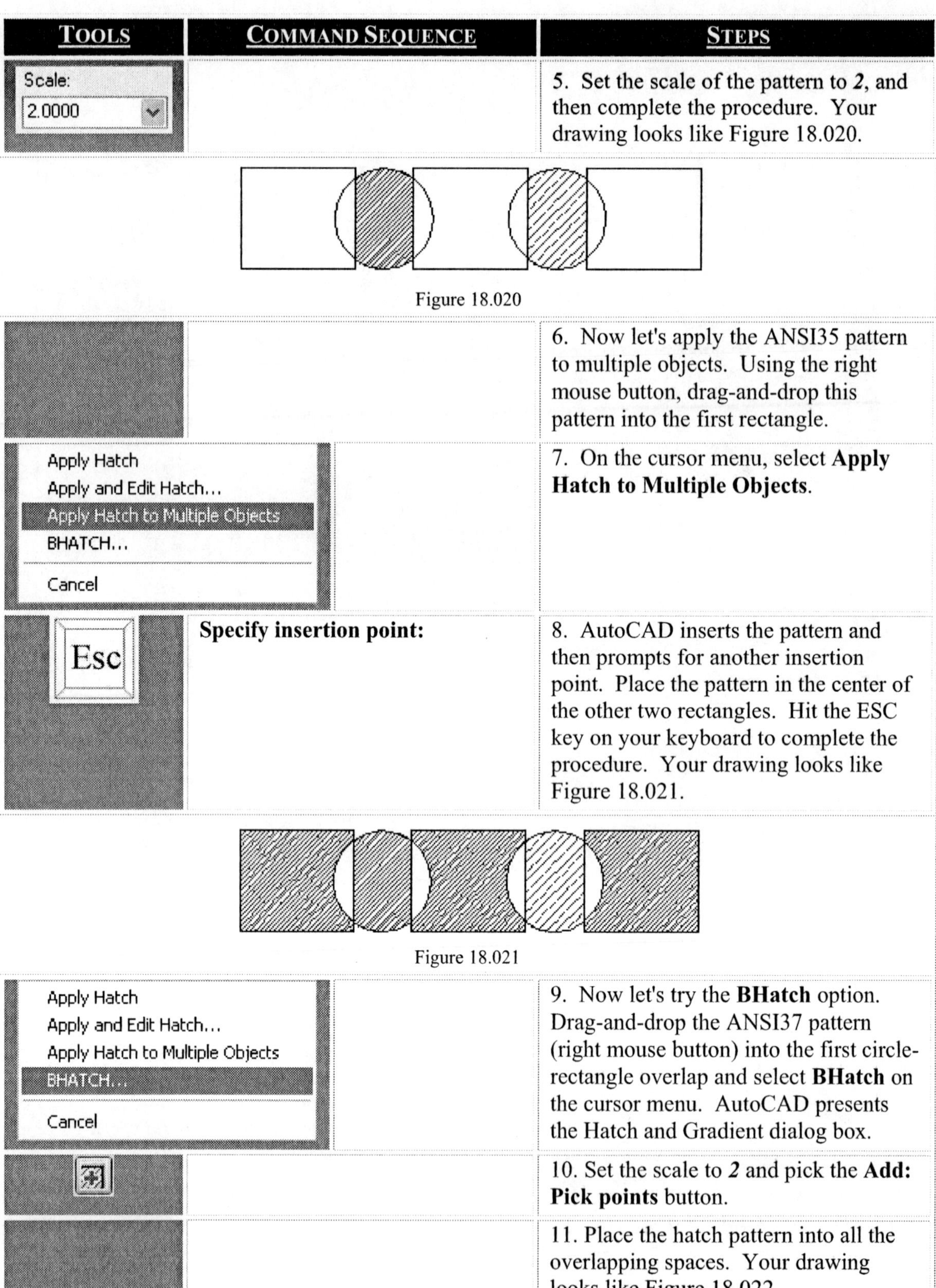

TOOLS	COMMAND SEQUENCE	STEPS
Scale: 2.0000		5. Set the scale of the pattern to ***2***, and then complete the procedure. Your drawing looks like Figure 18.020.
	Figure 18.020	
		6. Now let's apply the ANSI35 pattern to multiple objects. Using the right mouse button, drag-and-drop this pattern into the first rectangle.
Apply Hatch Apply and Edit Hatch... Apply Hatch to Multiple Objects BHATCH... Cancel		7. On the cursor menu, select **Apply Hatch to Multiple Objects**.
Esc	**Specify insertion point:**	8. AutoCAD inserts the pattern and then prompts for another insertion point. Place the pattern in the center of the other two rectangles. Hit the ESC key on your keyboard to complete the procedure. Your drawing looks like Figure 18.021.
	Figure 18.021	
Apply Hatch Apply and Edit Hatch... Apply Hatch to Multiple Objects BHATCH... Cancel		9. Now let's try the **BHatch** option. Drag-and-drop the ANSI37 pattern (right mouse button) into the first circle-rectangle overlap and select **BHatch** on the cursor menu. AutoCAD presents the Hatch and Gradient dialog box.
		10. Set the scale to ***2*** and pick the **Add: Pick points** button.
		11. Place the hatch pattern into all the overlapping spaces. Your drawing looks like Figure 18.022.

TOOLS	COMMAND SEQUENCE	STEPS
	Figure 18.022	
		12. Remember that you placed multiple patterns using the **Apply to Multiple Objects** option of the cursor menu in Steps 7 and 8. These are the patterns in the rectangles. You also placed several patterns at once in Step 11. Try to erase an individual pattern in a rectangle. Try to erase an individual in one of the overlapping spaces. Notice that the drag-and-drop procedure created separate pattern definitions that can be treated as individual objects. The Hatch and Gradient dialog box method did not.
	Command: ***e***	13. Erase the hatch patterns and close the ADC, but don't exit the drawing.

18.3.2 Using Tool Palettes to Hatch

Using tool palettes is a bit easier, although they're not radically different from the ADC methods for applying hatch patterns. The most obvious difference is that the patterns are already visible without having to scroll around looking for the pattern (.pat) file.

But a more important difference lies in the cursor menus. Whereas the ADC allows a right click drag-and-drop procedure to call a cursor menu with the various procedural options, the tool palettes has no right-click procedure … no application cursor menus. The tool palette procedure relies on the Properties palette to modify hatch pattern definitions before you insert them, or the ***Hatchedit*** command to modify patterns after they've been inserted.

Let's see how this works.

Do This: 18.3.2.1 Drag-and-Drop Hatching with Tool Palettes

I. Be sure you're still in the *d&d-hatch.dwg* file the C:\Steps\Lesson18 folder. If not, please open it now.

II. Open the Tool Palettes.

III. Follow these steps.

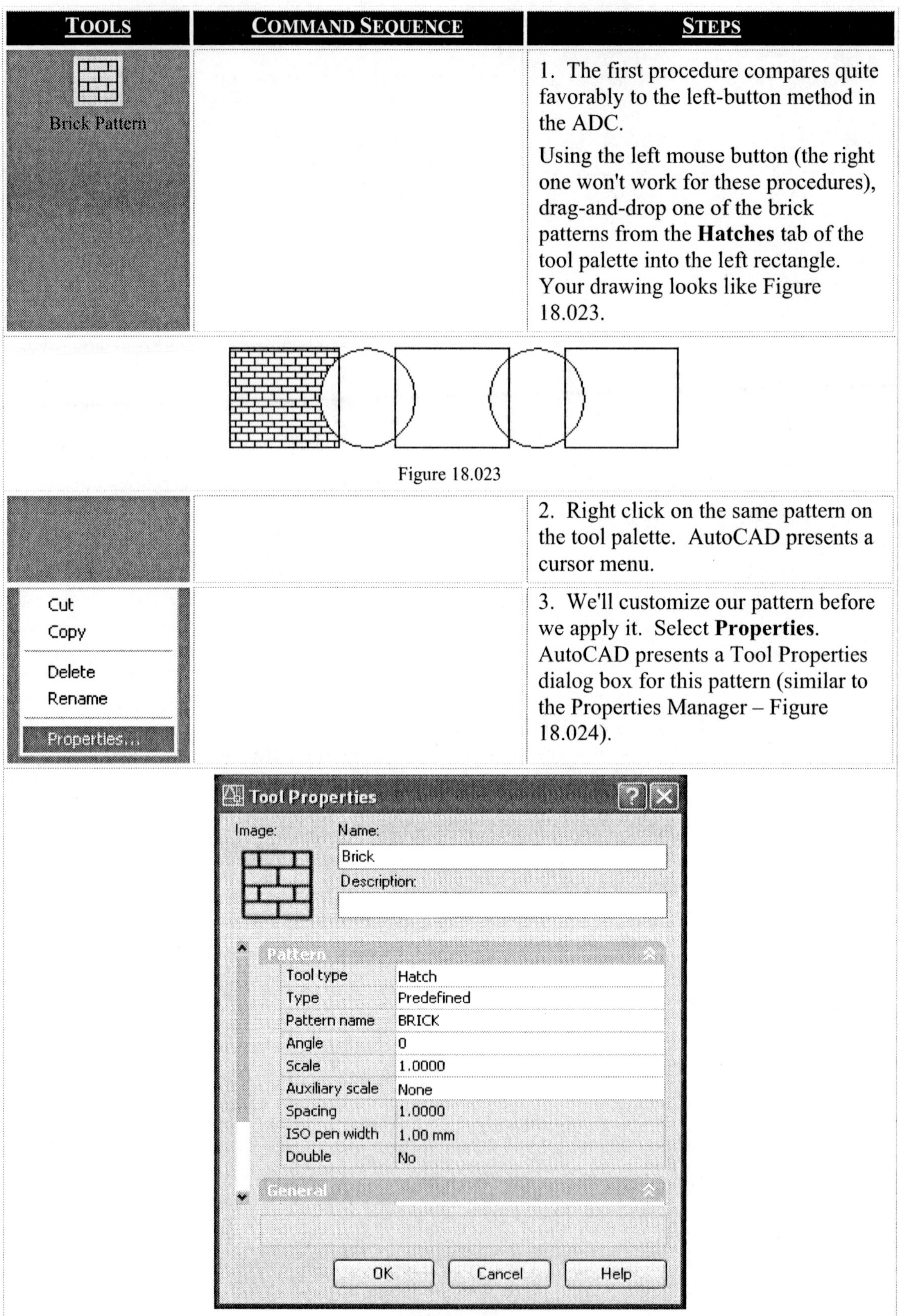

TOOLS	COMMAND SEQUENCE	STEPS
Brick Pattern		1. The first procedure compares quite favorably to the left-button method in the ADC. Using the left mouse button (the right one won't work for these procedures), drag-and-drop one of the brick patterns from the **Hatches** tab of the tool palette into the left rectangle. Your drawing looks like Figure 18.023.
	Figure 18.023	
		2. Right click on the same pattern on the tool palette. AutoCAD presents a cursor menu.
Cut Copy Delete Rename Properties...		3. We'll customize our pattern before we apply it. Select **Properties**. AutoCAD presents a Tool Properties dialog box for this pattern (similar to the Properties Manager – Figure 18.024).
	Figure 18.024	

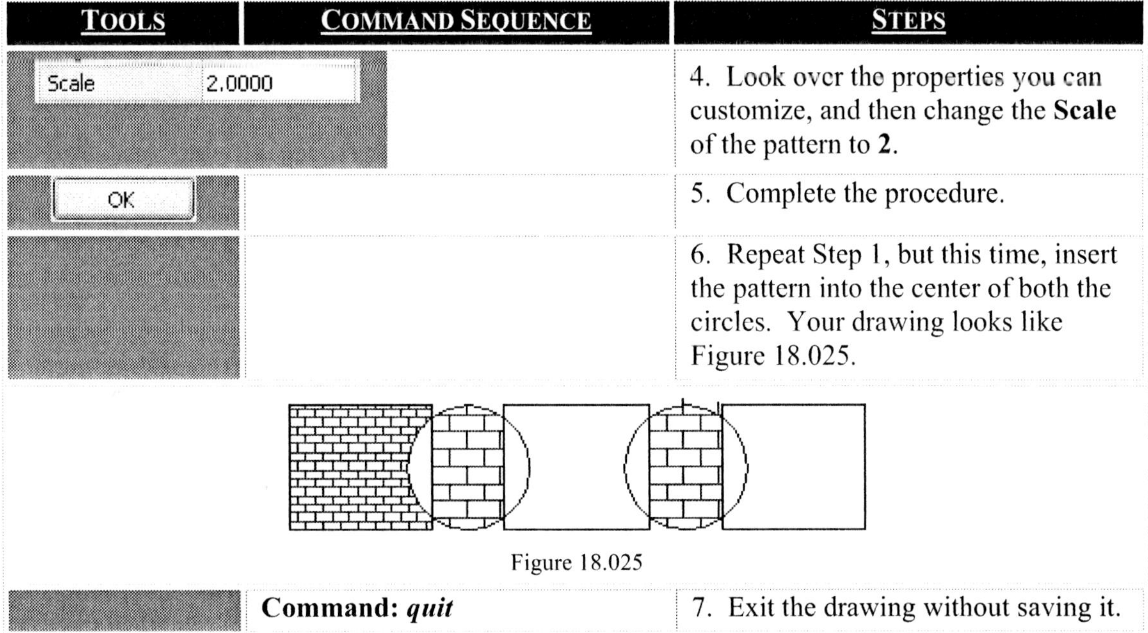

TOOLS	COMMAND SEQUENCE	STEPS
Scale 2.0000		4. Look over the properties you can customize, and then change the **Scale** of the pattern to **2**.
OK		5. Complete the procedure.
		6. Repeat Step 1, but this time, insert the pattern into the center of both the circles. Your drawing looks like Figure 18.025.
	Figure 18.025	
	Command: *quit*	7. Exit the drawing without saving it.

So which method do you prefer? Obviously, you prefer the easiest!

18.4 Extra Steps

Experiment with the command line approach to the ***Hatch*** command. Begin by placing a dash before the command (***-hatch***). (For a more detailed explanation of the command line approach, download *CmdLineHatch* from www.uneedcad.com/2006/Files.

18.5 What Have We Learned?

Classroom acquired skills are to the mind what paint is to pottery – nothing but surface fluff that fades and disappears with the passing of time. For the skills to become actual knowledge, they must be tempered into the mind's clay through the repeated pounding of experience.

PRACTICE PRACTICE PRACTICE

Anonymous

Items covered in this lesson include:

- *Hatching Tools:*
  - ***Hatch***
  - ***HatchEdit***
  - ***Drag and Drop Hatching***

By now you should be growing more comfortable with AutoCAD procedures and routines. You've passed beyond basic drawing and can create more complex objects in a few keystrokes or mouse picks. The one thing you still need – and need plenty of – is practice!

Work through the exercises at the end of this lesson. They may take a bit longer than earlier exercises, but that's because the drawings are becoming more complex. Additionally, I'm expecting more from you while providing less.

Our next two lessons will teach you to use the first tools that make AutoCAD something more than a very expensive drafting tool. We'll cover blocks in Lesson 19; we'll attach *information* to blocks in Lesson 20.

18.6 Exercises

1. Use the following information to create the drawing in Figure 18.029. Save the drawing as *MyTee* in the C:\Steps\Lesson18 folder.
   1.1. Layer Information (at right).
   1.2. Limits: 0,0 to 17,11
   1.3. Grid spacing = 1/4"
   1.4. Text sizes = 3/8", 1/4", 3/16", 1/8"
   1.5. Font: Times New Roman
   1.6. Hatching information
      1.6.1. Pattern = ANSI32
      1.6.2. Scale = 1"
      1.6.3. Angle = 0

LAYER NAME	COLOR	LINETYPE
0	7 (white)	Continuous
Border	5 (blue)	Continuous
Cl	3 (green)	Center
Dim	5 (blue)	Continuous
Hatch	32	Continuous
Marker	6 (magenta)	Continuous
Ob	1 (red)	Continuous
Text	6 (magenta)	Continuous

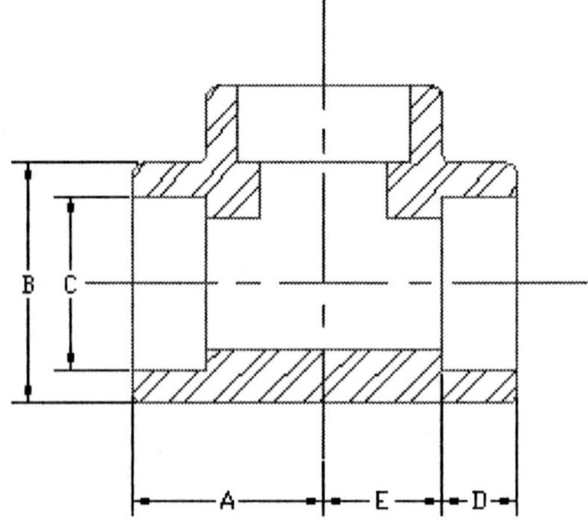

Figure 18.026

Dimensions (Inches)										
Nominal Pipe Size	1/8	1/4	1/2	3/4	1	1 1/4	1 1/2	2	2 1/2	3
A	7/8	7/8	1 1/8	1 5/16	1 1/2	1 3/4	2	2 3/8	3	3 3/8
B	29/32	29/32	1 5/16	1 9/16	1 3/4	2 7/32	2 1/2	3 1/32	3 5/8	4 5/16
C	.420	.555	.850	1.08	1.340	1.680	2	2.406	2.906	3.535
D	7/16	7/16	1/2	9/16	5/8	11/16	3/4	7/8	1 3/8	1 1/8
E	7/16	7/16	5/8	3/4	7/8	1 1/16	1 1/4	1 1/2	1 5/8	2 1/4

Figure 18.027

North Harris College				
Sample Piping Standard: Socket Weld Tee				
Drawn By: T. Jefferson		Checked By: B. Franklin		Project No.: 1001-A1A
Date: June 6, 1944	Scale: NTS		Approval: FDR	Sht: 1 of: 15

Figure 18.028

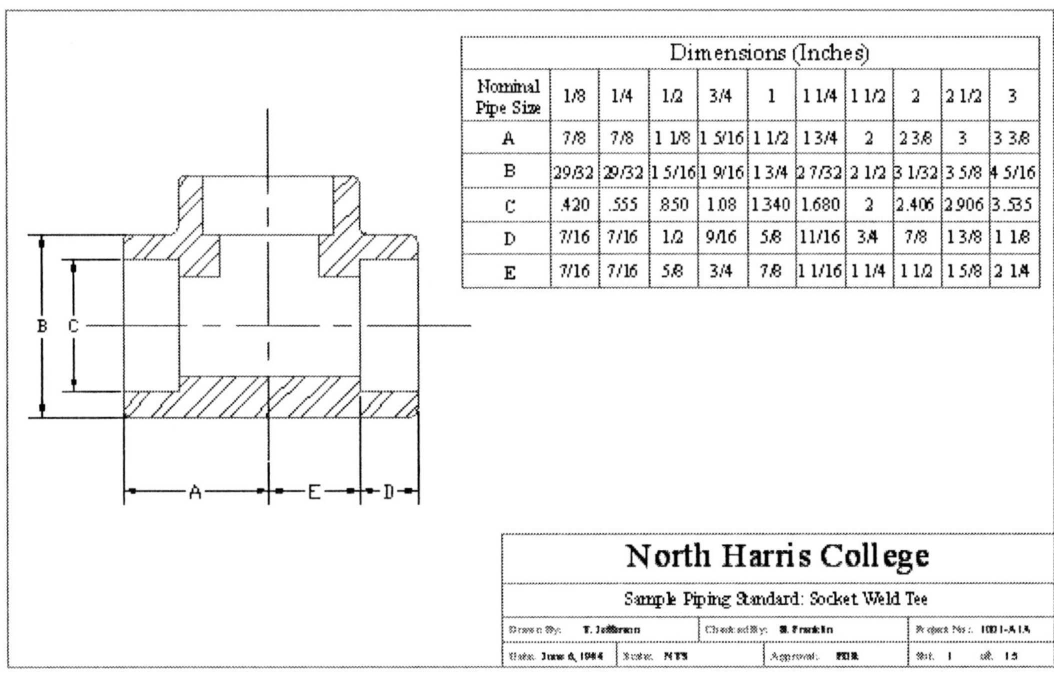

Dimensions (Inches)										
Nominal Pipe Size	1/8	1/4	1/2	3/4	1	1 1/4	1 1/2	2	2 1/2	3
A	7/8	7/8	1 1/8	1 5/16	1 1/2	1 3/4	2	2 3/8	3	3 3/8
B	29/32	29/32	1 5/16	1 9/16	1 3/4	2 7/32	2 1/2	3 1/32	3 5/8	4 5/16
C	.420	.555	.850	1.08	1.340	1.680	2	2.406	2.906	3.535
D	7/16	7/16	1/2	9/16	5/8	11/16	3/4	7/8	1 3/8	1 1/8
E	7/16	7/16	5/8	3/4	7/8	1 1/16	1 1/4	1 1/2	1 5/8	2 1/4

Figure 18.029

2. Start a new drawing from scratch.
   2.1. Create the following setup:
      2.1.1. Use a 1½"=1'-0" scale on an A-size sheet of paper (8½x11)
      2.1.2. Grid: 1" (snap as needed)
      2.1.3. The layers in the table.
   2.2. Use this information for the Grade hatching:
      Pattern: EARTH
      Scale: 8.0000
      Angle: 45
   2.3. Use this information for the sand hatching:
      Pattern: AR-SAND
      Scale: 0.5000
      Angle: 0

LAYER NAME	COLOR	LINETYPE
0	7 (white)	Continuous
Border	5 (blue)	Continuous
Cl	6 (magenta)	Center2
Dim	2 (yellow)	Continuous
Const	1 (red)	Continuous
Hidden	42	Hidden
Obj1	4 (cyan)	Continuous
Obj2	3 (green)	Continuous
Obj3	1 (red)	Continuous
Obj4	6 (magenta)	Continuous
Text	2 (yellow)	Continuous

2.4. Use the Times New Roman font. Large text should plot at ¼"; small text should plot at 1/8".

2.5. Create the Exterior Slab drawing shown in Figure 18.030. Save it as *MySlab* in the C:\Steps\Lesson18 folder.

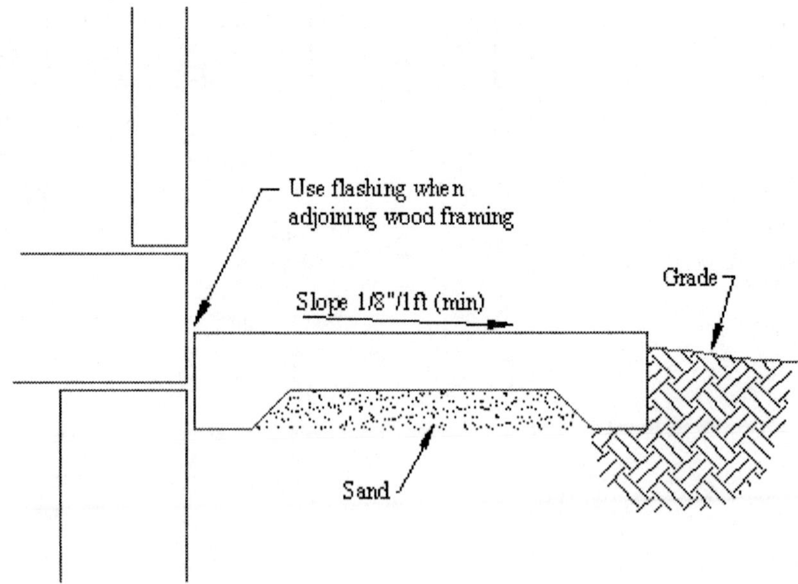

Exterior Slab

Figure 18.030: Exterior Slab

3. Start a new drawing from scratch. Using the same information you used in the *Exterior Slab* drawing in Exercise 2, create the *Concrete Pier Footing* drawing in Figure 18.031.

   3.1. Use this information to hatch the concrete:

   Pattern: AR-CONC

   Scale: 0.5000

   Angle: 0

   3.2. Save the drawing as *MyFooting* in the C:\Steps\Lesson18 folder.

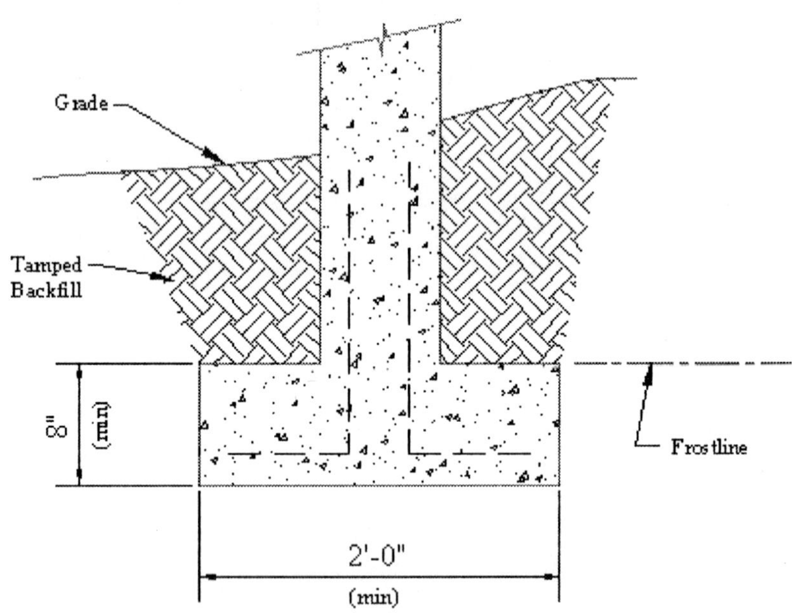

Concrete Pier Footing

Figure 18.031: Concrete Pier Footing

4. Open the *Cabin-hatch.dwg* file in the C:\Steps\Lesson18 folder. Use the following information to complete the drawing. The completed elevations are shown in Figures 18.032 & 18.033. (See if you can add a chimney on your own.)

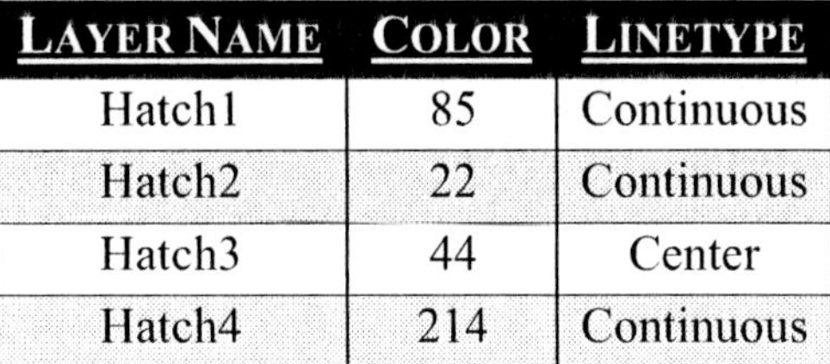

Layer Name	Color	Linetype
Hatch1	85	Continuous
Hatch2	22	Continuous
Hatch3	44	Center
Hatch4	214	Continuous

4.1. Create the additional layers shown.

4.2. Hatching information:

4.2.1. Doors:
Pattern: AR-RROOF
Scale = ¼"
Angle = 90°
Layer = Hatch3

4.2.2. Roof:
Pattern: AR-RSHKE
Scale = 1/16"
Angle = 0°
Layer = Hatch3

4.2.3. Facade:
Pattern: AR-BRELM
Scale = 1/8"
Angle = 0°
Layer = Hatch2

4.2.4. Curtains:
Pattern: STARS
Scale = 1"
Angle = 90°
Layer = Hatch4

4.2.5. Gables:
Pattern: ANSI31
Scale = 1"
Angle = 45°
Layer = Hatch2

4.2.6. Doorknobs are on the Hatch1 layer.

Figure 18.032: Front Elevation

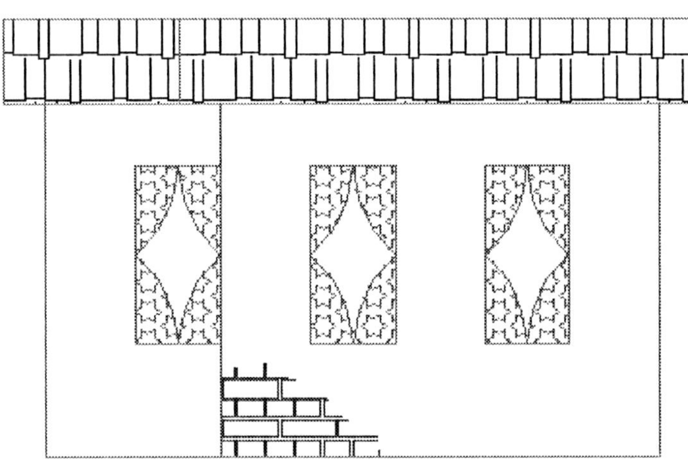

Figure 18.033: Side Elevation

5. Using what you've learned, create the drawings in Figures 18.034 to 18.039. The grid, where shown, is 2".

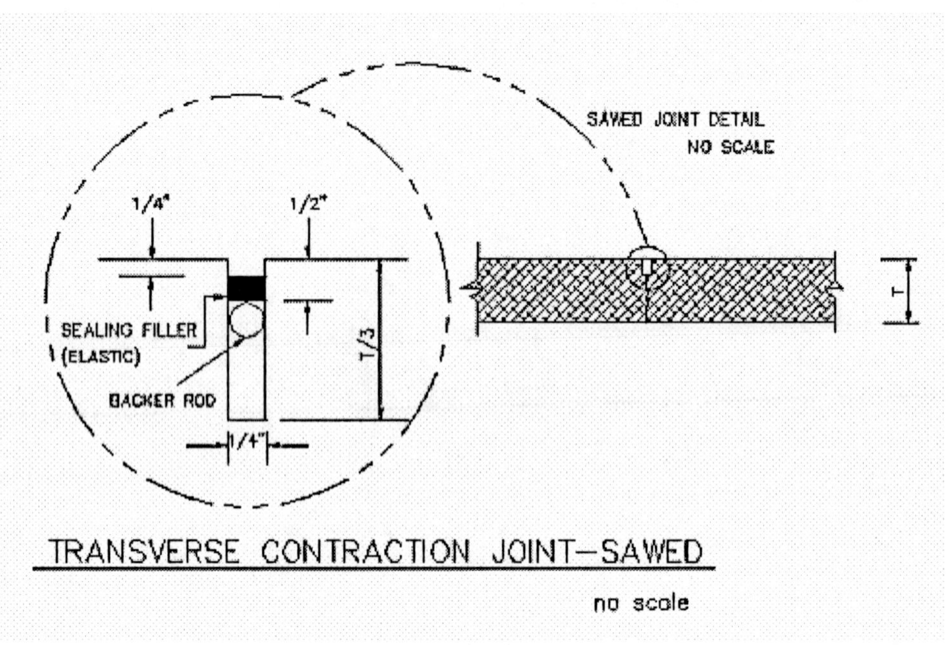

Figure 18.034: Transverse Contraction Joint

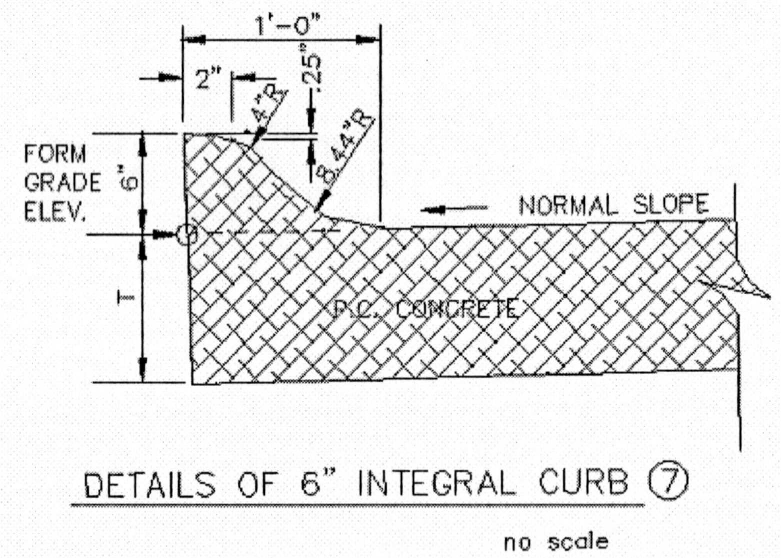

Figure 18.035: Integral Curb

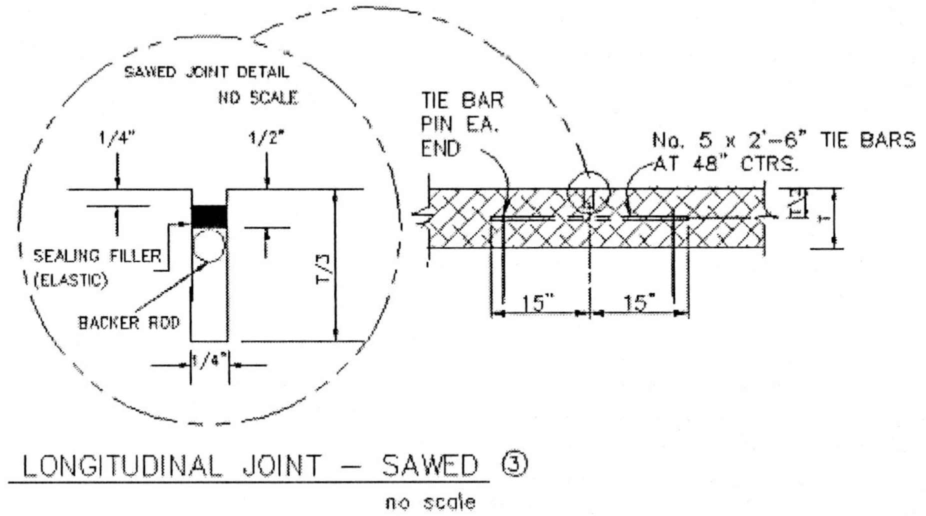

Figure 18.036: Longitudinal Joint

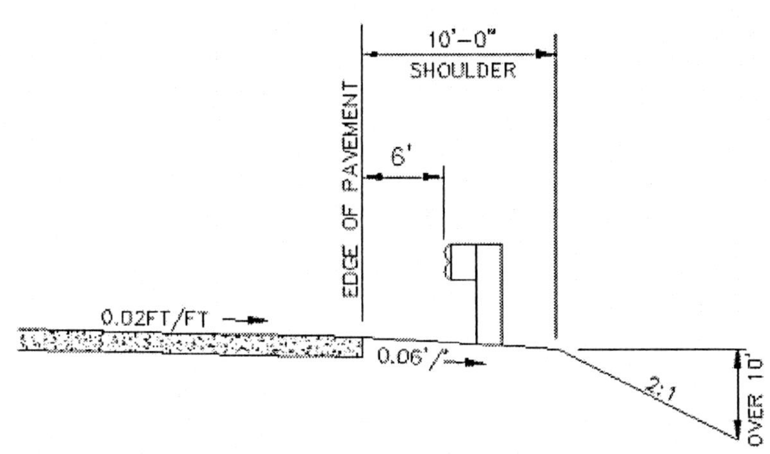

Figure 18.037: Guardrail Detail

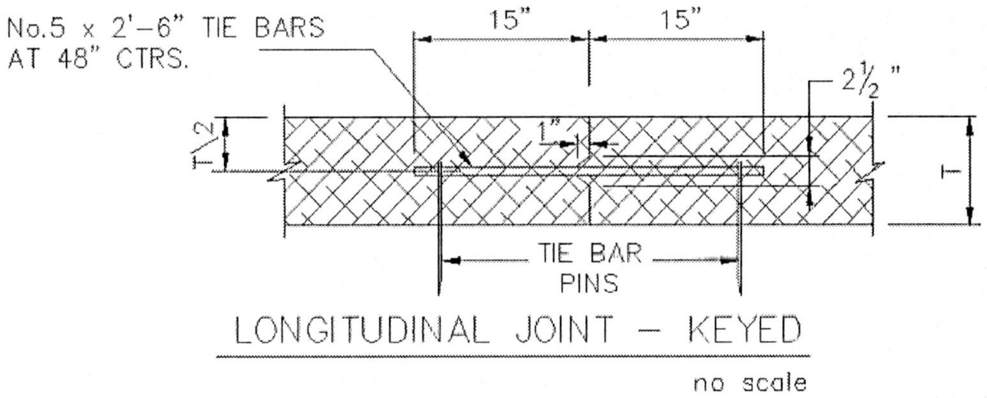

Figure 18.038: Longitudinal Joint

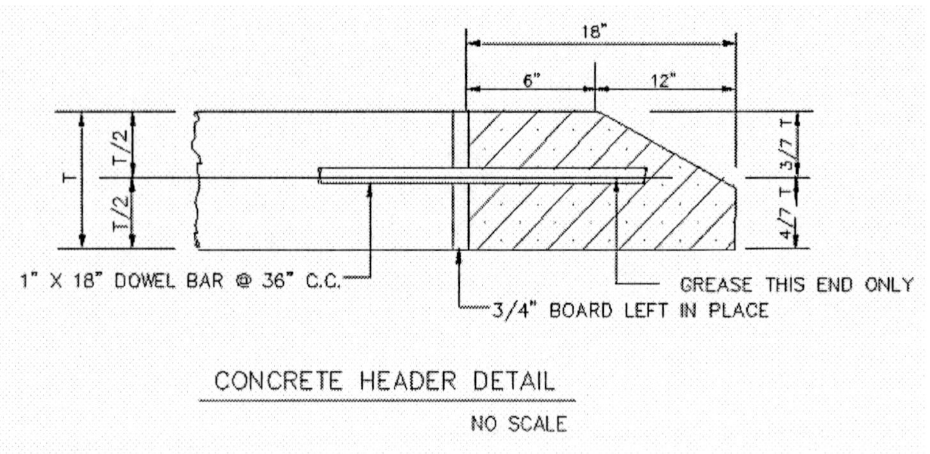

Figure 18.039: Concrete Header

6. Using what you've learned, create the drawing shown in Fig. 18.040.

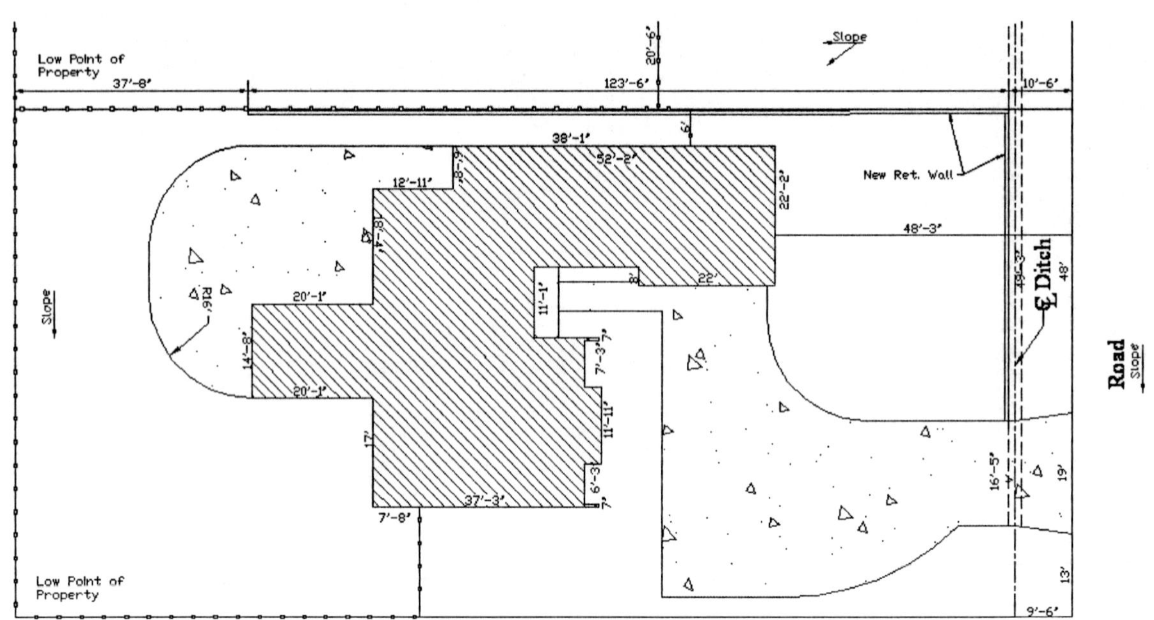

Fig. 18.040: Plot Plan

18.7 For Web-Based Review Questions, visit: http://www.uneedcad.com/2006/Files/06R18.pdf

Lesson 19

Following this lesson, you will:

- ✓ *Know how to create and manipulate Groups*
- ✓ *Know how to use blocks in a drawing*
  - o *The **Block** command*
  - o *The **WBlock** command*
  - o *The **Insert** Command*
- ✓ *Know how to create libraries of blocked objects*
- ✓ *Know how to share blocks between drawings using the AutoCAD Design Center and Tool Palettes*

Many as One – Groups and Blocks

*One of the great benefits of using a computer to create design plans lies in the ability of the operator to create something once, and then duplicate or manipulate it as desired. We've used several modification commands, techniques, and procedures throughout the course of this text and have become fairly comfortable with the basic tools. But there are still two modification routines that can increase speed and make your work easier. These are the **Group** and **Block** commands.*

We'll look at these in Lesson 19. Although they often behave in a similar manner, each has its niche in the drawing world and it'll be important to know when to use them. Then, in Lesson 20, we'll learn why blocks are one of the most valuable design tools ever created.

19.1 Paper Dolls: The *Group* Command

Have you ever done a furniture layout for an office or an equipment layout for a shop or plant? You may know then that the easiest way to accomplish the layout (in such a fashion that the equipment can be moved around as the plan develops) is to use the "paper dolls" approach. That is, you create a scaled drawing of the room or work area, make a blue line of it, and then move scaled representations (paper dolls) of the equipment around the blue line until you're satisfied with the locations. Once you're satisfied, you tape the dolls to the blue line for reference and draw the objects in your layout.

It's easy work *if* you keep the windows closed and nobody slams a door. A slight breeze, however, sends people scrambling for the paper dolls and mumbling things that might make a sailor blush. Of course, this is only after the hours spent reminiscing about kindergarten while cutting paper dolls out of construction paper.

Once again, AutoCAD has created tools that provide the benefits of construction paper and tape (combined with a few new benefits) while removing the hassles. Enter ***Groups***.

What is a group? Simply put, a group is a collection of objects treated as a single unit.

Let's take a look.

Do This: 19.1.1	**Working with Groups**

I. Open the *groups.dwg* file the C:\Steps\Lesson19 folder. The drawing looks like Figure 19.001.

II. Follow these steps.

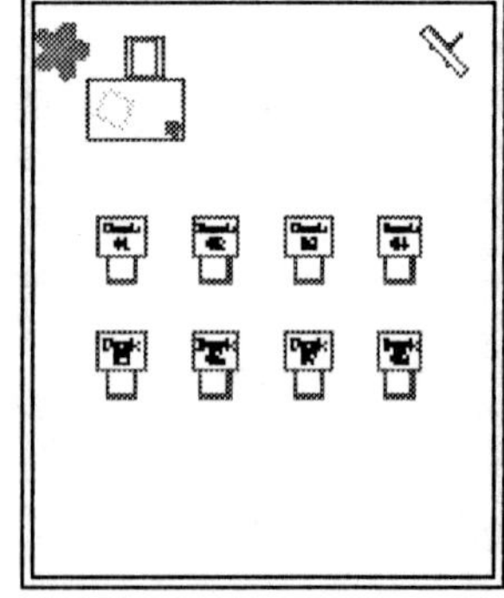

Figure 19.001

TOOLS	COMMAND SEQUENCE	STEPS
	Command: ***m***	1. We'll switch the tree (in the upper left corner of the screen) with the easel pad (in the upper right corner). Enter the ***Move*** command.
	Select objects: 80 found, 1 group **Select objects:** ***[enter]***	2. Select anywhere in the tree as shown in Figure 19.002. Complete the selection. (Notice how easy it is to select these 80 objects!)

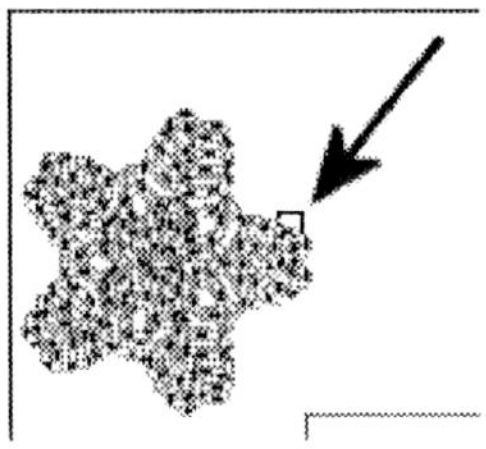

Figure 19.002

TOOLS	COMMAND SEQUENCE	STEPS
	Specify base point or [Displacement] <Displacement>: ***21',0*** **Specify second point or <use first point as displacement>:** ***[enter]***	3. Move the tree 21 feet to the right.
	Command: ***m***	4. Repeat Steps 1 through 3 to move the easel pad 21 feet to the left. Your drawing looks like Figure 19.003. Notice that, in each instance, you selected the objects with a single pick and AutoCAD indicated the number of objects *and the number of groups* found.

Figure 19.003

TOOLS	COMMAND SEQUENCE	STEPS
	Command: ***ro***	5. Now rotate the easel pad 90° to face the correct direction. This part of your drawing now looks like Figure 19.004.

TOOLS	COMMAND SEQUENCE	STEPS
	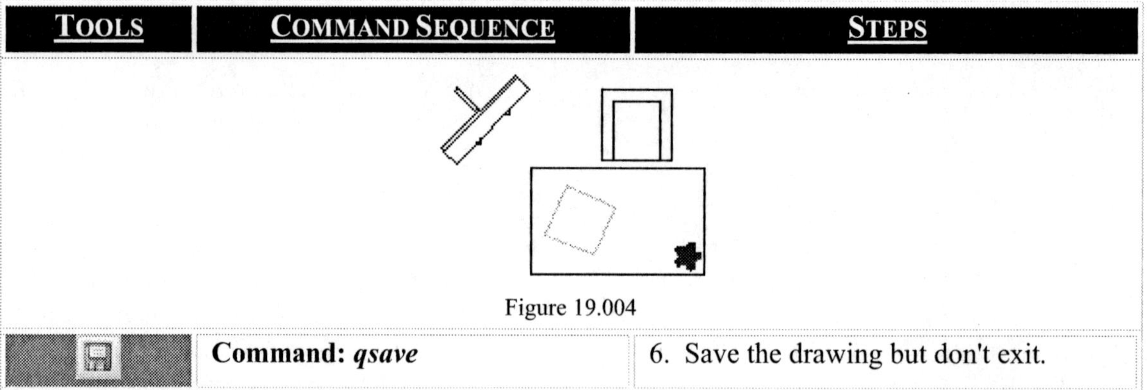 Figure 19.004	
	Command: ***qsave***	6. Save the drawing but don't exit.

You can see how easy it is to manipulate grouped objects. And before you ask, yes, you can manipulate individual objects within a group (but *not* within a block – well, at least not easily).

Let's take a look at how you can create groups yourself and at how you can work with individual parts of the group.

When you enter the ***Group*** command, AutoCAD provides the Object Grouping dialog box to assist you (Figure 19.005).

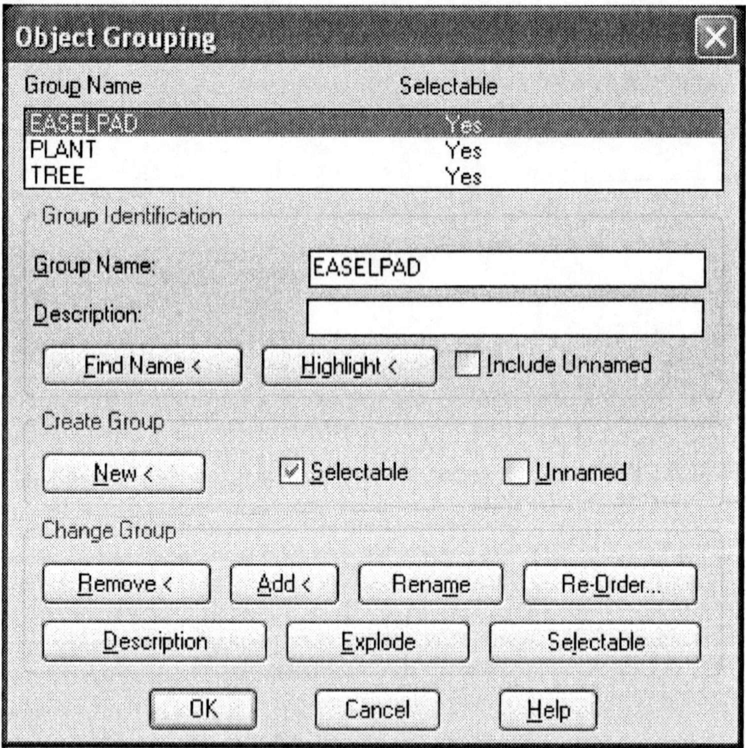

Figure 19.005

- The upper list box shows the names of existing groups (under **Group Name**) and whether or not the group is currently **Selectable (Yes** or **No**). Selectable simply means that you can manipulate the group as a single object. You'll want the group to be selectable to do what we did in the last exercise; but you won't want it selectable if you need to modify something within the group (like pruning the branches of the tree we moved). You can't change the **Selectable** setting in the list box. We'll see how to do that shortly.
- The **Group Identification** frame holds several useful items.
    - Appearing in the appropriate text box, you'll find the name and description (if any) of the group highlighted in the list box at the top of the dialog box. You'll begin to create a new group by typing a new **Group Name** and **Description** (if desired) into these boxes. (We'll create some new groups in our next exercise.)

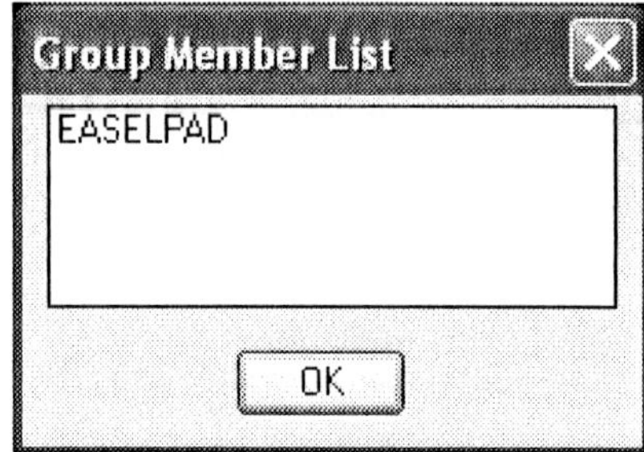

Figure 19.006

- To find the name of an existing group, begin by picking the **Find Name** button. AutoCAD returns to the graphics screen and prompts you to **Pick a member of a group**. It then displays the Group Member List Dialog box (Figure 19.006) showing a list of all the groups to which that object belongs.
- To find which objects belong to a certain group, begin by selecting the name of the group in the upper list box, and then pick the **Highlight** button. AutoCAD returns to the graphics screen, highlights all the objects belonging to that group, and presents a **Continue** button to return to the Object Grouping dialog box.
- Sitting inconspicuously in the lower right corner of the frame, you'll find a check box next to the words **Include Unnamed**. When a group is copied, the copy is also a group. You haven't named the copy, but AutoCAD has assigned a temporary name to it. Placing a check in this box tells AutoCAD to display the temporary names as well as the user-assigned names. You can then rename the copies to something more appropriate.

- You'll use tools in the **Create Group** frame to create a new group. After typing a name for your new group in the **Group Name** text box (or placing a check in the **Unnamed** check box if you want AutoCAD to assign the name), pick the **New** button. AutoCAD will return to the graphics screen and prompt **Select objects for grouping**. When you've finished selecting the objects, hit enter to return to the Object Grouping dialog box. Be sure there's a check in the **Selectable** check box if you want to manipulate the selected objects as a group.
- Use the seven buttons in the **Change Group** frame to modify a group. First, select the group to be modified in the list box. Then pick one of the buttons in the **Change Group** frame.
  - Add or remove objects from a group with the **Add** and **Remove** buttons.
  - Use the **Rename** button to change the name of a group. For example, to change the temporary name assigned by AutoCAD to a more recognizable name, highlight the temporary name in the list box, type the new name in the **Group Name** text box, and then pick the **Rename** button.
  - Type some text into the **Description** text box, and then pick the **Description** button to update the description of the highlighted group.
  - The **Explode** button will remove the definition of the group from the drawing's database. All objects in the group will then behave as individual objects (not as part of a group).
  - The **Selectable** button is a toggle for treating a group as a group or for suspending the group definition so you can modify one or more of the objects within the group. When **Selectable** is toggled off, the word **No** appears in the **Selectable** column of the list box, and all the objects within a group behave as individual objects. To manipulate the objects as part of the group, simply toggle **Selectable** back on.

- The **Re-Order…** button presents the Order Group dialog box (Figure 19.007). Here you can change the order in which AutoCAD reads the objects in a group. Type the number of the object you wish to change in the **Remove from position** text box. Type the position to which you wish to move the object in the **Enter new position number for the object** text box. Type the number or range of objects to reorder in the **Number of objects** text box.

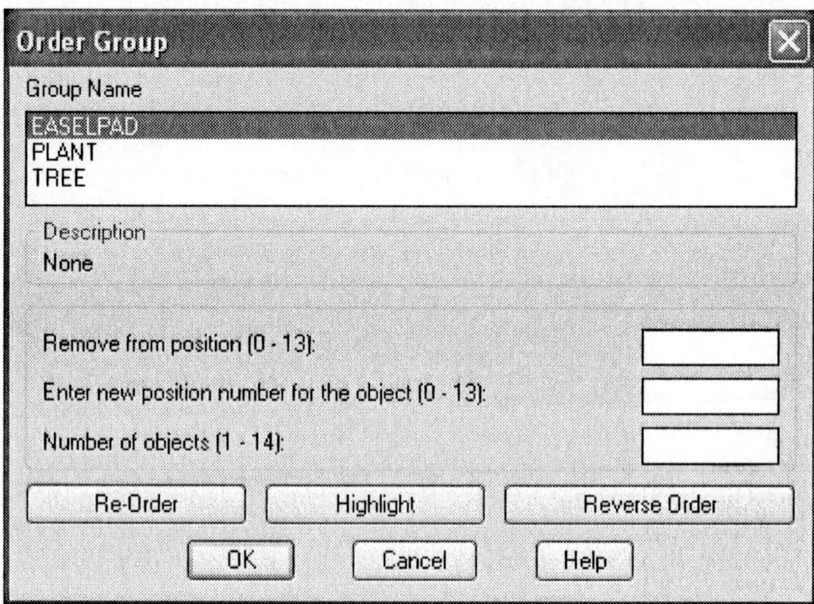

Figure 19.007

  Pick the **Reverse Order** button to simply reverse the order of the objects within the group.

> You'll rarely (if ever) need the **Order** options of the ***Group*** command. In the few brief years since AutoCAD included this tool, I haven't found a need or even a use for reordering objects in a group. However, this doesn't mean that you won't find a need or use. A corollary to AutoCAD's Redundancy Rule might be the Overkill Rule. Both rules simply and correctly state that *More is Better*. In other words, *if it might be useful, make it possible!*

If you're unsure of the position of the object you wish to reorder, pick the **Highlight** button. AutoCAD will present the Object Grouping counter shown in Figure 19.008. Pick the **Next/Previous** buttons to scroll through the objects making up the group. The number of the object will be indicated at the bottom of the dialog box.

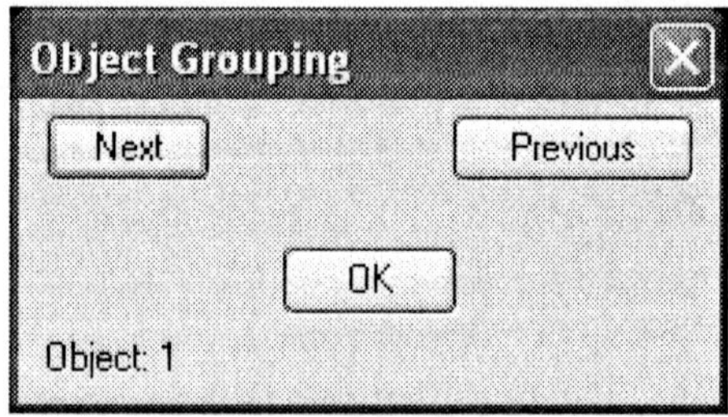

Figure 19.008

Let's play with the ***Group*** command!

Do This: 19.1.2	Creating and Manipulating Groups

I. Be sure you're still in the *groups.dwg* file the C:\Steps\Lesson19 folder. If not, please open it now.

II. Follow these steps.

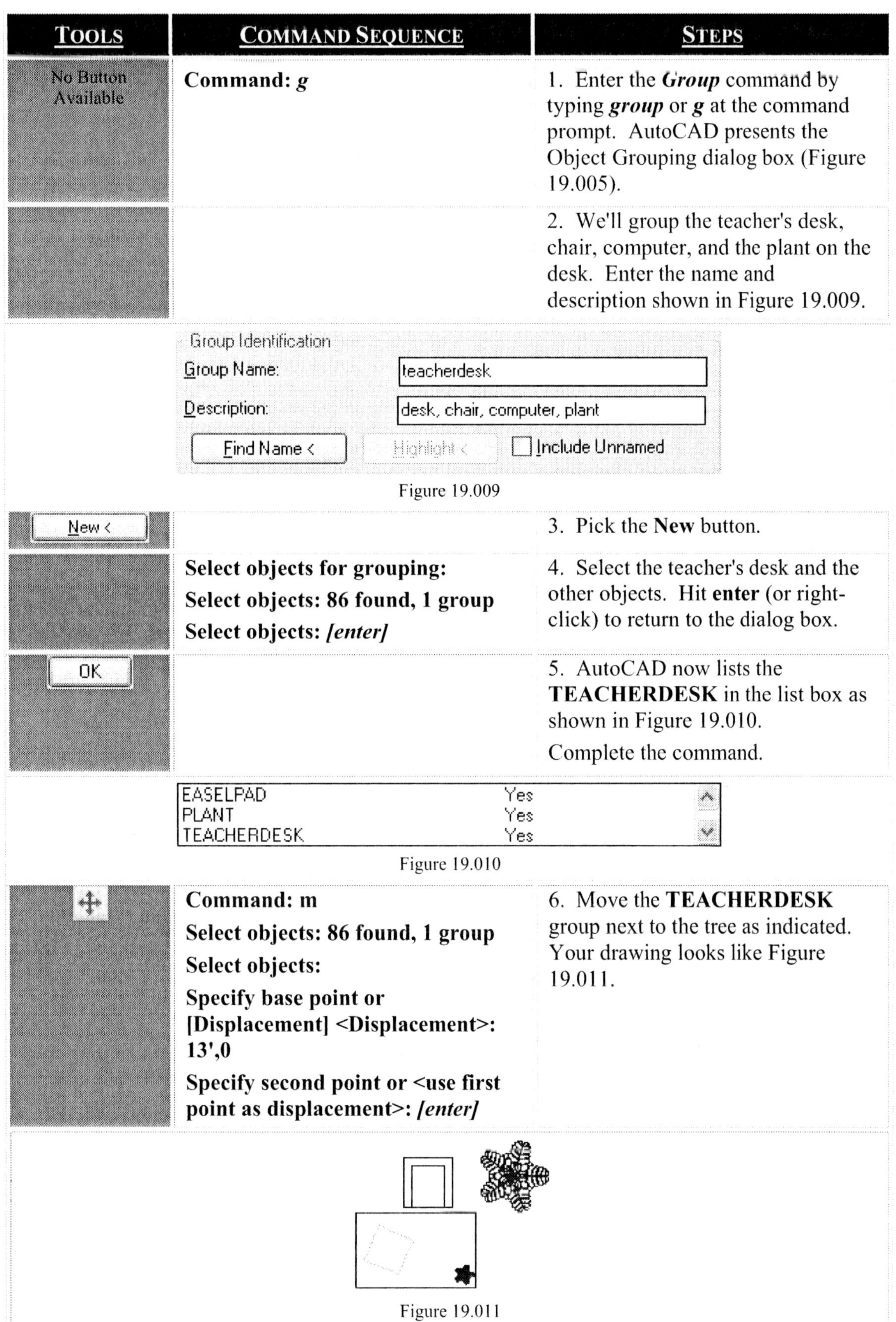

TOOLS	COMMAND SEQUENCE	STEPS
No Button Available	**Command: *g***	1. Enter the ***Group*** command by typing ***group*** or ***g*** at the command prompt. AutoCAD presents the Object Grouping dialog box (Figure 19.005).
		2. We'll group the teacher's desk, chair, computer, and the plant on the desk. Enter the name and description shown in Figure 19.009.
	Group Identification Group Name: teacherdesk Description: desk, chair, computer, plant Find Name < Highlight < Include Unnamed Figure 19.009	
New <		3. Pick the **New** button.
	Select objects for grouping: **Select objects: 86 found, 1 group** **Select objects: *[enter]***	4. Select the teacher's desk and the other objects. Hit **enter** (or right-click) to return to the dialog box.
OK		5. AutoCAD now lists the **TEACHERDESK** in the list box as shown in Figure 19.010. Complete the command.
	EASELPAD Yes PLANT Yes TEACHERDESK Yes Figure 19.010	
	Command: m **Select objects: 86 found, 1 group** **Select objects:** **Specify base point or [Displacement] <Displacement>: 13',0** **Specify second point or <use first point as displacement>: *[enter]***	6. Move the **TEACHERDESK** group next to the tree as indicated. Your drawing looks like Figure 19.011.
	Figure 19.011	

TOOLS	COMMAND SEQUENCE	STEPS
	Command: *g*	7. Reopen the Object Grouping dialog box.
Find Name <		8. Now we'll list all the groups to which an object belongs. Pick the **Find Name** button.
	Pick a member of a group.	9. AutoCAD returns to the graphics screen and prompts to **Pick a member of a group**. Pick the plant on the teacher's desk.
		10. AutoCAD presents the Group Member List dialog box (Figure 19.012) showing that the object selected belongs to the **Plant** and **Teacherdesk** groups. You see now that groups can be *nested* – that is, one group can contain another group. Objects can also be shared by more than one group. Pick the **OK** button to return to the Object Grouping dialog box.

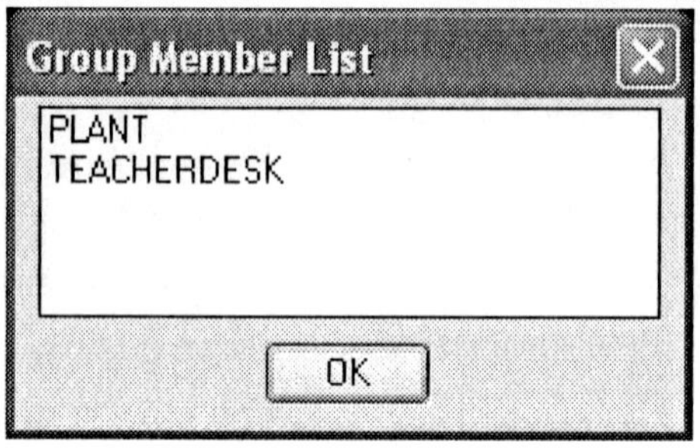

Figure 19.012

		11. Let's see which objects are in the **Plant** group. Pick **PLANT** in the list box. Notice that the name appears in the **Group Name** text box.
Highlight <		12. Pick the **Highlight** button. AutoCAD returns to the graphics screen and highlights the plant on the teacher's desk.
Continue		13. Return to the Object Grouping dialog box.
OK		14. Complete the command.

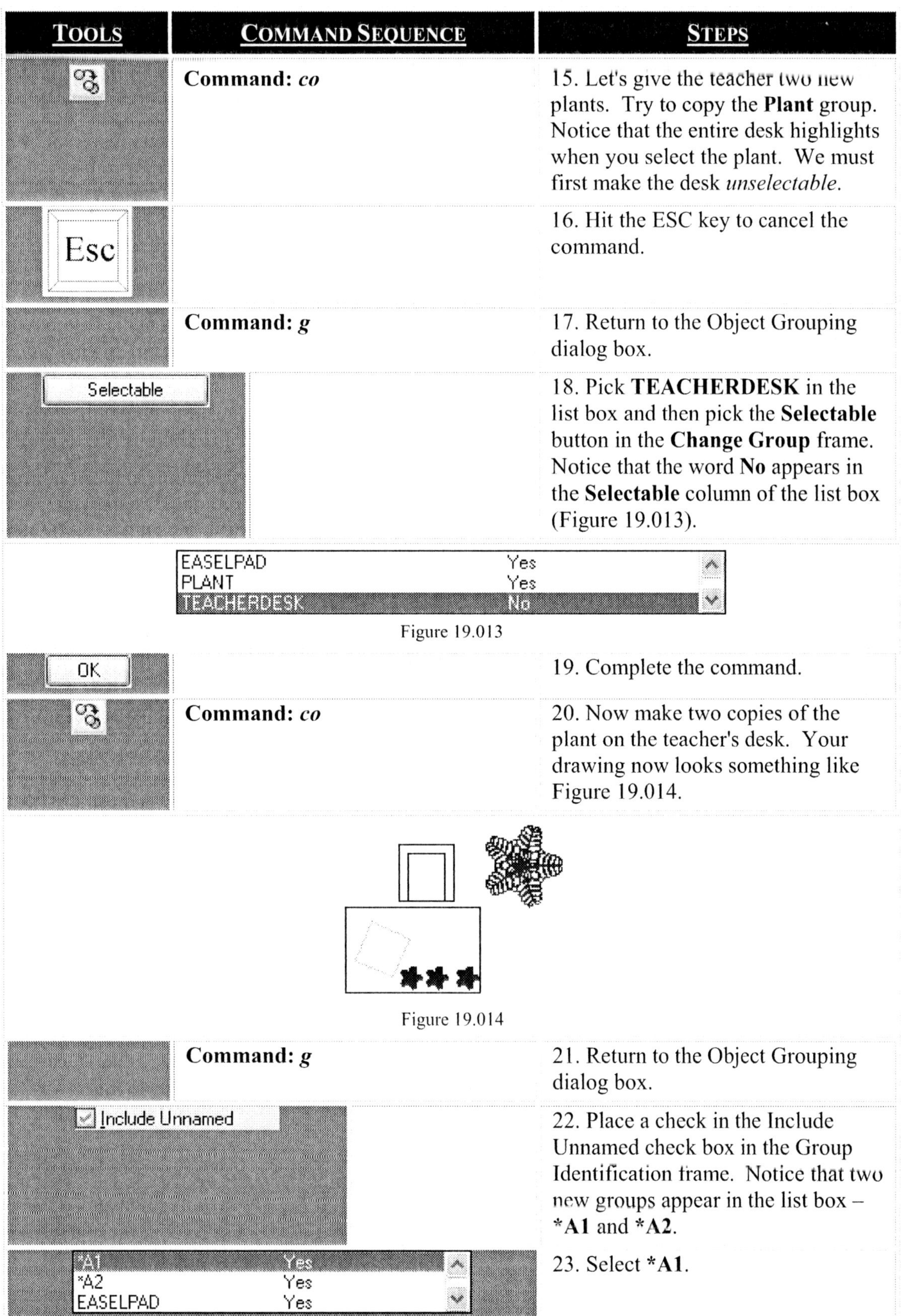

TOOLS	COMMAND SEQUENCE	STEPS
	Command: *co*	15. Let's give the teacher two new plants. Try to copy the **Plant** group. Notice that the entire desk highlights when you select the plant. We must first make the desk *unselectable*.
Esc		16. Hit the ESC key to cancel the command.
	Command: *g*	17. Return to the Object Grouping dialog box.
Selectable		18. Pick **TEACHERDESK** in the list box and then pick the **Selectable** button in the **Change Group** frame. Notice that the word **No** appears in the **Selectable** column of the list box (Figure 19.013).

EASELPAD	Yes
PLANT	Yes
TEACHERDESK	No

Figure 19.013

TOOLS	COMMAND SEQUENCE	STEPS
OK		19. Complete the command.
	Command: *co*	20. Now make two copies of the plant on the teacher's desk. Your drawing now looks something like Figure 19.014.

Figure 19.014

TOOLS	COMMAND SEQUENCE	STEPS
	Command: *g*	21. Return to the Object Grouping dialog box.
Include Unnamed		22. Place a check in the Include Unnamed check box in the Group Identification frame. Notice that two new groups appear in the list box – ***A1** and ***A2**.
*A1 Yes *A2 Yes EASELPAD Yes		23. Select ***A1**.

Tools	Command Sequence	Steps
Group Name: PlantB		24. Enter the name ***PlantB*** into the Group Name text box.
Rename		25. Now pick the **Rename** button. AutoCAD renames the group.
		26. Repeat Steps 22 through 25 to rename ***A2** to ***PlantC***.
		27. Now let's add these new plants to the **Teacherdesk** group. Select the **Teacherdesk** group in the list box (you may have to scroll down a bit to find it).
Add <		28. Pick the **Add** button in the **Change Group** frame.
	Select objects to add to group... **Select objects: 80 found, 1 group** **Select objects: 80 found, 1 group, 246 total** **Select objects: *[enter]***	29. AutoCAD returns to the graphics screen and prompts you to **Select objects to add to group**. Select the two new plants, and then return to the Object Grouping dialog box.
Selectable		30. Pick the **Selectable** button to make the **TEACHERDESK** group selectable again. Notice that the word **Yes** appears in the **Selectable** column of the list box.
OK		31. Complete the procedure.
	Command: *qsave*	32. Save the drawing but don't exit.

We've seen how groups can benefit our work by simplifying object selection and manipulation. We've also seen how to manage our groups through some of the buttons in the **Change Group** frame of the Object Grouping dialog box. Now let's remove a group definition from a drawing.

Do This: 19.1.3	Removing a Group Definition

I. Be sure you're still in the *groups.dwg* file the C:\Steps\Lesson19 folder. If not, please open it now.

II. Follow these steps.

Tools	Command Sequence	Steps
	Command: *g*	1. Enter the ***Group*** command.
EASELPAD Yes PLANT Yes PLANTB Yes		2. Select the **EASELPAD** group in the list box.

Tools	Command Sequence	Steps
Explode		3. Pick the **Explode** button in the **Change Group** frame. Notice that **Easelpad** disappears from the list box.
OK		4. Complete the command. AutoCAD returns to the graphics screen.
	Command: ***m***	5. Try to move the easel pad now. Notice that you can't select the entire pad with a single pick. The pad is no longer a group.
	Command: ***qsave***	6. Save the drawing and exit.

I've frequently used groups in my capacity as a piping designer to manipulate (particularly moving and copying) items such as control stations and pipe configurations. Architects and interior designers can also use groups as we've done in these exercises. Other disciplines can make use of groups when dealing with layouts, circuitry, boltholes, windows, and many other items.

The only limitations to groups are simple – their use is limited to a single drawing (you can't share groups between drawings), the group definition is permanently lost once the group is exploded or erased from a drawing, and you can't attach information to a group. To overcome these limitations, use blocks instead of groups.

19.2 Groups with Backbone – The *Block* Commands

No single aspect of CAD has served as a stronger selling point than blocks. In fact, all quality CAD systems have blocks (or cells, or something that behaves like blocks). No other single command or routine can speed the drawing process as well, and none has a greater potential for cost cutting or streamlining design management.

What is a block? A block is a single object made up of several other objects. You can manipulate blocks, like groups, as a single unit. But you can share blocks *between* drawings. More importantly, *blocks can contain user-defined data*. We'll discuss creation and manipulation of blocks here. In Lesson 20, we'll discuss attaching data to blocks and exporting that data to other computer applications (such as spreadsheets or databases).

> Be aware that much of the block details you will learn in the 2006 edition of the *One Step at a Time* series *does not hold true for earlier releases!* Dynamic blocks, as you will learn about them, are one of those rare giant leaps for Autodesk. (Be glad you're here!)

There are two important block commands – ***Block*** (which creates blocks within a drawing) and ***WBlock*** (which creates a block as a separate drawing file). Mercifully, both use dialog boxes. But to keep it even simpler, you'll use the ***Block*** command to create blocks and the ***WBlock*** command to copy your blocks into a *Folder library*.

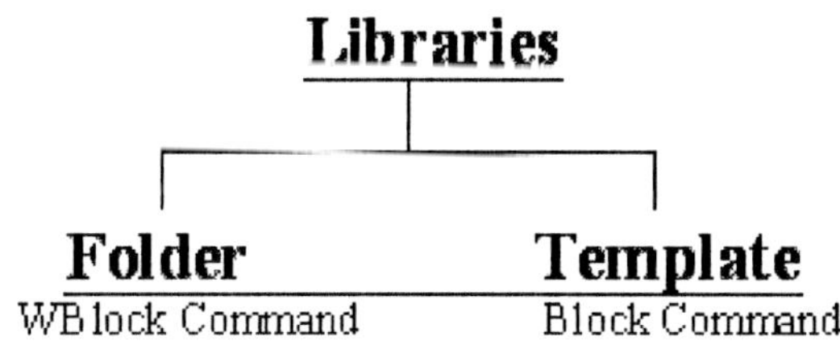

Figure 19.015

What's a library?

Groups of blocks are often assembled in useful packages called libraries (Figure 19.015). A library is a group of blocks used as inserts in a drawing. Use of blocked objects saves the time you might otherwise need to create the objects.

There are two types of libraries: *Template* files – associated with the ***Block*** command, and *Folders* – associated with the ***WBlock*** command. Both libraries are useful (each has its pluses and minuses), but each project should use only one type.

- The project guru (CAD coordinator) should create (or oversee) the folder library – a collection of standardized drawings to be used on the contract – and store it on a network. The path to the folder should be defined in the *Support File Search Path* section of the **Files** tab of the Options dialog box. This will make insertion much easier. [Note: The Options dialog box isn't a place for AutoCAD novices to experiment!]

  The folder library is easy for a single person (the guru) to maintain. Adding, deleting, or changing a project standard involves modifying only one file for each change.
- Blocks can be included as part of the templates used on a project (creating template libraries). Accessing blocks that are part of the original template is a bit faster than the folder method, but the size of the template can become quite large (heavy with block definitions) before any actual drafting begins. Additionally, any changes in project standards require that all the templates be updated. Even if the templates are centrally stored on a network, this may involve several files.

The decision as to which type of library to use should be universal for the project and is best made by the guru and the design supervisor. This doesn't mean that the operator can't create and use blocks on the fly. But the operator should take care not to duplicate (or overwrite) project standards.

> Most libraries consist of drawings associated with a single design discipline. For example, an architectural library may contain drawings of doors, windows, toilets, tubs, and so forth, whereas a piping library will contain drawings of valves, elbows, tees, etc. Library creation has become quite a business alongside CAD industries.

Another thing that must concern the CAD operator, both in the creation and insertion of blocks, is how blocks relate to layers. This can sound complicated, so let's use a chart (after all, a chart is worth a thousand words – give or take).

IF THE OBJECTS USED TO MAKE THE BLOCK ARE ON:	WHEN INSERTED, THE BLOCK HAS THE CHARACTERISTICS OF:	WHEN INSERTED, THE BLOCK EXISTS ON:
Layer 0	The current layer	The current layer
Any other layer	The layer on which it was created	The current layer

Let me try to explain this by using some examples (and fewer than a thousand words).

Generally speaking, you should always create objects for blocks on layer **0**. Then when inserting the block on another layer (let's say, layer **obj**), all the objects that went in to creating the block will appear on – and share the characteristics of – the current layer (layer **obj**). When this layer (**obj**) is frozen, turned off, or locked, the block will be affected accordingly.

Text might be an exception to this rule (and is rarely a good idea in a block – generally speaking). When part or all of the objects used to create a block exists on a layer other than 0 (say, **text**), those objects in the inserted block will appear with the characteristics of the layer on which they were created. (If that layer doesn't exist in the drawing, AutoCAD will create it.) This will be true regardless of the layer that's current (say, **obj**) when you insert the block. Now, when the **obj** layer is frozen, turned off, or locked, the block will be affected accordingly because the block exists on (was inserted on) layer **obj**. *Additionally*, when the text layer is frozen, turned off, or locked, the block will also be affected because that is the layer on which it was created.

Sound complicate? Use the chart!

19.2.1 Template Library Creation

We use the ***Block*** command to create template libraries or to create blocks on the fly. We'll use the ***WBlock*** command to convert template library blocks to folder libraries.

When completed, the newly defined block has become part of the current drawing's database and can be inserted into the current drawing at any time. Save this drawing as a template, and the block will be available to any drawing using this template.

Block presents the Block Definition dialog box (Figure 19.016) where you can enter the information you'll need to create a block.

- Place the name of the block in the **Name** control box.
- Although you can enter an insertion point's coordinates in the **Base Point** frame (X, Y, and Z text boxes), it's easier to use the **Pick point** button. AutoCAD hides the dialog box and prompts:

    Specify insertion base point:

    You can then pick a base point on the screen.
- Use the **Select Objects** button (in the **Objects** frame) to return to the graphics screen and select objects to include in the block. Alternately, you can use **Quick Select** filters by picking the "funnel" button to the right of **Select objects**.

    Once you've selected the objects, you must tell AutoCAD what to do with them after it makes the block. Simply place a bullet next to the appropriate option:

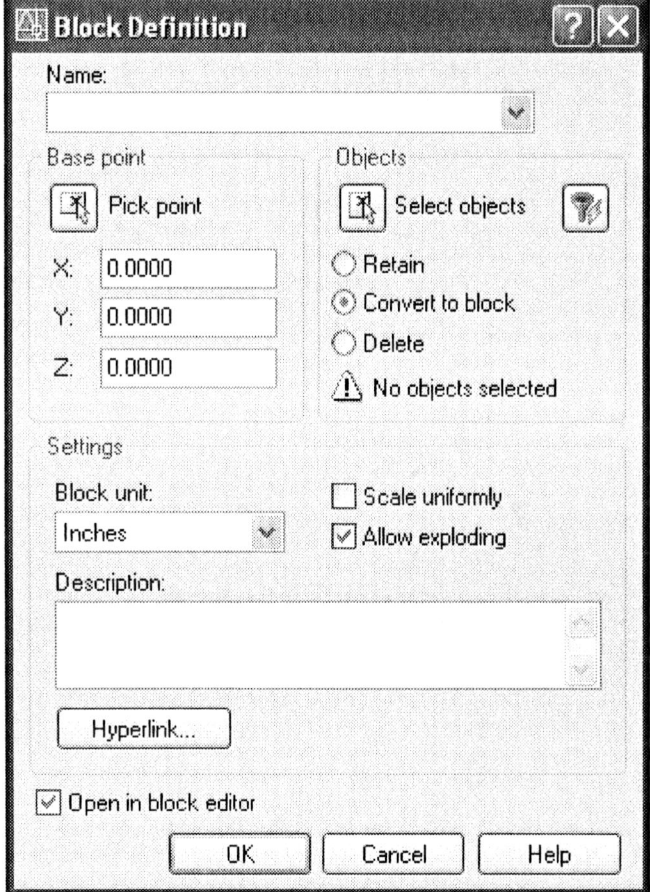

Figure 19.016

- o **Retain** tells AutoCAD to keep the selected objects in their current state. That is, AutoCAD won't automatically delete the objects after creating the block.

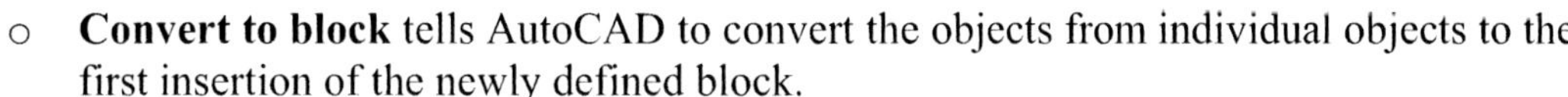

- o **Convert to block** tells AutoCAD to convert the objects from individual objects to the first insertion of the newly defined block.
- o **Delete** will delete the objects used to create the block.

- In the **Block unit** control box (**Settings** frame), you should define what units to use when inserting the block (preferably the units used by the drawing in which the block will be inserted). AutoCAD will use these units when it inserts a block via the ADC or tool palettes (more on this in Section 19.4.2).

  Place a check next to **Scale uniformly** to restrict scaling of the block to uniform X, Y, and Z scaling.

  Place a check next to **Allow exploding** if you wish to allow this option. Exploding a block loses all the block's definitions and leaves only the objects that went in to creating it.

  Enter a description of the block in the **Description** text box.

  The **Hyperlink** button at the bottom of the frame allows you to associate a hyperlink with the block using an Insert Hyperlink dialog box.
- The inconspicuous check box at the bottom of the dialog box – **Open in block editor** – provides access to a wonderful new world of block control! We'll discuss this in more detail in Section 19.3.

First, let's create some simple blocks. You can use simple blocks on the fly, but these instructions will also help to get your feet wet.

Do This: 19.2.1.1	**Creating Simple Blocks**

I. Open the *blocks.dwg* file the C:\Steps\Lesson19 folder. The drawing looks like Figure 19.017.

II. Follow these steps.

Figure 19.017

TOOLS	**COMMAND SEQUENCE**	**STEPS**
Make Block Button	**Command: *b***	1. (Refer to the door seen in the center of the drawing.) Enter the ***Block*** command by typing ***block*** or ***b*** at the command prompt. Alternately, you can pick the **Make Block** button on the Draw toolbar. AutoCAD presents the Block Definition dialog box (Figure 19.016).
Name: door		2. Enter the name (***door***) in the **Block name** text box.
		3. Pick the **Pick point** button. AutoCAD returns to the graphics screen.
	Specify insertion base point: _mid of	4. Pick the insertion point indicated in Figure 19.018. AutoCAD returns to the dialog box.

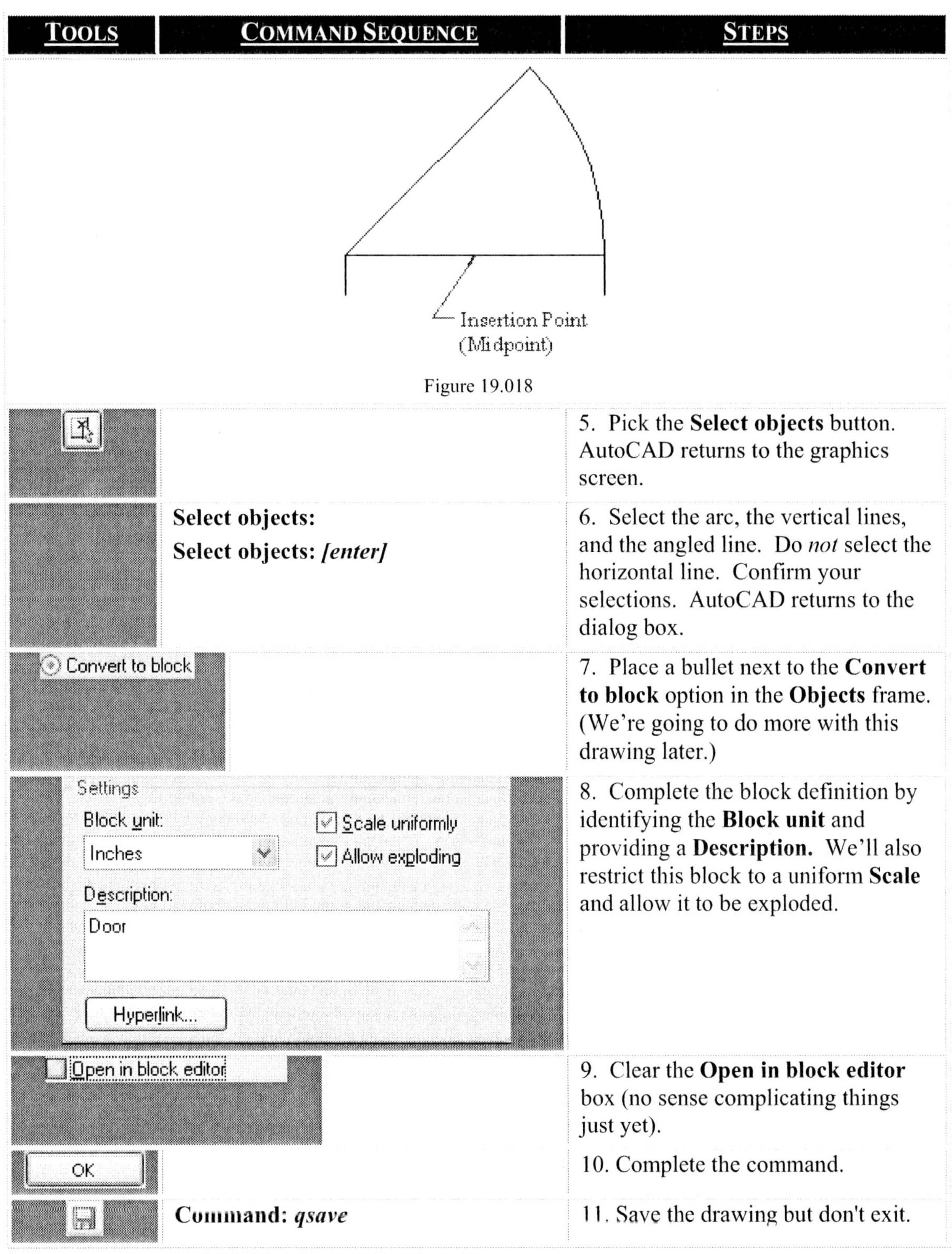

Figure 19.018

TOOLS	COMMAND SEQUENCE	STEPS
		5. Pick the **Select objects** button. AutoCAD returns to the graphics screen.
	Select objects: **Select objects: *[enter]***	6. Select the arc, the vertical lines, and the angled line. Do *not* select the horizontal line. Confirm your selections. AutoCAD returns to the dialog box.
Convert to block		7. Place a bullet next to the **Convert to block** option in the **Objects** frame. (We're going to do more with this drawing later.)
Settings Block unit: Inches Scale uniformly Allow exploding Description: Door Hyperlink...		8. Complete the block definition by identifying the **Block unit** and providing a **Description.** We'll also restrict this block to a uniform **Scale** and allow it to be exploded.
Open in block editor		9. Clear the **Open in block editor** box (no sense complicating things just yet).
OK		10. Complete the command.
	Command: *qsave*	11. Save the drawing but don't exit.

In this exercise, we've begun a template library. We could continue to add dozens of drawings as needed (deleting the drawings as we go). Then, when we've finished, we would save this drawing with the .dwt extension and use it as a template for any number of future drawings. But let's use what we have to start a Folder library.

19.2.2 Folder Library Creation

You'll use the ***WBlock*** (**WriteBlock**) command to create folder libraries. The procedure can be very similar to creating blocks, but it also allows you to convert template library files to folder library files.

As with the ***Block*** command, AutoCAD also provides a dialog box interface to ease creation of WBlocks. Access it by entering the ***WBlock*** command (or the ***W*** hotkey). The Write Block dialog box appears (Figure 19.019). Does it look familiar? It should. Two of the frames are identical to the Block Definition dialog box. Let's examine the other frames.

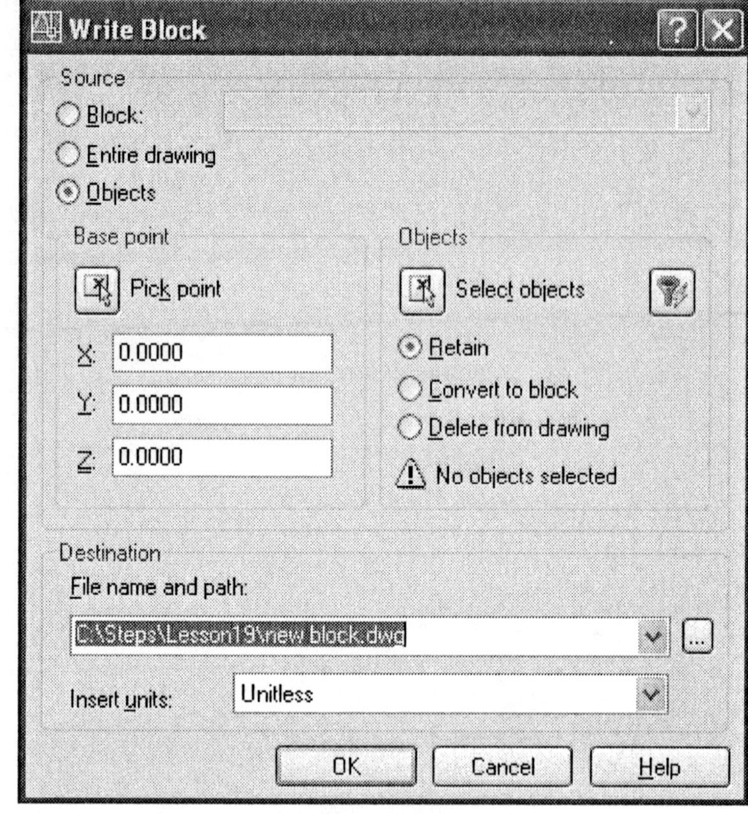

Figure 19.019

- In the **Source** frame, AutoCAD gives you three options:
    - The **Block** option opens the control box next to it. Here you can select from a list of blocks existing in the drawing to be saved as separate drawing files (WBlocks).
    - Of course, the **Entire drawing** option allows you to create a separate drawing file using all of the objects in the drawing.
    - The **Objects** option (the default) behaves like the ***Block*** command and allows you to select objects just as you did using the Block Definition dialog box.
- The **Base point** and **Objects** frames are identical to their namesakes found on the Block Definition dialog box.
- In the **Destination** frame, you'll:
    - name and locate the new block (**File name and path** text box).
    - identify the **Insert units** of the new block (this is the same thing as the **Block unit** found on the Block Definition dialog box).

In our next exercise, we'll create a WBlock to begin a folder library by converting the block created in our template library to a file we can use in our folder library.

Do This: 19.2.2.1 | **Creating Blocks for a Folder Library**

I. Be sure you're still in the *blocks.dwg* file the C:\Steps\Lesson19 folder. If not, please open it now.

II. Follow these steps.

TOOLS	COMMAND SEQUENCE	STEPS
	Command: ***w***	1. We'll use the ***WBlock*** command to export our earlier block to our Folder Library. Enter the ***WBlock*** command.
		2. (Refer to Figure 19.020.) Do this: a. Place the **Source** bullet in the **Block** option and then select **door** from the control box. (This is the block you created in our last exercise.) Notice that the **Base point** and **Objects** frames are no longer available. (This information was provided when you defined the original block.) b. Be sure the **Destination** information in your dialog box saves the new file as Door in the C:\Steps\Lesson19 folder. c. Pick the **OK** button to complete the command. How simple!

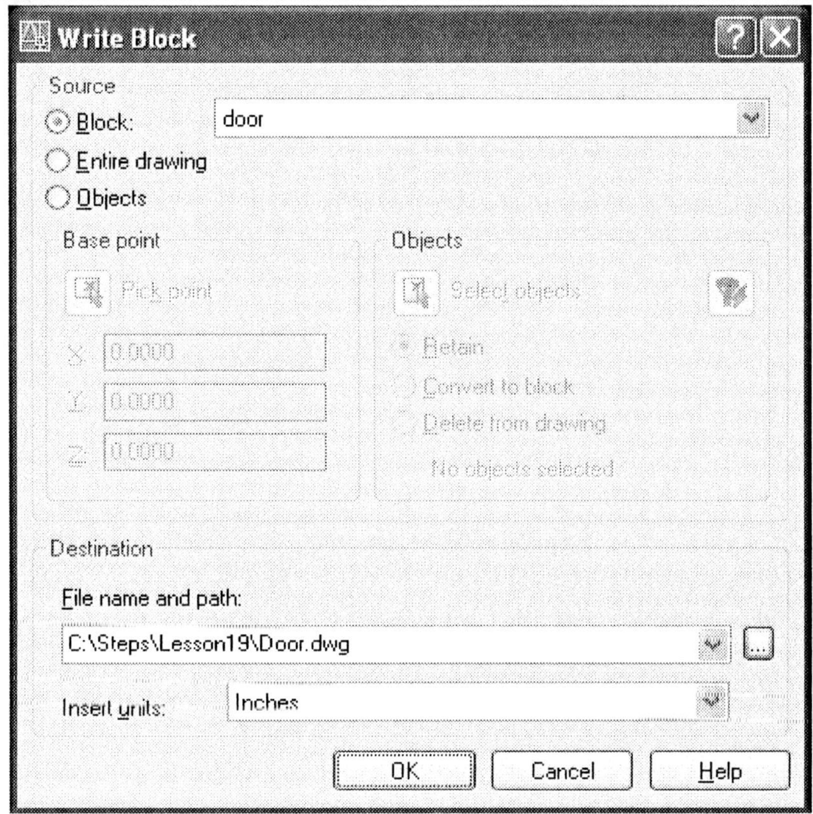

Figure 19.020

Tools	Command Sequence	Steps
	Command: ***qsave***	8. Save and close the drawing.

The block you just created will appear in the C:\Steps\Lesson19 folder as a new drawing that you can insert into other drawings as blocks!

19.2.3 Using Blocks in a Drawing – The *Insert* Command

Before we continue, we must know how to insert a block into a drawing once we've created it. We'll do this, appropriately enough, with the ***Insert*** command.

The ***Insert*** command calls the dialog box shown in Figure 19.021.

- The **Name** control box will list all of the blocks currently associated with the drawing (by definition, previous insertion, or template). To insert a WBlock not currently associated with the drawing, use the **Browse** button to locate the file. AutoCAD will show the path next to the **Path** statement.
- In the **Insertion point** frame, you can identify the **X/Y/Z** coordinates for the insertion or (preferably) leave the check in the **Specify On-screen** box. Then you can identify the insertion point on the screen with a mouse pick and OSNAP.

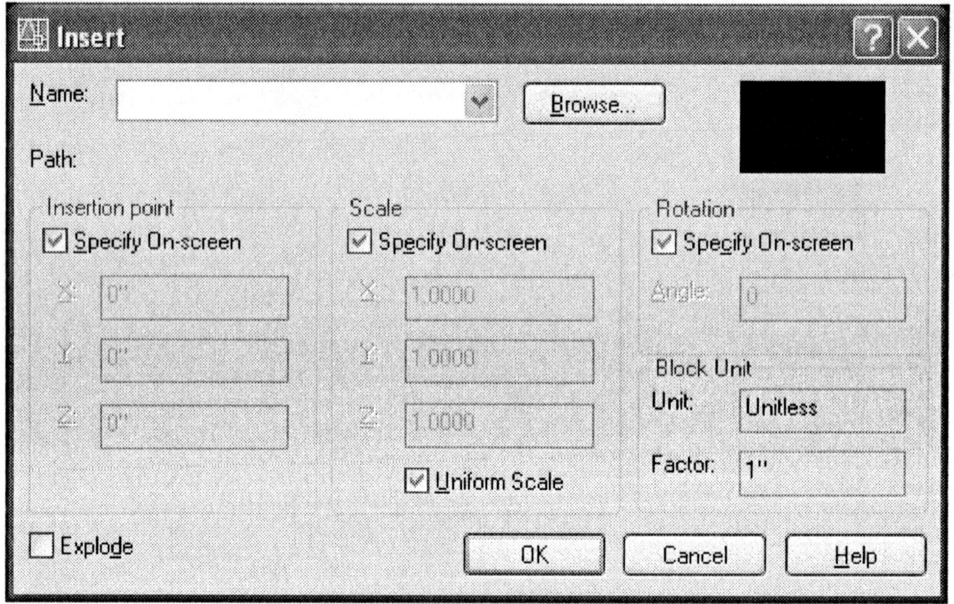

Figure 19.021

- The **Scale** frame also has a **Specify On-screen** box. But it may be preferable (unless you must see the scaled block to be sure of its size) to enter the **X/Y/Z** scale in the text boxes provided. A check in the **Uniform Scale** box will ensure the **X/Y/Z** scales remain proportional to the original block definition.
- The **Rotation** frame also has a **Specify On-screen** box. Like the **Scale** data, it's up to you to decide what's easiest to use.
- The **Block Unit** frame displays information about the block currently identified in the **Name** control box. This frame is informational only.

- The last item in the Insert dialog box – the **Explode** check box in the lower left corner – enables you to place all the objects of a block without the definition of the block. In other words, you can insert the block pre-exploded.

Let's insert a block into a drawing.

You can also access the ***Insert*** command from the Insert pull-down menu.

Do This: 19.2.3.1	Inserting Blocks

I. Open the *cab-pln.dwg* file the C:\Steps\Lesson19 folder. The drawing looks like Figure 19.022.

II. Follow these steps.

Figure 19.022

TOOLS	COMMAND SEQUENCE	STEPS
	Command: *z*	1. Adjust the display on your screen to see the front door opening (Figure 19.023).
	Figure 19.023	
Insert Block Button	**Command:** ***i***	2. Enter the ***Insert*** command by typing ***insert*** or ***i***. Alternately, you can pick the **Insert Block** button on the Draw toolbar. AutoCAD presents the Insert dialog box (Figure 19.021).
Browse...		3. We'll have to get our block. (It isn't part of this drawing yet.) Pick the **Browse** button.
Open		4. Navigate to the C:\Steps\ Lesson19 folder and select the *Door.dwg* file you created in Exercise 19.2.1.1. Pick the **Open** button. (AutoCAD returns to the Insert dialog box and displays the *Door* block in the **Name** control box.
		5. (Refer to Figure 19.024.) Be sure the **Insertion point**, **Scale**, and **Rotation** are set as indicated. (Be sure the **Explode** check box is empty.)

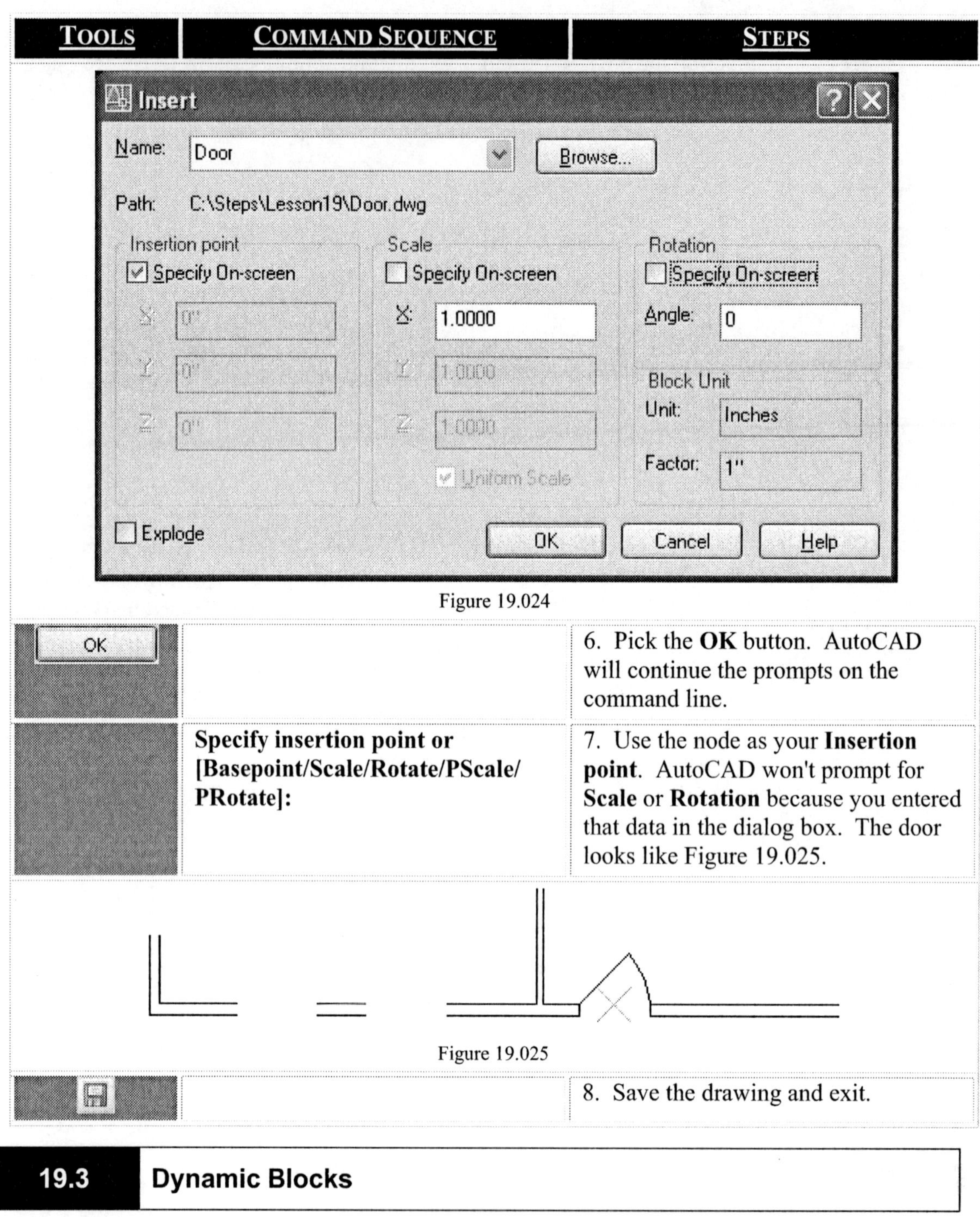

Figure 19.024

TOOLS	COMMAND SEQUENCE	STEPS
OK		6. Pick the **OK** button. AutoCAD will continue the prompts on the command line.
	Specify insertion point or [Basepoint/Scale/Rotate/PScale/PRotate]:	7. Use the node as your **Insertion point**. AutoCAD won't prompt for **Scale** or **Rotation** because you entered that data in the dialog box. The door looks like Figure 19.025.

Figure 19.025

TOOLS	COMMAND SEQUENCE	STEPS
		8. Save the drawing and exit.

19.3 Dynamic Blocks

Wow! Look what I made it do!

Novice CAD Operator

I've been working with AutoCAD now for about 16 years. They don't come up with new things anymore that really evoke a "way cool!" out of me (at least not very often), but dynamic blocks even make me capitalize the expression – *WAY COOL!*

Dynamic blocks will take a bit of time to master, but the time will be well spent.

What is a dynamic block?

Well, a dynamic block has at least one *parameter* (a tool that generally looks like a dimension but acts as a control for selected object properties). The CAD operator can manipulate the block objects associated with the parameter through grips which drive user-defined actions which, in turn, can change the geometry of the block.

By making them *dynamic*, AutoCAD has given us the power to manipulate the objects that compose a block. By manipulate, I mean that you can insert a single table & chairs combination (block), adjust its size, adjust its *style* (that's right, change the drafting symbol to any predefined style), flip parts of it, rotate parts of it, move parts around (like the chairs), and more! The same holds true for valve stations, doors and windows, electrical boxes, landscaping, and so forth! (*The dickens, you say!*)

The size of your libraries just got radically smaller!

As you can imagine, creating these blocks requires a bit more effort than the simple blocks you've already done. We'll do the work in the *block editor*. Remember that check box at the bottom of the Block dialog box? It takes you directly to the block editor. Alternately, you can get there by entering ***BEdit*** at the command prompt or by double-clicking on an existing block.

AutoCAD responds to the ***BEdit*** command with the Edit Block Definition dialog box (Figure 19.026). Pick the block you wish to edit from the list, and then pick the **OK** button to open the editor.

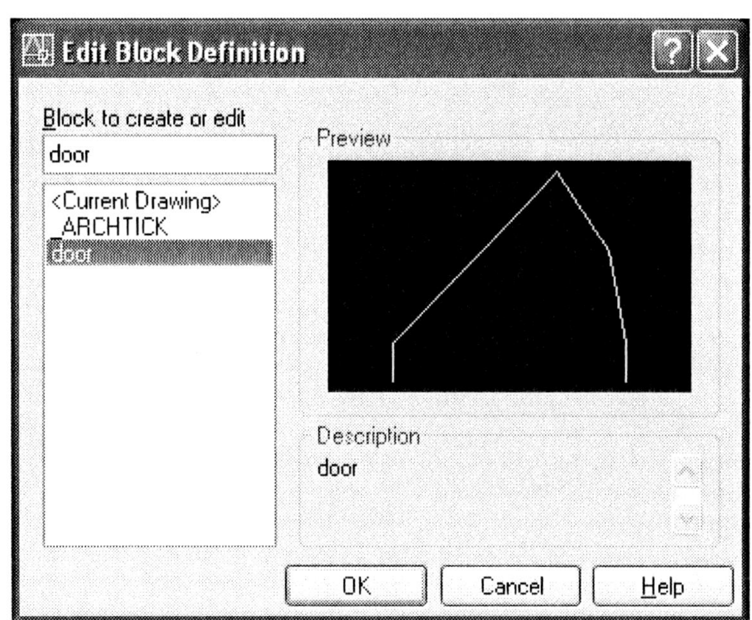

Figure 19.026

> When entering the Block Editor, you may encounter a message box inviting you to view a tutorial on dynamic block creation. Take a few minutes to look this over if you have the time. (I strongly recommend it; it'll make the rest of this section much easier to understand.)
>
> If you don't see the message box, you can find the tutorial by way of the Help pull down menu:
>
> *Help – New Features Workshop – Dynamic Blocks*

You'll immediately notice a marked change in your screen – the background becomes white, a new toolbar appears (Figure 19.027) and the Block Authoring Palettes appear (Figure 19.030). Let's spend a few minutes with each of these treasure houses of tools.

We'll begin at the left end of the new Block Authoring toolbar (Figure 19.027) and use a table for clarity.

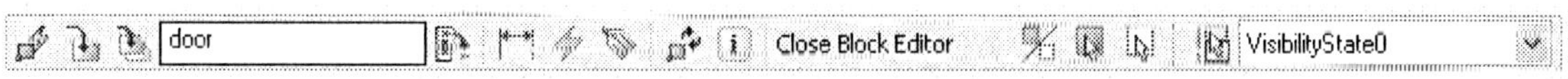

Figure 19.027

ITEM	DESCRIPTION
[icon]	The **Edit or Create Block Definition** button returns you to the Edit Block Definition dialog box (Figure 19.026).
[icon]	Use the **Save Block Definition** button to save your block work before exiting the block editor.
[icon]	Use the **Save Block As** button to save your work as a different block name before exiting the editor.
door	The **Block Name** box reminds you on which block you're working.
[icon]	The **Authoring Palettes** button toggles the display of the Block Authoring Palettes.
[icon]	The **Parameter** button enters the ***BParameter*** command. This is the keyboard approach to creating parameters in your block. The prompt looks like this: **Enter parameter type [Alignment/Base/pOint/Linear/Polar/Xy/ Rotation/Flip/Visibility/looKup]:** ***[select an option]*** You're probably better off using tools on the Block Authoring Palettes (which we'll examine shortly), but all the options appear in both locations.
[icon]	The **Action** button enters the ***BAction*** command. This is the keyboard approach to creating actions for your parameters. The prompt looks like this: **Select parameter:** ***[you must associate actions with parameters]*** **Enter action type [Array/Move/Scale/Stretch/Polar Stretch]:** ***[select an action to associate with the parameter]*** The prompts that follow will depend on the action you've selected.
[icon]	The **Define Attribute** button is the key to even richer possibilities within the world of blocks. We'll dedicate most of Lesson 20 to these!
[icon]	**Update Parameter and Action Text Size** simply regenerates the drawing.
[icon]	**Learn About Dynamic Blocks** launches the New Features Workshop – Dynamic Blocks introductory tutorial.
Close Block Editor	Use the **Close Block Editor** button to conclude your block editing session. If you haven't saved your work, AutoCAD will prompt you to do so. If you've already inserted blocks into the drawing, AutoCAD will display a message box giving you the opportunity to update the block definition for those blocks as well.
You could consider the remaining tools as part of a Visibility toolbar. Since they're next to the Block Authoring toolbar, however, and since we're here, we'll look at them now. These tools provide the method for toggling through styles of objects (simple round sinks vs. fancy oval sinks, desk chairs vs. kitchen chairs, etc.). The tools become available only when you've inserted a **Visibility** parameter into the block. (We'll do this in our next exercise.)	
[icon]	**Visibility Mode** serves as a toggle for the **BVMode** system variable. **On** (a setting of **1**) means that hidden objects will appear visible but dimmed. **Off** (a setting of **0**) means that hidden objects will not appear at all. This is a working tool and won't affect the actual insertion of the block.
[icons]	**Make Visible** and **Make Invisible** enable you to "add" and "remove" objects from your blocks. To enable your user to toggle between different styles of sinks (or other objects) within a single block, you'll draw both sinks and make one visible and the other invisible. You'll then associate the visibility with a visibility state.

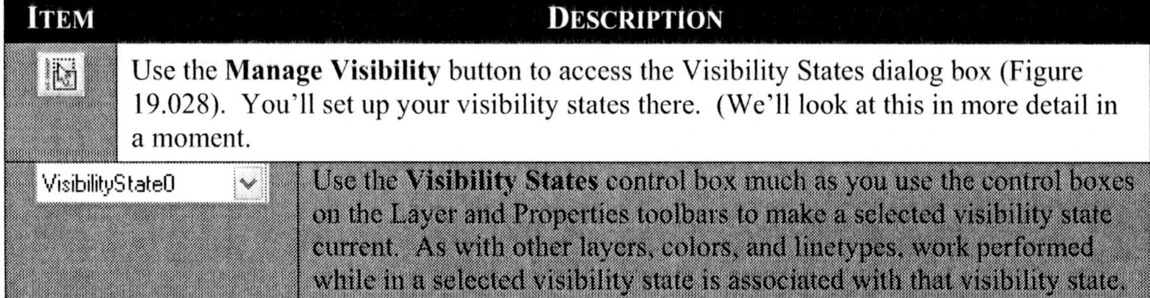

ITEM	DESCRIPTION
[Manage Visibility button icon]	Use the **Manage Visibility** button to access the Visibility States dialog box (Figure 19.028). You'll set up your visibility states there. (We'll look at this in more detail in a moment.
VisibilityState0	Use the **Visibility States** control box much as you use the control boxes on the Layer and Properties toolbars to make a selected visibility state current. As with other layers, colors, and linetypes, work performed while in a selected visibility state is associated with that visibility state.

Luckily, you won't find visibility states as complicated as layers. Take a look at the Visibility States dialog box (Figure 19.028). Most of it is fairly clear.

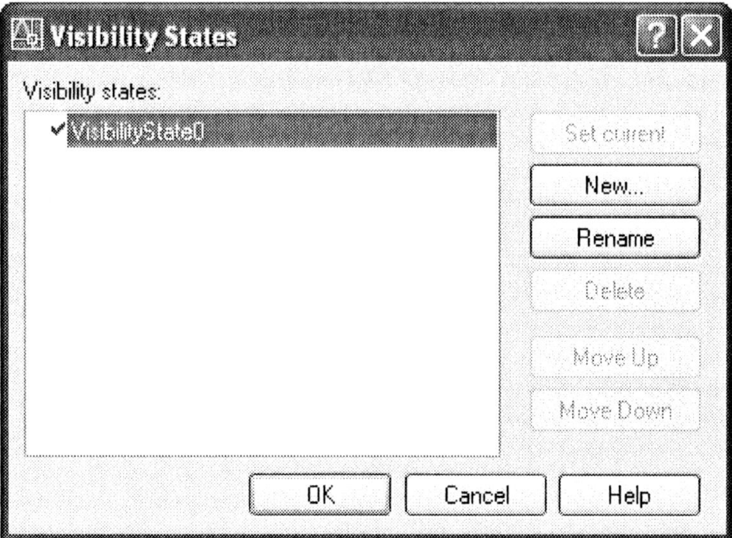

Figure 19.028

- The **Visibility states** list box lists all the states available in the block. Select one and use the **Set current** button to make it current.
- The buttons down the right side and across the bottom of the box are self-explanatory.
- The **New** button calls the New Visibility State dialog box (Figure 19.029). Here you'll name your new state and decide what, if anything, should be hidden in it. I recommend leaving the bullet next to **Leave visibility of existing objects unchanged in new state**. You can then adjust what is visible using the **Make Visible** and **Make Invisible** buttons on the toolbar.

Now let's look at Block Authoring Palettes (Figure 19.030).

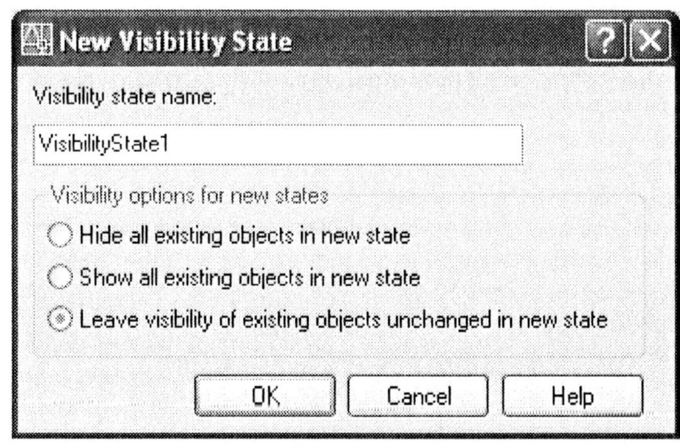

Figure 19.029

- We'll begin with the Parameters palette (Figure 19.030). Remember, for a block to be dynamic, it must contain at least one parameter (control object). The type of action you intend will govern which type of parameter you'll need to add. (All items on this palette invoke the associated option of the ***BParameter*** command.)

  We'll start at the top.

  - Associate a **Point Parameter** with a **Move** or **Stretch** operation, although it also works quite well for defining additional insertion points for your block. You can move or stretch specific points of the block when you've added a point parameter.

The **Point Parameter** will prompt:

Specify parameter location or [Name/Label/Chain/Description/Palette]: ***[locate the point]***

Specify label location: ***[locate the label – this can go anywhere but for organizational purposes, should go fairly close to the point]***

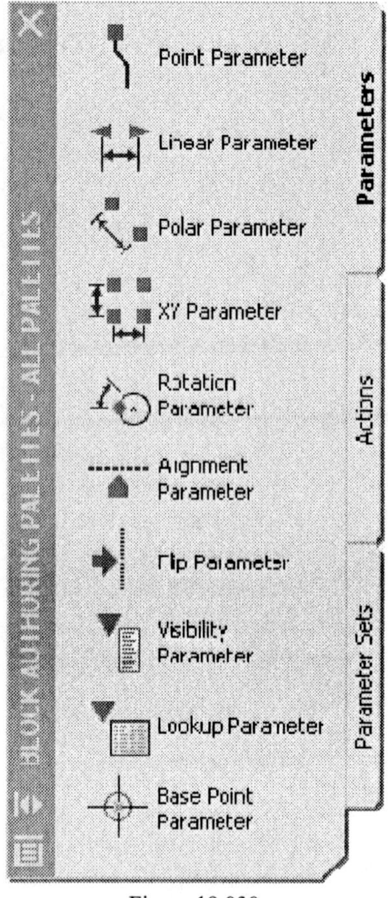

Figure 19.030

The first prompt offers you several options (which repeat for some of the other parameters).

- Assigning a **Name** to the parameter helps you locate it later in the Properties palette where you'll go to edit it.
- The **Label** should reflect the **Name**. The label helps you keep track of where you've located the parameter.
- You may find the **Chain** concept a bit difficult to understand at first. When you include the point parameter in the selection set of an action associated with a different parameter (call it parameter B), an edit of parameter B in the block will affect the point parameter. Now suppose you have a separate action associated with the point parameter. (That's two actions – the point parameter action and the parameter B action.) If the **Chain** option setting is **Yes**, any editing done with parameter B will also cause the action associated with the point parameter. If the **Chain** option setting is **No** (the default), the parameter B action will not cause the point parameter action to occur.
- Any **Description** you enter will appear in the Properties palette when you select the parameter in the block editor.
- The **Properties** option controls whether or not the parameter will appear in the Properties palette when the block is selected.

o Associate a **Linear Parameter** with a **Move**, **Stretch**, **Scale**, or **Array** action. You can move, stretch, scale, or array a group of objects when you've included a **Linear Parameter**. (Like a linear dimension, this is a workhorse. You'll use it as one way to resize tables, windows, doors, and other objects.) It prompts:

Specify start point or [Name/Label/Chain/Description/Base/Palette/Value set]: ***[pick the first endpoint of the parameter or another option]***

Specify endpoint: ***[pick the other endpoint of the parameter]***

Specify label location: ***[locate the label]***

You've seen most of the options of the first prompt, but let's look at the rest.

- The **Base** option will ask you for a **Base location** (either a **start point** or a **midpoint**). The **start point** will remain fixed when you edit the end points in the block editor. The **midpoint** will also remain fixed and both endpoints will react simultaneously to any editing.

- The **Value set** option provides a valuable key to block insertion. Its options include:
  - ∴ **None** means that a block edit of this parameter has no limits.
  - ∴ **List** means that, when a user edits the block, he can select from a list of available options (such as: window sizes, valve sizes, etc.).
  - ∴ **Increment** means that the user doesn't have to select from a list of different sizes, but resizing is restricted to incremental adjustments defined by the block editor. The editor can define the increment and a minimum and maximum adjustment.

- Associate a **Polar Parameter** with a **Move**, **Scale**, **Stretch**, **Polar Stretch**, or **Array** action. It's prompt is simple:

  Specify base point or [Name/Label/Chain/Description/Palette/Value set]: ***[pick base (or anchor) point of the parameter or another option]***

  Specify endpoint: ***[pick the other endpoint of the parameter]***

  Specify label location: ***[locate the label]***

You've already seen these options.

- Associate an **XY Parameter** with a **Move**, **Scale**, **Stretch**, or **Array** action. Use this parameter to move, scale, stretch, or array objects a set distance along the X- or Y-axis. (Set the distance with the **Value set** option.) It prompts:

  Specify base point or [Name/Label/Chain/Description/Palette/Value set]: ***[pick base point of the parameter or another option]***

  Specify endpoint: ***[pick a point that will define both the X- and Y-distance]***

- Associate a **Rotation Parameter** with a **Rotation** action only. Use it to rotate objects within a block (like the hands of a clock). It prompts:

  Specify base point or [Name/Label/Chain/Description/Palette/Value set]: ***[pick the base (or anchor) point of the parameter or another option]***

  Specify radius of parameter: ***[specify the radius or pick anywhere on the arc of the rotation]***

  Specify default rotation angle or [Base angle] <0>: ***[identify the base angle; zero indicates the current location of the object which will be rotated]***

  Specify label location: ***[locate the label]***

- You won't associate an **Alignment Parameter** with an action. Its location, however, is important as it will align the identified points with an object upon insertion. It prompts:

  Specify base point of alignment or [Name]: ***[pick a point along the path which will align with the drawing object]***

  Alignment type = Perpendicular

  Specify alignment direction or alignment type [Type] <Type>: ***[pick a second point along the path for a*** **Perpendicular** ***alignment or use the*** **Type** ***option to create a*** **Tangent** ***alignment]***

- Associate a **Flip Parameter** with a **Flip** action only. Use this to mirror a block insertion. It prompts:

  Specify base point of reflection line or [Name/Label/Description/Palette]: ***[pick a base point of the parameter (the first point of your mirror line) or another option]***

  Specify endpoint of reflection line: ***[pick a second point to identify the mirror line]***

  Specify label location: ***[locate the label]***

- Like the **Alignment Parameter**, you won't associate a **Visibility Parameter** with an action. It is, however, required to use Visibility States, which makes it required for a multiple styles block. It prompts:

  Specify parameter location or [Name/Label/Description/Palette]:

- Associate a **Lookup Parameter** with a **Lookup** action. This cool tool allows the user to select the size of an object from a lookup box. (We'll see this one in action in our exercise, too.) It prompts:

  Specify parameter location or [Name/Label/Description/Palette]:

  In this case, the location is fairly important as the grip for the lookup box will appear here.

- The **Base Point Parameter** is another that isn't associated with an action. It locates a point within the block which other objects in the block will use as a base point. It prompts:

  Specify parameter location:

- Next we'll look at the Actions Palette (Figure 19.031). Here, you'll assign actions to the parameters you added using the Parameters palette. This is the actual block modification setup. (All items on this palette invoke the associated option of the ***BAction*** command.)

  - You can associate the **Move Action** with a **Point**, **Linear**, **Polar**, or **XY** parameter. Use it to allow a user to move a block object(s). It prompts:

    Select parameter: ***[select the parameter with which you'll associate the action]***

    Specify parameter point to associate with action or enter [sTart point/Second point] <Second>: ***[pick one of the points of the parameter with which you'll associate the action – hit enter to use the second parameter point]***

    Specify selection set for action

    Select objects: ***[select the objects that will be affected by the action]***

    Select objects: ***[enter]***

    Specify action location or [Multiplier/Offset]: ***[locate the action symbol; you can locate it anywhere, but try to keep it close to the parameter for organizational purposes]***

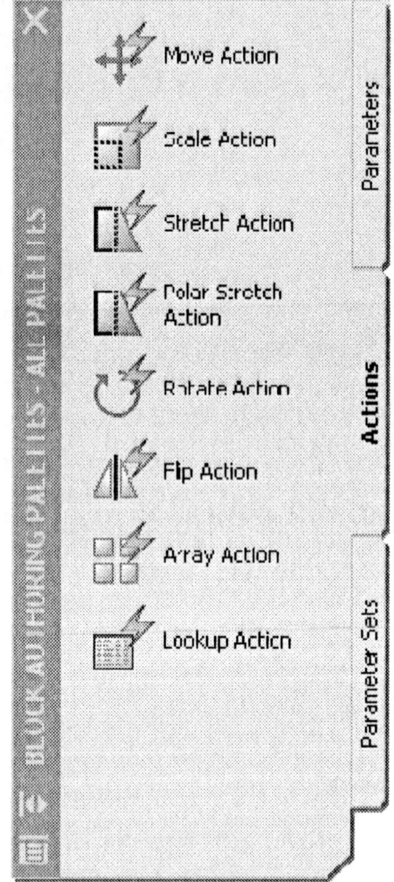

Figure 19.031

The second prompt allows you to select a **sTart point** or a **Second point**. You can ignore these options if you wish as the **sTart point** is the default and hitting ***enter*** will automatically select the **Second point** option.

You'll notice two other options – **Multiplier** and **Offset** – at the last prompt. When the action is triggered (when the user selects the associated grip), the **Multiplier** will multiply the action by a number you enter here. The **Offset** option has a similar result except that it factors the angle of the action by the number you enter in response to its prompt.

- You can associate the **Scale Action** with a **Linear**, **Polar**, or **XY** parameter. Use it to allow the CAD operator to scale selected objects within the block. **Scale Action** prompts:

  Select parameter: ***[select the parameter with which you'll associate the action]***

  Specify selection set for action

  Select objects: ***[select the objects that will be affected by the action]***

  Select objects: ***[enter]***

  Specify action location or [Base type]: ***[locate the action symbol; as always, you can locate it anywhere, but try to keep it close to the parameter for organizational purposes]***

  The only option that concerns you in this action is the **Base type** option of the last prompt. When selected, AutoCAD will prompt you to select either a **Dependent** base point (scaling done from the associated parameter's base point) or an **Independent** base point (scaling done from a user-identified base point).

- You can associate the **Stretch Action** with a **Point**, **Linear**, **Polar**, or **XY** parameter. Use it to allow the CAD operator to stretch selected objects within the block. **Stretch Action** prompts are similar to both the **Scale** and **Move Action** prompts:

  Select parameter: ***[select the parameter with which you'll associate the action]***

  Specify parameter point to associate with action or enter [sTart point/Second point] <Second>: ***[pick one of the points of the parameter with which you'll associate the action – hit enter to use the second parameter point]***

  Specify first corner of stretch frame or [CPolygon]: ***[create a typical crossing window]***

  Specify opposite corner:

  Specify objects to stretch

  Select objects: ***[select the objects to stretch]***

  Select objects: ***[enter]***

  Specify action location or [Multiplier/Offset]: ***[locate the action symbol]***

- You can associate the **Polar Stretch Action** only with a **Polar** parameter. Use it to allow the CAD operator to stretch selected objects within the block. **Polar Stretch Action** prompts are nearly identical to **Stretch Action** prompts:

  Select parameter: ***[select the Polar parameter with which you'll associate the action]***

  Specify parameter point to associate with action or enter [sTart point/Second point] <Second>: ***[pick one of the points of the parameter with which you'll associate the action – hit enter to use the second parameter point]***

  Specify first corner of stretch frame or [CPolygon]: ***[create a typical crossing window]***

  Specify opposite corner:

  Specify objects to stretch

  Select objects: ***[select the objects to stretch]***

  Select objects: ***[enter]***

  Specify objects to rotate only

  Select objects: ***[select objects that will rotate only (not stretch)]***

  Select objects: ***[enter]***

Specify action location or [Multiplier/Offset]: ***[locate the action symbol]***

- You can associate the **Rotate Action** only with a **Rotation** parameter. Use it to allow the CAD operator to rotate selected objects within the block. Compared to other actions, **Rotate Action** prompts are simple (and familiar):

  Select parameter: ***[select the Rotation parameter with which you'll associate the action]***

  Specify selection set for action

  Select objects: ***[select the objects that will rotate]***

  Select objects: ***[enter]***

  Specify action location or [Base type]: ***[locate the action symbol]***

- You can associate the **Flip Action** only with a **Flip** parameter. Use it to allow the CAD operator to "flip" or mirror objects within the block. This works much like the **Mirror** command (with the original objects removed). These prompts are also simple:

  Select parameter: ***[select the Flip parameter with which you'll associate the action]***

  Specify selection set for action

  Select objects: ***[select the objects that will flip]***

  Select objects: ***[enter]***

  Specify action location: ***[locate the action symbol]***

- You can associate the **Array Action** with a **Linear**, **Polar**, or **XY** parameter. Use it to allow the CAD operator to array selected objects within the block. **Array Action** prompts:

  Select parameter: ***[select the parameter with which you'll associate the action]***

  Specify selection set for action

  Select objects: ***[select the objects that will array]***

  Select objects: ***[enter]***

  Enter the distance between rows or specify unit cell (---): ***[as with the* Array *command, you must enter a distance between rows and cells; AutoCAD will limit the block object's array to these distances]***

  Enter the distance between columns (|||):

  Specify action location: ***[locate the action symbol]***

- You can associate the **Lookup Action** only with a **Lookup** parameter. Use it to allow the operator to select specific property values from a predefined list. **Lookup Action** prompts are very simple:

  Select parameter: ***[select the Lookup parameter with which you'll associate the action]***

  Specify action location: ***[locate the action symbol]***

  Once you've located the action symbol, AutoCAD presents the Property Lookup Table dialog box (Figure 19.032). Here you'll define the properties that will appear in the lookup box.

  - The name of the action associated with the table appears in the **Action name** box (upper left corner of the dialog box).

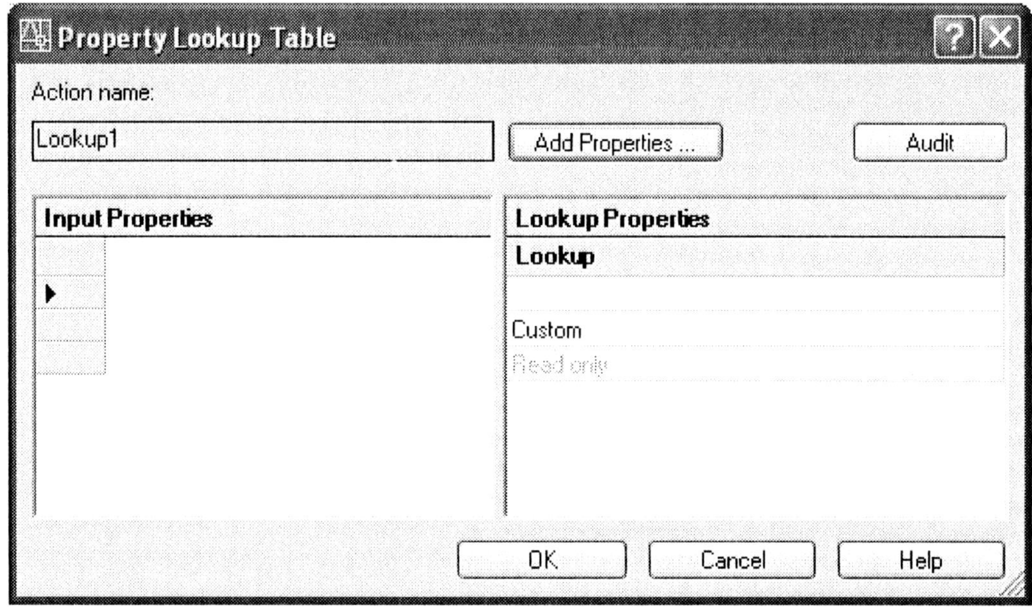

Figure 19.032

- The **Input Properties** list box contains columns of user-selected parameters associated with the dynamic block. When a parameter appears here, the corresponding name (found in the **Lookup Properties** list box) will appear in the lookup box.
- Use the **Add Properties** button to call the Add Properties dialog box. (Figure 19.033). Here you'll find a list of parameters already associated with the dynamic block. Select the property you'd like to add to the lookup box. (Use the **Add … properties** radio buttons to set what can be added to each of the list boxes.)

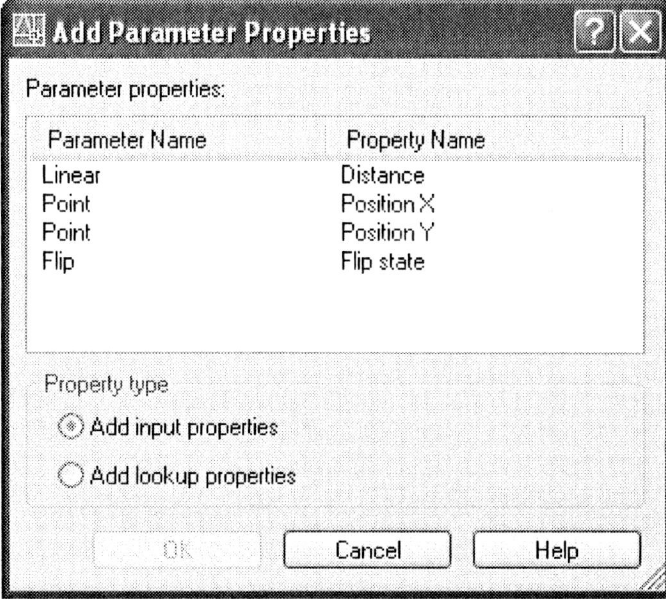

Figure 19.033

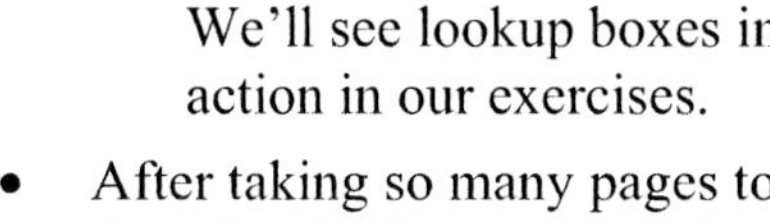

We'll see lookup boxes in action in our exercises.

- After taking so many pages to describe the Parameter and Action palettes, you might expect more from the Parameter Sets palette (Figure 19.034). These clever tools combine a parameter with an action, thus saving you the hassle of using both the Parameter and Action palette tools. (Notice the slider bar to the left; there are more tools available on the palette than can be shown here.)

Appendix G contains a chart to help you keep track of which actions and parameters can be paired.

Well that was a lot of pages of fun! I know, most of you fully understand dynamic blocks now, but let's try a couple exercises for those suffering that glazed look in their eyes.

In the next two exercises, we'll create three blocks – a door (we'll edit our door to make it much more efficient), a window, and a dining table.

- The window must be resizable. (We'll need 36" and 42" windows for the insertion exercise that follows.) We'll make it stretchable to predefined lengths.
- The door must be also resizable. (We'll need 30" and 36" doors.) We'll use a lookup box for this one. We must also be able to flip it to open in different directions. While we're there, let's give it another insertion point, too.
- The table will be our coup-de-grace. It'll be resizable to predefined lengths, have two styles of movable chairs, and align with a wall when we insert it.

Take a deep breath, put on some soft mood music, clear your calendar, and let's go …

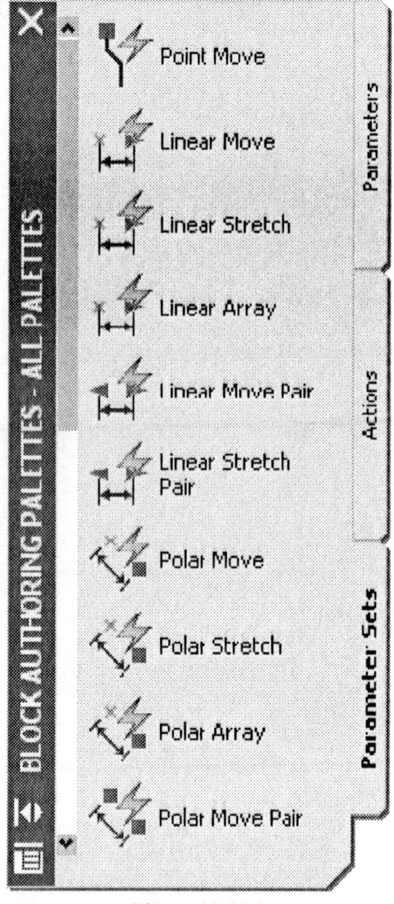

Figure 19.034

Do This: 19.3.1	Creating Dynamic Blocks

I. Reopen the *blocks.dwg* file the C:\Steps\Lesson19 folder.

II. Erase the horizontal line associated with the door block you created in Exercise 19.2.1.1.

III. Follow these steps.

TOOLS	COMMAND SEQUENCE	STEPS
	Command: *b*	1. Let's start with the easy one (the window), enter the ***Block*** command. AutoCAD presents the Block Definition dialog box (Figure 19.016.)

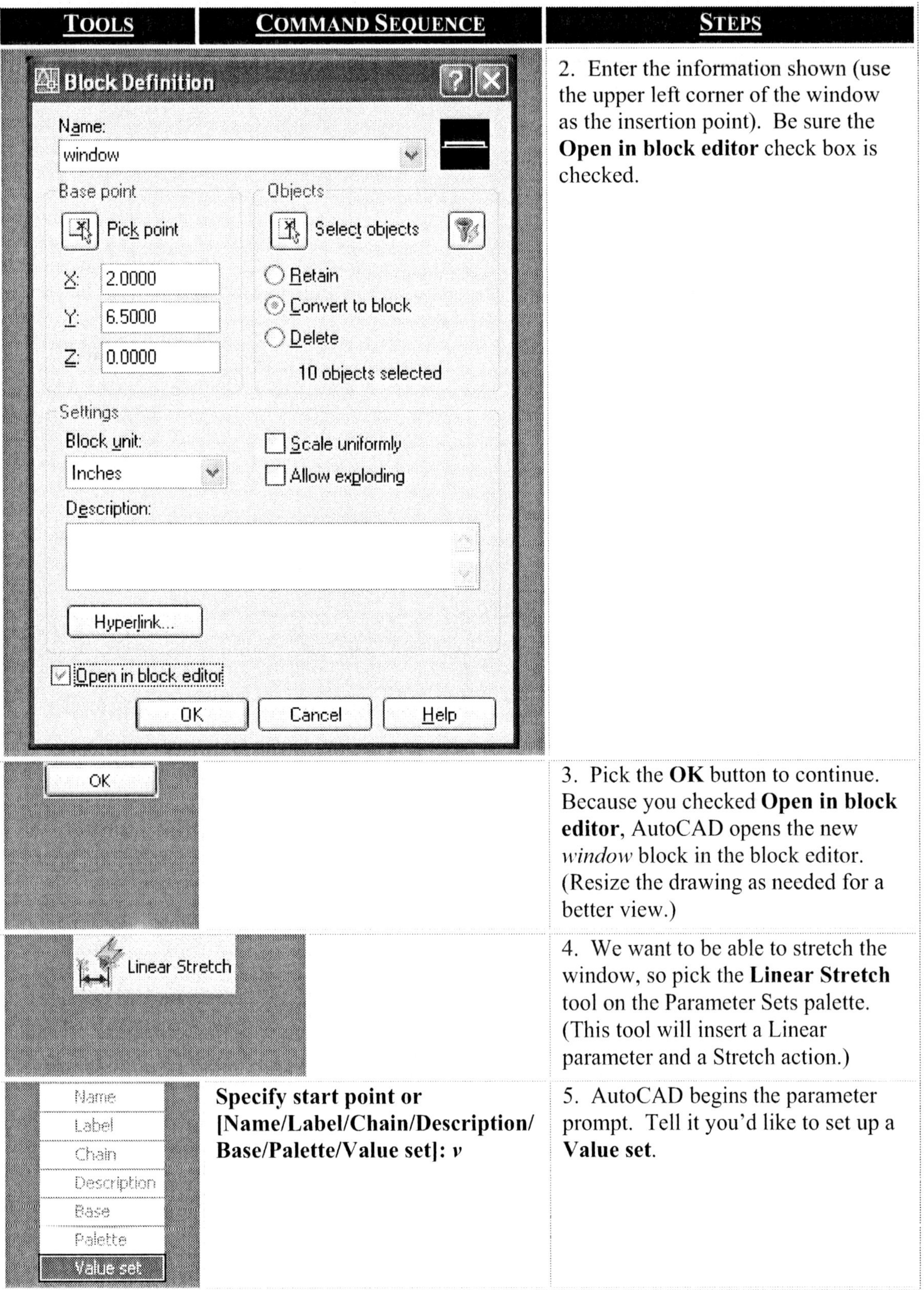

TOOLS	COMMAND SEQUENCE	STEPS
		2. Enter the information shown (use the upper left corner of the window as the insertion point). Be sure the **Open in block editor** check box is checked.
OK		3. Pick the **OK** button to continue. Because you checked **Open in block editor**, AutoCAD opens the new *window* block in the block editor. (Resize the drawing as needed for a better view.)
Linear Stretch		4. We want to be able to stretch the window, so pick the **Linear Stretch** tool on the Parameter Sets palette. (This tool will insert a Linear parameter and a Stretch action.)
Name Label Chain Description Base Palette Value set	**Specify start point or [Name/Label/Chain/Description/ Base/Palette/Value set]: *v***	5. AutoCAD begins the parameter prompt. Tell it you'd like to set up a **Value set**.

TOOLS	COMMAND SEQUENCE	STEPS
 None List • Increment	**Enter distance value set type [None/List/Increment] <None> :** ***i***	6. We'll use the **Incremental** option to limit the size of our window.
	Enter distance increment: ***3*** **Enter minimum distance:** ***24*** **Enter maximum distance:** ***42***	7. We'll allow windows from 24" to 42", sized in 3" increments.
	Specify start point or [Name/Label/Chain/Description/ Base/Palette/Value set]: **Specify endpoint:** **Specify label location:**	8. (Refer to Figure 19.035.) Now AutoCAD needs to know where to place the parameter. Place it as shown (start point on the left). When you use a parameter set, AutoCAD will locate the label for you.

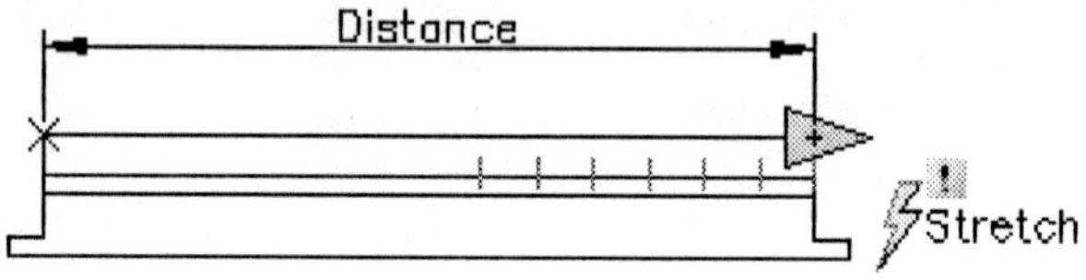

Distance

Stretch

Figure 19.035

Notice the increment identifiers locating the sizes you identified in Step 7. Notice also the **Stretch** label. The exclamation symbol indicates that you haven't identified the action yet. We'll do that now.

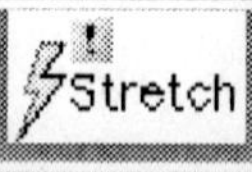 Stretch		9. Double click on the **Stretch** action label to define the action.
	Specify first corner of stretch frame or [CPolygon]: **Specify opposite corner:**	10. First, you'll create the stretch window (as you would with the ***Stretch*** command). Create the crossing window shown in Figure 19.036.

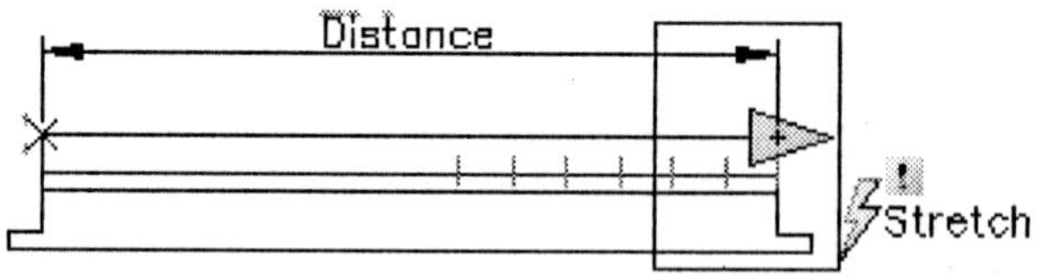

Distance

Stretch

Figure 19.036

	Specify objects to stretch **Select objects:** **Select objects:** ***[enter]***	11. Then you'll actually select the objects to stretch. Recreate the crossing window in Figure 19.036. (Hopefully, AutoCAD will correct this redundancy in future releases.)
 Stretch		12. Notice that the **Stretch** label no longer bears the exclamation point.

TOOLS	COMMAND SEQUENCE	STEPS
Close Block Editor		13. Save your work in the block editor. Then close the editor.
		14. Since you selected **Convert to block** in Step 2, AutoCAD has converted the window objects into a window block. Pick it now.
		15. Notice the grips on the window block (Figure 19.037). The arrow grip is a *block stretch* grip. Select it.

Figure 19.037

TOOLS	COMMAND SEQUENCE	STEPS
		16. Notice that when you selected the block stretch grip, AutoCAD showed you the available increments (Figure 19.038). Move the arrow back and forth. Notice that you can only resize the block to the available increments!

Figure 19.038

TOOLS	COMMAND SEQUENCE	STEPS
	Command: ***qsave***	17. Clear the grips and save the drawing. Don't exit.
No Button Available	**Command:** ***be***	18. Ready for something harder? Let's edit our door block to make it resizable … and flip-able. Double click on the door block you created in Exercise 19.2.1.1. (Alternately, you can enter the ***BEdit*** command.) Select the **door** block from the Edit Block Definition dialog box. AutoCAD opens the door block in the block editor.
Point Parameter		19. Let's start by adding a **Point** parameter that AutoCAD can use as a second insertion point. Pick **Point Parameter** on the Parameters palette.

TOOLS	COMMAND SEQUENCE	STEPS
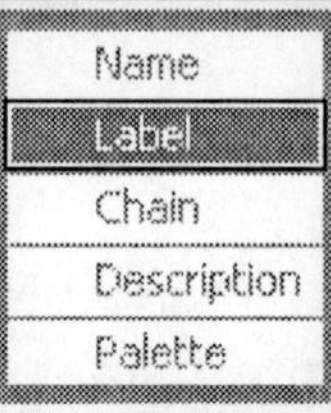 Name Label Chain Description Palette	**Specify parameter location or [Name/Label/Chain/Description/ Palette]:** ***L*** **Enter position property label <Position>:** ***Insertion Point 2***	20. Select the **Label** option, and call the parameter: **Insertion Point 2**.
	Specify parameter location or [Name/Label/Chain/Description/ Palette]: **Specify label location:**	21. Locate it as shown in Figure 19.039. As we have no action to associate with this parameter, we'll ignore the exclamation mark symbol.

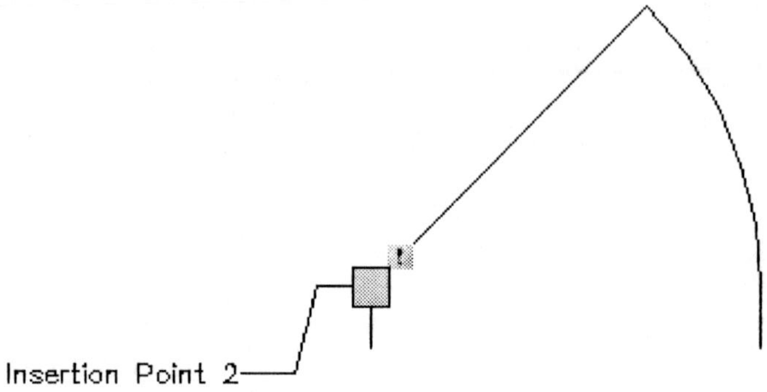

Insertion Point 2

Figure 19.039

TOOLS	COMMAND SEQUENCE	STEPS
 Flip Set		22. We'll make the door flip-able next. Select the **Flip Set** tool on the Parameter Sets palette. (You may have to scroll down a bit.)
	Specify base point of reflection line or [Name/Label/ Description/Palette]:	23. Use the midpoint of the eastern vertical line as the **base point of reflection**.
	Specify endpoint of reflection line: **Specify label location:**	24. Place the **endpoint of reflection line** (second point of the mirror line) anywhere to the west (use ORTHO). Locate the label as shown in Figure 19.040.

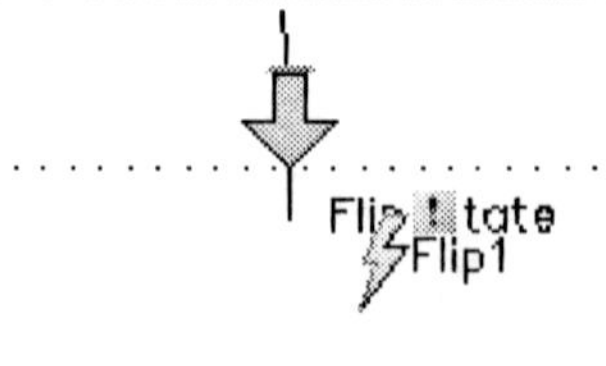

Flip1

Figure 19.040

TOOLS	COMMAND SEQUENCE	STEPS
 Flip1		25. We still need to define the **Flip** action. Double click on the action label.

TOOLS	COMMAND SEQUENCE	STEPS
	Specify selection set for action **Select objects:** ***all*** **Select objects:** ***[enter]***	26. Select all the objects in the block.
		27. Repeat Steps 23 through 27 using a **base point** midway between the midpoints of the two vertical lines. Make your **reflection line** vertical. (See Figure 19.041.)

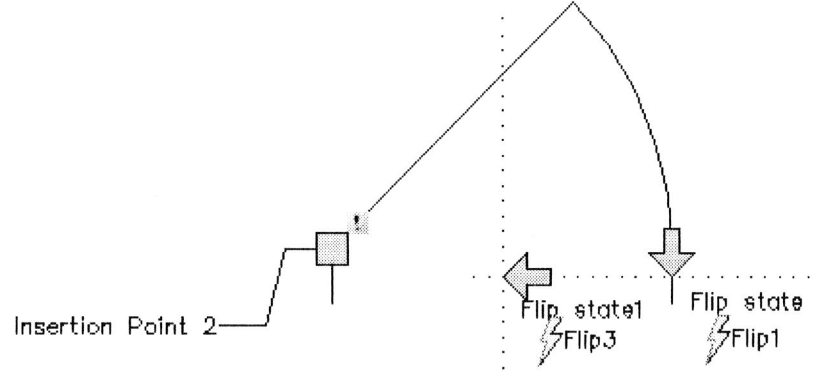

Figure 19.041

TOOLS	COMMAND SEQUENCE	STEPS
Linear Parameter		28. Now we'll make the block resizable and list the available sizes in a lookup box. Begin insertion of a Linear parameter. (Refer to Figure 19.042, and use **Linear Parameter** on the Parameter palette.)
None List Increment	**Specify start point or [Name/Label/Chain/ Description/Base/Palette/Value set]:** ***v*** **Enter distance value set type [None/List/Increment] <None> :** ***l***	29. This time, we'll use a **List Value set**. **List** is very similar to **Increment**, but it makes a list available for our use in the lookup box.
	Enter list of distance values (separated by commas): ***24,30,36***	30. Enter the values shown.
	Specify start point or [Name/Label/Chain/ Description/Base/Palette/Value set]: **Specify endpoint:** **Specify label location:**	31. Finally, locate the parameter as shown in Figure 19.042.

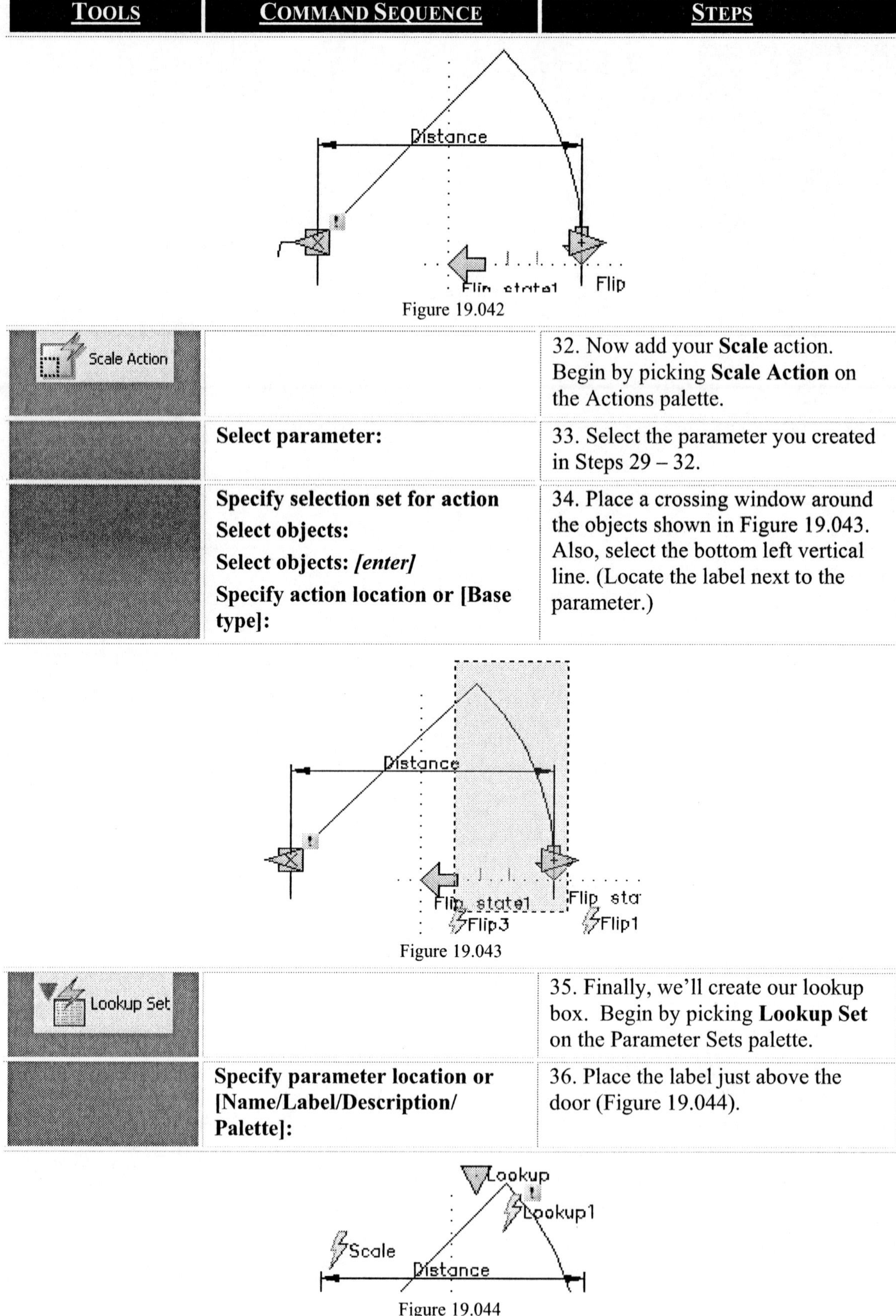

Figure 19.042

TOOLS	**COMMAND SEQUENCE**	**STEPS**
Scale Action		32. Now add your **Scale** action. Begin by picking **Scale Action** on the Actions palette.
	Select parameter:	33. Select the parameter you created in Steps 29 – 32.
	Specify selection set for action **Select objects:** **Select objects: *[enter]*** **Specify action location or [Base type]:**	34. Place a crossing window around the objects shown in Figure 19.043. Also, select the bottom left vertical line. (Locate the label next to the parameter.)

Figure 19.043

TOOLS	**COMMAND SEQUENCE**	**STEPS**
Lookup Set		35. Finally, we'll create our lookup box. Begin by picking **Lookup Set** on the Parameter Sets palette.
	Specify parameter location or [Name/Label/Description/ Palette]:	36. Place the label just above the door (Figure 19.044).

Figure 19.044

TOOLS	COMMAND SEQUENCE	STEPS
 Lookup1		37. Double click on the action label. AutoCAD opens the Properties Lookup Table dialog box (Figure 19.032).
 Add Properties ...		38. Pick the **Add Properties** button. AutoCAD opens the Add Parameter Properties dialog box (Figure 19.033).
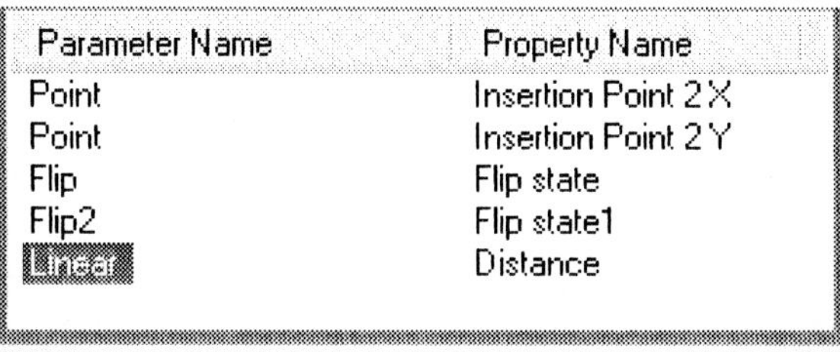 Parameter Name / Property Name Point / Insertion Point 2X Point / Insertion Point 2Y Flip / Flip state Flip2 / Flip state1 Linear / Distance		39. Pick the **Linear** parameter and then the **OK** button to return to the Properties Lookup Table dialog box.
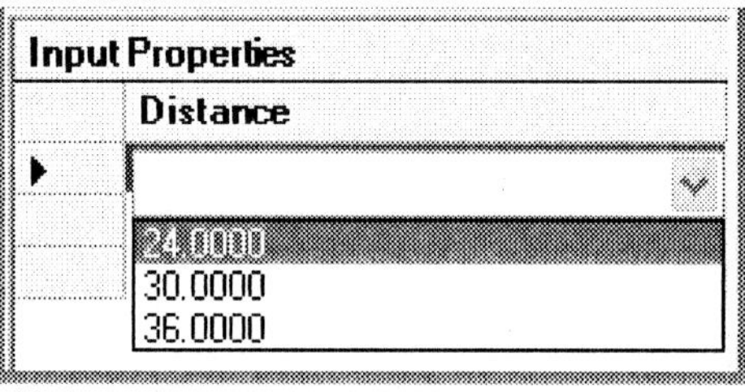 Input Properties Distance 24.0000 30.0000 36.0000		40. Under **Input Properties**, select the empty text box beside the arrow. A selection box will appear with the list you created in Step 31. Select the first item in the list.
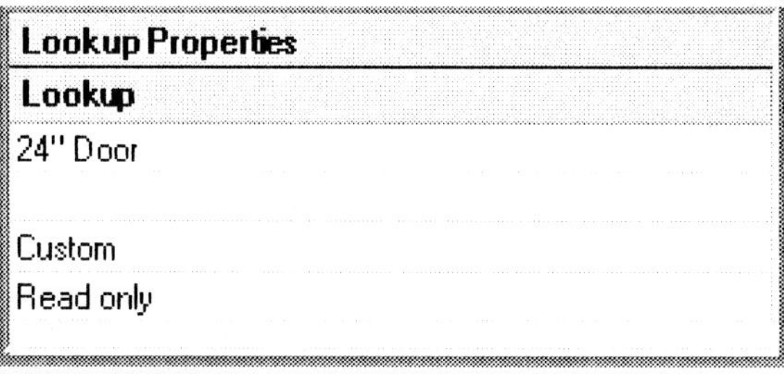 Lookup Properties Lookup 24" Door Custom Read only		41. In the corresponding row under Lookup Properties, enter ***24" Door***. (This is the text that will appear in the list box.)
		42. Repeat Steps 41 and 42 for the remaining items in the list.
		43. Finally, pick the **Read only** row under **Lookup Properties** and select **Allow reverse lookup** from the selection box that appears. (This step is necessary to make the list box available to the operator.) The box will look like Figure 19.045 when you've finished.

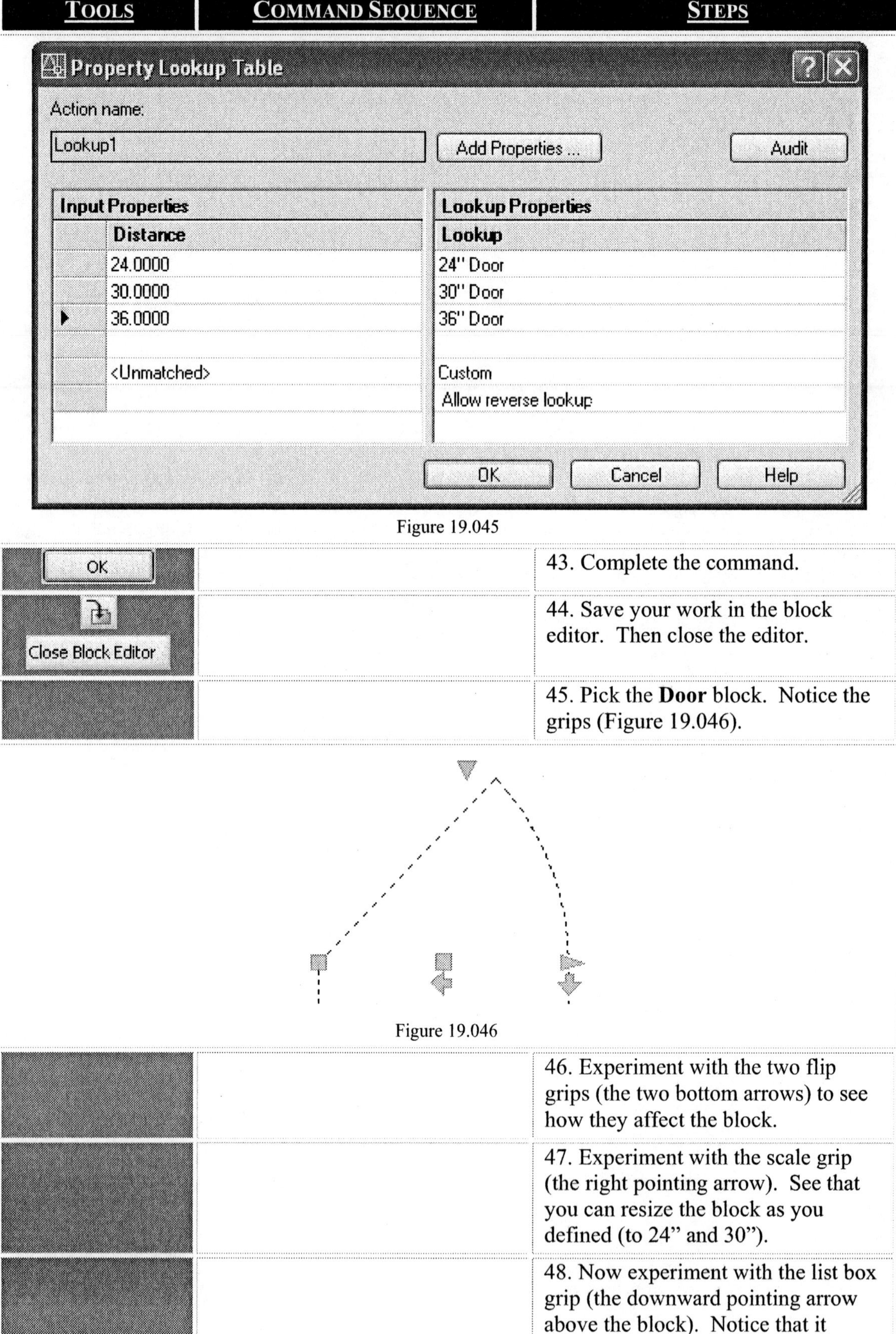

Figure 19.045

TOOLS	COMMAND SEQUENCE	STEPS
OK		43. Complete the command.
Close Block Editor		44. Save your work in the block editor. Then close the editor.
		45. Pick the **Door** block. Notice the grips (Figure 19.046).

Figure 19.046

TOOLS	COMMAND SEQUENCE	STEPS
		46. Experiment with the two flip grips (the two bottom arrows) to see how they affect the block.
		47. Experiment with the scale grip (the right pointing arrow). See that you can resize the block as you defined (to 24" and 30").
		48. Now experiment with the list box grip (the downward pointing arrow above the block). Notice that it

TOOLS	COMMAND SEQUENCE	STEPS
		shows the available sizes for the door (Figure 19.047). Notice also that you can resize the door by selecting the size you want.

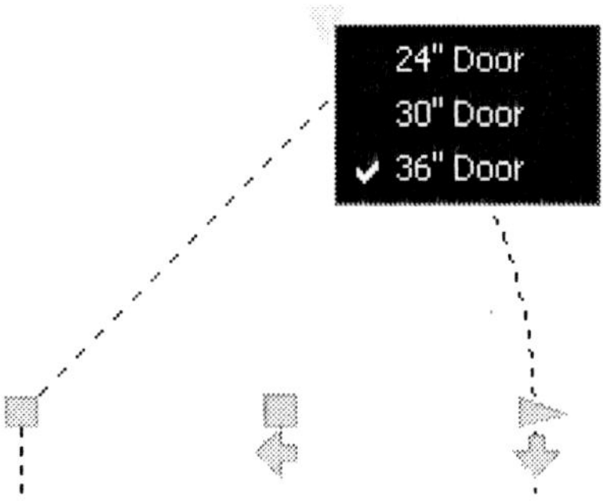

24" Door
30" Door
36" Door

Figure 19.047

TOOLS	COMMAND SEQUENCE	STEPS
	Command: ***i***	49. Begin to insert the *door* block. (Remove all checks in the Insert dialog box except the **Insertion point – Specify On-screen** box.)
		50. When AutoCAD prompts you for an insertion point (notice you're dragging the block on the screen), hit the CTRL key to toggle between the blocks insertion points.
		51. Abort the insertion.
	Command: ***qsave***	52. Save the drawing but don't exit.

Are you beginning to see the benefits of dynamic blocks? Let's move on to the next exercise – creating the dynamic table.

Do This: 19.3.2	Creating Dynamic Blocks (Continued)

I. Be sure you're still in the *blocks.dwg* file the C:\Steps\Lesson19 folder. If not, please open it now.

II. Restore the **Table** view.

III. Follow these steps.

TOOLS	COMMAND SEQUENCE	STEPS
	Command: ***be***	1. Enter the ***BEdit*** command and select the *table* block.

TOOLS	COMMAND SEQUENCE	STEPS
Linear Stretch		2. Create a **Linear Stretch** Parameter Set with Listed increments of 36, 48, 60, 72, and 84. Select the right end of the table to stretch. (Refer to our last exercise and to Figure 19.049 on the next page if you need assistance.)
Lookup Set		3. Create a **Lookup Set** to go with the Linear parameter list you created in Step 2.
Point Move		4. Now let's set up our block so we can move the chair around after it's inserted. Begin a **Point Move** Parameter Set.
	Specify parameter location or [Name/Label/Chain/ Description/ Palette]: *L* **Enter position property label <Position>: *Chair Location***	5. Call the parameter, ***Chair Location***.
	Specify parameter location or [Name/Label/Chain/ Description/ Palette]: _qua of **Specify label location:**	6. Place the parameter at the northern quadrant of the chair (Figure 19.048).

Figure 19.048

TOOLS	COMMAND SEQUENCE	STEPS
Move	**Specify selection set for action** **Select objects:**	7. Double click on the **Move** action, and create a selection set consisting of the objects that make up the chair. The drawing looks like Figure 19.049.

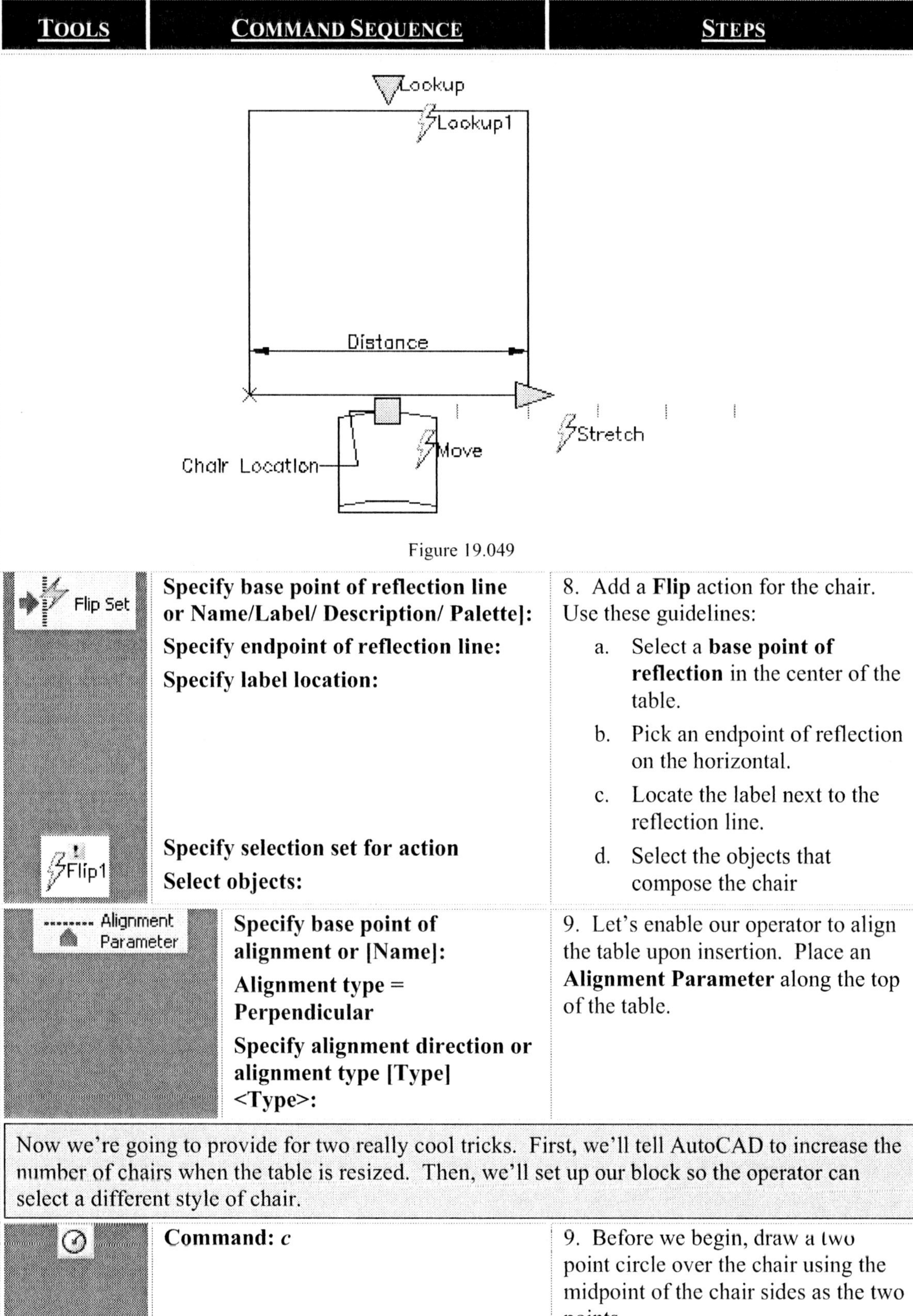

Figure 19.049

TOOLS	**COMMAND SEQUENCE**	**STEPS**
Flip Set Flip1	**Specify base point of reflection line or Name/Label/ Description/ Palette]:** **Specify endpoint of reflection line:** **Specify label location:** **Specify selection set for action** **Select objects:**	8. Add a **Flip** action for the chair. Use these guidelines: a. Select a **base point of reflection** in the center of the table. b. Pick an endpoint of reflection on the horizontal. c. Locate the label next to the reflection line. d. Select the objects that compose the chair
Alignment Parameter	**Specify base point of alignment or [Name]:** **Alignment type = Perpendicular** **Specify alignment direction or alignment type [Type] <Type>:**	9. Let's enable our operator to align the table upon insertion. Place an **Alignment Parameter** along the top of the table.

Now we're going to provide for two really cool tricks. First, we'll tell AutoCAD to increase the number of chairs when the table is resized. Then, we'll set up our block so the operator can select a different style of chair.

	Command: ***c***	9. Before we begin, draw a two point circle over the chair using the midpoint of the chair sides as the two points.

TOOLS	COMMAND SEQUENCE	STEPS
	Specify selection set for action object [New/Modify] <New>: _m **Select object to add to action set or [Remove]:** **Select object to add to action set or [Remove]:** ***[enter]***	10. Now here's a handy trick. We need to add the circle to the selection set for the **Flip** action. Double click on the action symbol. AutoCAD assumes you wish to add objects to the selection set and prompts you to do so. Select the circle.
		11. Repeat Step 10 to add the circle to the **Move** action next to the chair. (Isn't editing actions a breeze?!)
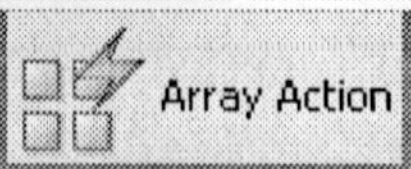 Array Action		12. We'll use the **Array** action with an existing parameter to have AutoCAD increase the number of chairs as the table stretches. Pick **Array Action** on the Action palette.
	Select parameter:	13. Select the Linear parameter you created in Step 2. (It looks like a **Distance** dimension.)
	Specify selection set for action **Select objects:** **Select objects:** ***[enter]***	14. Select the objects that compose the chair and the circle you drew in Step 9.
	Enter the distance between columns (|||): ***25*** **Specify action location:**	15. Tell AutoCAD to place the chairs 25" apart, and place the label next to the chair. (See Figure 19.049 for the current drawing.)

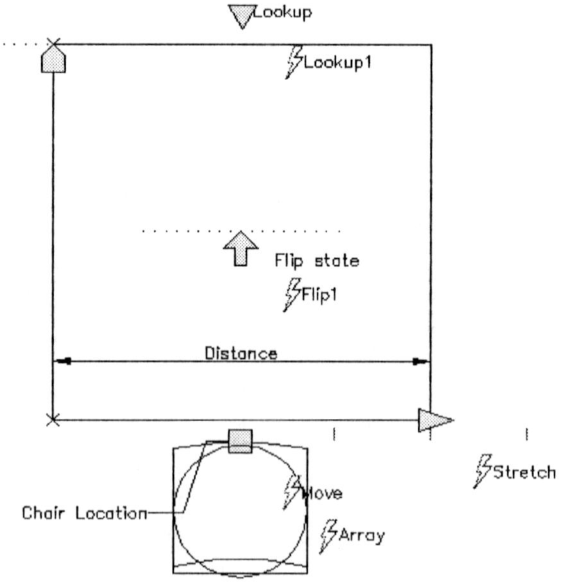

Figure 19.050

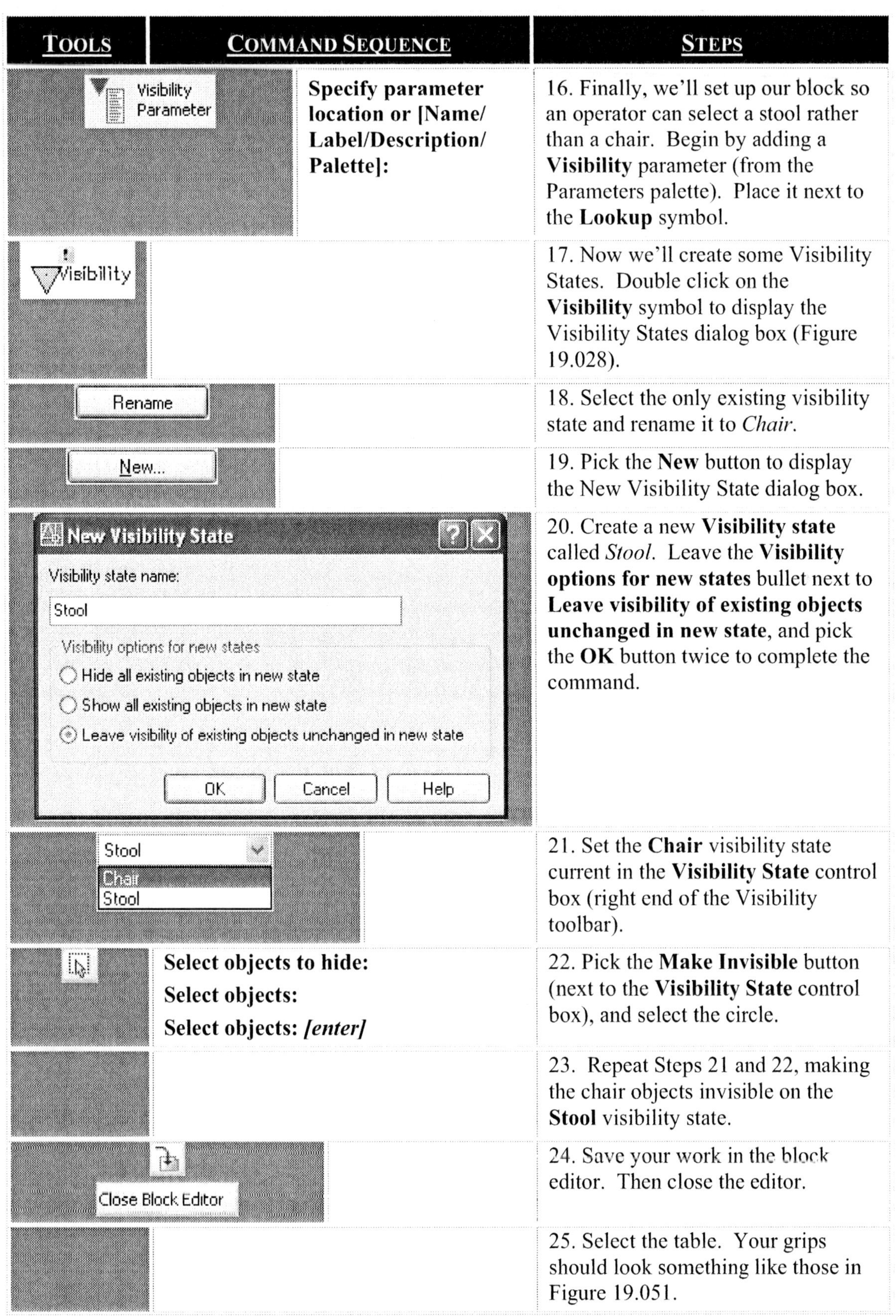

Tools	Command Sequence	Steps
Visibility Parameter	**Specify parameter location or [Name/ Label/Description/ Palette]:**	16. Finally, we'll set up our block so an operator can select a stool rather than a chair. Begin by adding a **Visibility** parameter (from the Parameters palette). Place it next to the **Lookup** symbol.
Visibility		17. Now we'll create some Visibility States. Double click on the **Visibility** symbol to display the Visibility States dialog box (Figure 19.028).
Rename		18. Select the only existing visibility state and rename it to *Chair*.
New...		19. Pick the **New** button to display the New Visibility State dialog box.
New Visibility State Visibility state name: Stool Visibility options for new states Hide all existing objects in new state Show all existing objects in new state Leave visibility of existing objects unchanged in new state OK Cancel Help		20. Create a new **Visibility state** called *Stool*. Leave the **Visibility options for new states** bullet next to **Leave visibility of existing objects unchanged in new state**, and pick the **OK** button twice to complete the command.
Stool Chair Stool		21. Set the **Chair** visibility state current in the **Visibility State** control box (right end of the Visibility toolbar).
	Select objects to hide: **Select objects:** **Select objects: *[enter]***	22. Pick the **Make Invisible** button (next to the **Visibility State** control box), and select the circle.
		23. Repeat Steps 21 and 22, making the chair objects invisible on the **Stool** visibility state.
Close Block Editor		24. Save your work in the block editor. Then close the editor.
		25. Select the table. Your grips should look something like those in Figure 19.051.

TOOLS	COMMAND SEQUENCE	STEPS
	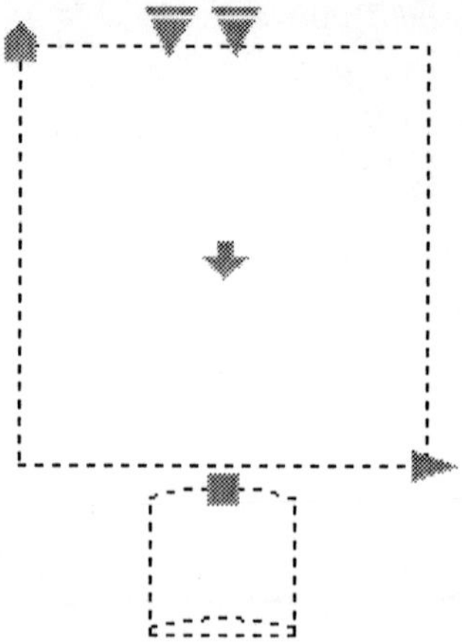 Figure 19.051	
		26. Experiment with flipping the chair (use the arrow grip in the center of the table).
		27. Experiment with the chair location (use the grip on the chair).
		28. Select the different table sizes from the list box grip (the down arrow on the left). Notice that AutoCAD adds more chairs as the table gets longer.
		29. Use the other down arrow grip to select the stool. Notice how the type of chair changes.
	**Command: *qsave***	30. Save the drawing.
		31. Use the ***WBlock*** command to save the blocks to the C:\Steps\Lesson19 folder. (Refer to Exercise 19.2.2.1 if you need help.)

Now use the blocks you've created to complete the *cab-pln.dwg* file you began earlier. It will look like Figure 19.052 when you've finished.

Let's take a look now at a couple other cool tools that make blocks nearly indispensable.

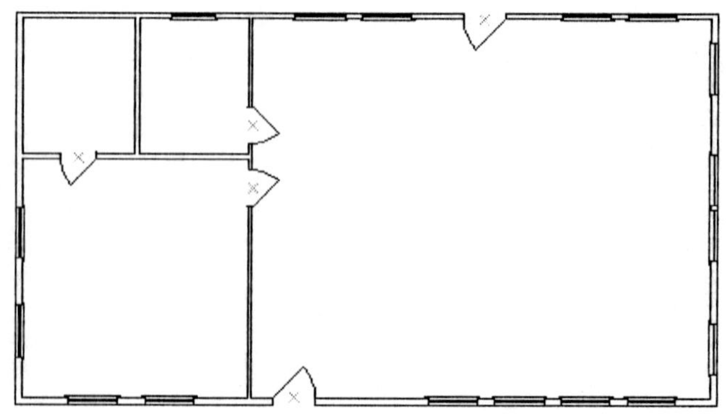

Figure 19.052

19.4 Other Insertion Methods

19.4.1 Getting Blocks from a Folder Library on a Web Site via AutoCAD's iDrop

AutoCAD has a marvelous toy called *iDrop*, and it bears closer examination before we proceed.

What is iDrop?

iDrop is the name given to a simple procedure for grabbing drawings (Write Blocks) from an iDrop enabled web site (folder) library and then dragging and dropping them into your drawing.

Why bother when I can create my own blocks?

Taking iDrop drawings from a manufacturer's site means that you have the exact item you want. It greatly reduces any possibility of error during the exchange of information between manufacturer and designer, including dimensional errors and engineering data provided through attributes. (We'll look more at attributes in Lesson 20.) It also saves the designer/draftsperson drawing time as well as research time.

Before you get too excited, however, let me give the downside. iDrop is fairly new. To date, not all manufacturers have iDrop-enabled blocks for you to use (although the list is growing). Additionally, the programmers at Autodesk designed the plug-in for Internet Explorer 5 or better. So you may need to change or upgrade your web browser. Finally, all insertions use a command line interface.

Let's take a look at that command line interface.

When you insert a iDrop, AutoCAD will prompt:

> **Specify insertion point or**
>
> **[Basepoint/Scale/X/Y/Z/Rotate/PScale/PX/PY/PZ/PRotate]:** ***[using coordinates or picking a point with the mouse, tell AutoCAD where to put the block (you're precisely locating the block's insertion point)]***

We're presented with a few options.

- AutoCAD asks for an **insertion point**. This sounds simple enough but the list of options that follows the prompt can be quite confusing. Let's take a look at these:
  - Selecting the **Basepoint** option will allow you to temporarily drop the block into the drawing where it's currently located. It then prompts:

    > **Specify base point:** ***[select a new base point]***

    AutoCAD will then allow you to insert the block using your new base point. (This procedure *does not* redefine the base point of the block.)
  - The first series of options (those without the "**P**" prefix) allows you to scale the block as it's inserted. **Scale** and **Rotate** do just what they say. **X/Y/Z** options allow you to scale along the selected axis.
  - The second series of option (those with the "**P**" prefix) does just what its counterparts without the **P** do, except that the scale or rotation is only for preview purposes.

Once you're ready, proceed with the next exercise. (This exercise requires Internet access and Internet Explorer.)

Do This: 19.4.1.1	iDrop and Block Insertions

I. Open the *cab-pln.dwg* file the C:\Steps\Lesson19 folder. We'll iDrop some bathroom fixtures from our uneedcad site.

II. Freeze the **MARKER** layer and create a new layer for fixtures. Make the new layer current.

III. Open Internet Explorer and go to this site: *http://www.uneedcad.com/2006.*

IV. Follow these steps.

TOOLS	COMMAND SEQUENCE	STEPS
		1. If your browser is maximized, pick the **Restore** button in the upper right corner of the window to float it over the AutoCAD window.
		2. Scroll down until you see the tub, sink, and WC (Figure 19.053).

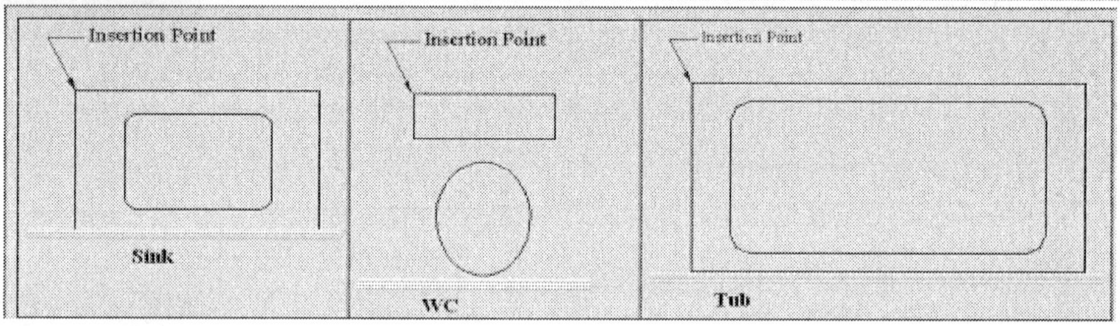

Insertion Point
Sink
Insertion Point
WC
Insertion Point
Tub

Figure 19.053

TOOLS	COMMAND SEQUENCE	STEPS
 iDrop Cursor		3. Notice the cursor when you pass over one of these items. It takes the shape of a tiny eyedropper.
		4. Pick anywhere in the AutoCAD window to make it active.
		5. Zoom in around the bathroom. Your screen should look something like Figure 19.054.

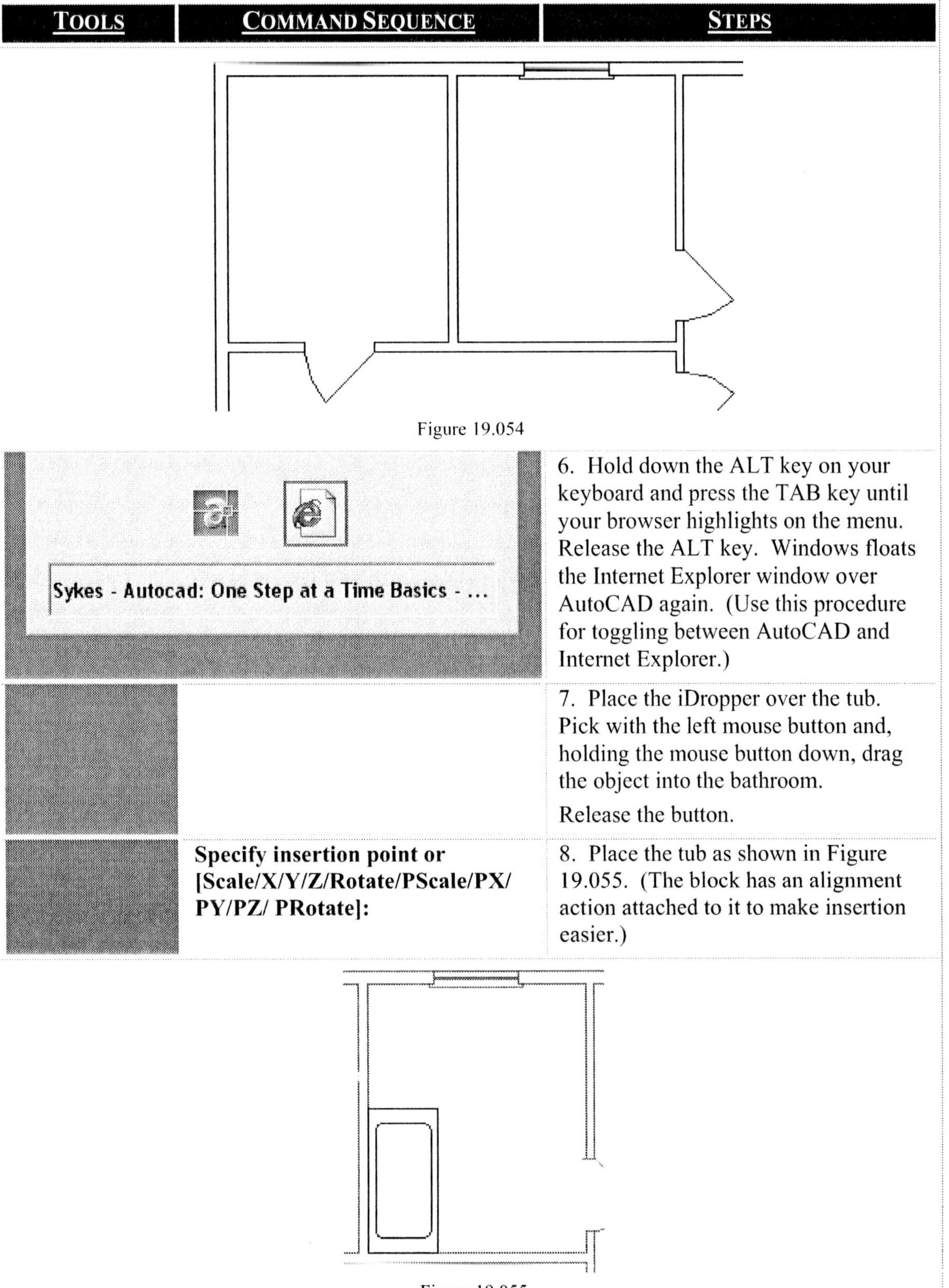

Tools	Command Sequence	Steps
	Figure 19.054	
		6. Hold down the ALT key on your keyboard and press the TAB key until your browser highlights on the menu. Release the ALT key. Windows floats the Internet Explorer window over AutoCAD again. (Use this procedure for toggling between AutoCAD and Internet Explorer.)
		7. Place the iDropper over the tub. Pick with the left mouse button and, holding the mouse button down, drag the object into the bathroom. Release the button.
	Specify insertion point or [Scale/X/Y/Z/Rotate/PScale/PX/ PY/PZ/ PRotate]:	8. Place the tub as shown in Figure 19.055. (The block has an alignment action attached to it to make insertion easier.)
	Figure 19.055	

Tools	Command Sequence	Steps
		9. Repeat Steps 6, 7, and 8 to insert the sink and WC. Then change the sink to **oval** and the WC to **Smooth**. Your drawing looks like Figure 19.056.

Figure 19.056

	Command: ***qsave***	10. Save your work. Close Internet Explorer.

19.4.2 Adding Blocks with the ADC or Tool Palettes

We first met the ADC (AutoCAD Design Center) back in Lesson 6 when we saw that we could share layer definitions between drawings. Well, sharing blocks between drawings is just as easy! In fact, with AutoCAD, you can view objects in a template library (or another drawing) as easily as you could view the different types of hatch patterns using the ***Hatch*** command.

In our next exercise, we'll take advantage of several things – first, we'll use the ADC to access a block on the web. We'll use the ADC to insert a block directly into our drawing (we'll use iDrop to do this); then we'll create a new tool palette in which to put our block so that we can access it more quickly and easily in the future (and to give us some experience creating tool palettes). Last, we'll use the tool palettes to insert another block into our drawing. (This exercise also requires Internet access.)

Let's give it a try.

Do This: 19.4.2.1 Sharing Blocks

I. Be sure you're still in the *cab-pln.dwg* file the C:\Steps\Lesson19 folder. If not, please open it now.

II. Zoom to display the bedroom (the large room to the left of the drawing).

III. Create a **Furniture** layer and make it current.

IV. Follow these steps.

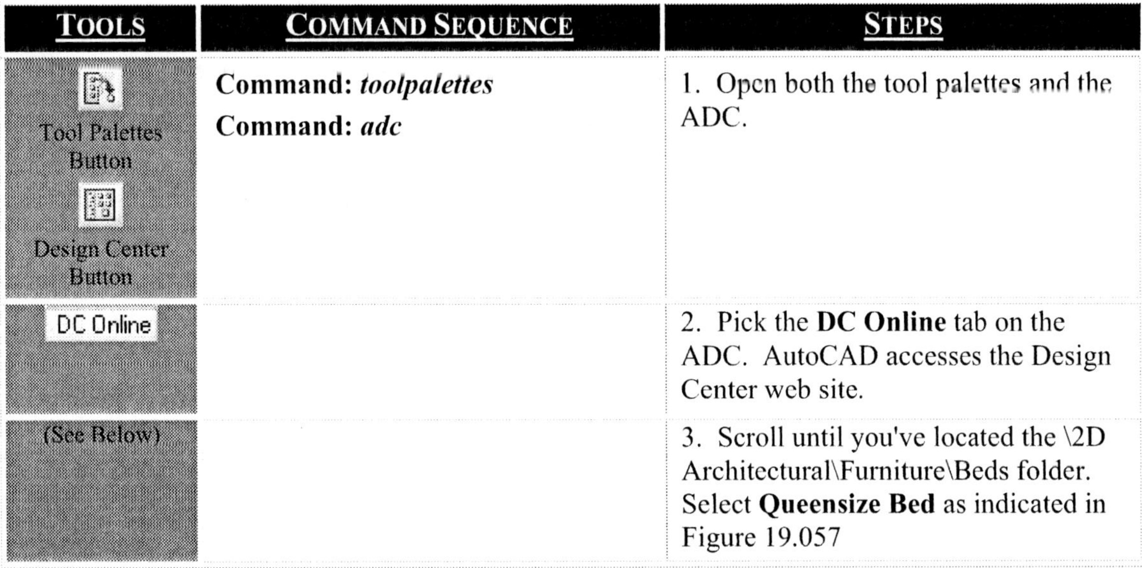

TOOLS	COMMAND SEQUENCE	STEPS
Tool Palettes Button Design Center Button	**Command:** ***toolpalettes*** **Command:** ***adc***	1. Open both the tool palettes and the ADC.
DC Online		2. Pick the **DC Online** tab on the ADC. AutoCAD accesses the Design Center web site.
(See Below)		3. Scroll until you've located the \2D Architectural\Furniture\Beds folder. Select **Queensize Bed** as indicated in Figure 19.057

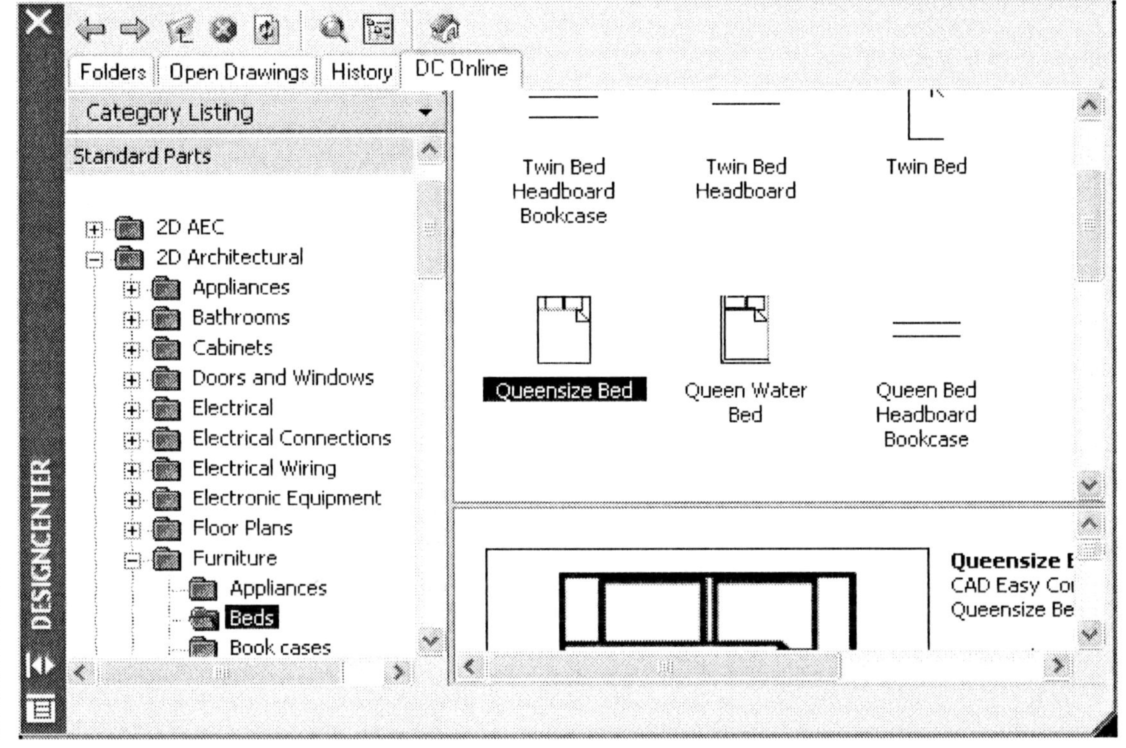

Figure 19.057

	Specify insertion point or [Scale/X/Y/Z/Rotate/PScale/PX/PY/PZ/PRotate]: ***r*** **Specify rotation angle:** ***270*** **Specify insertion point:**	4. Using the iDrop technique you learned in our last exercise, drag the bed and place it into the bedroom (Figure 19.058).

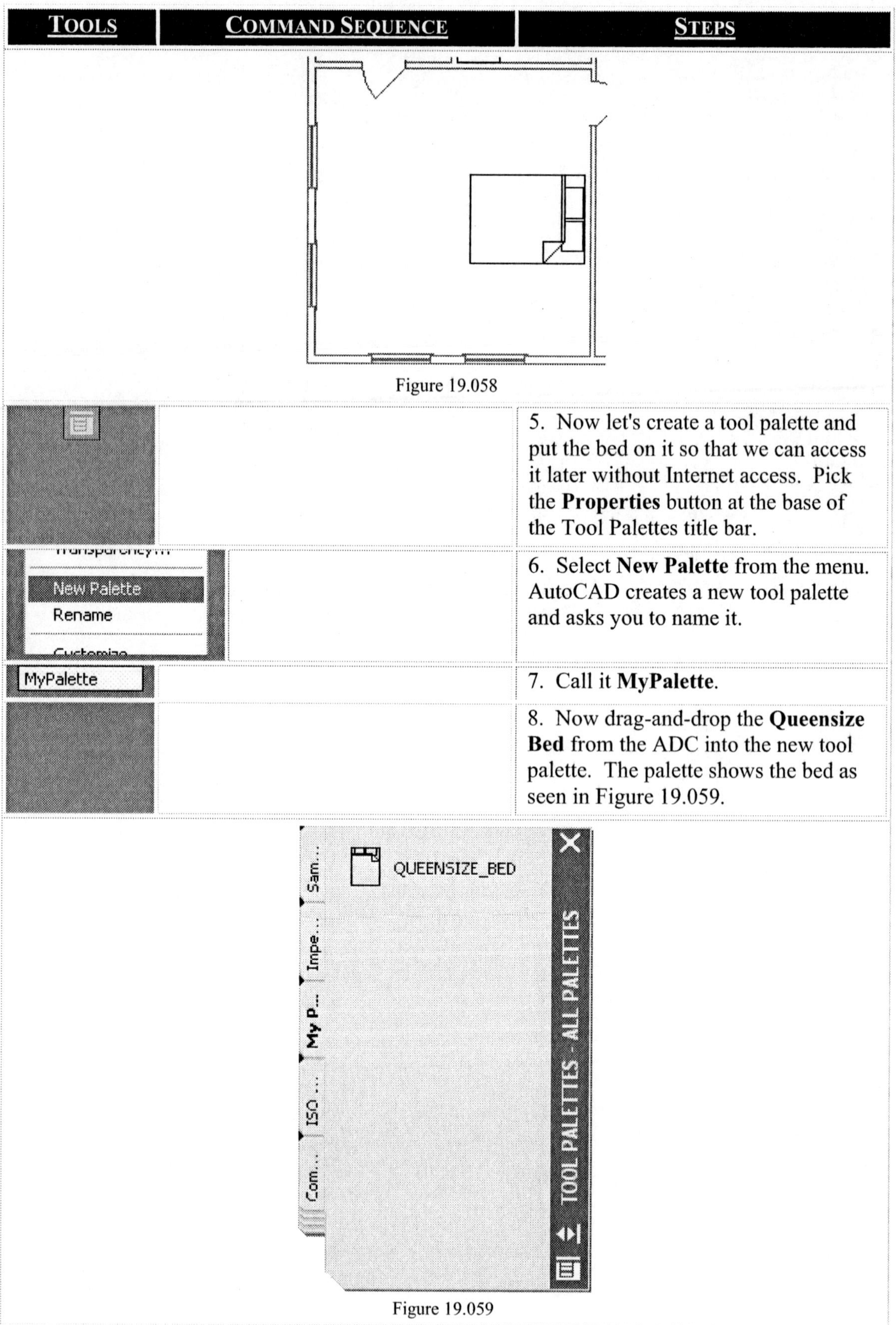

Tools	Command Sequence	Steps
		Figure 19.058
		5. Now let's create a tool palette and put the bed on it so that we can access it later without Internet access. Pick the **Properties** button at the base of the Tool Palettes title bar.
		6. Select **New Palette** from the menu. AutoCAD creates a new tool palette and asks you to name it.
		7. Call it **MyPalette**.
		8. Now drag-and-drop the **Queensize Bed** from the ADC into the new tool palette. The palette shows the bed as seen in Figure 19.059.
		Figure 19.059

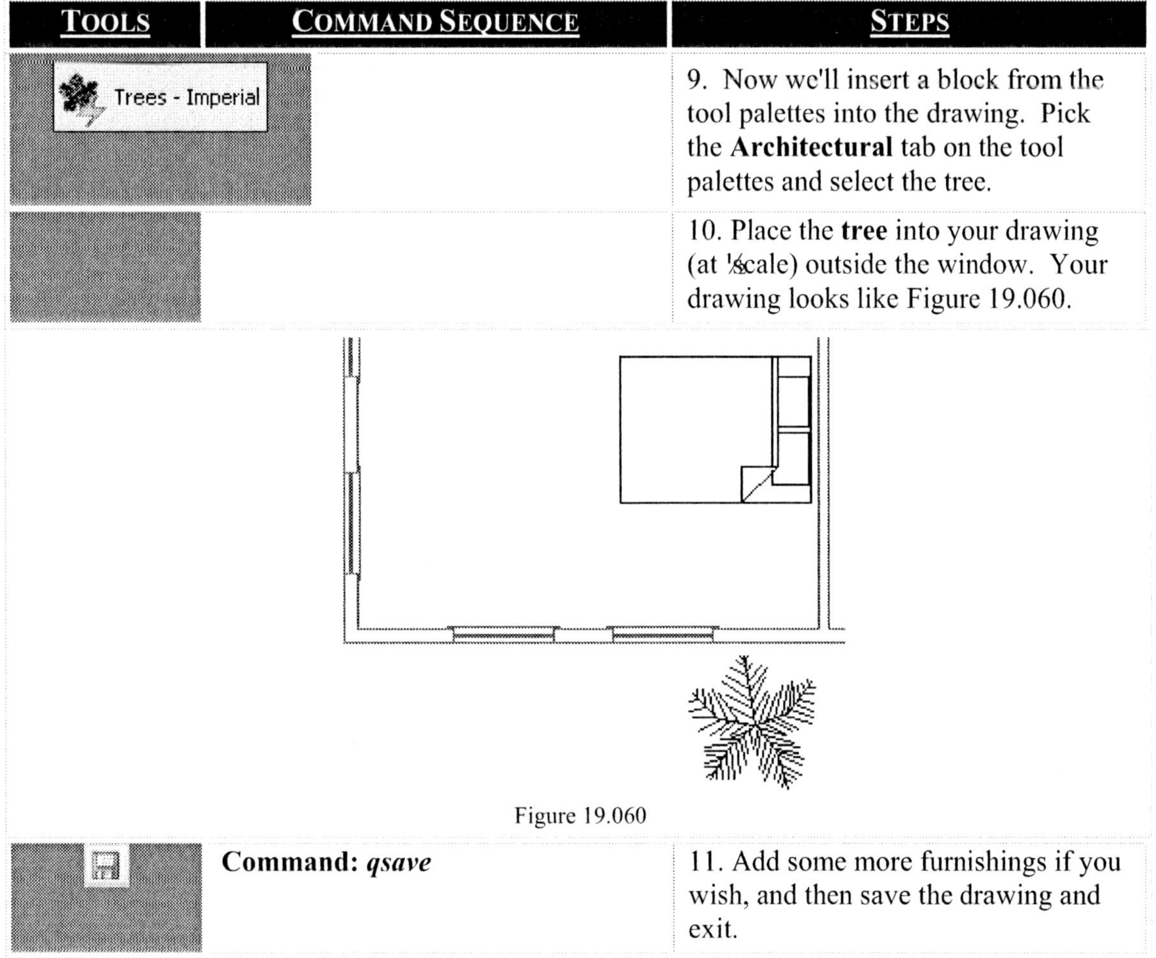

Tools	Command Sequence	Steps
Trees - Imperial		9. Now we'll insert a block from the tool palettes into the drawing. Pick the **Architectural** tab on the tool palettes and select the tree.
		10. Place the **tree** into your drawing (at ½scale) outside the window. Your drawing looks like Figure 19.060.

Figure 19.060

Tools	Command Sequence	Steps
	Command: ***qsave***	11. Add some more furnishings if you wish, and then save the drawing and exit.

These procedures save quite a bit of time by showing the CAD operator exactly what's available for insertion from any library!

19.5 Extra Steps

1. Familiarize yourself with the following chart to help you know when to use groups and when to use blocks.

Ability	Blocks	Groups
Can be shared between drawings	Yes	No
You can work on objects within the block/group	Yes	Yes
Can be treated as a single object	Yes	Yes
Can carry information (data)	Yes	No
Retrievable after erasure (without the Undo command)	Yes	No
May contain (other) blocks	Yes	Yes
May contain (other) groups	No	Yes

2. Experiment with inserting blocks into tables. Use the ***TInsert*** command. Use AutoCAD's Help menu if you have trouble.

19.6 What Have We Learned?

Items covered in this lesson include:

- *Working with groups*
- *Folder & template libraries*
- *Block creation, insertion, and editing*
- *Using iDrop, the ADC, and tool palettes to share blocks between drawings*
- *AutoCAD Commands:*
    - ***Block***
    - ***Explode***
    - ***WBlock***
    - ***Insert***
    - ***BEdit***
    - ***BParameter***
    - ***BAction***
    - ***BVMode***
    - ***TInsert***

After 18 lessons of learning *How*, we've begun to answer the question *Why*. *Why* is CAD a better design tool than paper and pencil? *Why* should I spend thousands of dollars to do on a computer what I can do for a lot less on a board? *Why* must I educate myself (or in many cases, reeducate myself) to work with a computer?

Hopefully, the answers began to dawn on many of you in this last lesson.

We'd already seen throughout this book that CAD drawings are neater and easier to read than many pen or pencil drawings. But up to the beginning of Lesson 18, it all seemed like a lot of work – often more than a comparable board drawing might require.

Then in Lesson 19, we found ways to manipulate large numbers of objects at once. With blocks, once created (or purchased), *no further drawing is necessary!* Additionally, a project (often a company and occasionally an entire industry) can expect standard symbols!

But believe it or not, we've only begun to scratch the surface of what we can accomplish using blocks. Wait until you see what we do in Lesson 20!

19.7 Exercises

1. Using the folder library we began in this lesson, place the doors and windows in the *flr-pln19.dwg* file located in the C:\Steps\Lesson19 folder. You'll need to create an additional block to complete the drawing. The details are shown in Figure 19.061. The completed floor plan is shown in Figure 19.062 (the dimension layer has been frozen for clarity).

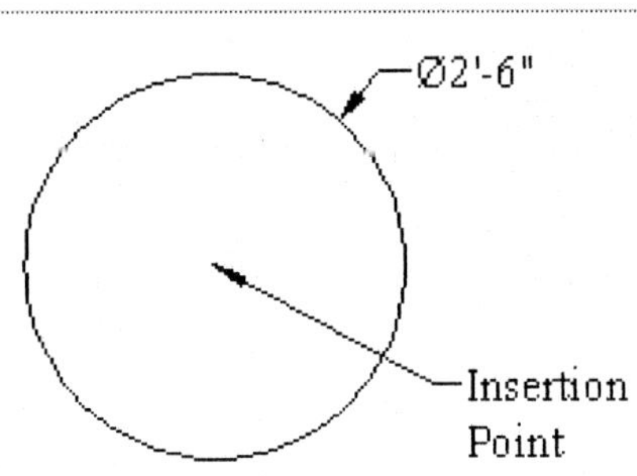

Figure 19.061: Water Heater

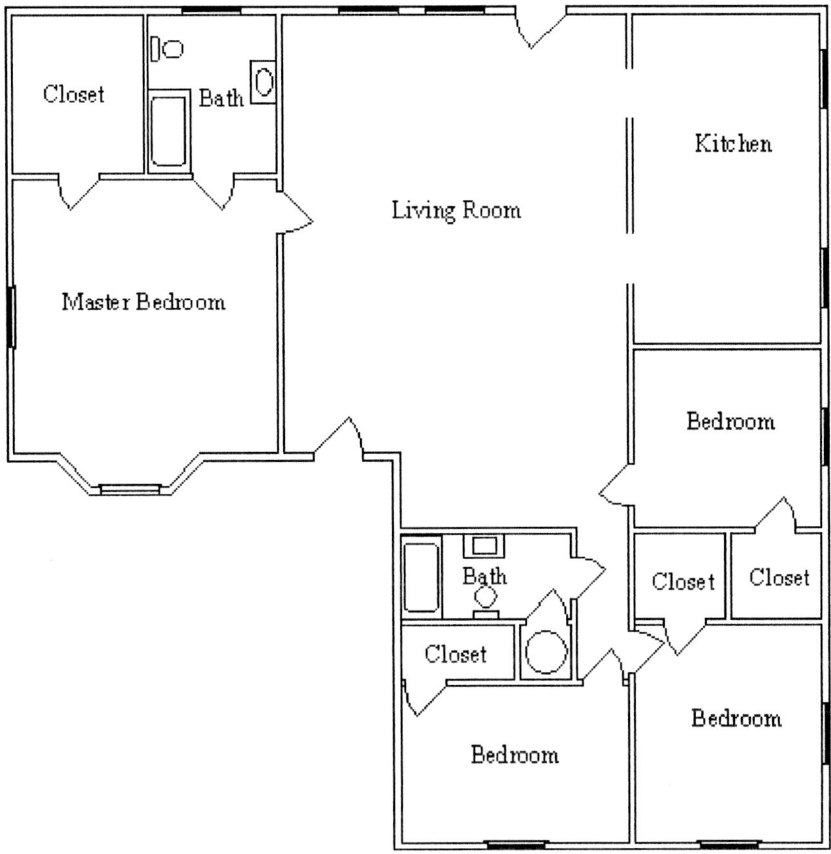

Figure 19.062: Completed Drawing

2. Start a new drawing from scratch.
    2.1. Set the limits for a full scale drawing on an 8½" x 11" sheet of paper.
    2.2. Grid: ¼"
    2.3. Create the layers indicated (all layers use a continuous linetype).
    2.4. Use the Times New Roman font. Text sizes are ¼", 0.2", and 1/8."
    2.5. Create the blocks shown in the *Legend* (Figure 19.063). (Remember to create all blocks on layer 0.)
    2.6. Create the drawing shown in Figure 19.063 (be sure to insert blocks on the appropriate layer). Use a table for the legend. Save it as *MyBridge* in the C:\Steps\Lesson19 folder.

LAYER NAME	COLOR
Battery	56
Border	5 (white)
Coil	4 (cyan)
Copperwire	3 (green)
Galvanometer	7 (white)
Pin	7 (white)
Resistor	6 (magenta)
Switch	1 (red)
Text	2 (yellow)

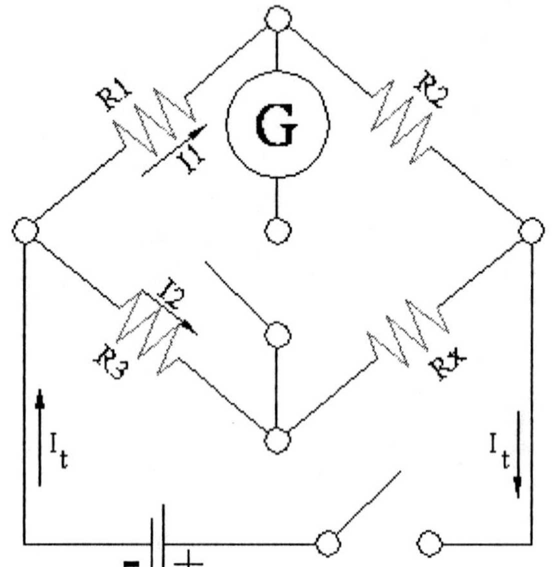

Legend	
	Battery
	Galvanometer
	Long Coil
	Pin
	Resistor
	Short Coil
	Switch

Figure 19.063: My Bridge

3. Start a new drawing from scratch.
    3.1. Repeat the setup you used for Exercise 2 with the following exceptions:
        3.1.1. Add a layer called *Loop* using color 32.
        3.1.2. Grid: ½
        3.1.3. Use the standard text style with ¼" and 0.2" text heights.
        3.1.4. Use the battery block you created in Exercise 2 and create a block for the wire loop.
    3.2. Create the *ElectroMagnet Circuitry* drawing shown in Figure 19.064. Save it as *MyMagnet* in the C:\Steps\Lesson19 folder.

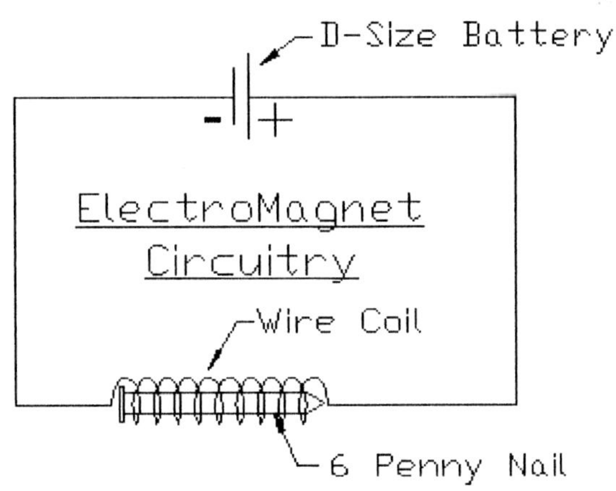

Figure 19.064: ElectroMagnet Circuitry

4. Using what you've learned, create the two drawings (Figs. 19.067 & 19.068). Use blocks whenever possible. Be sure to use appropriate layers and complete dimensioning as shown. The details shown in Figures 19.065 & 19.066 will help. Both drawings should plot on a scale of 3/8"=1'-0" on an 11" x 8½" sheet of paper. Use a title block.

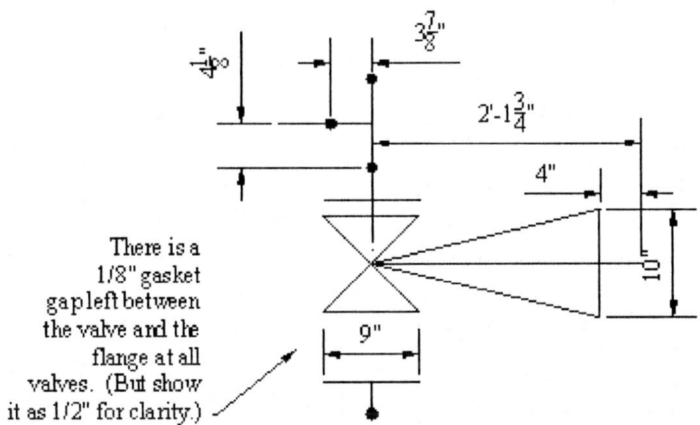

Figure 19.065

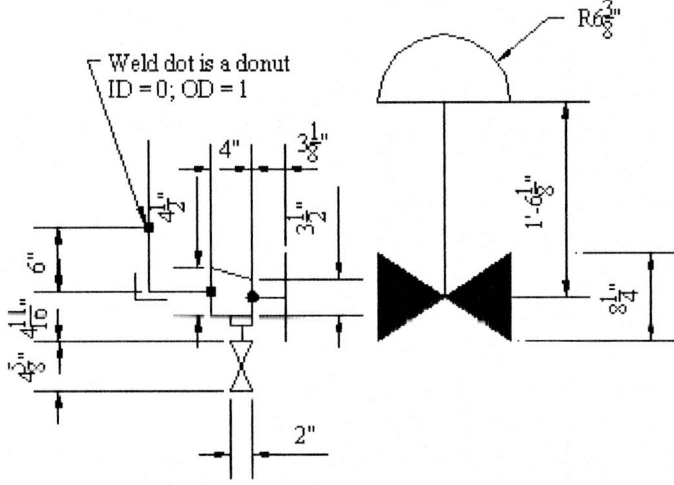

Figure 19.066

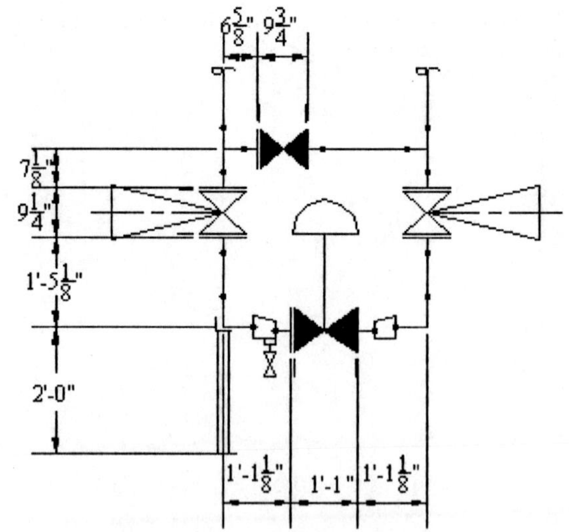

Figure 19.067: Control Station #1

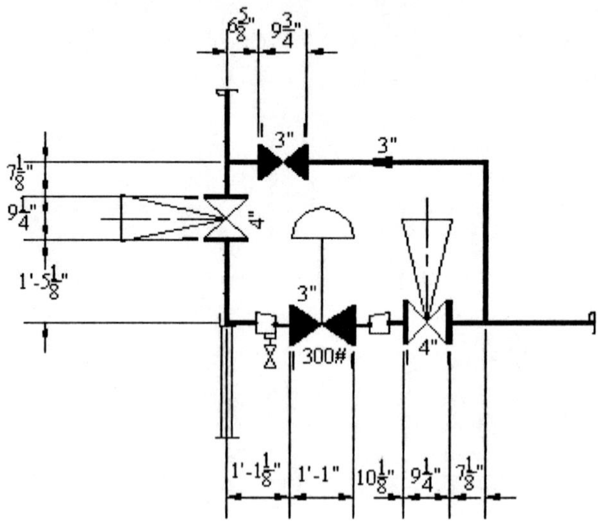

Figure 19.068: Control Station #2

5. Using blocks wherever possible, create the schematic drawing shown in Figure 19.069. Again, be sure to use appropriate layers. I used ½" grid marks.

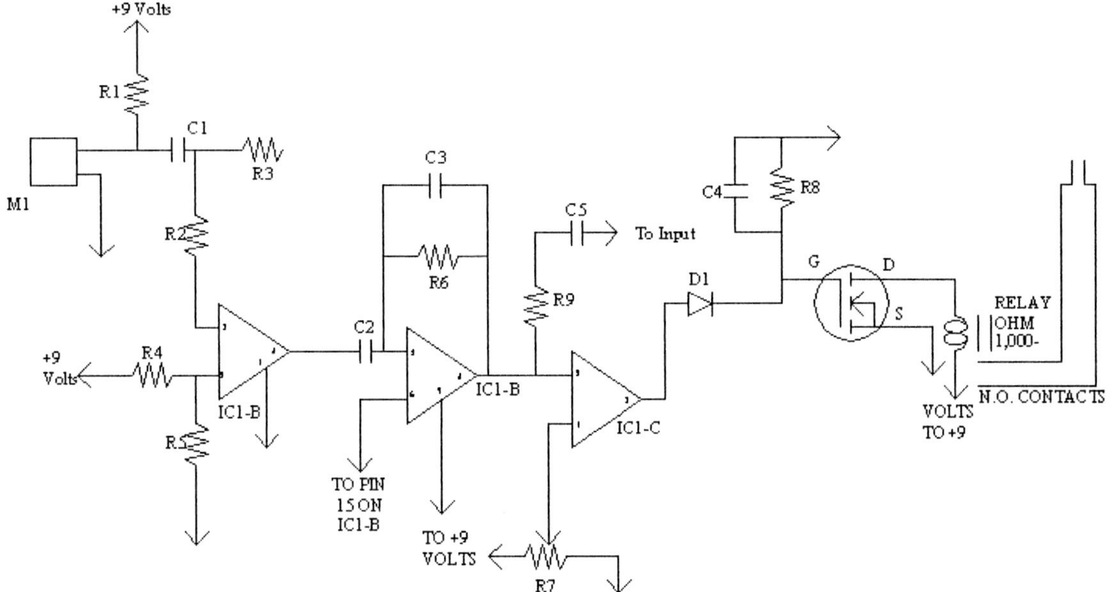

Figure 19.069: Schematic

6. Using blocks whenever possible, create the fireplace plans shown in Figures 19.070 and 19.071. The grid shown on each is 1".

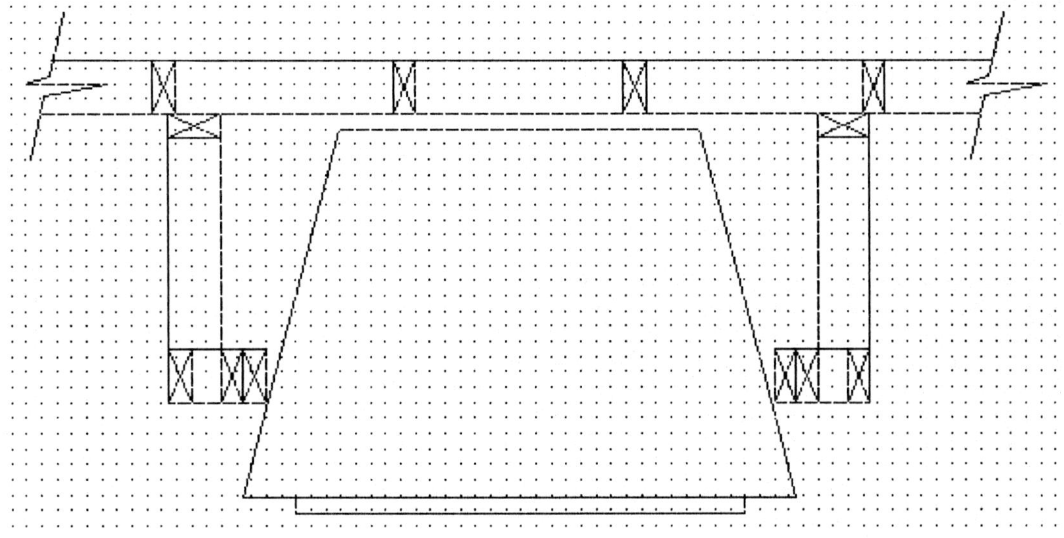

Figure 19.070: Fireplace Plan

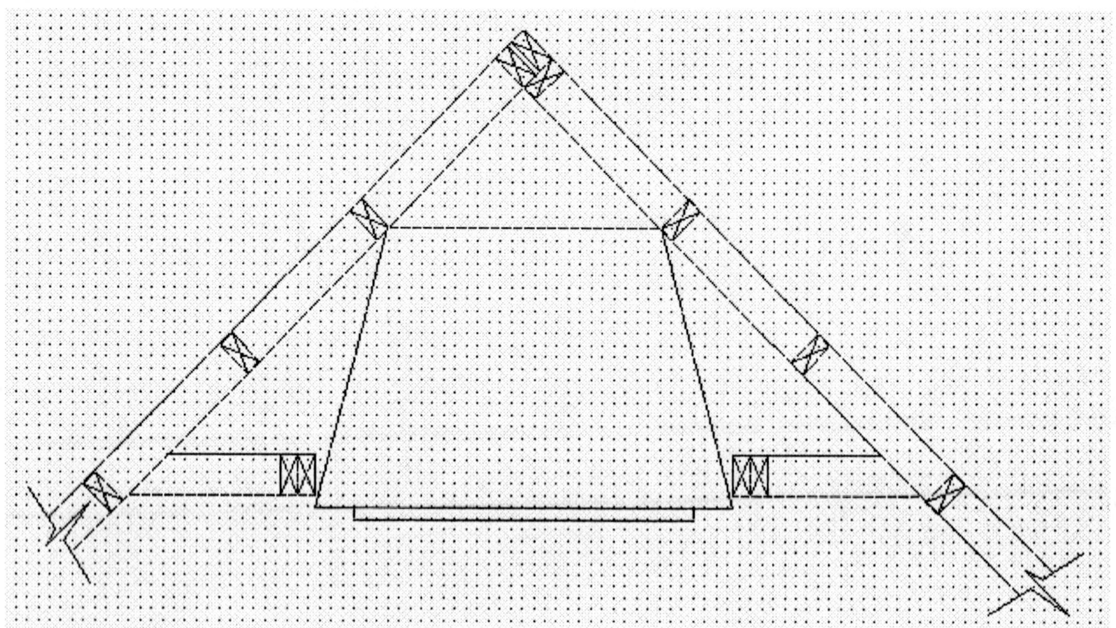

Figure 19.071: Fireplace Plan

19.6 For Web-Based Review Questions, visit: http://www.uneedcad.com/2006/Files/06R19.pdf

Following this lesson, you will:

- ✓ *Know how to create and manipulate Block Attributes*
  - o *The **Attdef** command*
- ✓ *Know how to insert blocks with attributes*
- ✓ *Know how to control the display of attributes*
  - o *The **Attdisp**, **Attreq**, and **Attdia** system variables*
- ✓ *Know how to edit attribute information*
  - o *The **-Attedit** command and the Properties palette*
- ✓ *Know how to redefine a block with attributes*
  - o *The Block Attribute Manager*
- ✓ *Know how to extract attribute data to another program or for a bill of materials*
- ✓ *The **Eattext** command*

Lesson 20 Advanced Blocks

One of the most important jobs a CAD operator may have involves the politics of convincing his or her supervisor (and often the supervisor's supervisor) of the importance of using AutoCAD as its creators intended. This will inevitably mean that the initial job setup will take more time than a non-CAD-oriented person might consider necessary. But the delay will be repaid "seven-fold" at the end of the project.

The operator might explain that AutoCAD isn't, as is commonly believed, simply a very expensive drafting tool. Rather, AutoCAD should be considered the backbone of the overall project. Indeed, a design properly created in AutoCAD serves not only as an outline for construction but also reduces material take-off and purchasing chores from weeks to minutes.

To cut large pieces of time from the end of the project, smaller pieces of time must be spent at the setup phase. Part of this time is required to create your libraries or to adjust purchased libraries to project standards. This adjustment should involve the addition of project-specific attributes to your blocks. You'll use these attributes to generate bills of materials and to share material information with material take-off (MTO) and purchasing programs.

This lesson will cover how to create and edit attributes and how to share attribute data with other programs.

Let's begin.

20.1 Creating Attributes

What exactly is an attribute?

Think of an attribute as a vessel that carries information. This information can be AutoCAD generated or user defined. We've learned that all objects in a drawing contain information kept in the drawing's database. This information identifies the object using such things as type, style, color, linetype, layer, position, and so forth. An attribute allows you to attach this information (and other types of information) to a block and to retrieve it later.

20.1.1 Defining Attributes

AutoCAD provides a simple, straightforward dialog box (Figure 20.001) for creating attributes. Access it from within Model Space or the block editor with the ***Attdef*** command (or the ***att*** hotkeys). Understanding this dialog box will go a long way toward helping you understand how attributes work.

Let's take a look.

- As you can see in the upper left frame (**Mode**), AutoCAD provides four modes from which to choose. These control how the attributes function. By default, all modes are toggled off (the check boxes are clear). Let's see what happens when you toggle each one on.
  - An **Invisible** attribute holds data that won't show on the screen or drawing. This setting is ideal for most information. (Use visible data for information you wish to see on the drawing – such as valve sizes or title block data.)
  - A **Constant** attribute contains information that doesn't change. AutoCAD won't prompt for this information when you insert the block, and you can't edit the value of the constant attribute after inserting the block.

- When you insert a block with an attribute that was created in **Verify** mode, AutoCAD will first prompt you to enter a value for the attribute and then prompt you again to *verify* that value.

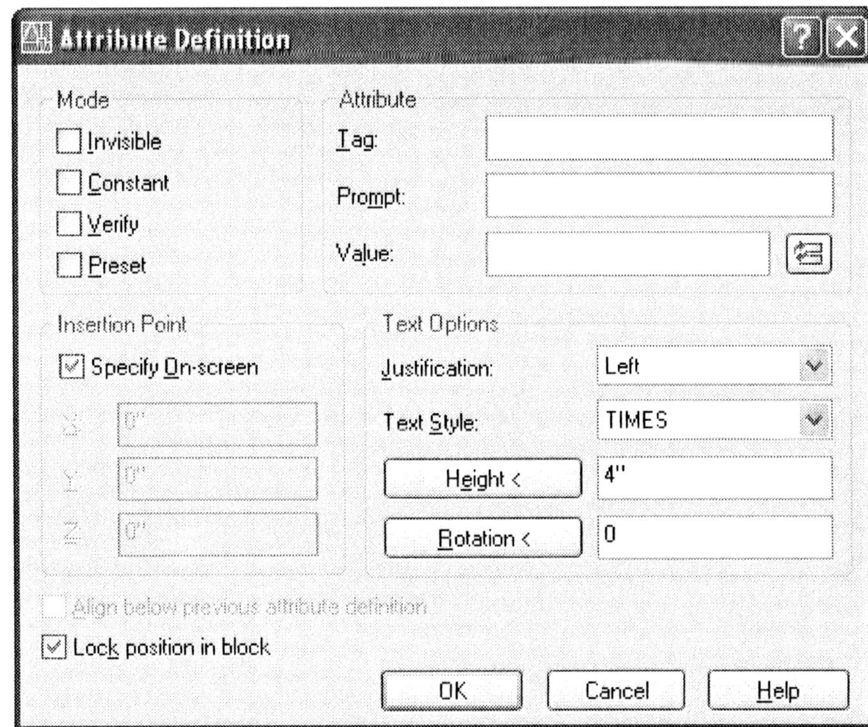

Figure 20.001

- AutoCAD won't prompt for an attribute value (except those requiring verification) when you create it in the **Preset** mode. AutoCAD assumes default values for all the attributes when the block is inserted.

- The **Attribute** frame provides a convenient location for you to easily place other important information.
  - Enter the name of the attribute in the **Tag** text box. Make this something simple but descriptive so that the operator can easily identify it.
  - Place the prompt – what you want AutoCAD to say when asking you for a value to assign to this attribute – in the **Prompt** text box. Follow the advice of the old English professor: "Be brilliant; be brief." (In other words, keep your prompts short, concise, and to the point.)
  - You can place a default value for the attribute in the **Value** text box. AutoCAD doesn't require a default value, but it'll provide you with the ability to respond to the prompt with an ***enter*** keystroke or a right click of the mouse.
  - To the right of the **Value** box, you'll find an **Insert field** button. This handy tool can even increase the incredible usefulness of attributes! Add a field into the **Value** box and AutoCAD will automatically update the attribute value even after you've inserted the block!
- The **Insertion Point** frame works exactly as it did on the Insert dialog box. But remember, this insertion is for the attribute not the block.
- In the **Text Options** frame, you'll use control boxes to select the **Justification** and **Style** of the attribute's text. You can also place the **Height** and **Rotation** of the text into the appropriate text box, or pick a button to select each from the screen.

- When creating several attributes, a check in the **Align below previous attribute** box will help keep the attributes organized.
- You can also **lock** [an attribute's] **position in** [a] **block**, although it's not always a good idea.

To edit or change an attribute before creating the block or within the block editor, use the standard text editor command (***DDEdit***) or double click on it. AutoCAD will present the Edit Attribute Definition dialog box shown here.

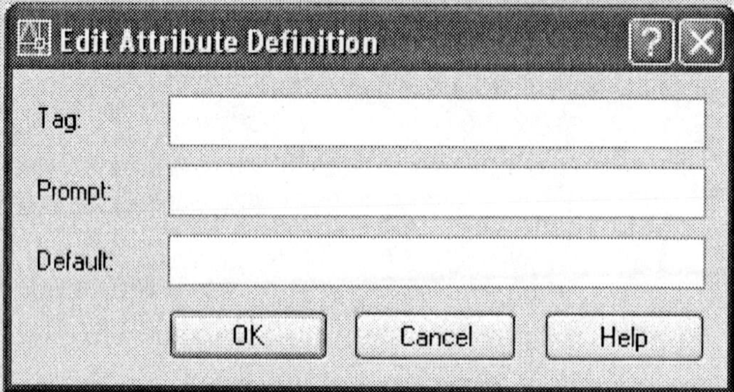

Here you can change the **Tag**, **Prompt**, or **Default** value. You can't change the mode of the attribute, however. You'll have to create a new attribute for that.

Remember this handy method when you have several similar attributes to create. Simply copy your attributes to the blocks you wish to create, edit them as needed, and then create the block.

Let's add some attributes to a few blocks.

You can create attributes before creating a block. Just include them in the objects selected to create the block.

You can also access the *Attdef* command from the Draw pull-down menu. Follow this path:
Draw – Block – Define Attributes…

Do This: 20.1.1.1	**Creating Attributes**

I. Open the *blocks-pipe2006.dwg* file the C:\Steps\Lesson20 folder. The drawing looks like Figure 20.003.

II. Follow these steps.

Note: If you discover an error in an attribute after you've created it, you can edit the definition with the Properties palette.

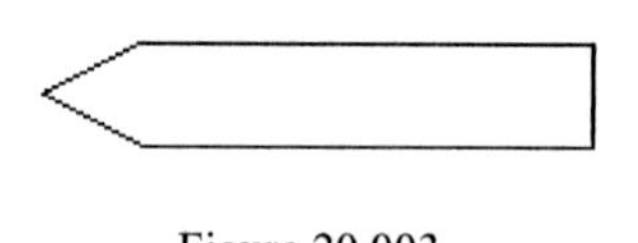

Figure 20.003

TOOLS	COMMAND SEQUENCE	STEPS
	Command: ***be***	1. Double click on the left valve (Figure 20.004), and open it in the block editor.

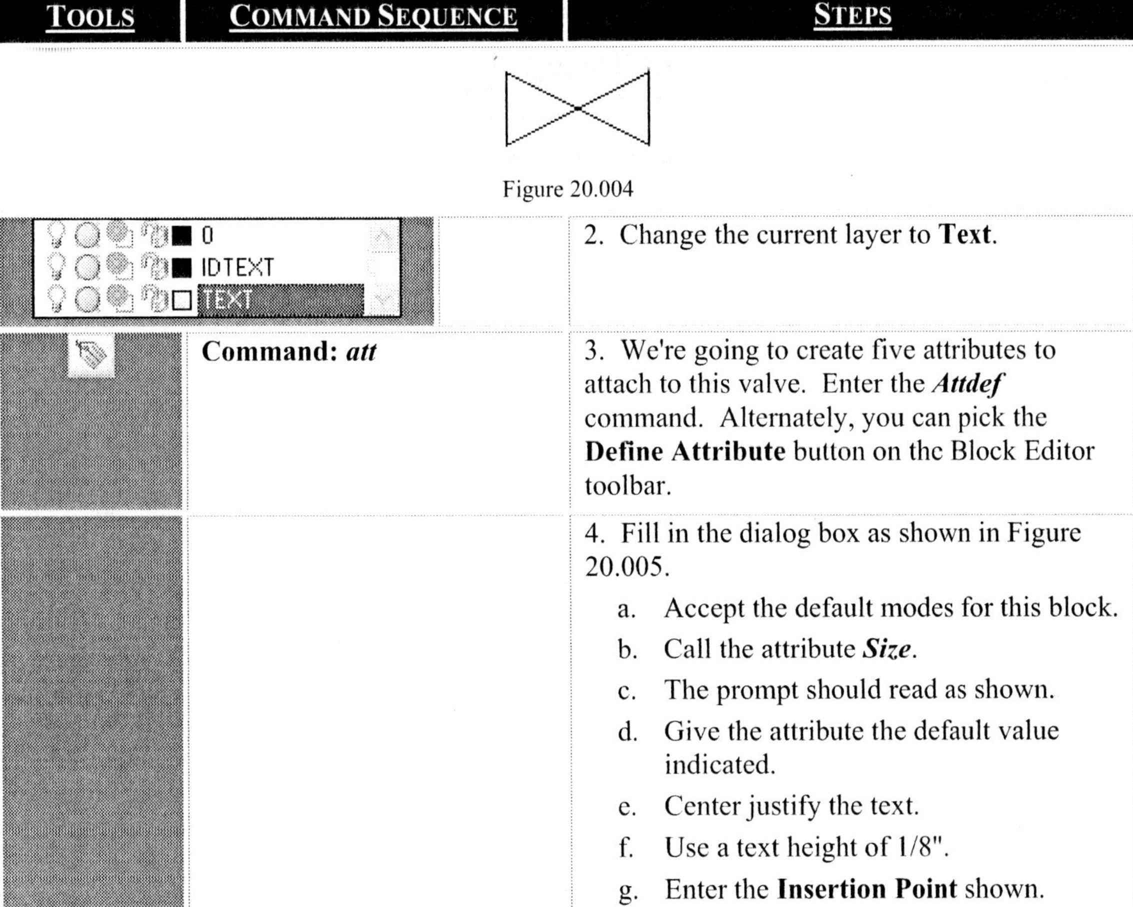

TOOLS	COMMAND SEQUENCE	STEPS
		Figure 20.004
		2. Change the current layer to **Text**.
	Command: *att*	3. We're going to create five attributes to attach to this valve. Enter the ***Attdef*** command. Alternately, you can pick the **Define Attribute** button on the Block Editor toolbar.
		4. Fill in the dialog box as shown in Figure 20.005. a. Accept the default modes for this block. b. Call the attribute ***Size***. c. The prompt should read as shown. d. Give the attribute the default value indicated. e. Center justify the text. f. Use a text height of 1/8". g. Enter the **Insertion Point** shown.

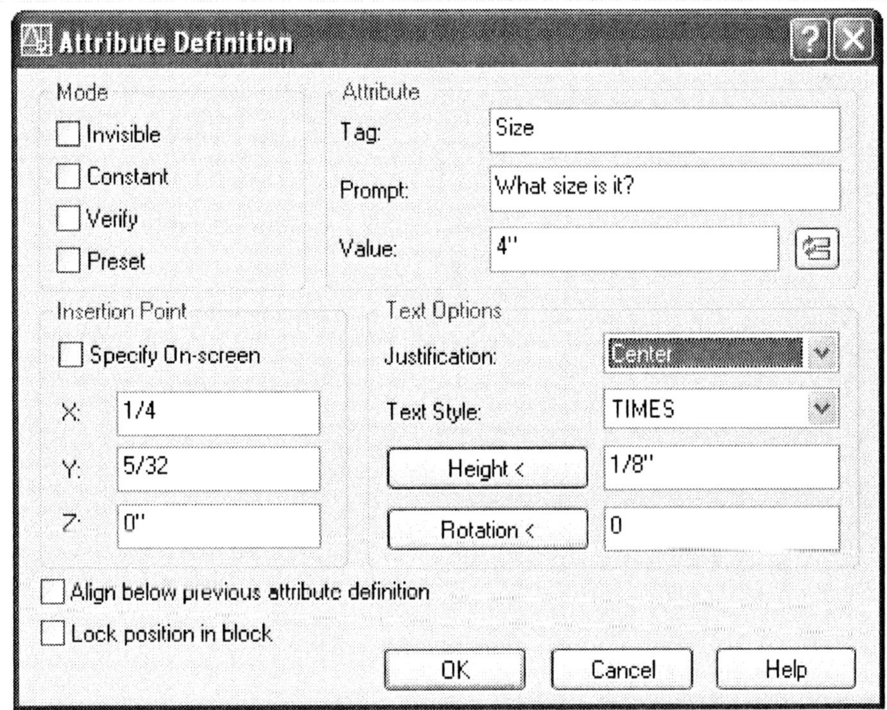

Figure 20.005

TOOLS	COMMAND SEQUENCE	STEPS
		5. Pick the **OK** button to complete your first attribute definition. Your screen should look like Figure 20.006.

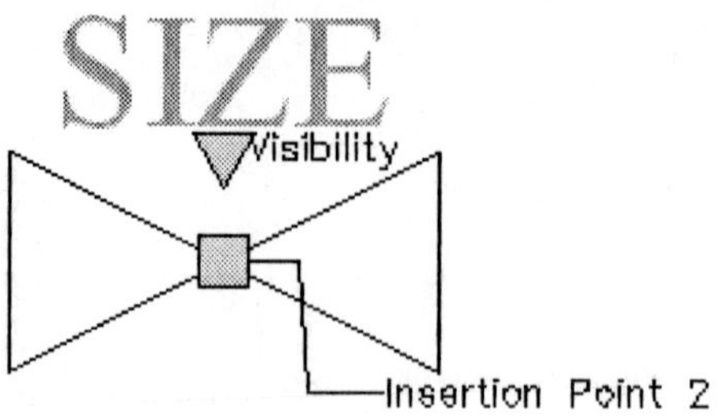

Figure 20.006

TOOLS	COMMAND SEQUENCE	STEPS
	**Command:** ***qsave***	6. Save the block and drawing but don't exit. (Update the reference when prompted.)
		7. Repeat Steps 3 through 6 to create a **Rating** attribute. All the modes for the attribute should be toggled off, the tag should be ***rating***, the prompt should read, ***What is the rating?***, and the default attribute value should be ***150#***. Center the tag below the valve at coordinates .25,-.25.

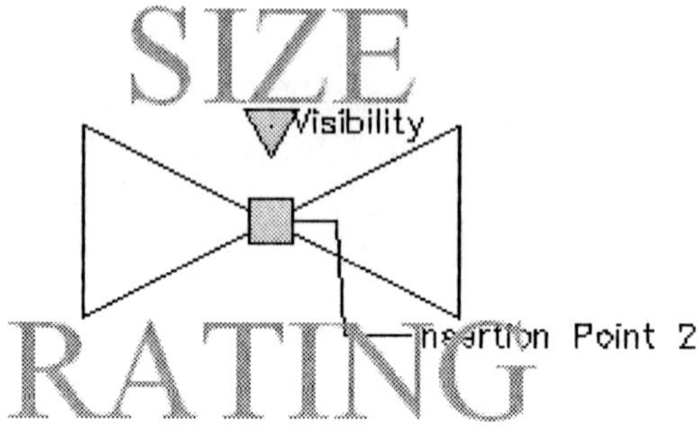

Figure 20.007

TOOLS	COMMAND SEQUENCE	STEPS
	Command: ***[enter]***	8. Now let's create a **Constant**, **Invisible** attribute. Repeat the ***Attdef*** command.

TOOLS	COMMAND SEQUENCE	STEPS

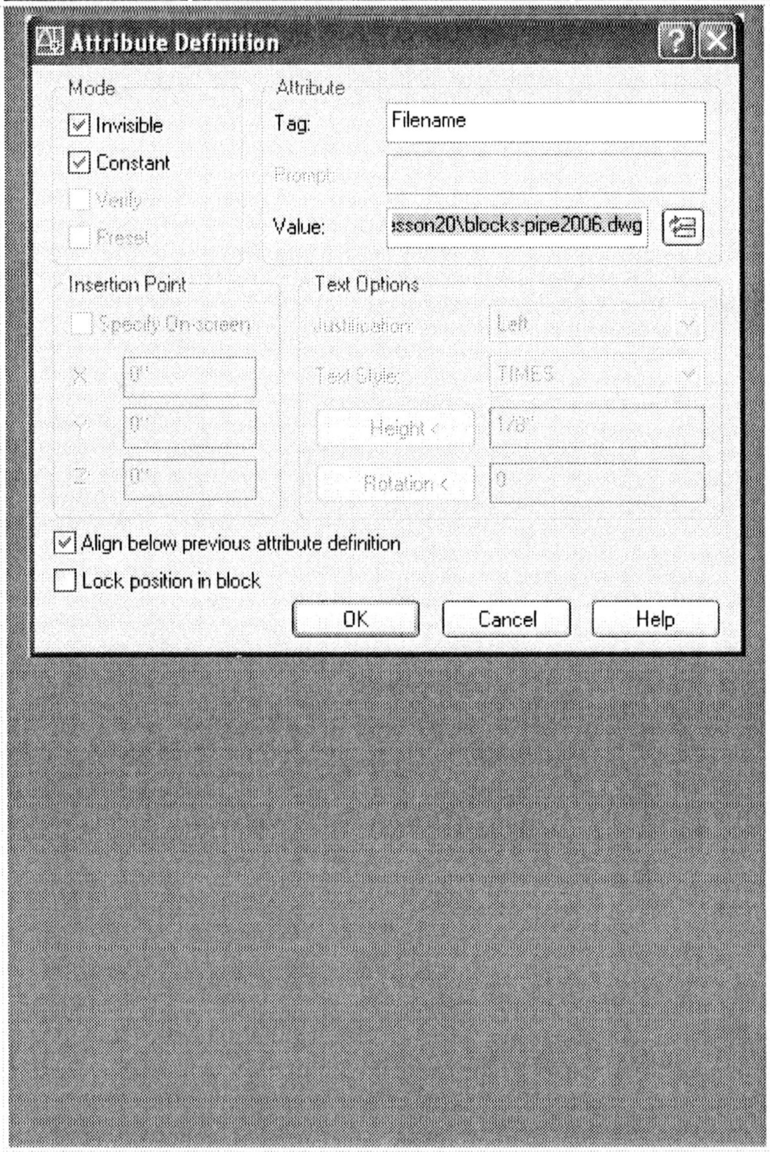

9. Create the settings shown.
   a. Begin by placing checks next to **Invisible** and **Constant**. Notice that the other modes become unavailable.
   b. Call the attribute ***Filename***. Notice that, with a constant attribute, you don't need a prompt.
   c. Pick the **Insert Field** button next to the **Value** control box.

      Select **Filename** in the **Field Names** box and use the **Lowercase** format (Figure 20.008).

      Pick the **OK** button to close the Field dialog box.
   d. Place a check in **the Align below previous attribute** definition option. Notice that AutoCAD removes the options to locate and define text types. It assumes this information from the previous definition.

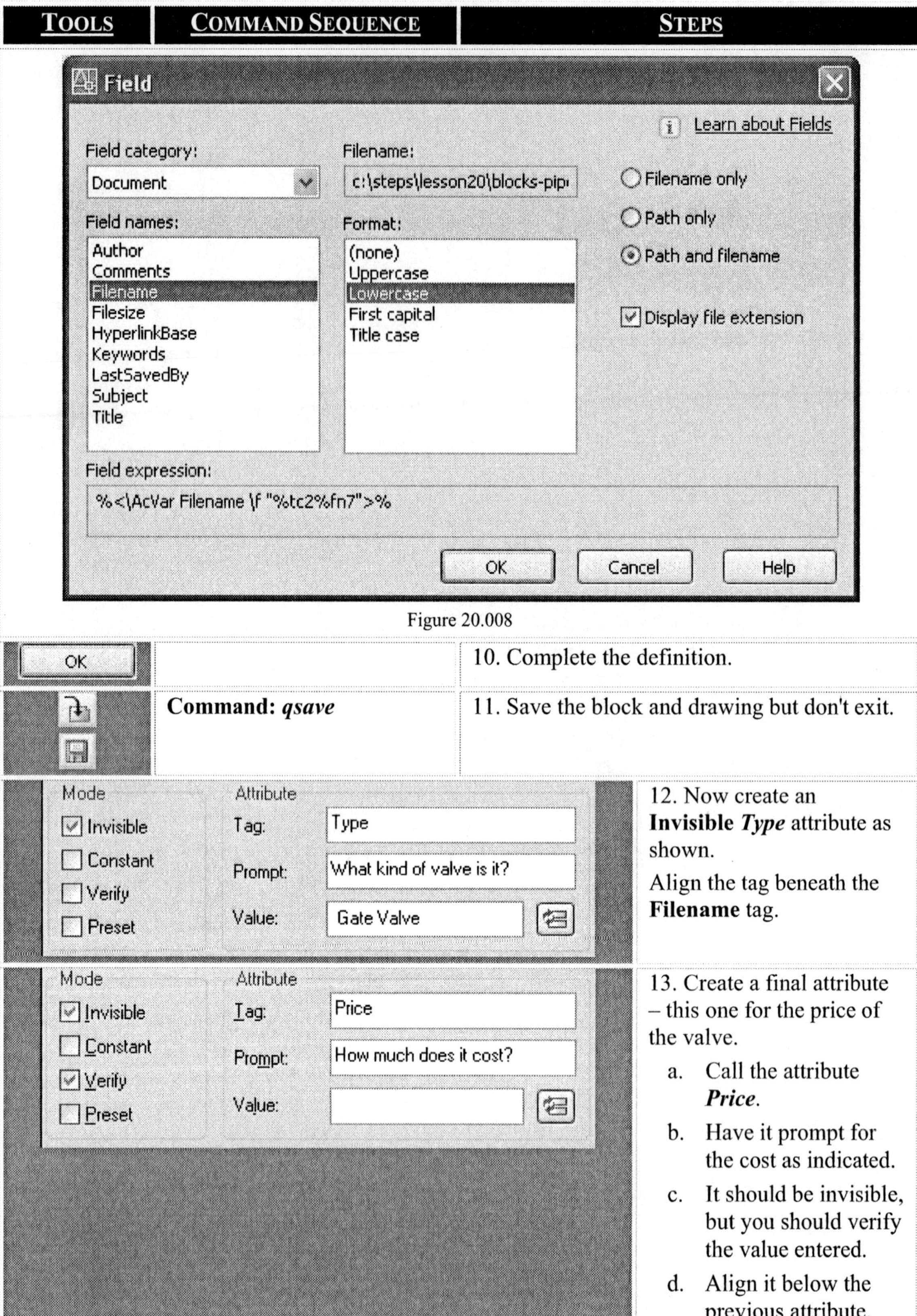

Figure 20.008

TOOLS	COMMAND SEQUENCE	STEPS
OK		10. Complete the definition.
	Command: *qsave*	11. Save the block and drawing but don't exit.
		12. Now create an **Invisible *Type*** attribute as shown. Align the tag beneath the **Filename** tag.
		13. Create a final attribute – this one for the price of the valve. a. Call the attribute ***Price***. b. Have it prompt for the cost as indicated. c. It should be invisible, but you should verify the value entered. d. Align it below the previous attribute.

TOOLS	COMMAND SEQUENCE	STEPS
	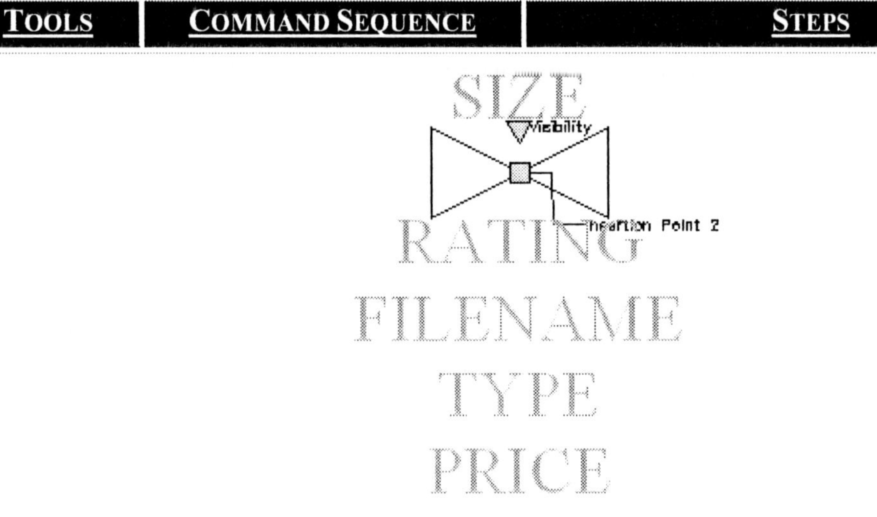 Figure 20.009	
	Command: ***qsave***	14. Save the block and drawing but don't exit.
Gate Valve Globe Valve Check Valve Control Valve		15. Notice that you've been working in the **Gate Valve** visibility state. (Look in the **Visibility State** control box.) Use the control box to change to the **Globe Valve** visibility state. Notice that all the attributes have disappeared! Let's fix that.
	Command: ***bvmode***	16. Toggle the **Visibility Mode** so that you can see the attributes. (They'll appear gray.)
		17. Now, with the **Globe Valve** visibility state current, use the **Make Visible** button to make the attributes visible.
		18. Repeat Step 17 for the **Check Valve** and **Control Valve** visibility states.
Close Block Editor		19. Save the block and close the block editor.
	Command: ***w***	20. WBlock the valve block as *Valve* to the C:\Steps\Lesson20 folder.
	Command: ***qsave***	21. Save the drawing but don't exit.

20.2 Inserting Attributed Blocks

When an attributed block is inserted into a drawing, the attribute prompts will follow the standard insertion prompts. This can occur in one of two ways – command line prompts or the Enter Attributes dialog box.

Let's look at the command line method first; then we'll look at the dialog box in Section 20.2.2.

AutoCAD includes a system variable – ***Attreq*** – which controls whether or not you'll be prompted for attribute values. If the variable is set to **1**, AutoCAD prompts on the command line or with a dialog box. If you set this system variable to **0**, however, AutoCAD won't prompt at all for attribute values and you must use the attribute editor to add the values.

Whether or not AutoCAD prompts for attribute values at the command line or with a dialog box is controlled by the ***Attdia*** system variable. A setting of **0** means that you'll receive prompts on the command line, whereas a setting a **1** calls a dialog box.

Do This: 20.2.1	Inserting Attributed Blocks Using the Command Line

I. Open the *pid-20.dwg* file the C:\Steps\Lesson20 folder. The drawing looks like Figure 20.2.1a.

II. Be sure the ***Attdia*** system variable is set to **0**. (This means that attribute prompts will appear on the command line.)

III. Set **VA** as the current layer.

IV. Follow these steps.

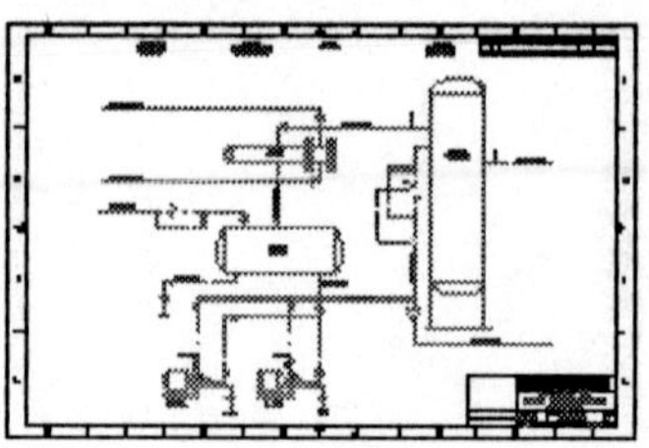

Figure 20.010

TOOLS	COMMAND SEQUENCE	STEPS
	Command: ***v***	1. Restore the **Cont_Station1** view. The view looks like Figure 20.011.
	Figure 20.011	
	Command: ***i***	2. Insert the block you created in the last exercise. (Find it in the C:\Steps\Lesson20 folder.) Insert it at the leftmost endpoint. Accept the default size and orientation.
	Enter attribute values **What size is it? <4">:** ***[enter]*** **What is the rating? <150#>:** ***[enter]*** **What kind of valve is it? <Gate Valve>:** ***[enter]*** **How much does it cost?:** ***55.00*** **Verify attribute values** **How much does it cost? <55.00>:** ***[enter]***	3. Once you've located the block, AutoCAD asks you to **Enter attribute values**. Accept the default **rating** and **size**, and enter a price of ***55.00***. (Note that you assigned these defaults in our last exercise.) *Notice that the prompts may appear in a different order. They should reflect the order in which you created them.*

Tools	Command Sequence	Steps
	Command: ***qsave***	4. Save the drawing but don't exit. It looks like Figure 20.012. Notice that the **Type**, **Filename**, and **Price** attributes aren't visible. Notice also that the valve assumed the characteristics defined by the **VA** layer, and the attribute text assumed the characteristics defined by this drawing's **Text** layer.
	Figure 20.012	
		5. Repeat Steps 3 through 6 to place the other block valve. The drawing looks like Figure 20.013. (Can you think of an easier way to have achieved the same results?*)
	Figure 20.013	
	Command: ***qsave***	6. Save the drawing but don't exit.

We'll look at the dialog box approach next. Note that, although the dialog box presents a comfortable user interface, familiarity with the command line approach will prove quite handy when you use AutoCAD's iDrop tools.

Do This: 20.2.2	Using a Dialog Box to Insert Attributed Blocks

I. Be sure you're still in the *pid-20.dwg* file the C:\Steps\Lesson20 folder.

II. Be sure the **Cont_Station1** view is still current.

III. Set the ***Attdia*** system variable to **1**. (This tells AutoCAD to use a dialog box for its attribute insertions.)

IV. Follow these steps.

* You could simply have copied the existing attributed valve

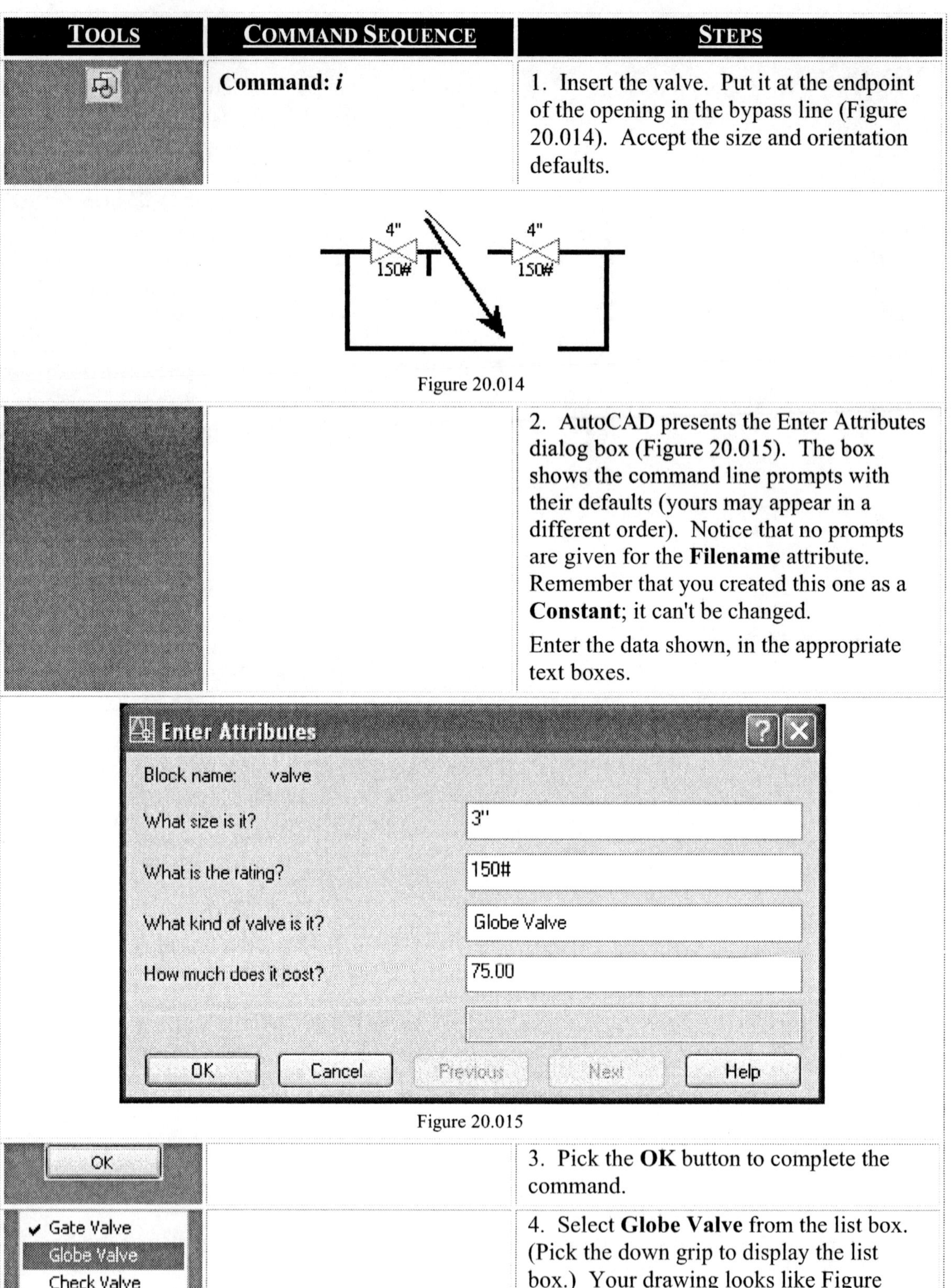

TOOLS	COMMAND SEQUENCE	STEPS
	Command: ***i***	1. Insert the valve. Put it at the endpoint of the opening in the bypass line (Figure 20.014). Accept the size and orientation defaults.

Figure 20.014

TOOLS	COMMAND SEQUENCE	STEPS
		2. AutoCAD presents the Enter Attributes dialog box (Figure 20.015). The box shows the command line prompts with their defaults (yours may appear in a different order). Notice that no prompts are given for the **Filename** attribute. Remember that you created this one as a **Constant**; it can't be changed. Enter the data shown, in the appropriate text boxes.

Figure 20.015

TOOLS	COMMAND SEQUENCE	STEPS
OK		3. Pick the **OK** button to complete the command.
Gate Valve Globe Valve Check Valve Control Valve		4. Select **Globe Valve** from the list box. (Pick the down grip to display the list box.) Your drawing looks like Figure 20.016.

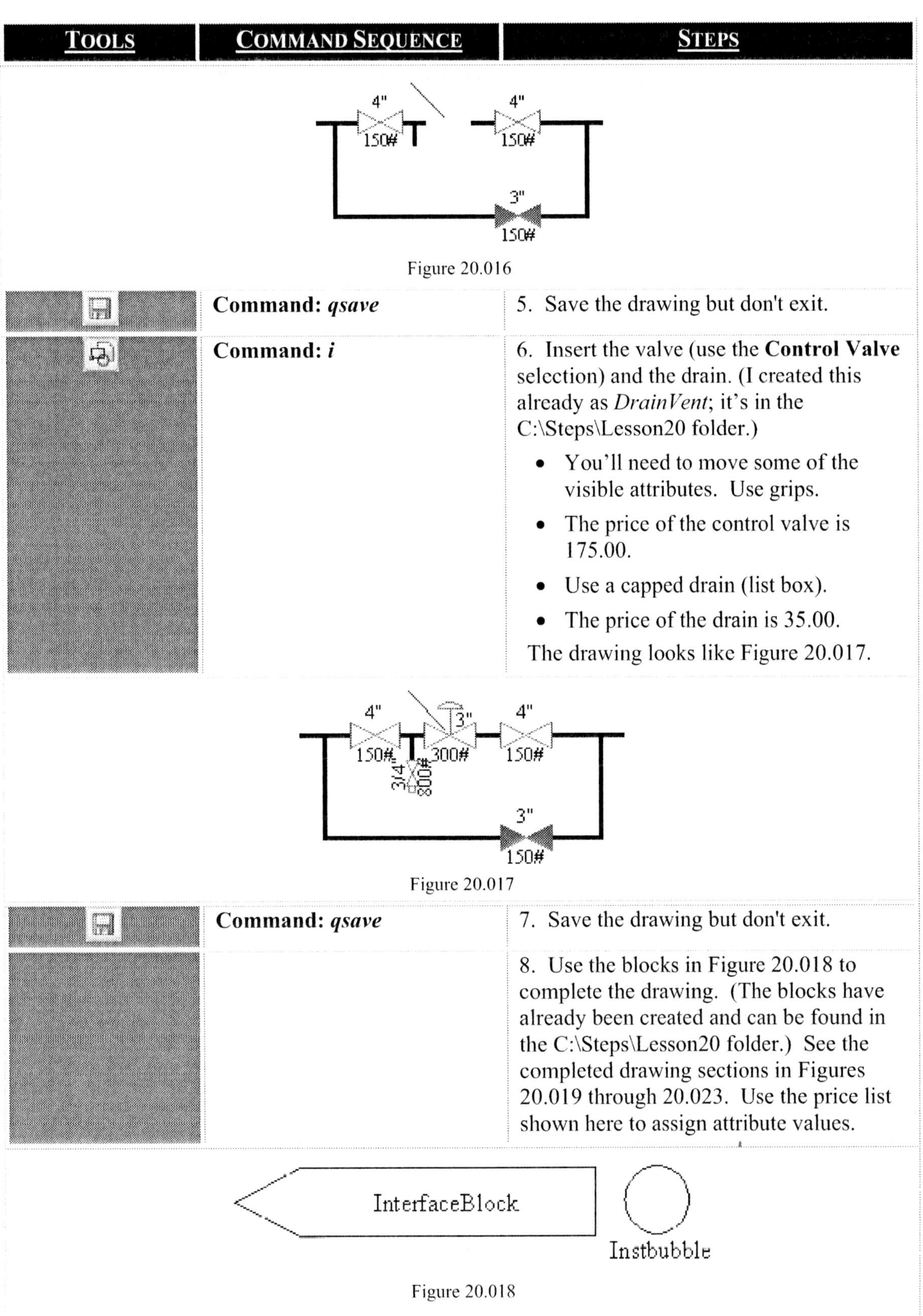

TOOLS	COMMAND SEQUENCE	STEPS
	Figure 20.016	
	Command: ***qsave***	5. Save the drawing but don't exit.
	Command: ***i***	6. Insert the valve (use the **Control Valve** selection) and the drain. (I created this already as *DrainVent*; it's in the C:\Steps\Lesson20 folder.) • You'll need to move some of the visible attributes. Use grips. • The price of the control valve is 175.00. • Use a capped drain (list box). • The price of the drain is 35.00. The drawing looks like Figure 20.017.
	Figure 20.017	
	Command: ***qsave***	7. Save the drawing but don't exit.
		8. Use the blocks in Figure 20.018 to complete the drawing. (The blocks have already been created and can be found in the C:\Steps\Lesson20 folder.) See the completed drawing sections in Figures 20.019 through 20.023. Use the price list shown here to assign attribute values.
	Figure 20.018	

TOOLS	COMMAND SEQUENCE	STEPS

SIZE/VALVE	GATE	GLOBE	CONTROL	CHECK
¾"	35.00			
2"	55.00			
4"	85.00	175.00	275.00	
6"	127.00			195.00
8"	385.00			
10"	585.00			

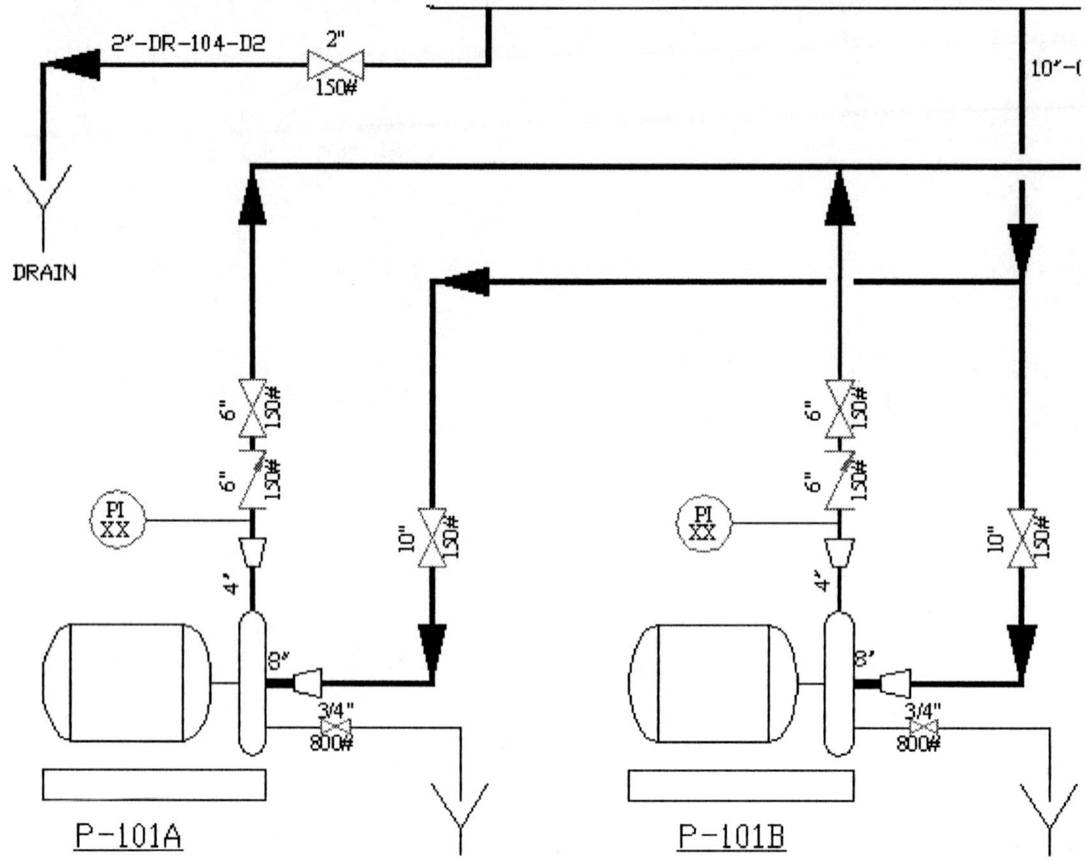

Figure 20.019

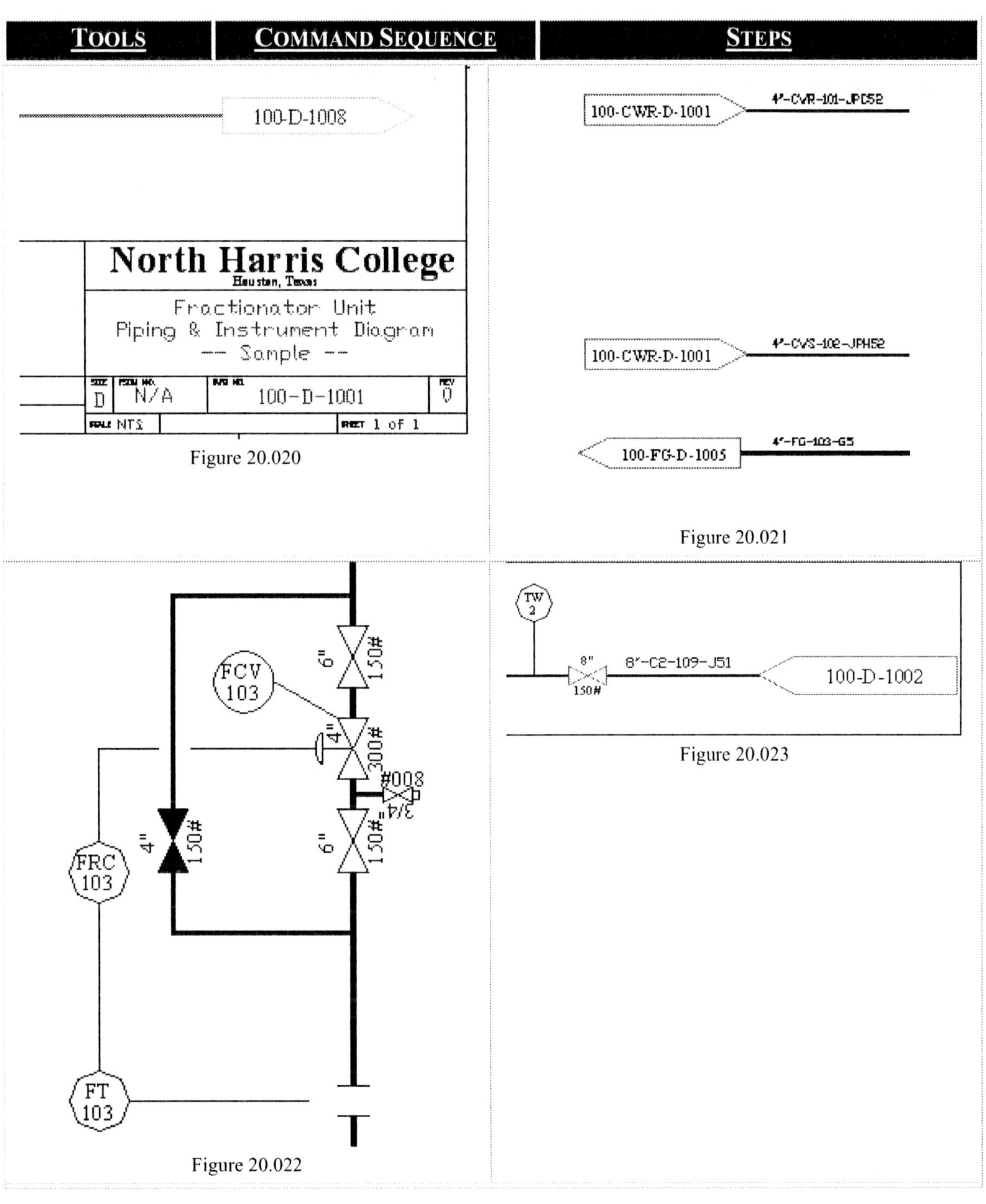

Figure 20.020

Figure 20.021

Figure 20.022

Figure 20.023

20.3 Editing Attributes

In previous editions of this text, I provided many pages of discussion for a couple block editing tools (***EAttEdit*** and ***DDAtte***). But this is a new release and blocks have become complicated enough without these monsters. So to keep life simple, I'm going to show you how to accomplish all the editing you'll need using a familiar tool – the Properties palette – and one really old command line tool – ***-ATTEdit*** (we'll need that one for universal changes).

For those of you who insist on doing things the hard way, I've placed this section of the '05 edition of *One Step at a Time* on the website. Go to: http://www.uneedcad.com/2006/Files. You'll find details on ***EAttEdit***, and ***DDAtte*** in a file called *EditingAttributes.pdf.* (Kock yourself out!)

20.3.1 Editing Attribute Values

Editing attribute values is as easy as calling the Properties palette.

Do This: 20.3.1.1 Editing Attribute Values

When we inserted the gate valves, we assigned a price value of 55.00. According to the chart at the end of our last exercise, the price should be 85.00. Let's fix that.

I. Be sure you're still in the *pid-20.dwg* file the C:\Steps\Lesson20 folder. If you haven't finished this one, open *pid-20 Phase 2-2006.dwg* instead.

II. Open the Properties palette and move it to the side of the screen.

III. Be sure the **Cont_Station1** view is current.

IV. Follow these steps.

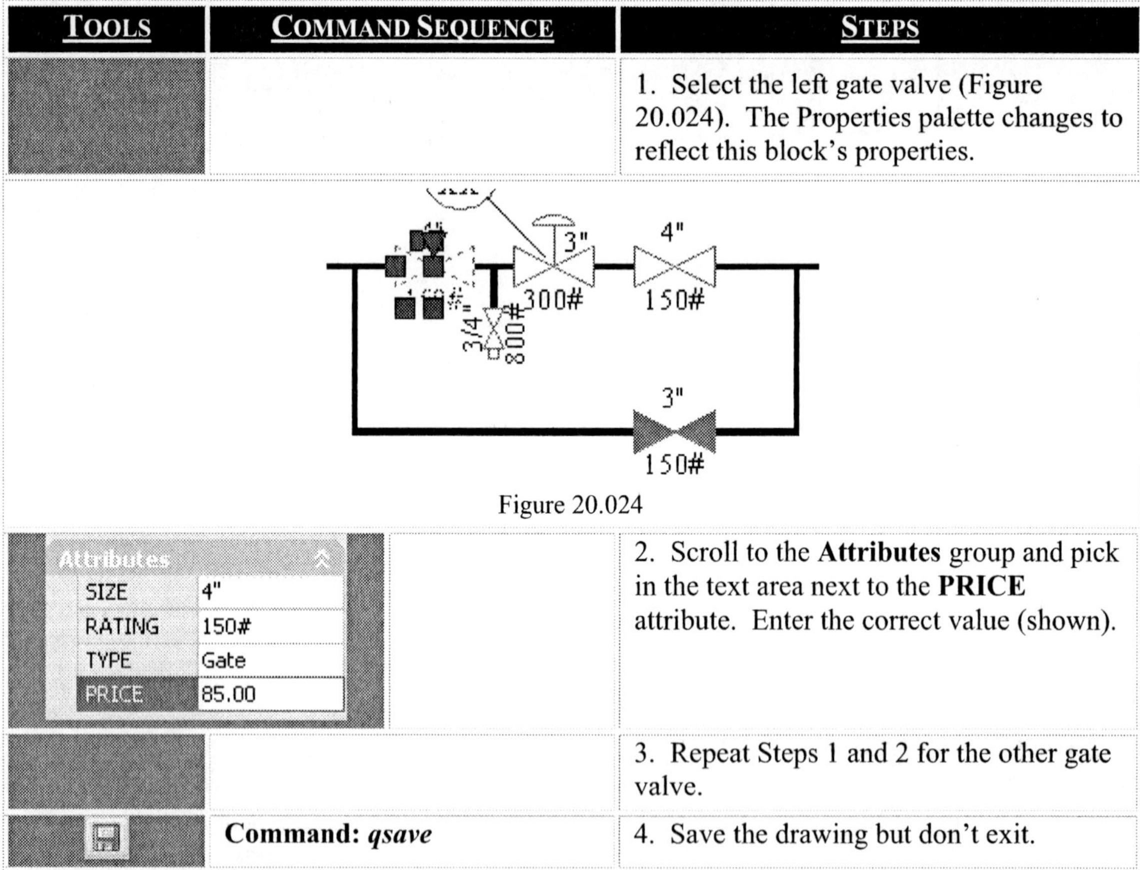

TOOLS	COMMAND SEQUENCE	STEPS
		1. Select the left gate valve (Figure 20.024). The Properties palette changes to reflect this block's properties.
Figure 20.024		
Attributes: SIZE 4"; RATING 150#; TYPE Gate; PRICE 85.00		2. Scroll to the **Attributes** group and pick in the text area next to the **PRICE** attribute. Enter the correct value (shown).
		3. Repeat Steps 1 and 2 for the other gate valve.
	Command: ***qsave***	4. Save the drawing but don't exit.

Was that easy enough for you? (That same exercise contained 11 steps when we discussed ***DDAtte*** and ***EAttEdit***.) Take a moment and look over the other properties listed in the palette. Remember, you can edit the white values; the gray values are informational.

But what if you have several attributes to edit at once?

It's possible, using an older command line AutoCAD tool, to edit the values and some of the properties of attributes in multiple insertions of a block. The command sequence is:

> **Command:** ***-attedit*** **(or** ***–ate*****)**
>
> **Edit attributes one at a time? [Yes/No] <Y>:** ***[enter]***
>
> **Enter block name specification <*>:** ***[enter]***
>
> **Enter attribute tag specification <*>:** ***[enter]***
>
> **Enter attribute value specification <*>:** ***[enter]***
>
> **Select Attributes:** ***[select the attributes to change]***
>
> **Select Attributes:** ***[enter to complete the selection set]***
>
> **1 attributes selected.** ***[AutoCAD reports how many attributes were selected]***
>
> **Enter an option [Value/Position/Height/Angle/Style/Layer/Color/Next] <N>:** ***[tell AutoCAD what you want to do]***

- The first option – **Edit attributes one at a time?** – allows you to change attributes globally (or several at once).
- The next three lines ask for some specifics about what you wish to edit. You can simply hit ***enter*** at each prompt if you'll edit the attributes individually. The default is to accept all selected attributes for possible editing. But you can use these prompts to act as filters in a global selection set. For example, you can edit just the gate valves in our *PID-20* drawing by responding ***valve*** to the **Enter block name specification** prompt.
- After you select the attributes to edit, AutoCAD presents a line of options to help specify what type of editing to perform.
    - The **Value** option allows you to change the value of the attribute. Use this if you need to globally change a value. For example, assume the price of 4" globe valves has just changed. You could edit your drawing globally to change the value of the **Price** attribute for all 4" globe valves. It's easier to use the Properties palette to change individual values.

> An easy way to see the values of all the attributes attached to a block is to set the **Attdisp** system variable to **On**. The command sequence looks like this:
>
> **Command:** ***attdisp***
>
> **Enter attribute visibility setting [Normal/ ON/OFF] <Normal>:** ***on***
>
> It can be useful to display all the attributes when searching for errors, but the display can quickly become quite crowded.
>
> - The **Normal** option tells AutoCAD to display only those attributes created with the **Invisible** mode off.
> - Turning **Off** the ***Attdisp*** tells AutoCAD to hide all the attributes regardless of the **Invisible** mode setting. This setting will speed regeneration, but be careful not to place objects where they'll overlap the attributes when they're displayed again.

-
    - The **Position** option comes in quite handy when the value of an attribute is physically too large to fit in the area allotted for it (it overlaps something else). The ***Move*** command will move the entire block, but the **Position** option of the ***Attedit*** command (command line method) allows you to move just a single attribute. (Then again, so do grips!)
    - The **Angle** option is also quite handy for making attributes read properly despite the insertion rotation of the block.

- The other options – **Height**, **Style**, **Layer**, and **Color** – allow you to edit these properties of attributes. If it's necessary to change any of these, however, it may be better to redefine the block(s) so that it inserts properly in the first place.

Let's try multiple attribute editing.

Do This: 20.3.1.2	Editing Attribute Values Globally

I. Be sure you're still in the *pid-20.dwg* file (*or pid-20 Phase2 -2006.dwg*) in the C:\Steps\Lesson20 folder.

II. Be sure the **Cont_Station1** view is still current.

III. Follow these steps.

TOOLS	COMMAND SEQUENCE	STEPS
No Button Available	**Command: *-ate***	1. Our project engineer has determined that this control station requires a higher rating for the block and bypass valves. Enter the ***-Attedit*** command.
	Edit attributes one at a time? [Yes/No] <Y>: *n* **Performing global editing of attribute values.**	2. We want to edit all the 150# valves. Tell AutoCAD that you don't want to **Edit attributes one at a time**. AutoCAD responds that this will be a global edit.
	Edit only attributes visible on screen? [Yes/No] <Y>: *[enter]*	3. We'll want only the valves on the screen to be affected by this editing.
	Enter block name specification <*>: *[enter]*	4. We'll be editing more than one type of block, so leave this default at the global setting.
	Enter attribute tag specification <*>: *rating*	5. We want to edit only the **RATING** attributes. If we tell AutoCAD this, it won't change any other type of attribute.
	Enter attribute value specification <*>: *[enter]*	6. We don't need any further filtering for our edit.
	Select Attributes: **Select Attributes: *[enter]***	7. Put a window around the entire control station; let AutoCAD sort things out for the **RATING** attributes.
	Enter string to change: *150#*	8. AutoCAD wants to know what to change …
	Enter new string: *300#*	9. … and what to make it. Your drawing looks like Figure 20.025.

Tools	Command Sequence	Steps
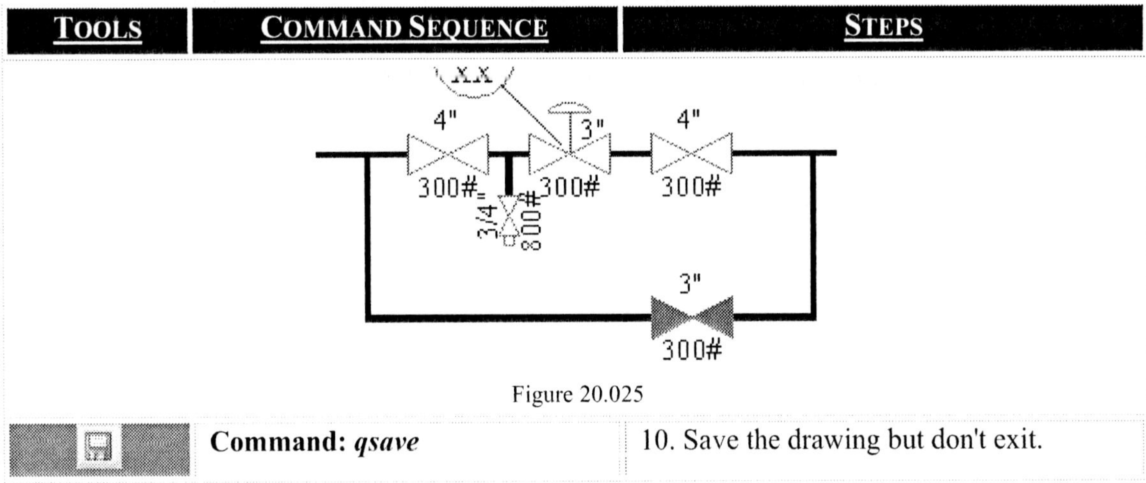		
	Figure 20.025	
	Command: ***qsave***	10. Save the drawing but don't exit.

Let's take a look at how we can edit an attribute's *definition* after creating the block.

20.3.2 Editing Attribute Definitions

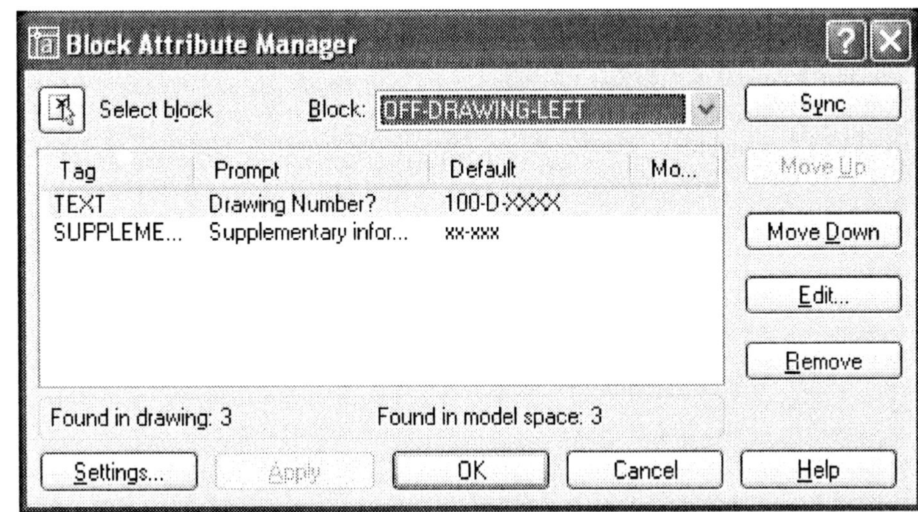

Figure 20.026

With the Block Attribute Manager (Figure 20.026), AutoCAD has made editing attribute properties after block creation almost easier than editing them before you make the block! Access the manager with the ***BAttMan*** command, but exercise some caution when editing block properties. Remember that *modifications may affect all insertions of the block (current and future).* Let's take a look.

- You'll probably notice the large list box first. Here AutoCAD lists the various attributes associated with the block shown in the **Block** control box above it. You can select another block from the control box, or you can use the **Select block** button to select a block from the drawing. The button is handy when you don't know the name of a particular block that needs editing.
- For its size, this dialog box contains quite a few buttons.
  - Use the **Sync** button to update all insertions of the selected block with the currently defined attribute definitions. AutoCAD does this automatically when you edit but provides this manual procedure for those who prefer it.

- AutoCAD lists the attributes in the list box in the order in which it prompts for values (when you insert the block). Use the **Move Up** and **Move Down** buttons to change the order of the prompts.
- Use the **Remove** button to remove an attribute from a block definition. Be careful with this one. By default, AutoCAD will remove the attribute definition *and values* from all the insertions in the drawing; you may lose some information.
- The **Apply** button (along the bottom of the box) applies your changes but leaves the dialog box open.
- The **OK** button also applies your changes but closes the dialog box.
- **Cancel** closes the dialog box without saving your changes.
- **Help** calls the Help dialog box.

- The two buttons we omitted – **Edit** and **Settings** – each call additional dialog boxes.
  - The **Edit** button calls the Edit Attribute dialog box (Figure 20.027). Its three tabs provide access to the attribute definitions.
    - The **Attribute** tab (shown) allows you to change the **Mode**, **Tag**, **Prompt**, and **Default** settings.
    - The **Text Options** tab (Figure 20.028) allows you to
    - change the **Text Style**, **Justification**, **Height**, **Rotation**, **Width Factor**, and **Oblique Angle**.
    - The **Properties** tab (Figure 20.029) allows you to change the **Layer**, **Linetype**, **Color**, **Lineweight**, and **Plot style**.

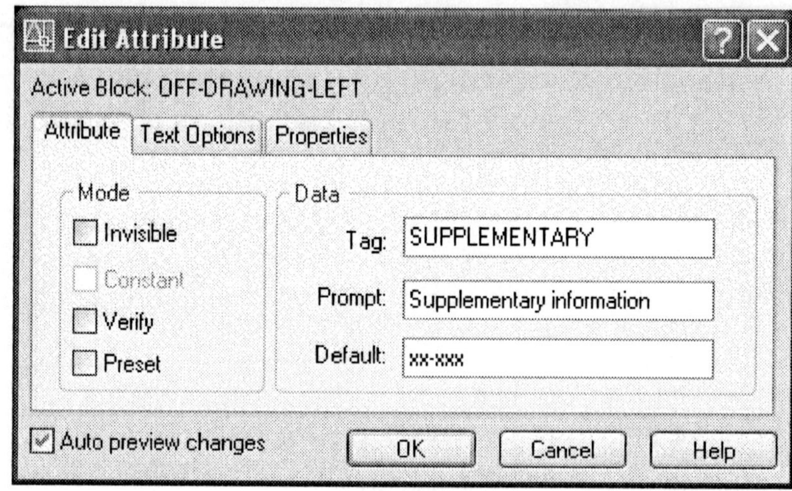

Figure 20.027

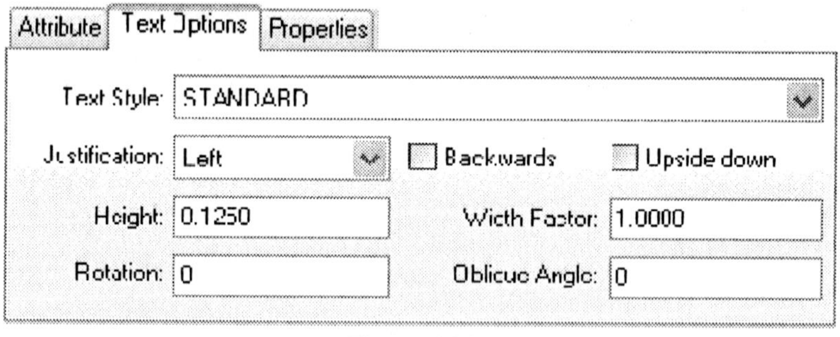

Figure 20.028

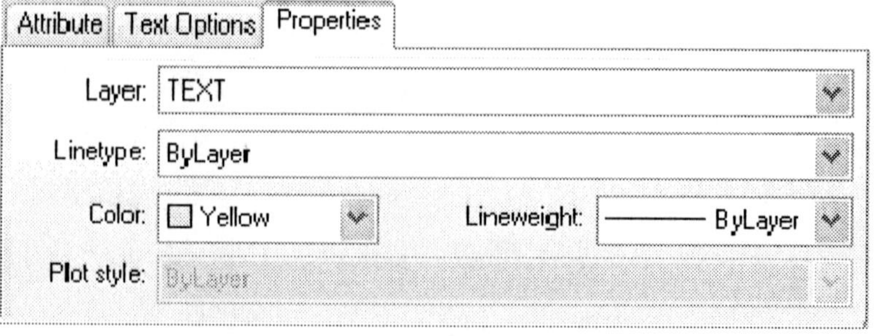

Figure 20.029

The bottom of the Edit Attributes dialog box contains a simple check box that might save you some time and grief. Put a check next to **Auto preview changes** and you can see the changes take place on your screen as you make them. This nifty tool enables you to catch errors before locking yourself into them.

- The **Settings** button (back on the Block Attribute Manager) calls the Settings dialog box (Figure 20.030). Here you can tell AutoCAD exactly what (and what not) to show in the Block Attribute Manager.

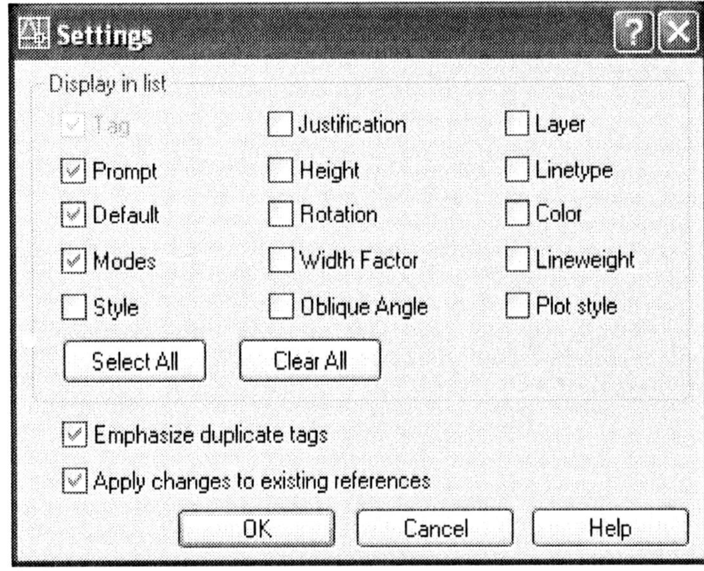

Figure 20.030

  - Use the check boxes in the **Display in list** frame to customize the list box of the Block Attribute Manager. A check next to an item tells AutoCAD to display that information in BAttMan's list box; a clear check box tells AutoCAD not to display it. When too many items are checked for AutoCAD to display them all, a scroll bar will appear in the bottom of the list box to allow you to see everything.
  - Use the **Emphasize duplicate tags** check box to have AutoCAD let you know if a block has attributes with duplicate tags in it. AutoCAD will highlight the duplications where they occur. When that happens, you might want to change one of the tags for clarity.
  - The purpose of **Apply changes to existing references** might seem a bit confusing, but understanding its use is quite important. A check next to this tool means that AutoCAD will update all current insertions of the block with the modifications you're making. Clear this box and AutoCAD will use the modifications for any new insertions but won't update existing blocks.

Let's see what BAttMan can do!

Do This: 20.3.2.1	Editing Attribute Definitions

I. Open the *pid-20-done.dwg* file the C:\Steps\Lesson20 folder.

II. Restore the I_O_LEFT view. Your drawing looks like Figure 20.031.

III. Follow these steps.

Figure 20.031

TOOLS	COMMAND SEQUENCE	STEPS
Block Attribute Manager Button	**Command: *battman***	1. Open the Block Attribute Manager by entering ***battman*** at the command prompt. Alternately, you can pick the **Block Attribute Manager** button on the Modify II toolbar.
Select Block Button		2. On the Block Attribute Manager, pick the **Select block** button.
	Select a block:	3. AutoCAD returns you to the graphics screen and prompts you to select a block. Select the upper block with the text that reads *100-CWR-D-1001*.
Tag / Prompt / Default / Mo... TEXT / Drawing Number? / 100-D-XXXX SUPPLEME... / Supplementary infor... / xx-xxx		4. Select the **TEXT** attribute.
Edit...		5. Pick the **Edit** button.
Text Options		6. AutoCAD presents the Edit Attribute dialog box (Figure 20.027). Go to the **Text Options** tab.
Text Style: TIMES		7. On the **Text Options** tab, change the **Text Style** to **TIMES**.
Properties		8. Go to the **Properties** tab.
Layer: TEXT		9. Notice that the attribute was placed on the **txt** layer rather than the **TEXT** layer that is standard in this drawing. Change it to the proper layer. (Be sure the **Color** control box is set to **ByLayer**.) If there's a check next to **Auto Preview Changes**, you can already see your changes.
OK		10. Pick the **OK** button to return to the Block Attribute Manager.
Edit...		11. Now let's do something about that extra attribute. Select the **Supplementary** attribute in the list box and then pick the **Edit** button.
Attribute		12. Go to the **Attribute** tab.

Tools	Command Sequence	Steps
Mode Invisible Constant Verify Preset		13. Rather than delete the extra attribute (there's always a chance we might need it later), we'll simply make it invisible. Place a check in the proper **Mode** box.
OK		14. Pick the **OK** button to return to the Block Attribute Manager, and again to complete the procedure.
	Command: *qsave*	15. Save the drawing.

Oh, yeah.

20.4 The Coup de Grace: Using Attribute Information in Bills of Materials, Spreadsheets, or Database Programs

This nifty stuff is guaranteed to move you to the head of the class!

One of the most useful and timesaving devices available to AutoCAD users lies in AutoCAD's ability to save steps along the road to project completion. In this section of our lesson, we'll discover how to use the information we've attached to our blocks. We'll extract the data into a table, *and* we'll simultaneously export the table and import it into a Microsoft Excel spreadsheet (for the folks in the Materials department).

> Again, there's an older procedure involving the ***ATText*** command. But I'm not even going to post that procedure as the one we're about to discuss is infinitely easier.

After so much work creating blocks, dynamic blocks, and attributes, extracting the data might seem almost anticlimactic. You just have to follow instructions in a wizard! (Access the wizard using the ***EAtText*** command.)

Let's give it a shot.

> You can also access the ***EAtText*** command using the Tools pull down menu. Follow this path:
>
> *Tools – Attribute Extraction*

Do This: 20.4.1 **Extracting Attribute Data**

I. Reopen the *pid-20 Phase 2-2006.dwg* file the C:\Steps\Lesson20 folder.

II. Set the **TEXT** layer current and zoom all.

III. Follow these steps.

Tools	Command Sequence	Steps
Attribute Extraction Button	**Command:** *eattext*	1. Enter the ***EAtText*** command. Alternately, you can pick the **Attribute Extraction** button on the Modify II toolbar. AutoCAD begins the Attribute Extraction wizard.

TOOLS	COMMAND SEQUENCE	STEPS
		2. You'll find two options on the Begin page (Figure 20.032): • **Create table or external file from scratch** • **Use template** You haven't created a template yet (although you'll have a chance soon), so select the **Create table** option, and the pick the **Next** button to continue.

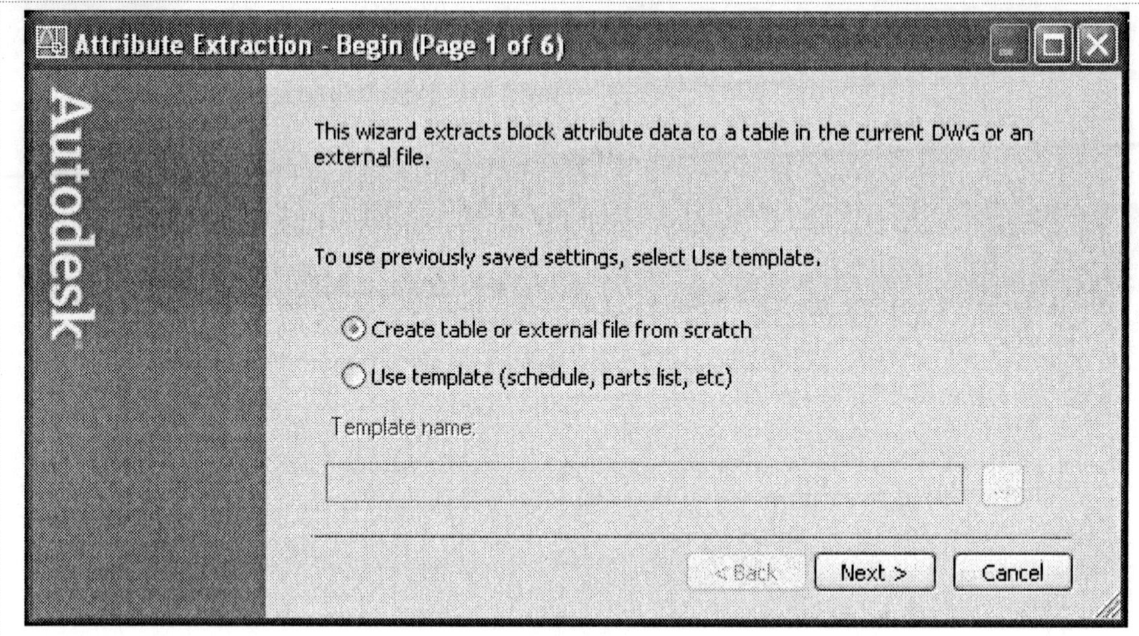

Figure 20.032

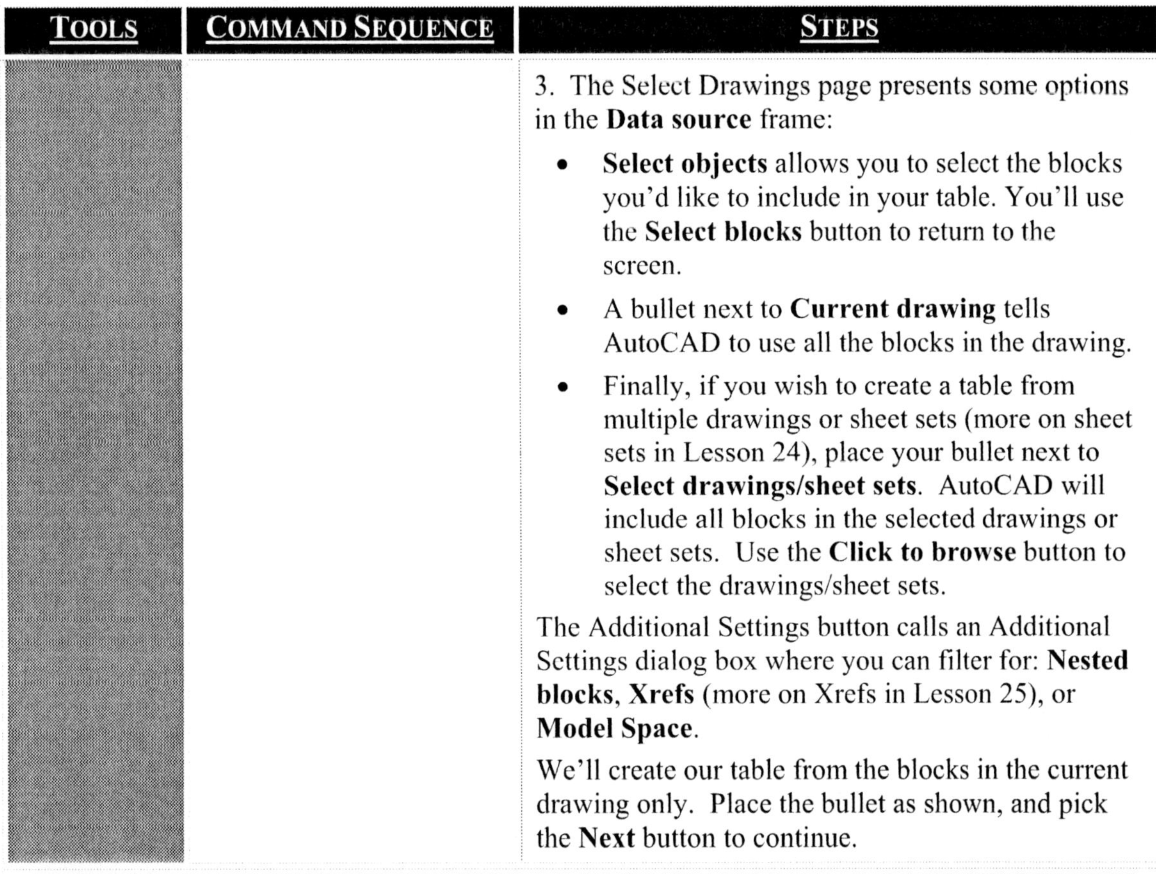

TOOLS	COMMAND SEQUENCE	STEPS
		3. The Select Drawings page presents some options in the **Data source** frame: • **Select objects** allows you to select the blocks you'd like to include in your table. You'll use the **Select blocks** button to return to the screen. • A bullet next to **Current drawing** tells AutoCAD to use all the blocks in the drawing. • Finally, if you wish to create a table from multiple drawings or sheet sets (more on sheet sets in Lesson 24), place your bullet next to **Select drawings/sheet sets**. AutoCAD will include all blocks in the selected drawings or sheet sets. Use the **Click to browse** button to select the drawings/sheet sets. The Additional Settings button calls an Additional Settings dialog box where you can filter for: **Nested blocks**, **Xrefs** (more on Xrefs in Lesson 25), or **Model Space**. We'll create our table from the blocks in the current drawing only. Place the bullet as shown, and pick the **Next** button to continue.

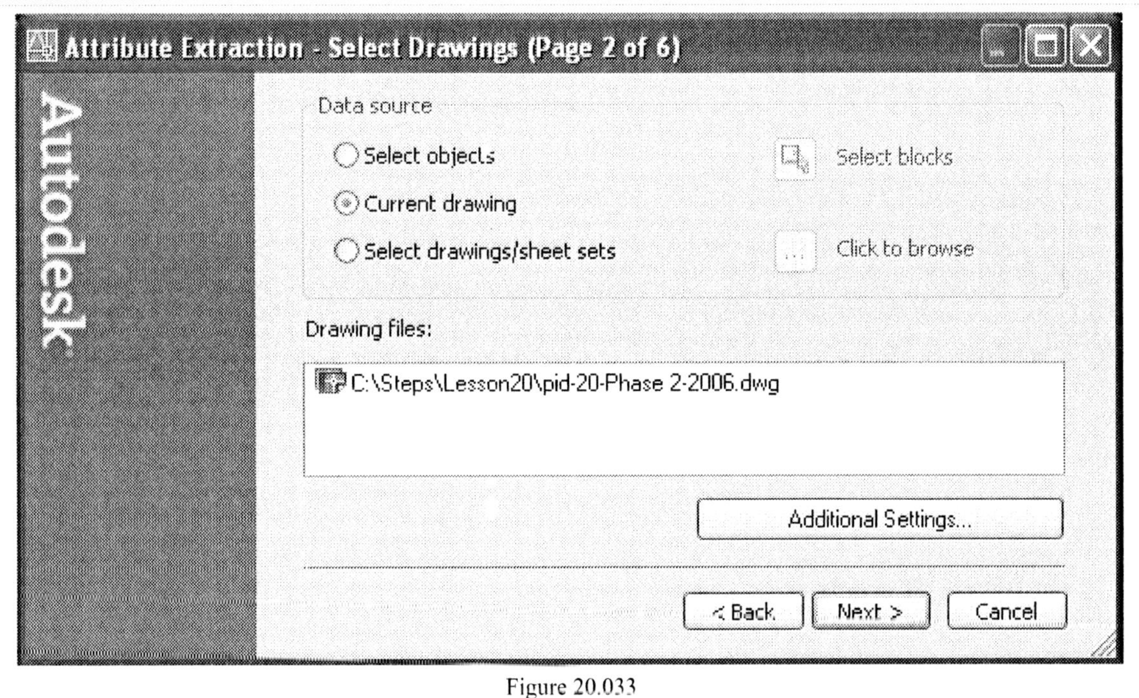

Figure 20.033

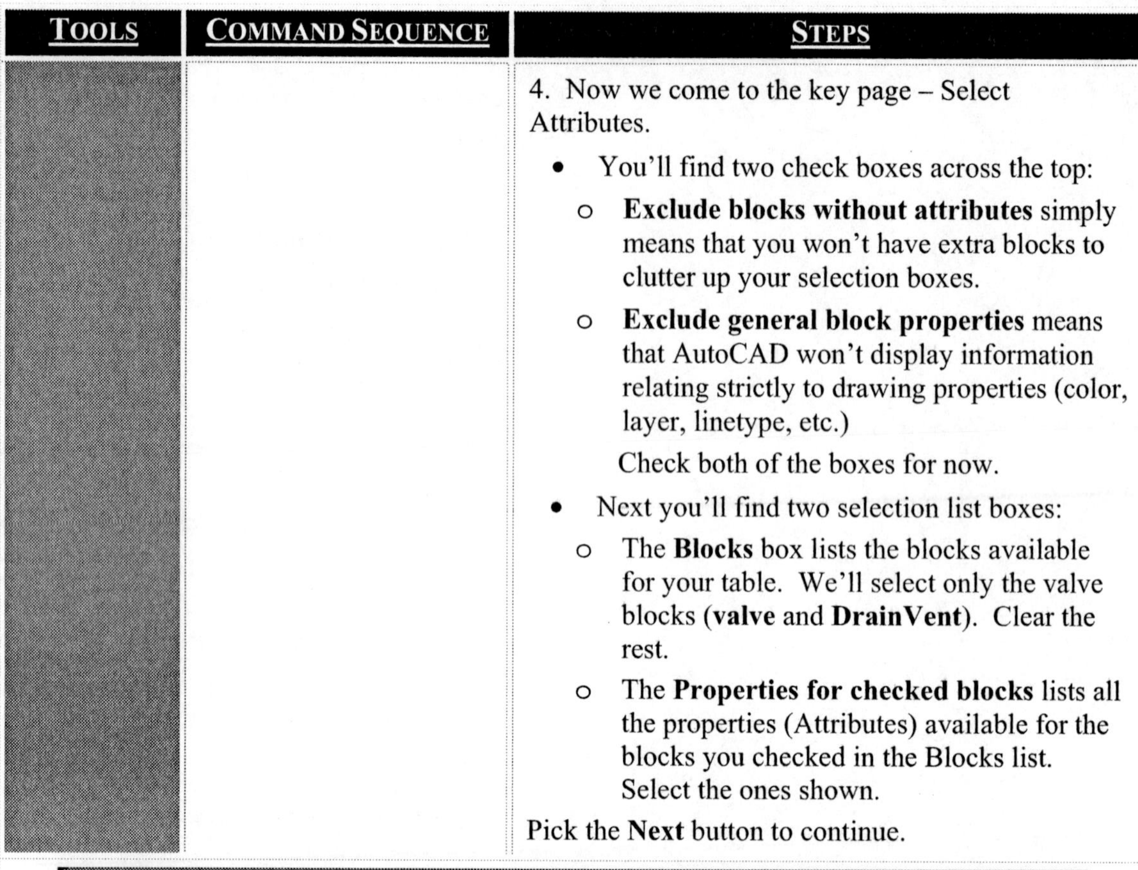

Tools	Command Sequence	Steps

4. Now we come to the key page – Select Attributes.

- You'll find two check boxes across the top:
  - **Exclude blocks without attributes** simply means that you won't have extra blocks to clutter up your selection boxes.
  - **Exclude general block properties** means that AutoCAD won't display information relating strictly to drawing properties (color, layer, linetype, etc.)

  Check both of the boxes for now.
- Next you'll find two selection list boxes:
  - The **Blocks** box lists the blocks available for your table. We'll select only the valve blocks (**valve** and **DrainVent**). Clear the rest.
  - The **Properties for checked blocks** lists all the properties (Attributes) available for the blocks you checked in the Blocks list. Select the ones shown.

Pick the **Next** button to continue.

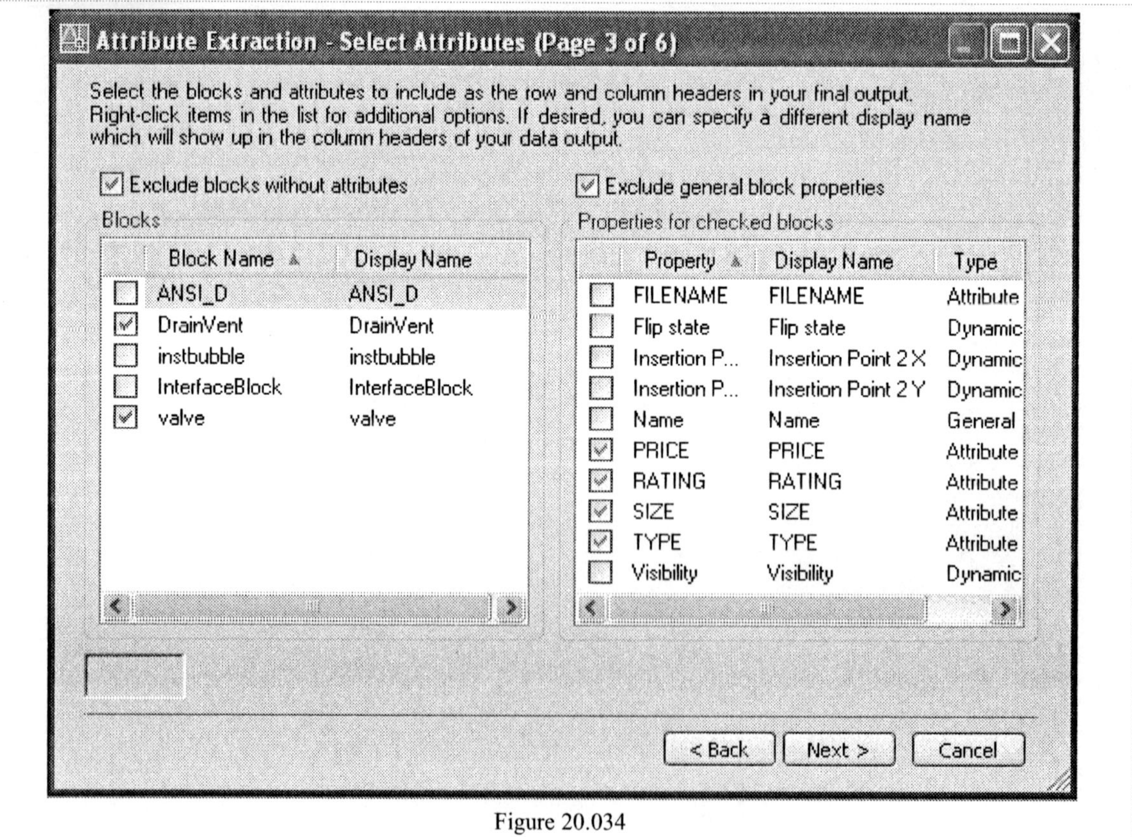

Figure 20.034

TOOLS	COMMAND SEQUENCE	STEPS

5. On the Finalize Output page, you'll set up your table's data.

- Adjust the grid by dragging the column headers to the desired position. Adjust yours to look like that in Figure 20.035.
- Adjust the order by picking in a column header – pick in **TYPE** until the arrow points upward, as shown.
- Below the list box, notice the **Extract attribute data to** frame. Here you'll tell AutoCAD to extract to a table or to an external file. Pick both.

  You'll have to pick the **...** button next to the text box to name and locate the extraction file. Your file type options include: **csv** (comma delimited format suitable for importing into many other applications), **xls** (Microsoft Excel file), **mdb** (Microsoft Access file), and **txt** (simple text file).

  Create the extraction file indicated.
- You can use the **Full Preview** button to see the data if you wish.

Pick the **Next** button to continue.

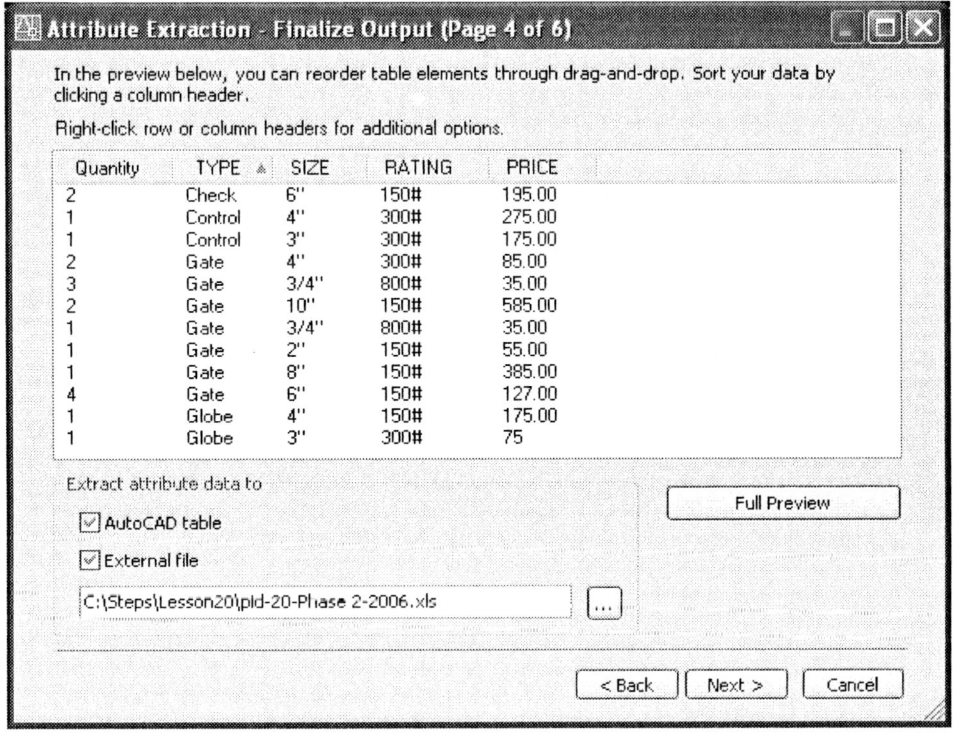

Figure 20.035

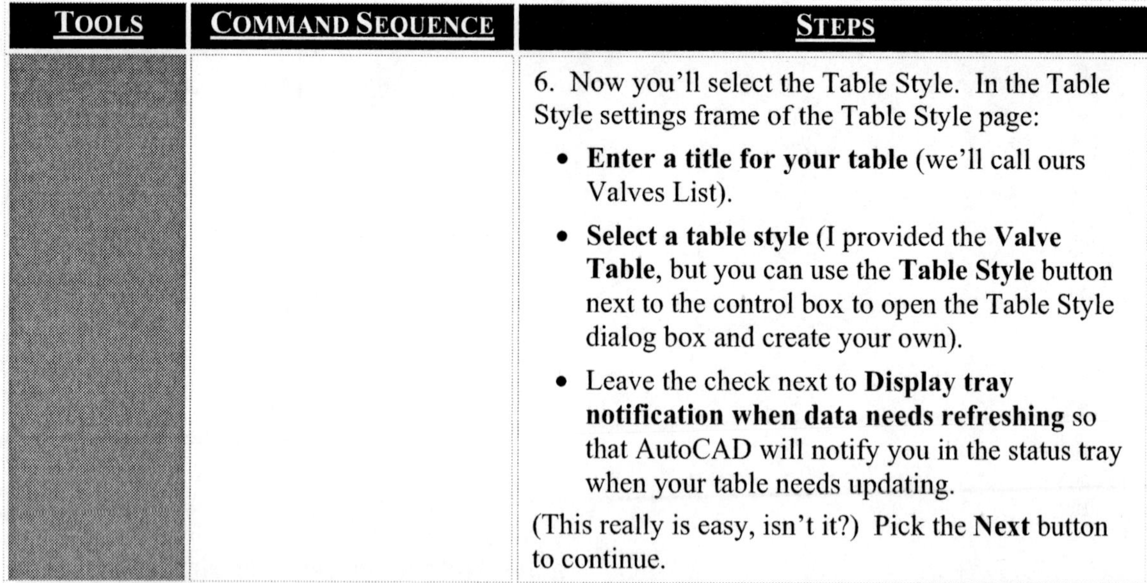

TOOLS	COMMAND SEQUENCE	STEPS
		6. Now you'll select the Table Style. In the Table Style settings frame of the Table Style page: • **Enter a title for your table** (we'll call ours Valves List). • **Select a table style** (I provided the **Valve Table**, but you can use the **Table Style** button next to the control box to open the Table Style dialog box and create your own). • Leave the check next to **Display tray notification when data needs refreshing** so that AutoCAD will notify you in the status tray when your table needs updating. (This really is easy, isn't it?) Pick the **Next** button to continue.

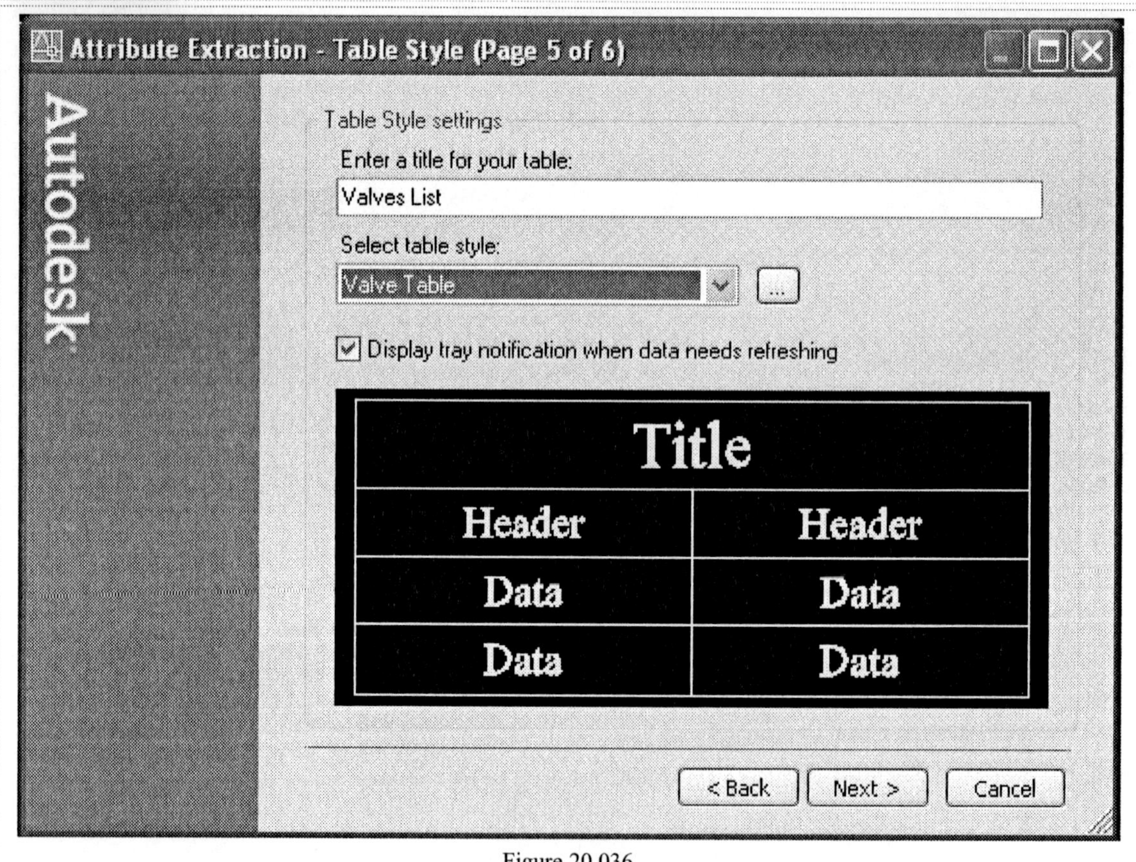

Figure 20.036

TOOLS	COMMAND SEQUENCE	STEPS
		7. The only option left is to save your setup as a template. Go ahead and do that now (pick the **Save template** button). Save the template as *PID-20.blk* to the C:\Steps\Lesson20 folder. Then pick the **Finish** button to insert the table. (As the window says, once you finish, AutoCAD will automatically generate your spreadsheet and place it in the appropriate folder.)

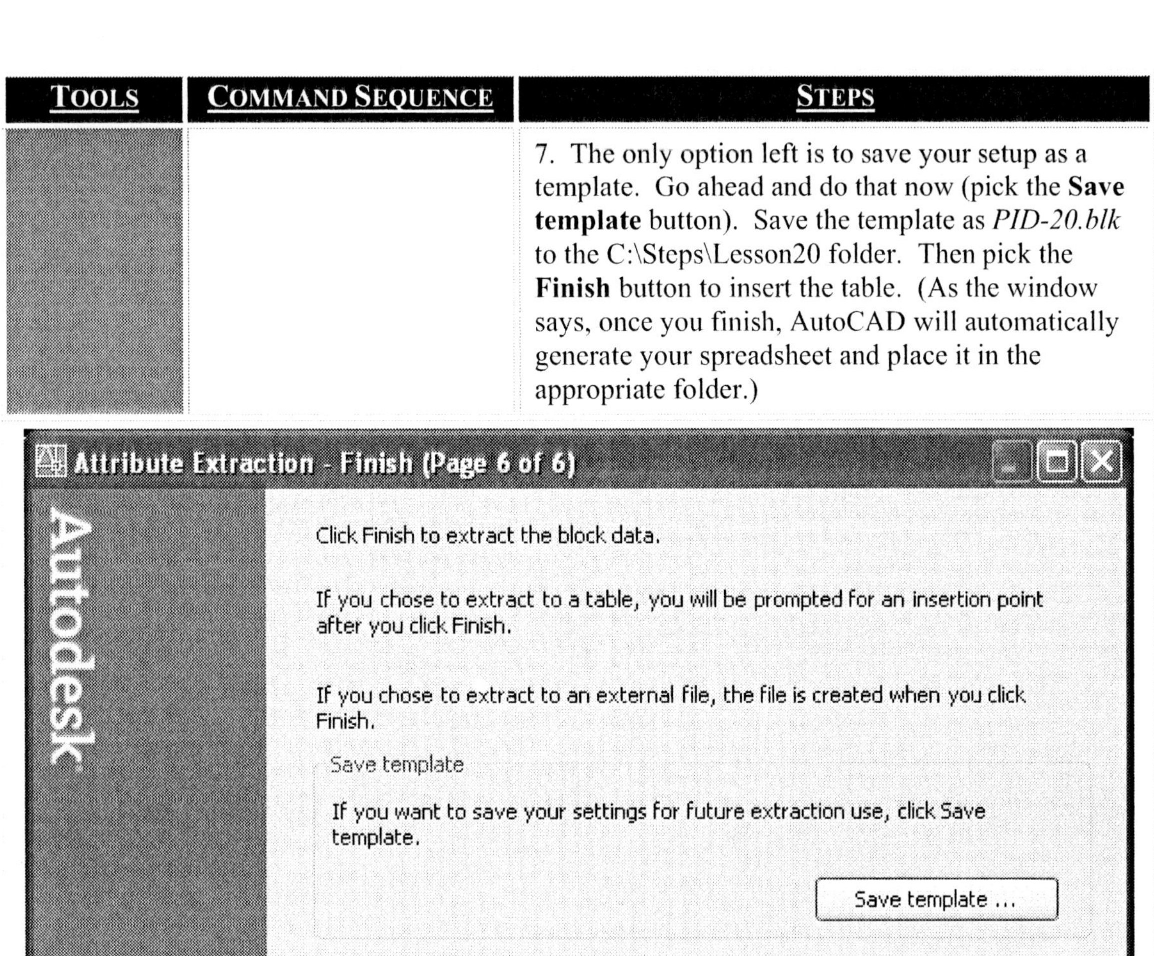

Figure 20.037

	External file "C:\Steps\Lesson20\pid-20-Phase 2-2006.xls" was successfully created. **Specify insertion point:** *3,7*	8. Locate the table around coordinates 3,7. The table looks like Figure 20.038.

TOOLS	COMMAND SEQUENCE	STEPS

Valves List

Quantity	TYPE	SIZE	RATING	PRICE
2	Check	6"	150#	195.00
1	Control	4"	300#	275.00
1	Control	3"	300#	175.00
2	Gate	4"	300#	85.00
4	Gate	6"	150#	127.00
2	Gate	10"	150#	585.00
1	Gate	2"	150#	55.00
3	Gate	3/4"	800#	35.00
1	Gate	3/4"	800#	35.00
1	Gate	8"	150#	385.00
1	Globe	4"	150#	175.00
1	Globe	3"	300#	75.00

Figure 20.038

	Command: ***qsave***	9. Save the drawing, but don't exit.

That may get a "way, cool," but you're not finished yet! Let's do one more thing.

Do This: 20.4.2	**Updating Attribute Data in a Table**

I. Continue in the *pid-20 Phase 2-2006.dwg* file.

II. Zoom in to the lower left quadrant of the screen so you can see the table and the pump next to it.

III. Follow these steps.

TOOLS	COMMAND SEQUENCE	STEPS
	Command: ***e***	1. Erase the ¾" drain valve indicated in Figure 20.039.

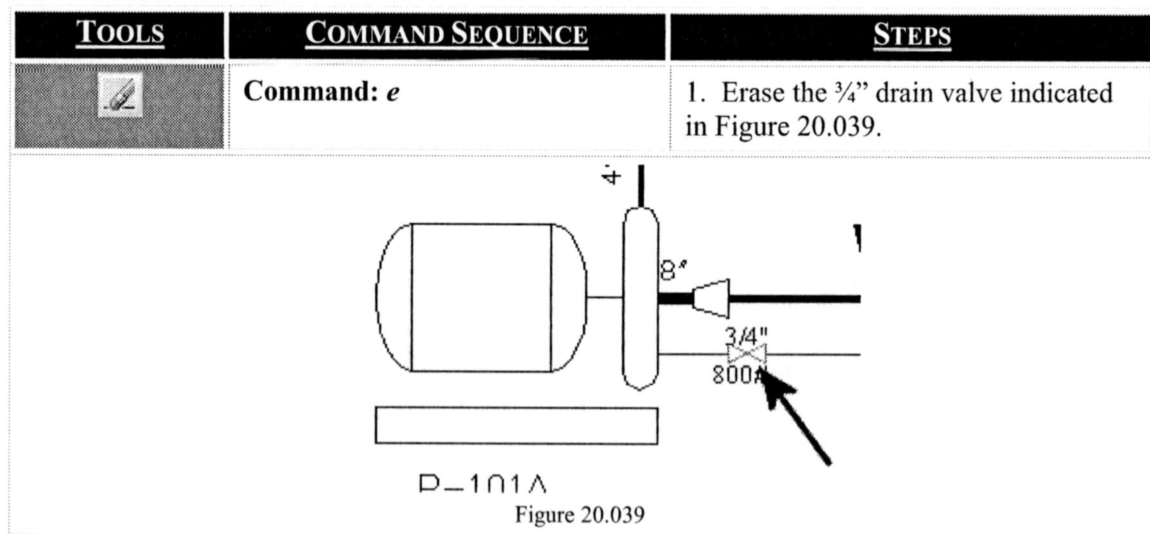

Figure 20.039

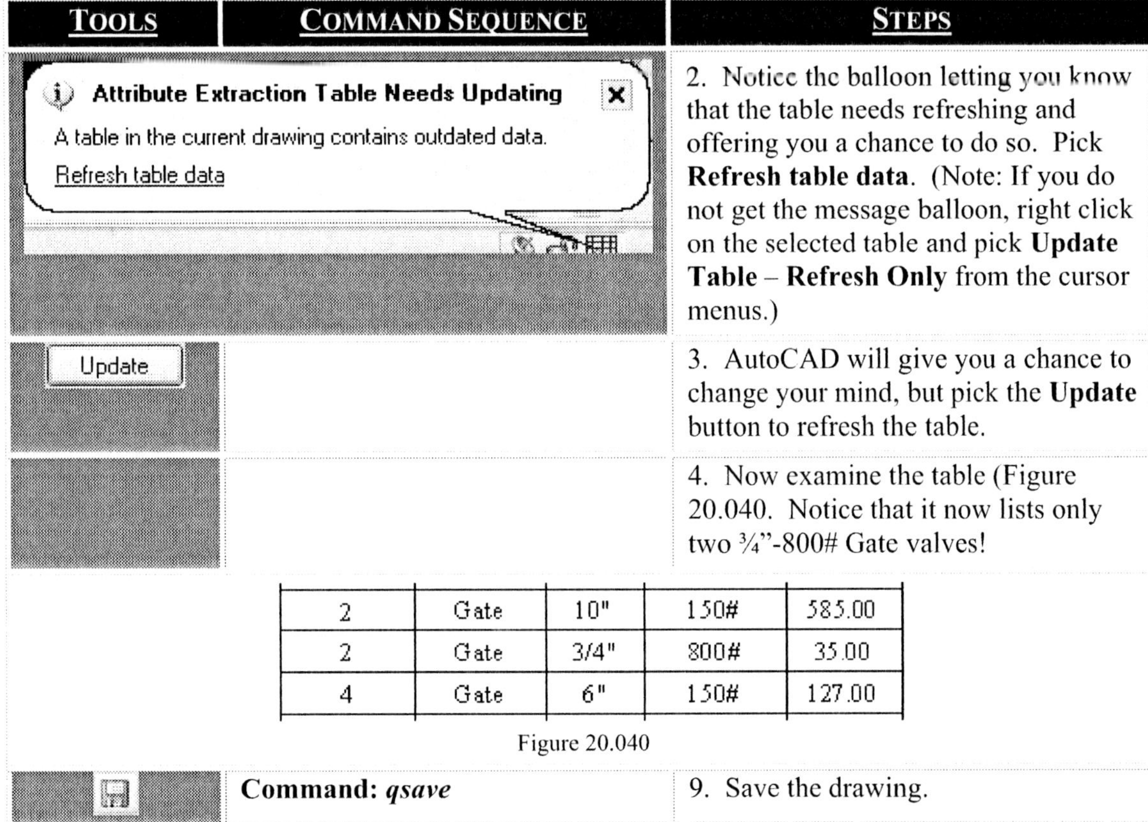

TOOLS	COMMAND SEQUENCE	STEPS
Attribute Extraction Table Needs Updating A table in the current drawing contains outdated data. Refresh table data		2. Notice the balloon letting you know that the table needs refreshing and offering you a chance to do so. Pick **Refresh table data**. (Note: If you do not get the message balloon, right click on the selected table and pick **Update Table – Refresh Only** from the cursor menus.)
Update		3. AutoCAD will give you a chance to change your mind, but pick the **Update** button to refresh the table.
		4. Now examine the table (Figure 20.040. Notice that it now lists only two ¾"-800# Gate valves!

2	Gate	10"	150#	585.00
2	Gate	3/4"	800#	35.00
4	Gate	6"	150#	127.00

Figure 20.040

TOOLS	COMMAND SEQUENCE	STEPS
	Command: ***qsave***	9. Save the drawing.

You can edit what you've created by selecting **Update Table – Edit Extraction Settings** from the cursor menu when you right click in the selected table.

Okay, now you can do the "Way, COOL!"

20.5 Extra Steps

Check out the Excel spreadsheet you created in Exercise 20.4.1 (if you have a copy of MS Excel). You'll notice a couple things:

- Both number columns (**Quantity** and **Price**) are formatted as text. You'll have to select the columns and use the Excel converter to turn the data into numbers so you (or your Materials rep.) can total the **Price** column.
- The quantity of ¾"-800# valves did not update as did the table in your drawing. You'll still have to notify the Materials folks when there's a change. (There's a thought for future releases; you listening, Autodesk?)

In Lesson 27, you'll see a method for dynamically tying block information to a database (the old Lesson 27). As I indicated, this tie is *dynamic* – that is, as you update the drawing, the database also updates. This procedure requires a tremendous amount of work both to create and then to maintain it. Personally, I prefer the methods outlined in this lesson, but take a look at Lesson 27 anyway. You never know …

20.6 What Have We Learned?

Items covered in this lesson include:

- *Creating, Inserting, and Manipulating Block Attributes*
  - ***Attdef***
  - ***Insert***
- *Attribute display commands:*
  - ***Attdia***
  - ***Attreq***
  - ***Attdisp***
- *Editing Attributes*
  - ***Attedit***
  - ***BAttMan***
  - *The Properties Palette*
- *Extracting Attribute Data*
  - ***Eattext***

In this lesson, we learned what makes AutoCAD worth the price you (or your company) paid for it. Here we saw how we can shave weeks from a project by spending a day or two in additional setup time. This savings translates into increased profit for the company by cutting production time (thus increasing the amount of work possible in a given period of time). It means more money for the trained operator because it's his or her training that makes the savings possible.

What we've done in this lesson is to cover the methods and techniques available that can accomplish these savings. But it's often up to you, the CAD operator and designer, to explain, demonstrate, and even sell these possibilities to the people and companies for whom you work. Remember that CAD is still relatively new to many people. They are relying on your expertise to show them what can be done!

20.7 Exercises

We're going to recreate the project we did in Lesson 19, but this time our blocks will contain attributes that we'll use to create a bill of materials for our drawing.

1. Begin by opening the *Blocks-arch-2006.dwg* file in the C:\Steps\Lesson20 folder. Notice that the drawings have already been created for you.

   1.1. Create attributes for each (on the **Text** layer) as indicated in the chart that follows. Use an **Invisible** mode for each (clear all other modes). Then WBlock each to the C:\Steps\Lesson20\Library folder (create this folder if it isn't already there). (Use the same insertion points you used in Lesson 21.)

BLOCK	TAG	PROMPT	DEFAULT VALUE	TEXT JUSTIFY
Door	Type	What type is it?	Flush	
Door	Size	What size is it?		Center
Door	Mfgr	Who made it?	Ideal	
Door	MfrID	What is the ID?		
Window	Type	What type is it?	DH	
Window	Size	What size is it?		Center
Window	Mfgr	Who made it?	Anderson	

Block	**Tag**	**Prompt**	**Default Value**	**Text Justify**
Window	MfrID	What is the ID?		
Sink	Type	What type is it?	Lav	
Sink	Size	What size is it?	18x30	
Sink	Mfgr	Who made it?	American	
Sink	MfrID	What is the ID?	W-POR-LA010	
Tub	Type	What type is it?	Tub	
Tub	Size	What size is it?	30x60	
Tub	Mfgr	Who made it?	American	
Tub	MfrID	What is the ID?	T/S030	
WC	Type	What type is it?	WC	
WC	Mfgr	Who made it?	American	
WC	MfrID	What is the ID?	W-POR-WC001	
WatrHtr	Type	What type is it?	WH	
WatrHtr	Size	What size is it?	50gal	
WatrHtr	Mfgr	Who made it?	American	
WatrHtr	MfrID	What is the ID?	E52	

1.2. Open the *FlrPln 20.dwg* file in the C:\Steps\Lesson20 folder.

1.3. Insert the blocks as shown in Figure 20.041 using the information in the following chart that follows.

1.3.1. The master bath window is 42x24

1.3.2. The bay window is 42x36

1.3.3. All other windows are 42x74

1.3.4. Outer wall doors are X-SOL-36 (solid core)

1.3.5. Inner wall doors are I-HOL-36 and I-HOL-30

1.3.6. Put a round WC in the mater bath and a smooth WC in the common bath

1.3.7. Put standard sinks in the master bath and an oval sink in the common bath

Block	**Type**	**Size**	**MfrID**
Door	Flush	36"	X-SOL-36
Door	Flush	36"	I-HOL-36
Door	Flush	30"	I-HOL-30
Window	DH	42x24	2-DH-S
Window	DH	42x35	2-DH-M
Window	DH	42x74	2-DH-L
Sink	Lav	18x30	W-POR-LA010
Sink	Lav	18x30	O-POR-LA010
Tub	Tub	30x60	T/S030
WC	WC		W-POR-001R
WC	WC		W-POR-001S

BLOCK	TYPE	SIZE	MFRID
WatrHtr	WH	50gal	E52

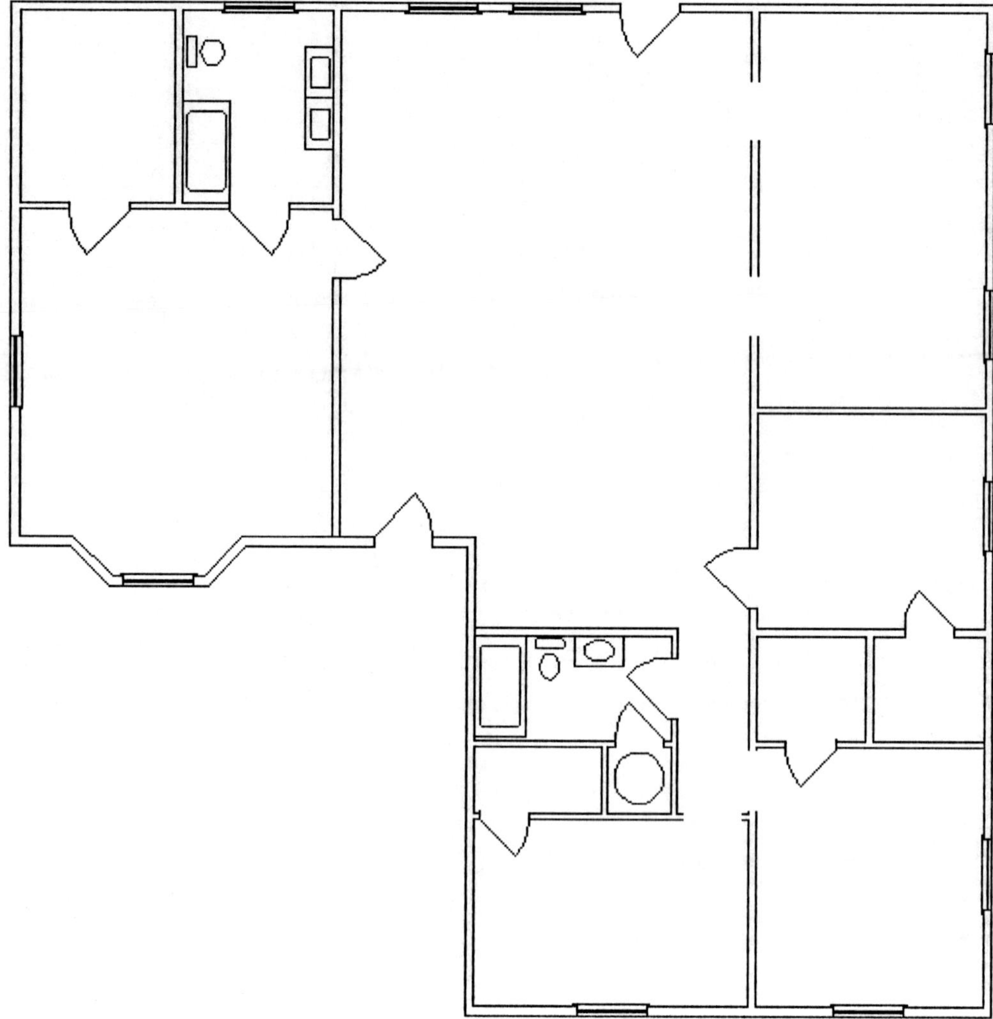

Figure 20.041

1.4. Save and close this drawing. (But we're not finished yet.)
1.5. Open the *Tara II Data Sheet* drawing.
1.6. Use the ADC to mine the *PID-20* drawing for the **Valve Table** table style.

Quantity	Name ▲	TYPE	SIZE	MFGR	MFRID
4	Door	Flush	30"	Ideal	I-HOL-30
5	Door	Flush	36"	Ideal	I-HOL-36
2	Door	Flush	36"	Ideal	X-SOL-36
3	Sink	Lav	18x30	American	W-POR-LA010
2	Tub	Tub	30x60	American	T/S030
1	WaterHtr	WH	50 gal	American	E52
1	WC	WC		American	W-POR-WC001R
1	WC	WC		American	W-POR-WC001S
1	window	DH	42x24	Anderson	2-DH-S
7	window	DH	42x74	Anderson	2-DH-L
1	window	DH	42x35	Anderson	2-DH-M
2	window	DH	42X74	Anderson	2-DH-L

Figure 20.042

1.7. Begin the attribute extraction procedure you did in Exercise 20.4.1. This time, however, tell AutoCAD to Select Drawings (Step 3) and select the *FlrPln20* drawing you just completed. Use the **Valve Table** style you imported from the PID-20 drawing.

1.8. Arrange the data as shown in Figure 20.042, and place it in the drawing between the other table and the notes.

1.9. Save the Data Sheet (Figure 20.043).

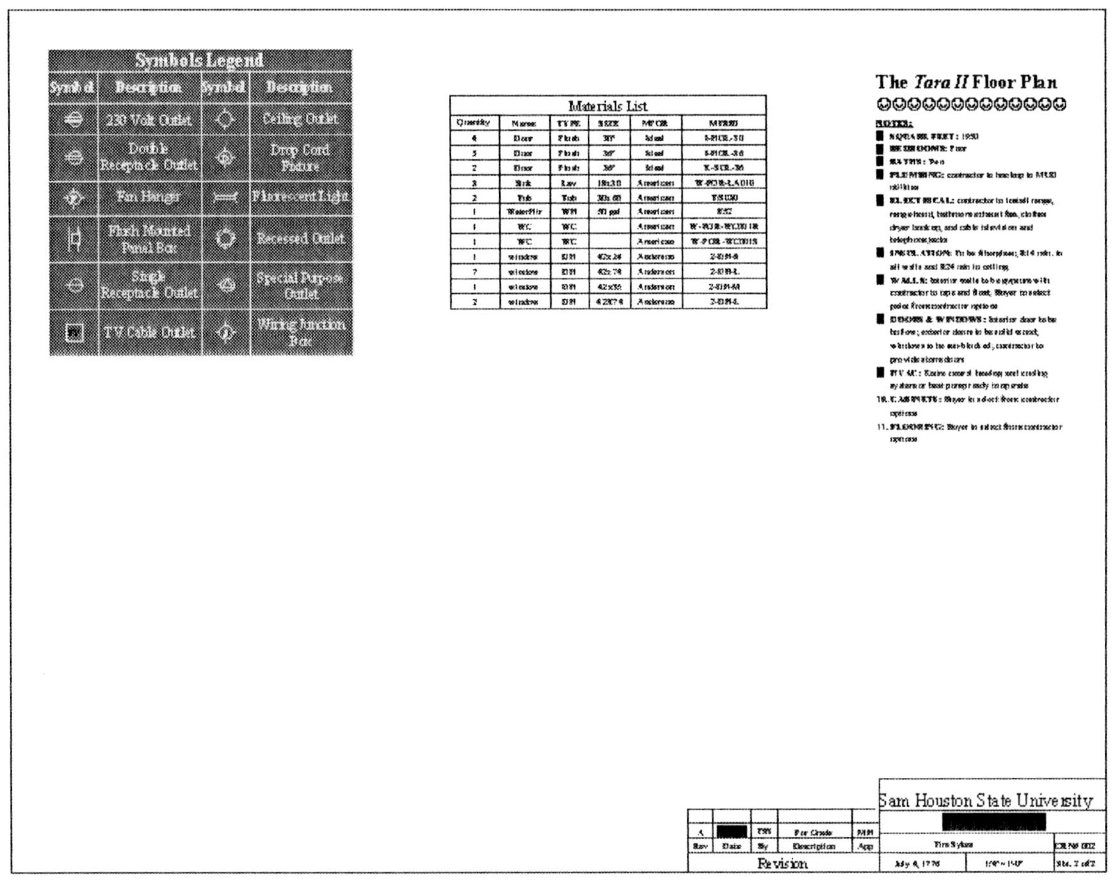

Figure 20.043

2. Using what you've learned, create the next drawing (Figure 20.045).
    2.1. Place the drawing on an appropriate title block (it was created on a 34"x22" sheet of paper and is NTS).
    2.2. Using attributes, create a BOM.

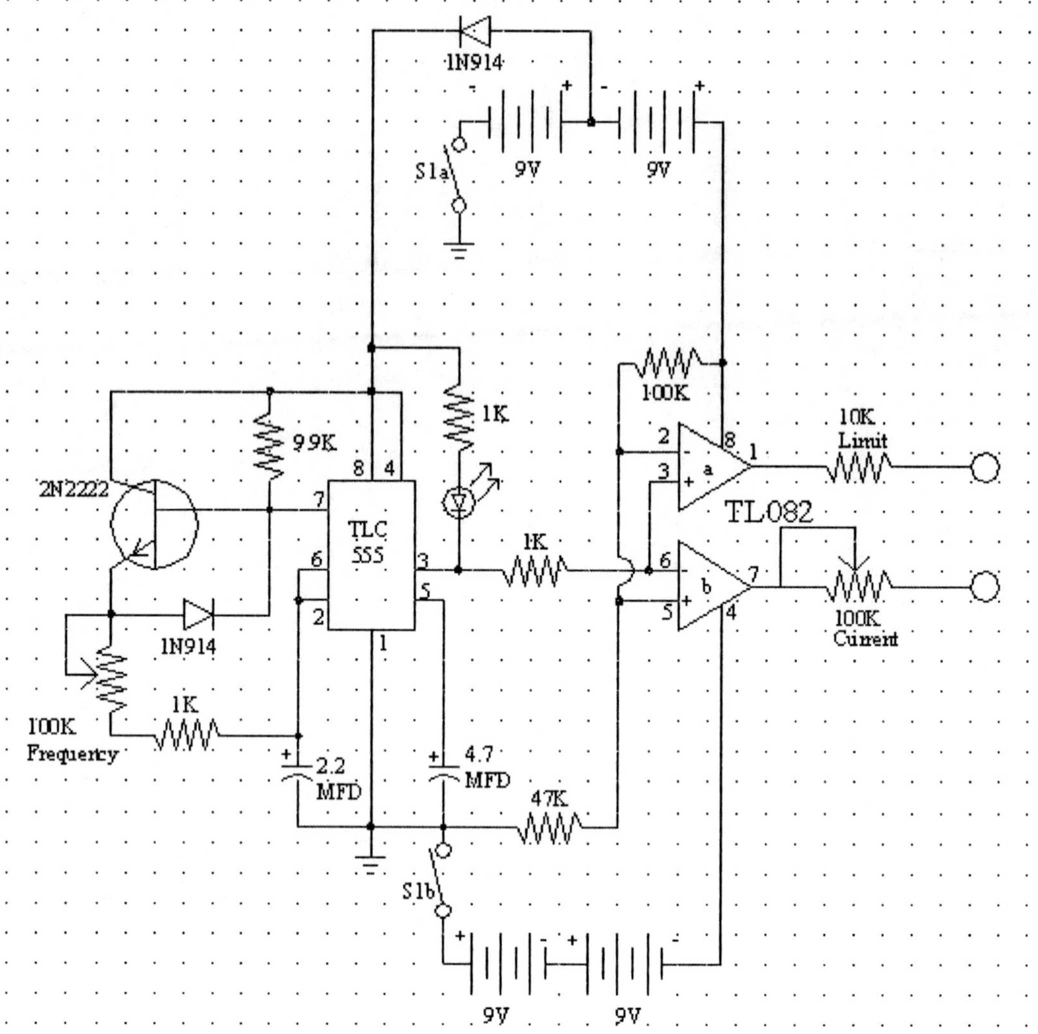

Figure 20.045
Design Courtesy of Thomas Miller or Richmond, Indiana

20.8 For Web-Based Review Questions, visit: http://www.uneedcad.com/2006/Files/06R20.pdf

Section V

Drawing Sharing, Display, and Arrangement

Lesson 21

Following this lesson, you will:

- ✓ *Know how to plot a drawing*
  - o *Setting up a drawing (page)*
  - o *Plotting*
- ✓ *Know how to plot multiple drawings at one time*
- ✓ *Know how to create an eTransmittal*
- ✓ *Know how to publish a drawing to the web*

Sharing Your Work with Others

A General Note to Students and Instructors:

Many instructors prefer to cover plotting early in a course; others prefer to cover it at the end. For this reason, we've made this lesson completely modular. The instructor might choose to cover this material earlier in the course.

However, I don't recommend covering this material later than this. Material in the next few chapters assumes familiarization with plotting.

Goods which are not shared are not goods.

Vernando de Rojas, **La Celestina**, *Act 1*

Sharing. This simple word might carry different meanings for different people. Indeed, it might mean something different for the same person depending on the circumstances.

*Certainly, you must share the results of your labor – at least if you want to get paid for it – and for this purpose, AutoCAD provides the tried-and-true **Plot** command as well as the eTransmit tools and the newer **Publish** command.*

*We'll start with the **Plot** command and explore the ways AutoCAD has provided for you to share the work and then share the fruit.*

Let's begin.

The terms print and plot are used interchangeably in industry – and in this lesson.

21.1 The Old-Fashioned Way – Putting It on Paper (Plotting)

It seems that we'll never escape our paper world!

Lamentations for a Pine Tree

Anonymous

The ironic thing about CAD is that, after all the wonders of the computer world have created this marvelous drawing; in the end, you still need that paper for construction. After all, it might be a bit clumsy to fold a PC and stick it in your tool belt down at the job site (and not many companies are ready to provide those cool pocket computers to their field workers … yet!)

Fortunately, AutoCAD has made it fairly painless to make the transfer from computer to paper. We'll use a series of dialog boxes that will guide us through the process – *One Step at a Time.*

Let's get started!

21.1.1 First Things First – Setting Up Your Printer (or Plotter)

Before actually printing a document in any application, you must first tell the application which printing device you'll use. The reasons are technical and involve those driver gizmos about which you've probably read. All printers ship with their own drivers. You must help the application – in this case, AutoCAD – to figure out which one to use.

Fortunately, that isn't as complicated as it might seem, and it only needs to be done once for each plotting device.

Since most people won't have plotters available to them, I've moved the printer/plotter setup section of this chapter to a supplemental pdf file. (Download *PlotterSetup.pdf* from here: *http://www.uneedcad.com/Files/PlotterSetup.pdf*) If you don't have a plotter, you can ignore it. If you or your company will use a plotter, you might want to go through those instructions first.

I must distinguish between printers and plotters here (as opposed to printing and plotting). *Printers* are comparatively inexpensive devices that usually sit on a desk or table and use letter or legal size paper. *Plotters* are much larger and are generally used to create drawings on C, D, or E size sheets of paper.

As a rule, AutoCAD can print to a printer using the computer's settings; you won't need to do any additional set up. Plotters, on the other hand, will require some efforts on your part.

21.1.2 Plot Styles

Believe it or not, there will be times when you must ask yourself, "Do I want to print it the way I drew it or some other way – different lineweights, linetypes, colors, etc.?" Personally, I've always been a firm advocate of *WYSIWYG* technology (see the insert), but there will be times when a change at plot time is necessary. (Some folks even prefer to set lineweights and linetypes at plot time!?) For example, my printer uses color. I like that, but I can't afford the cost of printer cartridges when I must print working drawings in full color. So I prefer to print in black-and-white until the final product is ready. With plot styles, I can do that without affecting the drawing. (Of course, for those of you who would rather wait until you create a plot to see what it looks like, you can always set weights and types using plot styles.)

WYSIWYG (pronounced "whiz-ee-wig") – literally, "What You See Is What You Get" – simply means that what appears on your screen is what will appear on your paper. This may seem obvious (and generally is for other types of documents). But some gurus prefer to assign (or change) such things as lineweights, linetypes, or colors at plot time rather than during the drawing setup.

As with plotters, you're fairly unlikely to need this information. However, I understand that once I say that .... Anyway, I've put details on setting up plot styles in a supplemental pdf file for those who'll need it. (*Download PlotStyleSetup.pdf* from here: *http://www.uneedcad.com/Files/PlotStyleSetup.pdf.*)

21.1.3 Setting Up the Page to Be Plotted

As with plotter setups and table setups, you don't absolutely have to know how to set up a page for printing/plotting. However, in this case, it's a good thing to know as it may save you a lot of time as using named page setups means that you won't have to repeat the setup every time you plot.

It isn't difficult; although it isn't as easy as the initial dialog box (the Page Setup Manager – Figure 21.001) might indicate.

When you access the Page Setup Manager with the ***PageSetup*** command (or by picking Page Setup Manager from the File pull down menu), AutoCAD presents Figure 21.001. Here you see two frames – one in which you'll work and one for information. Additionally, there are two fairly standard buttons and a check box.

- Most of your work will occur in the **Page setups** frame. Here, AutoCAD begins by telling you the **Current page setup** (**None** in our figure) and presents a list of existing setups from which you can select. Selecting a setup from the list means that your work here is finished. But if that was all there was to it, you wouldn't need those buttons down the side of the frame.
    - Use the **Set Current** button to use the selected setup to do your printing.

- The **New** and **Modify** buttons present dialog boxes. **New** gives you an opportunity to name the new setup before continuing (Figure 21.002). After you name the new setup, AutoCAD presents the Page Setup dialog box. (**Modify** takes you directly to the Page Setup dialog box and makes the selected setup's information available for modification.) We'll look at the Page Setup dialog box in more detail in a moment.

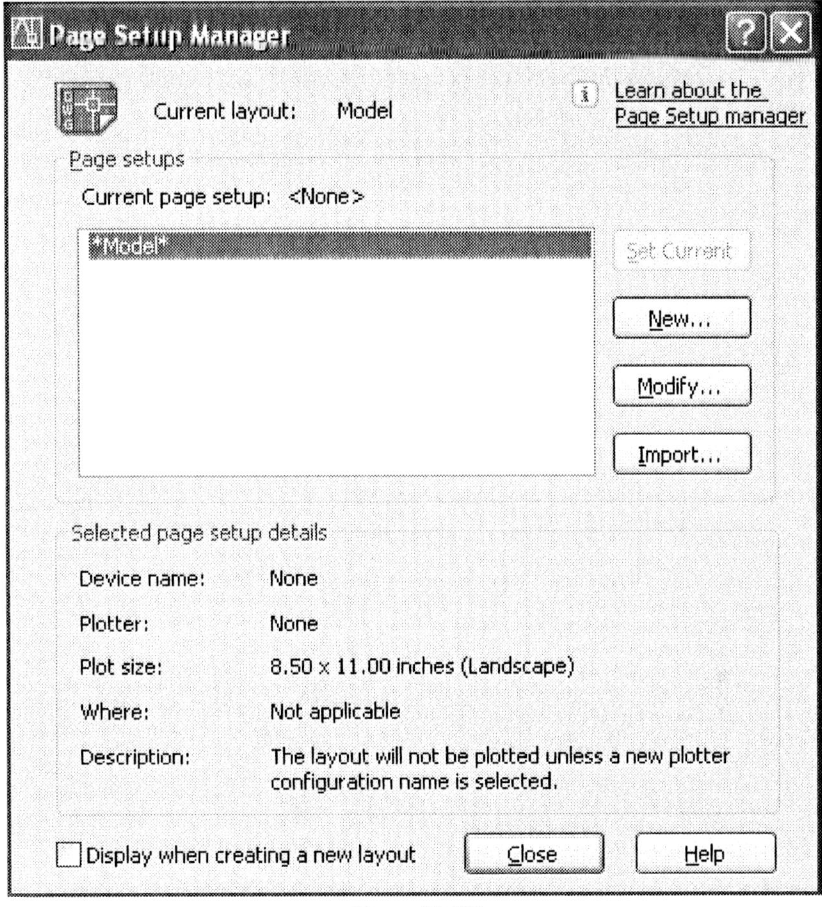

Figure 21.001

- **Import** allows you to take the page setup definition from another drawing and make it a definition in your drawing. You'll use a common Select File dialog box for this one and select a DWT file (a template).

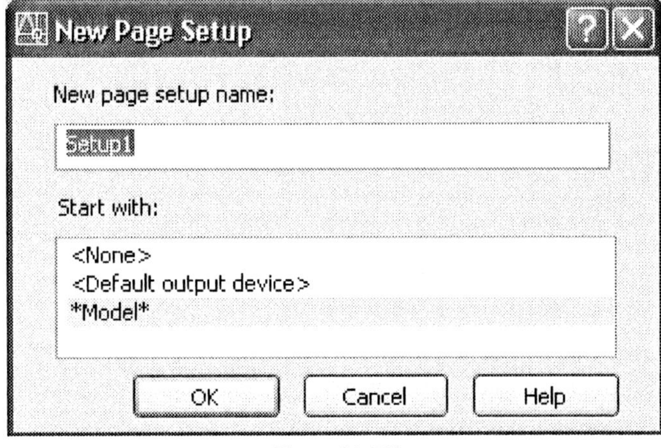

Figure 21.002

- The **Selected Page Setup Details** frame provides information about the selected setup. Use this information to be sure you've selected the correct setup for your plot.
- Placing a check next to **Display when creating a new layout** won't mean anything to you at this point – even if you've gone through the twenty chapters ahead of this one. It will, however, prove useful when you begin using Paper Space. We'll look at Paper Space in Lessons 22 and 23.

You can also remove a setup using the Page Setup Manager. Simply select the setup and use the DELETE key on your keyboard.

The important thing to remember about the manager you've just seen is that it provides only the opportunity to select an existing setup for use, or to create or modify a setup. It doesn't create the setup for you. You'll need the Page Setup dialog box for that (Figure 21.003) ... and it's a ten-frame doozy! Let's begin in the upper left corner and take a look.

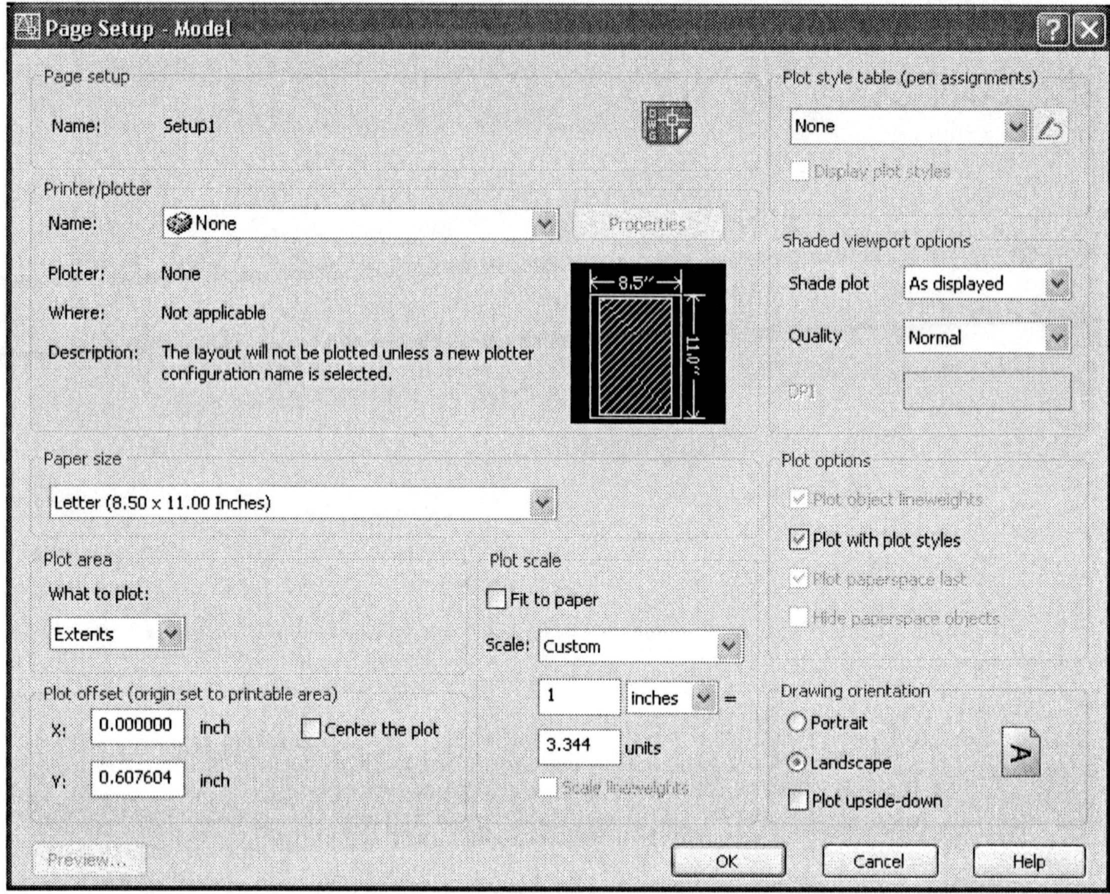

Figure 21.003

- The first frame – **Page setup** – is harmless enough. It tells you the name of the setup you're creating or modifying.
- The next frame down – **Printer/plotter** – allows you to select the device you'll use for this setup. Select the device from the **Name** drop down box and set any properties you want on the device via the **Properties** button just to the right of the list box. This is fairly simply stuff (and standard for most computer applications) as long as the device you want to use is on the list. If it isn't, you'll need to set it up. Refer to the plotter setup supplement for this.

  AutoCAD fills the rest of the frame with useful information about the selected device and the orientation of the setup.
- Below the **Printer/plotter** frame, you'll find the **Paper size** frame, which you'll use for selecting the size of the paper on which you wish to print.
- The **Plot area** frame also contains only a single drop down box. Use it to select exactly what you want to plot on the drawing. AutoCAD allows you to plot just the currently displayed portion of the drawing, the drawing's extents, limits, or an area defined by a window. (If you've opted to complete this lesson out of order, these options will become clearer as you complete the first few lessons.)

- Use the tools within the handy **Plot offset (origin set to printable area)** frame to adjust where your drawing lands on the page. I've found that a check in the box next to **Center the plot** works well for my printing, but you can adjust the position manually using the **X** and **Y** boxes if you wish.
- The **Plot scale** frame contains some critical options.
  - A check next to **Fit to paper** eliminates any effort to plot to scale and forces the drawing onto the page. The results are reduced/enlarged by ratio to fit on the paper. Use this setting for creating small, working drawings.
  - If you don't place a check in the **Fit to paper** box, AutoCAD allows you to select the scale from the **Scale** drop down box, or to enter a customized scale in the boxes below the drop down box.
  - **Scal**[ing] **lineweights** is a good idea if you've used lineweights in your drawing (Lesson 6).
- The **Plot style table (pen assignments)** frame (back at the top, on the right) allows you to select a style table. You can use plot style tables to convert a color drawing to black and white or to assign specific colors to specific pens on a multi-pen plotter. Use the **Edit** button next to the drop down selection box to modify the selected table. For more information on plot style tables, see the supplement.
- The next frame – **Shaded viewport options** – contains controls for plotting three-dimensional drawings. We'll discuss three-dimensional drawings, and viewports, in the *3D AutoCAD 2006: One Step at a Time* text. (Look for this one in the spring of 2005.) Don't mistake the **Quality** option as something that might be useful in a two-dimensional drawing; it controls quality of shaded or rendered three-dimensional objects.
- The **Plot options** frame provides four check boxes.
  - Use **Plot object lineweights** only if you've set the drawing up to use lineweights (Lesson 6). If you haven't, you can ignore this box.
  - Again, use **Plot with plotstyles** only if you've set up the drawing to use plot styles.
  - Normally, AutoCAD plots Paper Space objects first. If you prefer to plot Model Space objects first, place a check in the **Plot paperspace last** box. I haven't seen where this is necessary, but you might discover a need for it. (As I've mentioned, we'll discuss Paper Space in Lessons 22 and 23.)
- You'll tell AutoCAD how to position the drawing on the paper in the last frame (Whew!) – **Drawing orientation**. Your options are the standard **Portrait** and **Landscape** orientations, and a **Plot upside-down** option that you can use to print sepias.
- Finally, there's a **Preview** button at the bottom of the dialog box that will help you see what your settings will produce.

I know this has been a lot of material, but it might hearten you to know that it's less that has been required in previous releases. Let's set up a page and plot a drawing.

Do This: 21.1.3.1	**Setting Up a Page and Plotting**

I. Open the *pid-21.dwg* file in the C:\Steps\Lesson21 folder.

II. Follow these steps.

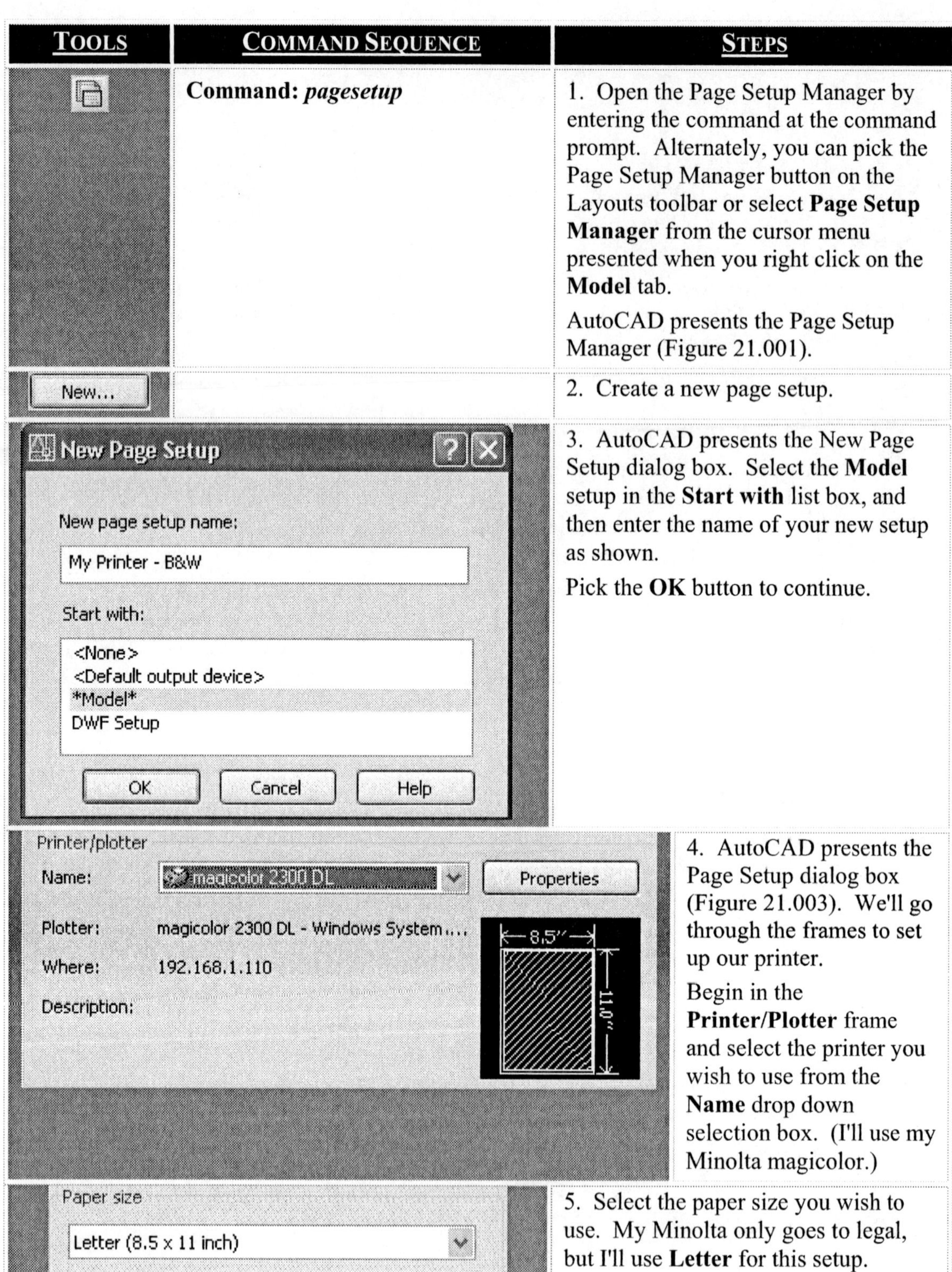

Tools	Command Sequence	Steps
	Command: ***pagesetup***	1. Open the Page Setup Manager by entering the command at the command prompt. Alternately, you can pick the Page Setup Manager button on the Layouts toolbar or select **Page Setup Manager** from the cursor menu presented when you right click on the **Model** tab. AutoCAD presents the Page Setup Manager (Figure 21.001).
New...		2. Create a new page setup.
		3. AutoCAD presents the New Page Setup dialog box. Select the **Model** setup in the **Start with** list box, and then enter the name of your new setup as shown. Pick the **OK** button to continue.
		4. AutoCAD presents the Page Setup dialog box (Figure 21.003). We'll go through the frames to set up our printer. Begin in the **Printer/Plotter** frame and select the printer you wish to use from the **Name** drop down selection box. (I'll use my Minolta magicolor.)
		5. Select the paper size you wish to use. My Minolta only goes to legal, but I'll use **Letter** for this setup.

TOOLS	COMMAND SEQUENCE	STEPS

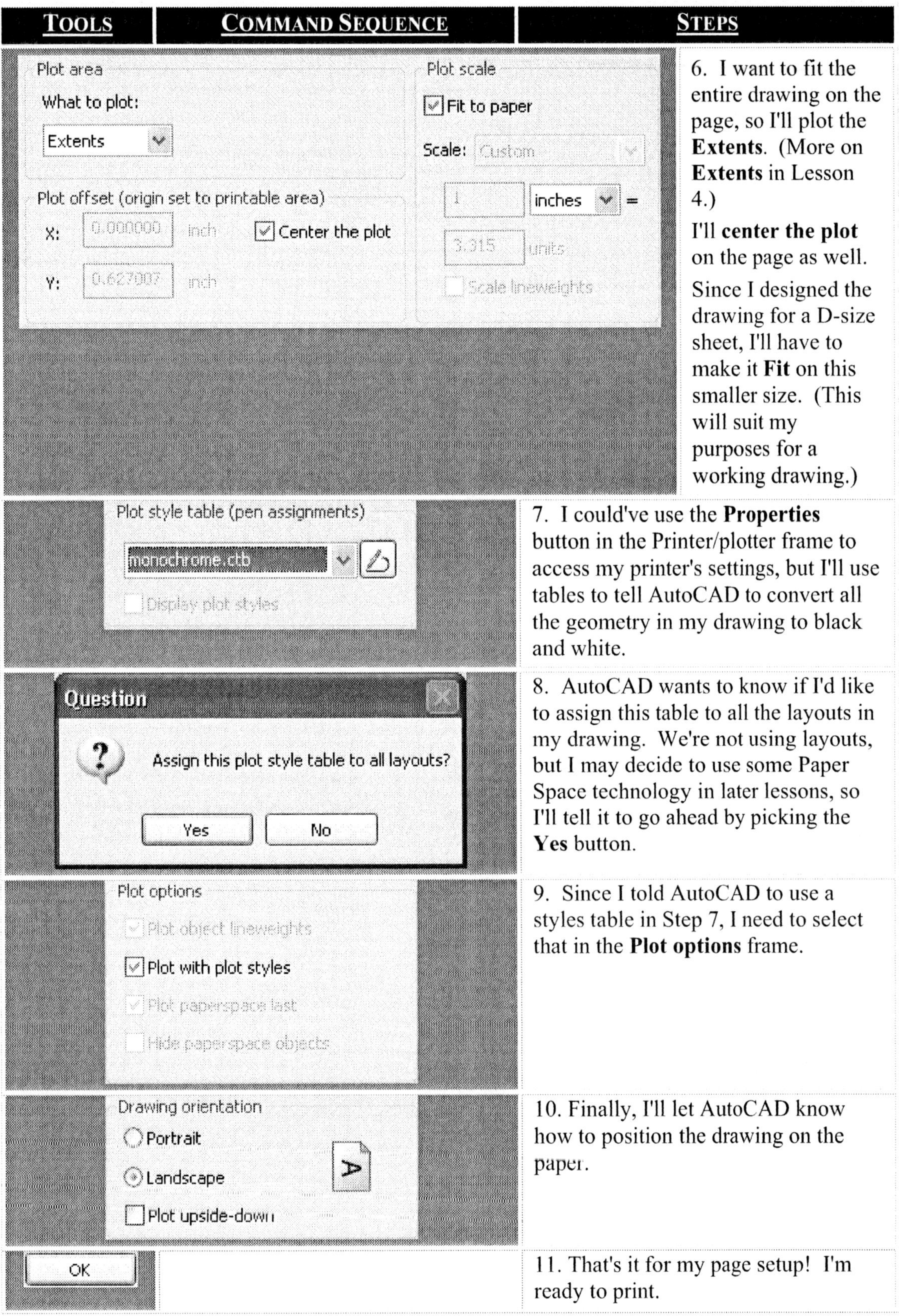

6. I want to fit the entire drawing on the page, so I'll plot the **Extents**. (More on **Extents** in Lesson 4.)

I'll **center the plot** on the page as well.

Since I designed the drawing for a D-size sheet, I'll have to make it **Fit** on this smaller size. (This will suit my purposes for a working drawing.)

7. I could've use the **Properties** button in the Printer/plotter frame to access my printer's settings, but I'll use tables to tell AutoCAD to convert all the geometry in my drawing to black and white.

8. AutoCAD wants to know if I'd like to assign this table to all the layouts in my drawing. We're not using layouts, but I may decide to use some Paper Space technology in later lessons, so I'll tell it to go ahead by picking the **Yes** button.

9. Since I told AutoCAD to use a styles table in Step 7, I need to select that in the **Plot options** frame.

10. Finally, I'll let AutoCAD know how to position the drawing on the paper.

11. That's it for my page setup! I'm ready to print.

Tools	**Command Sequence**	**Steps**
Set Current		12. Back at the Page Setup Manager, set the new style current (select it and pick the appropriate button).
Close		13. Close the Page Setup Manager.
	Command: ***print***	14. Now we can print the drawing. Enter the command at the command line. Alternately, you can pick the **Plot** button on the Standard toolbar or select **Plot** from the File pull down menu.
Preview...		15. Notice that the Plot dialog box is just a simplified version of the Page Setup dialog box. This time, however, because we set our new page setup as current (Step 12), all of our settings have been made for us. Use the **Preview** button to be sure that this setup will work for our drawing.
		16. Our drawing looks okay on the paper, so we'll pick the **Close Preview** button to leave the preview.
OK		17. Pick the **OK** button to start the print.
Plot and Publish Job Complete No errors or warnings found Click to view plot and publish details...		18. AutoCAD will let you know that it has completed your printing job. It'll also let you know of any problems! Pick the **X** to close the bubble.
	Command: ***qsave***	19. Save your drawing, but don't exit.

21.2 Sharing Your Drawing with the *Plot* Command – and *No Paper*!

"Gettin' paid a check's okay, I s'pose, 'cept it don't leave me nuttin' to jingle in my pocket."

from A Geezer's Lament

Anonymous

Ah, progress! Just as our poor geezer lost the joy of jingling pocket change, so we must eventually say goodbye to paper drawings – at least as much as we've said goodbye to cash!

AutoCAD has provided a special type of file that you can use to share design information via the Internet – without the need to send paper. This new file type also loads considerably faster than a drawing file, but it contains the ability to manipulate layers and views, and to be printed like any other web document.

AutoCAD called the file a Drawing Web Format file (DWF, pronounced "DWIF"), gave it the capability to contain hyperlink jumps (just like any other web document), and made its creation as simple as plotting a document (in fact, you use AutoCAD's ***Plot*** command to create it!).

> With Autodesk's DWF Composer, you can even use DWFs for review issues with clients. Visit the Autodesk website for more information on DWF Composer.

Let's see how it works.

21.2.1 Viewing a Drawing Web Format (DWF) File Using Your Browser

The AutoCAD installation includes a tool called the DWF Viewer. This tool, like its many predecessors, enables you to view an AutoCAD DWF file. The DWF file is a wonderful innovation that allows AutoCAD users – *and clients without access to the AutoCAD program* – to view AutoCAD drawings!

The DWF Viewer ships with the AutoCAD program, but for those clients who don't have access to AutoCAD, the viewer is a free download (2Mb) at the Autodesk web site: http://www.autodesk.com/. With the DWF Viewer, you can view files from within your browser or through the viewer program itself – the interface is the same.

Let's take a look.

Do This: 21.2.1.1 Viewing a DWF File

I. You can start a new drawing from scratch or continue from any drawing you have open.

II. Follow these steps.

TOOLS	COMMAND SEQUENCE	STEPS
Browse the Web Button	**Command:** ***browser*** **Enter Web location (URL) <http://www.autodesk.com>:** ***[enter]***	1. Launch your browser by entering the ***Browser*** command at the command line. Alternately, you can pick the **Browse the Web** button on the Web toolbar.
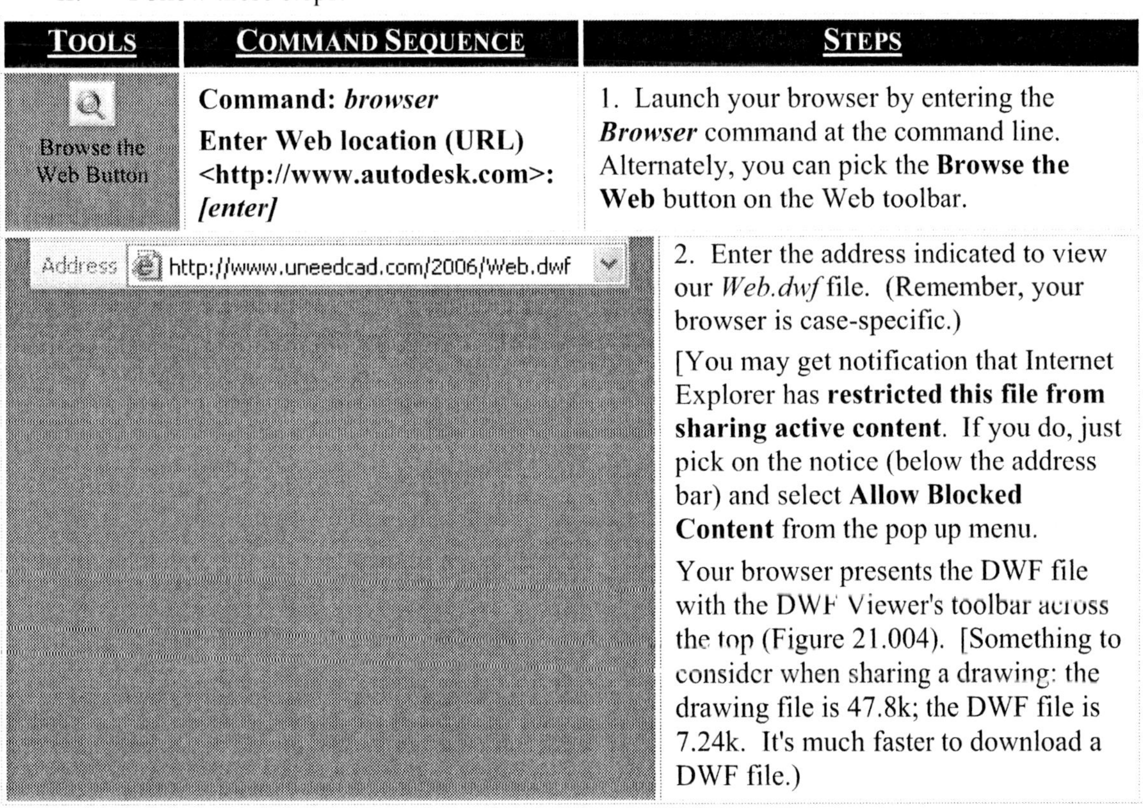		2. Enter the address indicated to view our *Web.dwf* file. (Remember, your browser is case-specific.) [You may get notification that Internet Explorer has **restricted this file from sharing active content**. If you do, just pick on the notice (below the address bar) and select **Allow Blocked Content** from the pop up menu. Your browser presents the DWF file with the DWF Viewer's toolbar across the top (Figure 21.004). [Something to consider when sharing a drawing: the drawing file is 47.8k; the DWF file is 7.24k. It's much faster to download a DWF file.)

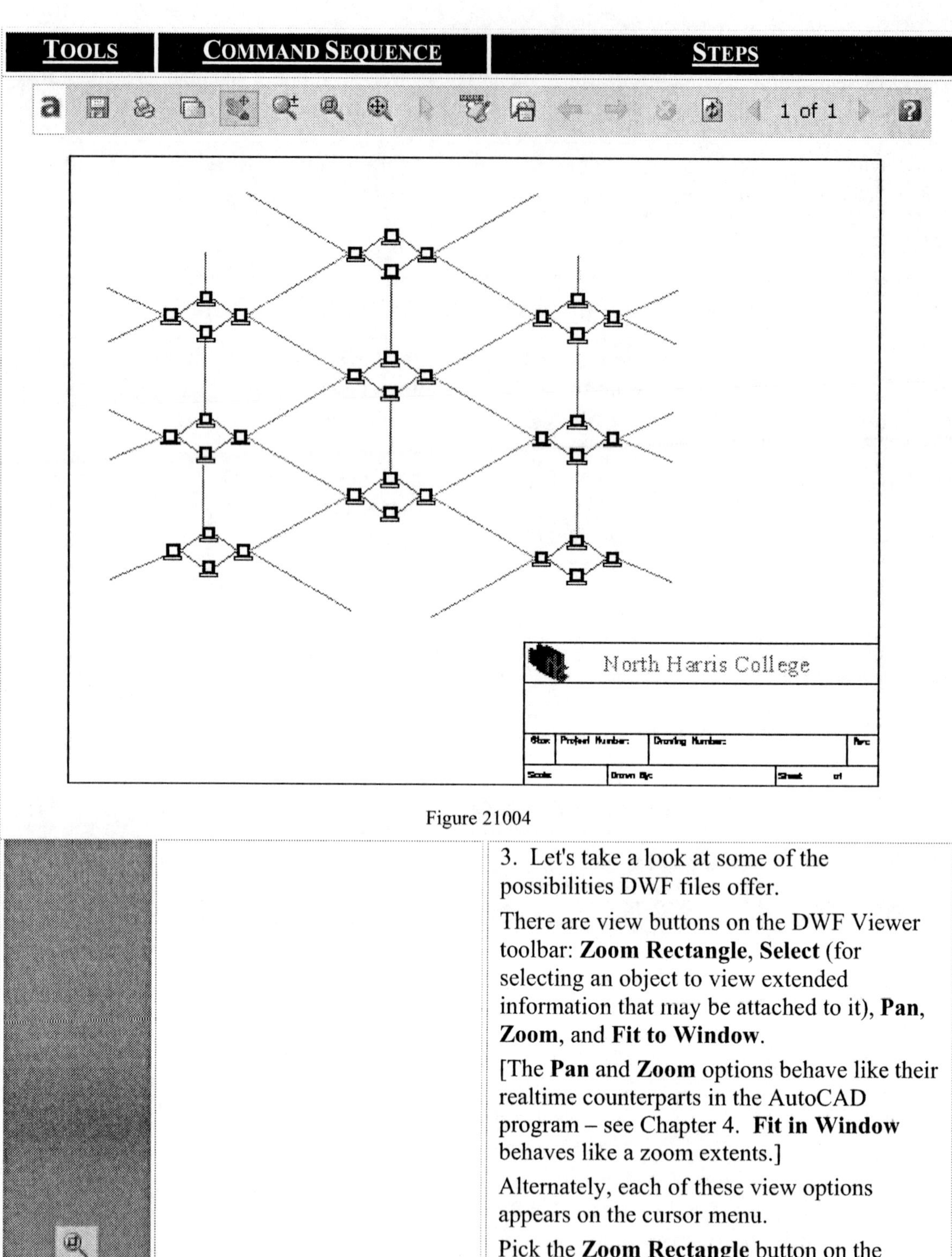

Figure 21004

Tools	Command Sequence	Steps
		3. Let's take a look at some of the possibilities DWF files offer. There are view buttons on the DWF Viewer toolbar: **Zoom Rectangle**, **Select** (for selecting an object to view extended information that may be attached to it), **Pan**, **Zoom**, and **Fit to Window**. [The **Pan** and **Zoom** options behave like their realtime counterparts in the AutoCAD program – see Chapter 4. **Fit in Window** behaves like a zoom extents.] Alternately, each of these view options appears on the cursor menu. Pick the **Zoom Rectangle** button on the toolbar.

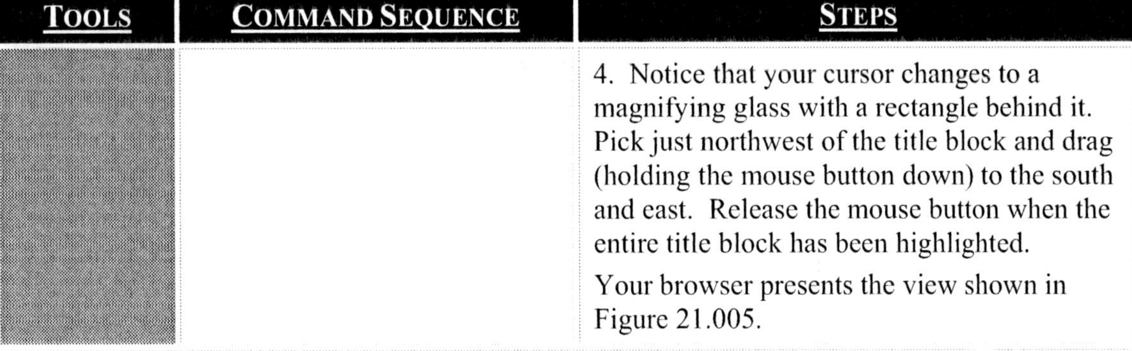

Tools	Command Sequence	Steps
		4. Notice that your cursor changes to a magnifying glass with a rectangle behind it. Pick just northwest of the title block and drag (holding the mouse button down) to the south and east. Release the mouse button when the entire title block has been highlighted. Your browser presents the view shown in Figure 21.005.

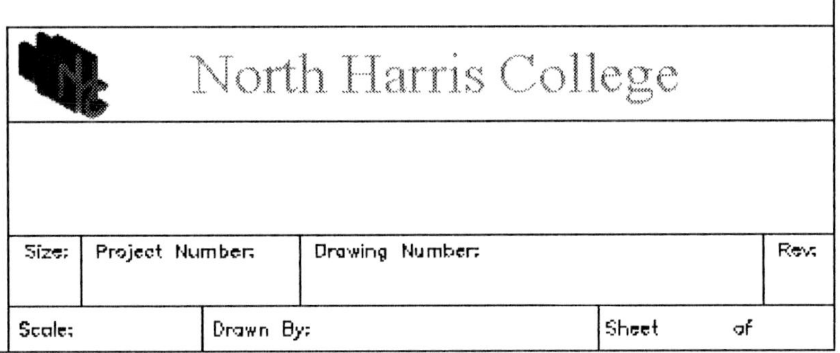

Figure 21.005

Tools	Command Sequence	Steps
		5. Notice that the magnifying glass cursor remains. You could continue to use **Zoom Rectangle** if you wished. Pick the **Fit to Window** button to return to the original view.
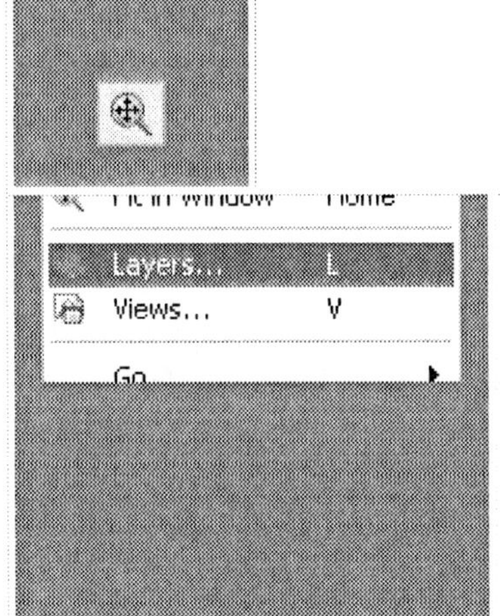		6. Let's take a look at the cursor window. Right-click and pick the **Layers** option. The DWF Viewer presents the Layers dialog box (Figure 21.006). Notice the light bulb symbol. When the symbol is yellow, objects residing on that layer are visible. Pick on a light bulb to turn it gray (**Off**). Objects residing on that layer are now hidden.

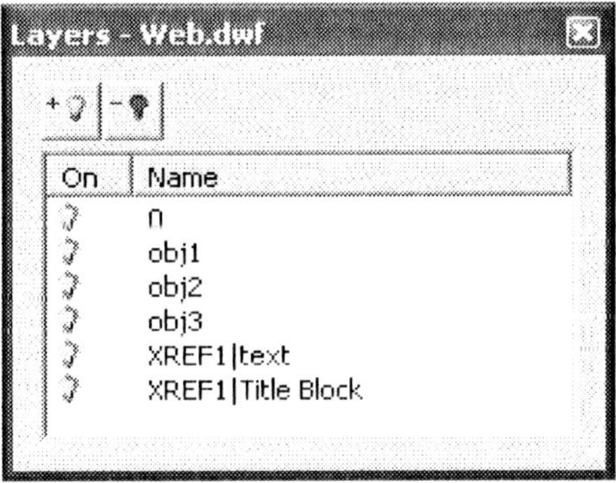

Figure 21.006

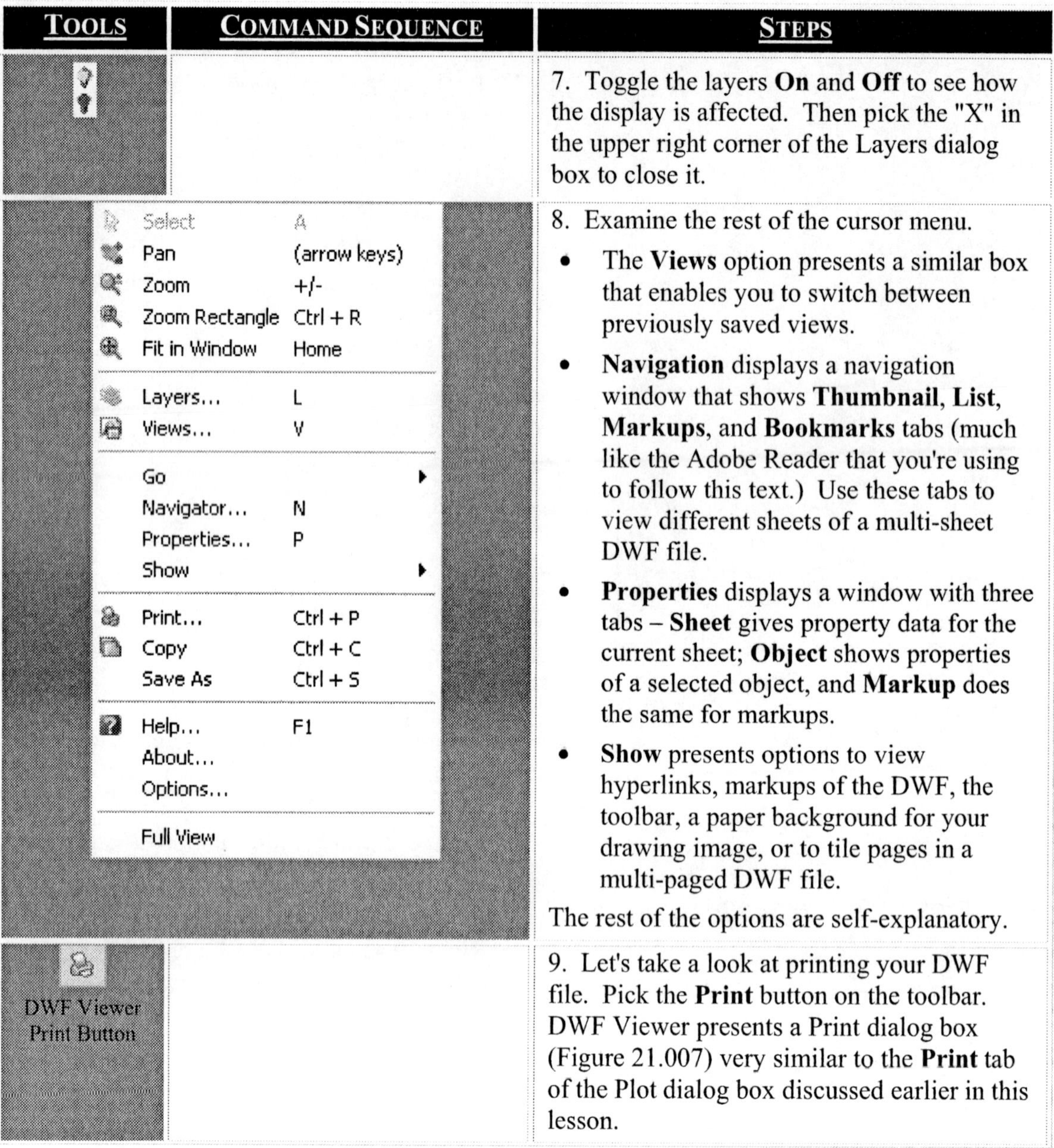

Tools	**Command Sequence**	**Steps**
		7. Toggle the layers **On** and **Off** to see how the display is affected. Then pick the "X" in the upper right corner of the Layers dialog box to close it.
		8. Examine the rest of the cursor menu. • The **Views** option presents a similar box that enables you to switch between previously saved views. • **Navigation** displays a navigation window that shows **Thumbnail**, **List**, **Markups**, and **Bookmarks** tabs (much like the Adobe Reader that you're using to follow this text.) Use these tabs to view different sheets of a multi-sheet DWF file. • **Properties** displays a window with three tabs – **Sheet** gives property data for the current sheet; **Object** shows properties of a selected object, and **Markup** does the same for markups. • **Show** presents options to view hyperlinks, markups of the DWF, the toolbar, a paper background for your drawing image, or to tile pages in a multi-paged DWF file. The rest of the options are self-explanatory.
DWF Viewer Print Button		9. Let's take a look at printing your DWF file. Pick the **Print** button on the toolbar. DWF Viewer presents a Print dialog box (Figure 21.007) very similar to the **Print** tab of the Plot dialog box discussed earlier in this lesson.

TOOLS	COMMAND SEQUENCE	STEPS

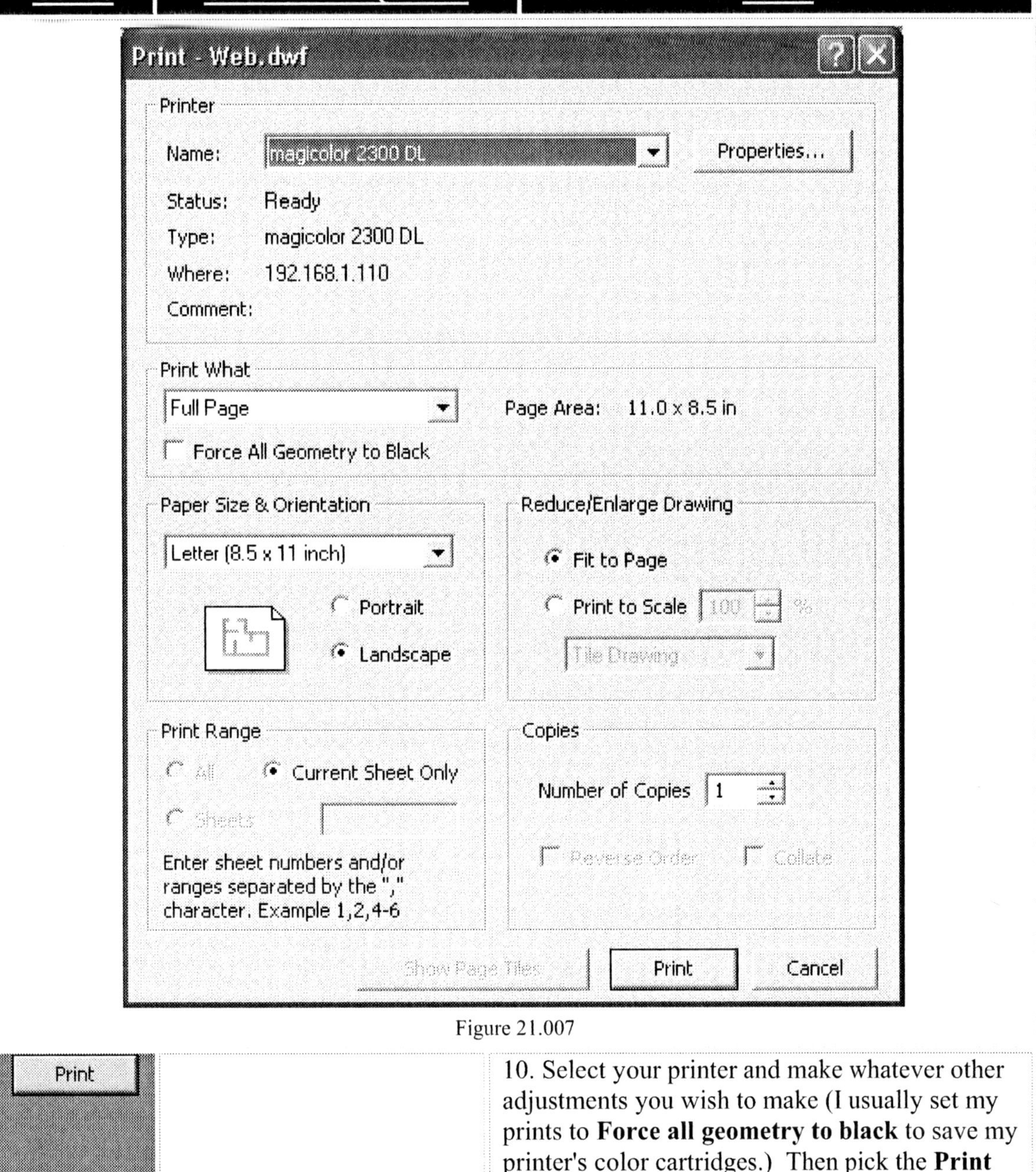

Figure 21.007

TOOLS	COMMAND SEQUENCE	STEPS
Print		10. Select your printer and make whatever other adjustments you wish to make (I usually set my prints to **Force all geometry to black** to save my printer's color cartridges.) Then pick the **Print** button. DWF Viewer prints your drawing.

The rest of the menu options are self-explanatory. Use the **Help** option if you have any problems with these.

You can also copy the DWF file from the web site to your hard drive using the **Copy** option on the cursor menu.

So, now you can see what a remarkable tool a DWF file can be – shared information without compromising the security of your drawing files! Let's create a DWF file for ourselves.

21.2.2 Multiple Plots and Creating a DWF File – with Hyperlinks!

In previous versions of AutoCAD, we created DWF files using some different settings in our plotting procedure. It was simply a question of selecting the DWF device on the **Plot Device** tab of the Plot dialog box.

We can still use this approach – simply select the **DWF6** plotting device – or we can opt for the new ***Publish*** command and dialog box (Figure 21.008).

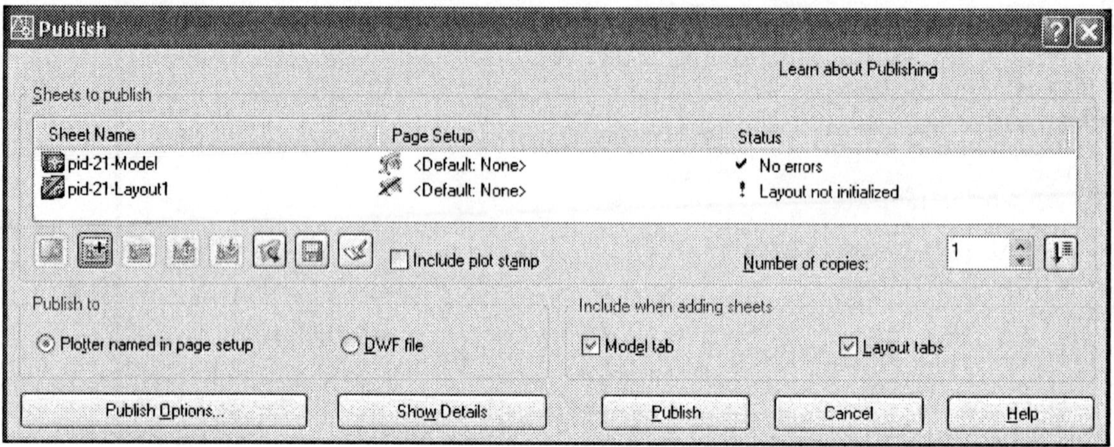

Figure 21.008

Let's take a look.

- The first thing you see – the **Sheets to publish** list box – shows the various sheets associated with the current drawing file, their current page setups, and their status. As we haven't discussed Paper Space and **Layout** tabs yet, we'll concentrate on the **Model** sheet.
- Below the list box, you'll find several buttons and a couple frames. Let's look at these.

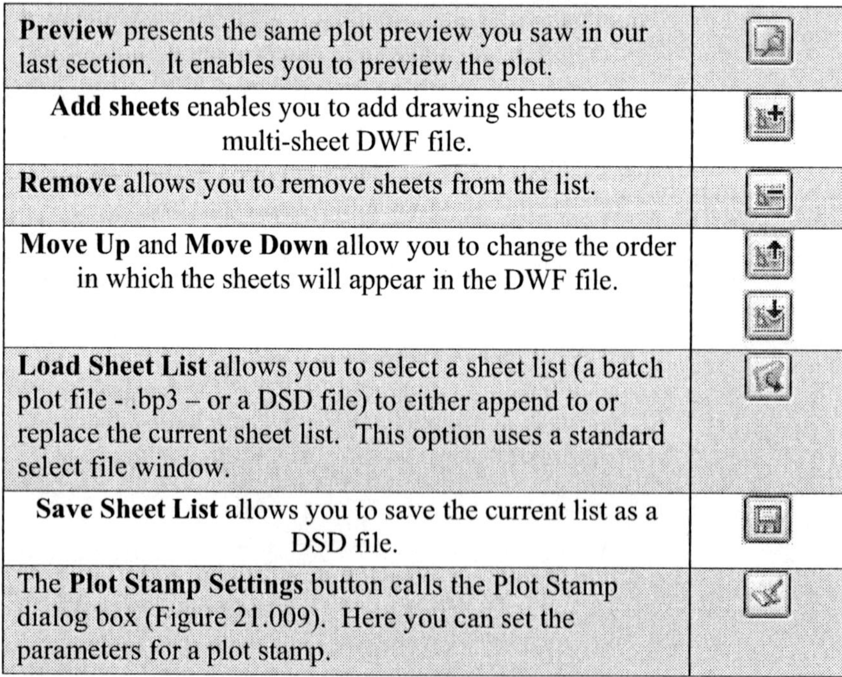

Preview presents the same plot preview you saw in our last section. It enables you to preview the plot.	
Add sheets enables you to add drawing sheets to the multi-sheet DWF file.	
Remove allows you to remove sheets from the list.	
Move Up and **Move Down** allow you to change the order in which the sheets will appear in the DWF file.	
Load Sheet List allows you to select a sheet list (a batch plot file - .bp3 – or a DSD file) to either append to or replace the current sheet list. This option uses a standard select file window.	
Save Sheet List allows you to save the current list as a DSD file.	
The **Plot Stamp Settings** button calls the Plot Stamp dialog box (Figure 21.009). Here you can set the parameters for a plot stamp.	

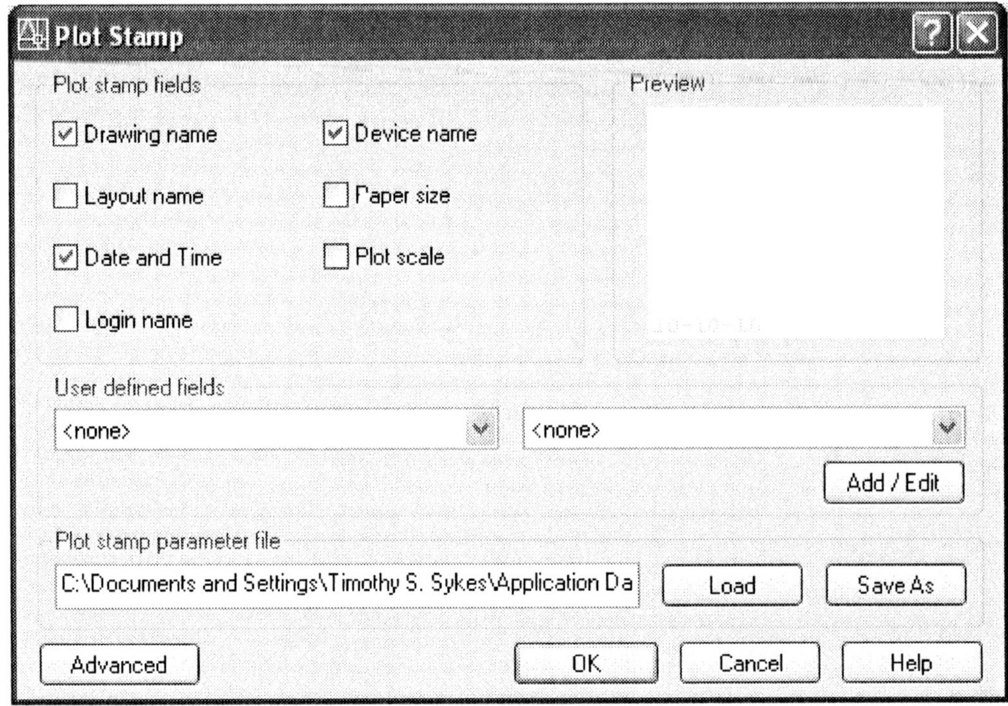

Figure 21.009

- Turn the plot stamp on by putting a check in the **Include plot stamp** check box (Publish dialog box).
- Use the **Number of copies** box to plot multiple copies of a drawing.
- You have a couple choices to make in the **Publish to** frame. You can plot to the device in the selected setup (**Plotter named in page setup** column); or you can create a **DWF file**.
- In the **Include when adding sheets** frame, you'll tell AutoCAD what to include in your plot – either the **Model tab** (where you've been working thus far in this text), the Layout tabs (Paper Space) or both.
- Use the **Publish Options** button to tell AutoCAD where to place the DWF file.
- The **Show Details** button presents two data frames for the selected sheet.
- Finally, the **Publish** button tells AutoCAD to proceed with the plot.

21.2.3 Hyperlinks

If you plan to use hyperlinks in your DWF file, you must assign them before plotting. Let's look at how to do that now.

Begin by entering the ***Hyperlink*** command and selecting the object(s) to which you want to assign the jump (the thing you want to pick to go to another web address). AutoCAD will present the Insert Hyperlink dialog box (Figure 21.010).

The dialog box looks considerably more complicated than it actually is. Let's look at one piece at a time.

- At the top of the dialog box, you'll find a text box with the words **Text to display** next to it. What you enter here will display in a small tooltip whenever a viewer passes his cursor over the hyperlink.

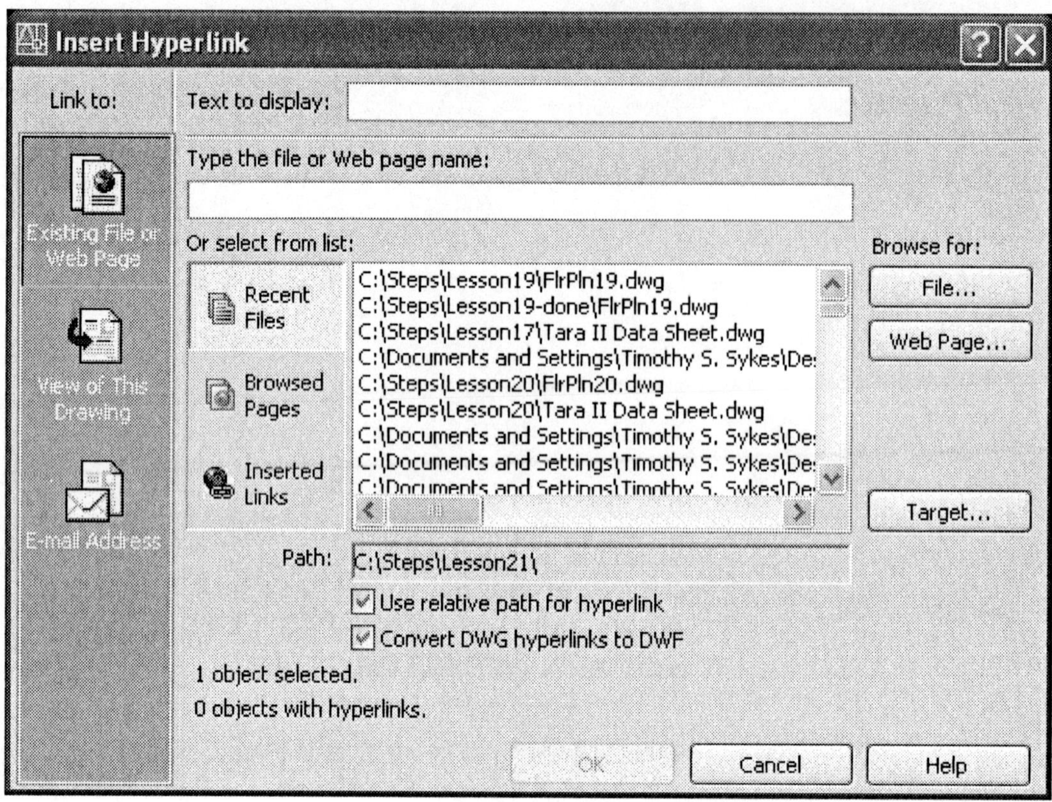

Figure 21.010

- Down the left side of the box, you'll see three **Link to** picks. These control the methods you'll use to identify the target hyperlink (the place to which you wish to jump).
- The first **Link to** pick – **Existing File or Web Page** – provides the dialog shown in Figure 21.010. Use it to create a link to a file, layout, or web site that already exists. (The other links change the dialog box as you'll see shortly.) Let's look at how to do this.
  - Below the **Text to display** box, you see a **Type the file or Web page name** text box. This provides the key to your hyperlink and the easy way to identify your web site or target file. Enter the page name and address of the target site in this box.
  - In the **Or select from list** box, AutoCAD has provided a selection list from which you can pick the data that will go into the **Type the file or Web page name** text box. Selecting a target here saves you from having to type in a target (and deal with typos). Three option buttons help organize your choices into these groups:

    Recent Files – files you've recently opened in AutoCAD.

    Browsed Pages – Internet pages to which you've browsed.

    Inserted Links – recently inserted hyperlinks.

    Each of these option buttons changes the list to accommodate the choice.
  - To the right of the list box are three buttons that also provide an easy method of filling the **Type the file or Web page name** text box.
    - The **File** button opens a standard Open dialog box where you can select the name of the target file.
    - The **Web Page** button works just like the **File** button but opens AutoCAD's browser where you'll select the name of the target web site.

- The **Target** button allows you to select a layout or preset view within the drawing as a target.

- The second **Link to** pick – **View of This Drawing** – provides the same thing the **Target** button provides when the **Existing file or Web page** button has been selected.
- With the last **Link to** pick – **Email Address** – you can place a hyperlink in the drawing that will allow the reader to send an email to a predefined address. AutoCAD provides the simple interface shown in Figure 21.011 for this task. (It even provides a list of recently used email addresses from which to choose.)

E-mail address:

Subject:

Recently used e-mail addresses:

Figure 21.011

Let's create a DWF file with a hyperlink.

Do This: 21.2.2.1	Creating a DWF File with Links

I. Be sure you're still in the *pid-21.dwg* file in the C:\Steps\Lesson21 folder. If not, please open it now.

II. Zoom in around the title block.

III. Follow these steps.

TOOLS	COMMAND SEQUENCE	STEPS
No Button Available	**Command:** ***hyperlink***	1. First, we must create our hyperlinks. Enter the ***Hyperlink*** command.
	Select objects:	2. Select the **North Harris College** text in the title block. (Remember to hit ***enter*** to complete the selection set.)
Text to display: North Harris College Website Type the file or Web page name: http://nhc.nhmccd.edu		3. Link to the North Harris College web site by entering the web address in the **Type the file or Web page name** text box as shown. (The address is: *http://nhc.nhmccd.edu.*) Notice that the name appears in the **Text to Display** text box as well. You can change this to something more descriptive or simply leave it as is. (I'll call it *North Harris College Website.*)
OK		4. Pick the **OK** button to complete the command.
		5. Now let's provide an email hyperlink. Repeat Step 1, but select the name in the title block. (Zoom as necessary.)

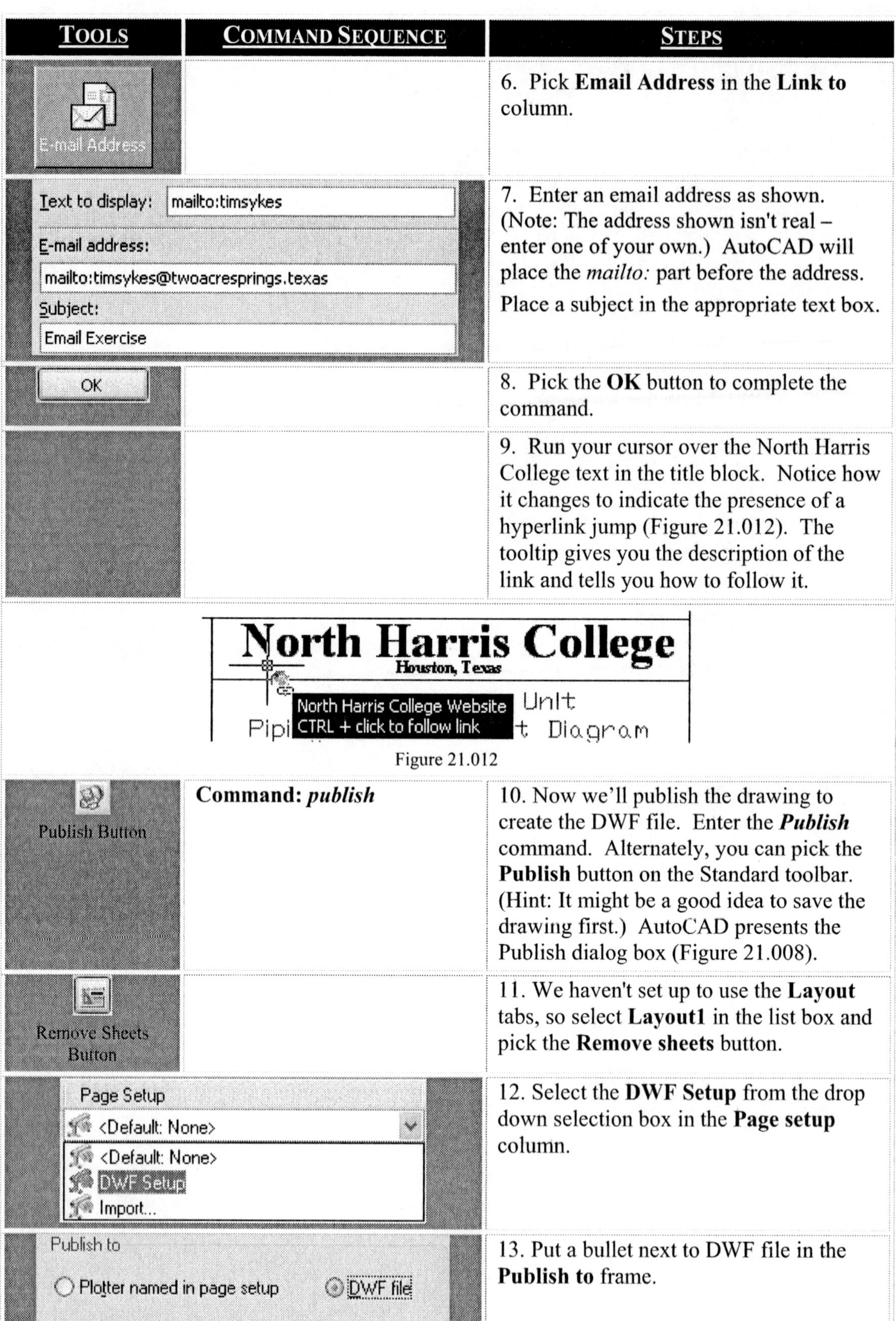

Tools	Command Sequence	Steps
E-mail Address		6. Pick **Email Address** in the **Link to** column.
Text to display: mailto:timsykes E-mail address: mailto:timsykes@twoacresprings.texas Subject: Email Exercise		7. Enter an email address as shown. (Note: The address shown isn't real – enter one of your own.) AutoCAD will place the *mailto:* part before the address. Place a subject in the appropriate text box.
OK		8. Pick the **OK** button to complete the command.
		9. Run your cursor over the North Harris College text in the title block. Notice how it changes to indicate the presence of a hyperlink jump (Figure 21.012). The tooltip gives you the description of the link and tells you how to follow it.
North Harris College Houston, Texas North Harris College Website CTRL + click to follow link Unit Pipi t Diagram Figure 21.012		
Publish Button	**Command:** ***publish***	10. Now we'll publish the drawing to create the DWF file. Enter the ***Publish*** command. Alternately, you can pick the **Publish** button on the Standard toolbar. (Hint: It might be a good idea to save the drawing first.) AutoCAD presents the Publish dialog box (Figure 21.008).
Remove Sheets Button		11. We haven't set up to use the **Layout** tabs, so select **Layout1** in the list box and pick the **Remove sheets** button.
Page Setup <Default: None> <Default: None> DWF Setup Import...		12. Select the **DWF Setup** from the drop down selection box in the **Page setup** column.
Publish to Plotter named in page setup DWF file		13. Put a bullet next to DWF file in the **Publish to** frame.

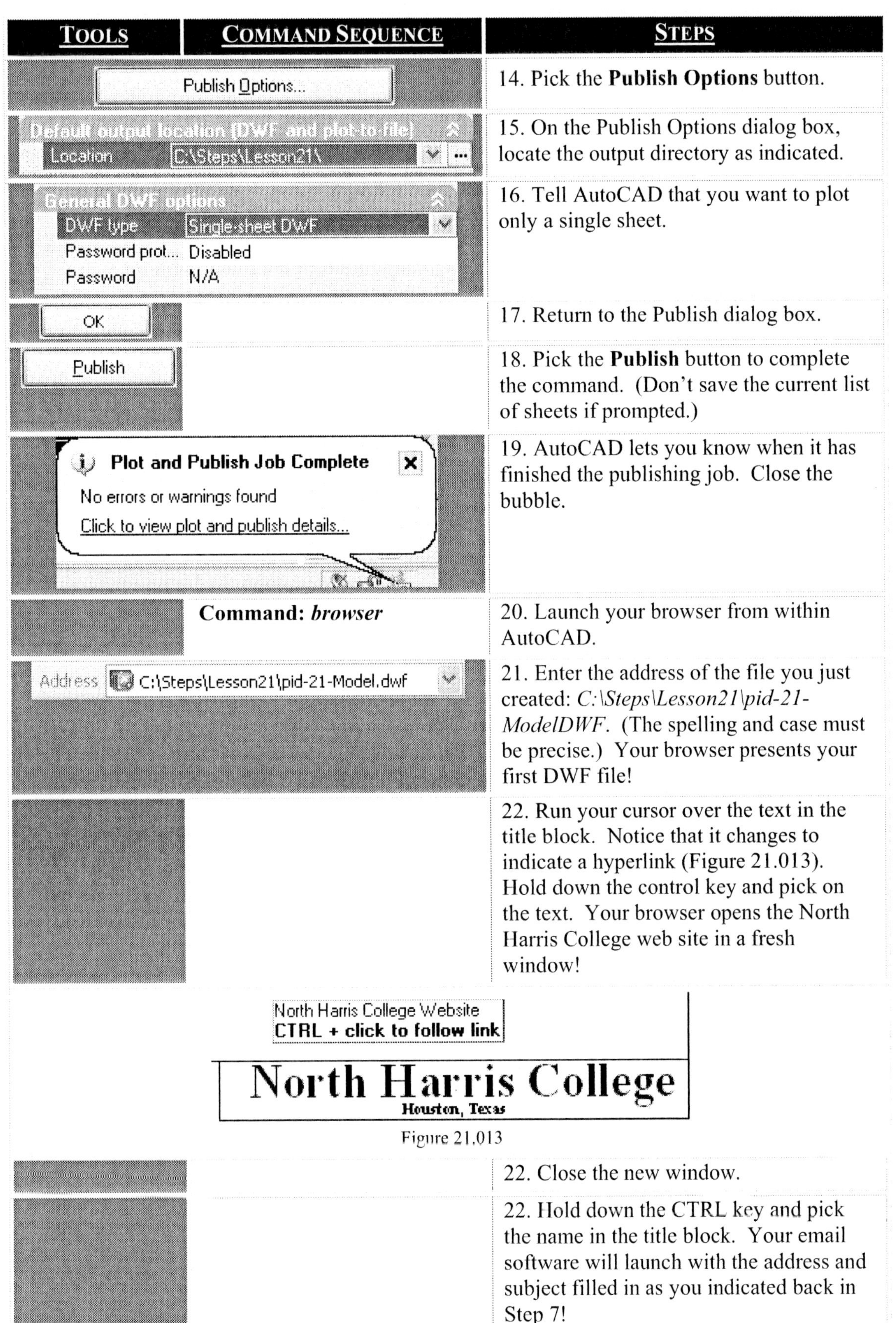

Tools	**Command Sequence**	**Steps**
Publish Options...		14. Pick the **Publish Options** button.
Default output location (DWF and plot-to-file) Location C:\Steps\Lesson21\		15. On the Publish Options dialog box, locate the output directory as indicated.
General DWF options DWF type Single-sheet DWF Password prot... Disabled Password N/A		16. Tell AutoCAD that you want to plot only a single sheet.
OK		17. Return to the Publish dialog box.
Publish		18. Pick the **Publish** button to complete the command. (Don't save the current list of sheets if prompted.)
Plot and Publish Job Complete No errors or warnings found Click to view plot and publish details...		19. AutoCAD lets you know when it has finished the publishing job. Close the bubble.
	Command: *browser*	20. Launch your browser from within AutoCAD.
Address C:\Steps\Lesson21\pid-21-Model.dwf		21. Enter the address of the file you just created: *C:\Steps\Lesson21\pid-21-ModelDWF*. (The spelling and case must be precise.) Your browser presents your first DWF file!
		22. Run your cursor over the text in the title block. Notice that it changes to indicate a hyperlink (Figure 21.013). Hold down the control key and pick on the text. Your browser opens the North Harris College web site in a fresh window!

Figure 21.013

		22. Close the new window.
		22. Hold down the CTRL key and pick the name in the title block. Your email software will launch with the address and subject filled in as you indicated back in Step 7!

TOOLS	COMMAND SEQUENCE	STEPS
		23. Close all the windows except AutoCAD.
	Command: *qsave*	25. Save your drawing but don't exit.

Wow!

21.2.4 AutoCAD can Create Full Web Pages, Too!

Your efforts so far in this section have been to create and manipulate files that a programmer can place at a web site for you. But AutoCAD has also provided a way to cut that middleman – the extremely well paid web-programmer – out of the loop and save yourself (or The Company) some money. With the *Publish to Web* tool, AutoCAD enables you to create (or edit) your own web page! The tool even works in the form of a wizard so that you can do the job in no time at all!

Let's take a look.

Do This: 21.2.4.1 Creating Your Own Web Page

I. Be sure you're still in the *pid-21.dwg* file in the C:\Steps\Lesson21 folder. If not, please open it now.

II. Follow these steps.

TOOLS	CMD SEQUENCE	STEPS
No Button Available	**Command:** ***publishtoweb***	1. Begin by entering the ***PublishToWeb*** command at the command prompt. AutoCAD begins the Publish to Web wizard with the dialog box shown in Step 2. Alternately, you can select **Publish to Web** from the File pull down menu.
		2. Notice that AutoCAD allows you the option of creating a new web page or editing an existing page (Figure 21.014). The second option will come in handy when you need to make adjustments to an existing page. We'll **Create** [a] **New Web Page** for now. Be sure the bullet is next to that option and pick the **Next** button to continue. (Note: This tool will work only on a saved drawing.)

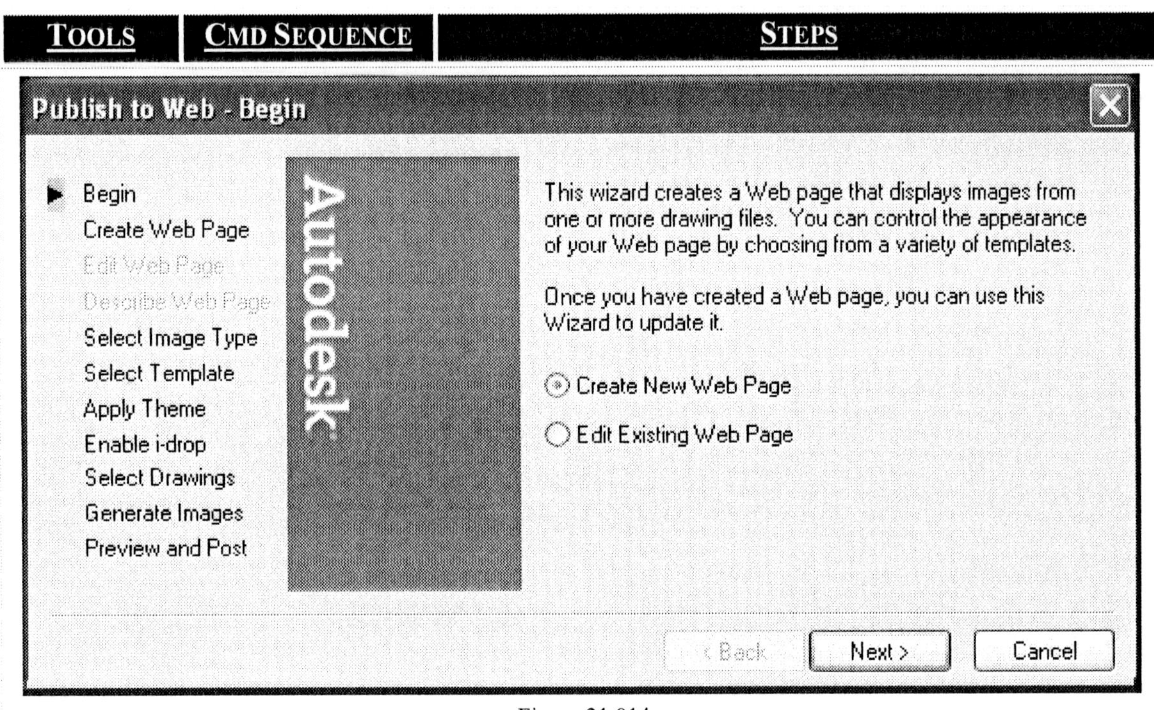

Figure 21.014

TOOLS	CMD SEQUENCE	STEPS
		3. AutoCAD presents the Create Web Page dialog box (Figure 21.015). Here you'll name your web page. AutoCAD will create a new subfolder with the name of the web page. • To begin, enter the name of your web page as indicated (I'll call mine *PID21WebPage*). Don't place a file extension on the name; AutoCAD will do that for you. (Note: Don't use spaces in the name of the page. Although they won't bother AutoCAD, the Internet won't like them.) • Use the browse button (**...**) to locate the web page folder in the C:\Steps\Lesson21 folder. • Add the description shown in the figure. • Pick the **Next** button to continue.

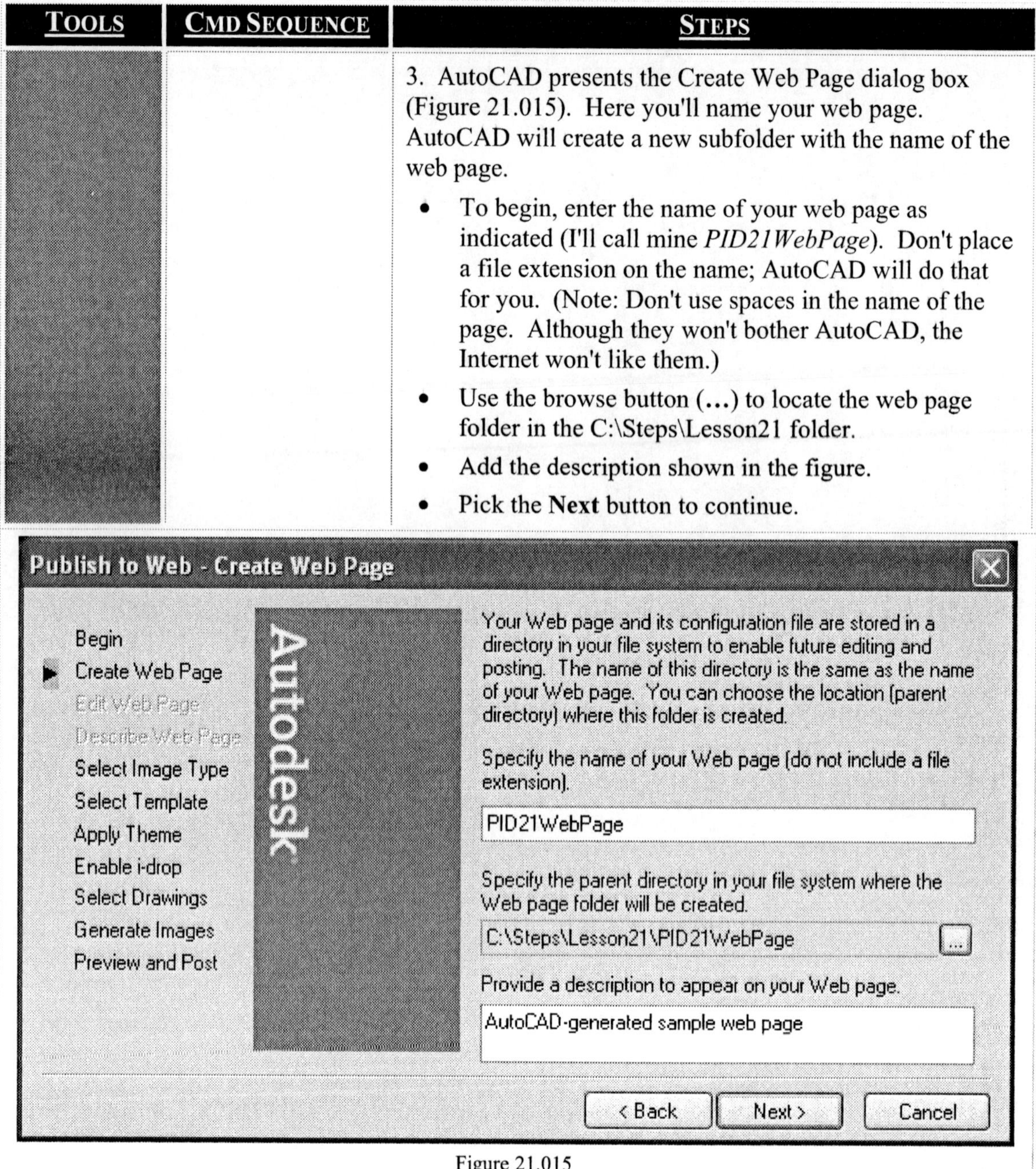

Figure 21.015

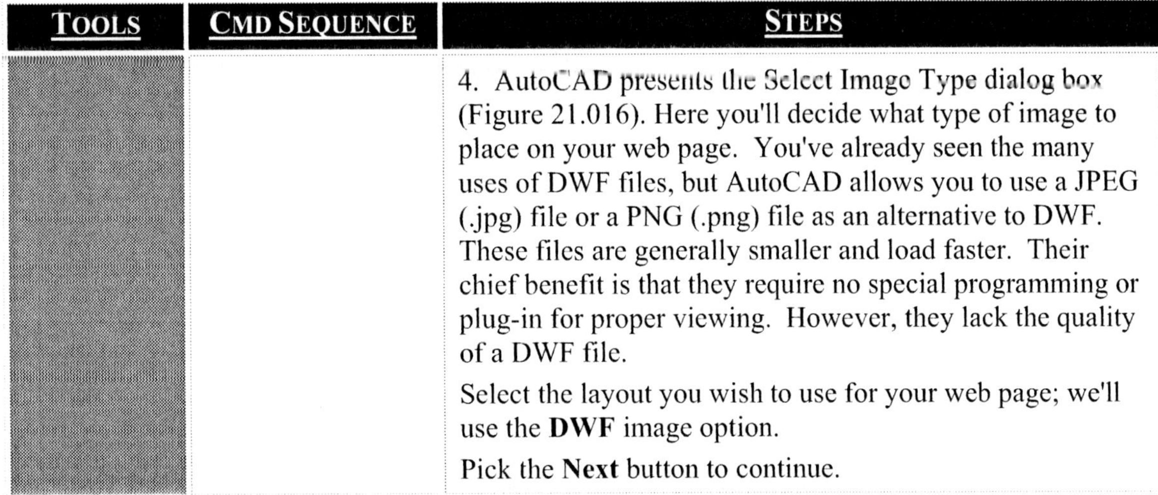

TOOLS	CMD SEQUENCE	STEPS
		4. AutoCAD presents the Select Image Type dialog box (Figure 21.016). Here you'll decide what type of image to place on your web page. You've already seen the many uses of DWF files, but AutoCAD allows you to use a JPEG (.jpg) file or a PNG (.png) file as an alternative to DWF. These files are generally smaller and load faster. Their chief benefit is that they require no special programming or plug-in for proper viewing. However, they lack the quality of a DWF file. Select the layout you wish to use for your web page; we'll use the **DWF** image option. Pick the **Next** button to continue.

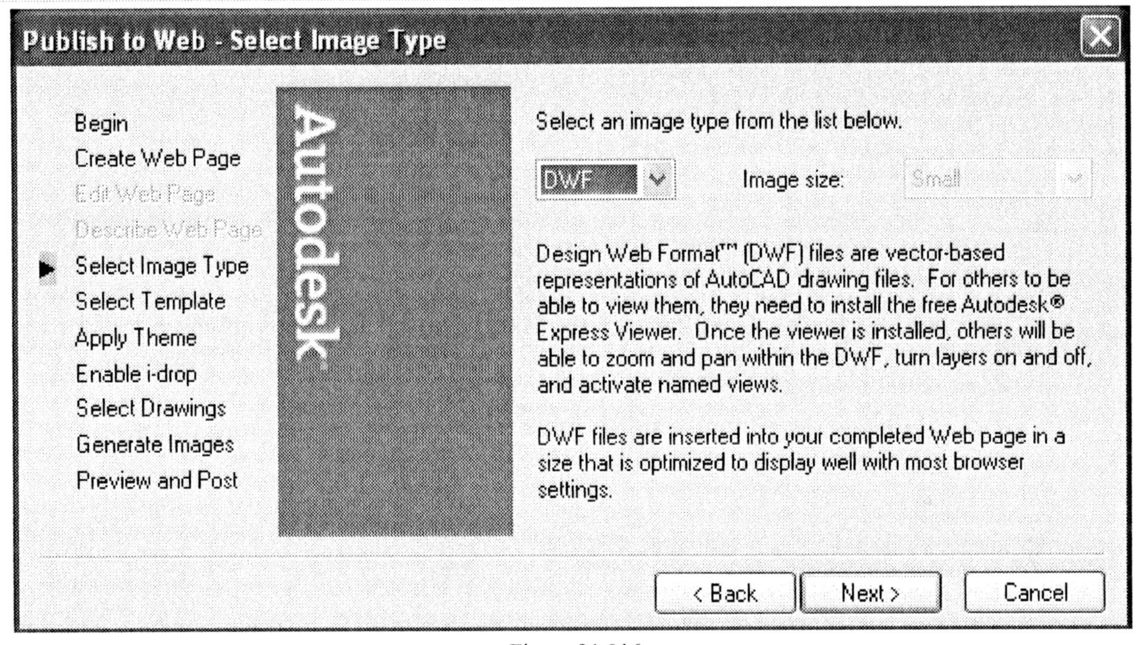

Figure 21.016

		5. Now AutoCAD wants to know how to lay out your web page (Figure 21.017). Pick each of the four options to view samples of the layouts, and then select **List Plus Summary**. Pick the **Next** button to continue.

TOOLS	CMD SEQUENCE	STEPS

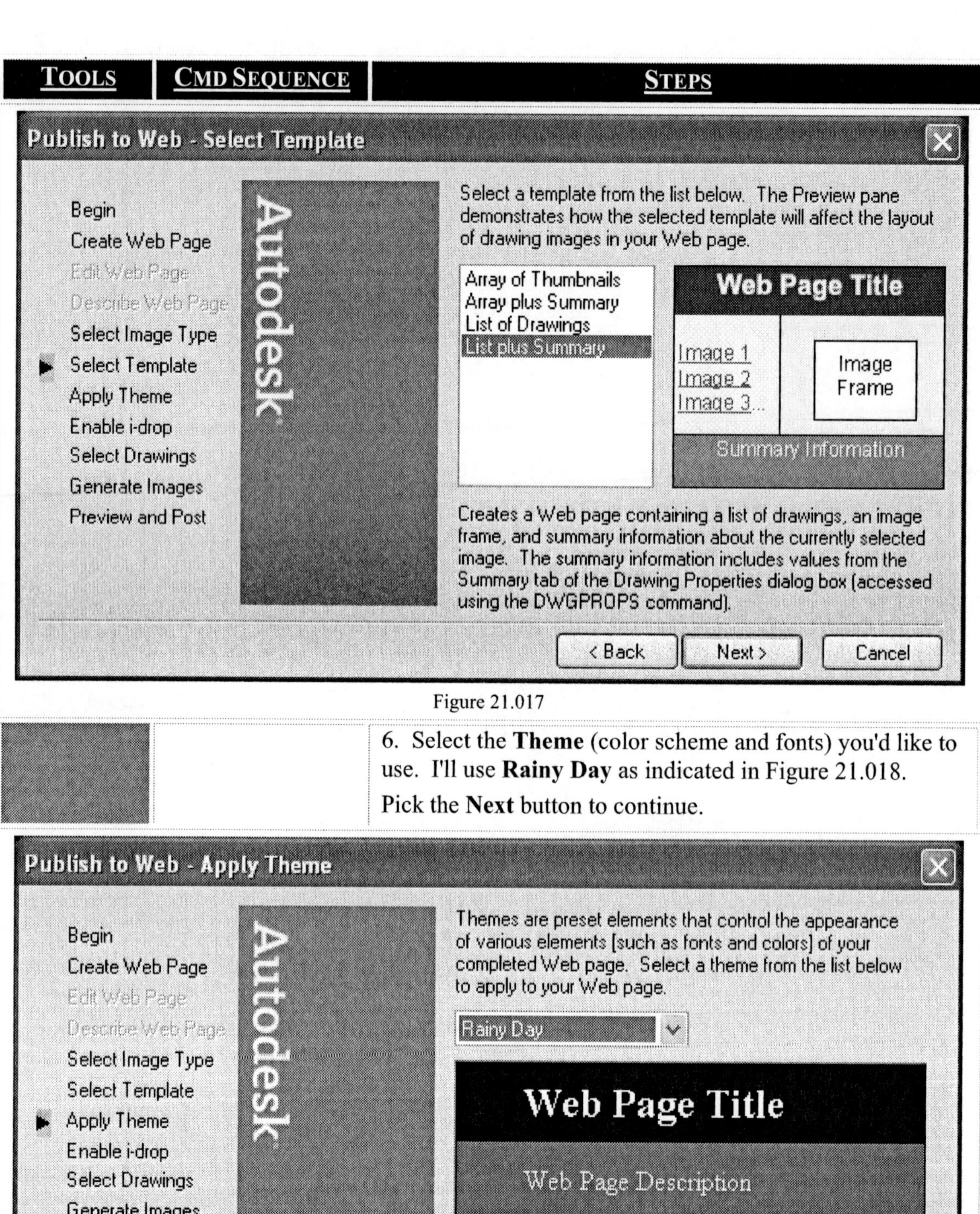

Figure 21.017

6. Select the **Theme** (color scheme and fonts) you'd like to use. I'll use **Rainy Day** as indicated in Figure 21.018.

Pick the **Next** button to continue.

Figure 21.018

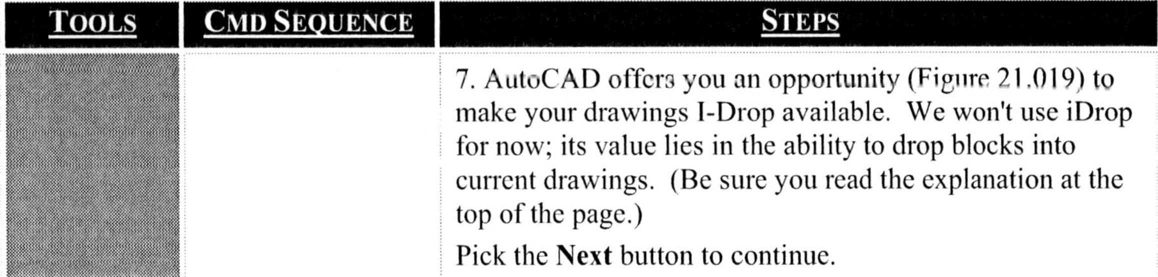

Tools	Cmd Sequence	Steps
		7. AutoCAD offers you an opportunity (Figure 21.019) to make your drawings I-Drop available. We won't use iDrop for now; its value lies in the ability to drop blocks into current drawings. (Be sure you read the explanation at the top of the page.) Pick the **Next** button to continue.

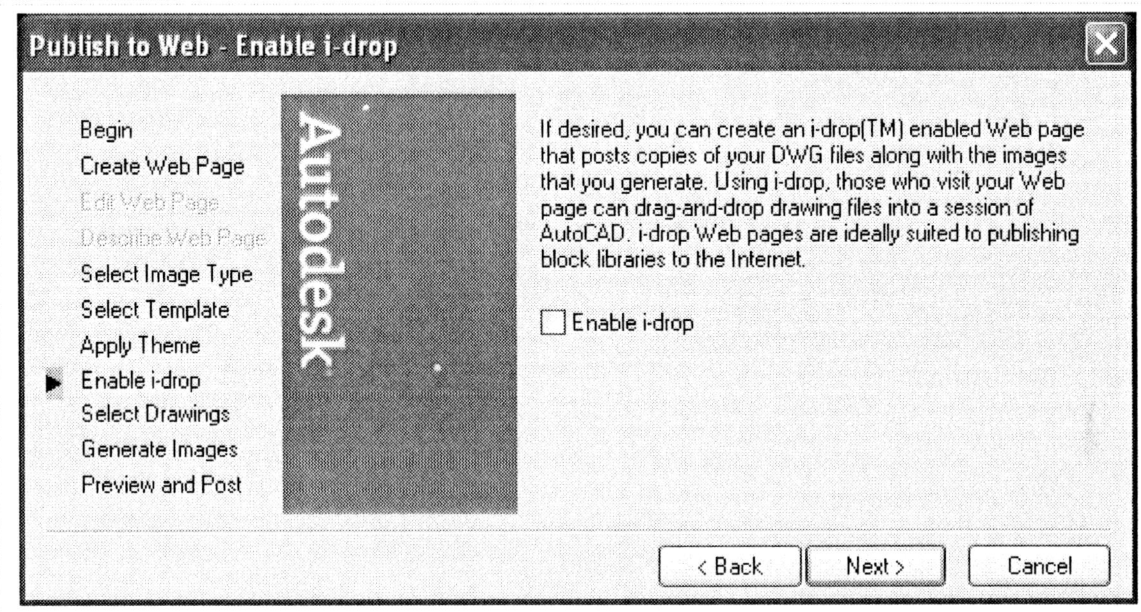

Figure 21.019

TOOLS	CMD SEQUENCE	STEPS
		8. AutoCAD needs to know what to include in your web page (Figure 21.020). • In the **Label** text box, enter a label for the image selected. • The **Description** box allows you to annotate the image. Place a description there as indicated.

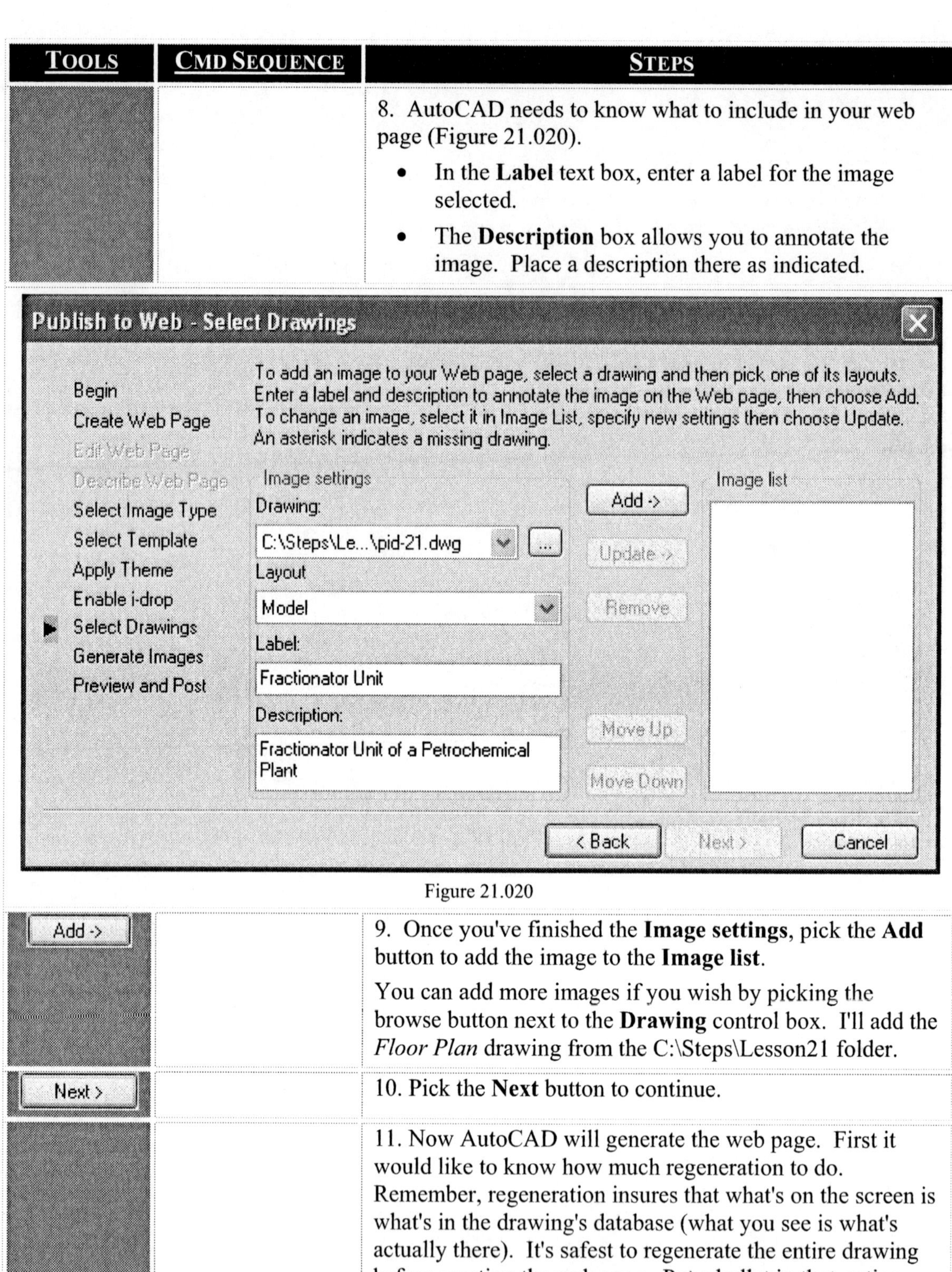

Figure 21.020

TOOLS	CMD SEQUENCE	STEPS
Add ->		9. Once you've finished the **Image settings**, pick the **Add** button to add the image to the **Image list**. You can add more images if you wish by picking the browse button next to the **Drawing** control box. I'll add the *Floor Plan* drawing from the C:\Steps\Lesson21 folder.
Next >		10. Pick the **Next** button to continue.
		11. Now AutoCAD will generate the web page. First it would like to know how much regeneration to do. Remember, regeneration insures that what's on the screen is what's in the drawing's database (what you see is what's actually there). It's safest to regenerate the entire drawing before creating the web page. Put a bullet in that option (Figure 21.021) and pick the **Next** button to continue.

TOOLS	CMD SEQUENCE	STEPS

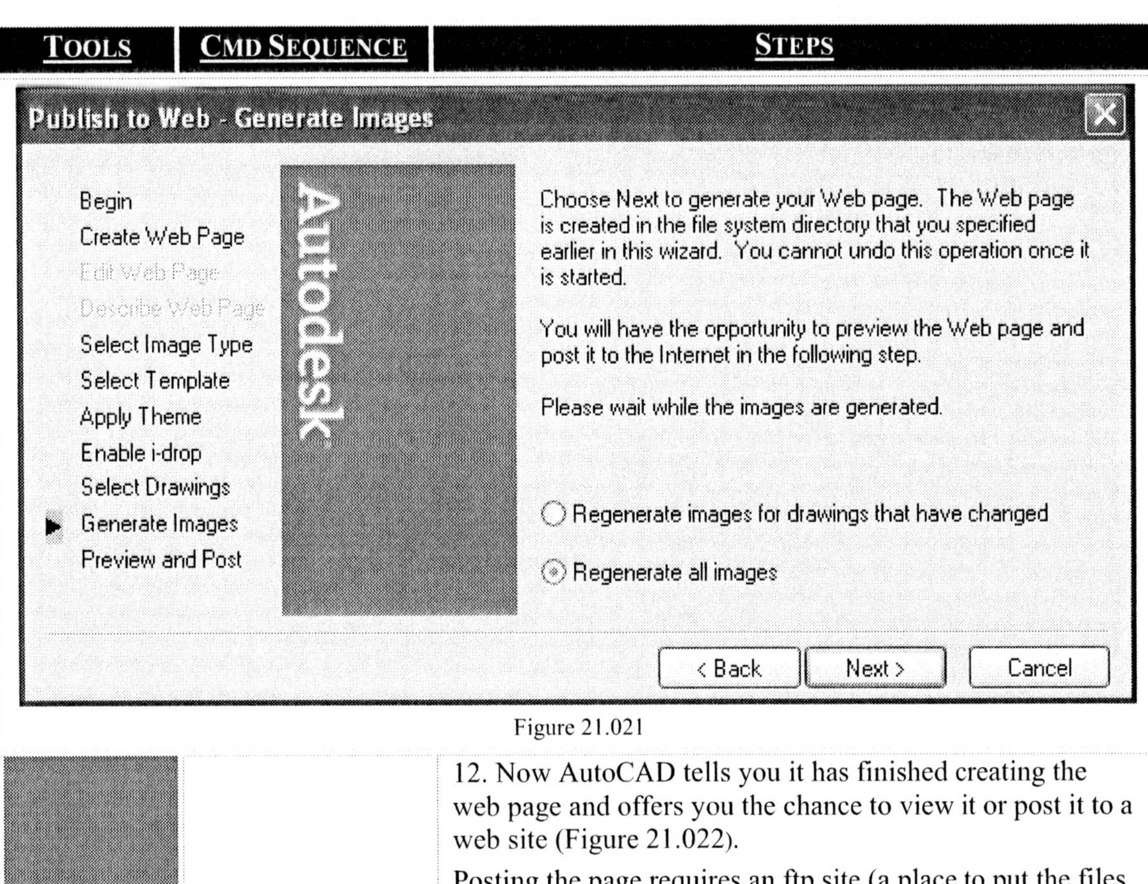

Figure 21.021

		12. Now AutoCAD tells you it has finished creating the web page and offers you the chance to view it or post it to a web site (Figure 21.022). Posting the page requires an ftp site (a place to put the files on the Internet or an Intranet) – usually involving permissions and passwords. If you don't post it now, you can always post it later by copying all the files created during this procedure (found in the folder you told AutoCAD to create earlier) to the web site. For now, pick the **Preview** button to see your new web page.

TOOLS	CMD SEQUENCE	STEPS

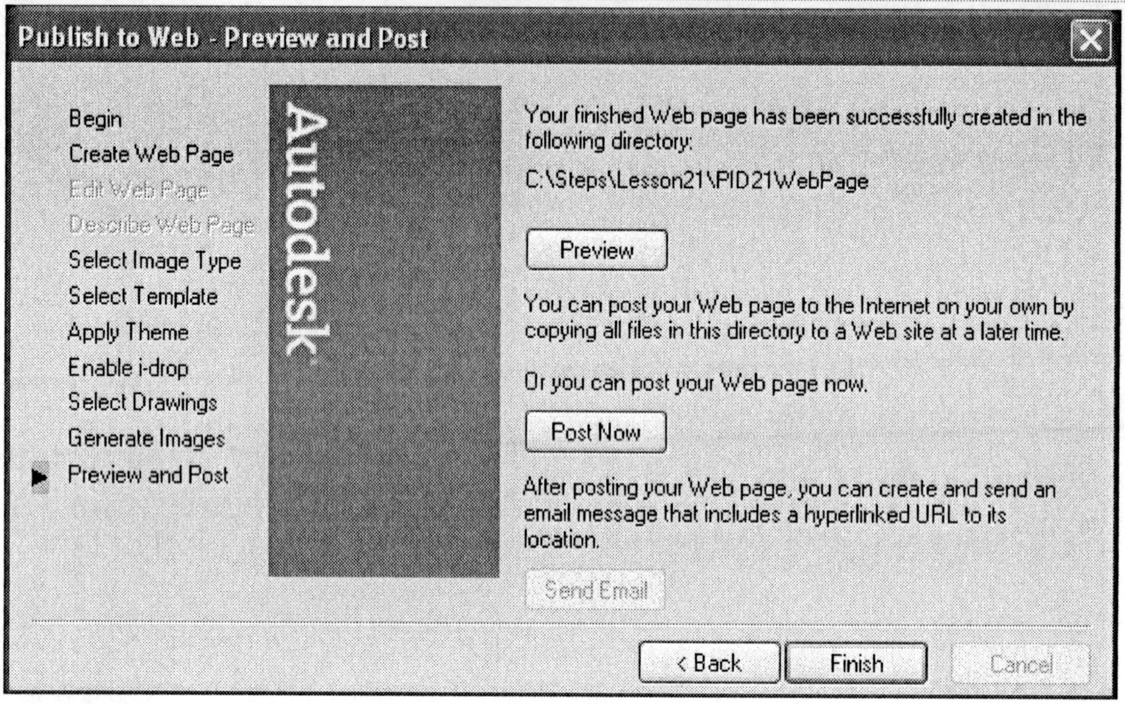

Publish to Web - Preview and Post

Begin
Create Web Page
Edit Web Page
Describe Web Page
Select Image Type
Select Template
Apply Theme
Enable i-drop
Select Drawings
Generate Images
Preview and Post

Autodesk

Your finished Web page has been successfully created in the following directory:
C:\Steps\Lesson21\PID21WebPage
Preview
You can post your Web page to the Internet on your own by copying all files in this directory to a Web site at a later time.
Or you can post your Web page now.
Post Now
After posting your Web page, you can create and send an email message that includes a hyperlinked URL to its location.
Send Email
< Back | Finish | Cancel

Figure 21.022

TOOLS	CMD SEQUENCE	STEPS
		13. Take a few minutes to explore the web page. Notice that the hyperlink jumps you created in our last exercise still work here (you can create hyperlinks prior to creating a web page just as you did prior to creating the DWF file).
Finish		14. When you've finished with the web page, close your browser and pick the **Finish** button on the wizard.
	Command: *qsave*	15. Save your drawing but don't exit.

21.3 Sending the Package over the Internet with *eTransmit*

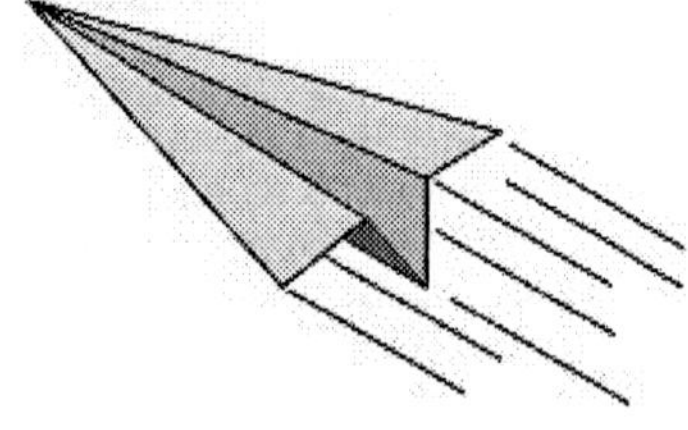

Times will undoubtedly occur when you need to share an actual drawing file with someone – that is, you'll need to send the drawing to someone for changes or even as a final product to a client. In the past, difficulties have occasionally arisen with incompatible or missing support files (such as fonts, linetypes, and so forth). At other times, you may need to share secure data with a client or co-worker and posting information to a web site simply won't do. With AutoCAD's **eTransmit** tool, these difficulties need no longer concern you.

eTransmit groups a drawing file with all the necessary support files (and any other files you wish to attach) into a single self-extracting executable or .zip file. You can protect this data with an encrypted password and transmit it to a friend or client via web site, email, CD, or even a good old-fashioned floppy disk!

To make things even easier, AutoCAD uses a dialog box (Figure 21.023) to help create the transmittal. Just answer a few questions!

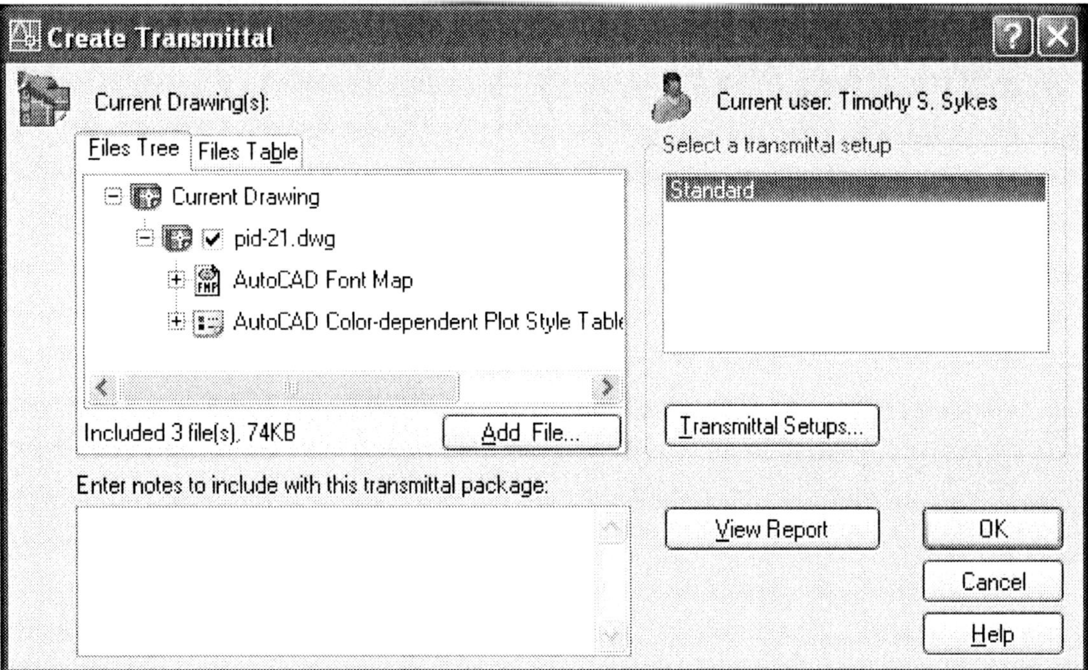

Figure 21.023

Let's take a look.

The Create Transmittal dialog box presented by the ***eTransmit*** command contains two tabs. (Note: There will be a third tab – Sheets – when sheet sets are open. More on sheet sets in Lesson 24.)

- The **File Tree** tab displays all the files included in the transmittal.
- The **Files Table** tab displays the same thing, but in table format.
- Use the **Add File** button at the bottom of the tab to add files to the transmittal using a standard Open File dialog box.
- Below the tabs, you'll find a text box. Use this to **Enter notes to include with this transmittal package**.
- Just to the right of the notes text box, AutoCAD has placed a **View Report** button. This will present the report that'll accompany your eTransmittal. The report contains details about what AutoCAD has included in the transmittal. You can save this file or print it for your records.
- Above the **View Report** button is the **Select a transmittal setup** frame. Here, you'll select the format for your transmittal, or pick the **Transmittal Setups** button to create a new one.

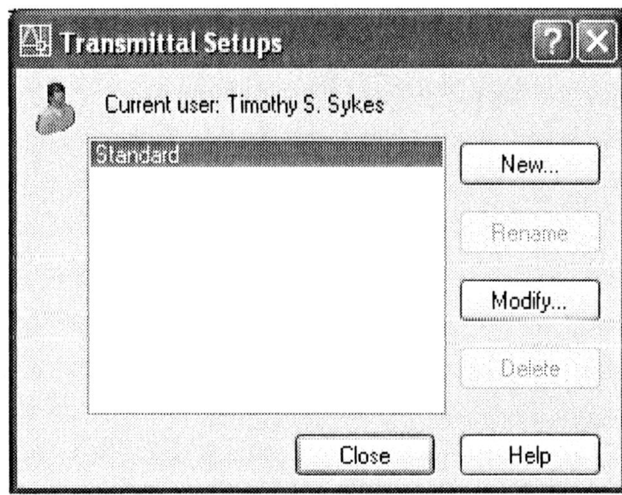

Figure 21.024

To set up a transmittal, you'll follow a procedure very similar to that which you used to set up a dimension style or a page (for plotting).

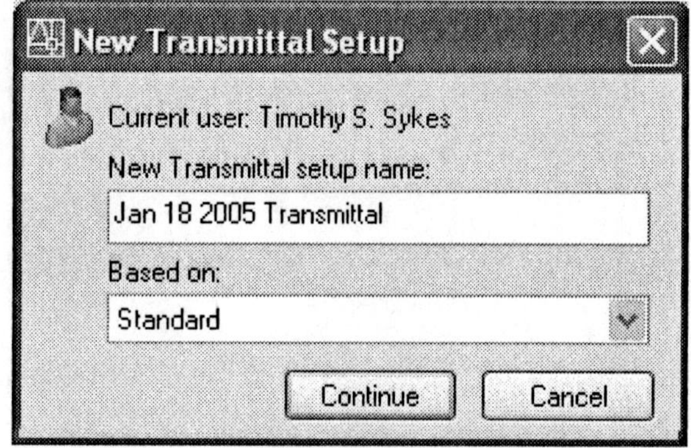

Figure 21.025

The first thing you'll see after you pick the **Transmittal Setups** button is the Transmittal Setups dialog box (Figure 21.024). Use the buttons on the right of this box to create a **New** transmittal, **Rename** an existing transmittal, **Modify** an existing transmittal, or **Delete** an existing transmittal.

- The **New** button calls the New Transmittal Setup dialog box (Figure 21.025). Use this to name the new transmittal (use something that you can trace later). You can even base the settings for the new transmittal on those of an existing transmittal by selecting the existing one from the **Based on** list box.
- The **Continue** button on the New Transmittal Setup dialog box calls the Modify Transmittal Setup dialog box (Figure 21.026). (Note: The **Modify** button on the Transmittal Setups dialog box will take you directly to the Modify Transmittal Setup dialog box.)

  Let's look at this frightening dialog box!

  - The **Transmittal type and location** frame (at top) provides many options:
    - Select the type of transmittal (how it will be compressed for electronic transmittal) from the **Transmittal package type** drop down list box. Your options include:

      Self-extracting executable (*.exe) files. This option compresses all files into a single file with an EXE extension. Executing this file (double-clicking on it) will cause it to extract (decompress) the files necessary to open and edit your drawing.

      Folder (set of files). This option copies all the necessary files for opening and editing your drawing into a single folder. You can copy this folder to a disk or web site for your client or co-worker to retrieve.

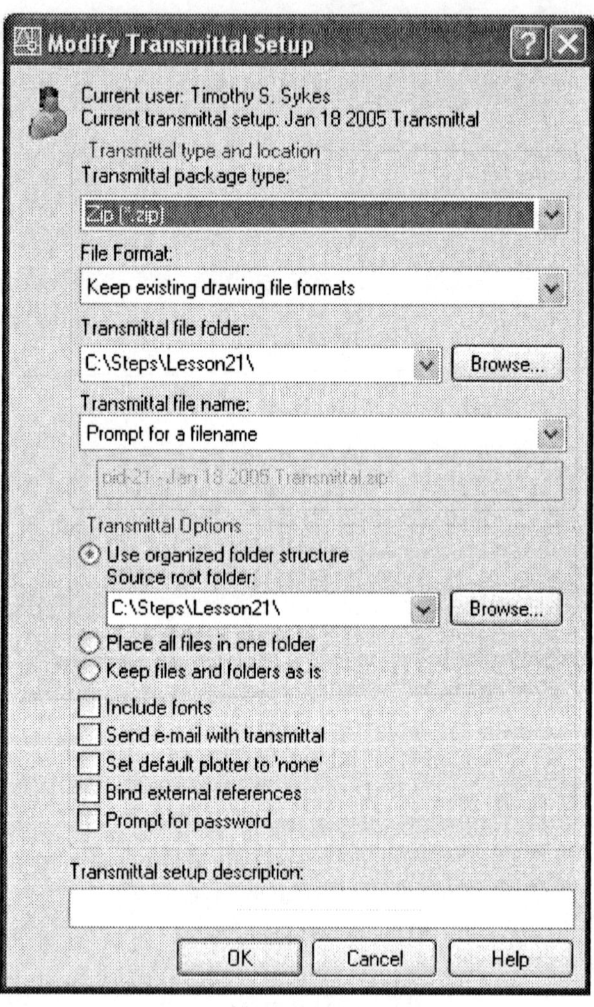

Figure 21.026

Zip (*.zip) files. Like self-extracting executable files, zip files compress the appropriate files into a single file (this time with a ZIP extension). Most Windows operating systems can read the zip file, or you can pick up an application (*WinZip* or *Zip*) to extract the files.

- Use the **File format** list box to change the drawing file type to be more compatible with previous releases of AutoCAD (if necessary).
- The **Transmittal file folder** is where AutoCAD will create the transmittal. Use the **Browse** button to select an alternate location.
- Your best option in the **Transmittal file name** box is the default (**Prompt for a file name**). The **Overwrite if necessary** option means that you'll run the risk of accidentally overwriting an existing transmittal; the **Increment file name if necessary** option means that you may end up with a lot of unnecessary files on your computer.
- The last box in the **Transmittal type and location** frame simply lists the name of the transmittal.

- The second frame – **Transmittal options** – requires that you make some formatting decisions.
  - **Use organized folder structure** forces AutoCAD to use the folder structure for the files being transmitted.
  - The **Source root folder** is the relative path for drawing-dependent files (like Xrefs or images – we'll see more on Xrefs and images in later lessons).
  - **Place all files in one folder** negates the previous options and forces AutoCAD to include all transmittal files in a single folder.
  - **Keep files and folders as is** negates the previous options and tells AutoCAD to retain the existing hierarchical structure of transmitted files. (Don't use this one if you intend to save the transmittal package to an Internet location.)
  - A check next to **Include fonts** tells AutoCAD to transmit the fonts used in the drawing with the package. This isn't necessary unless you've used some non-standard fonts in your drawing.
  - **Send email with transmittal** means that AutoCAD will launch your email program so that you can send an email with the transmittal as an attachment.
  - It's a courtesy to **Set default plotter to none** before sending the transmittal. Your printer/plotter settings won't mean anything to your client (unless he happens to be using the same printer/plotter).
  - We'll learn about Xrefs and binding Xrefs in Lesson 25. For now, you can ignore this option.
  - **Prompt for password** is yet another acknowledgement of the paranoia of most companies. Adding a password to your package insures that no one but your designated recipient can open it.
- Use the **Transmittal setup description** box to give a brief description of this setup. AutoCAD will present this in the Create Transmittal dialog box when you select this setup.

JEEPERS; that was a lot of information!

Let's create an eTransmittal.

Do This: 21.3.1	Creating an eTransmittal

I. Be sure you're still in the *pid-21.dwg* file in the C:\Steps\Lesson21 folder. If not, please open it now.

II. Follow these steps.

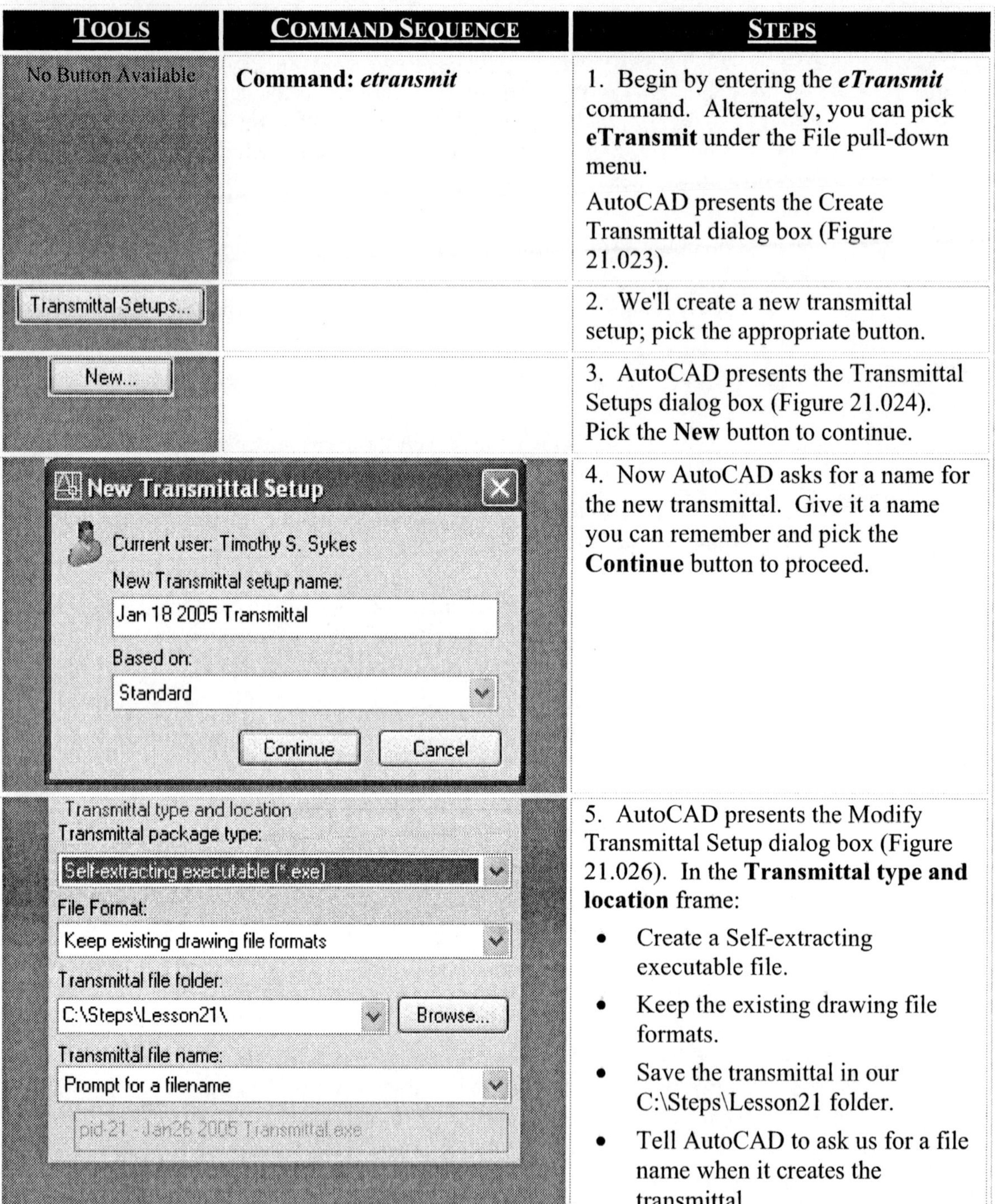

TOOLS	COMMAND SEQUENCE	STEPS
No Button Available	**Command:** ***etransmit***	1. Begin by entering the ***eTransmit*** command. Alternately, you can pick **eTransmit** under the File pull-down menu. AutoCAD presents the Create Transmittal dialog box (Figure 21.023).
Transmittal Setups...		2. We'll create a new transmittal setup; pick the appropriate button.
New...		3. AutoCAD presents the Transmittal Setups dialog box (Figure 21.024). Pick the **New** button to continue.
New Transmittal Setup Current user: Timothy S. Sykes New Transmittal setup name: Jan 18 2005 Transmittal Based on: Standard Continue Cancel		4. Now AutoCAD asks for a name for the new transmittal. Give it a name you can remember and pick the **Continue** button to proceed.
Transmittal type and location Transmittal package type: Self-extracting executable (*.exe) File Format: Keep existing drawing file formats Transmittal file folder: C:\Steps\Lesson21\ Browse... Transmittal file name: Prompt for a filename pid-21 - Jan26 2005 Transmittal.exe		5. AutoCAD presents the Modify Transmittal Setup dialog box (Figure 21.026). In the **Transmittal type and location** frame: • Create a Self-extracting executable file. • Keep the existing drawing file formats. • Save the transmittal in our C:\Steps\Lesson21 folder. • Tell AutoCAD to ask us for a file name when it creates the transmittal.

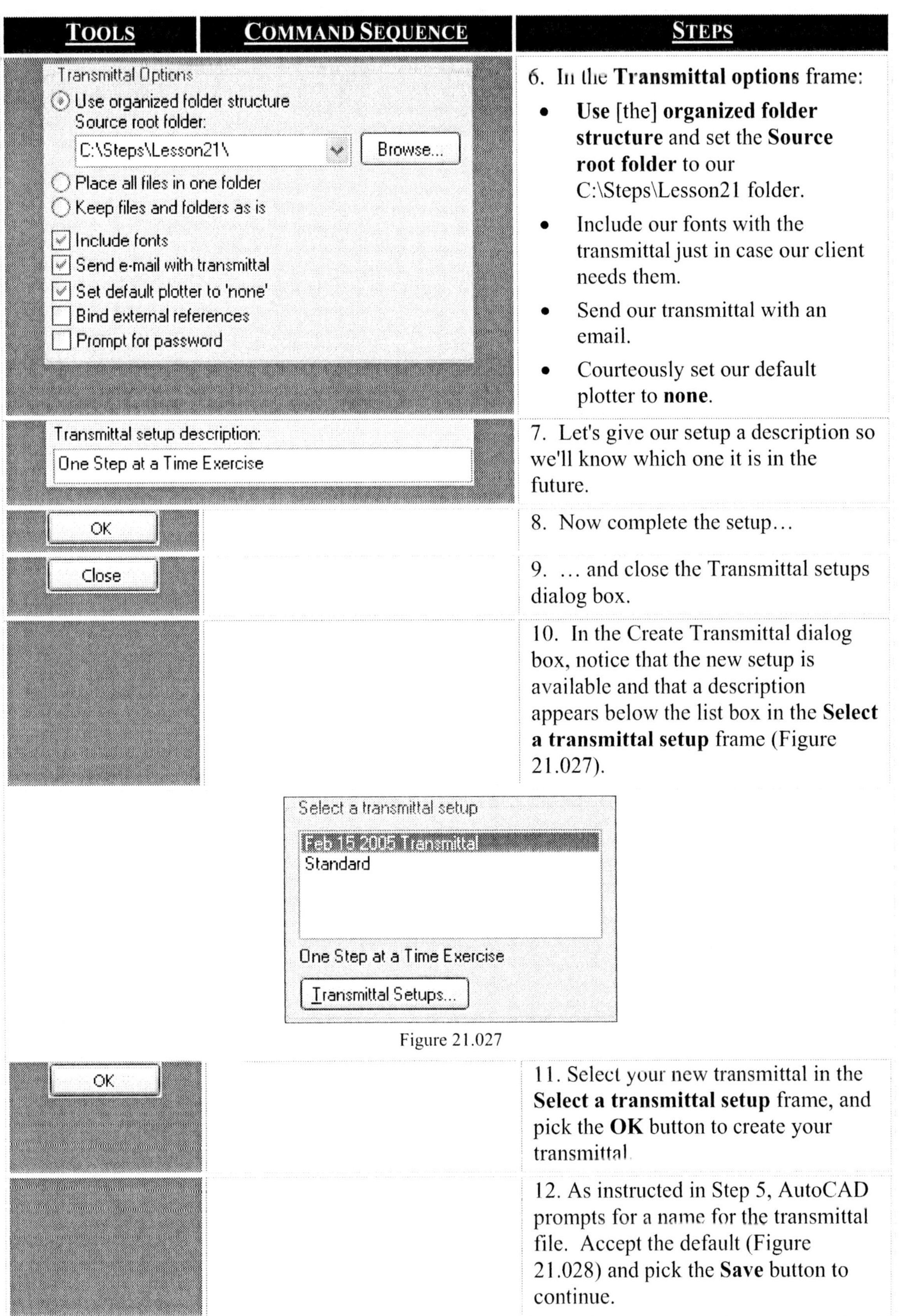

TOOLS	COMMAND SEQUENCE	STEPS
Transmittal Options: Use organized folder structure; Source root folder: C:\Steps\Lesson21\ [Browse...]; Place all files in one folder; Keep files and folders as is; Include fonts; Send e-mail with transmittal; Set default plotter to 'none'; Bind external references; Prompt for password		6. In the **Transmittal options** frame: • **Use** [the] **organized folder structure** and set the **Source root folder** to our C:\Steps\Lesson21 folder. • Include our fonts with the transmittal just in case our client needs them. • Send our transmittal with an email. • Courteously set our default plotter to **none**.
Transmittal setup description: One Step at a Time Exercise		7. Let's give our setup a description so we'll know which one it is in the future.
OK		8. Now complete the setup…
Close		9. … and close the Transmittal setups dialog box.
		10. In the Create Transmittal dialog box, notice that the new setup is available and that a description appears below the list box in the **Select a transmittal setup** frame (Figure 21.027).

Figure 21.027

TOOLS	COMMAND SEQUENCE	STEPS
OK		11. Select your new transmittal in the **Select a transmittal setup** frame, and pick the **OK** button to create your transmittal.
		12. As instructed in Step 5, AutoCAD prompts for a name for the transmittal file. Accept the default (Figure 21.028) and pick the **Save** button to continue.

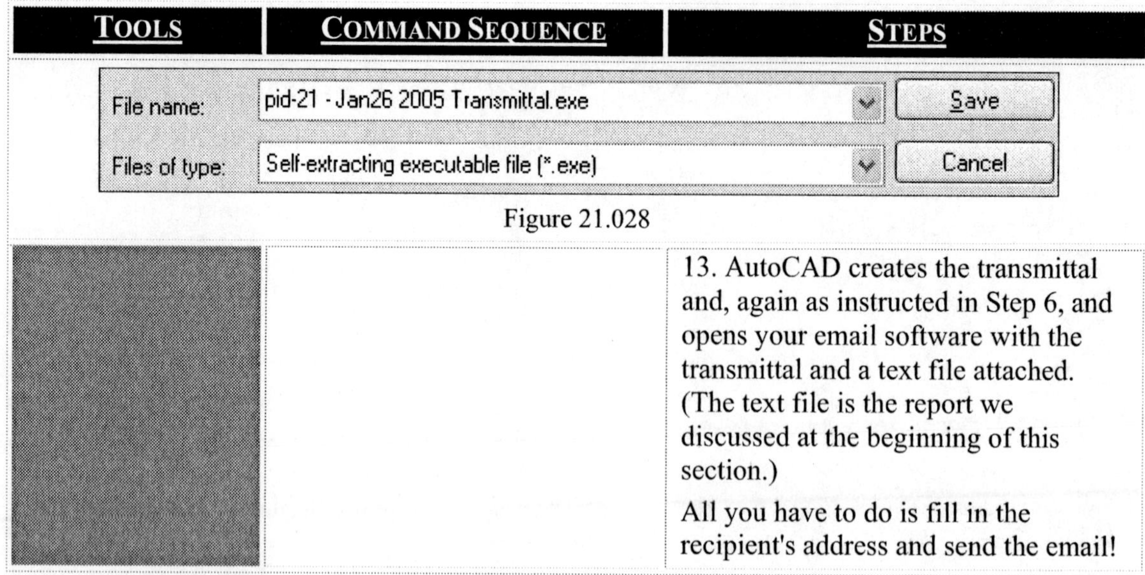

Figure 21.028

13. AutoCAD creates the transmittal and, again as instructed in Step 6, and opens your email software with the transmittal and a text file attached. (The text file is the report we discussed at the beginning of this section.)

All you have to do is fill in the recipient's address and send the email!

The recipient of the transmittal will receive a file that, once executed, will create a folder with all the files and data required for your client to open, read, and modify the drawing you've sent him! (If you want to check this out, the files are located in the C:\Steps\Lesson21 folder. Feel free to execute it; for this exercise, I'd extract the files to a separate directory just to see exactly what was included in it.)

21.4 Extra Steps

- If you haven't looked at the supplementary material for this lesson, it would be helpful for you to do so.
- Autodesk offers a unique approach to sharing project drawings and other information. It works something like a web host and operates for an addition fee. Visit their Buzzsaw site (http://usa.autodesk.com/) for more information.

21.5 What Have We Learned?

Items covered in this lesson include:

- *Setting up a printer/plotter*
- *Setting up a Plot Style*
- *Setting up a drawing page*
- *Creating an eTransmittal*
- *Creating a DWF file*
- *Adding hyperlinks to a drawing*
- *Creating a web page through AutoCAD*
- *AutoCAD plot commands:*
  - ***Pagesetup***
  - ***Plot & Print***
  - ***Browser***
  - ***Hyperlink***
  - ***PublishToWeb***
  - ***Publish***
  - ***eTransmit***

I strongly suggest printing at least two of the assignments for each of the lessons you'll complete throughout the remainder of this text. Then, when you've finished the course, review this lesson once again. After all, you really can't roll up the PC and stick it in your tool belt down at the job site. Your drawings must, eventually, be put on paper.

21.6 Exercises

*Before trying these exercises, familiarize yourself with your printer and / or plotter by reading the appropriate manuals.

1. If you've a plotter available, plot the *Floor Plan* drawing found in the C:\Steps\Lesson21 folder. Use these parameters:
   - Plot to a ¼"=1'-0" scale;
   - Plot to a C-size (22"x17") sheet of paper.
2. Using a printer, plot the *Floor Plan* drawing to fit on a 17" x 11" sheet of paper.
3. Using a printer, plot the *Floor Plan* drawing to fit on a 11" x 8.5" sheet of paper.
4. Create a hyperlink from the title of the *Floor Plan* drawing to your company's or school's web site.
5. Create a DWF file for the *Floor Plan* drawing.
6. Create a web page for the *Floor Plan* drawing.
7. If you've a plotter available, plot the *Pipe Plan* drawing found in the C:\Steps\Lesson21 folder. Use these parameters:
   - Plot to a 3/8"=1'-0" scale;
   - Plot to a D-size (36"x24") sheet of paper.
8. Using a printer, plot the *Piping Plan* drawing to fit on a 17" x 11" sheet of paper.
9. Using a printer, plot the *Piping Plan* drawing to fit on a 11" x 8.5" sheet of paper.
10. Create a hyperlink from the title of the *Piping Plan* drawing to your company or school web site.
11. Create a DWF file for the *Piping Plan* drawing.
12. Create a web page for the *Piping Plan* drawing.
13. Print each of the drawings you created in Lesson 20 to fit on 11" x 8.5" sheets of paper.

21.7 For Web-Based Review Questions, visit: http://www.uneedcad.com/2006/Files/06R21.pdf

Lesson 22

Following this lesson, you will:

- ✓ *Be familiar with Viewports*
- ✓ *Know the difference between Model Space and Paper Space*
- ✓ *Know how to set up a drawing in the Paper Space environment*

Space for a New Beginning

By now, you've printed (or plotted) a drawing in Model Space. You understand, then, the complexity of the mathematics involved ...

- *How large is the area to plot?*
- *How large is the paper?*
- *At what scale will I want to plot?*

... and a host of other questions that must be answered. And then you have to consider stuff like text and dimensions – plotted size and drawing scale factor. AGHH!

Does it have to be that difficult!?

The answer is a resounding, NO! ("Now I tell you!")

We begin this section of our text by simplifying these tasks with a remarkable tool called Paper Space.

When it comes to drawing display and arrangement, there exist two distinct groups of CAD operators – those who've used Paper Space and would never use anything else, and those who (generally for lack of training) haven't used Paper Space.

This lesson will familiarize you (painlessly) to the wonders of Paper Space and Viewports so that you may join the ranks of enlightened operators! To keep it simple, we'll remain in the two-dimensional world throughout this lesson. However, you'll continue to discover the benefits of these tools even as you explore the third dimension in our next text – 3D AutoCAD 2006: One Step at a Time.

Let's begin by answering the basic questions.

22.1 Understanding the Terminology

What is a viewport?

My *New American Dictionary* defines a port as a window in the side of a ship. Similarly, a viewport is a window into your drawing.

If you imagine viewing an object that's resting in the center of a box through holes in the sides, top, and bottom of the box, you'll get a fairly good idea of what viewports are. Essentially, viewports are openings into your drawing, each presenting a different view of the drawn object(s).

AutoCAD provides two types of viewport from which to choose – simple *tiled* viewports and more complex *floating* (or untiled) viewports. We'll look at each of these.

What is Paper Space?

Paper Space is a plotting tool. (You'll like this one!) It provides a method for creating a finished drawing that uses more than one scale and/or view of a drawing. In other words, this is how you can create a drawing with separate details shown at larger scales for ease of viewing (and dimensioning).

You'll create the drawing as you always have – in *Model Space* (the *space* where you create your drawing or three-dimensional *model*). But before you plot, you'll place the drawing and details in their own spaces on an imaginary sheet of *paper*.

How do I know which space I'm using?

There are a few ways to know.

First, look at the UCS icon. The standard XY icon (Figure 22.001) indicates Model Space; the triangular icon (Figure 22.002) indicates Paper Space.

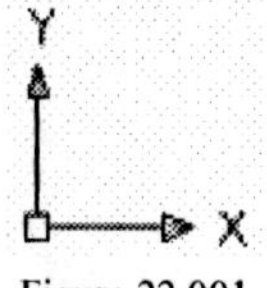

Figure 22.001

If you have the UCS icon turned off, you can look at the **Model/Paper** toggle on the status bar. If **MODEL** appears, you're in Model Space. Conversely, if **PAPER** appears, you're in Paper Space.

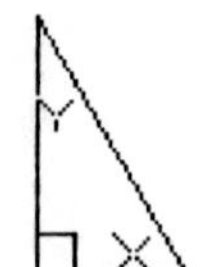

Figure 22.002

How do I switch between Model Space and Paper Space?

The keyboard approach is simply to type ***MSpace*** (or ***MS***) for Model Space or ***PSpace*** (or ***PS***) for Paper Space at the command prompt. Alternately, you can pick the toggle on the status bar.

All of this will become clearer as we proceed.

22.2 Using Tiled Viewports

Use tiled viewports in Model Space (what you might at this point consider "normal" drawing space) to enhance your ability to see several parts of the drawing at once. This ability will become particularly important when drawing in three dimensions. You can place a three-dimensional view of the object in one viewport while drawing on a single, two-dimensional plane (one side of the object) in another.

Create tiled viewports using the Viewports dialog box (Figure 22.003). Access the dialog box using either the ***Viewports*** or ***VPorts*** command.

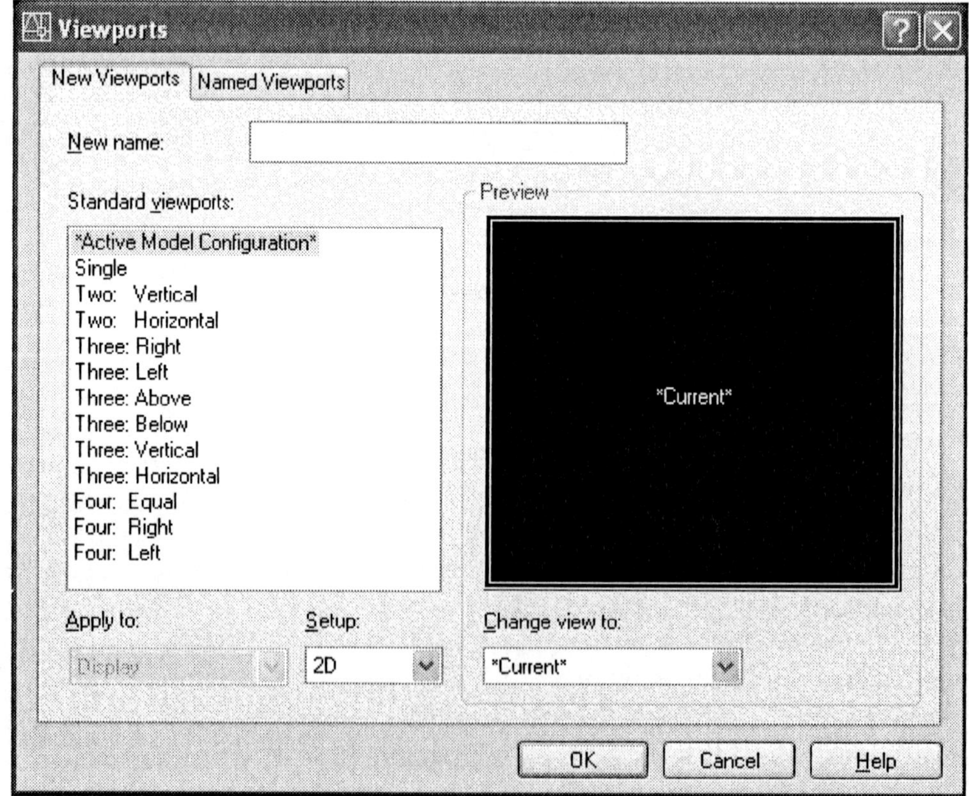

Figure 22.003

Let's look at our options.

The names of the two tabs indicate their function; use **New Viewports** to create new viewports and **Named Viewports** to activate or set current a saved viewport configuration.

We'll begin with the **New Viewports** tab.

- Place a name or title in the **New name** text box at the top if you wish to save a current configuration. (You won't need to use a name if you don't want to save the configuration.) You'll be able to recall your configuration later using the **Change view to** control box (lower-right) or the **Named Viewports** tab.
- The **Standard viewports** list box provides a list of the more common viewport setups. Select each and see the configuration in the **Preview** frame.
- Once you've selected a viewport configuration, you can choose to apply your selection to the **Display** or the **Current Viewport** using the **Apply to** control box. Using the **Display** option will replace the drawing's current configuration with the new selection. Using the **Current Viewport** option will place the new configuration inside the currently active viewport. This is how you customize your viewports.
- The **Setup** control box offers two choices: **2D** or **3D**.
  - The **2D** option will place the drawing's current view in each of the viewports.
  - The **3D** option will create the viewports using standard 3D views (top, front, side, isometric).

  Once selected, you can adjust the view using display commands (***Zoom***, ***Pan***, ***View***).
- The **Named Viewports** tab (Figure 22.004) presents the **Named viewports** list box and a **Preview** frame.

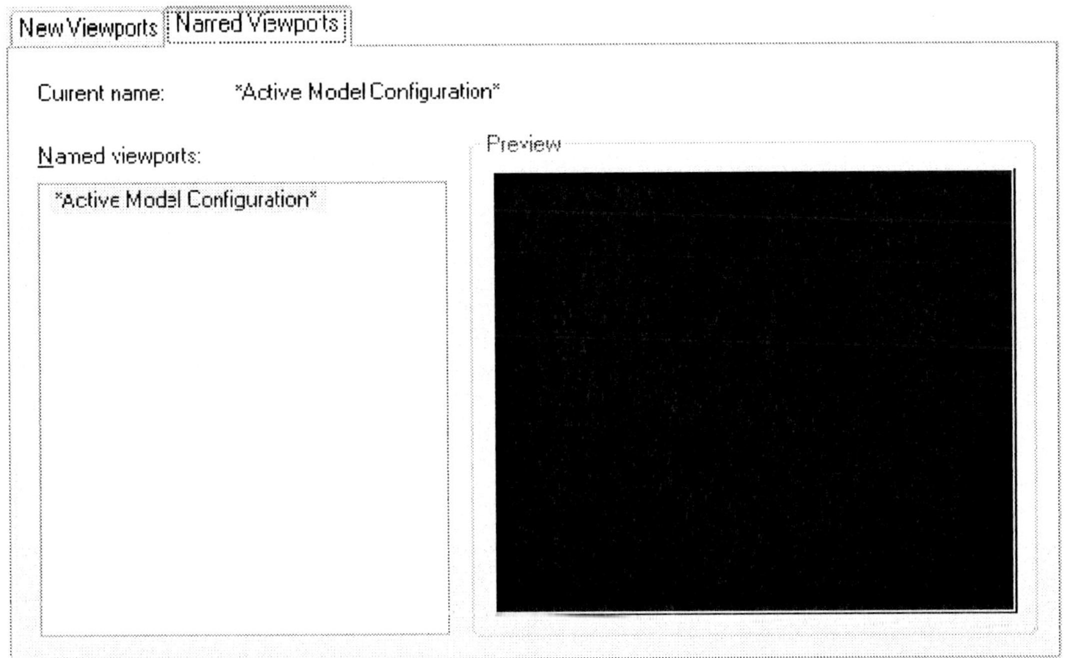

Figure 22.004

  - The **Named viewports** list box offers the names of any viewport configurations that have been saved. You can set a viewport configuration current by selecting its name and picking the **OK** button.
  - The **Preview** frame allows you to see the setup of the selected viewport configuration.

Let's experiment a bit.

> You can also access the Viewports dialog box by selecting it from the pull-down menus. Follow this path:
>
> *View – Viewports – New [or Named] Viewports ...*

Do This: 22.2.1	**Working with Tiled Viewports**

I. Open the *flr-pln22a.dwg* file in the C:\Steps\Lesson22 folder. The drawing looks like Figure 22.005.

II. Follow these steps.

Figure 22.005

TOOLS	COMMAND SEQUENCE	STEPS
Display Viewports Dialog Button	**Command: *vports***	1. We'll begin by creating some viewports. Enter the ***Viewports*** command by typing ***viewports*** or ***vports*** at the command prompt. Alternately, you can pick the **Display Viewports Dialog** button on either the Viewports or the Layouts toolbar.
		2. Select the **Three: Right** configuration. Notice the **Preview** window (Figure 22.006).

Standard viewports:
Active Model Configuration
Single
Two: Vertical
Two: Horizontal
Three: Right
Three: Left
Three: Above
Three: Below
Three: Vertical
Three: Horizontal
Four: Equal
Four: Right
Four: Left

Preview
Current
Current
Current

Figure 22.006

TOOLS	COMMAND SEQUENCE	STEPS
OK		3. Pick the **OK** button to continue. Your drawing looks like Figure 22.007.

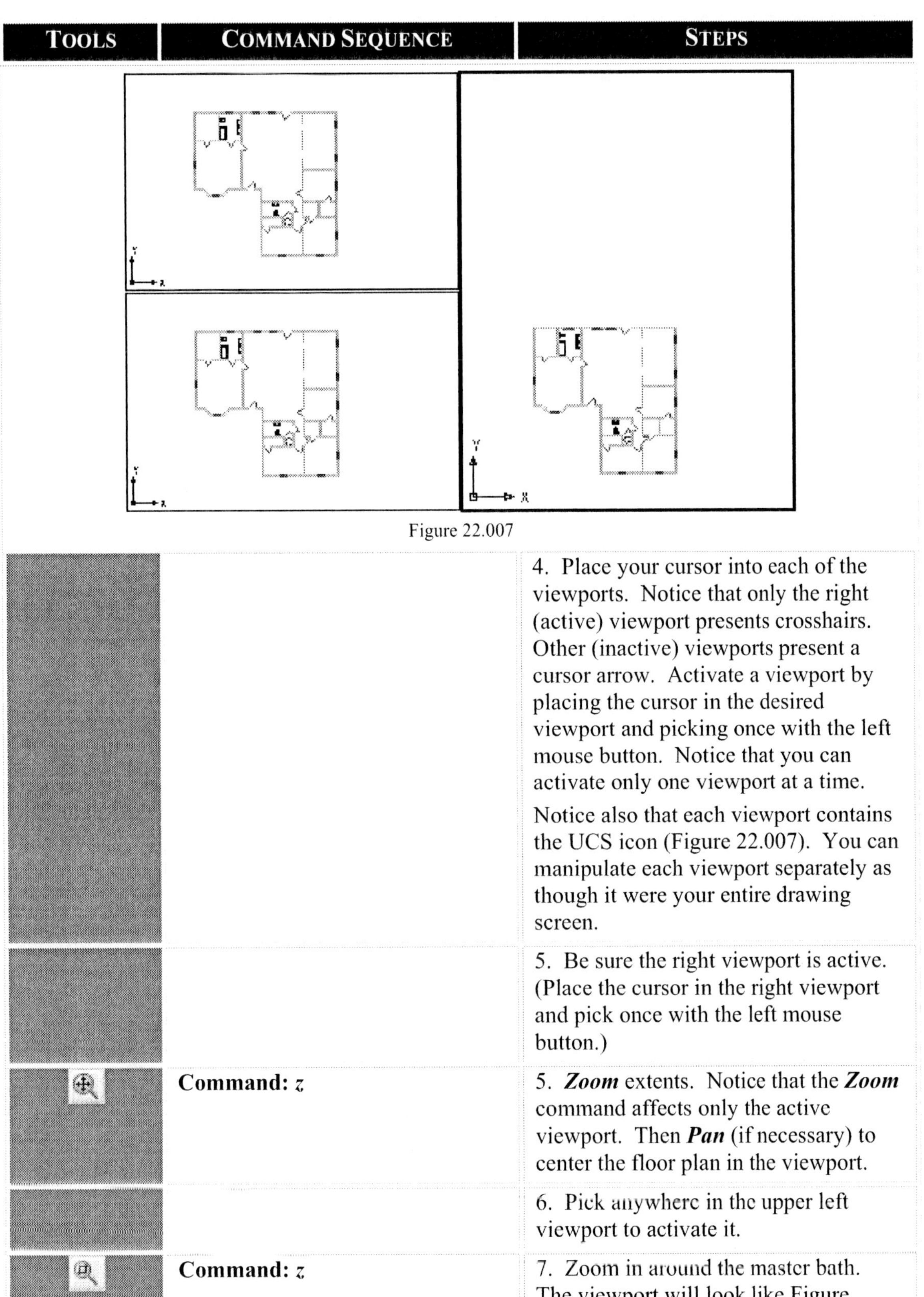

Figure 22.007

TOOLS	COMMAND SEQUENCE	STEPS
		4. Place your cursor into each of the viewports. Notice that only the right (active) viewport presents crosshairs. Other (inactive) viewports present a cursor arrow. Activate a viewport by placing the cursor in the desired viewport and picking once with the left mouse button. Notice that you can activate only one viewport at a time. Notice also that each viewport contains the UCS icon (Figure 22.007). You can manipulate each viewport separately as though it were your entire drawing screen.
		5. Be sure the right viewport is active. (Place the cursor in the right viewport and pick once with the left mouse button.)
	Command: *z*	5. ***Zoom*** extents. Notice that the ***Zoom*** command affects only the active viewport. Then ***Pan*** (if necessary) to center the floor plan in the viewport.
		6. Pick anywhere in the upper left viewport to activate it.
	Command: *z*	7. Zoom in around the master bath. The viewport will look like Figure 22.008.

TOOLS	COMMAND SEQUENCE	STEPS
	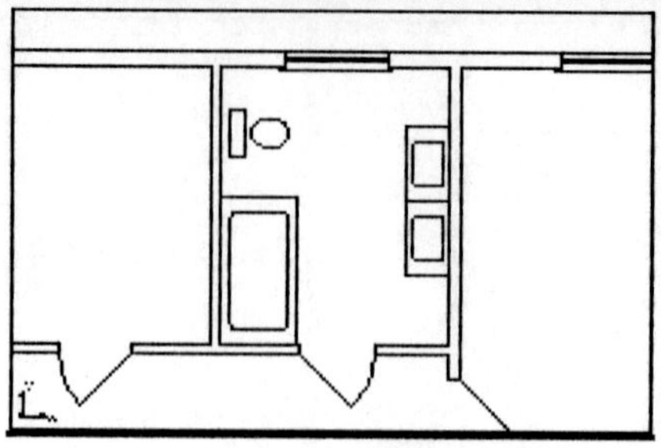 Figure 22.008	
		8. Now activate the lower left viewport.
	**Command:** ***z***	9. Zoom in around the common bath (Figure 22.009).
	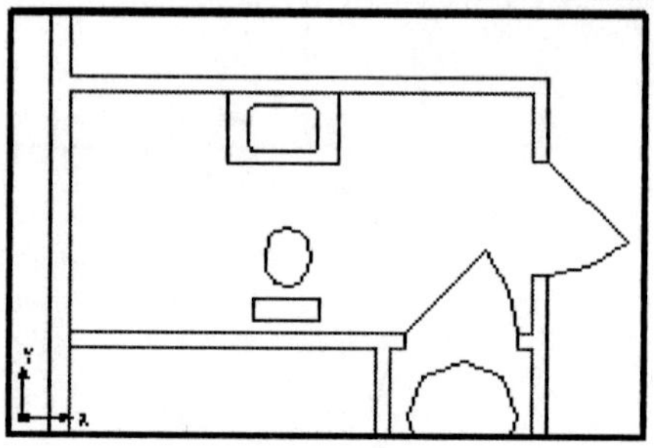 Figure 22.009	
	**Command:** ***co***	10. Let's place a tub in the common bath. Enter the ***Copy*** command.
	Select objects: **Specify base point or [Displacement] <Displacement>: _endp of**	11. Pick once in the upper left viewport to activate it; then select the bathtub. Select the lower left endpoint of the tub as your base point.
	Specify second point or <use first point as displacement>: _endp of	12. Pick once in the lower left viewport to activate it, and then place the tub in the lower left corner of the bathroom. Your screen now looks like Figure 22.010. Notice that the changes are reflected in the right viewport as well as the lower left.

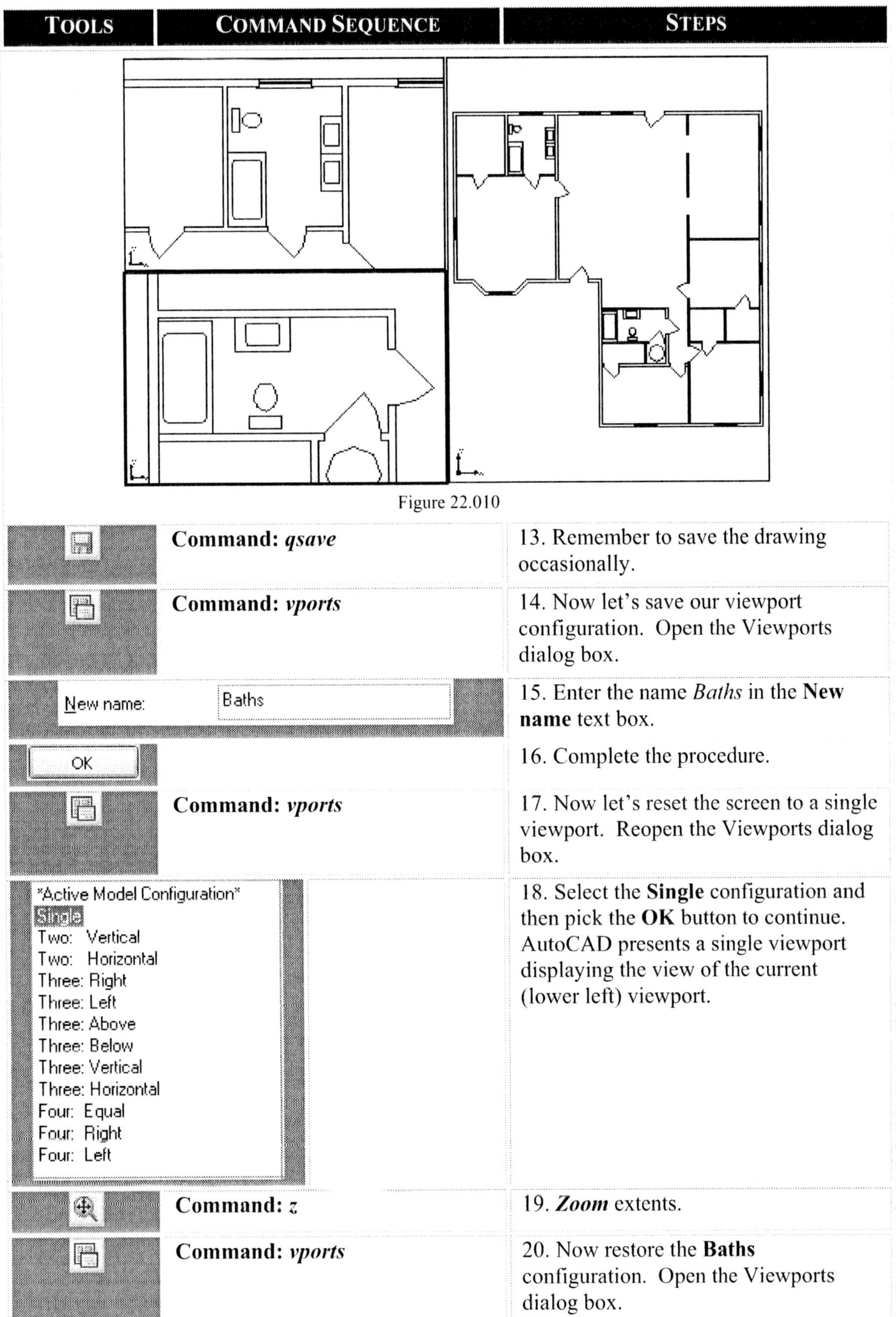

Figure 22.010

Tools	Command Sequence	Steps
	Command: ***qsave***	13. Remember to save the drawing occasionally.
	Command: ***vports***	14. Now let's save our viewport configuration. Open the Viewports dialog box.
New name: Baths		15. Enter the name *Baths* in the **New name** text box.
OK		16. Complete the procedure.
	Command: ***vports***	17. Now let's reset the screen to a single viewport. Reopen the Viewports dialog box.
Active Model Configuration Single Two: Vertical Two: Horizontal Three: Right Three: Left Three: Above Three: Below Three: Vertical Three: Horizontal Four: Equal Four: Right Four: Left		18. Select the **Single** configuration and then pick the **OK** button to continue. AutoCAD presents a single viewport displaying the view of the current (lower left) viewport.
	Command: ***z***	19. ***Zoom*** extents.
	Command: ***vports***	20. Now restore the **Baths** configuration. Open the Viewports dialog box.

Tools	Command Sequence	Steps
		21. Pick the **Named Viewports** tab and select the **Baths** configuration in the **Named viewports** list box (Figure 22.011).

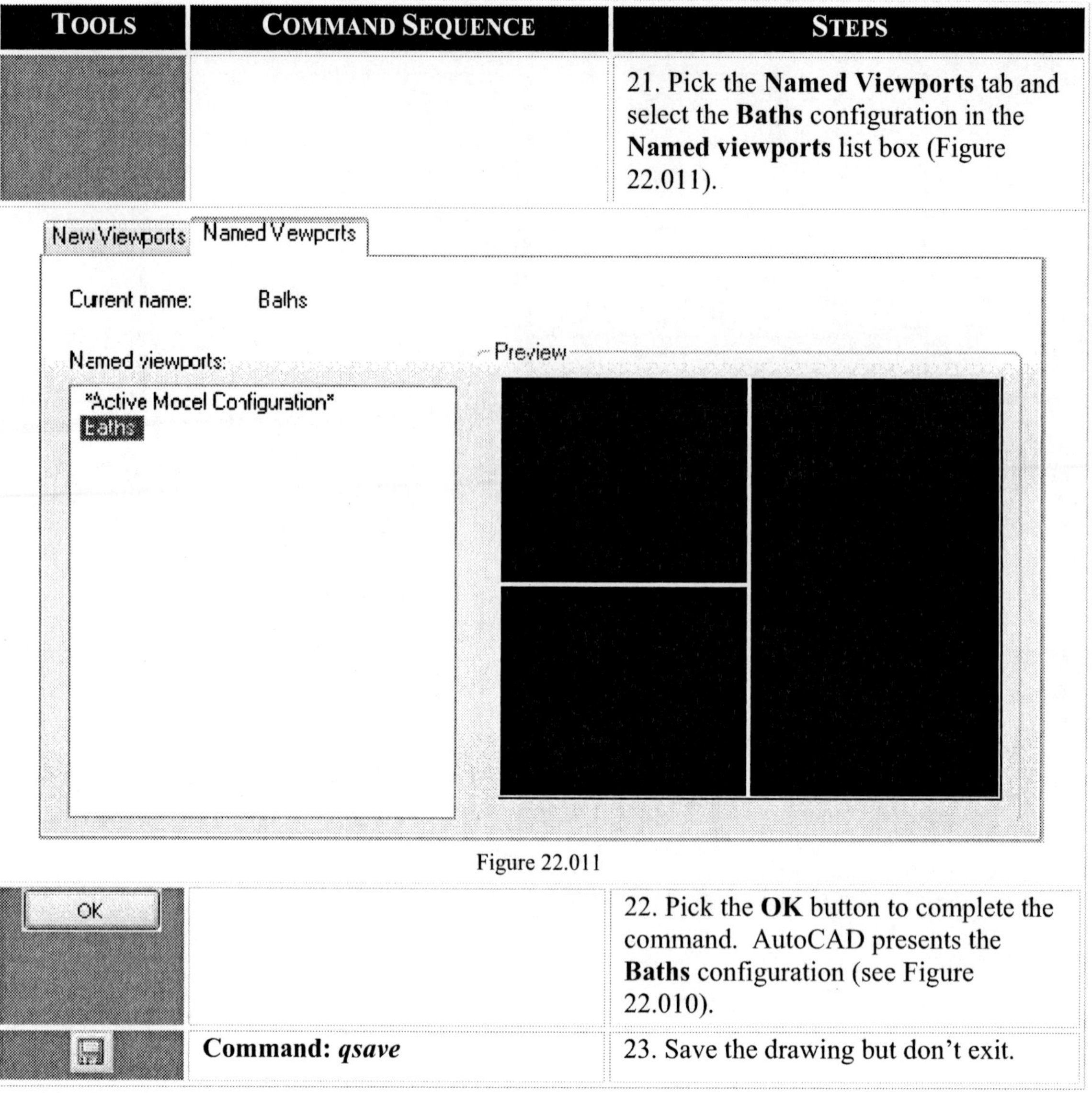

Figure 22.011

Tools	Command Sequence	Steps
OK		22. Pick the **OK** button to complete the command. AutoCAD presents the **Baths** configuration (see Figure 22.010).
	Command: ***qsave***	23. Save the drawing but don't exit.

You can see the benefits of using viewports when manipulating several smaller parts of your drawing at one time. But when we consider the limitations of tiled viewports, we can see that they were designed as drawing aids, not plotting tools.

Some things to remember about tiled viewports include:

- Tiled viewports were designed for use in Model Space.
- Tiled viewports are not objects and won't plot. Your plot will show only the view in the *active* viewport.
- Only one viewport is active at a time. This means that you can draw only in one viewport at a time, but you can activate a new viewport transparently (while using another command).
- The active viewport will show crosshairs while inactive viewports will show a cursor. Place the cursor in the viewport you wish to activate and click once to activate it.
- Layers behave universally in tiled viewports. You can't freeze or thaw a layer just for one viewport as you can with floating viewports. (You'll see how to use layers in floating viewports in Lesson 23.)

- While you can control the number and position of tiled viewports, you can't easily control the size. You can't control the shape at all (all tiled viewports are rectangular).
- You can create viewports within viewports, but you should consider the size of the viewports and the size of your monitor before attempting this.
- Manipulation of viewports doesn't affect the actual drawing.

To see how you can use viewports to assist in plotting a drawing that uses multiple scales, we'll take a look at floating viewports in Section 22.4. But first, we must set up our Paper Space environment.

> You'll occasionally see the term *Paper Space* written as *paperspace*. Both refer to the same thing, though *paperspace* is generally a programmer's term.

22.3 Setting Up a Paper Space Environment

Entering Paper Space is as easy as picking a **Layout** tab just above the command line. When you select a **Layout** tab for the first time, AutoCAD will create a single floating viewport in the center of the page.

Like Model Space, Paper Space must be set up. But it's quite a bit easier with Paper Space. Let's set up a Paper Space layout for our floor plan.

> Note: This procedure will utilize my printer. You may have to adjust the settings to match your printer or plotter setup.

Do This: 22.3.1 Creating a Paper Space Layout

I. Be sure you're still in the *flr-pln22a.dwg* file in the C:\Steps\Lesson22 folder. If not, please open it now.

II. Set **VPORTS** as the current layer.

III. Follow these steps.

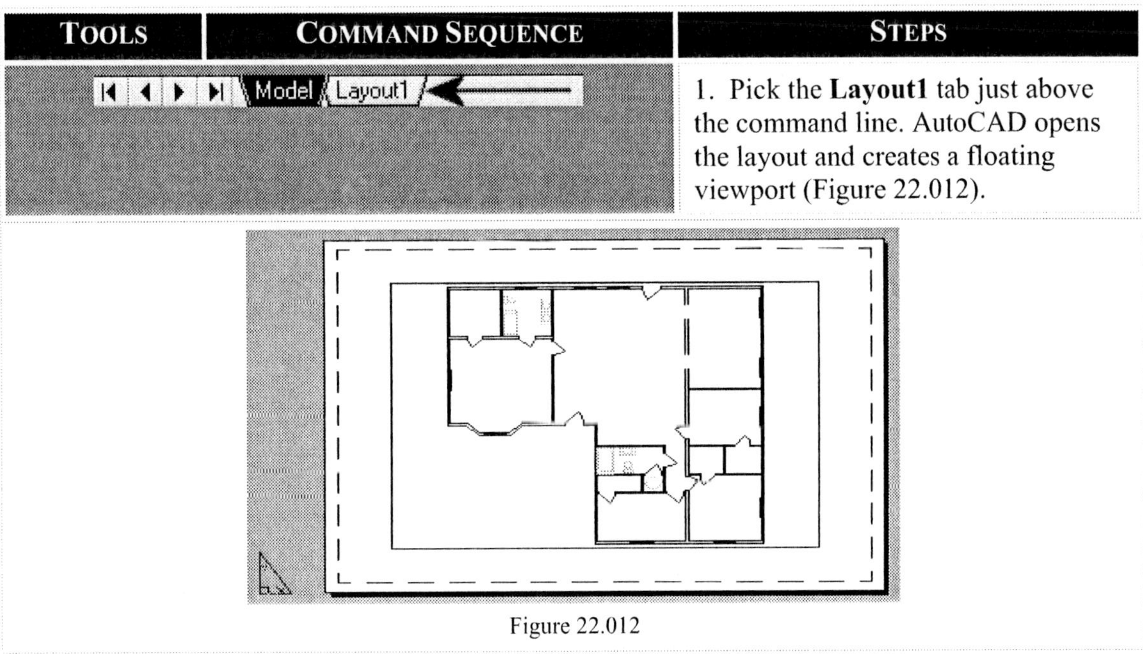

TOOLS	COMMAND SEQUENCE	STEPS
		1. Pick the **Layout1** tab just above the command line. AutoCAD opens the layout and creates a floating viewport (Figure 22.012).

Figure 22.012

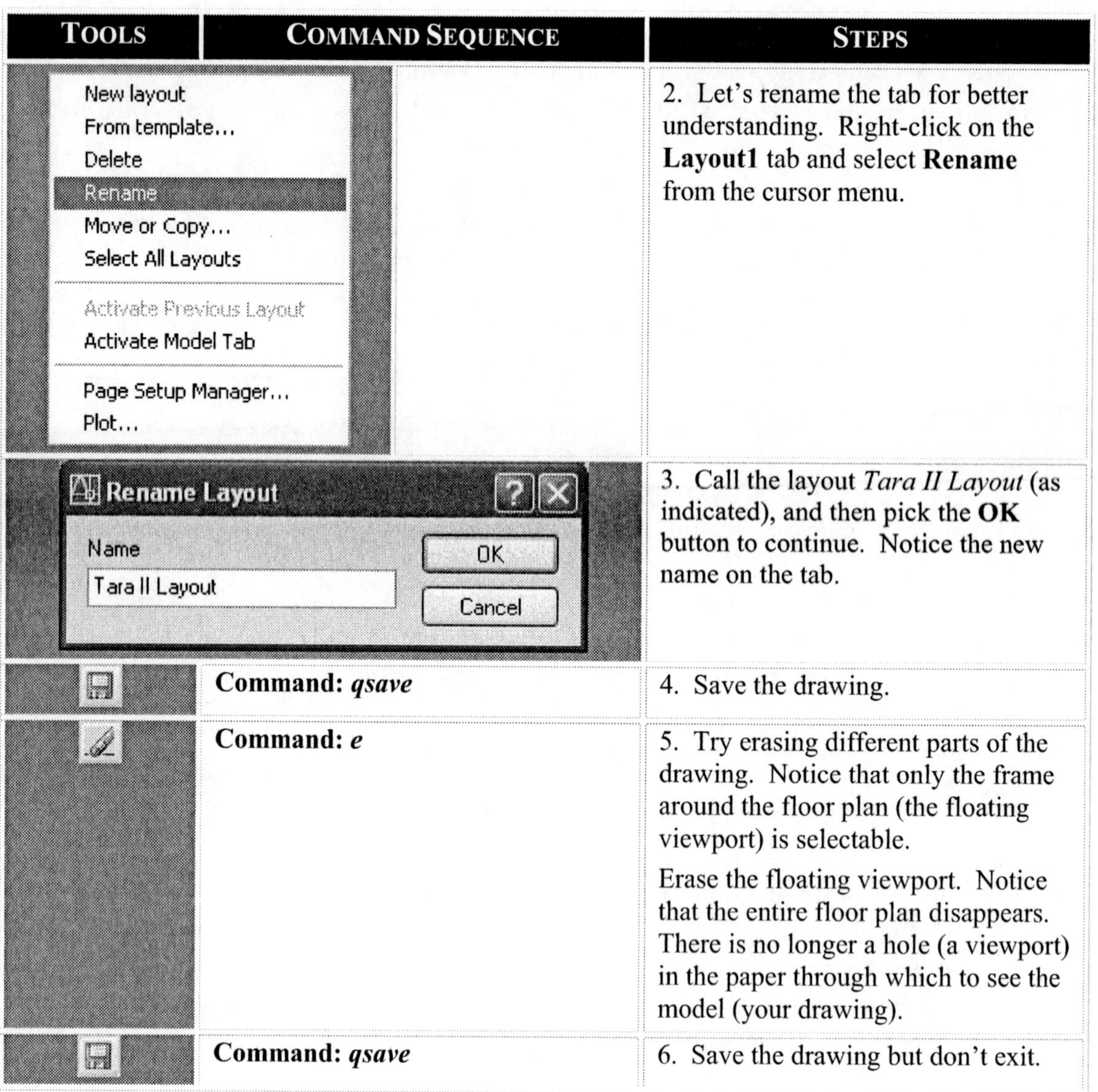

TOOLS	COMMAND SEQUENCE	STEPS
New layout From template... Delete Rename Move or Copy... Select All Layouts Activate Previous Layout Activate Model Tab Page Setup Manager... Plot...		2. Let's rename the tab for better understanding. Right-click on the **Layout1** tab and select **Rename** from the cursor menu.
Rename Layout Name Tara II Layout OK Cancel		3. Call the layout *Tara II Layout* (as indicated), and then pick the **OK** button to continue. Notice the new name on the tab.
	Command: ***qsave***	4. Save the drawing.
	Command: ***e***	5. Try erasing different parts of the drawing. Notice that only the frame around the floor plan (the floating viewport) is selectable. Erase the floating viewport. Notice that the entire floor plan disappears. There is no longer a hole (a viewport) in the paper through which to see the model (your drawing).
	Command: ***qsave***	6. Save the drawing but don't exit.

You've seen how to start a Paper Space layout – just go to the **Layout** tab and let AutoCAD do the rest. AutoCAD presents a sheet of paper with a floating viewport (a hole in the page) that's the only thing that exists on the page. (The dashed outline shows the margins of the working area on the page.)

You can place objects on the paper that won't affect the model (title block, text, and so forth). Alternately, you can return to Model Space to work on the model. You can even work on the model through the viewport by entering the ***MSpace*** command! We'll look at this in more detail in later sections of this lesson; but first, let's examine floating viewports.

> You can have more than one layout in your drawing – each set up differently for different printing needs. Use the ***Layout*** command to add, remove, or copy layout tabs. It presents the following options:
>
> **Command:** ***layout***
>
> **Enter layout option [Copy/Delete/New/Template/Rename/SAveas/Set/?] <set>:**
>
> Most of these options are self-explanatory. However, the **Save** option might not do what you expect. It replaces the default layout with the current setup (all future layouts will begin with the

current setup).

An easier approach than the command line is simply to right-click on a tab and select the desired option from the cursor menu.

22.4 Using Floating Viewports

Floating, or untiled, viewports, although more complex than tiled viewports, offer considerably more flexibility. But how are floating viewports different from tiled viewports? Let's take a look.

As we saw in Section 22.2, AutoCAD designed tiled viewports as *drawing* tools for a Model Space environment. Tiled viewports act like holes in an imaginary box through which you view different parts of your drawing. The location and size of the hole determine what you see, how much you *see*, and at what angle you see the drawing objects. Tiled viewports don't affect how the drawing will be plotted.

Floating viewports were designed as *plotting* tools in a Paper Space environment. Floating viewports also act like holes, but this time they're holes in a sheet of paper covering the drawing objects. The location and size of floating viewport holes determine what will be *plotted*, how much will be plotted, and at what angle the drawing objects will be plotted.

Some things to remember about floating viewports include:

- Floating viewports are objects and can be moved, stretched, and erased like any other object on a drawing. Consequently, you can place them on a separate layer that can be frozen at plot time.
- Unlike tiled viewports, floating viewports don't have to be rectangular.
- Floating viewports can overlap.
- You can control layers within each viewport independently of the rest of the drawing. This is a key benefit since you often won't want details shown in one viewport reflected in another.
- Use floating viewports to show different views of one or more objects on a single plot.
- Like tiled viewports, only one floating viewport is active at a time.
- Floating viewports live in Paper Space (on a **Layout** tab). Although they're not available in Model Space, you can work in Model Space *through* a floating viewport (much as a doctor works on a kidney or gall bladder through a hole in the skin).
- Sizing text on Paper Space is really quite easy. Since you're working on the actual plotted page, simply enter the text at the desired plotted size. No need for scale factors!

22.4.1 Creating Floating Viewports Using *MView*

Creating floating viewports using the ***MView*** command appears more daunting than it actually is. The command sequence looks like this:

Command: *mview* (or *mv*)

Specify corner of viewport or

[ON/OFF/Fit/Shadeplot/Lock/Object/Polygonal/Restore/2/3/4] <Fit>: *[begin a window]*

Specify opposite corner: *[complete the window]*

Let's look at each option.

- The **ON/OFF** options allow you to "open" or "close" the viewport through which you see the drawing. If the viewport is **OFF**, it's closed and you can't see through it. Thus, that part of the drawing is hidden.
- When you select one of these options, AutoCAD will prompt you to select the viewport to turn **ON** or **OFF**.
- The **Fit** option will create a single, maximum-size floating viewport within the display area.
- **Shadeplot** controls exactly what plots within a viewport. It prompts

  Shade plot? [As displayed/Wireframe/ Hidden/Rendered] <As displayed>:

  - **As displayed**, of course, plots the viewport as is.
  - **Wireframe** refers to a type of three-dimensional drawing. You'll learn more about that in the *3D AutoCAD 2006:One Step at a Time* text.
  - **Hidden** allows you to remove hidden lines from the selected viewport during plotting. These are not lines drawn using a hidden linetype, but lines "hidden" or behind other lines or objects in three-dimensional space.
  - **Rendered** refers to a shading technique used on three-dimensional objects. Again, you'll learn more about that in the 3D text.
- The **Lock** option allows you to lock a viewport. It prompts

  Viewport View Locking [ON/OFF]: ***[enter ON or OFF]***

  Select objects: ***[select the viewport to lock or unlock]***

  When a viewport is locked, you can't (intentionally or accidentally) change the scale factor within it. This is a handy tool if you intend to work on the Model Space within a viewport.
- The **Object** option allows you to select any existing closed polyline, ellipse, spline, region, or circle (existing in Paper Space) and turn it into a floating viewport.
- The **Polygonal** option allows you to create a floating viewport with any number of sizes and in any shape. It prompts

  Specify start point: ***[pick a start point]***

  Specify next point or [Arc/Length/Undo]: ***[create the shape just as you would a polyline]***
- The **2/3/4** options tell AutoCAD to create two, three, or four viewports. AutoCAD will prompt you to locate the viewports.
- **Restore** is a very useful tool. It allows you to translate tiled viewports into floating viewport objects. When selected, AutoCAD allows you to enter the name of a saved tiled configuration or to translate the current tiled configuration into floating viewports.
- Of course the default option – **Specify corner of viewport** – allows you to manually create viewports one at a time.

Let's insert a title block into our drawing and then set up some floating viewports.

Do This: 22.4.1.1	**Creating Floating Viewports**

I. Be sure you're still in the *flr-pln22a.dwg* file in the C:\Steps\Lesson22 folder. If not, please open it now.

II. Set the **BORDER** layer current.

III. Follow these steps.

TOOLS	COMMAND SEQUENCE	STEPS
	Command: ***i***	1. Insert the *ANSI-A title block* drawing that came with AutoCAD. (Find it in the **Documents and Settings\[Timothy S. Sykes]\Application Data\Autodesk\AutoCAD 2006\R16.0\enu\Template** folder. (This is on a Windows XP computer.) Put it at the 0,0 coordinates.
		2. Set the **VPORTS** layer current.
No Button Available	**Command:** ***mv***	3. Enter the ***MView*** command by typing ***mview*** or ***mv*** at the prompt.
	Specify corner of viewport or [ON/OFF/Fit/Shadeplot/Lock/ Object/Polygonal/Restore/2/3/4] <Fit>: ***.5,7.5*** **Specify opposite corner:** ***4.75,4.25***	4. Place the first floating viewport as indicated.
	Command: ***[enter]*** **Specify corner of viewport or [ON/OFF/Fit/Shadeplot/Lock/ Object/Polygonal/Restore/2/3/4] <Fit>:** ***5,6.5*** **Specify opposite corner:** ***10,2.5***	5. Place a second floating viewport as indicated. Your drawing now looks like Figure 22.013.

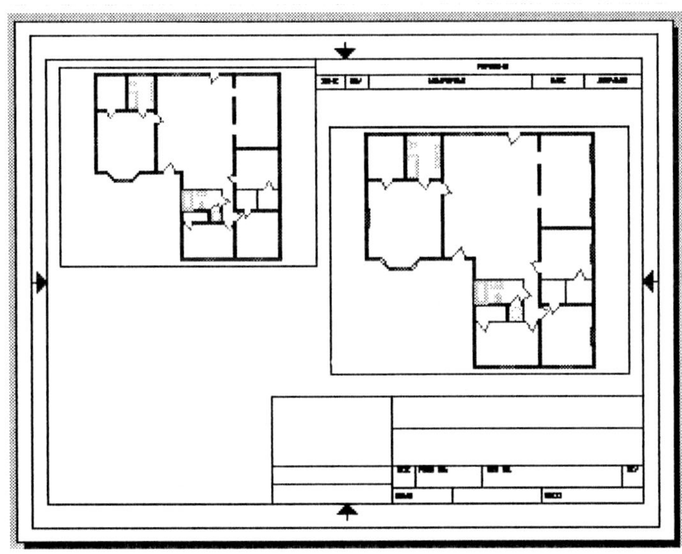

Figure 22.013

<table>
<tr><th>TOOLS</th><th>COMMAND SEQUENCE</th><th>STEPS</th></tr>
<tr><td></td><td>Command: c
Specify center point for circle or [3P/2P/Ttr (tan tan radius)]: 2.25,2.25
Specify radius of circle or [Diameter]: 1.75</td><td>6. Now let’s make a nonrectangular viewport – the easy way. Draw a circle as indicated.</td></tr>
<tr><td></td><td>Command: mv</td><td>7. Now we’ll convert the circle to a floating viewport. Enter the MView command.</td></tr>
<tr><td rowspan="2"> 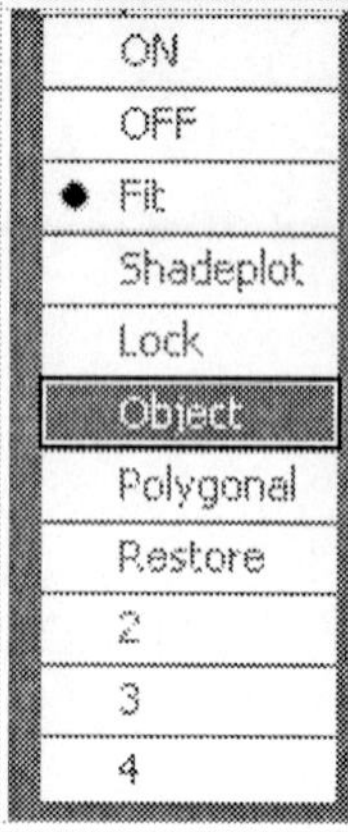ON
OFF
• Fit
Shadeplot
Lock
Object
Polygonal
Restore
2
3
4</td><td>Specify corner of viewport or [ON/OFF/Fit/Shadeplot/ Lock/Object/Polygonal/ Restore/2/3/4] <Fit>: o</td><td>8. Use the Object option.</td></tr>
<tr><td>Select object to clip viewport:</td><td>9. Select the circle. Your drawing now looks like Figure 22.014. Notice that the round viewport shows only part of the drawing. It began with the full drawing and then clipped away the part that didn’t fit into the circle.</td></tr>
<tr><td colspan="3">Figure 22.014</td></tr>
<tr><td></td><td>Command: qsave</td><td>10. Save the drawing but don’t exit.</td></tr>
</table>

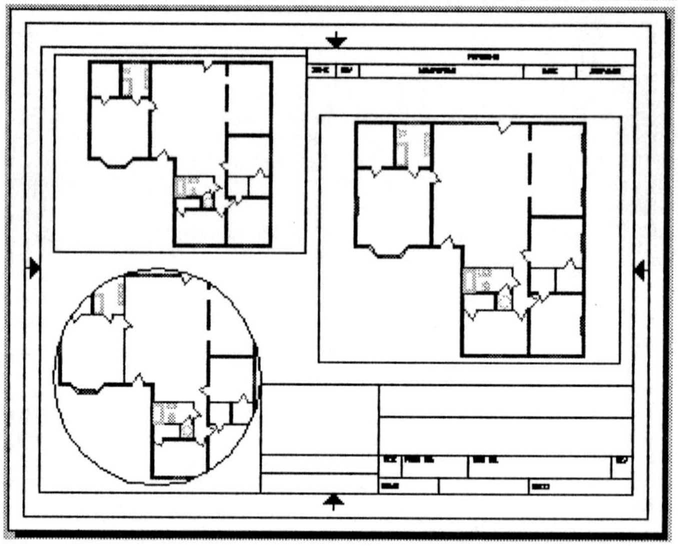

22.4.2 The Viewports Toolbar

The one common thread that permeates the thrills of life – your first kiss, your first child, your first paycheck ...– is that each results from the ***discovery*** *of something new and wonderful.*

Never miss an opportunity to explore or you may miss an opportunity to discover.

Anonymous

We've made a good start with Paper Space and floating viewports. But have you discovered the viewports toolbar yet (Figure 22.015)?

Figure 22.015

This handy item provides single-button selection of some of the ***MView*** options as well as some other tools.

Let's take a look.

- The first button – **Display Viewports Dialog** – does just that. It displays the Viewports dialog box that we used to create tiled viewports in Section 22.2 of this lesson. You can also use this dialog box to create *floating* viewports in Paper Space! Simply follow the same procedures you learned for tiled viewports.

  (Notice that the viewports dialog box presented when in Paper Space doesn't have the **New name** text box. Floating viewport configurations are saved as layouts.)
- The second button – **Single Viewport** – enables you to create a single viewport much as you created the first two viewports in our last exercise.
- The third button – **Polygonal Viewport** – allows you to create a viewport with any number of sizes and in any shape by executing the **Polygon** option of the ***MView*** command.
- The fourth button – **Convert Object to Viewport** – executes the **Object** option of the ***MView*** command as we did in our last exercise.
- The last button – **Clip Existing Viewport** – is a modifying tool used to redefine viewport boundaries. We'll learn more about it in Lesson 23.
- On the right end of the toolbar, you'll find the **Viewport Scale** control box. You'll use this to set the scale of the image seen through the floating viewport. We'll look at this procedure next.

22.4.3 Adjusting the Views in Floating Viewports

Once you've created floating viewports, you'll need to adjust what you see through them. This means adjusting the scale and then panning to achieve the appropriate view for your plot. Before we do either, we must tell AutoCAD to allow us to work in the Model Space we see through the floating viewport. Do this by simply entering ***MSpace*** or ***MS*** at the command prompt and then selecting the viewport you wish to use (see the insert below).

> To toggle between Paper Space and Model Space, simply type ***PSpace*** (or ***ps***) or ***MSpace*** (or ***ms***) at the command prompt. Alternately, you can pick on **PAPER** or **MODEL** on the status bar. You can also double-click in a Paper Space area to activate Paper Space, or in a viewport to activate Model Space (simultaneously making that viewport current).

We'll begin by setting the scale for the viewport. AutoCAD provides two methods of doing this – the **XP** option of the ***Zoom*** command, or the **Viewport Scale** control box on the Viewports toolbar.

- The Zoom Approach: While at the ***Zoom*** prompt, simply type ***1/[SF]xp*** (where ***SF*** is the scale factor for the scale you wish to use in this particular viewport – refer to Appendix A).
- The Control Box Approach: Pick the down arrow and select the appropriate scale. Alternately, you can type a scale into the box.

Let's try it.

Do This: 22.4.3.1	**Scaling Floating Viewports**

I. Be sure you're still in the *flr-pln22a.dwg* file in the C:\Steps\Lesson22 folder. If not, please open it now.

II. Follow these steps.

TOOLS	COMMAND SEQUENCE	STEPS
PAPER	**Command: *ms***	1. Open Model Space by typing ***mspace*** or ***ms*** at the command prompt. Alternately, you can pick **PAPER** on the status bar.
		2. Select anywhere in the upper left viewport to activate it. Notice that the boundary darkens to indicate that it's active.
	Command: *p*	3. Use the ***Pan*** command to center the master bath in the viewport.
	Command: *z*	4. Now we'll set the scale for this viewport. Enter the ***Zoom*** command.
	Specify corner of window, enter a scale factor (nX or nXP), or [All/Center/Dynamic/Extents/ Previous/Scale/Window/ Object] <real time>: *1/48xp*	5. We wish to set the scale of this viewport to ¼"=1'-0". The scale factor for this scale is 48 (see Appendix A). So enter the scale factor, as shown, using the ***xp*** suffix to indicate that you are scaling Paper Space. AutoCAD scales the viewport. (You may have to pan slightly to center the view again.) This viewport now looks like Figure 22.016.
	Figure 22.016	
		6. Now let's use the control box method. Pick anywhere in the right viewport to activate it.

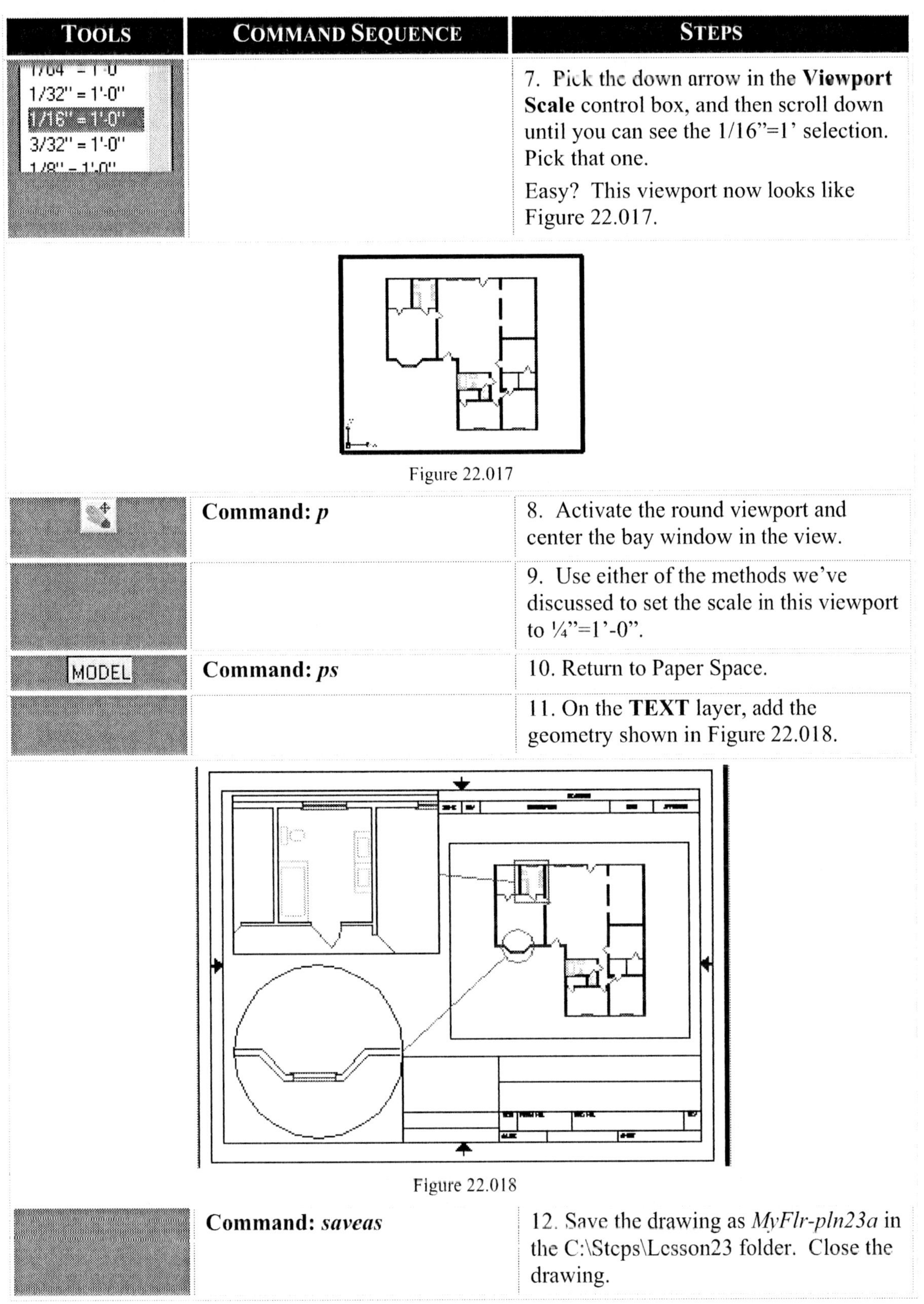

Tools	Command Sequence	Steps
1/32" = 1'-0" 1/16" = 1'-0" 3/32" = 1'-0"		7. Pick the down arrow in the **Viewport Scale** control box, and then scroll down until you can see the 1/16"=1' selection. Pick that one. Easy? This viewport now looks like Figure 22.017.

Figure 22.017

Tools	Command Sequence	Steps
	Command: ***p***	8. Activate the round viewport and center the bay window in the view.
		9. Use either of the methods we've discussed to set the scale in this viewport to ¼"=1'-0".
MODEL	**Command:** ***ps***	10. Return to Paper Space.
		11. On the **TEXT** layer, add the geometry shown in Figure 22.018.

Figure 22.018

Tools	Command Sequence	Steps
	Command: ***saveas***	12. Save the drawing as *MyFlr-pln23a* in the C:\Steps\Lesson23 folder. Close the drawing.

The drawing now shows the full plan at a 1/16"-1'-0" scale and the common bathroom and bay window at a ¼"=1'-0" scale.

We've completed the Paper Space setup of our drawing. Let's review what we've accomplished.

- We began with a floor plan drawn in Model Space. The limits of Model Space had been set to produce a ¼"=1'-0" drawing on a C-size sheet of paper.
- We opened the layout tab of our drawing and set it up to print our Model Space drawing on an A-size sheet (AutoCAD's default). We used an AutoCAD title block designed for this page size and added three floating viewports – two rectangular and one converted object (circle).
- We set different views of the same model in each of the floating viewports – each viewport having its own scale.

22.5 And Now the Easy Way – The *LayoutWizard* Command

We've explored several steps in creating and setting up a Paper Space layout. But as you know, I always save the best for last.

I briefly discussed the ***Layout*** command in Section 22.3. That command allowed you to create new layouts. But AutoCAD's Layout Wizard does the same thing and more!

Using the ***LayoutWizard*** command, you can create a new layout and set it up as well.

Let's take a look at the wizard.

Do This: 22.5.1 Using the Layout Wizard

I. Open the *flr-pln22b.dwg* file in the C:\Steps\Lesson22 folder. This is the same file as *flr-pln22a*, but hasn't had the layout set up yet.

II. Set the **VPORTS** layer current.

III. Follow these steps.

TOOLS	CMD SEQUENCE	STEPS
No Button Available	**Command:** ***layoutwizard***	1. Enter the ***LayoutWizard*** command by typing ***layoutwizard*** at the command prompt. Alternately, you can use the Tools pull-down menu. Follow this path: *Tools – Wizards – Create Layout...*
		2. AutoCAD presents the Create Layout – Begin dialog box (Figure 22.019). Enter the name *My Wizard Layout* in the text box as shown. Pick the **Next** button to continue.

Tools	Cmd Sequence	Steps

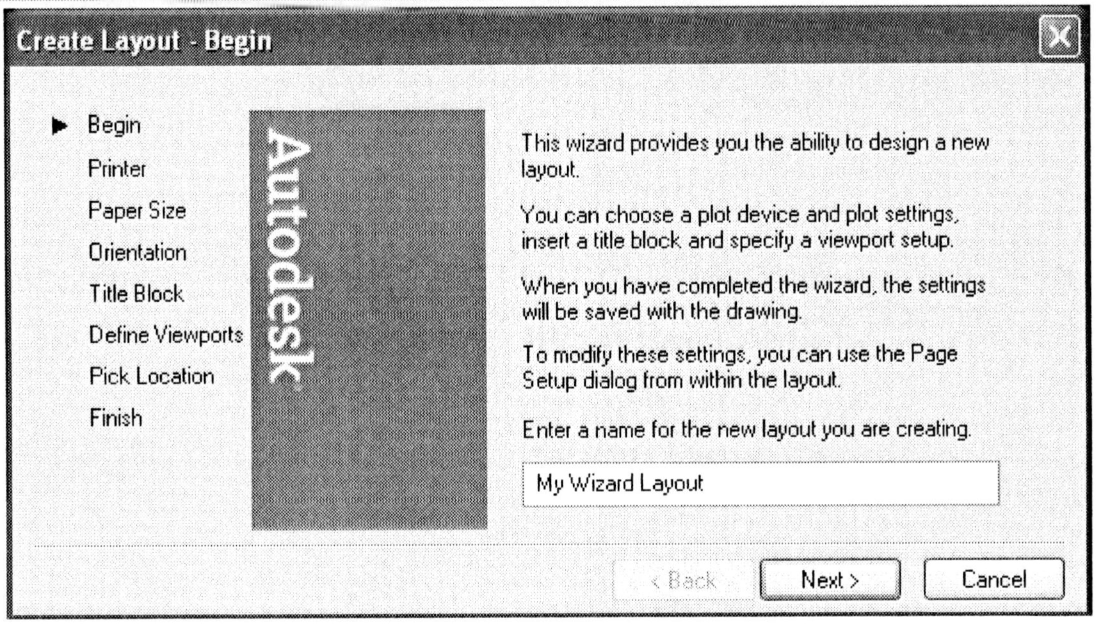

Create Layout - Begin
Begin
Printer
Paper Size
Orientation
Title Block
Define Viewports
Pick Location
Finish
Autodesk
This wizard provides you the ability to design a new layout.
You can choose a plot device and plot settings, insert a title block and specify a viewport setup.
When you have completed the wizard, the settings will be saved with the drawing.
To modify these settings, you can use the Page Setup dialog from within the layout.
Enter a name for the new layout you are creating.
My Wizard Layout
< Back
Next >
Cancel

Figure 22.019

		3. Select the printer or plotter you wish to use (Figure 22.020). (Your options may differ from mine.) Pick the **Next** button to continue.

Create Layout - Printer
Begin
Printer
Paper Size
Orientation
Title Block
Define Viewports
Pick Location
Finish
Autodesk
Select a configured plotter for the new layout.
None
Microsoft Office Document Image Writer
magicolor 2300 DL
Lexmark X63
Auto Microsoft Office Document Image Writer on LIS.
Auto magicolor 2300 DL on LISA
Auto Adobe PDF on LISA
Adobe PDF
PublishToWeb JPG.pc3
PublishToWeb PNG.pc3
Default Windows System Printer.pc3
DWF6 ePlot.pc3
< Back
Next >
Cancel

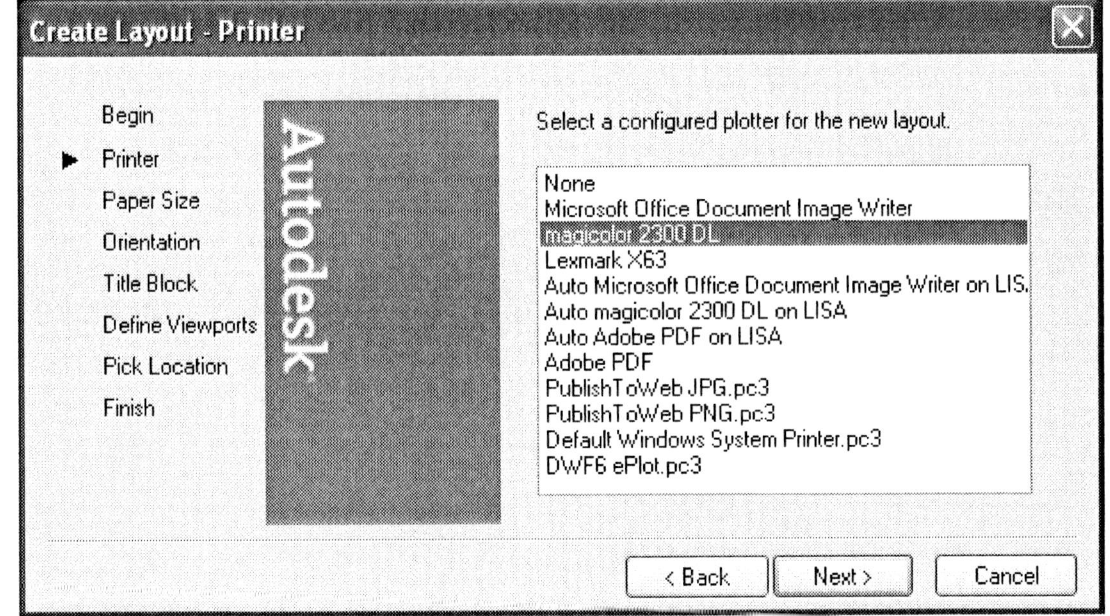

Figure 22.020

		4. Select a paper size for the layout (I'll use the **8½" x 11"** size). Remember to tell AutoCAD to set up the layout in **Inches** or **Millimeters**. Here we'll use **Inches** (Figure 22.021). Pick the **Next** button to continue.

TOOLS	CMD SEQUENCE	STEPS

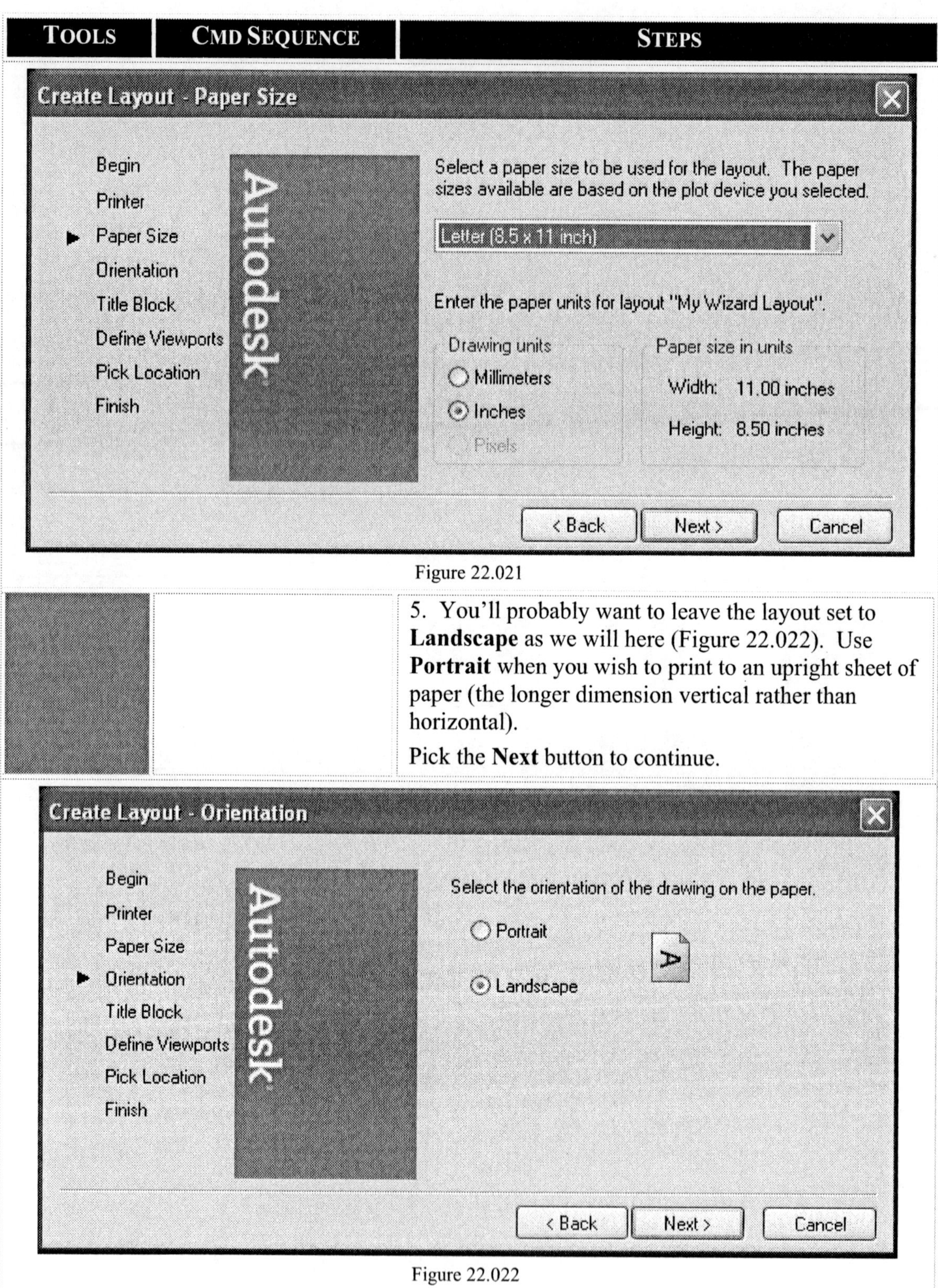

Figure 22.021

5. You'll probably want to leave the layout set to **Landscape** as we will here (Figure 22.022). Use **Portrait** when you wish to print to an upright sheet of paper (the longer dimension vertical rather than horizontal).

Pick the **Next** button to continue.

Figure 22.022

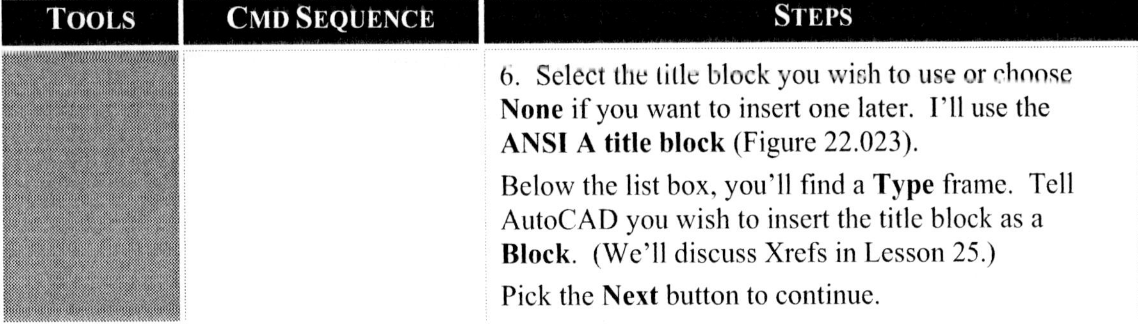

TOOLS	CMD SEQUENCE	STEPS
		6. Select the title block you wish to use or choose **None** if you want to insert one later. I'll use the **ANSI A title block** (Figure 22.023). Below the list box, you'll find a **Type** frame. Tell AutoCAD you wish to insert the title block as a **Block**. (We'll discuss Xrefs in Lesson 25.) Pick the **Next** button to continue.

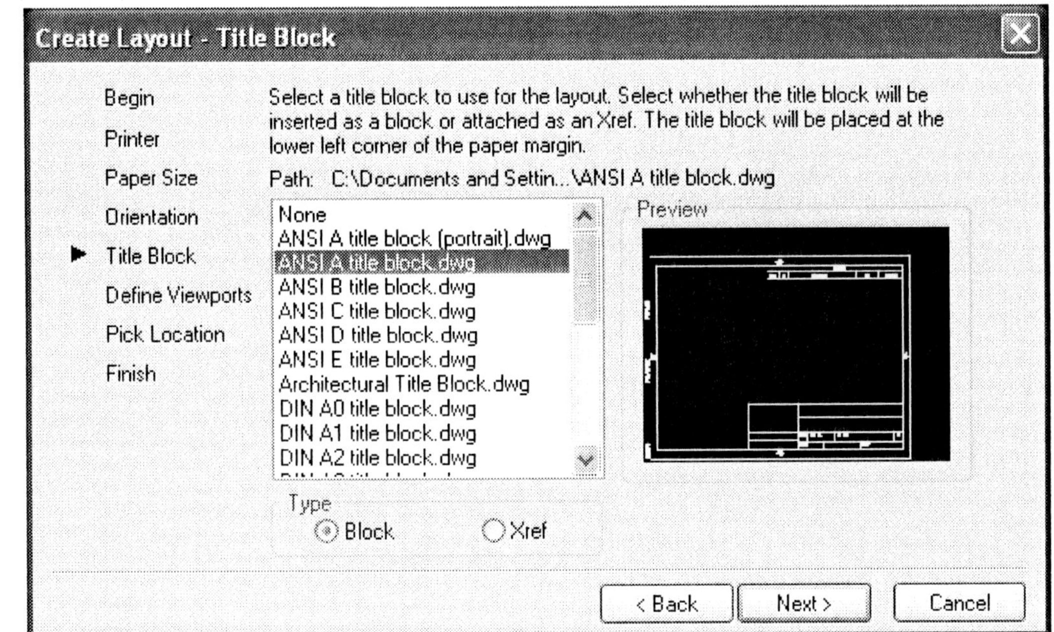

Figure 22.023

		7. Now we can create a rough setup for our viewports. In the **Viewport setup** frame (Figure 22.024), select the **Single** option to create a single viewport. You can use the other options to create the standard three-dimensional engineering views (four viewports – three with orthographic views and one three-dimensional view) or an **Array** of viewports. The **Array** option displays the **Rows/Columns** and **Spacing** boxes below the **Viewport setup** frame. In the **Viewport scale** control box, set the scale for our single viewport as 1/16"=1'-0". Pick the **Next** button to continue.

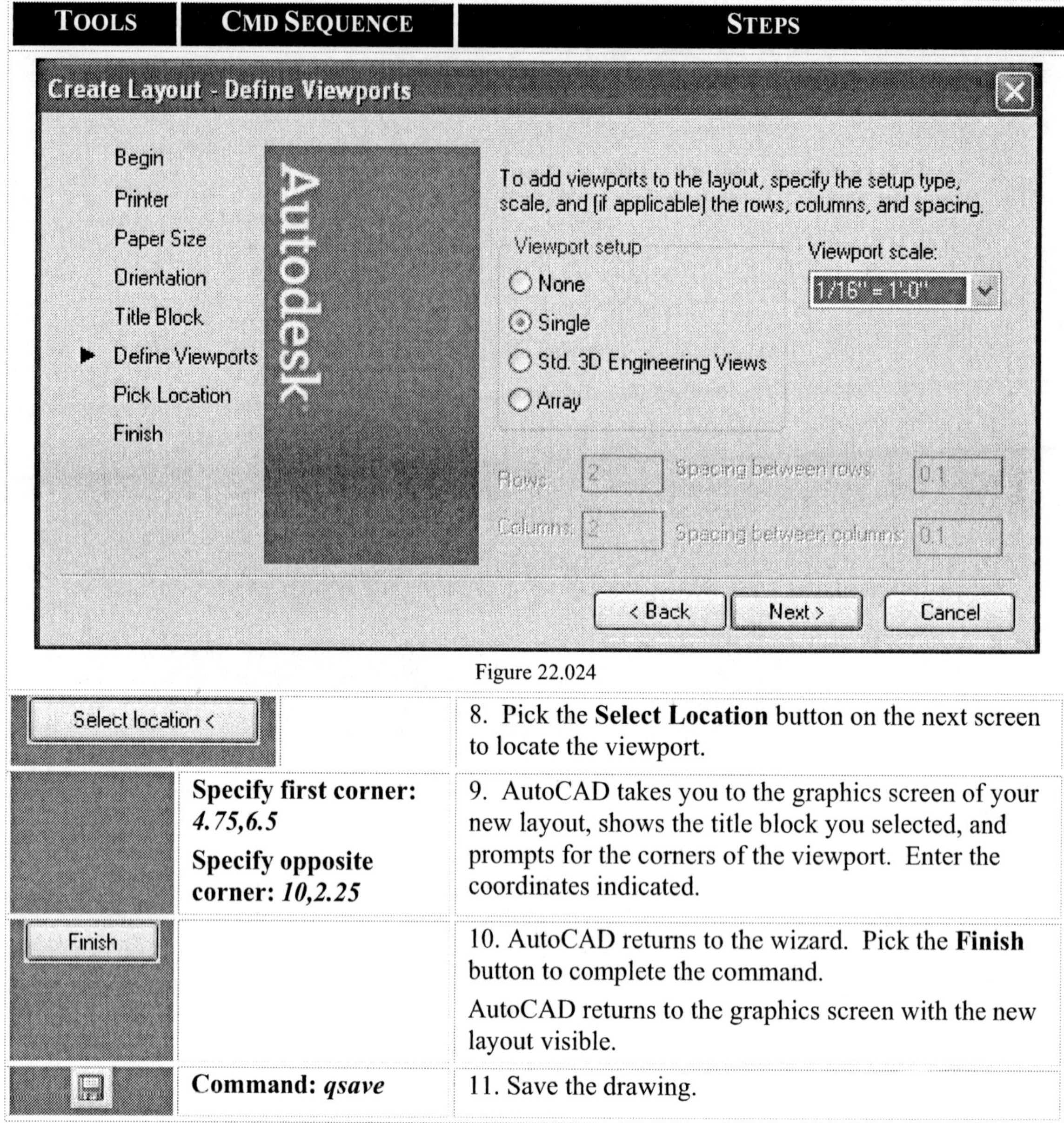

Figure 22.024

TOOLS	CMD SEQUENCE	STEPS
Select location <		8. Pick the **Select Location** button on the next screen to locate the viewport.
	Specify first corner: ***4.75,6.5*** **Specify opposite corner:** ***10,2.25***	9. AutoCAD takes you to the graphics screen of your new layout, shows the title block you selected, and prompts for the corners of the viewport. Enter the coordinates indicated.
Finish		10. AutoCAD returns to the wizard. Pick the **Finish** button to complete the command. AutoCAD returns to the graphics screen with the new layout visible.
	Command: ***qsave***	11. Save the drawing.

Wasn't that easier than our previous exercises? You can use the ***MView*** command to add additional viewports as desired, but the bulk of the work has been accomplished in fewer steps and with less effort.

How will you set up your layouts?

We've accomplished quite a lot in such a short lesson. But we haven't finished learning the basics of Paper Space. We must consider how dimensions, layers, text, and plotting relate to Paper Space, as well as some methods of editing our layout. We'll look at these in Lesson 23, but for now, let's take time for some projects.

We've used the ***MView*** command to set up our floating viewports. We've also seen an easier approach to creating layouts – using the ***LayoutWizard*** command. But wait! There is another approach.

AutoCAD provides a method that incorporates all aspects of Paper Space setup into a single command – the ***MVSetup*** command. You may experiment with this command if you like, but be warned that consolidation doesn't always make a task easier! We'll explore ***MVSetup*** as an editing tool in Lesson 23.

22.6 Extra Steps

If you have access to a printer or plotter, try to plot the results of the last exercise. Don't worry if you have problems; we'll cover plotting in Paper Space in Lesson 23. This is just a preview.

Some important things to remember when plotting include:

- Be sure to plot the **My Wizard Layout** tab.
- Plot to a 1=1 scale.
- Use an A-size sheet of paper (ANSI A is 11" x 8½").

Examine the scale. Designers use Paper Space to create drawings at industry standard scales while showing details at whatever scale is necessary for clarity.

22.7 What Have We Learned?

Items covered in this lesson include:

- *Tiled viewports (Model Space)*
- *Floating viewports (Paper Space)*
- *The Layout Wizard*
- *Commands:*
  - ***PSpace***
  - ***MSpace***
  - ***Viewports***
  - ***MView***

We've seen the basic setup of Paper Space in two-dimensional drawings.

While the setup may seem somewhat confusing at first, the benefits of practice can't be overemphasized. In the two-dimensional world, Paper Space provides convenience when using multiple drawing scales and details. In the three-dimensional world, you'll find Paper Space an essential tool for printing the same object from different angles simultaneously!

Try some of the exercises at the end of this lesson to make yourself more comfortable with Paper Space. Then move on to the next lesson where you'll discover more about how to work in Paper Space.

22.8 Exercises

1. Open the *needle.dwg* file in the C:\Steps\Lesson22 folder. Create the drawing configuration for plotting found in Figure 22.025. Some helpful information includes:
   1.1. The page size is A4 (metric – 210mm x 297mm).
   1.2. The title block is the *ISO-A4* file found in AutoCAD's Template folder. (You may need to adjust its position on the sheet.)
   1.3. The title block text is attributed.
   1.4. Watch your layers (place viewports on the **VPorts** layer).
   1.5. The radius of the large circle is 60mm; the radius of the smaller circle is 36mm.
   1.6. Remember that floating viewports can overlap.
   1.7. The scale of each viewport (from top to bottom) is 10:1, 8:1, 2:1.
   1.8. Fill in the title block as desired.
   1.9. Save the drawing as *MyNeedle* in the C:\Steps\Lesson23 folder.

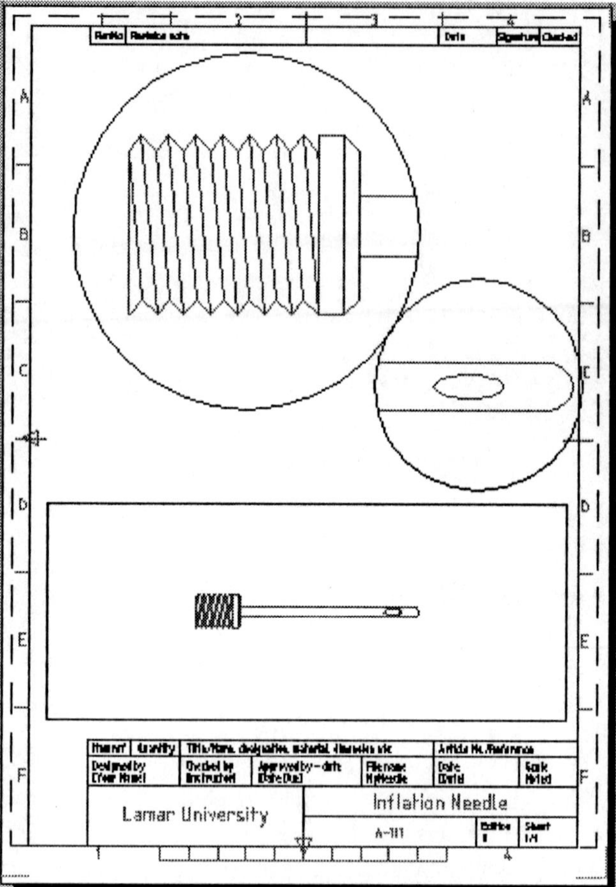

Figure 22.025: Inflation Needle

2. Open the *cable splitter.dwg* file in the C:\Steps\Lesson22 folder. Create the drawing configuration for plotting found in Figure 22.026. Some helpful information includes:
   2.1. The page size is 11 x 8½".
   2.2. Watch your layers (place viewports on the **VPorts** layer).
   2.3. The radius of the circle is 1.75".
   2.4. The title block is the *ANSI A title block* file found in AutoCAD's Template folder.
   2.5. The scale of each viewport is 4:1 (upper left), 4:1 (lower left), and 1:1 (right).
   2.6. Fill in the title block as desired.
   2.7. Save the drawing as *MySplitter* in the C:\Steps\Lesson23 folder.

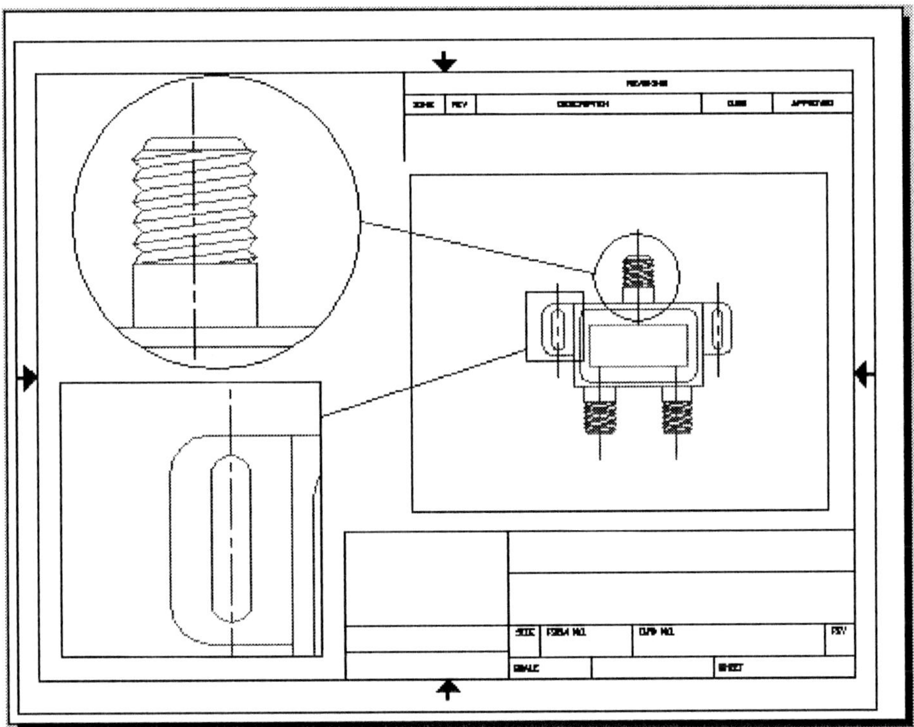

Figure 22.026: Cable Splitter.dwg

3. Open the *glass cutter.dwg* file in the C:\Steps\Lesson22 folder. Create the drawing configuration for plotting found in Figure 22.027. Some helpful information includes:
    3.1. The page size is 11" x 8½".
    3.2. Watch your layers (place viewports on the **VPorts** layer).
    3.3. The radius of the circle is 1.25".
    3.4. The title block is the *ANSI A title block* file found in AutoCAD's Template folder.
    3.5. The scale of each viewport is 4:1 (upper left), 2:1 (upper right), and 1:2 (lower).
    3.6. Fill in the title block as desired.
    3.7. Save the drawing as *MyCutter* in the C:\Steps\Lesson23 folder.

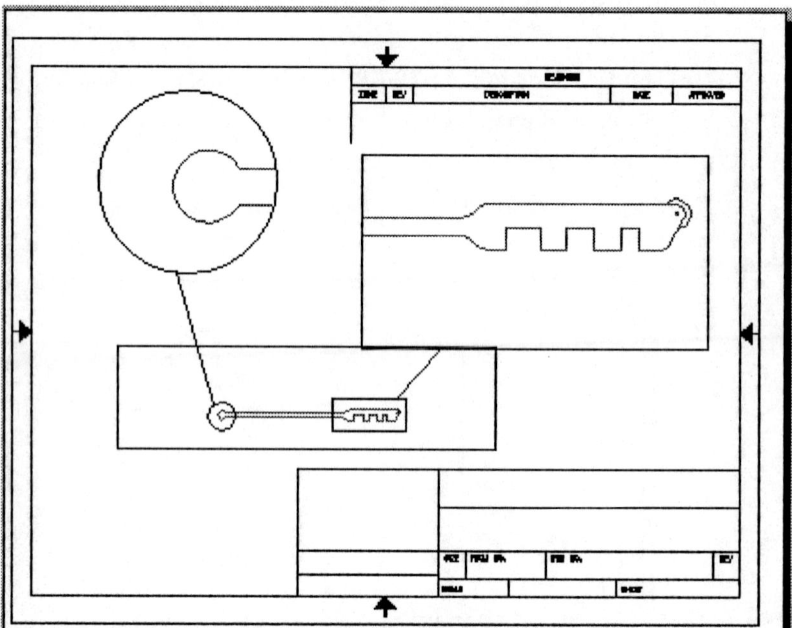

Figure 22027: Glass Cutter

4. Open the *spice rack.dwg* file in the C:\Steps\Lesson22 folder. Create the drawing configuration for plotting found in Figure 22.028. Some helpful information includes:
   4.1. The page size is 11" x 8½".
   4.2. Watch your layers (place viewports on the **VPorts** layer).
   4.3. The title block is the *ANSI A title block* file found in AutoCAD's Template folder.
   4.4. The scale of each viewport is 1:1 (upper left), 1:1 (lower left), and 6"=1' (right).
   4.5. Fill in the title block as desired.
   4.6. Save the drawing as *My Spice Rack* in the C:\Steps\Lesson23 folder.

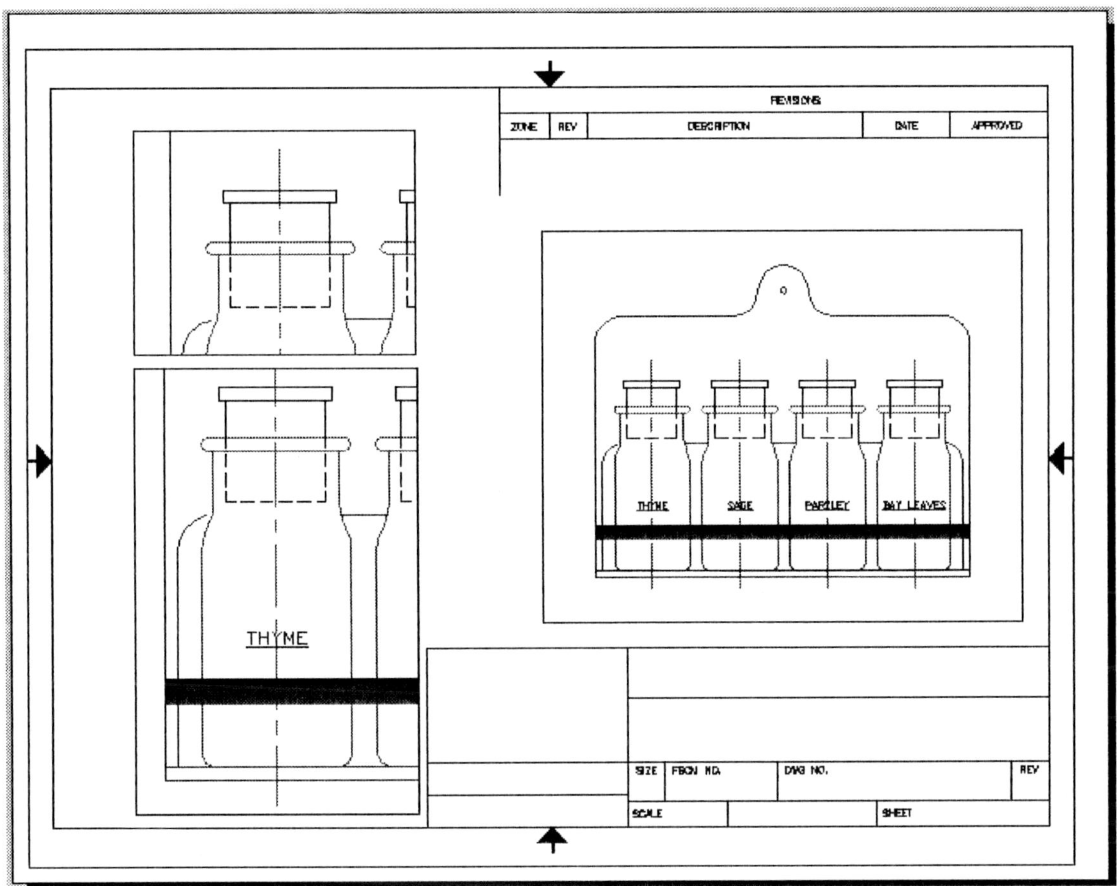

Figure 22.028: Spice Rack

5. Open the *motor-assbly.dwg* file in the C:\Steps\Lesson22 folder. Create the drawing configuration for plotting found in Figure 22.029. Some helpful information includes:
   5.1. The page size is 17" x 11". (Hint: If your printer won't support this sheet size, set up the page using **NONE** as the printer. AutoCAD will then make all of the sheet sizes available to you.)
   5.2. Watch your layers (place viewports on the **VPorts** layer).
   5.3. The title block is the *ANSI B title block* file found in AutoCAD's Template folder.
   5.4. The scale of each viewport is 1:2 (upper left), 1:2 (lower left), and 1:2 (right).
   5.5. Fill in the title block as desired.
   5.6. Save the drawing as *MyAssbly* in the C:\Steps\Lesson23 folder.

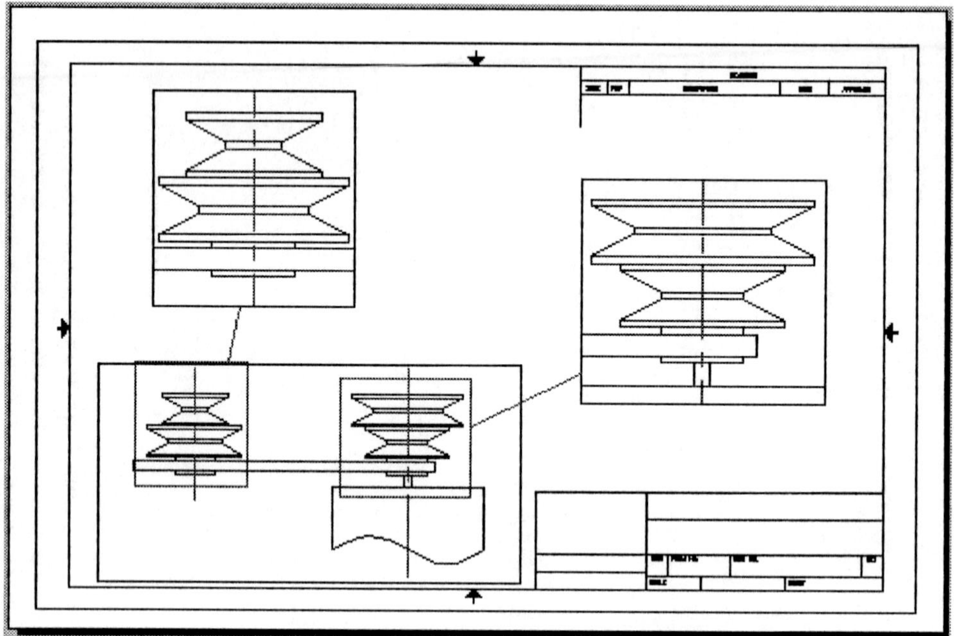

Figure 22.029: Motor Assembly

6. Open the *remote22.dwg* file in the C:\Steps\Lesson22 folder. Create the drawing configuration for plotting found in Figure 22.030. Some helpful information includes:
    6.1. The page size is 11" x 8½".
    6.2. Watch your layers (place viewports on the **VPorts** layer).
    6.3. The title block is the *ANSI A title block* file found in AutoCAD's Template folder.
    6.4. The scale of each viewport is 1:1 (upper left, center left, lower left), and 1:2 (right).
    6.5. Fill in the title block as desired.
    6.6. Save the drawing as *MyRemote* in the C:\Steps\Lesson23 folder.

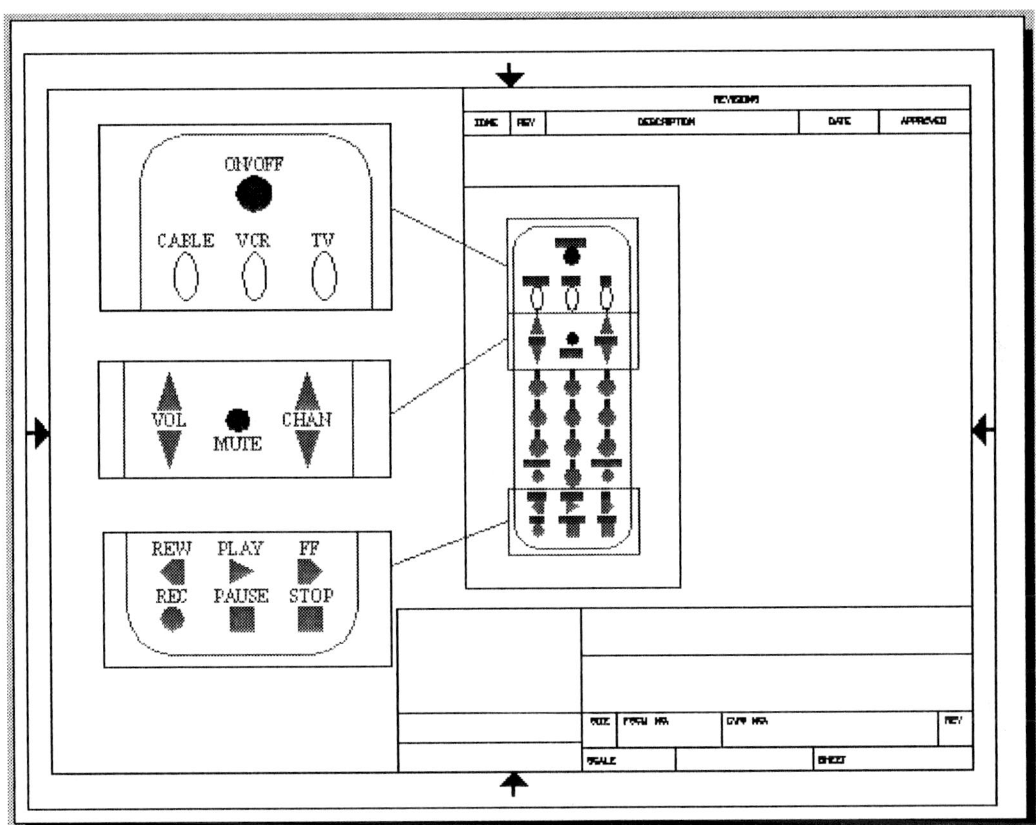

Figure 22.030: Remote

7. Open the *Cabin.dwg* file in the C:\Steps\Lesson22 folder. Create the drawing configuration for plotting found in Figure 22.031. Some helpful information includes:
   7.1. The page size is 34" x 22".
   7.2. Watch your layers (place viewports on the **VPorts** layer).
   7.3. The title block is the *ANSI D title block* file found in AutoCAD's Template folder.
   7.4. The scale of each viewport is 1:1 (upper left and upper right), and 6"=1' (lower left and lower right).
   7.5. Fill in the title block as desired.
   7.6. Save the drawing as *MyCabin* in the C:\Steps\Lesson23 folder.

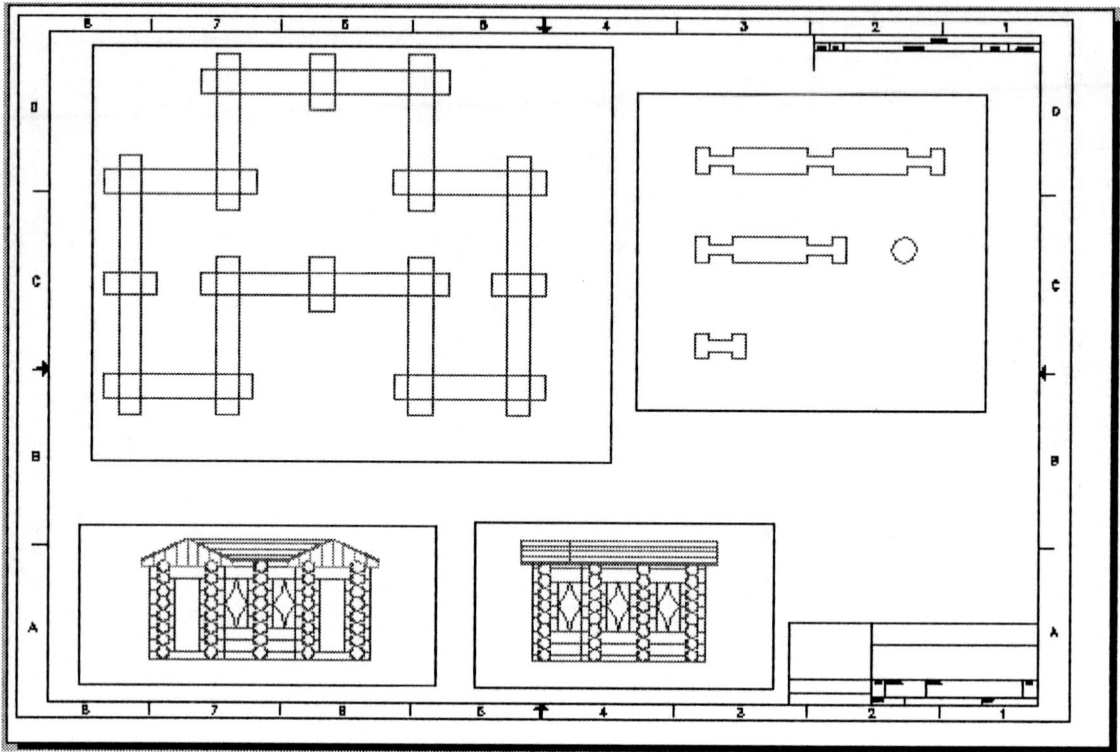

Figure 22.031: Cabin

8. Open the *Piping plan 22.dwg* file in the C:\Steps2\Lesson22 folder. Create the drawing configuration for plotting found in Figure 22.032. Some helpful information includes:
   8.1. The page size is 34" x 22".
   8.2. Watch your layers (place viewports on the **VPorts** layer).
   8.3. The title block is the *ANSI D title block* file found in AutoCAD's Template folder.
   8.4. The scale of each viewport is 3/8"=1' (main), and ¾"=1' (detail).
   8.5. Fill in the title block as desired.
   8.6. Save the drawing as *My Piping Plan* in the C:\Steps\Lesson23 folder.

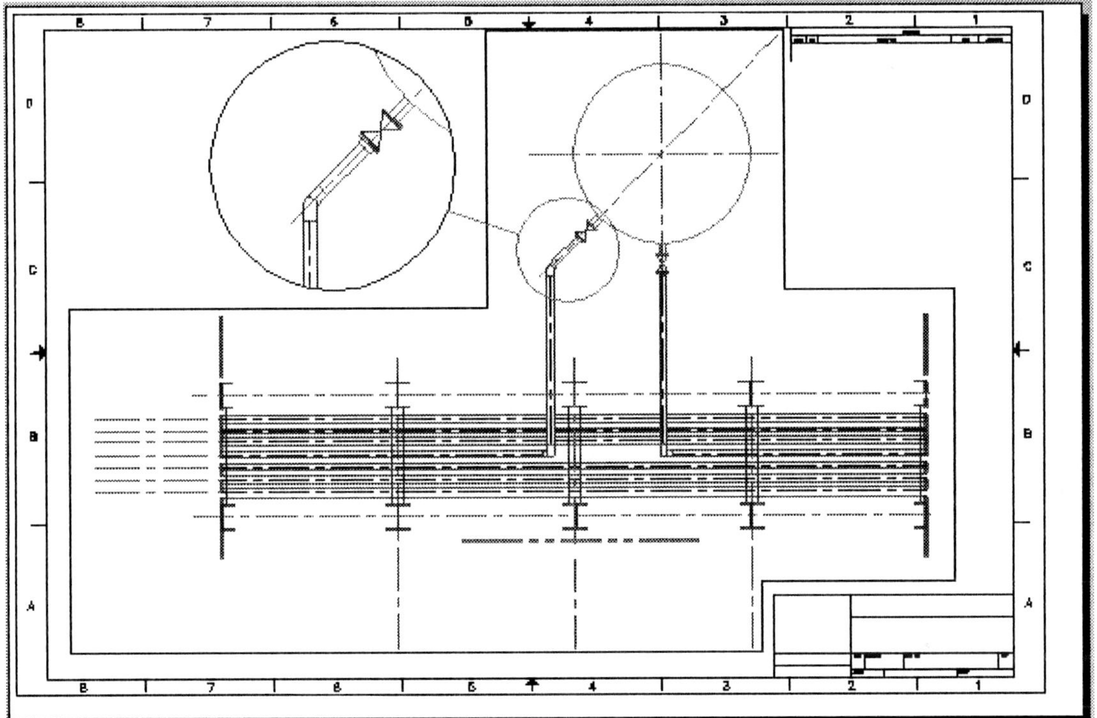

Figure 22.032: Piping Plan 1

22.9 **For Web-Based Review Questions, visit: http://www.uneedcad.com/2006/Files/06R22.pdf**

Lesson 23

Following this lesson, you will:

- ✓ *Know how to work with a Paper Space drawing*
  - *Know how to use layers in Paper Space*
  - *Know how to use text in Paper Space*
  - *Know how to dimension in Paper Space*
  - *Know how to plot a Paper Space drawing*
- ✓ *Know how to use **MVSetup** as a floating viewport editor*
- ✓ *Know how to use **Regenall** and **Redrawall** to refresh viewports*

The New Beginning Continues ...

You've seen how to show a drawing (a model) at different scales on the same page. But what'll happen to text and dimensions when the scale changes? What'll happen when you need to show information in a detail that you don't want to see on the plan (after all, that's why we use details)?

Up until now, you've determined text and dimension sizes using a mathematical formula based on the desired size at plot time and the drawing scale factor. An undiscovered error in your math might have wreaked havoc when you went to plot the drawing and discovered that all the text and dimension elements had to be resized.

In creating Paper Space, AutoCAD took these problems into consideration and provided some clever solutions. In Lesson 23, we'll investigate these solutions as well as some tricks to control the display both inside and outside of your viewports.

Let's begin.

23.1 Dimensioning and Paper Space

AutoCAD has two ways to create dimensions when Paper Space is involved – the *Olde Way* and the *New Way*. The *Olde Way* takes considerably more work and will, no doubt, eventually pass the way of Beta VCRs and the two-dollar bill. Still, you'll probably find yourself editing older drawings from time to time; knowledge of how it was done "in olden times" will be beneficial. You'll almost certainly prefer the New Way.

Let's take a look at both.

23.1.1 Dimensioning and Paper Space – the Olde Way

The Olde Way of setting up dimensioning for a Paper Space drawing is almost identical to setting up dimensioning for Model Space. The subtle difference involves the scale factor on the **Fit** tab of the Dimension Style Manager. For Model Space dimensioning, you must enter the scale factor, but for Paper Space dimensioning, you have to put a check in the **Scale dimensions to layout (paperspace)** check box. AutoCAD will scale the arrowheads, text, and other dimension objects accordingly.

The confusing part is answering the question of just where to place the dimensions. When thinking about dimensioning and Paper Space, it helps to remember that old adage: *Dance with the one what brung you*. In other words, if you draw it in Model Space, place your dimensions in Model Space; if you draw it in Paper Space, place your dimensions in Paper Space.

This will become clearer with an example. Let's step back in time, play some Beatles tunes on the 8-track, and try one.

Do This: 23.1.1.1 Adding Paper Space Dimensions – The Olde Way

I. Open the *MyFlr-pln23a.dwg* file in the C:\Steps\Lesson23 folder. (If this drawing wasn't completed in the last chapter, open the *flr-pln23a.dwg* file instead.)

II. Set the **DIM** layer current.

III. Follow these steps.

TOOLS	COMMAND SEQUENCE	STEPS
	Command: *ms*	1. Double click in the upper left viewport to activate it in Model Space.

Tools	Command Sequence	Steps
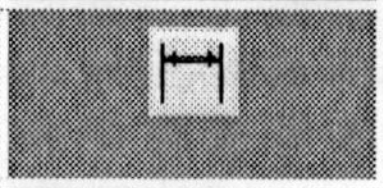	**Command:** ***ddim***	2. Call the Dimension Style Manager.
 ARCH Angular STANDARD		3. Select the **Arch** parent style…
 Modify...		4. …and pick the **Modify** button.
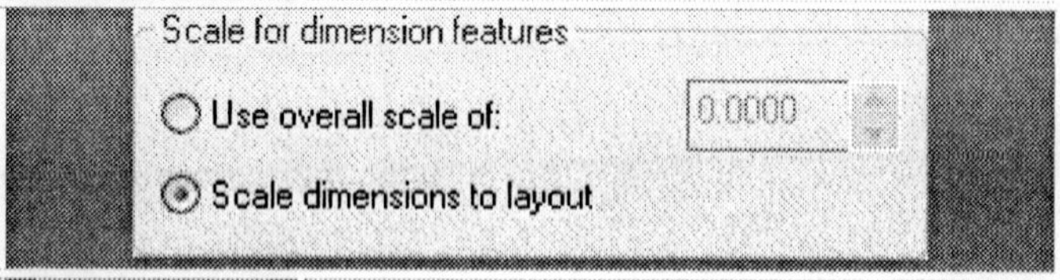 Scale for dimension features Use overall scale of: 0.0000 Scale dimensions to layout		5. In the **Scale for dimension features** frame of the **Fit** tab, place a bullet next to **Scale dimensions to layout**.
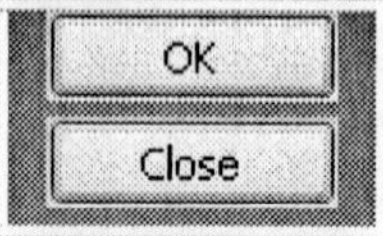 OK Close		6. Pick the **OK** button and then the **Close** button to continue. (The rest of the setup has been done for you.)
		7. Place the dimensions shown in Figure 23.001. (Use grips or the ***Stretch*** command to adjust the size and shape of the viewport as necessary.)

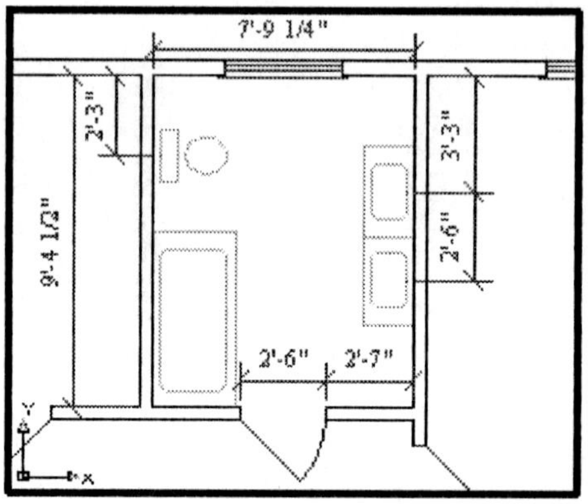

Figure 23.001

		8. Now place the dimensions in the round viewport as shown in Figure 23.002. (Hint: You may have to use ***DimTedit*** to help you.)

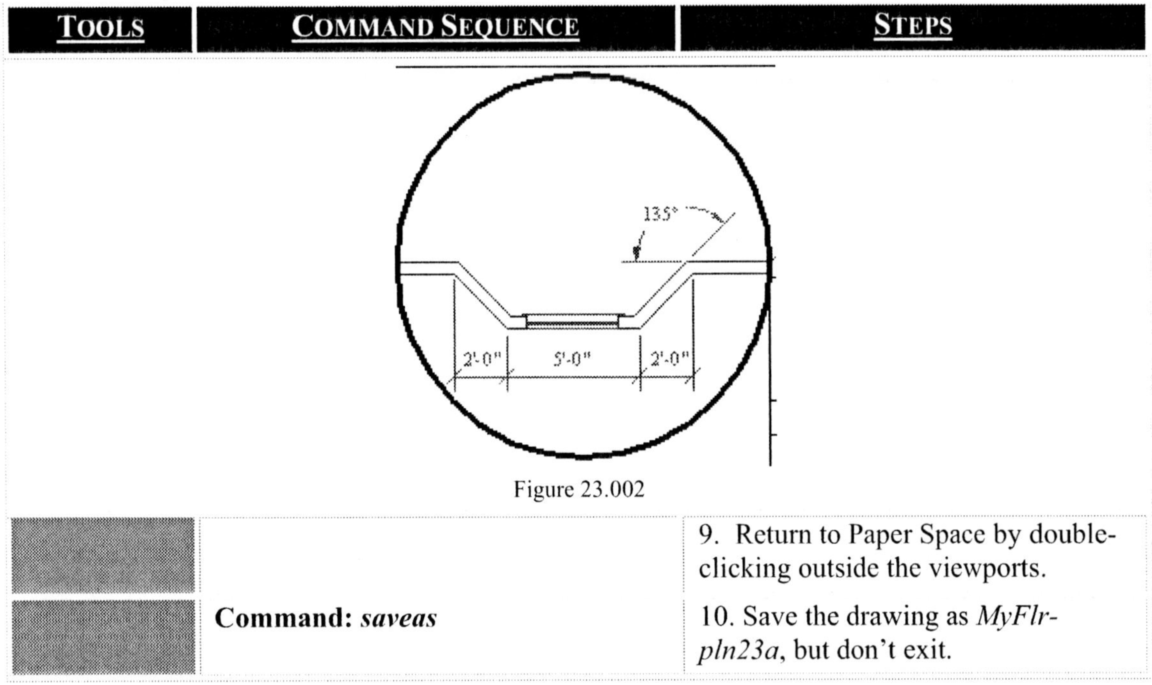

Figure 23.002

Tools	Command Sequence	Steps
		9. Return to Paper Space by double-clicking outside the viewports.
	Command: ***saveas***	10. Save the drawing as *MyFlr-pln23a*, but don't exit.

You'll find a useful tool on the status bar next to the Paper/Model toggle. Use the **Minimize Viewport** button to toggle between the view in an active viewport and the same view on the **Model** tab. Use the arrows on the sides to toggle between viewport views while still on the **Model** tab.	 Minimize Viewport Button

As you can see, the only problem presented by dimensioning in Paper Space was one of room. But if dimensions didn't fit into the viewport, you could use standard modifying tools (grips or the ***Stretch*** command) to resize it. (Remember that the viewport exists in Paper Space. So any modifying on the viewport itself must be done there.)

Did you notice that the dimensions appeared not only in the active viewport but also in the other viewports as well? (Look in the large viewport where you can see both the bath and bay window.) This presented a problem that users of older AutoCAD releases would fix with careful manipulation of layers. Regardless of how you place dimensions, the techniques used to manipulate those layers are still quite useful today for a host of other reasons. You'll learn the how-tos of layers in Paper Space in Section 23.2, but first, let's take a look at the modern approach to Paper Space dimensioning.

23.1.2 Dimensioning and Paper Space – the New Way

Despite the name, the new way of Paper Space dimensioning really involves no new techniques at all. With some programming adjustments, you simply place dimensions in Paper Space rather than Model Space (regardless of where the objects to be dimensioned reside). AutoCAD automatically interprets in which space the objects exist and adjusts the dimension accordingly. Using this new program, all dimensions exist in Paper Space – even if the object dimensioned exists in Model Space.

You should remember some general rules when using this new approach:

- The **Dimassoc** system variable must be set to **2**. Since this is the default for new drawings, you won't have a problem with them. However, if you're working with a drawing created in an earlier release, you'll have to change the variable setting.

- The new programming may have a problem recognizing multilines. If this occurs, you'll find it necessary to either explode the multilines or use the Olde Way as detailed in Section 23.1.1.

Do This: 23.1.2.1	Adding Paper Space Dimensions – The New Way

I. Open the *flr-pln23a-new.dwg* file in the C:\Steps\Lesson23 folder.

II. Be sure the **Dimassoc** system variable is set to **2**.

III. Be sure you're in Paper Space (the toggle on the status bar should read **PAPER**).

IV. Follow these steps.

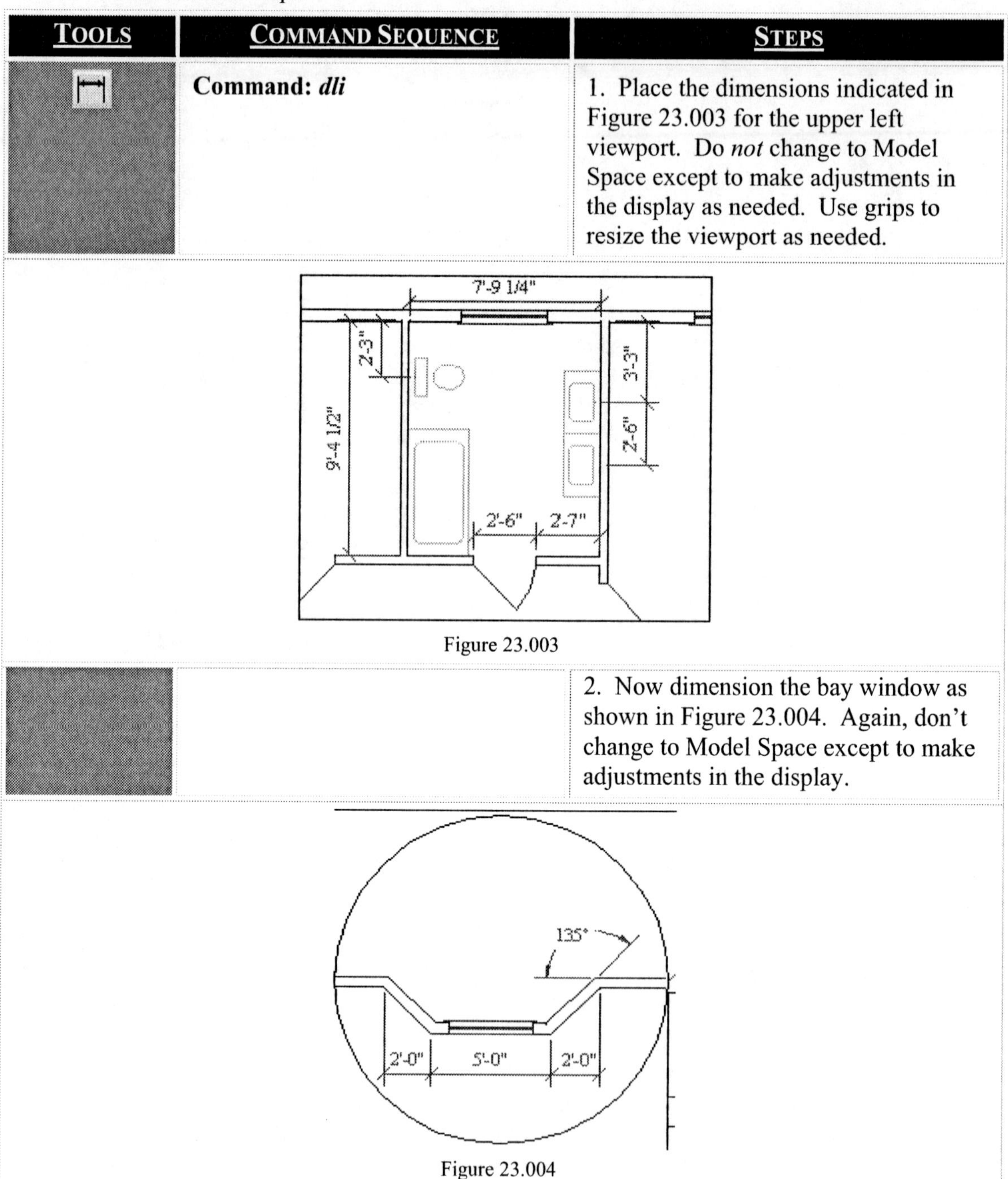

TOOLS	COMMAND SEQUENCE	STEPS
	Command: *dli*	1. Place the dimensions indicated in Figure 23.003 for the upper left viewport. Do *not* change to Model Space except to make adjustments in the display as needed. Use grips to resize the viewport as needed.

Figure 23.003

TOOLS	COMMAND SEQUENCE	STEPS
		2. Now dimension the bay window as shown in Figure 23.004. Again, don't change to Model Space except to make adjustments in the display.

Figure 23.004

TOOLS	COMMAND SEQUENCE	STEPS
		3. Now Zoom all and look at the drawing. Compare it to the drawing you did in the last exercise (reopen that drawing if necessary and view the two side by side).
	Command: ***qsave***	4. Save the drawing and exit.

Did you notice the difference between the two drawings?

You should have seen that the dimensions placed in the first exercise appeared both in the viewport being dimensioned and in the full viewport at right. This happens because the dimensions exist in Model Space, which appears through the viewports. In the drawing you created in the second exercise, the dimensions appear only in the viewports where you created them. These dimensions, although detailing objects that live in Model Space, exist in Paper Space.

It won't be necessary to manipulate layers to hide dimensions in the second drawing, but you'll have to do so in the first. You'll see how in our next section.

23.2 The Benefits of Layers in Paper Space

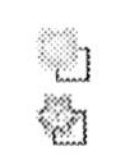

Figure 23.005

One of the real wonders of Paper Space has to be the ability to manipulate layers in a single viewport independently of other viewports. In other words, you can freeze (or thaw) layers in one viewport while leaving them thawed (or frozen) in another! The trick lies in using the ***VPLayer*** command instead of the ***Layer*** command in your manipulations. Alternately, you can use the **Freeze or Thaw in Current Viewport** column on the **Layer Control** box. The symbols for thawed or frozen layers in the current viewport can be seen in Figure 23.005.

The ***VPLayer*** command sequence goes like this:

> **Command:** ***vplayer***
>
> **Enter an option [?/Freeze/Thaw/Reset/ Newfrz/Vpvisdflt]:** ***[tell AutoCAD what you want to do]***

Let's look at each option.

- The **?** option prompts you to select a viewport. Then AutoCAD shows the layers that are frozen in that particular viewport. If the command is given from Model Space, AutoCAD will switch to Paper Space just long enough to complete the procedure.
- The **Freeze/Thaw** options allow you to enter the name(s) of a layer(s), and then prompts you to select the viewports in which the layer(s) will be frozen or thawed. The command sequence looks like this:

  > **Enter layer name(s) to freeze or <select objects>:**
  >
  > **Enter an option [All/Select/Current] <Current>:** ***[tell AutoCAD to freeze/thaw the layer in all the viewports, Selected viewports, or the Current viewport]***

- The **Reset** option sets layers to their default settings. Use the **Vpvisdflt** option to create the default settings. The **Vpvisdflt** option will prompt as follows:

  > **Enter layer name(s) to change viewport visibility or <select objects>:** ***[name the layer(s) – use commas to separate several layer names]***
  >
  > **Enter a viewport visibility option [Frozen/Thawed] <Thawed>:** ***[tell AutoCAD how you wish this layer to behave by default]***

- The **Newfrz** option will create a new layer that is frozen in all viewports.

Let's take a look at how layers interact with viewports.

Do This: 23.2.1	Manipulating Layers in Floating Viewports

I. Go back to the *MyFlr-pln23a.dwg* file in the C:\Steps\Lesson23 folder. Reopen it if necessary.

II. Be sure you're in Paper Space.

III. Follow these steps.

TOOLS	COMMAND SEQUENCE	STEPS
No Button Available	**Command:** ***vplayer***	1. Enter the ***VPLayer*** command. There's no hotkey, button, or pull-down menu selection for this command.
? Freeze Thaw Reset Newfrz Vpvisdflt	**Enter an option [?/Freeze/Thaw/Reset/ Newfrz/Vpvisdflt]:** ***f*** **Enter layer name(s) to freeze or <select objects>:** ***dim,fixtures***	2. Tell AutoCAD you wish to freeze the **DIM** and **FIXTURES** layers.
	Enter an option [All/Select/Current] <Current>: ***s*** **Select objects:** ***[select the right viewport]***	3. AutoCAD asks you to identify the viewport in which you want the layers frozen. Tell it that you'll select one, and then select the right viewport.
	Select objects: ***[enter]*** **Enter an option [?/Freeze/Thaw/Reset/Newfrz/ Vpvisdflt]:** ***[enter]***	4. Confirm the selection and complete the command. The drawing now looks like Figure 23.006.

TOOLS	COMMAND SEQUENCE	STEPS

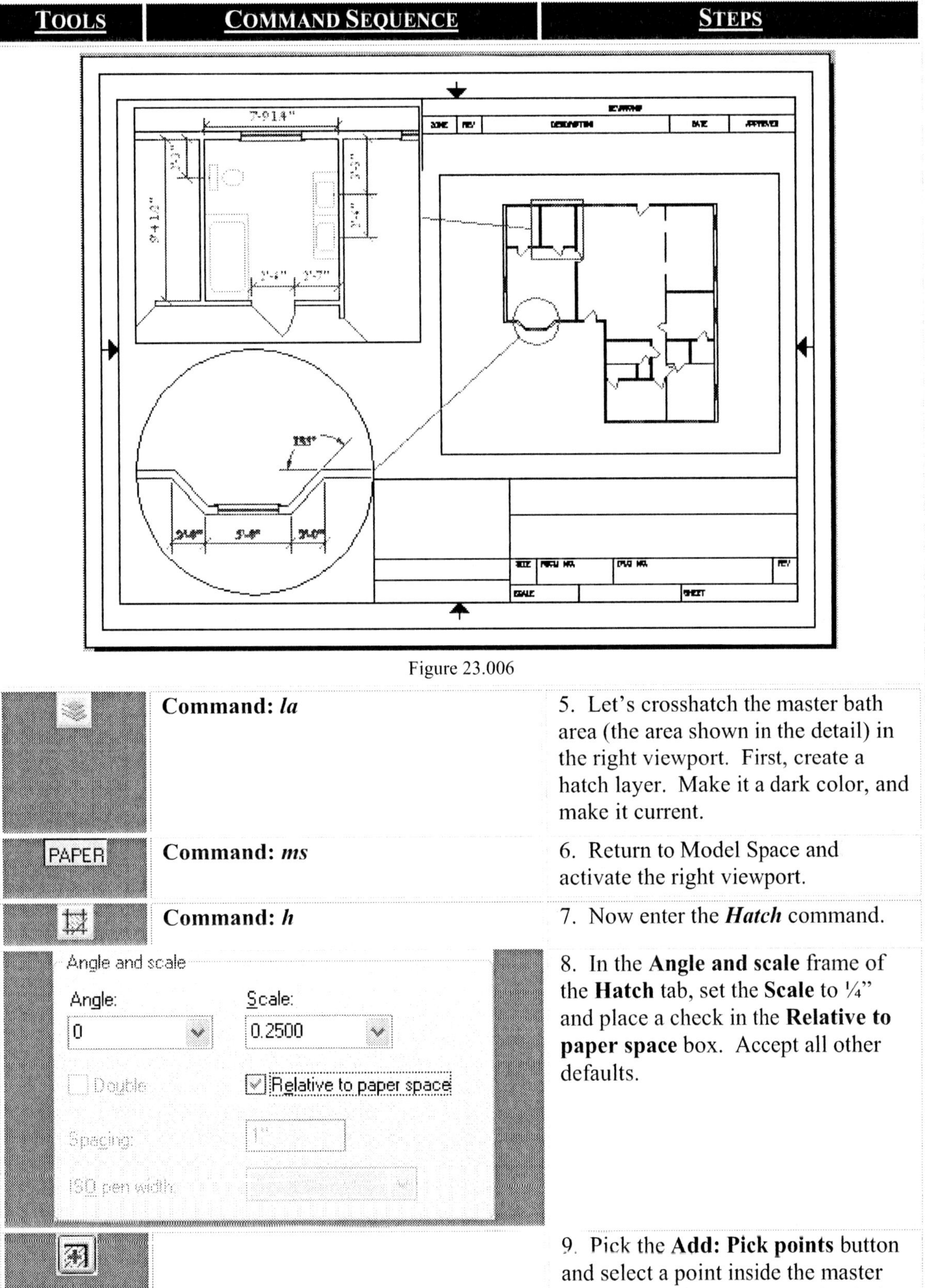

Figure 23.006

TOOLS	COMMAND SEQUENCE	STEPS
	Command: ***la***	5. Let's crosshatch the master bath area (the area shown in the detail) in the right viewport. First, create a hatch layer. Make it a dark color, and make it current.
PAPER	**Command:** ***ms***	6. Return to Model Space and activate the right viewport.
	Command: ***h***	7. Now enter the ***Hatch*** command.
Angle and scale Angle: 0 Scale: 0.2500 Double Relative to paper space Spacing: 1" ISO pen width:		8. In the **Angle and scale** frame of the **Hatch** tab, set the **Scale** to ¼" and place a check in the **Relative to paper space** box. Accept all other defaults.
		9. Pick the **Add: Pick points** button and select a point inside the master bath. Hit ***enter*** to return to the dialog box.

TOOLS	COMMAND SEQUENCE	STEPS
OK		10. Pick the **OK** button to continue. Notice that the hatch pattern appears in both viewports that show the master bath.
		11. Let's try an easier way to freeze layers. Make the upper left viewport current.
0 BORDER Defpoints DIM DOORS FIXTURES Hatch TEXT Title Block VPORTS WALLS WINDOWS		12. Now use the viewport toggle in the **Layer Control** box to freeze the **Hatch** layer in the current viewport. Your drawing looks like Figure 23.007.

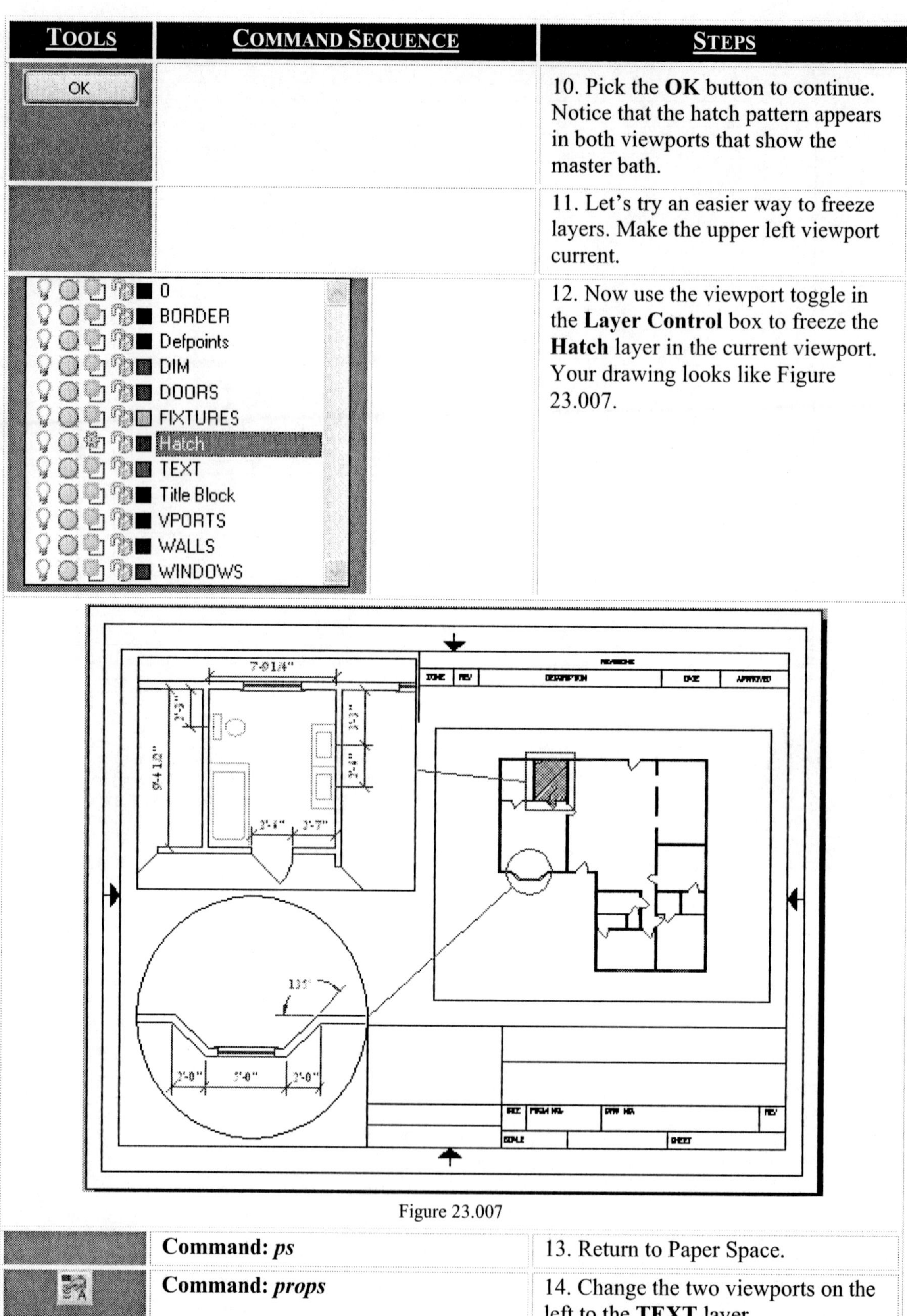

Figure 23.007

TOOLS	COMMAND SEQUENCE	STEPS
	Command: ***ps***	13. Return to Paper Space.
	Command: ***props***	14. Change the two viewports on the left to the **TEXT** layer.

Tools	Command Sequence	Steps
		15. Now freeze the **VPORTS** layer. Your drawing now looks like Figure 23.008.

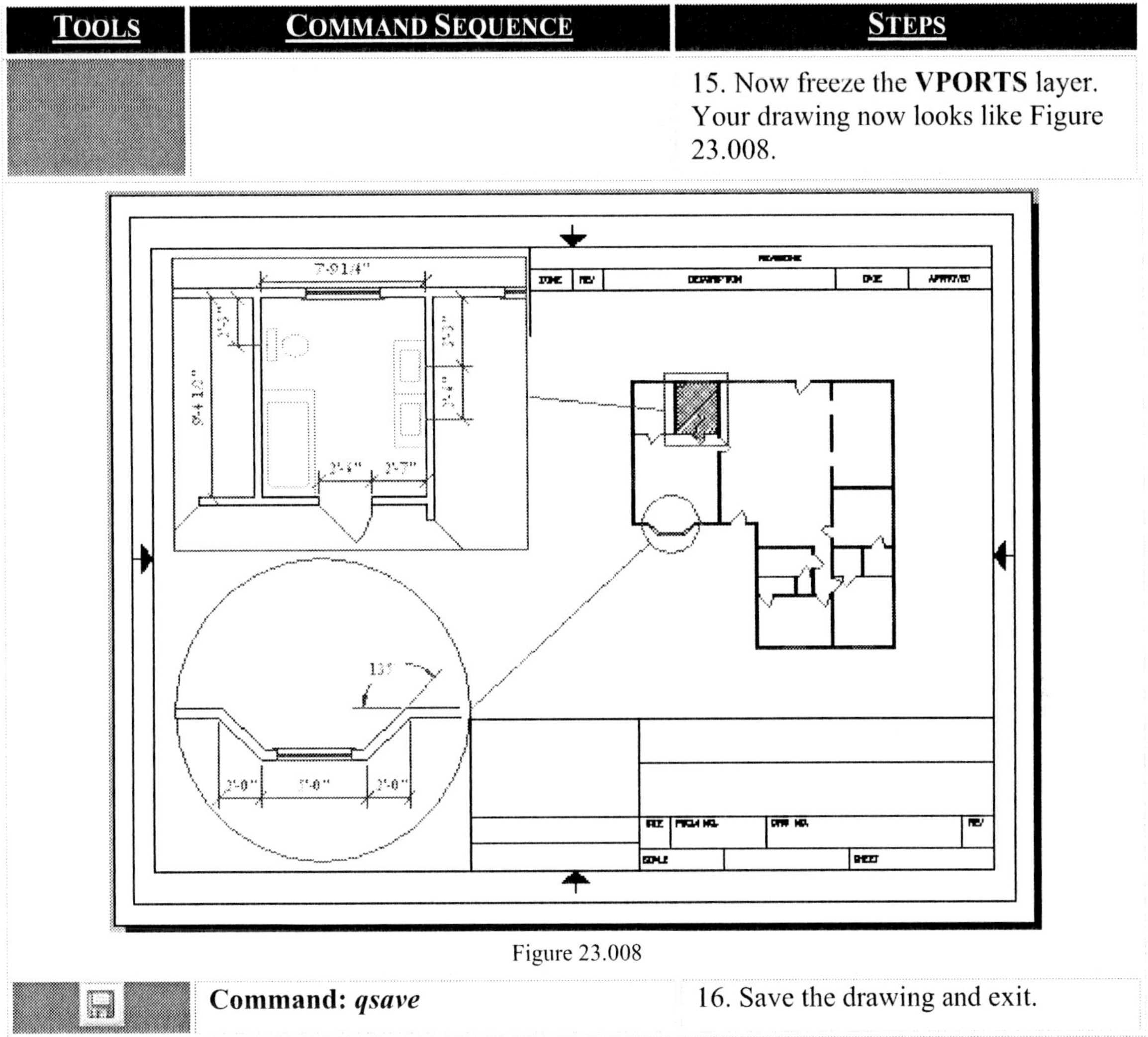

Figure 23.008

Tools	Command Sequence	Steps
	Command: ***qsave***	16. Save the drawing and exit.

This is a much finer image for plotting, but there's still more to do. We must add some callouts to the drawing before we plot it.

23.3 Using Text in Paper Space

In a drawing that uses Paper Space, place all text in Paper Space unless it's part of the model. The reasoning behind this general rule is this: *Placing text in Paper Space is easier than placing text in Model Space.*

Let me explain.

Remember how difficult you found sizing text in Model Space? You had to consider the size that you wanted the text to be at plot time and the scale at which you would plot. Then you had to work some mathematical wizardry to determine the size of the text to use in your drawing. You had to do all of this before placing any text.

Try this formula to determine text height in Paper Space:

The height you want the text to be when you plot = the height you make your text

It just can't get any simpler than that!

But wait! AutoCAD has included a tool that greatly simplifies the Paper Space to Model Space (and vice versa) translation of text sizes. When you determine that text simply must go into Model Space, use the ***SpaceTrans*** command to help you determine its size. This transparent command works anytime AutoCAD asks you for a size. Look at its sequence (this sequence is seen when the command is given from Model Space):

Command: ***dt***

Current text style: "TIMES" Text height: 0'-0"

Specify start point of text or [Justify/Style]:

Specify height <0'-0">: ***'spacetrans***

>>Specify paper space distance <1">: ***[tell AutoCAD how large you'd like the text to be in Paper Space]***

Resuming TEXT command.

Specify height <0'-0">: ***[AutoCAD automatically translates the size into Model Space increments]***

Specify rotation angle of text <0>: ***[continue with the* Text *command]***

Enter text:

Spacetrans determines the appropriate Model Space size for the text and responds to the Specify height prompt for you. (The prompts are slightly different when translating from Paper Space to Model Space.)

Note: **Spacetrans** is *not* available on the **Model** tab. (Oh, *that's* why we didn't cover it earlier!)

You'll see this in action in our next exercise. Let's add a bit of text to our drawing.

Do This: 23.3.1	Adding Text in Paper Space

I. Open the *flr-pln23b-new.dwg* file in the C:\Steps\Lesson23 folder.

II. Be sure you're in Paper Space.

III. Follow these steps.

TOOLS	COMMAND SEQUENCE	STEPS
AI	**Command:** ***dt***	1. On the **TEXT** layer, add the callouts shown in Figure 23.009. Large text is 3/16" and smaller text is 1/8". (Use the **Times** text style that has already been set up for you.)

TOOLS	COMMAND SEQUENCE	STEPS

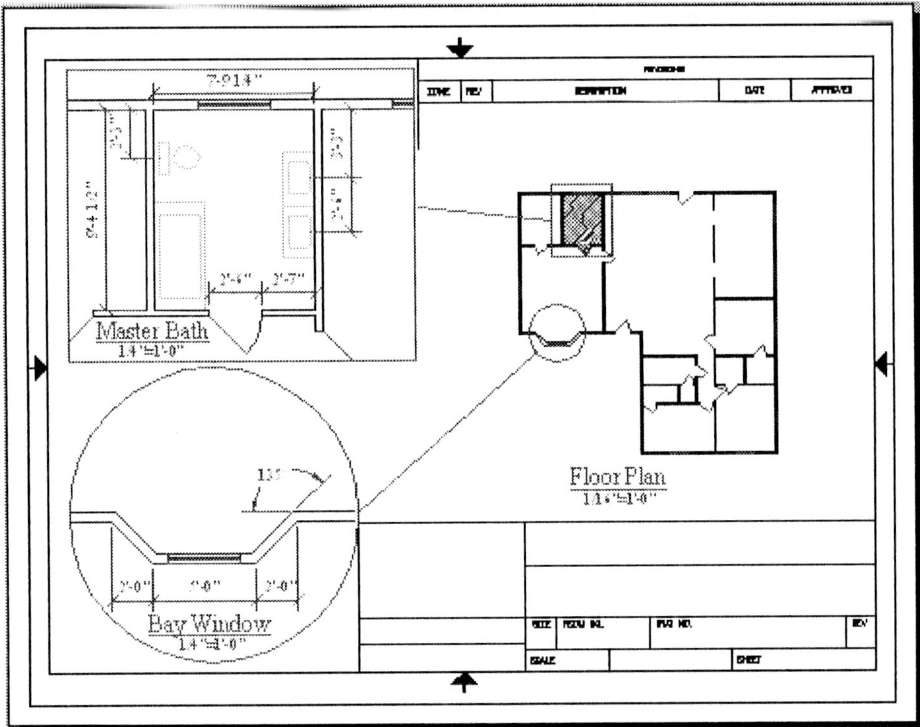

Figure 23.009

2. Now fill out the title block as shown in Figure 23.010. Text sizes are ¼", 3/16", and 1/8". Feel free to use your own school's name.

Figure 23.010 (title block text)

Lamar University

Tara II Building Design
Sample Layout

AutoCAD Text
One Step at a Time

SIZE A | FSCM NO. XX-1b | DWG NO. A-231 | REV 0

SCALE Noted | [Your Name] | SHEET 1 of 1

Figure 23.010

TOOLS	COMMAND SEQUENCE	STEPS
	Command: ***qsave***	3. Save the drawing but don't exit.
PAPER	**Command:** ***ms***	4. Now let's add some text to Model Space. We'll have AutoCAD size it for us. First, activate Model Space and make the right viewport current.
AI	**Command:** ***dt*** **Current text style: "TIMES"** **Text height: 0'-0 1/8"** **Specify start point of text or [Justify/ Style]:** ***c*** **Specify center point of text:**	5. Begin the ***Text*** command and center the text in the den (refer to Figure 23.011).

Tools	Command Sequence	Steps
	Specify height <0'-0 1/8">: ***'spacetrans***	6. Now enter the ***SpaceTrans*** command transparently.
	>>Specify paper space distance <1">: ***3/32*** **Resuming TEXT command.** **Specify height <0'-0 1/8">: 18.00000000**	7. Tell AutoCAD to make the text height 3/32". AutoCAD makes the translation and enters the text height for you.
	Specify rotation angle of text <0>: ***[enter]***	8. Complete the command, entering the text ***Den*** as shown in Figure 23.011.

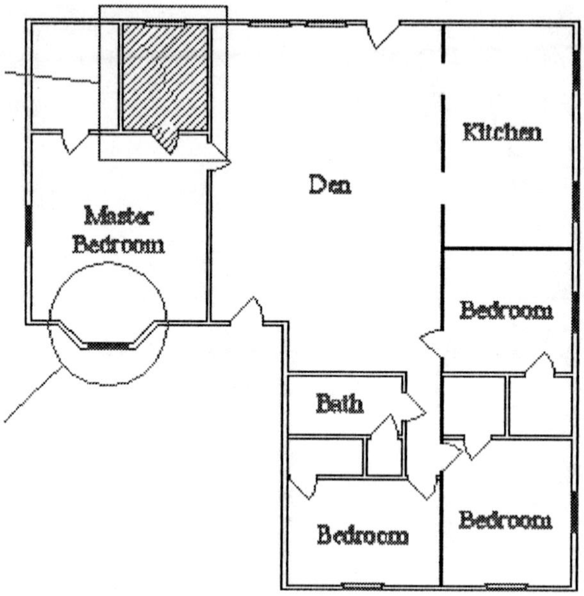

Figure 23.011

		9. Complete the text entries as detailed in Figure 23.011.
	Command: ***qsave***	10. Save the drawing.

Take a moment and toggle between the **Model** tab and the Layout (**Tara II Layout**) tab of your drawing. Notice which objects exist as part of the model and which don't. Only those objects that you created through the viewports in Model Space exist on the **Model** tab. Everything else exists as part of the paper on which you'll plot your model.

Once the dimensions are drawn and the text placed – the *i*'s dotted and the *t*'s crossed – it's time to plot the drawing. Let's look at that next.

23.4 Plotting the Layout

It's funny that, after all the setting up, creating, and manipulating, it always comes back to getting it on paper. Perhaps that's why AutoCAD has put so much time and money into making printing as user-friendly as possible.

Printing a layout isn't very different from printing Model Space (although it is a bit easier). Let's print our floor plan layout.

Do This: 23.4.1	Printing/Plotting the Layout

I. Be sure you're still in the *flr-pln23b-new.dwg* file in the C:\Steps\Lesson23 folder. If not, please open it now.

II. Follow these steps.

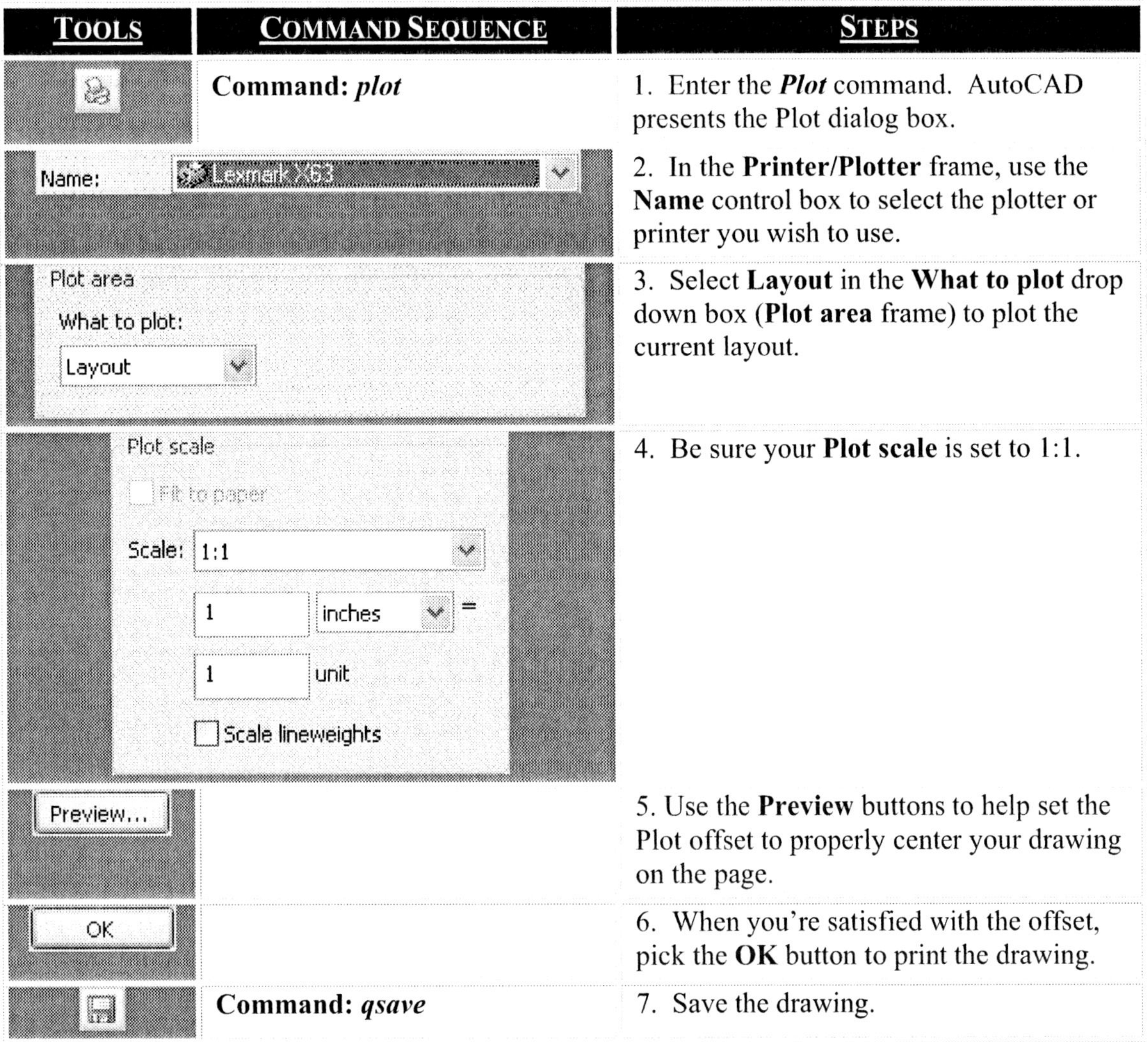

TOOLS	COMMAND SEQUENCE	STEPS
	Command: ***plot***	1. Enter the ***Plot*** command. AutoCAD presents the Plot dialog box.
Name: Lexmark X63		2. In the **Printer/Plotter** frame, use the **Name** control box to select the plotter or printer you wish to use.
Plot area What to plot: Layout		3. Select **Layout** in the **What to plot** drop down box (**Plot area** frame) to plot the current layout.
Plot scale Fit to paper Scale: 1:1 1 inches = 1 unit Scale lineweights		4. Be sure your **Plot scale** is set to 1:1.
Preview...		5. Use the **Preview** buttons to help set the Plot offset to properly center your drawing on the page.
OK		6. When you're satisfied with the offset, pick the **OK** button to print the drawing.
	Command: ***qsave***	7. Save the drawing.

Use a drafting scale to check the dimensions on your plot. How did you do?

As with any print job, it's inevitable that something must be modified after the plot. Despite the ability to preview a drawing before plotting, some things simply don't show up until you see it on paper.

You can make changes in Model Space through the viewports or on the **Model** tab. You can make changes in Paper Space on the **Layout** tab. However, changes to the viewports themselves may require some additional tools. We'll look at these next.

23.5 Tweaking the Layout

Generally speaking, modifying the layout is as easy as modifying any other part of a drawing. The basic modifying tools – ***Move***, ***Copy***, ***Stretch***, and so forth – will work in Paper Space as well as Model Space. However, adjusting the view through a viewport or adjusting the shape or scale of a viewport will require some new modifying procedures. These include two commands: ***MVSetup*** and ***VPClip***.

23.5.1 Modifying Viewports with the *MVSetup* Command

AutoCAD originally designed the ***MVSetup*** command to perform the same function as the layout wizard. Using the single ***MVSetup*** command, we can insert the title block and create/scale the viewports just as we did with the wizard. But the wizard is so much easier to use than ***MVSetup***'s command line approach that ***MVSetup*** might have been removed. But AutoCAD chose to leave it (it's so hard to lose a good tool) because of its use as a modifying tool.

We'll look at all parts of the ***MVSetup*** command, but we'll use the command as a modifying tool.

The command sequence looks like this:

> **Command:** ***mvsetup***
>
> **Enable paper space? [No/Yes] <Y>:**

When entered while on the **Model** tab, the ***MVSetup*** command initially asks if you wish to enable Paper Space. What follows depends on your answer.

- If you respond ***No***, you'll set up the drawing for Model Space. AutoCAD prompts as follows:

  Enter units type [Scientific/Decimal/Engineering/Architectural/Metric]:

  Tell AutoCAD which type of units you wish to use. AutoCAD will respond with a list of scale factors available. Select one. Then AutoCAD will ask for the width and height of the sheet of paper to which you will plot. When it has all the information, it will place a polyline border around the limits of the drawing.

  This approach is a bit quicker for someone who is comfortable with AutoCAD and the keyboard, but an AutoCAD novice might wish to use the **Setup Wizard** in lieu of the command line.

- If you respond ***Yes*** to the **Enable paper space** prompt (or if you enter the command while on a layout tab), AutoCAD flips to the first layout tab, creates a single viewport (if none currently exist), and then prompts as follows:

  Enter an option [Align/Create/Scale viewports/Options/Title block/Undo]:

  The first line simply lets you know what AutoCAD is doing.

  The last line presents several options. These include:

  - The **Align** option allows you to align a view in one viewport with the view in another.
  - **Create** allows you to create (or delete) floating viewports. It prompts:

    Enter option [Delete objects/Create viewports/Undo] <Create>:

    - The **Delete objects** option, of course, allows you to remove a viewport.
    - The default option – **Create** – offers these choices:
      - **Available layout options: . . .**

        0: None ***[for no viewports]***

        1: Single ***[for a single viewport]***

2: **Std. Engineering** ***[This option creates four viewports with standard three-dimensional views (plan, front, side, isometric).]***

3: **Array of Viewports** ***[This option allows you to create a rectangular array of viewports – you define the number of rows and columns to use and the spacing between them]***

- **Enter layout number to load or [Redisplay]:** ***[Make your selection or hit enter to return to MVSetup's first option line.]***

- Scaling the viewports can be done one at a time or uniformly. You'll find setting the scale one viewport at a time more easily accomplished using the **Viewport Scale** control box on the Viewports toolbar, or the ***Zoom*** command. If you select more than one viewport to scale, AutoCAD will prompt as follows:

  Set zoom scale factors for viewports. Interactively/<Uniform>:

  Set the ratio of paper space units to model space units...

  Enter the number of paper space units <1.0>: ***[usually hit enter]***

  Enter the number of model space units <1.0>: ***[enter a scale factor]***

- The **Options** prompt allows you to set the following:

  Enter an option [Layer/LImits/Units/ Xref] <exit>:

  Most of these are obvious. You can set the current layer and Paper Space units, or you can allow AutoCAD to set the limits according to the drawing you've created. (We'll look at Xrefs in Lesson 25.)

- The **Title Block** option allows you to insert a title block in Paper Space.

Let's change the scale in one of our viewports. We'll use the ***MVSetup*** command to change the actual scale. Then we'll use more conventional commands to adjust the viewport.

Do This: 23.5.1.1	Using MVSetup as a Modifying Tool

I. Be sure you're still in the *flr-pln23b-new.dwg* file in the C:\Steps\Lesson23 folder. If not, please open it now.

II. Follow these steps.

TOOLS	COMMAND SEQUENCE	STEPS
No Button Available	**Command:** ***mvsetup***	1. Enter the ***MVsetup*** command.
Align Create Scale viewports Options Title block Undo	**Enter an option [Align/Create/Scale viewports/Options/Title block/Undo]:** ***S*** **Select the viewports to scale...** **Select objects:** ***[select the upper left viewport]*** **Select objects:** ***[enter]***	2. Choose the **Scale viewports** option and select the upper left viewport (the master bath). Hit ***enter*** to complete the selection.
	Set the ratio of paper space units to model space units... **Enter the number of paper space units <1.0>:** ***[enter]***	3. Now you'll set the ratio of Paper Space to Model Space. Accept **1** as the number of **paper space units**.

TOOLS	COMMAND SEQUENCE	STEPS
	Enter the number of model space units <1.0>: ***64***	4. We'll change the scale from ¼"=1'-0" to 3/16"=1'-0". Enter the scale factor for the 3/16" scale (***64***). Notice how everything is rescaled.
	Enter an option [Align/Create/Scale viewports/Options/Title block/Undo]: ***[enter]***	5. Complete the command. Notice that the dimensions automatically update – even though they're in Paper Space.
	Command: ***dimtedit***	6. Use ***DimTedit*** or grips to adjust the locations of the dimensions as needed.
		7. Using grips or other modifying tools, resize and reposition the viewport. Then edit the text as shown in Figure 23.012.

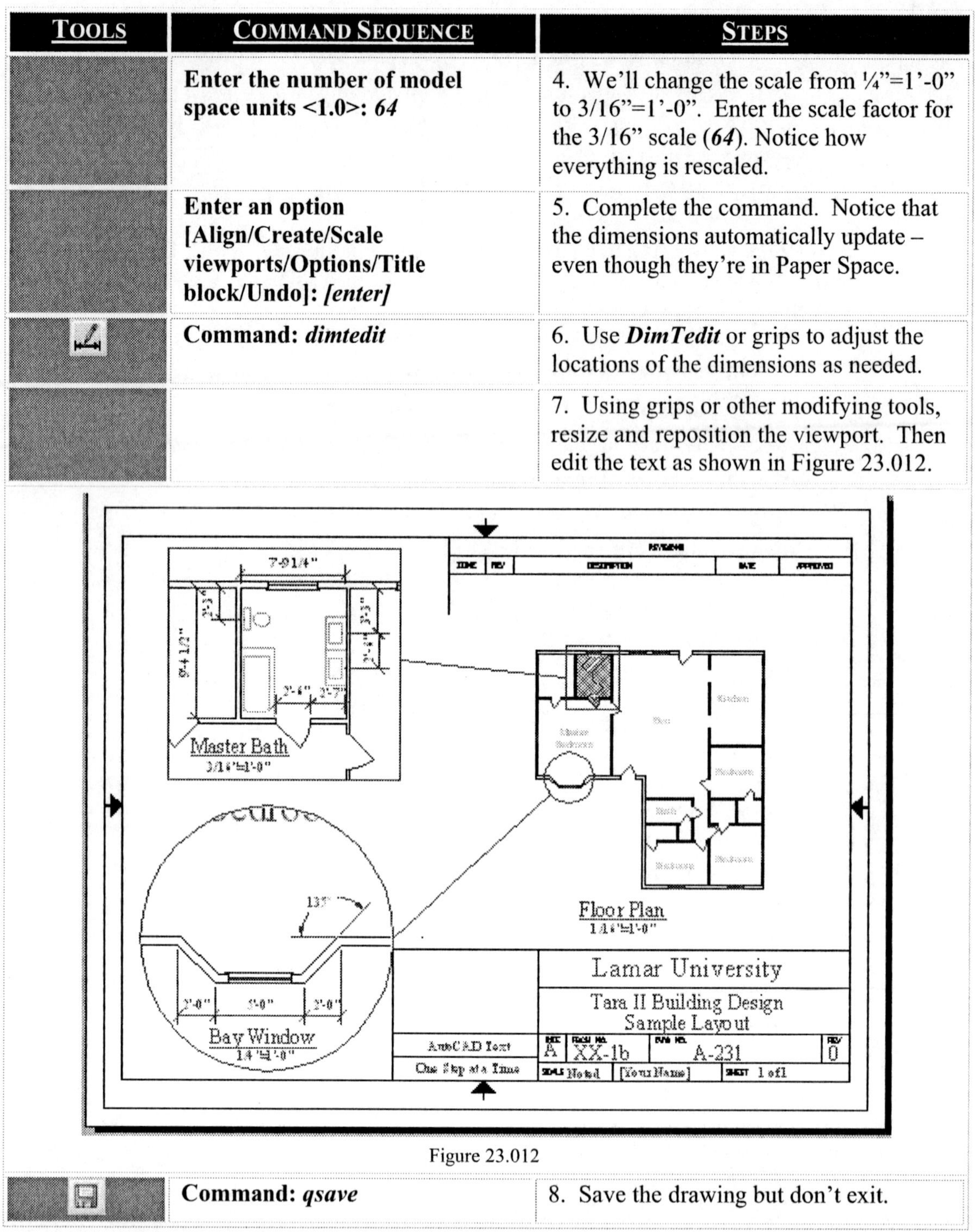

Figure 23.012

TOOLS	COMMAND SEQUENCE	STEPS
	Command: ***qsave***	8. Save the drawing but don't exit.

> When working with several viewports, you may notice that the ***Redraw*** and ***Regen*** commands only affect the one that is currently active. To use these commands to refresh all of the viewport simultaneously, use the ***Redrawall*** and ***Regenall*** commands.

Now that we've created our viewports and set up Paper Space, let's see what comes next.

23.5.2 Changing the Shape of a Viewport with the *VPClip* Command

Occasionally you'll discover that the shape you chose for your viewport doesn't satisfy the needs of that particular view. If you created the viewport using the **Object** option of the ***MView*** command to convert a polygon, closed polyline, or spline to a viewport, you can use the ***PEdit*** or ***Splinedit*** commands to reshape the viewport. If you used any other method to create the viewport, modifying the shape won't be so easy.

Fortunately, AutoCAD has provided the ***VPClip*** command. You can use this to reshape the view in a standard rectangular viewport. The command sequence looks like this:

> **Command:** ***vpclip***
>
> **Select viewport to clip:** ***[pick the viewport you wish to reshape (clip)]***
>
> **Select clipping object or [Polygonal/Delete] <Polygonal>:** ***[enter]***
>
> **Specify start point:**
>
> **Specify next point or [Arc/Length/Undo]:** ***[this line operates like the* PLine *command and repeats until the polyline is closed]***

Let's look at each of the prompts.

- The first line is simple enough. It asks which viewport you wish to clip. Select one.
- The next line gives you a couple options:
  - The default option – **Polygonal** – allows you to place the clipping border manually with a closed polyline (a polygon).
  - The **Delete** option allows you to remove a clipping border. It'll return the view to its original shape.
  - Enter **S** to use the **Select clipping object** option (or just select the object) if you've created a new boundary around the view using a polyline, spline, and so forth. It prompts:

    Select object to clip viewport:

    Simply select the object you wish to use as the new viewport.

> You can also access the ***VPClip*** command by selecting the viewport to clip, opening the cursor menu, and selecting **Viewport**.

Let's clip the round viewport in our drawing. (Notice that it has some unwanted text in it.)

Do This: 23.5.2.1	**Reshaping a Viewport**

I. Be sure you're still in the *flr-pln23b-new.dwg* file in the C:\Steps\Lesson23 folder. If not, please open it now.

II. Be sure you're in Paper Space and the **VPORTS** layer is thawed and current.

III. Follow these steps.

TOOLS	COMMAND SEQUENCE	STEPS
	Command: ***rec***	1. Draw a rectangle around the bay window similar to the one shown in Figure 23.013.

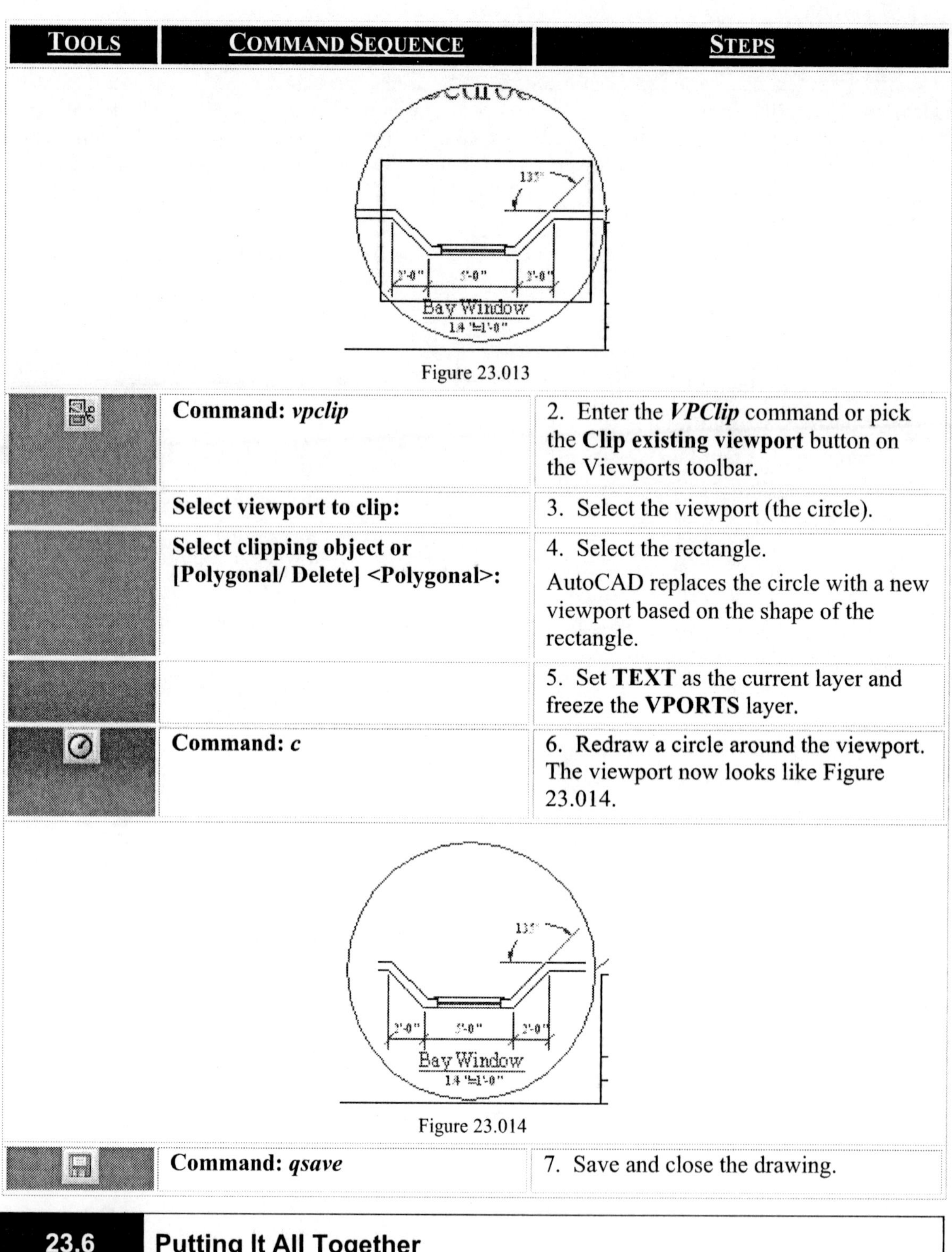

TOOLS	COMMAND SEQUENCE	STEPS
	Figure 23.013	
	Command: ***vpclip***	2. Enter the ***VPClip*** command or pick the **Clip existing viewport** button on the Viewports toolbar.
	Select viewport to clip:	3. Select the viewport (the circle).
	Select clipping object or [Polygonal/ Delete] <Polygonal>:	4. Select the rectangle. AutoCAD replaces the circle with a new viewport based on the shape of the rectangle.
		5. Set **TEXT** as the current layer and freeze the **VPORTS** layer.
	Command: ***c***	6. Redraw a circle around the viewport. The viewport now looks like Figure 23.014.
	Figure 23.014	
	Command: ***qsave***	7. Save and close the drawing.

23.6 Putting It All Together

We've learned quite a bit about Paper Space and viewports. Let's try a project from the beginning (well, almost the beginning – I'll provide the drawing).

Do This: 23.6.1	From Setup to Plot – A Project

I. Open the *table saw.dwg* file in the C:\Steps\Lesson23 folder. The drawing looks like Figure 23.015. (I've hidden the grid for clarity.)

II. Set the **VPORTS** layer current.

III. Follow these steps.

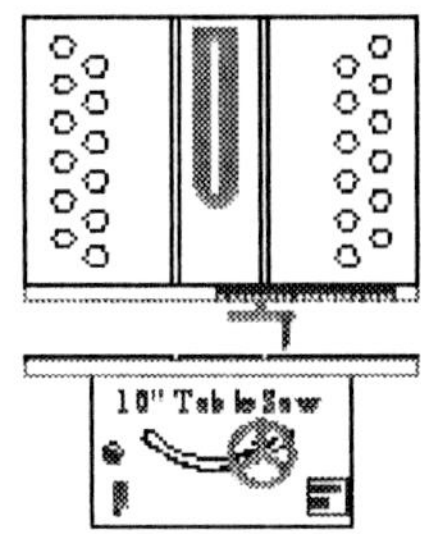

Figure 23.015

TOOLS	COMMAND SEQUENCE	STEPS
No Button Available	**Command: *layoutwizard***	1. Let's start the easy way. Enter the ***LayoutWizard*** command.
	Enter a name for the new layout you are creating. MasterLayout	2. Call the layout *MasterLayout.* Pick the **Next** button to continue.
	None Microsoft Office Document Image Writer magicolor 2300 DL Lexmark X63 Auto Microsoft Office Document Image Writer on LIS. Auto magicolor 2300 DL on LISA Auto Adobe PDF on LISA Adobe PDF PublishToWeb JPG.pc3 PublishToWeb PNG.pc3 Default Windows System Printer.pc3 DWF6 ePlot.pc3	3. Select a plotter if one is available. Otherwise, select **None**. Pick the **Next** button to continue.
	Select a paper size to be used for the layout. The paper sizes available are based on the plot device you selected. ANSI D (22.00 x 34.00 Inches) Enter the paper units for layout "MasterLayout". Drawing units: Millimeters, Inches, Pixels Paper size in units: Width: 34.00 inches, Height: 22.00 inches	4. Select an **ANSI D** size sheet and use **Inches** for your drawing units. Pick the **Next** button to continue.
	Select the orientation of the drawing on the paper. Portrait Landscape A	5. Tell AutoCAD to plot a **Landscape** drawing. Pick the **Next** button to continue.

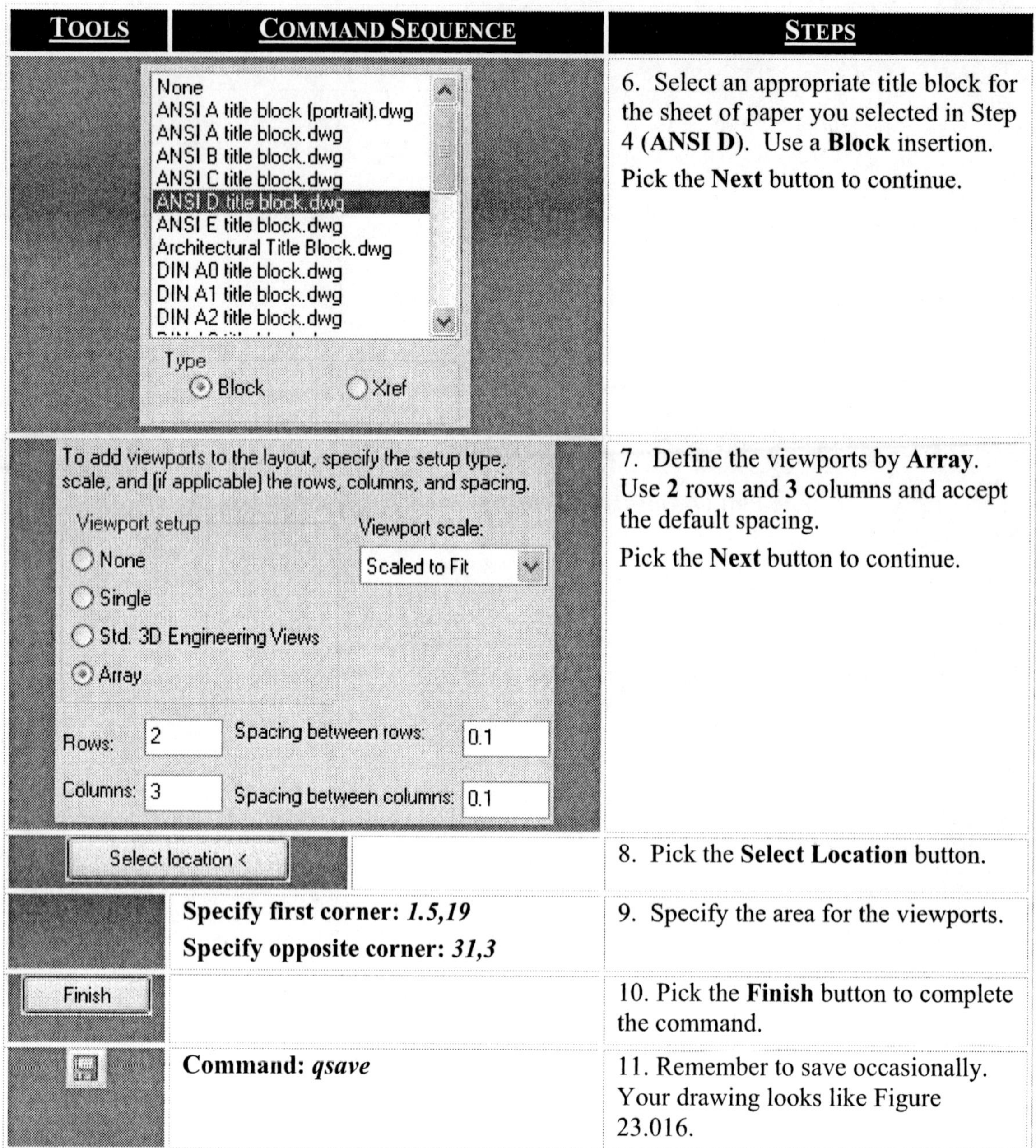

TOOLS	COMMAND SEQUENCE	STEPS
None ANSI A title block (portrait).dwg ANSI A title block.dwg ANSI B title block.dwg ANSI C title block.dwg ANSI D title block.dwg ANSI E title block.dwg Architectural Title Block.dwg DIN A0 title block.dwg DIN A1 title block.dwg DIN A2 title block.dwg Type Block Xref		6. Select an appropriate title block for the sheet of paper you selected in Step 4 (**ANSI D**). Use a **Block** insertion. Pick the **Next** button to continue.
To add viewports to the layout, specify the setup type, scale, and (if applicable) the rows, columns, and spacing. Viewport setup: None, Single, Std. 3D Engineering Views, Array Viewport scale: Scaled to Fit Rows: 2 Spacing between rows: 0.1 Columns: 3 Spacing between columns: 0.1		7. Define the viewports by **Array**. Use **2** rows and **3** columns and accept the default spacing. Pick the **Next** button to continue.
Select location <		8. Pick the **Select Location** button.
	Specify first corner: ***1.5,19*** **Specify opposite corner:** ***31,3***	9. Specify the area for the viewports.
Finish		10. Pick the **Finish** button to complete the command.
	Command: ***qsave***	11. Remember to save occasionally. Your drawing looks like Figure 23.016.

Tools	Command Sequence	Steps

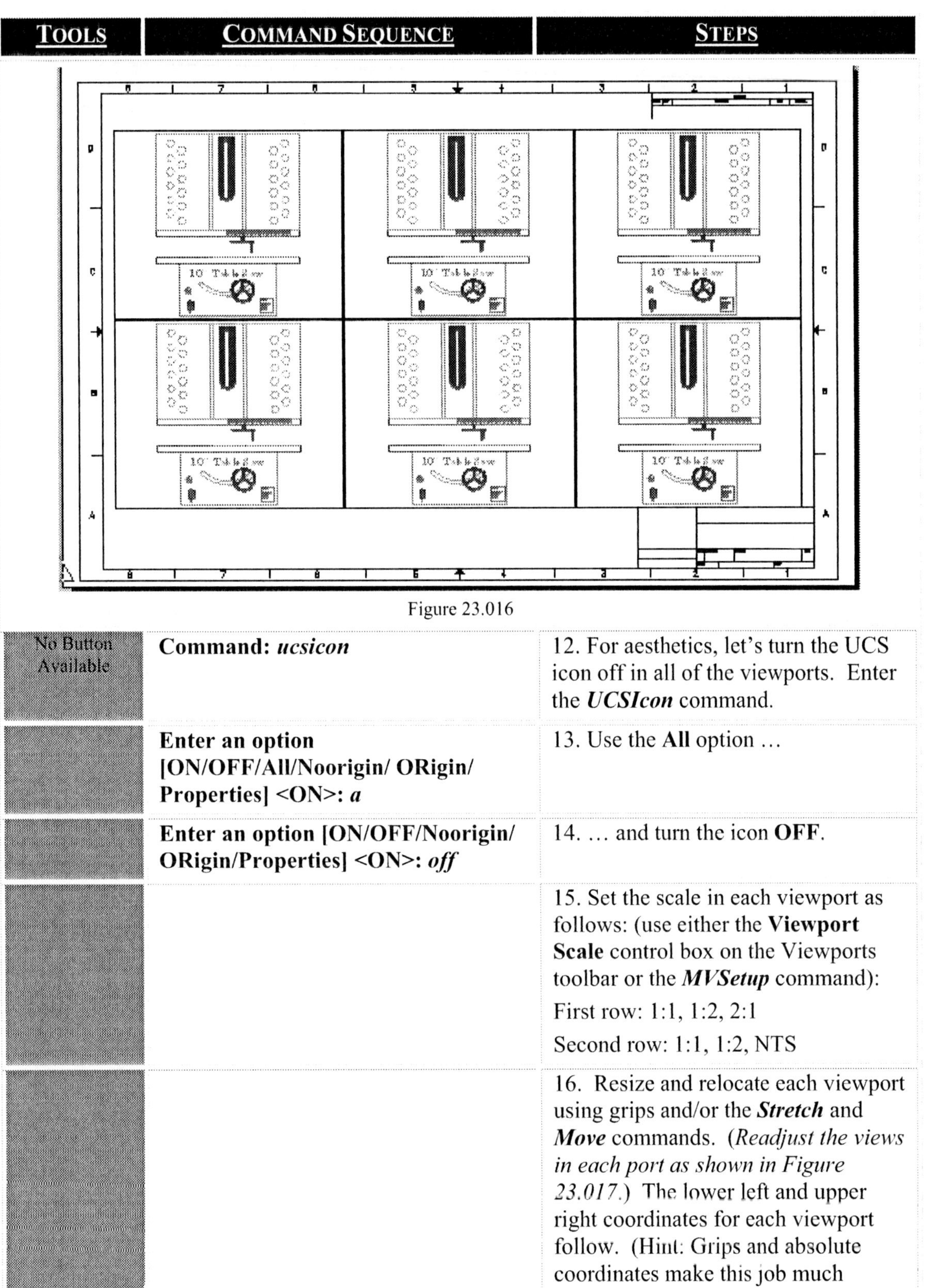

Figure 23.016

Tools	Command Sequence	Steps
No Button Available	**Command:** ***ucsicon***	12. For aesthetics, let's turn the UCS icon off in all of the viewports. Enter the ***UCSIcon*** command.
	Enter an option [ON/OFF/All/Noorigin/ ORigin/ Properties] <ON>: ***a***	13. Use the **All** option …
	Enter an option [ON/OFF/Noorigin/ ORigin/Properties] <ON>: ***off***	14. … and turn the icon **OFF**.
		15. Set the scale in each viewport as follows: (use either the **Viewport Scale** control box on the Viewports toolbar or the ***MVSetup*** command): First row: 1:1, 1:2, 2:1 Second row: 1:1, 1:2, NTS
		16. Resize and relocate each viewport using grips and/or the ***Stretch*** and ***Move*** commands. (*Readjust the views in each port as shown in Figure 23.017.*) The lower left and upper right coordinates for each viewport follow. (Hint: Grips and absolute coordinates make this job much easier.)

TOOLS	COMMAND SEQUENCE	STEPS

VIEWPORT (ROW/COL)	HANDWHEEL PLAN (1/1)	SAW PLAN (1/2)	SWITCH (1/3)	HANDWHEEL ELEV. (2/1)	SAW ELEV. (2/2)	SPEC. PLATE (2/3)
Lower left coordinate	1.5,15.1	7.25,8.25	2,1.75	1.5,10	7.25,1	23.75,4
Upper right coordinate	7.75,19	23.5,20	5.75,7.75	7.75,15	23.5,11	31,11.75

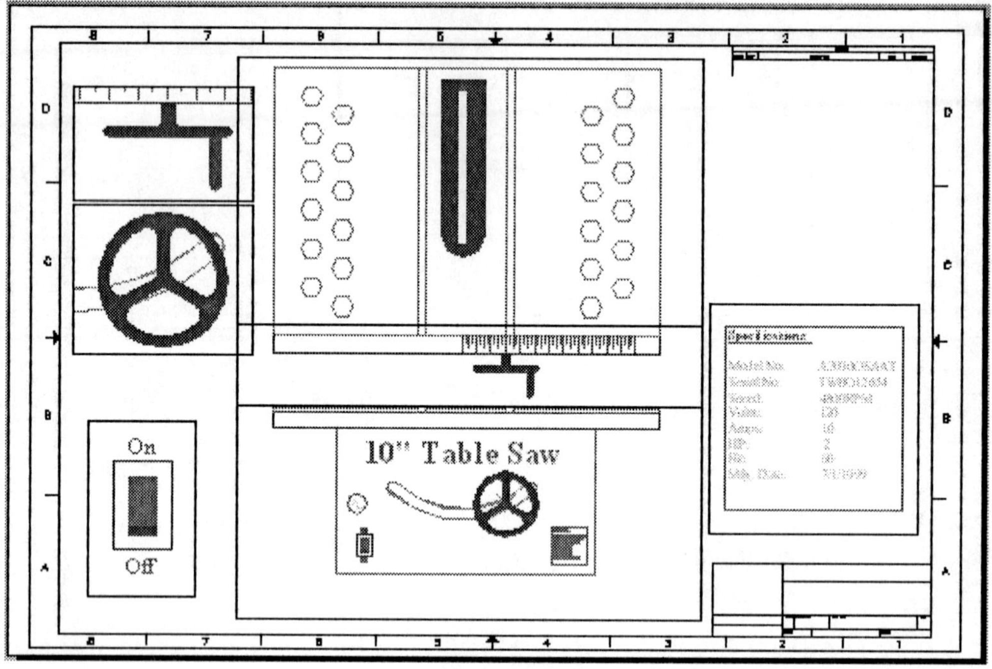

Figure 23.017

	Command: ***vplayer***	17. Use the ***VPLayer*** command to freeze unwanted layers as follows. (Hint: It might be faster to freeze all layers with the * and then thaw the few you wish visible.)

VIEWPORT:	HANDWHEEL – PLAN & ELEV.	SWITCH	SAW – PLAN & ELEV.	SPECS
Freeze All Layers Except:	Obj3 Obj3a	Obj2 Obj2a Obj3 Text	(Don't freeze any layers)	Text

	Command: ***qsave***	18. Remember to save occasionally. Your drawing looks like Figure 23.018.

Tools	Command Sequence	Steps

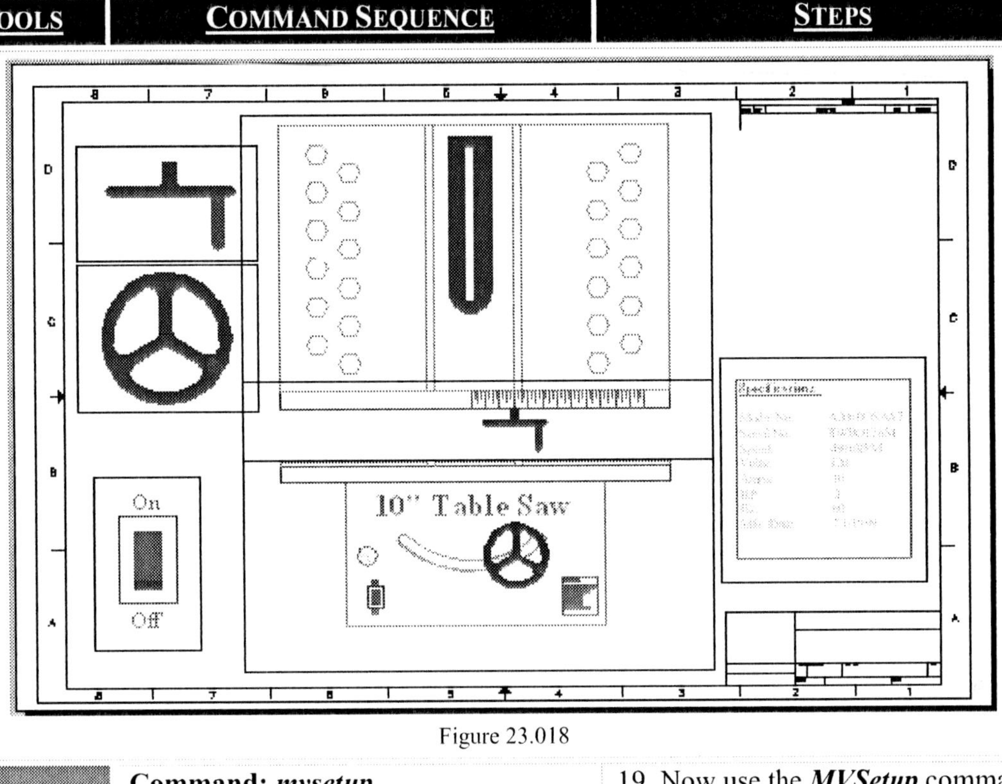

Figure 23.018

Tools	Command Sequence	Steps
	Command: ***mvsetup***	19. Now use the ***MVSetup*** command to align the views in the handwheel plan and elevation. Begin by entering the command.
Align Create Scale viewports Options Title block Undo	**Enter an option [Align/Create/ Scale viewports/ Options/Title block/Undo]:** ***a***	20. Select the **Align** option.
Angled Horizontal Vertical alignment Rotate view Undo	**Enter an option [Angled/Horizontal/Vertical alignment/Rotate view/Undo]:** ***v***	21. We'll align the objects vertically.
	Specify basepoint: _qua of	22. Select the leftmost quadrant of the handwheel in the plan view …
	Specify point in viewport to be panned: _qua of	23. … and the corresponding quadrant in the elevation view.
	Enter an option [Angled/Horizontal/ Vertical alignment/Rotate view/Undo]: ***[enter]*** **Enter an option [Align/Create/Scale viewports/ Options/Title block/Undo]:** ***[enter]***	24. Complete the command.

TOOLS	COMMAND SEQUENCE	STEPS
	Command: ***[enter]***	25. Repeat Steps 19 through 24 to align the plan and elevation views of the saw.
	Command: ***rec***	26. We'll use the ***VPClip*** command to set the saw plan and elevation viewports so that all you see is the plan in the plan viewport and the elevation in the elevation viewport. Begin by drawing a rectangle around the elevation in the bottom viewport as seen in Figure 23.019. (Be sure you're in Paper Space and that the **vports** layer is current.)

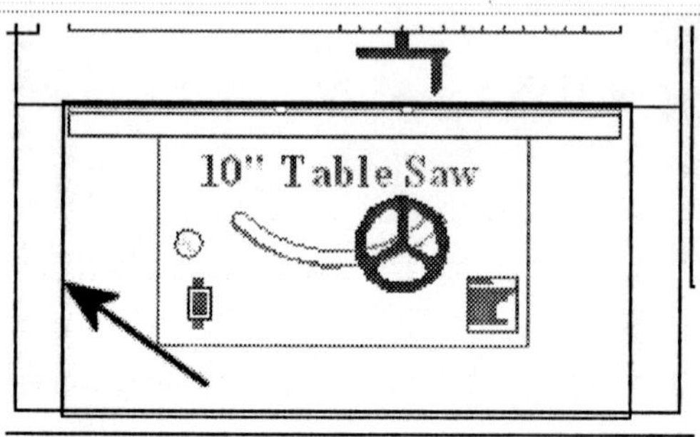

Figure 23.019

TOOLS	COMMAND SEQUENCE	STEPS
	Command: ***vpclip***	27. Enter the ***VPClip*** command.
	Select viewport to clip:	28. Select the viewport with the saw elevation in it.
	Select clipping object or [Polygonal] <Polygonal>:	29. Select the polyline you drew in Step 26.
		30. Move the title block to the **Title Block** layer. Set the **text** layer current and freeze the **vports** layer.
	Command: ***qsave***	31. Remember to save occasionally. Your drawing looks like Figure 23.020.

TOOLS	COMMAND SEQUENCE	STEPS

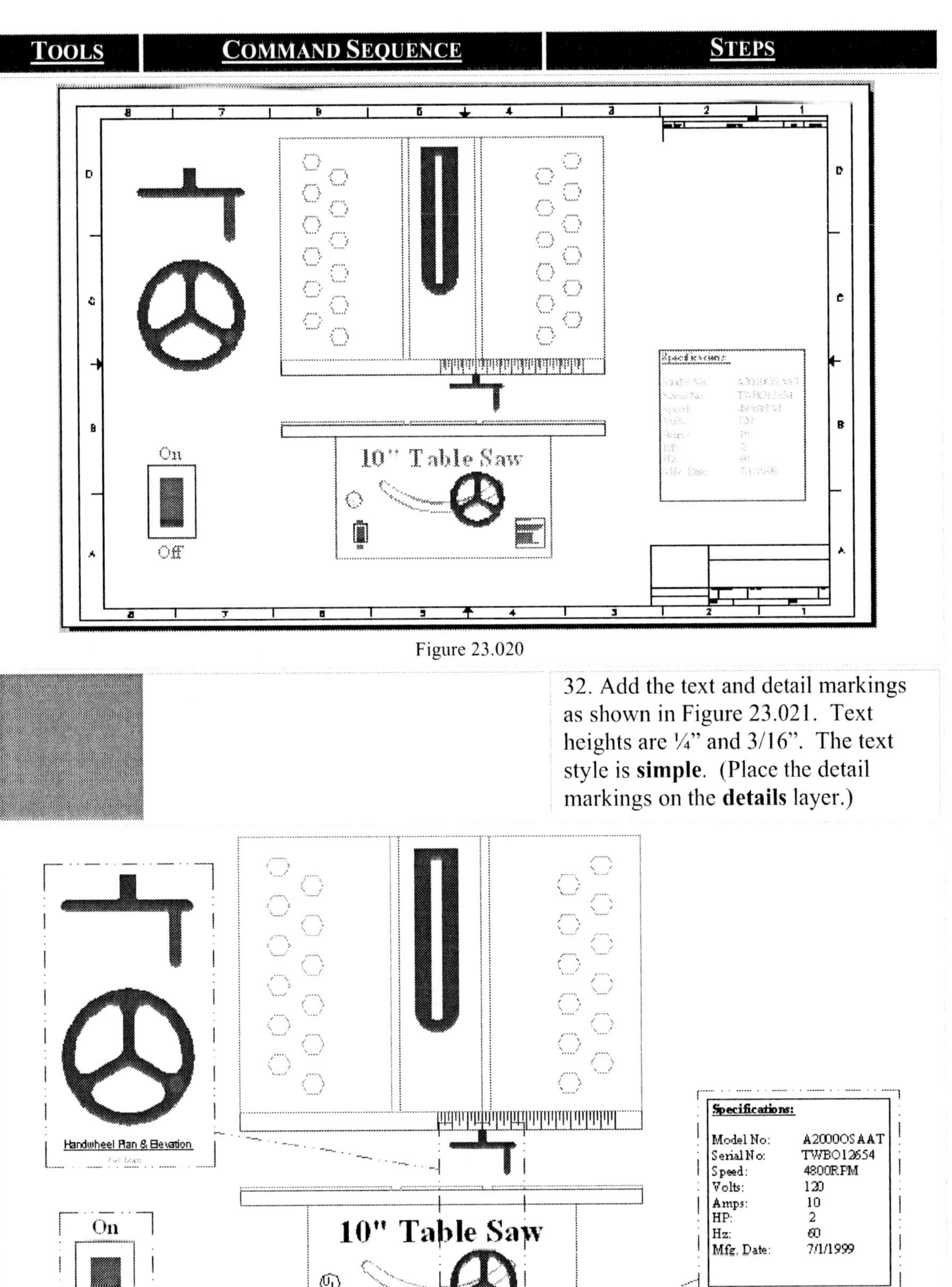

Figure 23.020

32. Add the text and detail markings as shown in Figure 23.021. Text heights are ¼" and 3/16". The text style is **simple**. (Place the detail markings on the **details** layer.)

Figure 23.021

TOOLS	COMMAND SEQUENCE	STEPS
		33. Fill in the title block as shown in Figure 23.022. Text sizes are ¼", 3/16", and 1/8". Styles are **Timesbold** and **Times**.

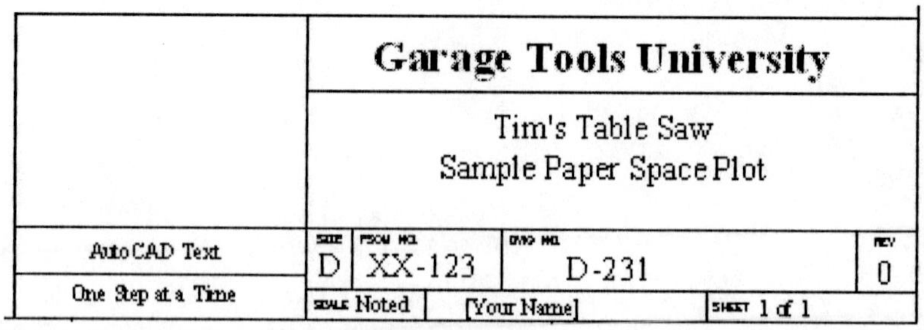

Garage Tools University			
Tim's Table Saw Sample Paper Space Plot			
AutoCAD Text	SIZE D	FSCM NO. XX-123	DWG NO. D-231	REV 0
One Step at a Time	SCALE Noted	[Your Name]	SHEET 1 of 1	

Figure 23.022

TOOLS	COMMAND SEQUENCE	STEPS
	Command: ***qsave***	34. Remember to save occasionally.
	Command: ***plot***	35. Now we must plot the drawing. (Note: If you haven't a plotter available, you can print to your own printer – just make sure you print to fit.) Begin by entering the ***Plot*** command.
		36. Your Plot dialog box should resemble the one in Figure 23.023. (Note: I'm printing to fit on a printer, as I don't have a plotter available.) Your plotter may vary and the **Plot offset** may vary. Use the **Preview** button to be sure you have set up the plot correctly and then plot the drawing.

Tools	Command Sequence	Steps

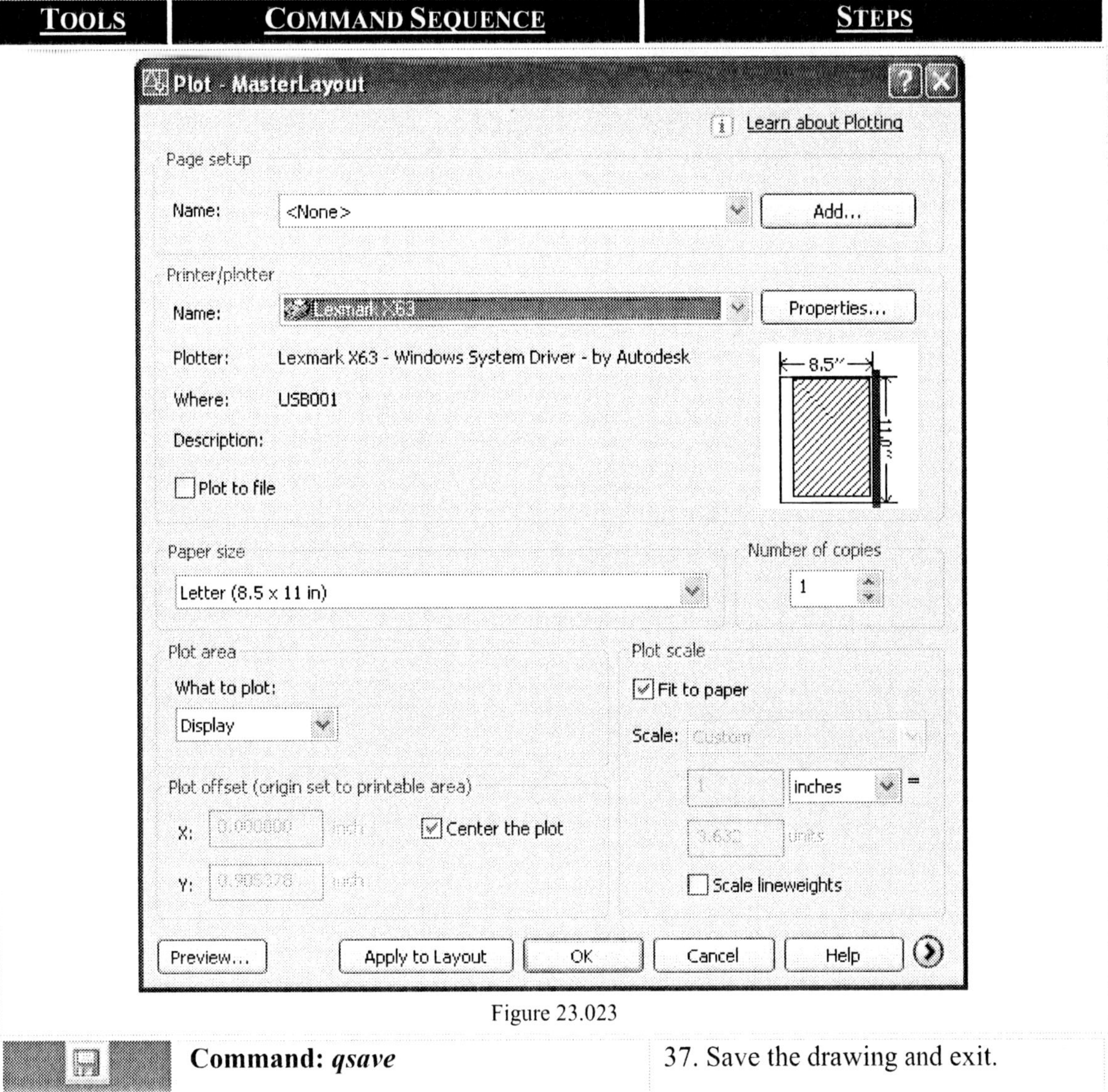

Figure 23.023

	Command: ***qsave***	37. Save the drawing and exit.

How was that? Just 37 easy steps to completion!

I know what that sounds like, but most of these steps will become second nature in time. Where it probably took 45 minutes to complete the exercise, with experience it'll take about 15 minutes to complete a similar project. This text can help you acquire some of that experience. Try some of the projects at the end of this lesson!

23.7 Extra Steps

- Try setting up and plotting some of your own drawings in a Paper Space environment.
- Try plotting the drawing from Exercise 23.6.1 to **Fit** on an 11" x 8½" sheet of paper.

23.8 What Have We Learned?

Items covered in this lesson include:

- *Using layers in Paper Space*

- *How to use text in Paper Space*
- *How to dimension in Paper Space*
- *How to plot a Paper Space drawing*
- *Commands*
    - ***MVsetup***
    - ***VPLayer***
    - ***VPClip***
    - ***Regenall***
    - ***Redrawall***
    - ***Spacetrans***

Remember the first paragraphs of Lesson 22? You may now step into that group of CAD operators who have used Paper Space and would never use anything else!

In Paper Space, you've taken your first steps into a whole new AutoCAD world! With experience, you'll soon wonder why we don't teach Paper Space from the beginning. But think back to what you knew when you began your first AutoCAD class. So much of what you learned in the last two lessons requires that you already have a foundation in the basics. And now, with Paper Space (and viewports) under your belt, you have a foundation for what comes next.

23.9 Exercises

1. Open the *MyNeedle.dwg* file in the C:\Steps\Lesson23 folder. (If that drawing isn't there, use the *needle 23.dwg* file in the same folder.) Create the drawing configuration for plotting found in Figure 23.024. Some helpful information includes:
    1.1. The text height is 5mm and 2.5mm; the font is Times New Roman.
    1.2. The title block text is attributed.
    1.3. I used two dimension layers (create new layers as required).
    1.4. Dimension text is 3mm.
    1.5. Remember that Floating viewports can overlap.
    1.6. Save the drawing as *MyNeedle23.dwg* in the C:\Steps\Lesson23 folder.

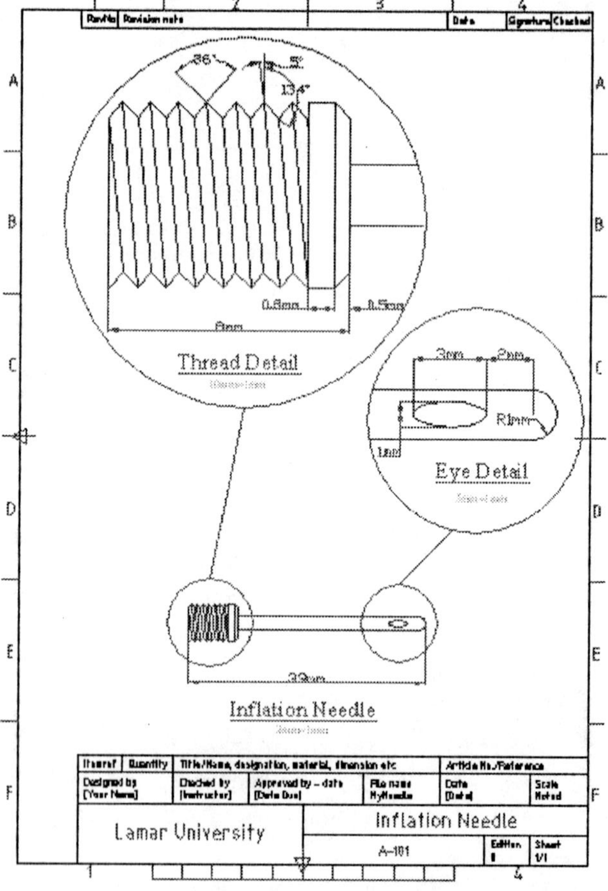

Figure 23.024: *Needle.dwg*

2. Open the *MySplitter.dwg* file in the C:\Steps\Lesson23 folder. (If this drawing isn't there, open the *cable splitter 23.dwg* file instead.) Create the drawing configuration for plotting found in Figure 23.025. Some helpful information includes:
   2.1. The text height is 3/16" and 1/8"; the font is Times New Roman.
   2.2. The title block text is ¼", 3/16", and 1/8"; the font is Times New Roman.
   2.3. I used two dimension layers (create new layers as required).
   2.4. Dimension text is 1/8".
   2.5. Remember that floating viewports can overlap.
   2.6. Save the drawing as *MySplitter23.dwg* in the C:\Steps\Lesson23 folder.

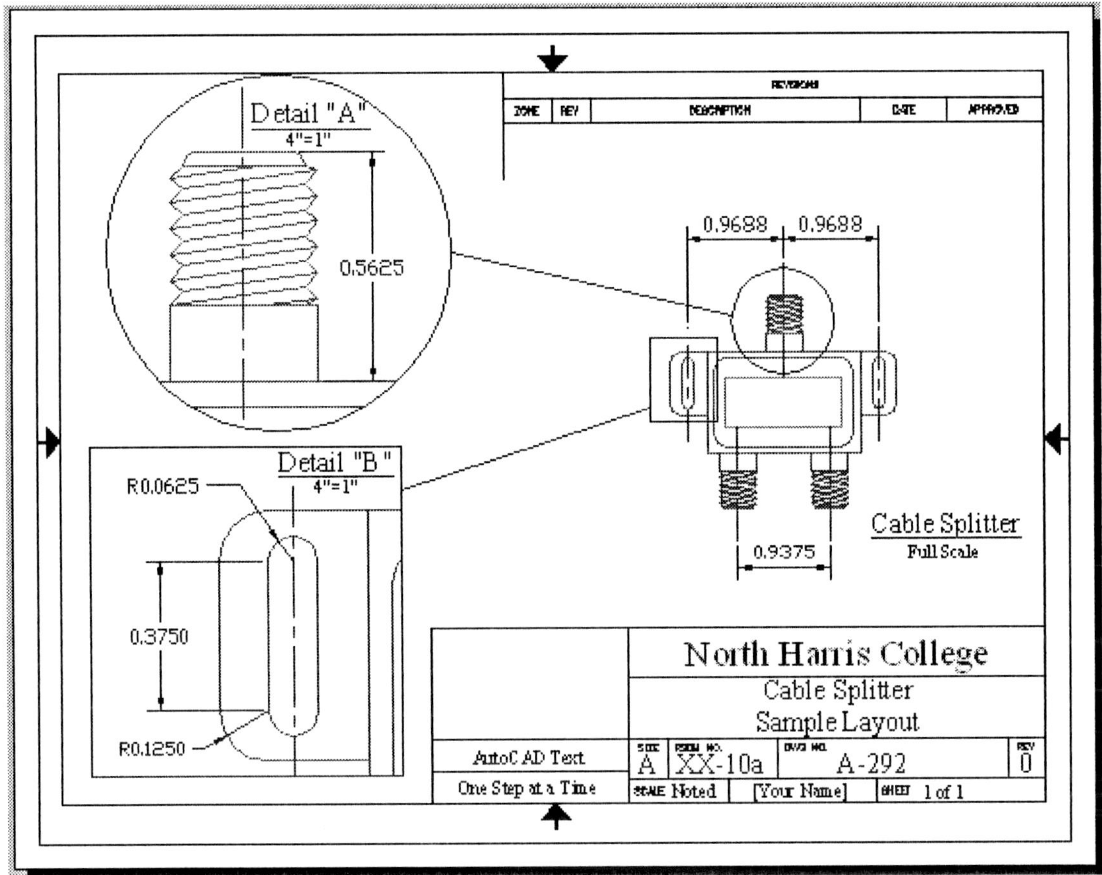

Figure 23.025: *Cable Splitter.dwg*

3. Open the *MyCutter.dwg* file in the C:\Steps\Lesson23 folder. (If this drawing isn't there, open the *glass cutter 23.dwg* file instead.) Create the drawing configuration for plotting found in Figure 23.026. Some helpful information includes:
   3.1. The text height is 3/16" and 1/8"; the font is Times New Roman.
   3.2. The title block text is ¼", 3/16", and 1/8"; the font is Times New Roman.
   3.3. I used two dimension layers (create new layers as required).
   3.4. Dimension text is 1/8".
   3.5. Remember that floating viewports can overlap.
   3.6. Save the drawing as *MyCutter23.dwg* in the C:\Steps\Lesson23 folder.

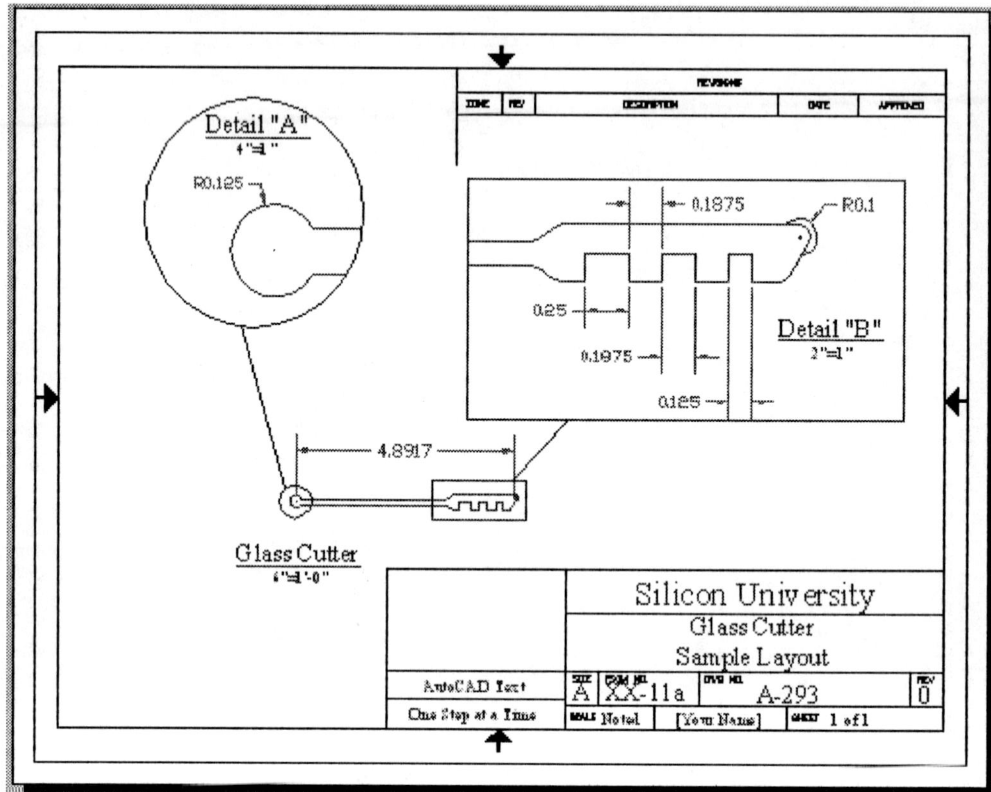

Figure 23.026: *Glass Cutter.dwg*

4. Open the *My Spice Rack.dwg* file in the C:\Steps\Lesson23 folder. (If this drawing isn't there, open the *Spice Rack 23.dwg* file instead.) Create the drawing configuration for plotting found in Figure 23.027. Some helpful information includes:
   4.1. The text height is 3/16" and 1/8"; the font is Txt.
   4.2. The title block text is ¼", 3/16", and 1/8"; the font is Times New Roman.
   4.3. I used three dimension layers (create new layers as required).
   4.4. Dimension text is 1/8".
   4.5. Align the bottle and cap.
   4.6. Save the drawing as *My Spice Rack 23.dwg* in the C:\Steps\Lesson23 folder.

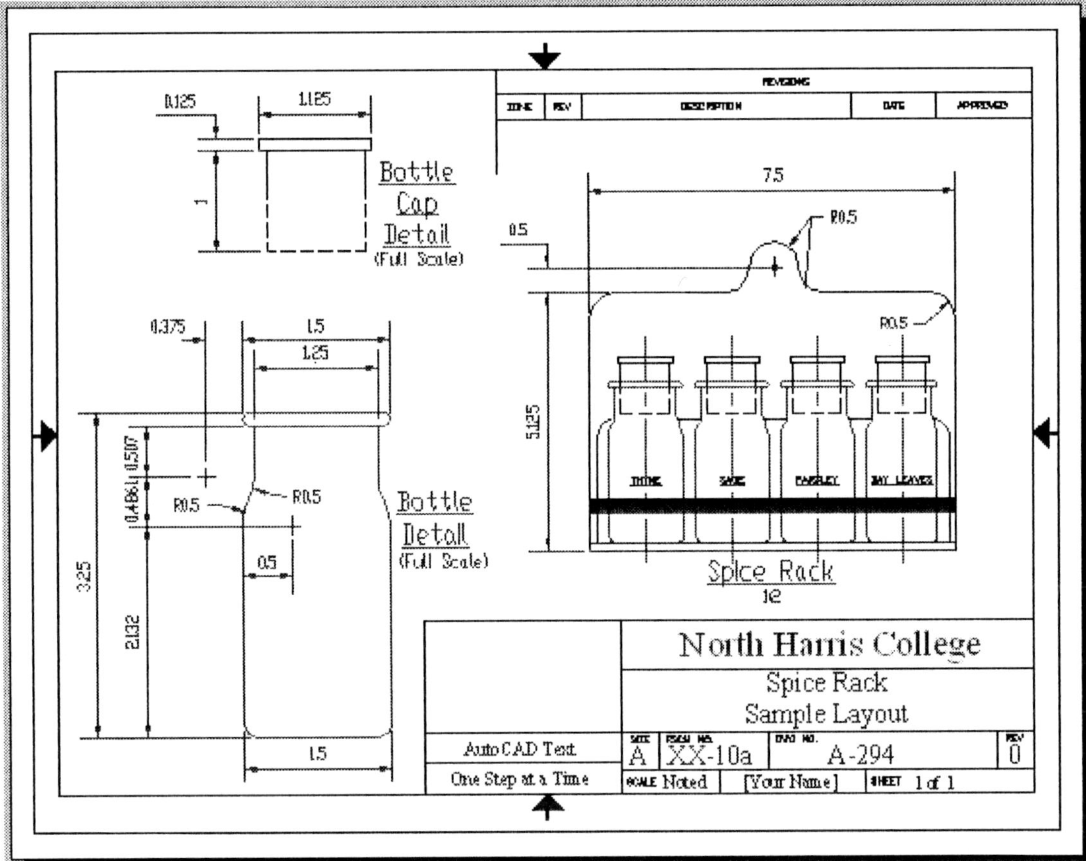

Figure 23.027: Spice Rack

5. Open the *MyAssbly.dwg* file in the C:\Steps\Lesson23 folder. (If this drawing isn't there, open the *motor assbly 23.dwg* file instead.) Create the drawing configuration for plotting found in Figure 23.028. Some helpful information includes:
   5.1. The text height is 3/16" and 1/8"; the font is Times New Roman.
   5.2. The title block text is ¼", 3/16", and 1/8"; the font is Times New Roman.
   5.3. I used three dimension layers (create new layers as required).
   5.4. Dimension text is 1/8".
   5.5. Save the drawing as *MyAssbly23.dwg* in the C:\Steps\Lesson23 folder.

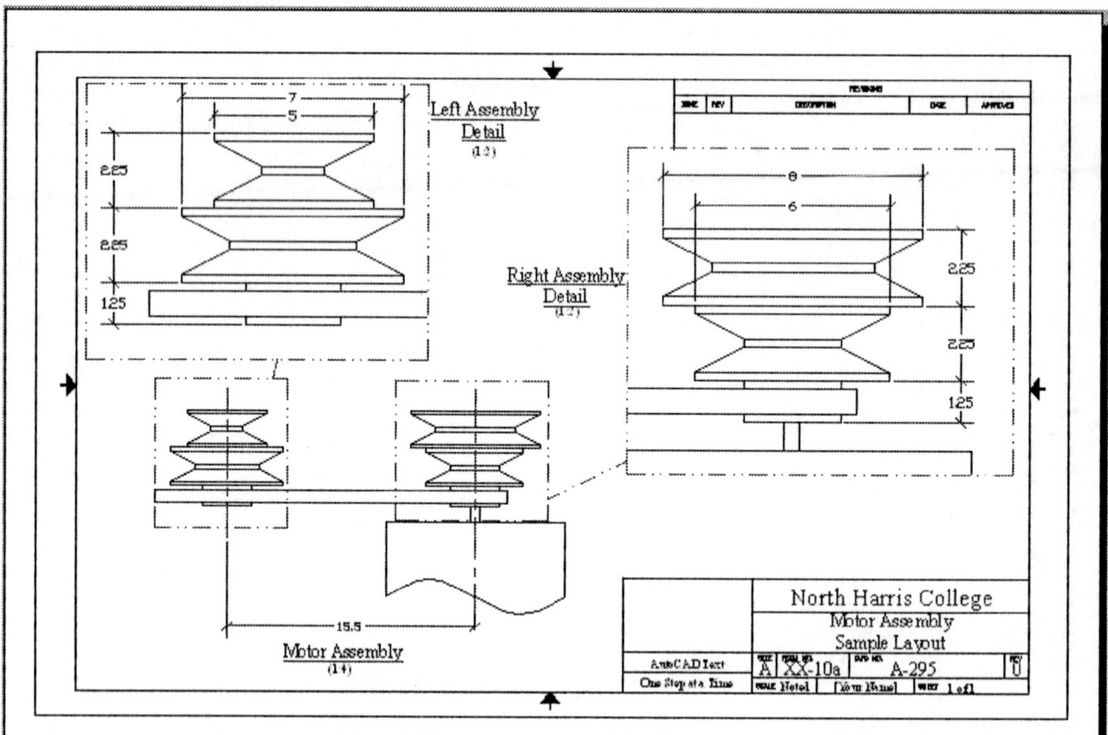

Figure 23.028: Motor Assembly

6. Open the *My Pipng Plan.dwg* file in the C:\Steps\Lesson23 folder. (If this drawing isn't there, open the *Piping plan 23.dwg* file instead.) Create the drawing configuration for plotting found in Figure 23.029. Some helpful information includes:
   6.1. The text height is 3/16" and 1/8"; the font is Times New Roman.
   6.2. The title block text is ¼", 3/16", and 1/8"; the font is Times New Roman.
   6.3. I used two dimension layers (create new layers as required).
   6.4. Dimension text is 1/8".
   6.5. Save the drawing as *MyPipingPlan23.dwg* in the C:\Steps\Lesson23 folder.

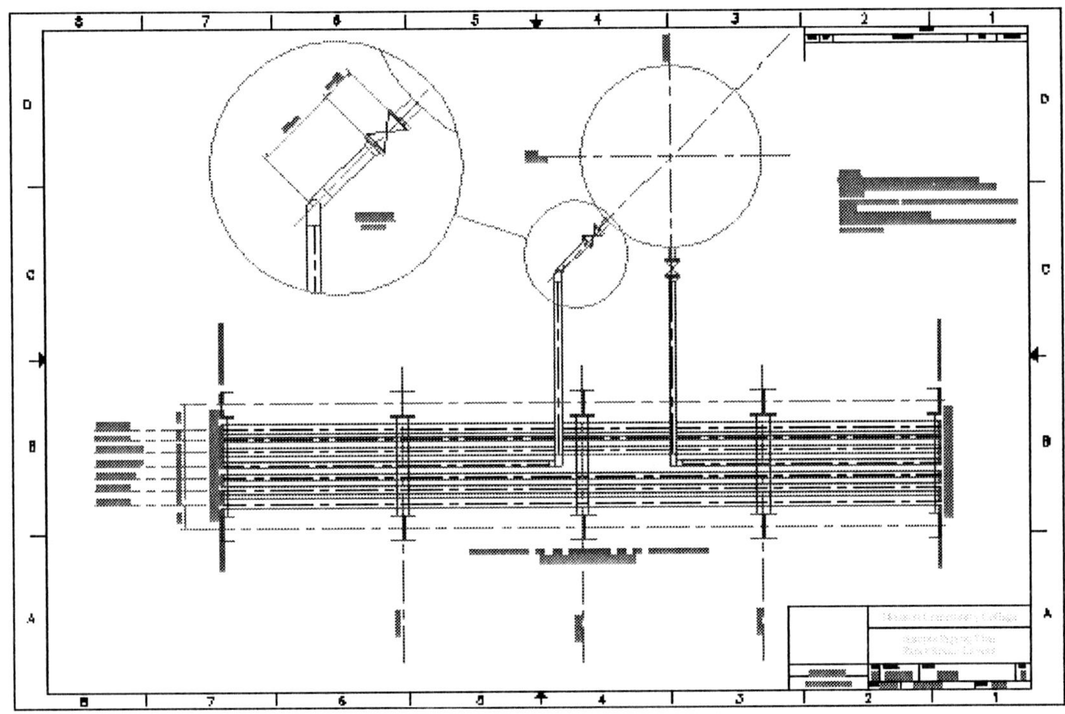

Figure 23.029: Piping Plan

NOTES:
1. High and low point vents and drains required on all pipe.
2. See drawings *SPC4001* through *SPC 40009* for Piping Support Standards.
3. See drawings *INS2022* through *INS2025* for Instrumentation Installation Details.
4. **Hold drawing for Stress Analysis.**
5. See customer spec *TXCO502331-103a/b* for construction specifications.
6. HPFS is 101'-0"

Figure 23.030

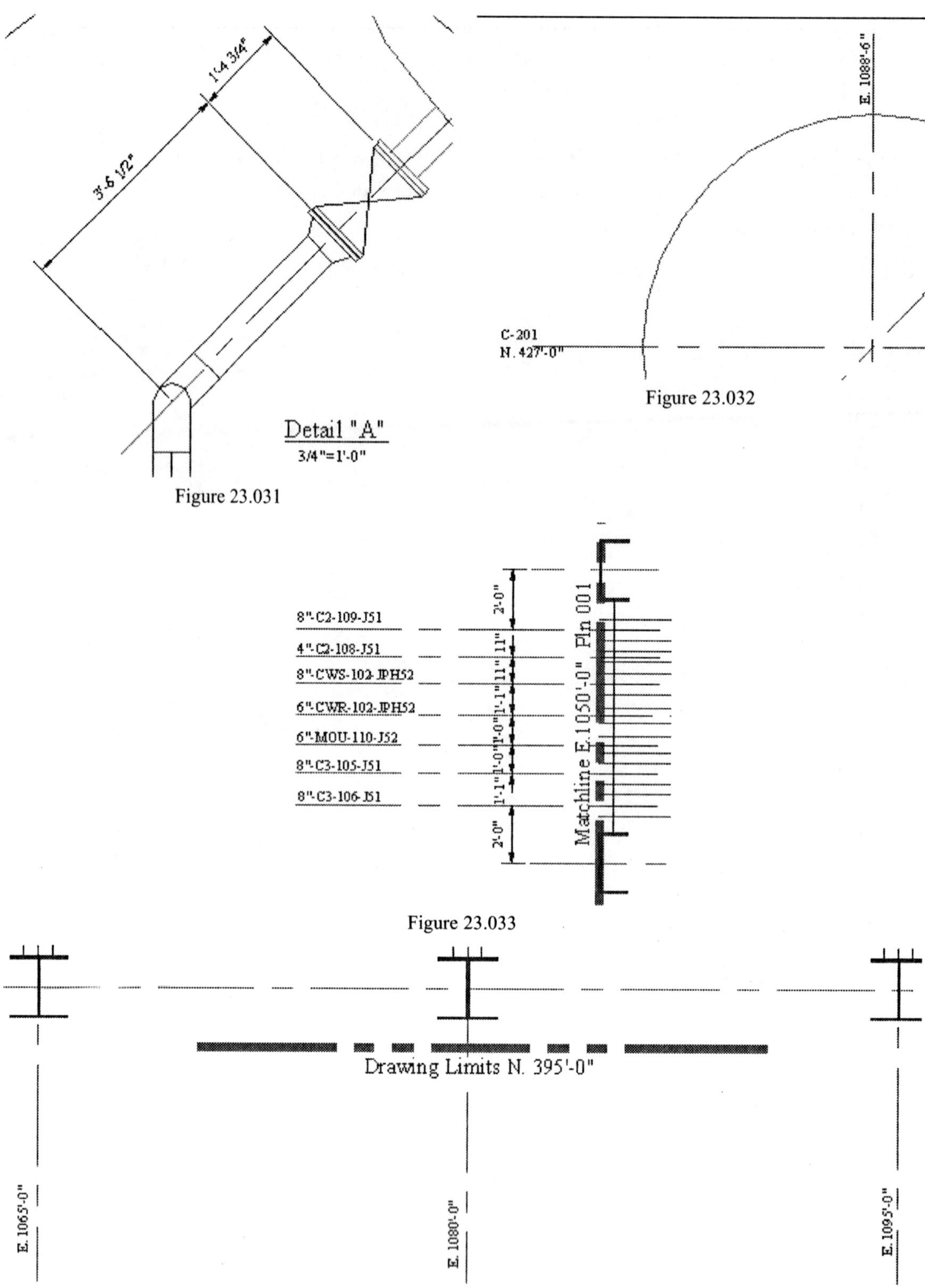

Figure 23.031

Figure 23.032

Figure 23.033

Figure 23.034

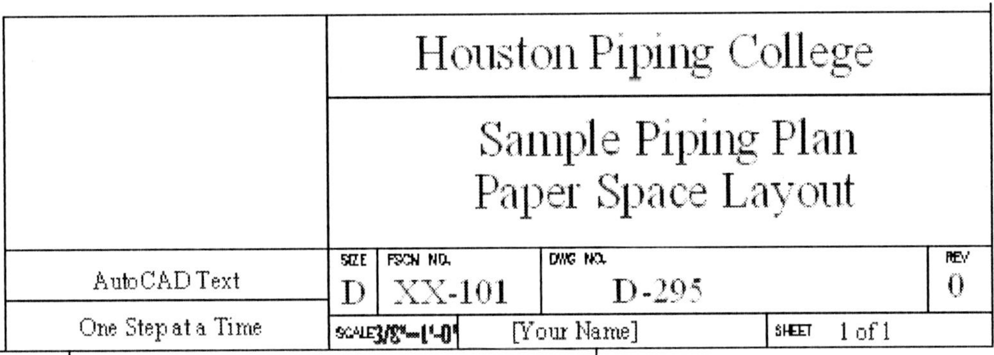

Figure 23.035

7. Open the *drillguide23.dwg* file in the C:\Steps\Lesson23 folder. Create the drawing configuration for plotting found in Figure 23.036. Some helpful information includes:
   7.1. The title block is the *ANSI B title block* file found in AutoCAD's Template folder.
   7.2. The text height is 3/16" and 1/8"; the font is Times New Roman.
   7.3. The title block text is ¼", 3/16", and 1/8"; the font is Times New Roman.
   7.4. I used three dimension layers (create new layers as required).
   7.5. Dimension text is 1/8".
   7.6. Save the drawing as *MyDrillGuide.dwg* in the C:\Steps\Lesson23 folder.

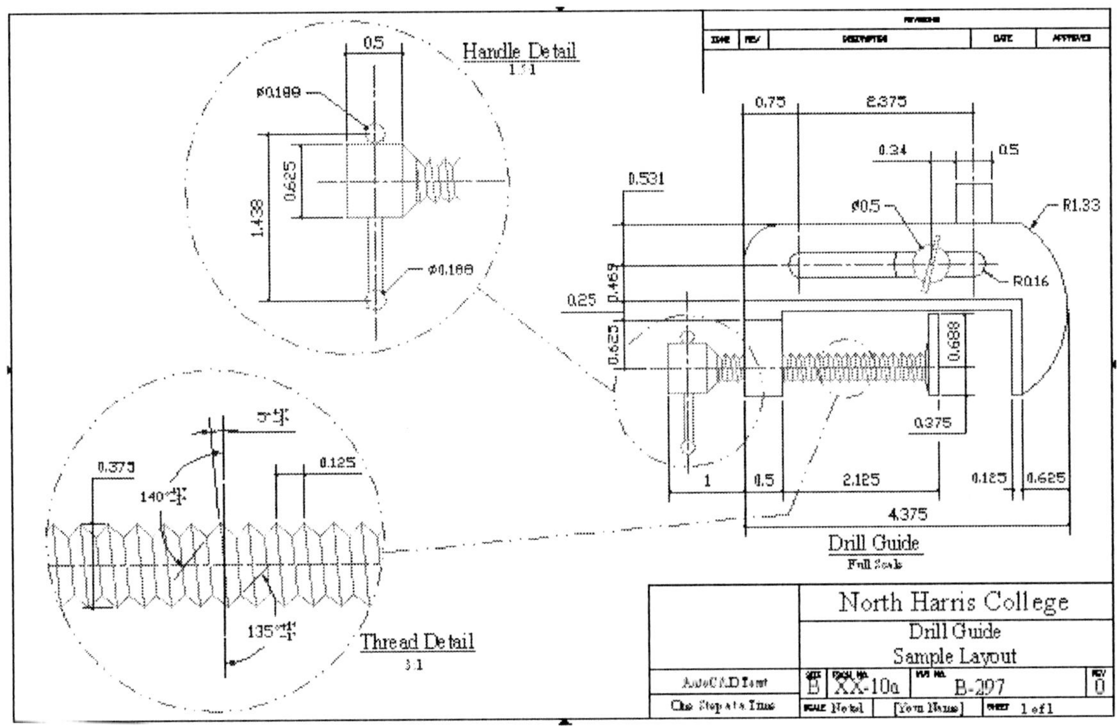

Figure 23.036: Drill Guide

8. Open the *Sawed Joint.dwg* file in the C:\Steps\Lesson23 folder. Create the drawing configuration for plotting found in Figure 23.037. Some helpful information includes:
   8.1. The title block is the *ANSI A title block (portrait)* file found in AutoCAD's Template folder.
   8.2. The text height is 3/16" and 1/8"; the font is Times New Roman.
   8.3. The title block text is ¼", 3/16", and 1/8"; the font is Times New Roman.
   8.4. I used two dimension layers (create new layers as required).
   8.5. Dimension text is 1/8".
   8.6. Save the drawing as *MyJoint.dwg* in the C:\Steps\Lesson23 folder.

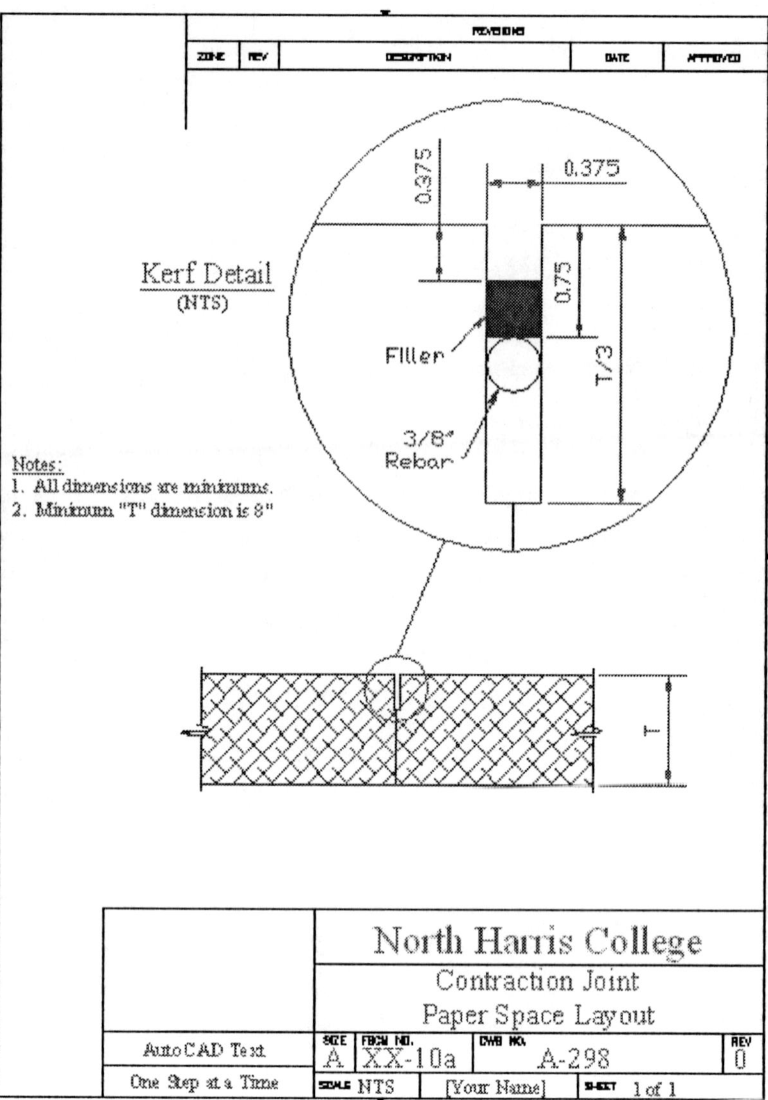

23.10 For Web-Based Review Questions, visit: http://www.uneedcad.com/2006/Files/06R23.pdf

Lesson 24

Following this lesson, you will:

- ✓ *Know how to organize your Paper Space Drawings into Drawing (Sheet) Sets*
  - o ***SheetSet***
  - o ***NewSheetSet***
  - o ***OpenSheetSet***
- ✓ *Know how to transmit your sheet set to a client*
- ✓ *Know how to archive a project*
- ✓ *Know how to create multiple-sheet DWF files*

Drawing Sheet Sets

If the last couple lessons frightened you or you didn't see where Paper Space would do you any good, you can skip this chapter altogether. If, on the other hand, you saw the potential of this remarkable "plotting tool", then by all means, please continue. What you find in Lesson 24 will place the icing on the cake of your Paper Space aspirations! (Be warned, however; if you have an employer who lacks foresight – as many do – he or she will no doubt resist sheet sets. They are, after all, the bane of the sedentary boss ... they're an innovation – something completely new!)

24.1 Sheet Sets – A Primer

Knowledge isn't what you know ... it's what you know how to find out!

Hickory

Let me warn you before we start; the Sheet Sets palette, although benign in appearance, contains an amazing amount of opportunity (as you can tell from the amount of explanation before we even begin our first exercise). But don't feel as though you have to learn it all at once; take your time and repeat a section if you become confused. Remember what Hickory said at the beginning of this section. In other words, keep this text handy and make reference to it when you need help!

AutoCAD doesn't make it easy to find a definition for sheet sets. In fact, the Preview Guide refers both to drawing sets and sheet sets, but further reading indicates that both names essentially refer to the same thing (but like *print* and *plot*, don't expect them to settle on one name any time soon!). That being said, "sets" actually include both drawings and "sheets" (or Paper Space layouts).

So, what exactly are drawing/sheet sets?

Often, you'll find yourself with a bundle of drawings that need to be numbered and cataloged properly so that you (and your client) can keep track of them. Usually, this means keeping a log of some sort with drawing numbers assigned by discipline, and then running plots that we store in separate drawers of a large cabinet ... or folders on someone's hard drive (or network).

Sheet sets (we'll settle on one name to keep it simple) are a systematic approach to organizing the package you're creating for your client – plans, details, electrical, plumbing, data sheets, etc. Further, the Sheet Set Manager greatly simplifies locating, opening, and editing any drawing or any layout in the set.

In this lesson, I'll walk you through the set up and use of sheet sets using the Sheet Set Manager. But bear in mind that this relatively new tool warrants greater exploration than we can do in these few pages. Once you've gotten your feet wet, feel free to head on into the deep end of the pool. (By now, you should be able to swim fairly well!)

24.2	Using the Sheet Set Manager to Organize Your Project
24.2.1	The Sheet List Tab

Unlike other managers, the Sheet Set Manager appears as a palette (Figure 24.001). (This should probably fill us with a sense of foreboding for what other managers will look like in future releases.) This handy palette – accessed with the ***SheetSet*** command or ***SSM*** hotkeys – will prove its value in more complex projects.

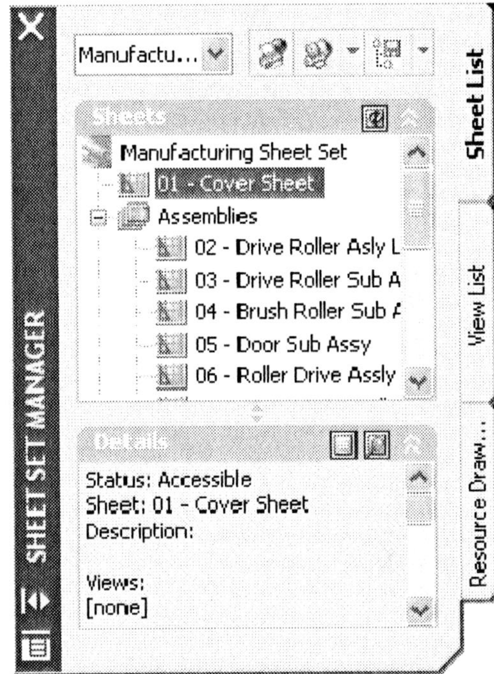

Figure 24.001

Let's take a look at its three tabs.

- The **Sheet List** tab (Figure 24.001) presents a list of the sheets in the set (under the **Sheets** heading), and either specific information about the selected sheet (**Details**) or a preview of the drawing (**Preview**). You can decide which of the latter two you'll see by picking the appropriate button on the title bar of the lower section. Right-click on any selected sheet and pick open to open the drawing to that layout.

  The top of this tab presents a selection box and three buttons.

  - Use the selection box to **Open** an existing set, create a **New Sheet Set** (to launch the New Sheet Set wizard – see Exercise 24.2.1.1), or view a list of **Recent**[ly] opened sets.
  - The first button – **Publish to DWF** – works much like a print button except that it tells AutoCAD to create a DWF file. This button works automatically and uses the defaults set up in the **Publish** command.
  - The second button – **Publish** – calls a cursor menu (Figure 24.002) with several options.

Publish to DWF
Publish to Plotter
Publish using Page Setup Override ▸

Include Plot Stamp
Plot Stamp Settings...

Manage Page Setups...
Sheet Set Publish Options ...
Publish Dialog Box ...

Figure 24.002

    - **Publish to DWF** operates the same as the button to the left. **Publish to Plotter** does the same thing, but plots to the default plotter.
    - **Publish using Page Setup Override** publishes the sheet using the selected overrides. The overrides come from drawing templates with their own setups.
    - The toggle **Include Plot Stamp** tells AutoCAD whether or not to place a stamp on the plot you're about to make.
    - **Plot Stamp Settings** calls the Plot Stamp dialog box that will help you set up the stamp. (For more on the Plot Stamp dialog box, see Section 21.2.2.)
    - **Manage Page Setups** displays the Page Setup Manager. (For more on the Page Setup Manager, see Section 21.1.3.)

- **Sheet Set Publish Options** calls the Publish Options dialog box but the settings are specific to the current sheet set. (For more on the Publish Options dialog box, see Section 21.2.2.)
- Finally, **Publish Dialog Box** calls the Publish dialog box (Section 21.2.2).

- The last button on the **Sheet List** tab – **Sheet Selections** – enables you to either **Manage** or **Create** sheet selections. Use this tool to group several selected sheets for simultaneous publishing or transmitting action. AutoCAD will ask you for a name for the sheet selection. (Use something descriptive as there is no opportunity to describe the set anywhere else.) Once you've identified the sheet selection, you can publish or transmit the grouping. Use the **Manage** option to rename or delete the sheet selection.
- The **Sheets** list box presents a list of the drawings and sheets (layouts) currently listed in the sheet set. AutoCAD presents the cursor menu shown in Figure 24.003 when you right-click on one of the listings. (Note: The options will vary according to where your cursor is when you right-click. I produced the menu in the image by right-clicking on the sheet set name – at the top of the palette.) Let's look at these options.

Figure 24.003

- Use **Close Sheet Set** to close the current sheet set. You can't delete the DST file (sheet set data file – the file that contains the setup information for your sheet set) while the sheet set is open.
- Create a **New Sheet** set with the next option. First, create your new drawing with a layout, and then this option will present the New Sheet dialog box (Figure 24.004), which will allow you to number and identify (**File name**) the new sheet in the current set.

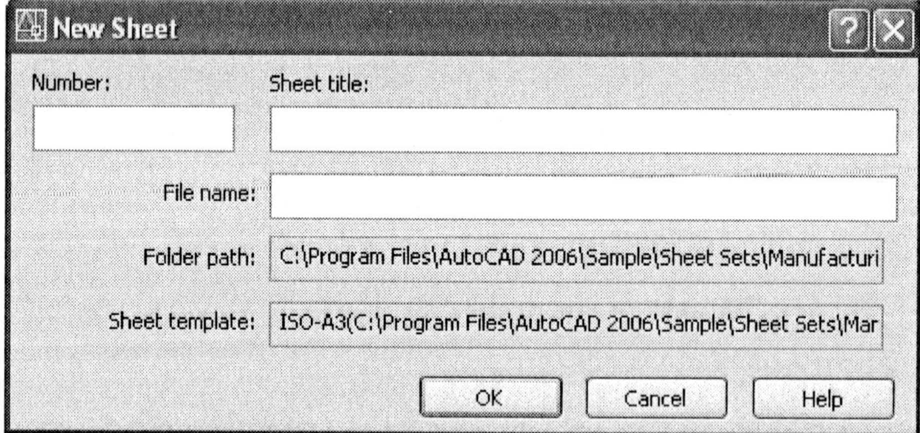

Figure 24.004

- Use the **New Subset** option to call the Subset Properties dialog box (Figure 24.005). It'll help organize your list with a subset of an existing set. The Subset Properties dialog box provides options for naming (**Subset name**), storing (**Store new sheet DWG files in**), and even providing a template to create the new subset (**Sheet creation template for subset**). A check in the **Prompt for template** box tells AutoCAD to ignore the default template and ask you which template to use. A check next to **Create folders relative to parent subset storage location** helps you better organize your efforts.

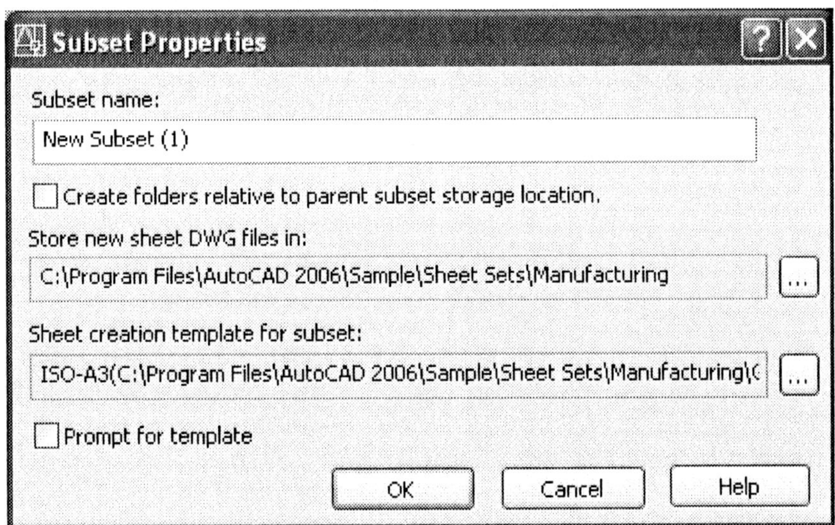

Figure 24.005

- **Import Layout as Sheet** presents another dialog box (Figure 24.006). Use the **Browse for Drawings** button to select drawings to include in your sheet set. Once you've selected drawings, the list box will provide the layout names available for import. Put a check next to those rows that contain layouts you want to use.

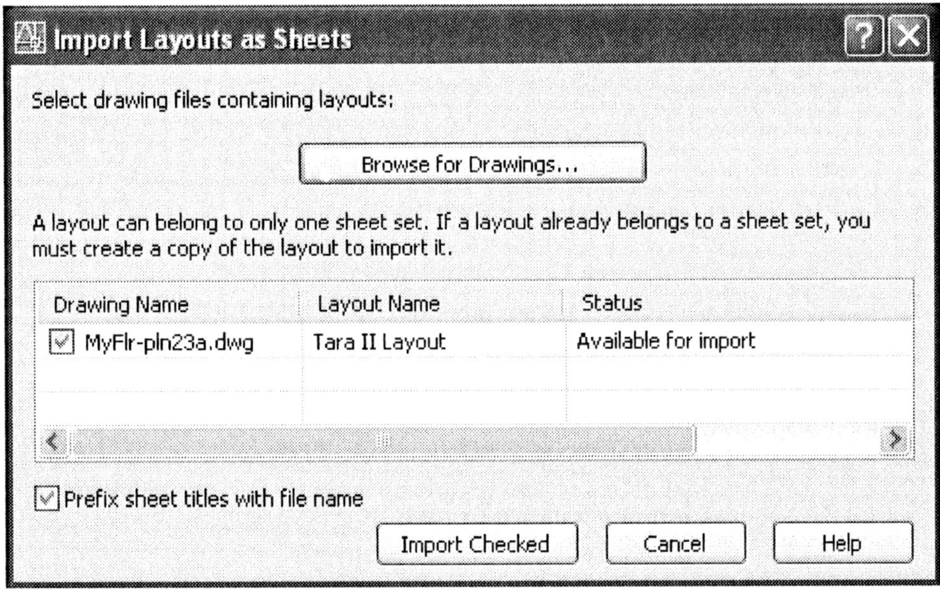

Figure 24.006

- **Resave All Sheets** opens and saves all the sheets associated with the sheet set. Use this tool to save any new sheet set information to the sheets, but be sure all the sheets are closed first.
- The **Publish** option presents the same cursor menu seen in Figure 24.002.
- **eTransmit** presents the Create Transmittal dialog box we discussed in Section 21.3.

- **Transmittal Setups** presents the Transmittal Setup dialog box. We also discussed this one in Section 21.3.
- Use **Insert Sheet List Table** to insert a table listing the sheets in the set. You'll usually insert this table on the data sheet for a project. (You can use the ***SheetSet*** command to accomplish the same purpose.) AutoCAD simplifies this procedure with a dialog box.
- The **Properties** option will display a Properties dialog box with information about the sheet set or the selected sheet.
- **Archive** presents the Archive a Sheet Set dialog box (Figure 24.007). (Reach the same dialog box with the ***Archive*** command.) You can use this to archive (store) all the drawings associated with a project at critical stages (Issued for Approval, Issued for Construction, Issued for Review, and so forth).

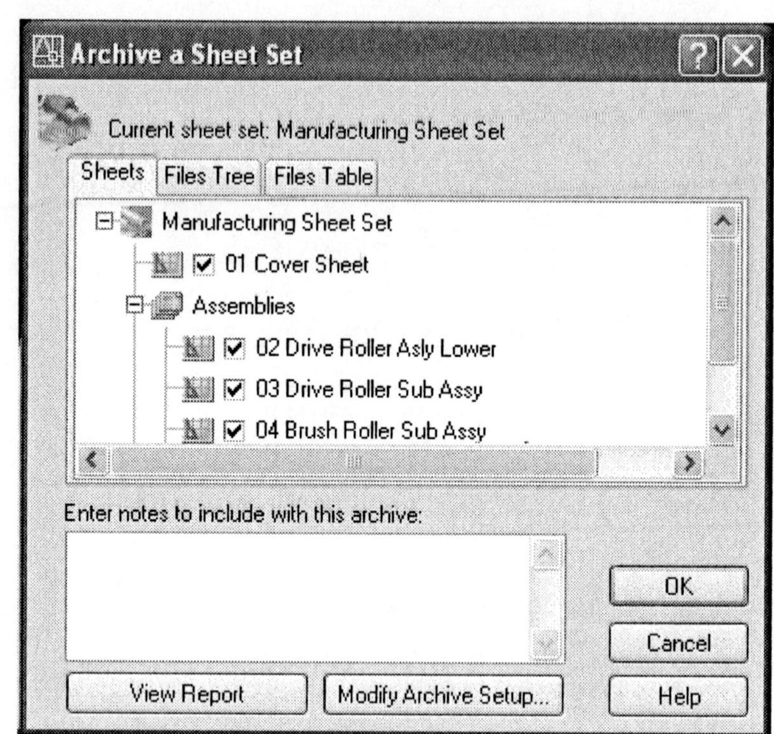

Figure 24.007

You'll notice three tabs in this dialog box. The first, **Sheets**, creates an archive package from your sheet set. The other two list the files in that package – the **Files Tree** tab does it in a tree view while the **Files Table** tab does it in a table view. You can remove any sheet or file by removing the check in the box to its left.

Use **Enter notes to include with this archive** to add your own notes to the report that accompanies the archive. (The **View Report** button will display the report for you.)

The **Modify Archive Setup** button calls the Modify Archive Setup dialog box (Figure 24.008. This box is almost identical to the Modify Transmittal Setup dialog box we discussed in Section 21.3. Please refer to that section for explanations of the various options.

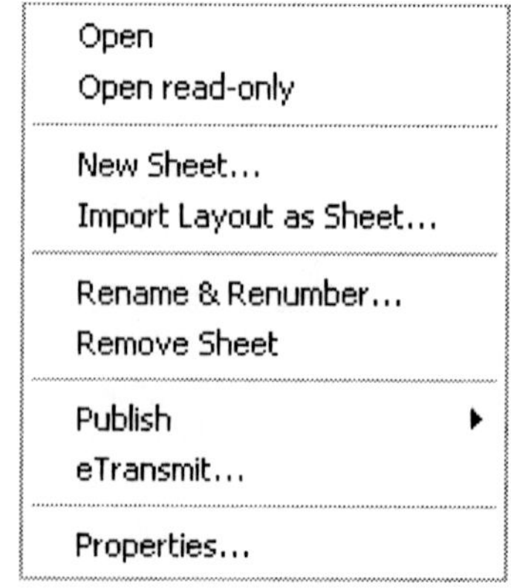

Figure 24.009

- The cursor menu presented when you right-click over a sheet in the sheet set looks like Figure 24.009 (next page). We haven't discussed two of these options.
  - The **Rename and Renumber** option calls a dialog box similar to the New Sheet dialog box (Figure 24.004). Here, however, you have a couple check boxes that enable you to **Rename associated drawing file to match sheet set title** or to **Prefix** [a] **sheet number to** [the] **file name.**
  - **Remove Sheet** removes the selected sheet from the set; it does not delete the drawing.

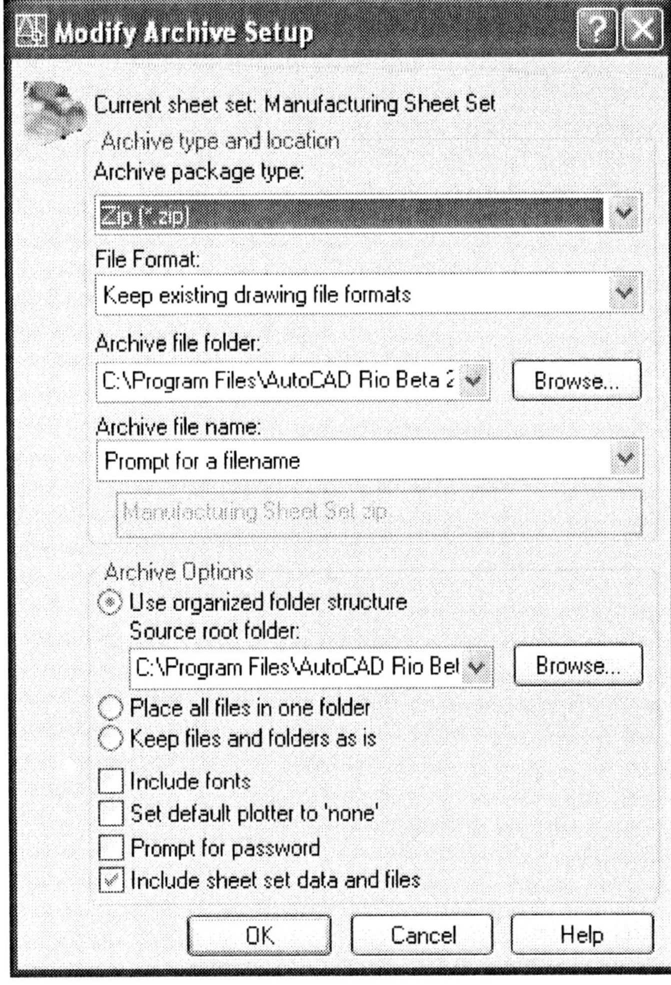

Figure 24.008

That's a tremendous amount of material for the first tab of a palette! But wait, there's more to come! (This might be a good time to shake the cobwebs loose and go get some coffee before you continue.)

Let's try an exercise with what we've learned so far.

Do This: 24.2.1.1	Creating Sheet Set

I. Open the *Tara II Data Sheet* drawing in the C:\Steps\Lesson24\Sheet Sets folder. Notice that I've set this drawing up in Paper Space. We'll create a sheet set for this project.

II. Follow these steps.

TOOLS	COMMAND SEQUENCE	STEPS
Sheet Set Manager Button	**Command:** ***ssm***	1. Open the Sheet Set Manager. You can use the command prompt or the **Sheet Set Manager** button on the Standard toolbar.

TOOLS	COMMAND SEQUENCE	STEPS
	Command: ***newsheetset***	2. We'll use the Create Sheet Set wizard. You can start it by either entering the ***NewSheetSet*** command at the command line, or selecting **New Sheet Set** from the drop down selection box at the top of the palette.
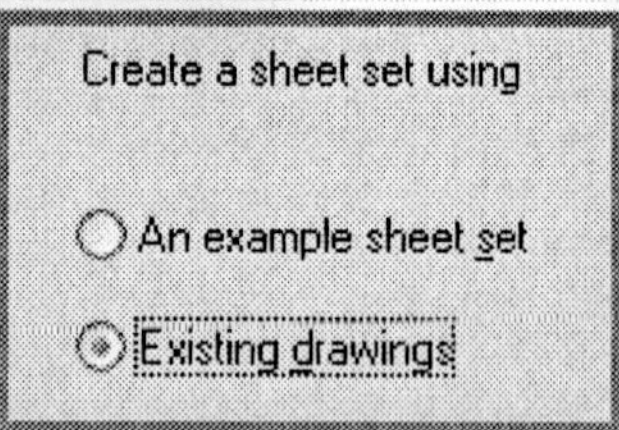 Create a sheet set using An example sheet set Existing drawings		3. AutoCAD begins the New Sheet wizard with an option to create your new sheet set using **Existing drawings** or **An example sheet set**. Using existing drawings allows you to select a folder(s) with files in it. AutoCAD will use the layouts from these drawings in the new sheet set. Using **An example sheet set** tells AutoCAD to use the structure from the sample in creating the structure for the new set. It won't add any drawings to your set. We'll use the **Existing drawings** option for this exercise. Pick the **Next** button to continue.
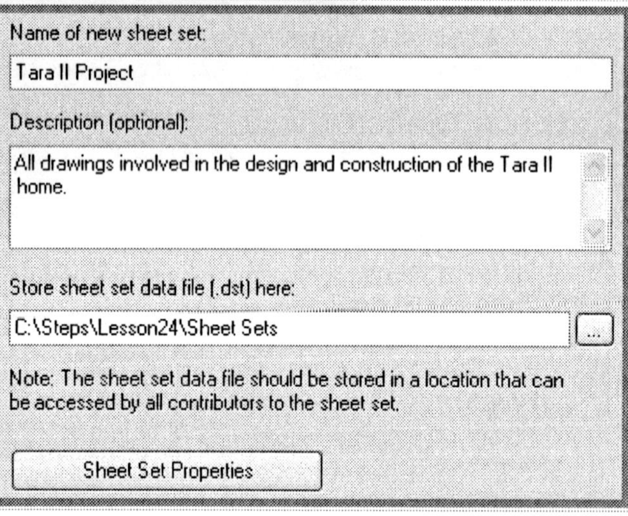 Name of new sheet set: Tara II Project Description (optional): All drawings involved in the design and construction of the Tara II home. Store sheet set data file (.dst) here: C:\Steps\Lesson24\Sheet Sets Note: The sheet set data file should be stored in a location that can be accessed by all contributors to the sheet set. Sheet Set Properties		4. On the second page of our wizard, we can name the new set (call it ***Tara II Project***). Add a description if you wish and tell AutoCAD where to store the data file for the sheet set (store yours in the C:\Steps\Lesson24\Sheet Sets folder). Notice the **Sheet Set Properties** button. Use this to create custom properties for your project. (We'll ignore it for this exercise.) Pick the **Next** button to continue.

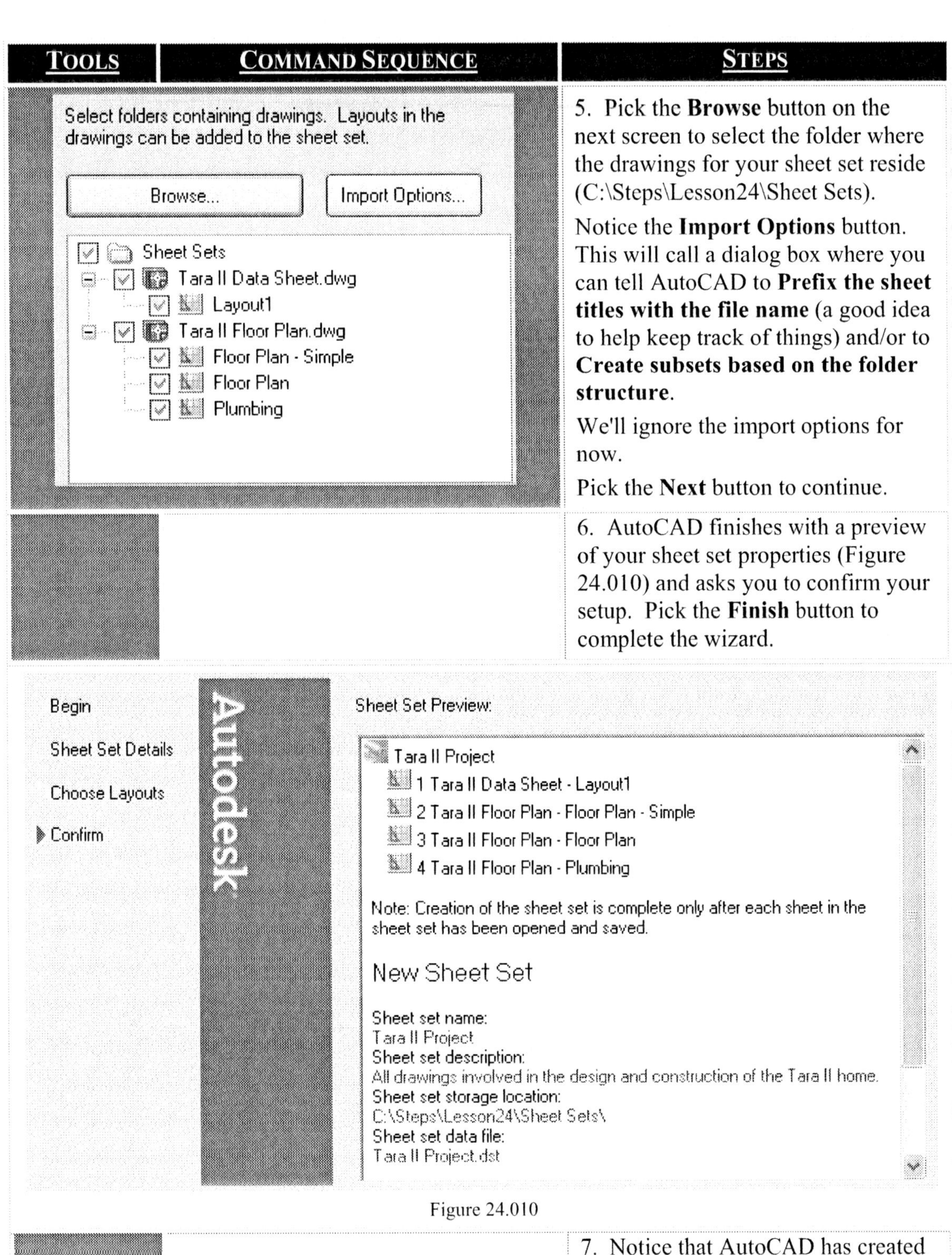

TOOLS	COMMAND SEQUENCE	STEPS
		5. Pick the **Browse** button on the next screen to select the folder where the drawings for your sheet set reside (C:\Steps\Lesson24\Sheet Sets). Notice the **Import Options** button. This will call a dialog box where you can tell AutoCAD to **Prefix the sheet titles with the file name** (a good idea to help keep track of things) and/or to **Create subsets based on the folder structure**. We'll ignore the import options for now. Pick the **Next** button to continue.
		6. AutoCAD finishes with a preview of your sheet set properties (Figure 24.010) and asks you to confirm your setup. Pick the **Finish** button to complete the wizard.

Figure 24.010

		7. Notice that AutoCAD has created your sheet set (Figure 24.011).

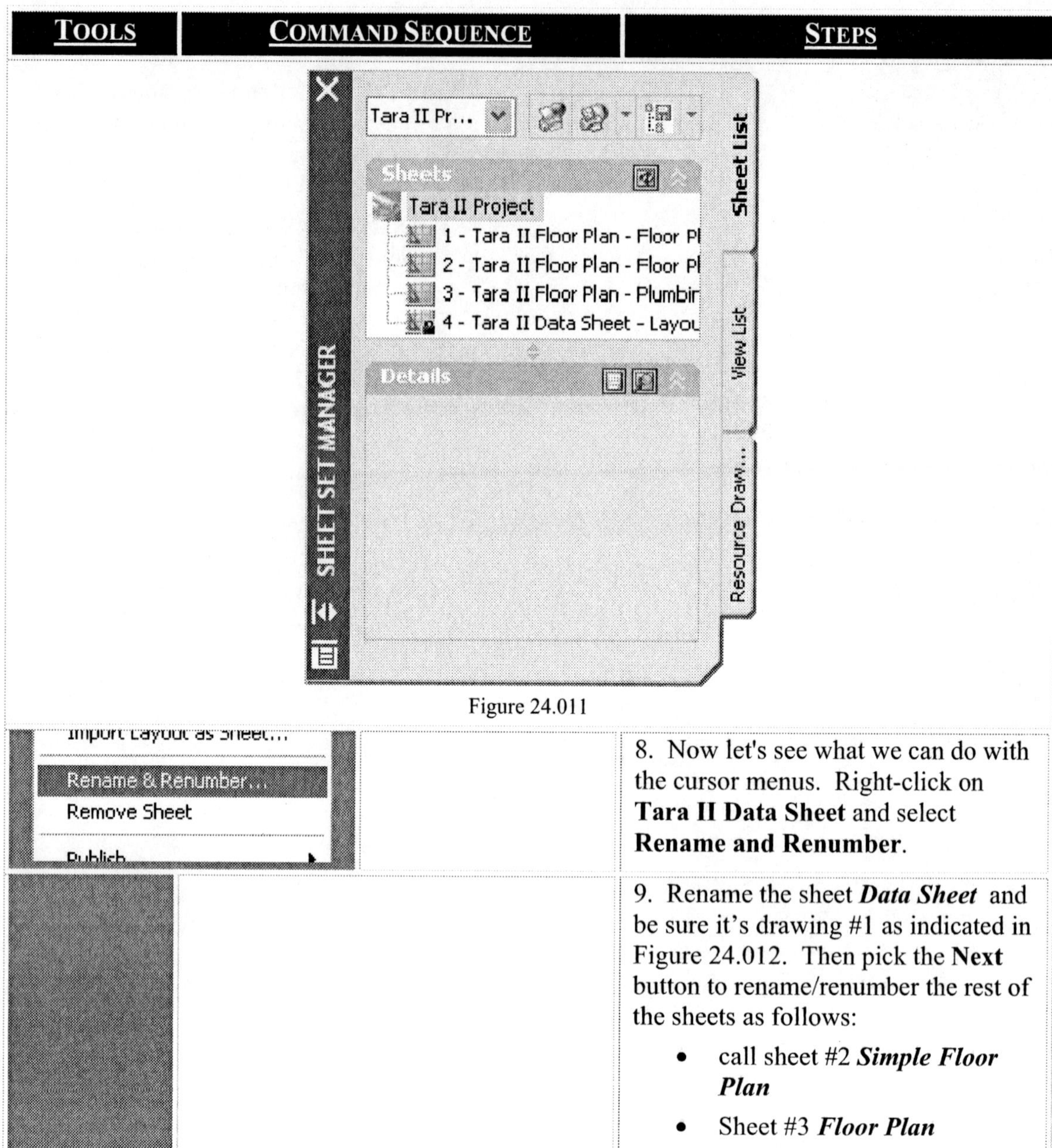

Figure 24.011

Tools	Command Sequence	Steps
		8. Now let's see what we can do with the cursor menus. Right-click on **Tara II Data Sheet** and select **Rename and Renumber**.
		9. Rename the sheet ***Data Sheet*** and be sure it's drawing #1 as indicated in Figure 24.012. Then pick the **Next** button to rename/renumber the rest of the sheets as follows: • call sheet #2 ***Simple Floor Plan*** • Sheet #3 ***Floor Plan*** • Sheet #4 ***Plumbing***

Tools	Command Sequence	Steps

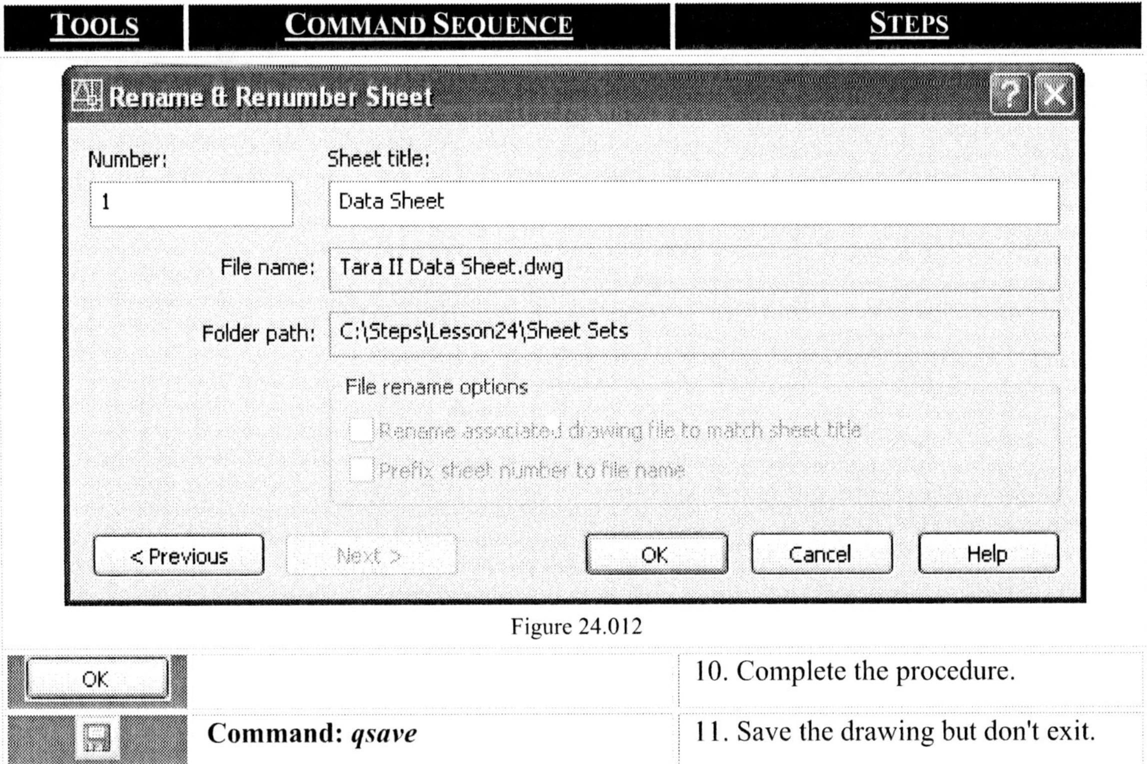

Figure 24.012

Tools	Command Sequence	Steps
OK		10. Complete the procedure.
	Command: ***qsave***	11. Save the drawing but don't exit.

In this exercise, AutoCAD has created a sheet set using the two drawings available in the C:\Steps\Lesson24\Sheet Sets folder (*Tara II Data Sheet.dwg* and *Tara II Floor Plan*). Bear in mind that I created both with Paper Space layouts (these are versions of the files you've been using), views, and blocks. But this simple four-step wizard has done so much more than is readily visible.

Take a moment and explore the **Sheet List** in the light of what we've discussed so far. Then let's continue our discussion and see what else this complex tool has to offer!

24.2.2 The View List Tab

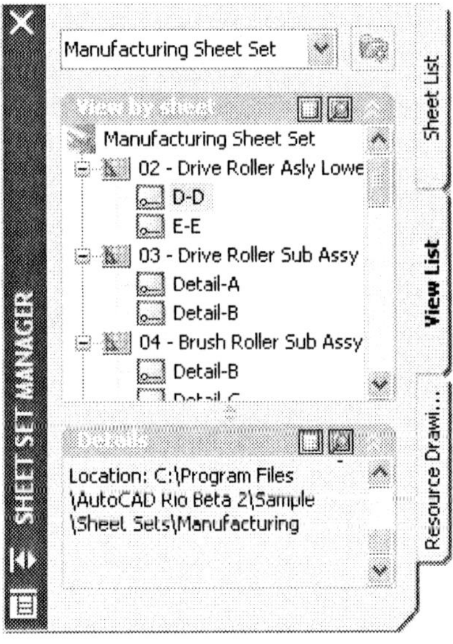

Figure 24.013

The **View List** tab of the Sheet Set Manager (Figure 24.013) presents a list of available views. In the upper list box (**View by sheet**), AutoCAD organizes the views under the name of the sheets in the set. Use the two buttons on the section's title bar to toggle between **Views by sheet** and **Views by category**. You can even use the button at the top of the palette (**New View Category**) to create your own categories. Once you have your own category, just drag and drop the views where you want them.

You can also use this tab to mine drawings for their blocks (and use the blocks in the current drawing).

Let's look at the three cursor menus for this tab.

- The first (Figure 24.014) displays when you right-click on the title of the sheet set. Use this one to either create a **New View Category** (just as the button does) or to check the **Properties** of the sheet set.

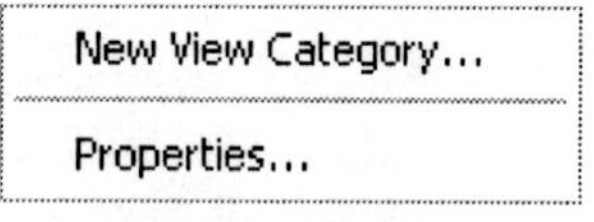

Figure 24.014

If you select the **New View Category** option (or pick the button at the top of the palette), AutoCAD will present the View Category dialog box (Figure 24.015). Here you can name your new category (**Category name** text box) or **Select the callout blocks to be used in this category**. The list box shows the blocks that are currently available in the sheet set. Use the **Add Blocks** button to add additional blocks or remove existing ones (you'll see this in our next exercise).

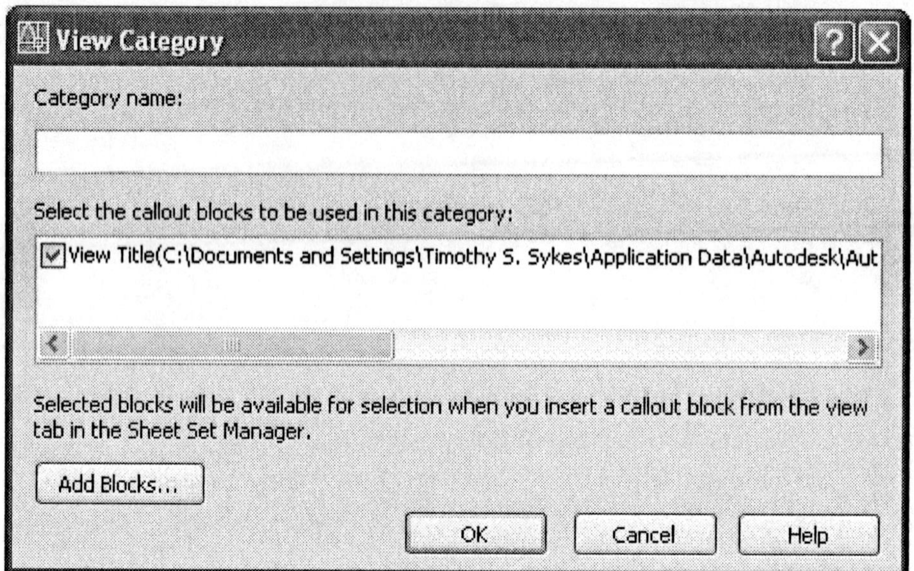

Figure 24.015

- The second cursor menu (Figure 24.016) appears when you right-click on one of the folders. Use it to **Rename** a category, **Remove** [a] **Category**, or view the **Properties** of that category. You can also add blocks to the category via the Properties dialog box.

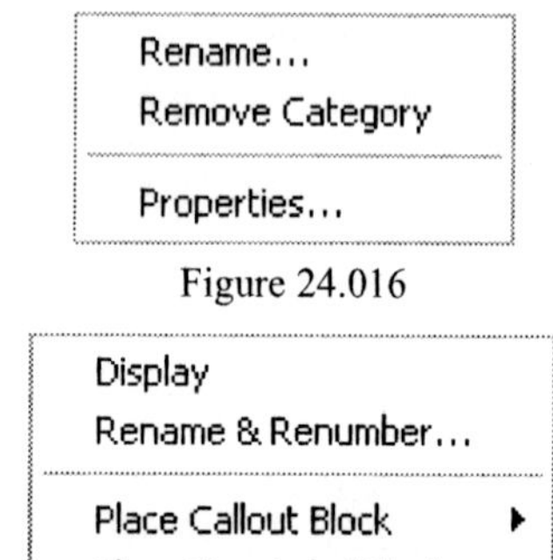

Figure 24.016

- The last (Figure 24.017) appears when you right-click on one of the views.
  - o The **Display** option is one of AutoCAD's finest. It opens the appropriate drawing with the selected view displayed. How's that for handy?! (Show some restraint with this one. You can wind up with several drawings open at once … and wonder why your system has slowed so much!)

Display
Rename & Renumber...
Place Callout Block
Place View Label Block

Figure 24.017

  - o **Rename and Renumber** (when selected from this menu) will present the Rename and Renumber dialog box seen in Figure 24.018. Here you can rename and/or renumber the selected view.

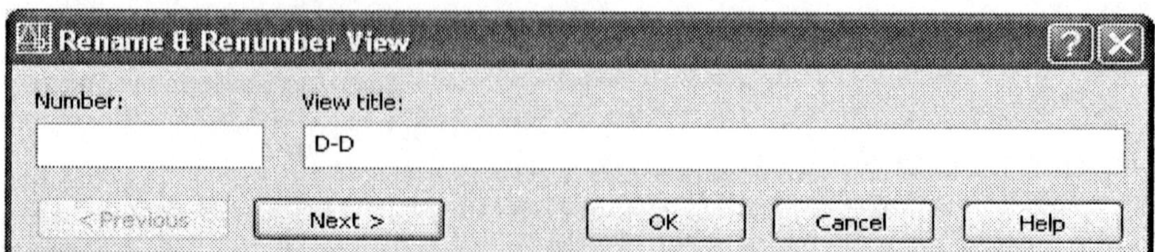

Figure 24.018

- **Place Callout Block** presents a list of blocks available from the sheet set drawing that contains the selected view. You can insert these blocks into the current drawing. If no blocks are available, AutoCAD displays a **Select Blocks** option. Use this to call the View Category dialog box (Figure 24.015). From there, pick the **Add Blocks** button to add blocks to the list.
- The **Place View Label Block** inserts a standard view label (we'll see this in our next exercise).

Let's try another exercise before we continue to the last tab.

Do This: 24.2.2.1	Working with the Views List Tab

I. Begin a new drawing from scratch.

II. Use architectural units and set the limits for a C-size sheet of paper (upper left limits of 88',68').

III. Follow these steps.

TOOLS	COMMAND SEQUENCE	STEPS
	Command: ***opensheetset***	1. If the Tara II sheet set isn't open, use the drop down selection box at the top of the palette to open it. (Select **Open** from the list, navigate to the C:\Steps\Lesson24\Sheet Sets folder, and then select the *Tara II Project.dst* file.) Alternately, you can use the ***OpenSheetSet*** command.
		2. Pick the **View List** tab to place it on top and then the **View by category** button to adjust the list. Notice the categories with and without a list of views. Let's make these more manageable.
		3. Use the cursor menu to **Renumber and Rename** the three views in the Border Data category as follows: • rename **FP - Block Border Data** to **Floor Plan Title Block**; make it **#001**; • rename **FP – Simple Title and Revision Block** to **Simple Plan Title Block**; make it **#002**; • rename **Plumbing – Block Border Data** to **Plumbing Title Block**; make it **#003**.
New View Category... Properties...		4. Right click on the **Project** title and select **New View Category**.

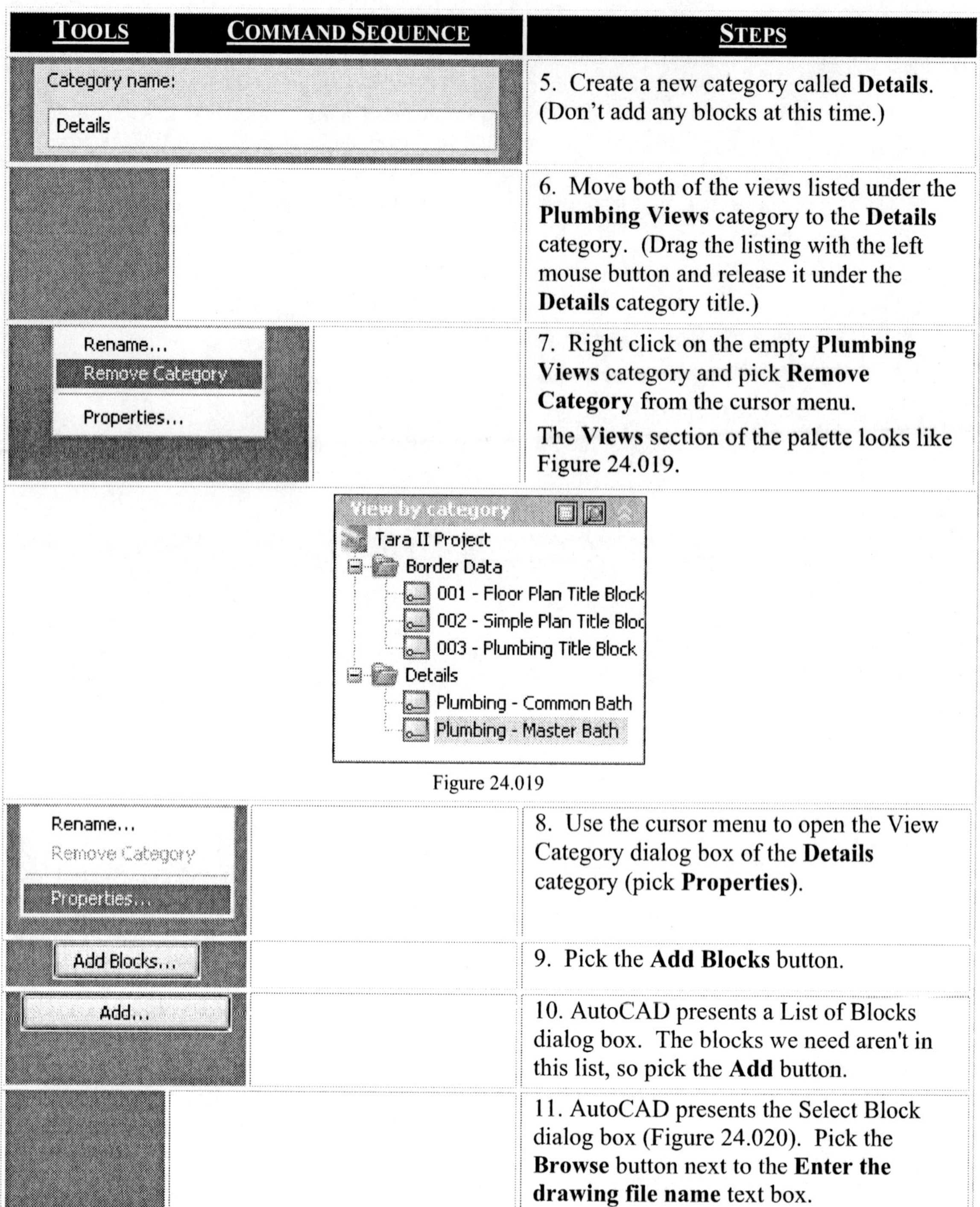

TOOLS	COMMAND SEQUENCE	STEPS
		5. Create a new category called **Details**. (Don't add any blocks at this time.)
		6. Move both of the views listed under the **Plumbing Views** category to the **Details** category. (Drag the listing with the left mouse button and release it under the **Details** category title.)
		7. Right click on the empty **Plumbing Views** category and pick **Remove Category** from the cursor menu. The **Views** section of the palette looks like Figure 24.019.
	Figure 24.019	
		8. Use the cursor menu to open the View Category dialog box of the **Details** category (pick **Properties**).
		9. Pick the **Add Blocks** button.
		10. AutoCAD presents a List of Blocks dialog box. The blocks we need aren't in this list, so pick the **Add** button.
		11. AutoCAD presents the Select Block dialog box (Figure 24.020). Pick the **Browse** button next to the **Enter the drawing file name** text box.

TOOLS	COMMAND SEQUENCE	STEPS

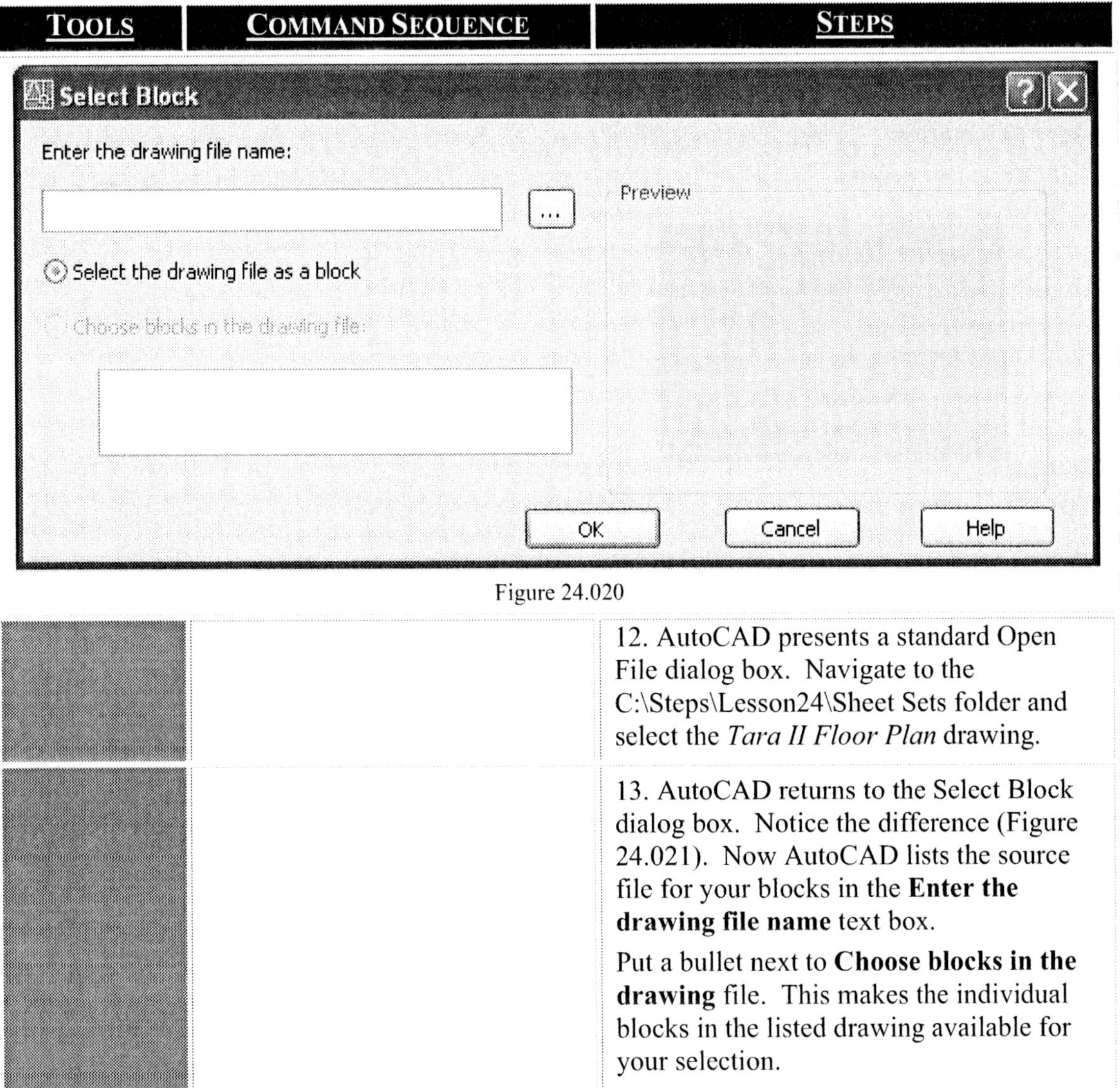

Figure 24.020

		12. AutoCAD presents a standard Open File dialog box. Navigate to the C:\Steps\Lesson24\Sheet Sets folder and select the *Tara II Floor Plan* drawing.
		13. AutoCAD returns to the Select Block dialog box. Notice the difference (Figure 24.021). Now AutoCAD lists the source file for your blocks in the **Enter the drawing file name** text box. Put a bullet next to **Choose blocks in the drawing** file. This makes the individual blocks in the listed drawing available for your selection. Select the **Sink**, **Tub**, and **WC**, as shown. Pick the **OK** button here and on the List of Blocks dialog box to return to the View Category dialog box.

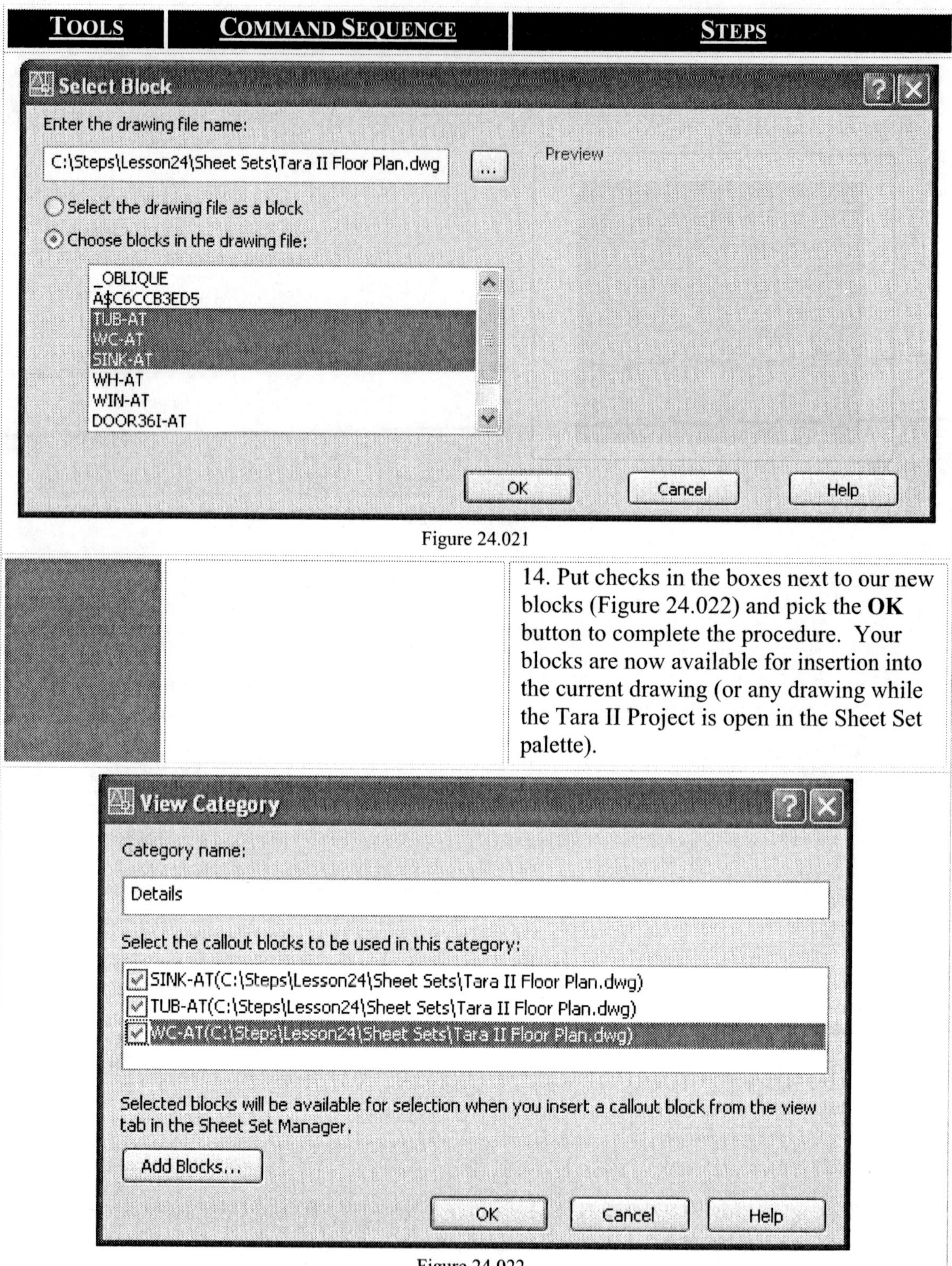

TOOLS	COMMAND SEQUENCE	STEPS

Figure 24.021

		14. Put checks in the boxes next to our new blocks (Figure 24.022) and pick the **OK** button to complete the procedure. Your blocks are now available for insertion into the current drawing (or any drawing while the Tara II Project is open in the Sheet Set palette).

Figure 24.022

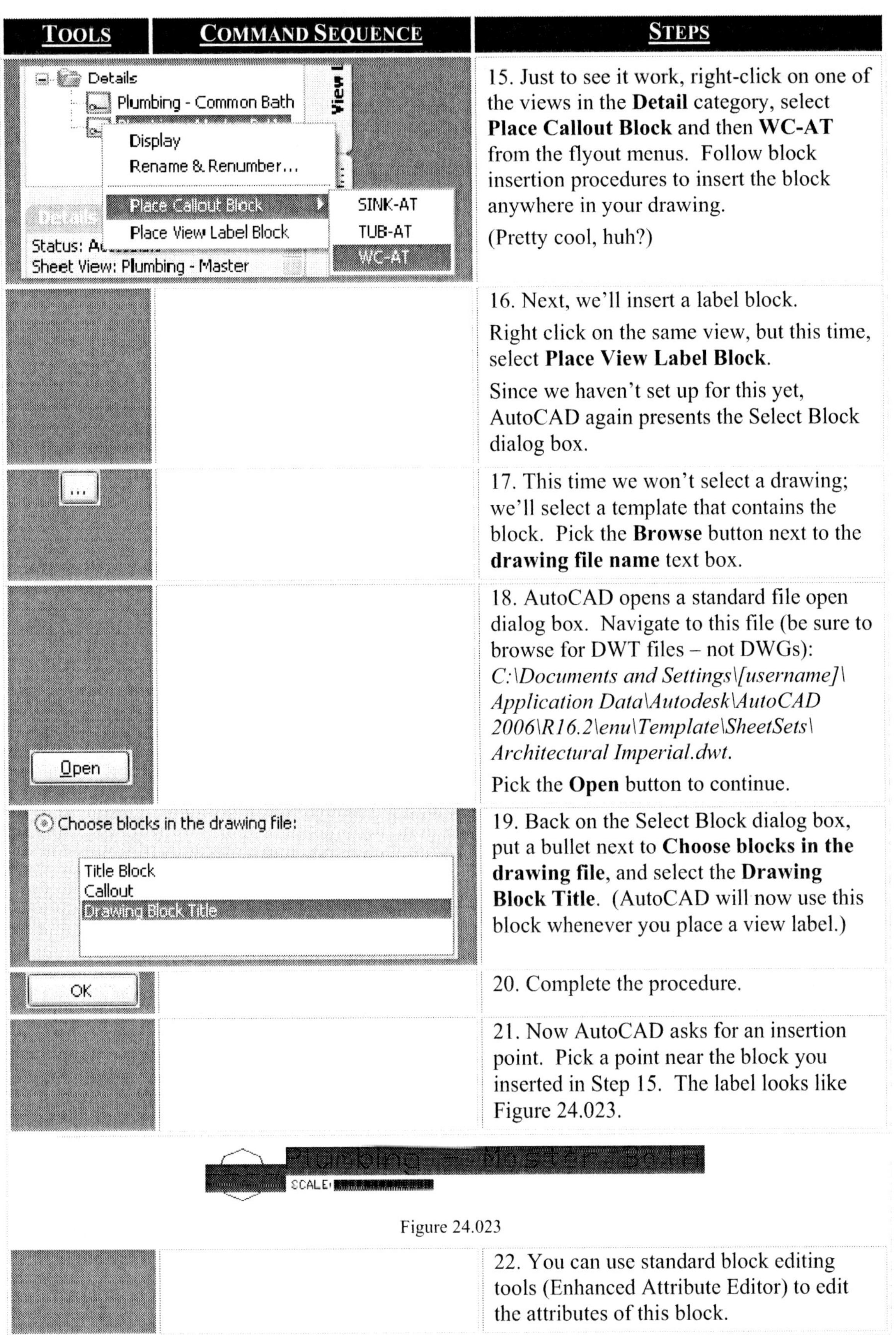

TOOLS	COMMAND SEQUENCE	STEPS
Details; Plumbing - Common Bath; Display; Rename & Renumber...; Place Callout Block; Place View Label Block; Status:; Sheet View: Plumbing - Master	SINK-AT; TUB-AT; WC-AT	15. Just to see it work, right-click on one of the views in the **Detail** category, select **Place Callout Block** and then **WC-AT** from the flyout menus. Follow block insertion procedures to insert the block anywhere in your drawing. (Pretty cool, huh?)
		16. Next, we'll insert a label block. Right click on the same view, but this time, select **Place View Label Block**. Since we haven't set up for this yet, AutoCAD again presents the Select Block dialog box.
...		17. This time we won't select a drawing; we'll select a template that contains the block. Pick the **Browse** button next to the **drawing file name** text box.
Open		18. AutoCAD opens a standard file open dialog box. Navigate to this file (be sure to browse for DWT files – not DWGs): *C:\Documents and Settings\[username]\ Application Data\Autodesk\AutoCAD 2006\R16.2\enu\Template\SheetSets\ Architectural Imperial.dwt.* Pick the **Open** button to continue.
Choose blocks in the drawing file: Title Block; Callout; Drawing Block Title		19. Back on the Select Block dialog box, put a bullet next to **Choose blocks in the drawing file**, and select the **Drawing Block Title**. (AutoCAD will now use this block whenever you place a view label.)
OK		20. Complete the procedure.
		21. Now AutoCAD asks for an insertion point. Pick a point near the block you inserted in Step 15. The label looks like Figure 24.023.

Figure 24.023

		22. You can use standard block editing tools (Enhanced Attribute Editor) to edit the attributes of this block.

Wasn't that neat? Of course, you won't have to do the setup in Steps 17 through 20 every time.

24.2.3	The Resource Drawings Tab

One more tab! And we can relax … this one's fairly easy.

The **Resource Drawings** tab (Figure 24.024) contains a single option – **Add New Location**. You'll use this to add the location (folder) where you've located additional drawings that you wish to be associated with the current sheet set.

In our next exercise, we'll use this third tab to add an additional folder to our sheet set. Then we'll import a layout into our sheet set and place a sheet list onto our *Tara II Data Sheet*.

Let's begin.

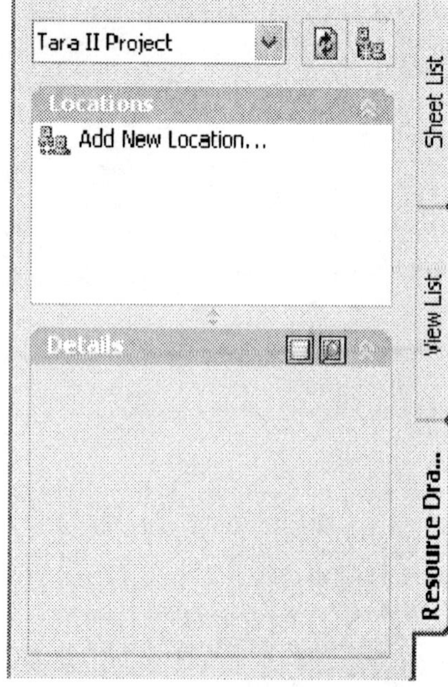

Figure 24.024

Do This: 24.2.3.1	Working with the Resource Drawing Tab & Some Final Touches

I. Be sure you're in the *Tara II Data Sheet* drawing in the C:\Steps\Lesson24\Sheet Sets folder. If not, please open it now.

II. Set the **TEXT** layer current, and pick on the **Resource Drawings** tab to put it on top of the Sheet Set palette.

III. Follow these steps.

Tools	Command Sequence	Steps
		1. First, let's associate the new folder. Double-click on the **Add New Location** option in the **Locations** list box. Alternately, you can pick the **Add New Location** button at the top of the palette.
Open		2. AutoCAD presents a standard Open dialog box. Navigate to the C:\Steps\Lesson24\ Resource Drawings folder and pick the **Open** button. Notice that the palette now shows the new folder and the drawing file within it (Figure 24.025). This drawing is now associated with the sheet set and may be plotted, archived, or transmitted with it.

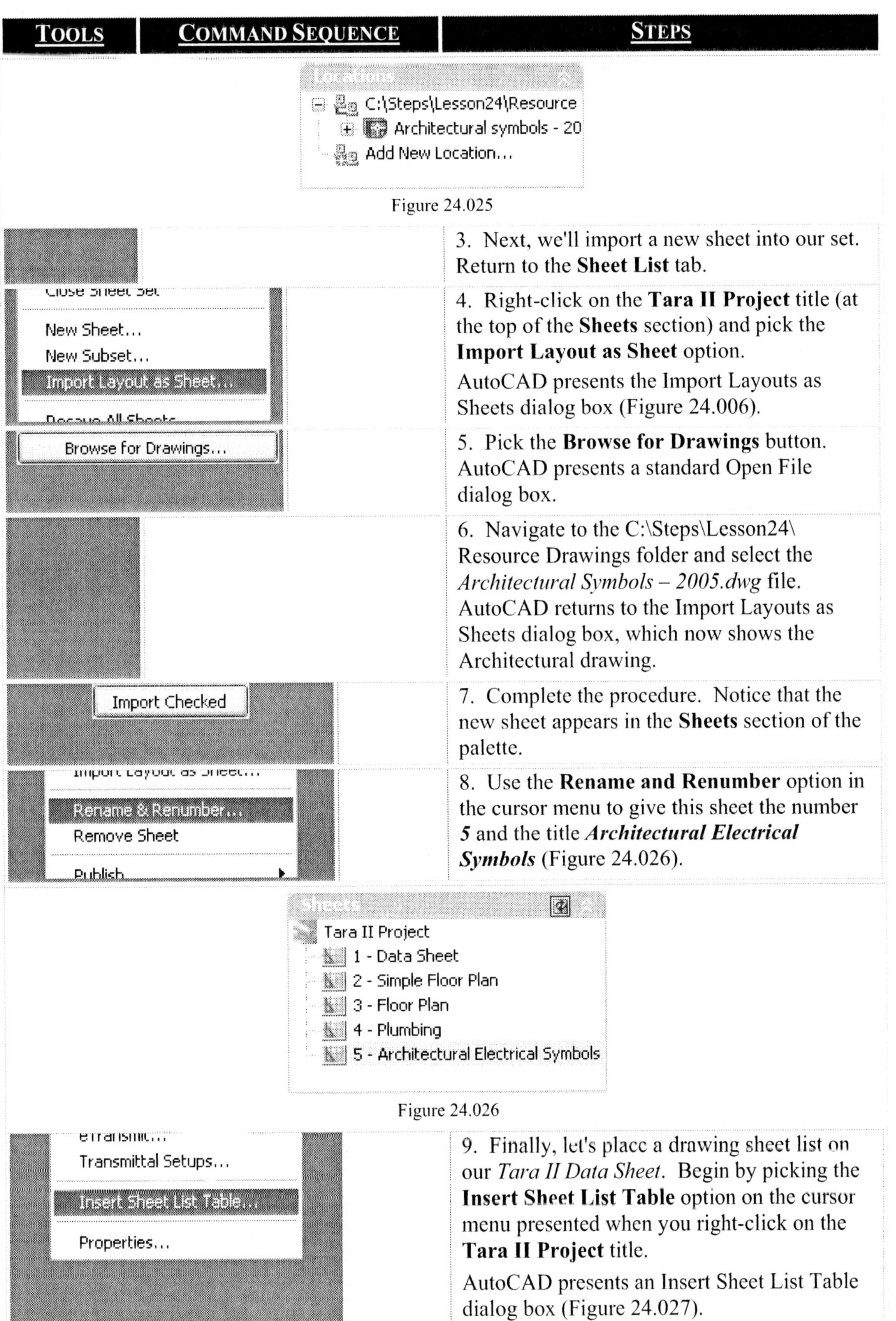

TOOLS	COMMAND SEQUENCE	STEPS

Figure 24.025

TOOLS	COMMAND SEQUENCE	STEPS
		3. Next, we'll import a new sheet into our set. Return to the **Sheet List** tab.
New Sheet... New Subset... Import Layout as Sheet...		4. Right-click on the **Tara II Project** title (at the top of the **Sheets** section) and pick the **Import Layout as Sheet** option. AutoCAD presents the Import Layouts as Sheets dialog box (Figure 24.006).
Browse for Drawings...		5. Pick the **Browse for Drawings** button. AutoCAD presents a standard Open File dialog box.
		6. Navigate to the C:\Steps\Lesson24\ Resource Drawings folder and select the *Architectural Symbols – 2005.dwg* file. AutoCAD returns to the Import Layouts as Sheets dialog box, which now shows the Architectural drawing.
Import Checked		7. Complete the procedure. Notice that the new sheet appears in the **Sheets** section of the palette.
Rename & Renumber... Remove Sheet Publish		8. Use the **Rename and Renumber** option in the cursor menu to give this sheet the number ***5*** and the title ***Architectural Electrical Symbols*** (Figure 24.026).

Figure 24.026

TOOLS	COMMAND SEQUENCE	STEPS
Transmittal Setups... Insert Sheet List Table... Properties...		9. Finally, let's place a drawing sheet list on our *Tara II Data Sheet*. Begin by picking the **Insert Sheet List Table** option on the cursor menu presented when you right-click on the **Tara II Project** title. AutoCAD presents an Insert Sheet List Table dialog box (Figure 24.027).

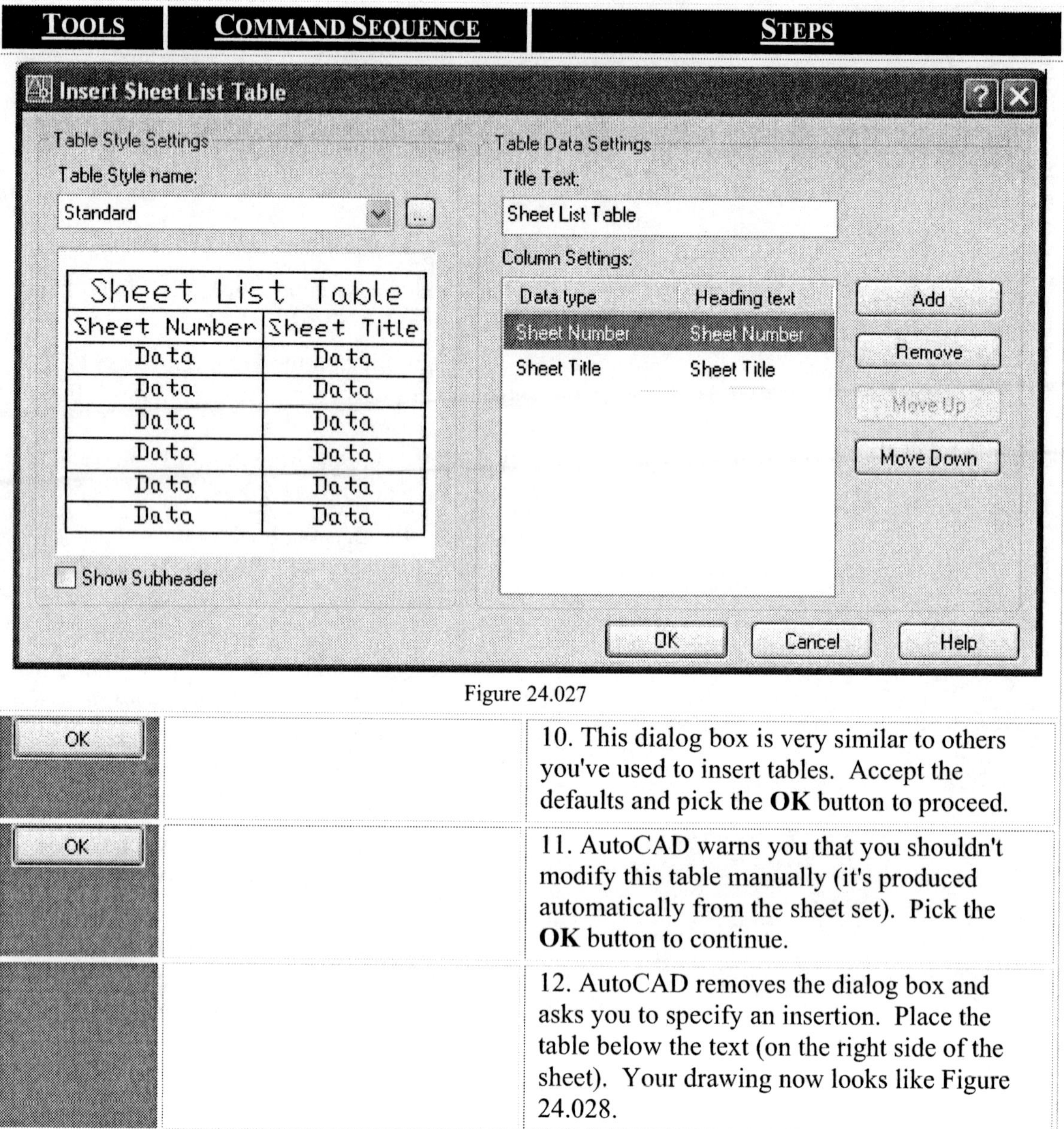

Figure 24.027

TOOLS	COMMAND SEQUENCE	STEPS
OK		10. This dialog box is very similar to others you've used to insert tables. Accept the defaults and pick the **OK** button to proceed.
OK		11. AutoCAD warns you that you shouldn't modify this table manually (it's produced automatically from the sheet set). Pick the **OK** button to continue.
		12. AutoCAD removes the dialog box and asks you to specify an insertion. Place the table below the text (on the right side of the sheet). Your drawing now looks like Figure 24.028.

TOOLS	COMMAND SEQUENCE	STEPS

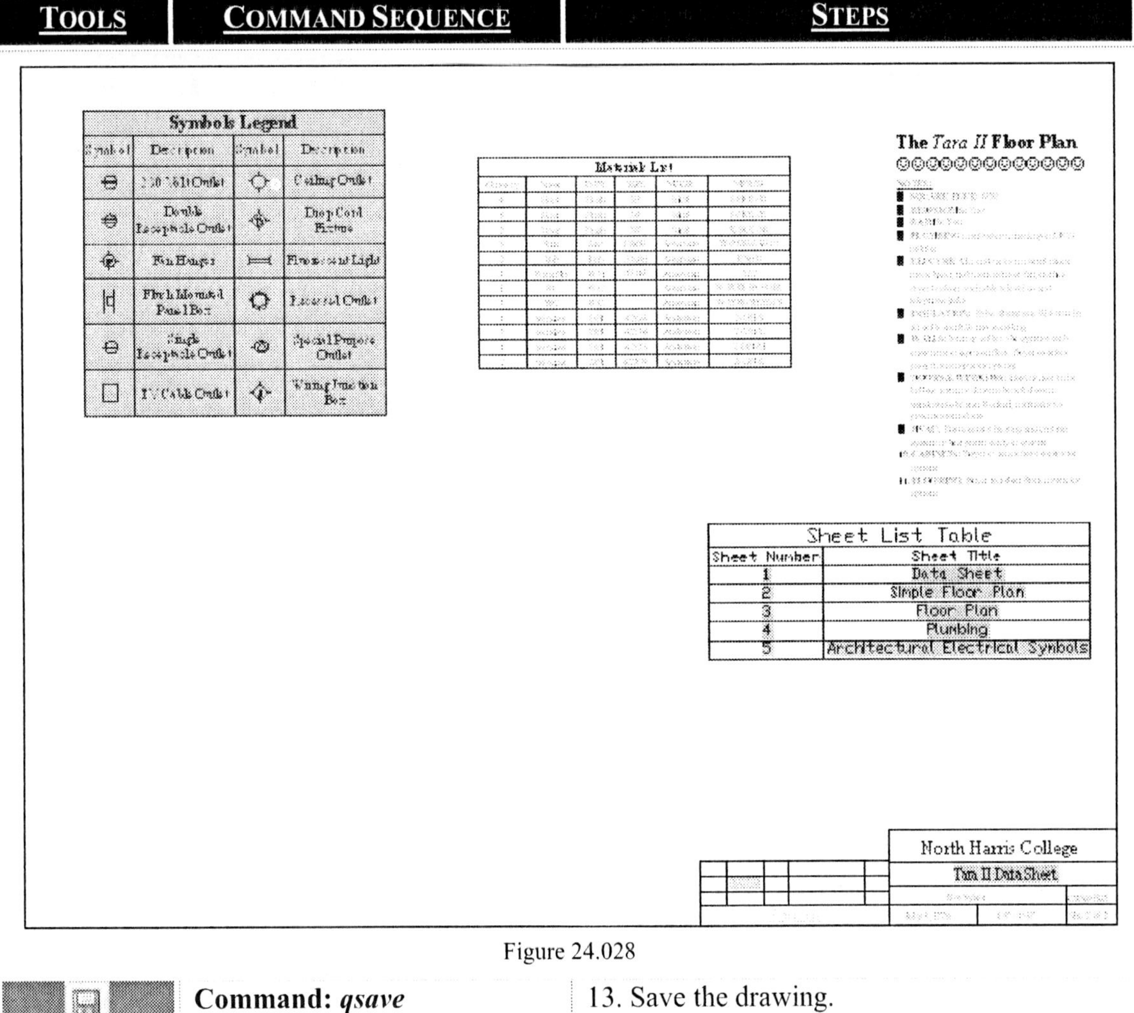

Figure 24.028

	Command: ***qsave***	13. Save the drawing.

Did you notice that the table is filled with fields that contain hyperlink jumps? You can (CTRL+) pick on any of them to open the listed drawing!

24.3 Using Your Sheet Sets to Share Information

You've seen how to set up your sheet sets, but what's the purpose? Aside from making the transition between drawings and sharing blocks (which you do as easily with other tools), what good are sheet sets?

Sheet sets help you share *project* information (as opposed to information about a specific drawing or discipline). Use them to communicate project status to clients or employers and to archive your project at predetermined stages of development.

Let's do some exercises that'll walk you through plotting (as we don't have a plotter, we'll plot to a DWF), transmitting information to our client/employer, and archiving our project.

Do This: 24.3.1	**Sharing Information with Sheet Sets – Creating a Multi-Sheet DWF File**

I. Be sure you're in the *Tara II Data Sheet* drawing in the C:\Steps\Lesson24\Sheet Sets folder. If not, please open it now.

II. Be sure the Sheet Set Manager and the **Tara II Project** are open.

III. Follow these steps.

TOOLS	COMMAND SEQUENCE	STEPS
		1. We'll begin by creating a DWF file. Right-click on the project title and select the **Publish** option from the cursor menu (Figure 24.029). Then pick the **Publish to DWF** option from the Publish menu. AutoCAD presents a standard Select File Dialog box.

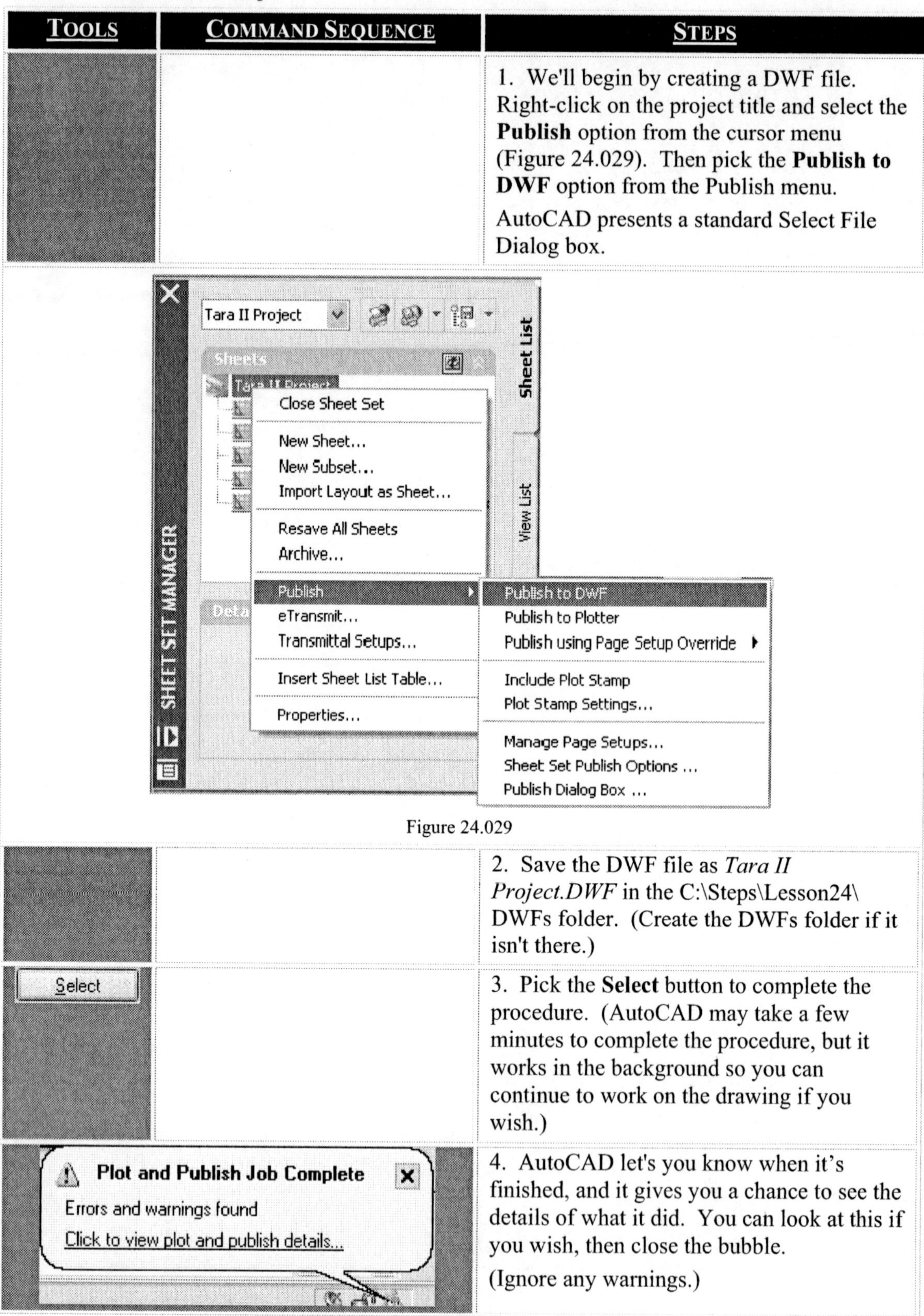

Figure 24.029

TOOLS	COMMAND SEQUENCE	STEPS
		2. Save the DWF file as *Tara II Project.DWF* in the C:\Steps\Lesson24\ DWFs folder. (Create the DWFs folder if it isn't there.)
Select		3. Pick the **Select** button to complete the procedure. (AutoCAD may take a few minutes to complete the procedure, but it works in the background so you can continue to work on the drawing if you wish.)
Plot and Publish Job Complete Errors and warnings found Click to view plot and publish details...		4. AutoCAD let's you know when it's finished, and it gives you a chance to see the details of what it did. You can look at this if you wish, then close the bubble. (Ignore any warnings.)

Tools	Command Sequence	Steps
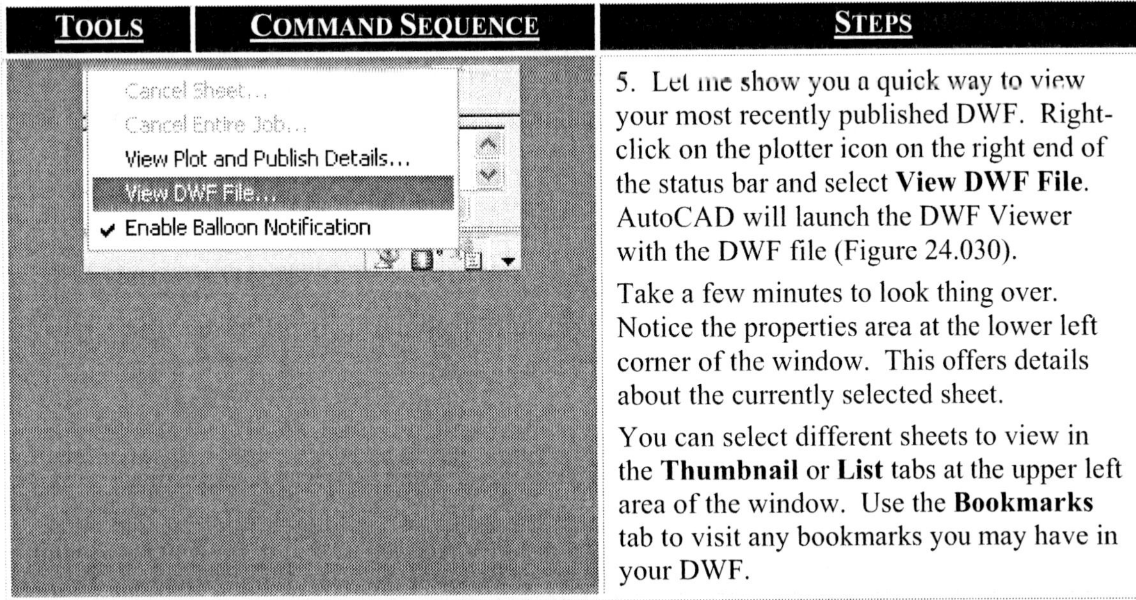		5. Let me show you a quick way to view your most recently published DWF. Right-click on the plotter icon on the right end of the status bar and select **View DWF File**. AutoCAD will launch the DWF Viewer with the DWF file (Figure 24.030). Take a few minutes to look thing over. Notice the properties area at the lower left corner of the window. This offers details about the currently selected sheet. You can select different sheets to view in the **Thumbnail** or **List** tabs at the upper left area of the window. Use the **Bookmarks** tab to visit any bookmarks you may have in your DWF.

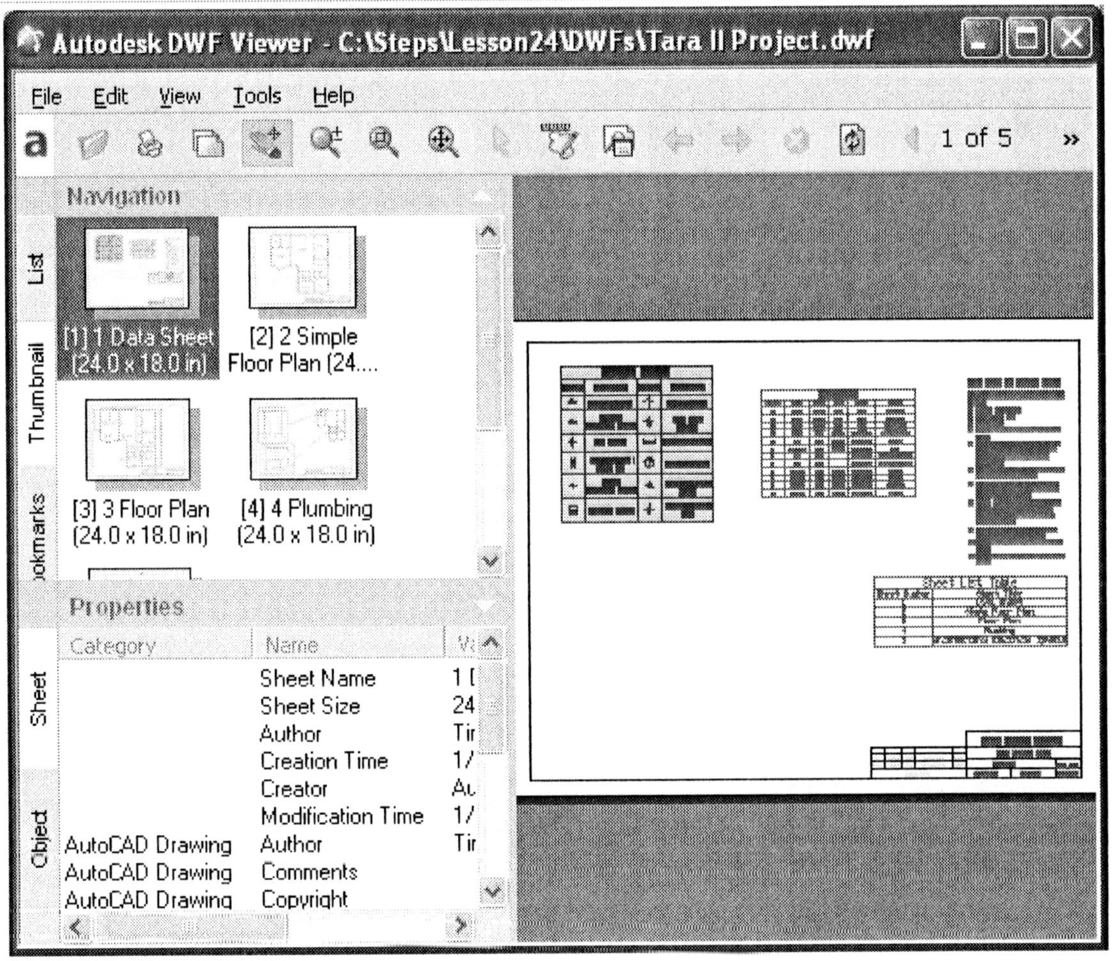

Figure 24.030

		6. Exit the viewer.

You see that creating a DWF file for a multi-sheet set is really quite easy. But remember that the Publish to DWF option uses defaults set up in the Publish dialog box, so you'll need to go there to change any settings.

The client liked our project; so let's transmit it to him.

Do This: 24.3.2	Sharing Information with Sheet Sets – Using eTransmit for a Multi-Sheet Set

I. Be sure you're in the *Tara II Data Sheet* drawing in the C:\Steps\Lesson24\Sheet Sets folder. If not, please open it now.

II. Be sure the Sheet Set Manager and the **Tara II Project** are open.

III. Follow these steps.

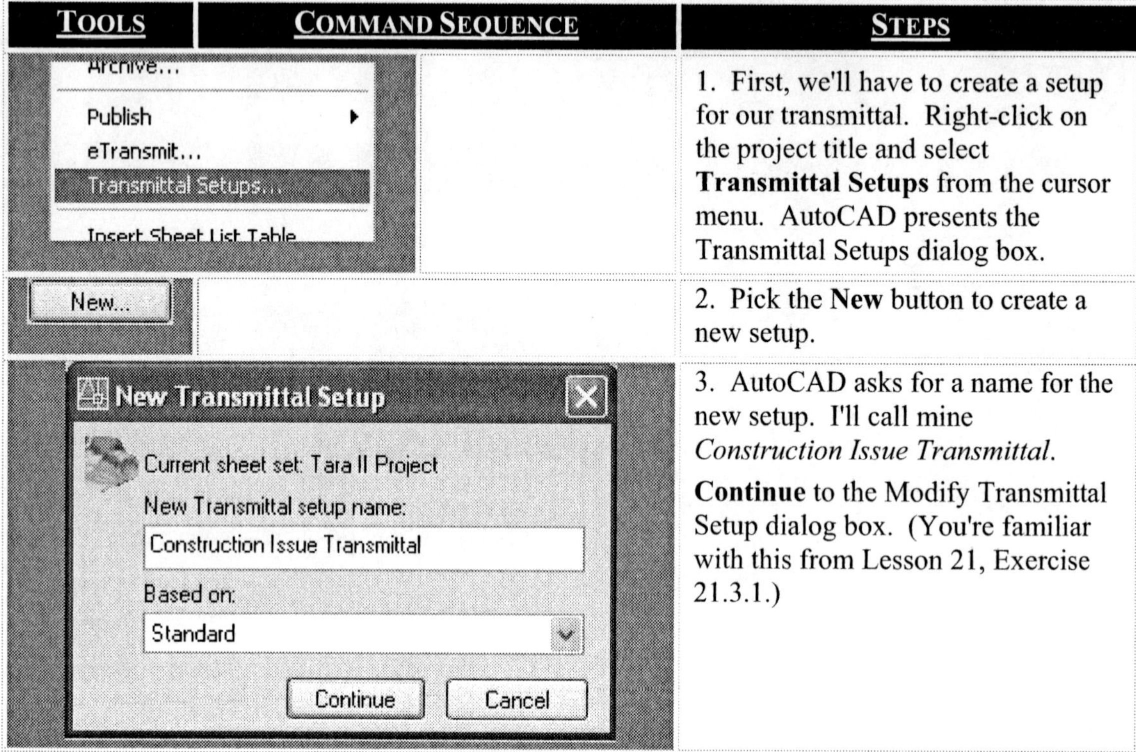

TOOLS	COMMAND SEQUENCE	STEPS
		1. First, we'll have to create a setup for our transmittal. Right-click on the project title and select **Transmittal Setups** from the cursor menu. AutoCAD presents the Transmittal Setups dialog box.
		2. Pick the **New** button to create a new setup.
		3. AutoCAD asks for a name for the new setup. I'll call mine *Construction Issue Transmittal*. **Continue** to the Modify Transmittal Setup dialog box. (You're familiar with this from Lesson 21, Exercise 21.3.1.)

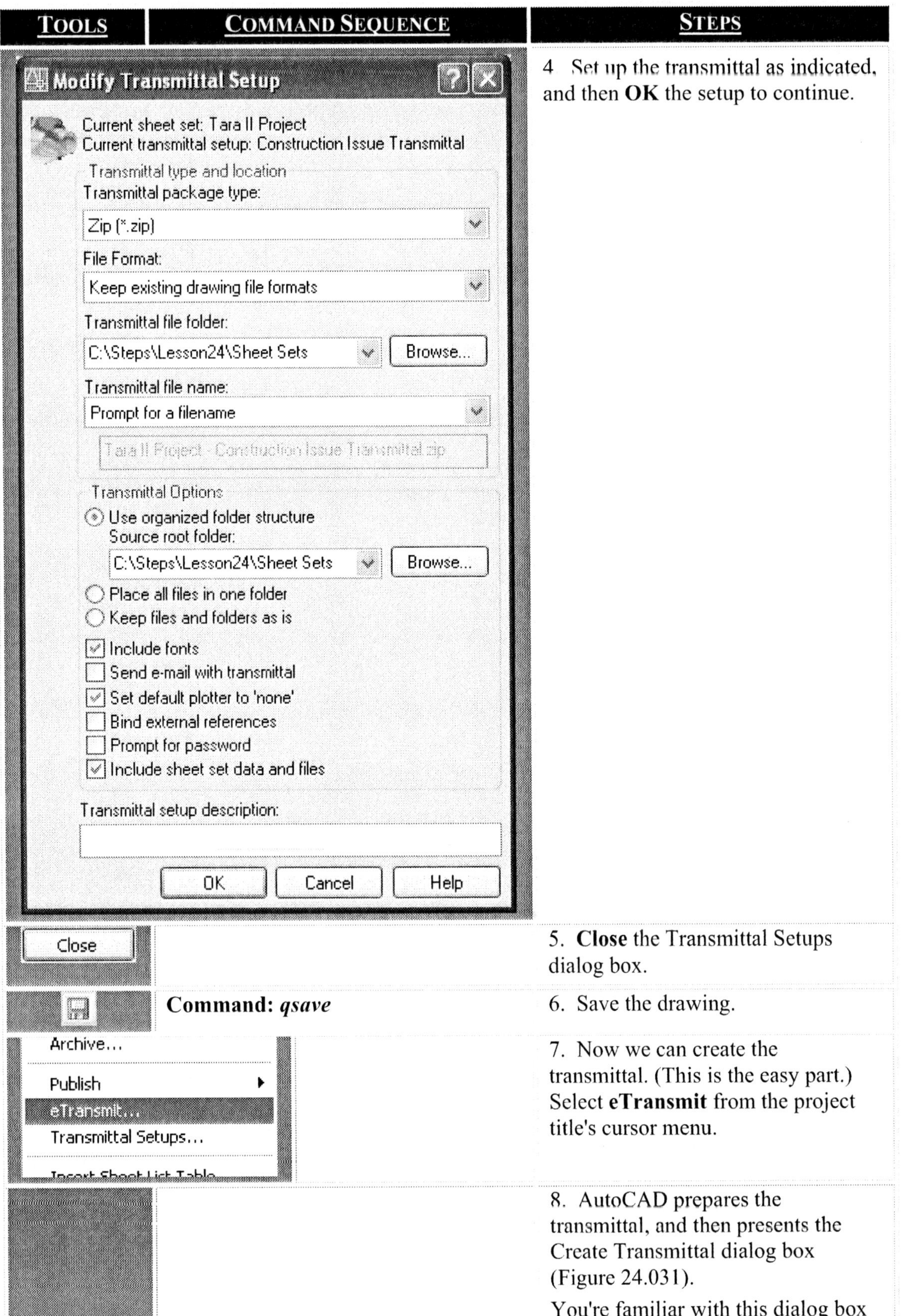

TOOLS	COMMAND SEQUENCE	STEPS
		4. Set up the transmittal as indicated, and then **OK** the setup to continue.
		5. **Close** the Transmittal Setups dialog box.
	Command: ***qsave***	6. Save the drawing.
		7. Now we can create the transmittal. (This is the easy part.) Select **eTransmit** from the project title's cursor menu.
		8. AutoCAD prepares the transmittal, and then presents the Create Transmittal dialog box (Figure 24.031). You're familiar with this dialog box

Tools	Command Sequence	Steps
		from your studies in Lesson 21, but notice that AutoCAD has included a **Sheets** tab. This tab lists the drawings that AutoCAD will include in the transmittal (you can remove the check from the check box to exclude a drawing). Notice that not all of the sheets have checks. These sheets are included as layouts in a checked drawing. Select the **Construction Issue Transmittal** setup (or whatever setup you created) and pick the **OK** button to continue.

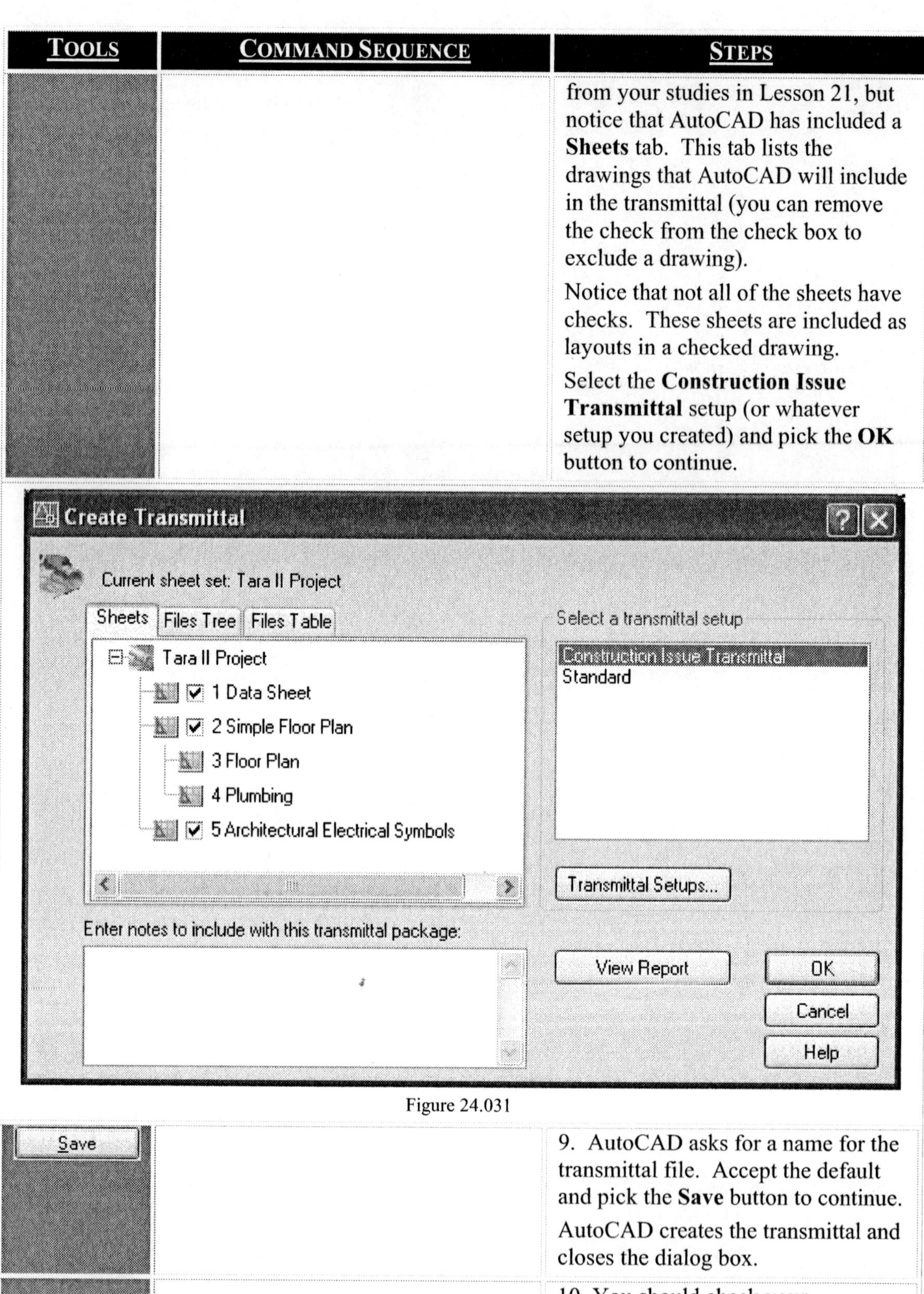

Figure 24.031

Tools	Command Sequence	Steps
Save		9. AutoCAD asks for a name for the transmittal file. Accept the default and pick the **Save** button to continue. AutoCAD creates the transmittal and closes the dialog box.
		10. You should check your transmittal before sending it. Go to the C:\Steps\Lesson24\Sheet Sets folder to make sure your transmittal file was created. (You can open it if

TOOLS	COMMAND SEQUENCE	STEPS
		you have a program capable of opening a zip file, and check the files that were included.)

Okay, we've plotted our project (created a DWF) and sent it to the client. Now we need to archive it – put it away so we can start working on something else.

Here we go.

Do This: 24.3.3	Sharing Information with Sheet Sets – Archiving Your Project

I. Be sure you're in the *Tara II Data Sheet* drawing in the C:\Steps\Lesson24\Sheet Sets folder. If not, please open it now.

II. Be sure the Sheet Set Manager and the **Tara II Project** are open.

III. Follow these steps.

TOOLS	COMMAND SEQUENCE	STEPS
Resave All Sheets Archive...		1. Select **Archive** from the project title's cursor menu. AutoCAD presents the Archive a Sheet Set dialog box.
Modify Archive Setup...		2. We'll need to set up the archive so pick the **Modify Archive Setup** button.

Tools	**Command Sequence**	**Steps**
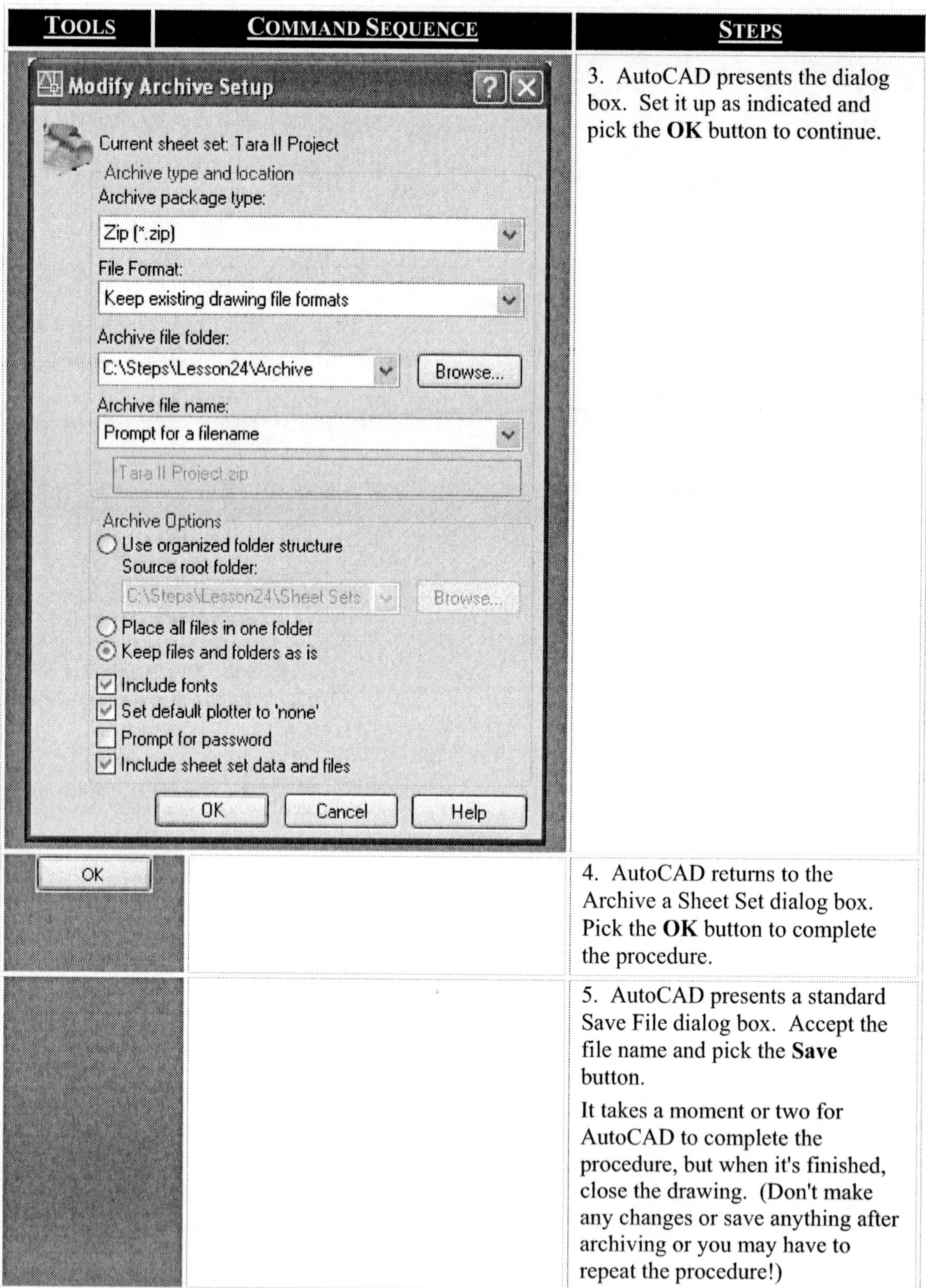		3. AutoCAD presents the dialog box. Set it up as indicated and pick the **OK** button to continue.
OK		4. AutoCAD returns to the Archive a Sheet Set dialog box. Pick the **OK** button to complete the procedure.
		5. AutoCAD presents a standard Save File dialog box. Accept the file name and pick the **Save** button. It takes a moment or two for AutoCAD to complete the procedure, but when it's finished, close the drawing. (Don't make any changes or save anything after archiving or you may have to repeat the procedure!)

24.4 Extra Steps

- Since this is a fairly new tool, call up AutoCAD's help window and explore the entries under the **Sheet Set** category.
- Launch the New Features Workshop under the Help pull down menu and let AutoCAD walk you through the Sheet Set tutorials. (There's nothing quite like a demonstration to help you see things you might have missed!)

24.5 What Have We Learned?

Items covered in this lesson include:

- *Sheet Sets*
    - o *creation*
    - o *transmittals*
    - o *archiving*
    - o *publishing*

This has been a tough lesson. For a palette with such a simple appearance, AutoCAD has created a bit of a monster … but like Godzilla, it's a monster that can be quite helpful. (Okay, so Godzilla helped mostly in urban renewal efforts for a model Tokyo … but you get the idea.)

I do encourage you to take some time to get comfortable with sheet sets. Like most complex tools, those who demonstrate mastery are the ones who make the money.

This completes the fifth section of our text (whew!). Our next (last!) section will explain how AutoCAD gets along with others (including other AutoCAD programs).

24.6 Exercises

Open the *Sample Unit Data Sheet* in the C:\Steps\Lesson24\Exercises folder. Follow these instructions.

1. Add the tables shown in Figures 24.032, 24.033, 24.034, and 24.035.
    1.1. Items in the **Reference Drawings** table are hyperlink jumps to their respective drawings. The *Sample Unit.dwg* file is in the C:\Steps\Lesson24\Exercises folder; the other two drawings are in the C:\Steps\Lesson24\Exercise Resource Drawings folder.
    1.2. Locate the **Reference Drawings** table in the upper right corner of the drawing.
    1.3. Locate the **Revision block** next to the title block.
    1.4. Position the other tables as you wish. (All blocks are part of the drawing.)

0	2-6-04	TS	Issued for Approval	BB
Rev	Date	By	Description	App
Revisions				

Figure 24.032

Reference Drawings
Sample Unit.dwg
Piping Symbols Detail Sheet.dwg
Welding Symbols Detail Sheet.dwg

Figure 24033

Piping Symbols Legend	
Symbol	Description
	Concentric Reducer
	Concentric Swage
	Cross
	Eccentric Reducer
	Gate Valve
	Socket Weld Swage
	Socket Weld Tee
	Socket Weld Union
	Tee
	Union

Figure 24.034

Welding Symbols Legend	
Symbol	Description
	Bevel Both Sides
	Bevel
	Fillet
	Fillet Both Sides
	Flush
	Plug
	Scarf
	Scarf Both Sides
	Square
	Square Both Sides
	V
	V Both Sides

Figure 24.035

2. Create a sheet set called *Sample Unit Project*, and include all the files in the C:\Steps\Lesson24\Exercises folder. (Store the .dst files in the same folder.)
3. Add the two drawings in the C:\Steps\Lesson24\Exercises Resource Drawings folder as resource drawings.
4. Publish the sheet set to a printer/plotter.
5. Publish the sheet set to a DWF file.
6. Transmit the set as an executable file to your home email address or your instructor.
7. Archive the sheet set in a .zip file.

24.7 For Web-Based Review Questions, visit: http://www.uneedcad.com/2006/Files/06R24.pdf

Section IV
Interfaces

Chapter 25: Externally Referenced Drawings

Chapter 26: Other Application Files and AutoCAD

Chapter 27: Databases and AutoCAD

Lesson 25

Following this lesson, you will:

- ✓ *Know how to reference one drawing from another*
  - *Know how to use the Xref Manager*
  - *Know how to attach, detach, and overlay a reference drawing*
  - *Know how to clip a reference to see just what you want to see*
  - *Understand reference drawings' dependent symbols*
  - *Know how to load, unload, and reload a reference*
  - *Know how to edit a referenced drawing from within the primary drawing*
- ✓ *Know how to open a referenced drawing from within the primary drawing*
- ✓ *Know how to permanently bind a referenced drawing to the primary drawing*

Externally Referenced Drawings

Think way back to our discussion of layers in Lesson 6. I explained layers by referring to the presentation method Encyclopedia Britannica *used to detail the human body (plastic overlays with the different systems of the body). This is also the idea behind externally referenced drawings – Xrefs.*

There is, however, quite a difference between layers and Xrefs. We use layers, as you know, to control the display of, and differentiate between, objects in a drawing (much as we used linetypes and widths on the drawing board). On the other hand, we use Xrefs to save drawing time and computer memory by sharing information (much as Britannica *shared the outline of the human body among the various system overlays).*

> When working with Xrefs, file location is a critical consideration. For the exercises in this lesson to work properly with the files provided, the files must be located in one of two places:
>
> 1. The best location is the C:\Steps\Lesson25 folder. This site has been thoroughly tested to be sure the files work properly.
> 2. The files may be placed on a network or other location *provided the path is defined in the **Project File Search Path*** (**Files** tab of the Options dialog box). If you're not comfortable with the Options dialog box, however, and don't have a CAD guru who can help, *please don't attempt to make changes in the Options dialog box.* Use the first choice instead.

25.1 Working with Externally Referenced Drawings – Xrefs

Exactly what are Xrefs?

Xrefs – externally referenced drawings – are drawings called into another drawing as a referenced background or object. They are, in fact, quite similar to blocks with some notable exceptions:

- Unlike blocks, Xrefs don't occupy space within a drawing. That is, the drawing won't increase in size (at least not appreciably) with the inclusion of an Xref.
- Whereas a block may contain attributed information, an Xref can't. However, the referenced file may contain blocks with attributes, and the values of these attributes may be extracted from the primary drawing (the one doing the referencing).
- The primary drawing automatically reloads the referenced drawing whenever the primary drawing is accessed. Additionally, when the referenced drawing is updated, AutoCAD will let you know with an information bubble in the lower right corner of the window. So, the reference is as current as the last time the primary drawing was opened.

What are the benefits of using Xrefs?

- An important benefit of using Xrefs is that another operator may edit the referenced drawing without tying up your primary drawing. The changes he makes become available to you as soon as you reload the reference.
- Like blocks, any number of primary drawings may use a single referenced drawing. But unlike blocks, updating the references is automatic.

  Consider a refinery unit. Each unit requires civil, structural, piping, and electrical plans. Generally, the structural designer will copy the civil drawing for a "foundation" for his work. Likewise, the piper and electrical designer will use the structural plan. Changes to the structural plan may go unnoticed for days or weeks by others (unless some extraordinary communication occurs). However, if the pipers and electrical designers Xref the structural plan,

  - they won't have to draw the background themselves, and
  - they'll be automatically notified of any changes made to the referenced drawing, and

- any changes made by the structural designer will automatically show on the others' drawings with the next loading or reloading.

Let's take a look at how to use Xrefs.

25.1.1 Attaching and Detaching Xrefs to Your Drawing

Although you can use individual commands for each manipulation of a referenced drawing, AutoCAD provides a manager-type dialog box – the Xref Manager (Figure 25.001) – to help with Xrefs.

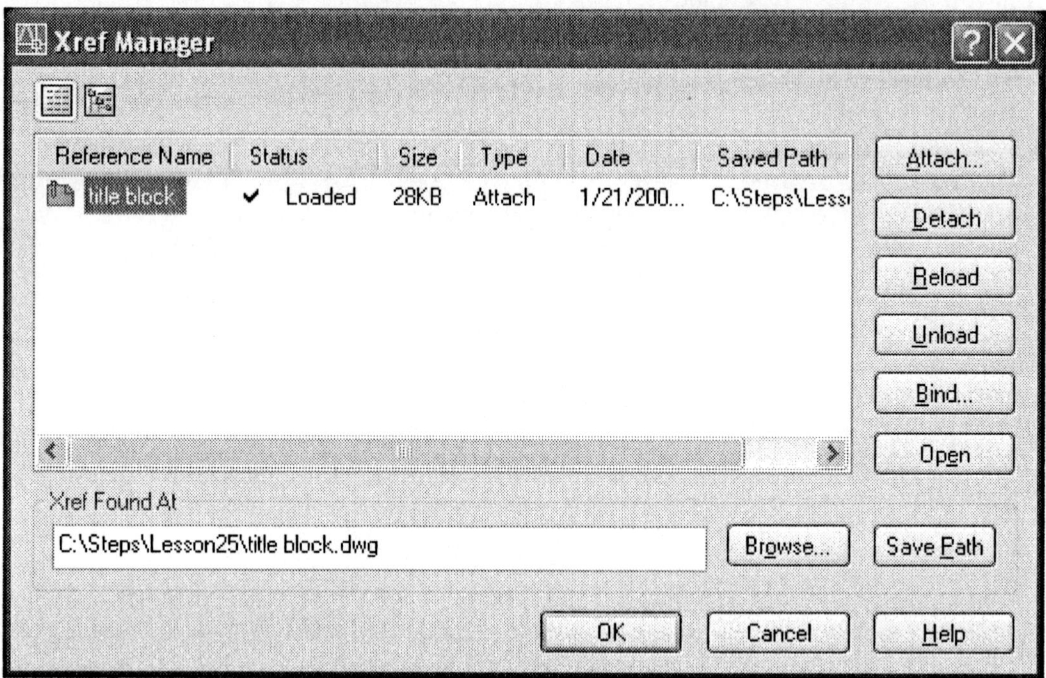

Figure 25.001

Let's take a look.

- AutoCAD allows you to view the items in the list box using either a **List View** (the default) or a **Tree View**. Toggle between types of views using the buttons in the upper left corner of the manager. (We'll use the default list view in this lesson).
- In the list box, AutoCAD provides several columns of information:
  - The **Reference Name** is the file name of the referenced drawing.
  - The drawing's **Status** will fall into one of several categories:
    - **Loaded** simply means that the drawing is currently attached.
    - An **Unloaded** reference will be removed from the primary drawing once the Xref Manager is closed. This isn't a permanent condition. The reference remains intact and may be reloaded as desired.
    - A **Reload** designation means that AutoCAD will reload that reference when the Xref Manager closes.
    - An **Unreferenced** drawing is attached to the primary drawing but has been erased.

- A drawing that no longer resides in the folder from which it was originally referenced (or in the search path defined in the Options dialog box) is marked in the **Status** column as **Not Found**.
- If AutoCAD can't read the referenced drawing, it marks it as **Unresolved**.
- Xrefs can be nested. An **Orphaned** drawing was nested into a reference that is unreferenced, unloaded, or not found.

o The **Size** column indicates the size of the referenced drawing.

o You can either **Attach** or **Overlay** a reference (see the **Type** column). An attached drawing will go with the primary drawing if another drawing references it; an overlaid drawing won't (more on this in Section 25.1.4).

o The **Date** column indicates when the referenced drawing was last modified.

o The **Saved Path** column is a bit misleading. The path refers to the location of the drawing when it was originally referenced but *not necessarily where the reference is found.* Let me explain.

When AutoCAD begins a drawing, it searches for a referenced drawing in the **Saved Path** location. If it doesn't find it there, it searches the **Project File Search Path** defined in the Options dialog box. Then it searches the folder in which the current drawing resides. It'll use the first file it finds with the appropriate name regardless of its location. But it won't change the information in the **Saved Path**.

The **Project File Search Path** is defined on the **Files** tab of the Options dialog box (Figure 25.002). Pick the "+" beside the **Project File Search Path** listing to see the folders AutoCAD will search. To add a folder, select the **Project File Search Path** listing and pick the **Add** button. AutoCAD will add a listing, and you must type in the desired name.

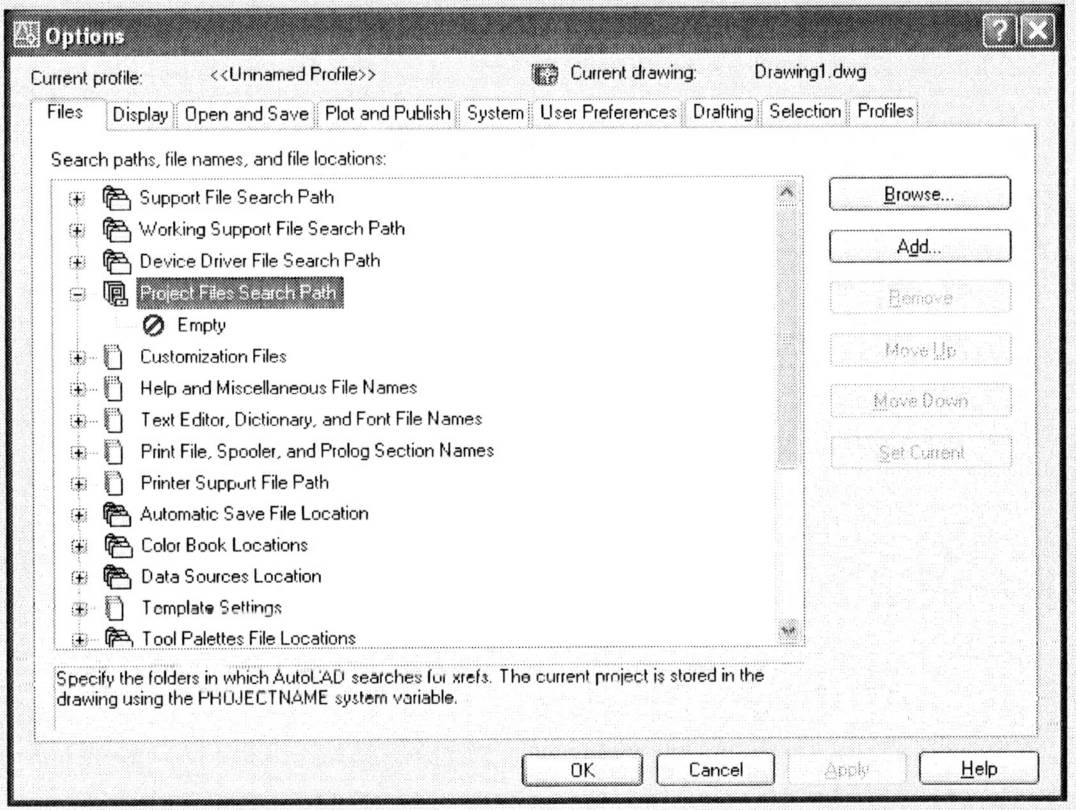

Figure 25.002

Then pick the plus beside the new project name, double-click on the **Empty** slot, and select the folder you wish to add to the search path.

Warning: Don't make changes in the Options dialog box without first consulting the CAD guru on your project.

- Down the right side of the Xref Manager (Figure 25.001), you'll find six buttons.
  - The **Attach** button begins the ***XAttach*** command.

    The ***XAttach*** command begins with a standard Select File dialog box. There you'll follow the path to the file you wish to reference. Once you've selected a file and picked the **Open** button (on the Select File dialog box), AutoCAD presents the External Reference dialog box (Figure 25.003).

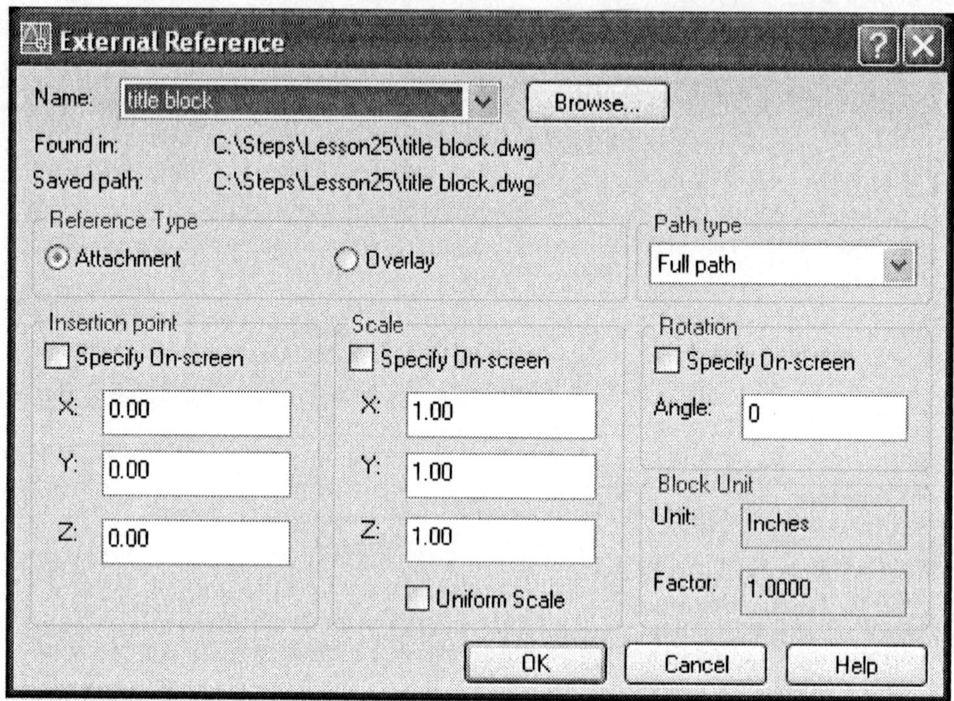

Figure 25.003

    - The **Name** control box indicates the file you're attaching. You may pick the **Browse** button to select another file.
    - In the **Reference Type** frame, tell AutoCAD if you want your reference to be an **Attachment** or **Overlay**.
    - The **Path type** provides three options to make location of the reference a bit easier.
      - ∴ Using **Full path** (the default) means that AutoCAD will use the full path (drive & location) when searching for the reference.
      - ∴ The **Relative path** option tells AutoCAD that the referenced file may be located in a subfolder of the folder in which the primary drawing is located. Relative paths won't work if the referenced drawing is on another drive.
      - ∴ **No path** means that the referenced drawing must be located in the same folder as the primary drawing or in a path identified in the **Project File Search Path** in the Options dialog box.

- The **Insertion**, **Scale**, and **Rotation** frames are identical to their counterparts on the Insert dialog box.

  - Use the **Detach** button (back on the Xref Manager) to remove references to the selected drawing. AutoCAD will detach the drawing when the Xref Manager closes. (Note: You can't detach a nested reference. You must detach its primary drawing.)
  - **Unload** a drawing to remove a reference that you may want to use later. Unloading doesn't permanently remove the reference from the drawing, but it does remove it from display.
  - The **Reload** button marks the selected file for reloading when the Xref Manager closes. Use this button to update a reference without having to reopen your primary drawing, or to display an unloaded drawing.
  - Use the **Bind** button to permanently attach a reference to a primary drawing. (This isn't the same as the ***XBind*** command, which we'll discuss in Section 25.1.3.) AutoCAD presents the Bind Xrefs dialog box (Figure 25.004) with two options.

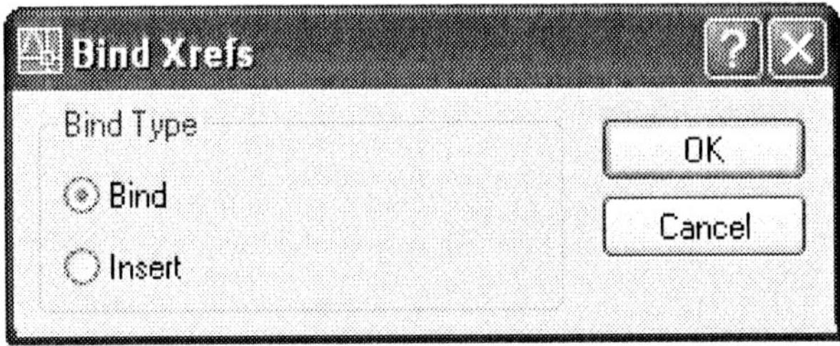

Figure 25.004

    As referenced information, dependent symbols are identified by the name of the referenced drawing followed by a bar and the symbol's name (i.e., **board|slots** is the **slots** layer on the referenced *board* drawing). The two options in the Bind Xrefs dialog box determine how Xref dependent symbols will be treated.

    > *Dependent symbols* are the layers, blocks, text styles, dimension styles, and linetypes that are part of a referenced drawing. To be available in the primary drawing, these symbols require that the referenced drawing be attached.

    - **Bind**ing a referenced drawing causes AutoCAD to rename the dependent symbol but retain the referenced drawing's name in the new name. Thus, the **board|slots** layer will become **board0slots**. This approach means that you'll always be able to trace where the symbol originated. [If the **board0slots** already exists, the number between the dollar signs increases (**board1slots**, **board2slots**, etc.).]
    - **Insert**ing a referenced drawing changes the referenced drawing into a block with the name of the referenced drawing becoming the name of the block. Dependent symbols become a part of the drawing but drop the name of the referenced drawing (i.e., **board|slots** becomes **slots**).
  - The **Open** button opens the selected reference for editing in a new AutoCAD window when the Xref Manager closes. This provides a simple way to edit the reference (we'll look at another way later in this lesson).

- The **Xref Found At** frame indicates where the selected drawing was found when AutoCAD loaded. This is where AutoCAD actually found the drawing and may not be the same as the saved path.
  - Use the **Browse** button to select a different copy of the selected drawing to reference.
  - Use the **Save Path** button to redefine the saved path of the selected drawing to that shown in the **Xref Found At** box.

Whew! That was a lot of material to cover! Let's try our hands at Xref-ing.

Here's the scenario for this lesson:

Your employer is developing a new product – a kit designed to help children learn about electricity. The kit will contain a circuit board where the child can attach a battery pack, switches, lights, resistors, and a galvanometer (kids love those big scientific words). The kit must be capable of creating any of several different wiring layouts.

Your job is to lay out some wiring diagrams of things the child can build using the objects listed. You have the initial board and component designs from the engineer, but some of these objects may change as the project develops. You don't have time to wait for engineering (what a surprise!), so you'll begin your layouts now using Xrefs so you can easily modify the component designs as they develop.

You can also access the Xref Manager by selecting **Xref Manager**, or the ***XAttach*** command by selecting **External Reference** on the Insert pull-down menu.

Do This: 25.1.1.1	**Working with Xrefs**

I. Start a new drawing using the *Start* template found in the C:\Steps\Lesson25 folder.

II. Save the drawing as *MyBoard* in the C:\Steps\Lesson25 folder.

III. Follow these steps.

TOOLS	COMMAND SEQUENCE	STEPS
Xref Manager Button	**Command:** ***xr***	1. We'll begin by referencing our title block. Enter the ***Xref*** command. Alternately, you can pick the **Xref Manager** button on the Reference toolbar.
Attach...		2. AutoCAD presents the Xref Manager. Pick the **Attach** button.
		3. AutoCAD presents the Select Reference File dialog box. Select the *title block.dwg* file in the C:\Steps\Lesson25 folder. (Double-click on the file name or pick the **Open** button to continue.)
		4. AutoCAD presents the External Reference dialog box. Be sure the selections match those shown in Figure 25.005. • Use the **Attachment Reference Type** and a **Relative path.** • Remove the checks from the boxes in the three lower frames. Pick the **OK** button to continue.

TOOLS	COMMAND SEQUENCE	STEPS

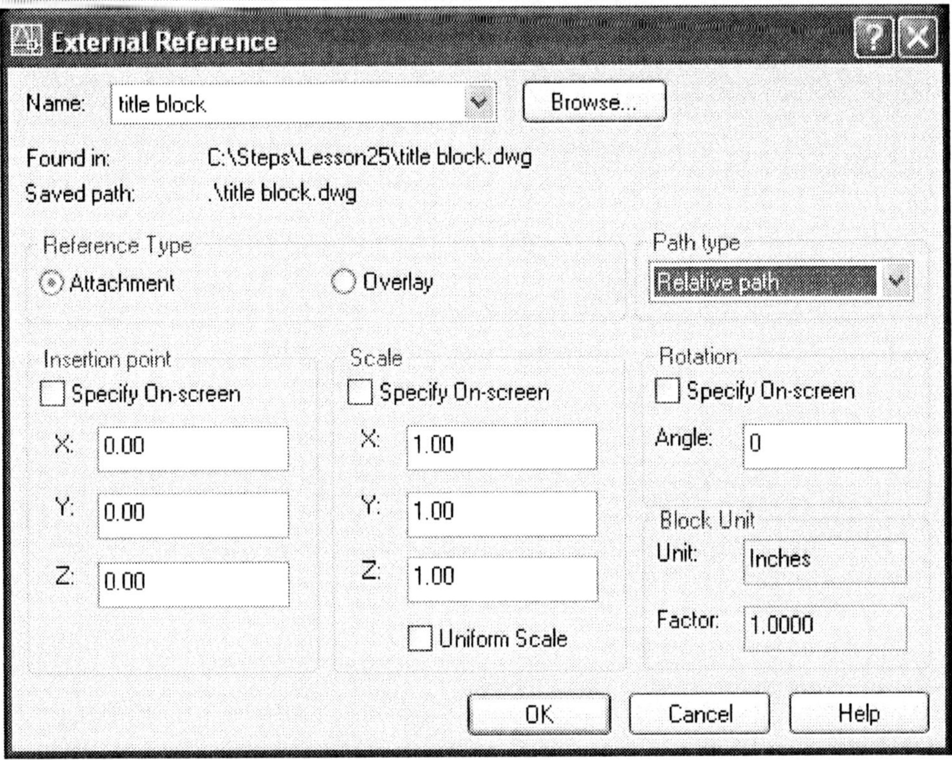

Figure 25.005

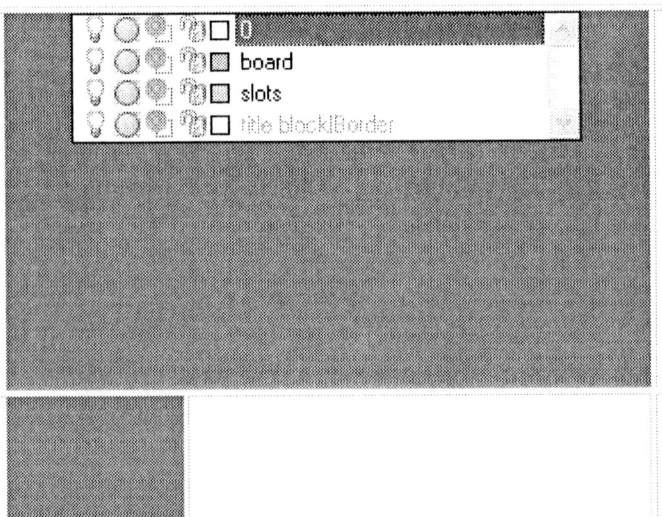

5. Check the **Layer** control box. Notice that AutoCAD has added the layer **title block|Border**. (The other layers were part of the template.) This is the layer on which the title block was created and has been referenced with the drawing. Notice that the layer is gray – you can turn it off, freeze it, lock it, or plot it; but it can't be made current. Nor can you draw on this layer, as it isn't actually part of the primary drawing.

6. Draw the board shown in Figure 25.006.

- The rectangle's corners are at coordinates ***1,1*** and ***8.5,9***.
- The fillets are ½".
- There are 15 rows and 14 columns of slots.
- The board is on the **board** layer.
- The slots are on the **slots** layer.
- The slots are 3/16"dia., ½" apart, and begin at coordinate ***1.5,1.5***.

TOOLS	COMMAND SEQUENCE	STEPS

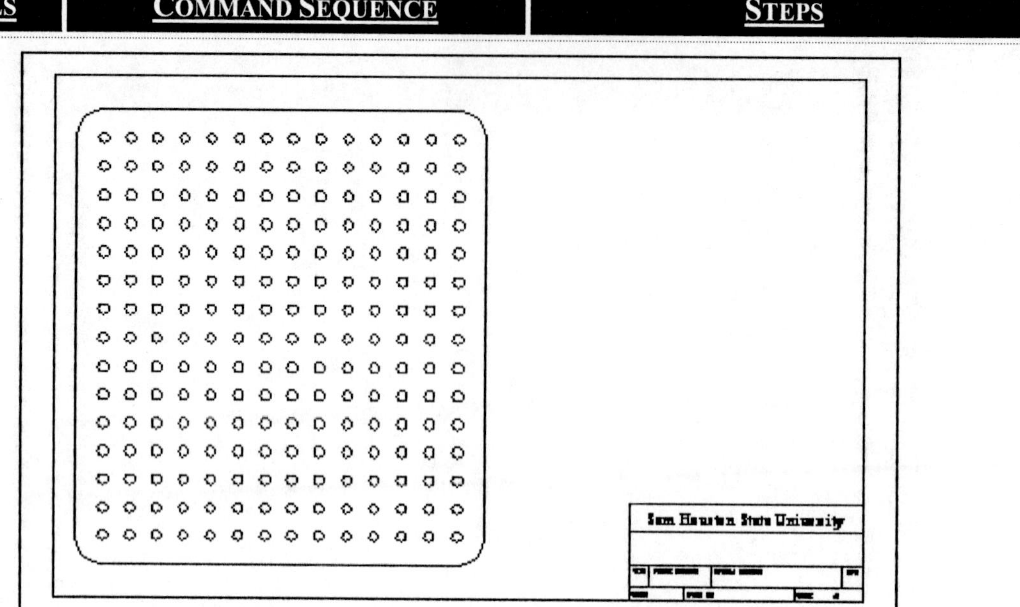

Figure 25.006

TOOLS	COMMAND SEQUENCE	STEPS
	Command: ***qsave*** **Command:** ***close***	7. Save the drawing and close it.
		8. Start a new drawing using the Start template found in the C:\Steps\Lesson25 folder. Save the drawing as *MyCircuit1* in the C:\Steps\Lesson25 folder.
		9. Repeat Steps 1 to 4, but this time, reference the *MyBoard.dwg* you created earlier in this lesson. (If you have a problem with this one, you can attach the *board.dwg* file instead.)
	Command: ***qsave***	10. Save the drawing.
External Reference Button	**Command:** *xa*	11. Using the ***XAttach*** command, we'll attach the battery and switch drawings. Begin by entering the ***XAttach*** command. Alternately, you can pick the **External Reference** button on the Reference toolbar. (You'll notice that this procedure is identical to the one we used to attach the *MyBoard.dwg* file except that we skip the Xref Manager.)
		12. Repeat Step 3, but this time, select the *battery.dwg* file.
		13. Insert the file at coordinates ***2.5,4*** as shown in Figure 25.007.

TOOLS	COMMAND SEQUENCE	STEPS

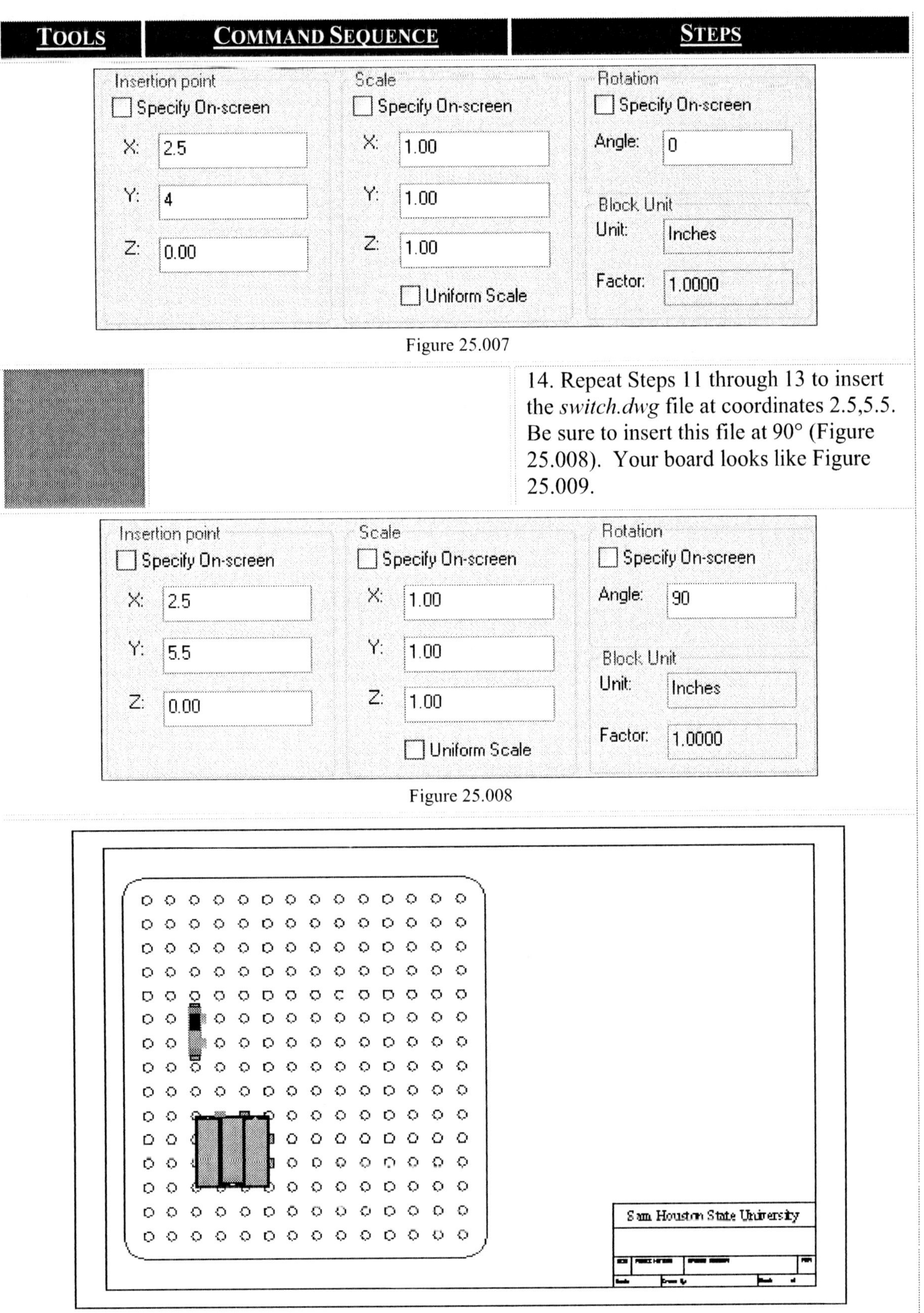

Figure 25.007

14. Repeat Steps 11 through 13 to insert the *switch.dwg* file at coordinates 2.5,5.5. Be sure to insert this file at 90° (Figure 25.008). Your board looks like Figure 25.009.

Figure 25.008

Figure 25.009

TOOLS	COMMAND SEQUENCE	STEPS
	Command: ***qsave***	15. Save the drawing but don't exit.

Notice the two pairs of wire connections on both the switch and the battery. Our engineers haven't decided where to put the single required pair, so they've created two for now. We have a fair idea which ones they'll eventually use, but we don't want to change the actual component drawings yet. We can, however, alter the reference to show only those connections we want to show.

25.1.2 Removing Part of a Reference – the *XClip* Command

You'll use a tool called ***XClip*** to remove part of a reference drawing. The command sequence looks like this:

> **Command:** *xclip* **(or** *xc***)**
>
> **Select objects:** ***[select the reference(s) to clip]***
>
> **Select objects:** ***[enter]***
>
> **Enter clipping option**
>
> **[ON/OFF/Clipdepth/Delete/generate Polyline/New boundary] <New>:** ***[tell AutoCAD what you want to do – accept the default to clip a reference]***
>
> **Specify clipping boundary:**
>
> **[Select polyline/Polygonal/Rectangular] <Rectangular>:** ***[tell AutoCAD what type of clipping boundary you wish to use]***

- The **ON/OFF** options determine whether AutoCAD will present only those portions of the referenced drawing visible through the clipping window (**ON**) or the entire referenced drawing (**OFF**).
- **Clipdepth** allows you to set the front/back clipping planes of three-dimensional objects. A two-dimensional boundary must exist before you can define front or back clip points. Identify the clip points by coordinate or distance from the two-dimensional clipping boundary.
- Use **Delete** to remove a boundary.
- **Generate Polyline** will automatically draw a polyline along the clipping boundary. Again, a boundary must exist before AutoCAD can generate the polyline.
- **New boundary** (the default) permits you to identify a new clipping boundary.

> AutoCAD provides a system variable to allow you to see the boundary even when it isn't a polyline. The system variable is **XClipFrame**. A setting of **0** (the default) means the boundaries will be hidden. A setting of **1** will show the boundaries. AutoCAD provides a button – **Frame** – on the Reference toolbar to help you toggle the system variable on and off.

The next line of options (**[Select polyline/Polygonal/ Rectangular] <Rectangular>:**) offers some choices for how to create the new boundary.

- Use the **Select polyline** option to use an existing polyline to define the boundary. The polyline doesn't have to be closed, but it must not intersect itself. (To create a "round" clipping boundary, use a polygon with a large number of sides.)
- Use the **Polygonal** option to create a multisided or nonlinear shape for a boundary (much like using a poly-window to create a selection set).
- Use the **Rectangular** option (the default) to use a window to define the clipping boundary.

We'll remove the extra wire connectors from the views of our battery and switch.

> You can also access the ***XClip*** command on the Modify pull-down menu. Follow this path:
> *Modify – Clip – Xref*

Do This: 25.1.2.1	**Clipping Xrefs**

I. Be sure you're still in the *MyCircuit1.dwg* file. If not, please open it now.

II. This exercise is easier if you zoom in around the battery and switch.

III. Follow these steps.

TOOLS	COMMAND SEQUENCE	STEPS
Xref Button	**Command:** *xc*	1. Enter the ***XClip*** command. Alternately, you can pick the **Xref** button on the Reference toolbar.
	Select objects: **Select objects: *[enter]***	2. Select the battery.
	Enter clipping option [ON/OFF/Clipdepth/Delete/ generate Polyline/New boundary] <New>: *[enter]*	3. Accept the default **New boundary** option.
	Specify clipping boundary: [Select polyline/Polygonal/ Rectangular] <Rectangular>: *[enter]*	4. Tell AutoCAD that you'll create a **Rectangular** clipping boundary (the default).
	Specify first corner: _endp of	5. Place the first corner at the lower right corner of the battery (use OSNAPs).
	Specify opposite corner:	6. … and the opposite corner northward and westward of the battery. AutoCAD clips the reference, and the battery now looks like Figure 25.010. (Note that you haven't actually modified the battery, just how much of it you can see through the reference window.)
	Figure 25.010	
		7. Repeat Steps 1 to 6 to clip the side connections from the switch. Your board looks like Figure 25.011.

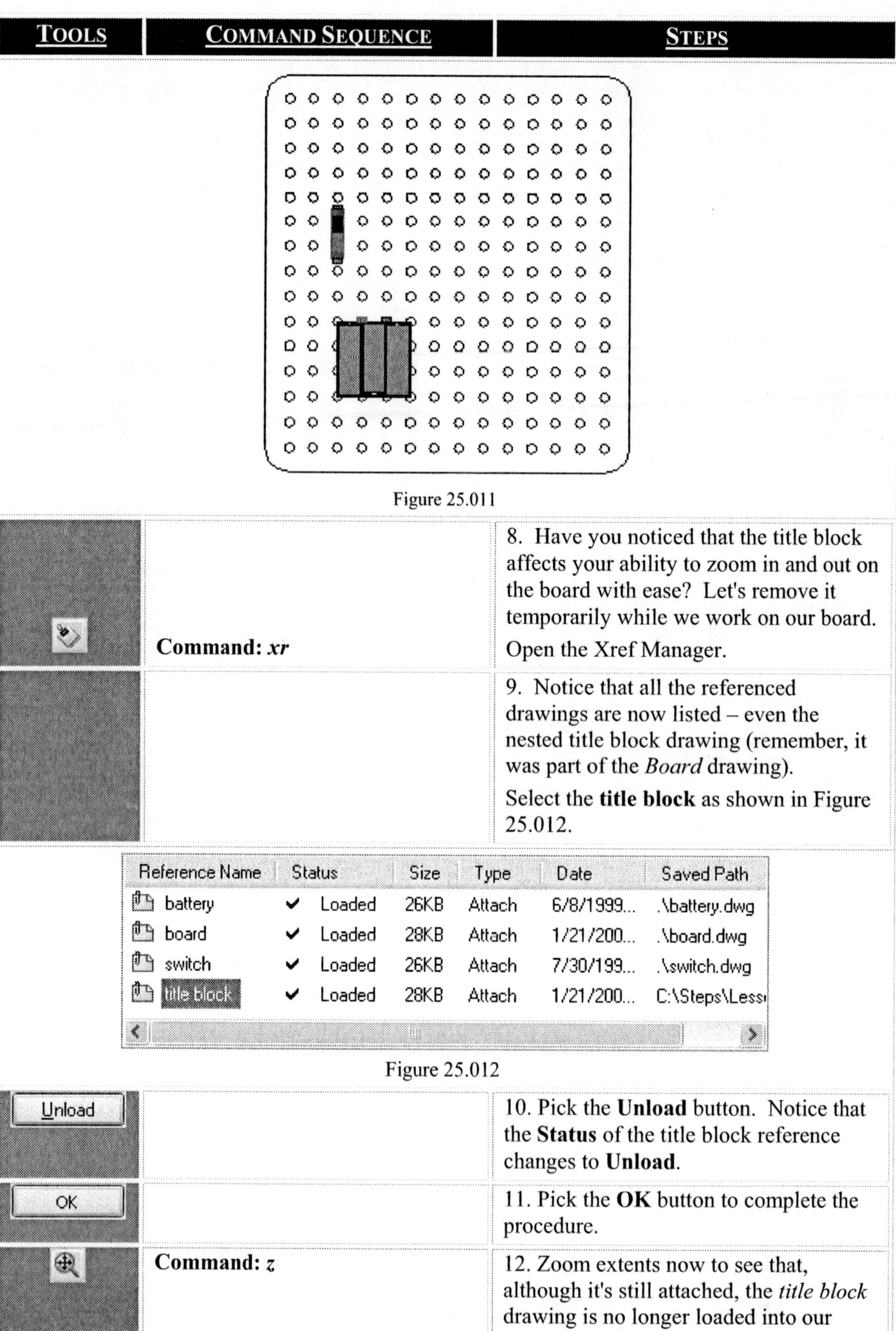

TOOLS	COMMAND SEQUENCE	STEPS

Figure 25.011

TOOLS	COMMAND SEQUENCE	STEPS
	Command: *xr*	8. Have you noticed that the title block affects your ability to zoom in and out on the board with ease? Let's remove it temporarily while we work on our board. Open the Xref Manager.
		9. Notice that all the referenced drawings are now listed – even the nested title block drawing (remember, it was part of the *Board* drawing). Select the **title block** as shown in Figure 25.012.

Reference Name	Status	Size	Type	Date	Saved Path
battery	✔ Loaded	26KB	Attach	6/8/1999...	.\battery.dwg
board	✔ Loaded	28KB	Attach	1/21/200...	.\board.dwg
switch	✔ Loaded	26KB	Attach	7/30/199...	.\switch.dwg
title block	✔ Loaded	28KB	Attach	1/21/200...	C:\Steps\Less

Figure 25.012

TOOLS	COMMAND SEQUENCE	STEPS
Unload		10. Pick the **Unload** button. Notice that the **Status** of the title block reference changes to **Unload**.
OK		11. Pick the **OK** button to complete the procedure.
	Command: *z*	12. Zoom extents now to see that, although it's still attached, the *title block* drawing is no longer loaded into our *MyCircuit1* drawing.

TOOLS	COMMAND SEQUENCE	STEPS
	Command: ***qsave***	13. Save the drawing but don't exit.

25.1.3 Xrefs and Dependent Symbols

AutoCAD allows two methods of permanently attaching referenced drawing data to the primary file – Binding and Xbinding. You'll use the **Bind** button on the Xref Manager to permanently attach, or bind, an entire referenced drawing to the primary drawing. We discussed this in Section 25.1.1 and will demonstrate it in Section 25.4. But you can also attach parts (specific dependent symbols) of the referenced drawing individually to the primary drawing. The command for this is ***Xbind*** (or ***xb***), and it presents the Xbind dialog box (Figure 25.013).

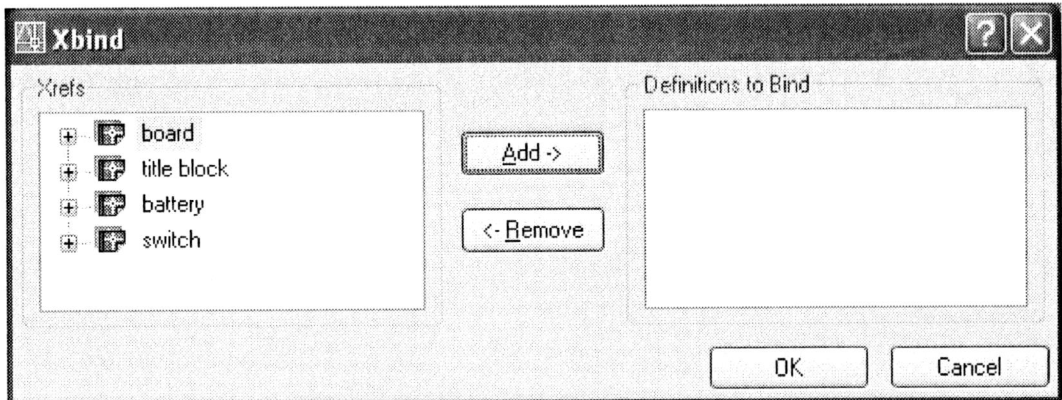

Figure 25.013

The Xbind dialog box is one of AutoCAD's easiest. Simply select the dependent symbol you wish to bind in the Xrefs frame, pick the **Add** button, and **OK** your changes!

Let's try one. The battery drawing has a **wire** layer and a **times** text style; we'll add these to our primary file.

> You can also access the ***Xbind*** command on the Modify pull-down menu. Follow this path:
> *Modify – Object – External Reference – Bind...*

Do This: 25.1.3.1 — Xbinding Dependent Symbols

I. Be sure you're still in the *MyCircuit1.dwg* file. If not, please open it now.

II. Follow these steps.

TOOLS	COMMAND SEQUENCE	STEPS
Bind Button	**Command:** ***xb***	1. Enter the ***Xbind*** command. Alternately, you can pick the **Bind** button on the Reference toolbar.

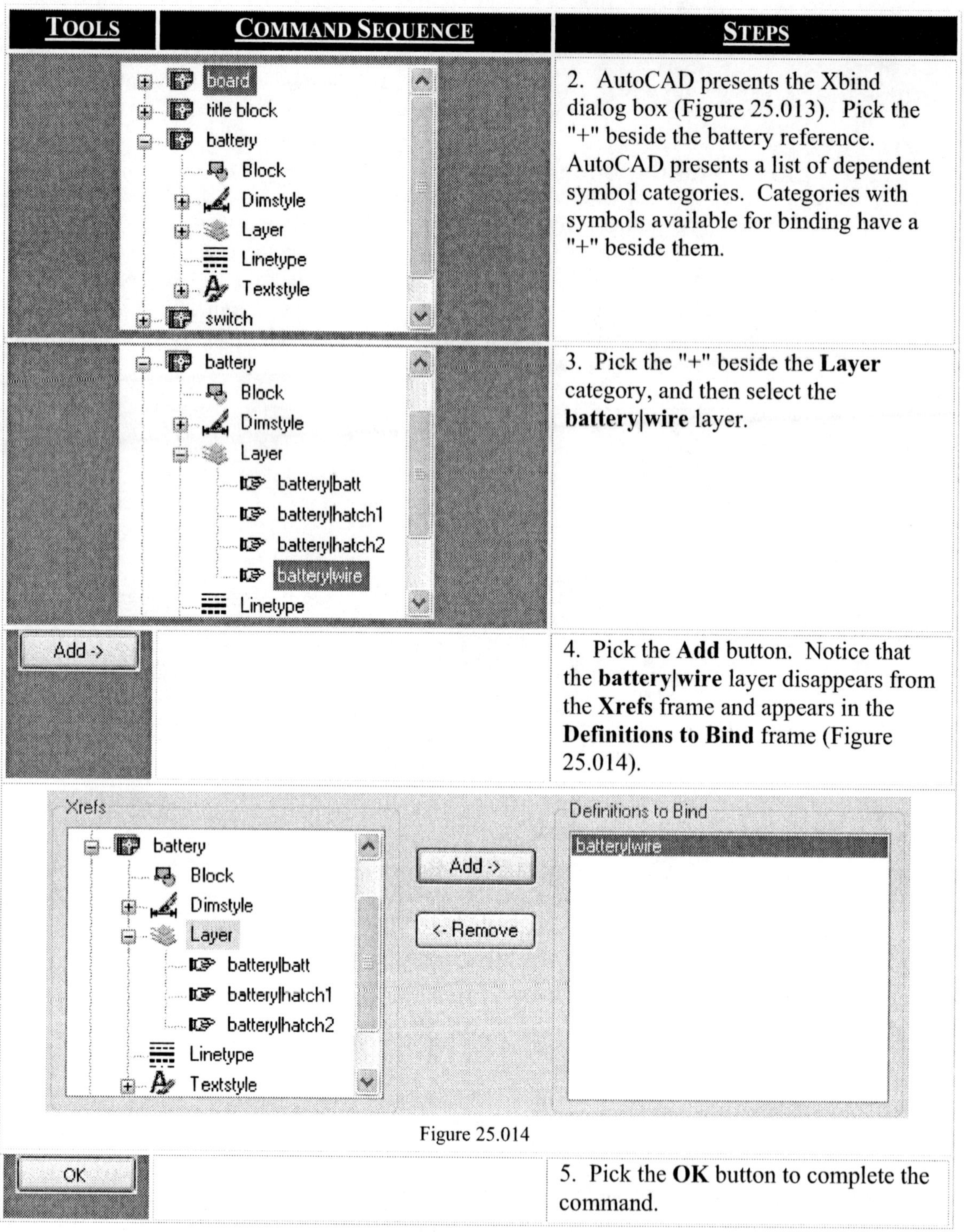

TOOLS	COMMAND SEQUENCE	STEPS
		2. AutoCAD presents the Xbind dialog box (Figure 25.013). Pick the "+" beside the battery reference. AutoCAD presents a list of dependent symbol categories. Categories with symbols available for binding have a "+" beside them.
		3. Pick the "+" beside the **Layer** category, and then select the **battery|wire** layer.
Add ->		4. Pick the **Add** button. Notice that the **battery|wire** layer disappears from the **Xrefs** frame and appears in the **Definitions to Bind** frame (Figure 25.014).

Figure 25.014

TOOLS	COMMAND SEQUENCE	STEPS
OK		5. Pick the **OK** button to complete the command.

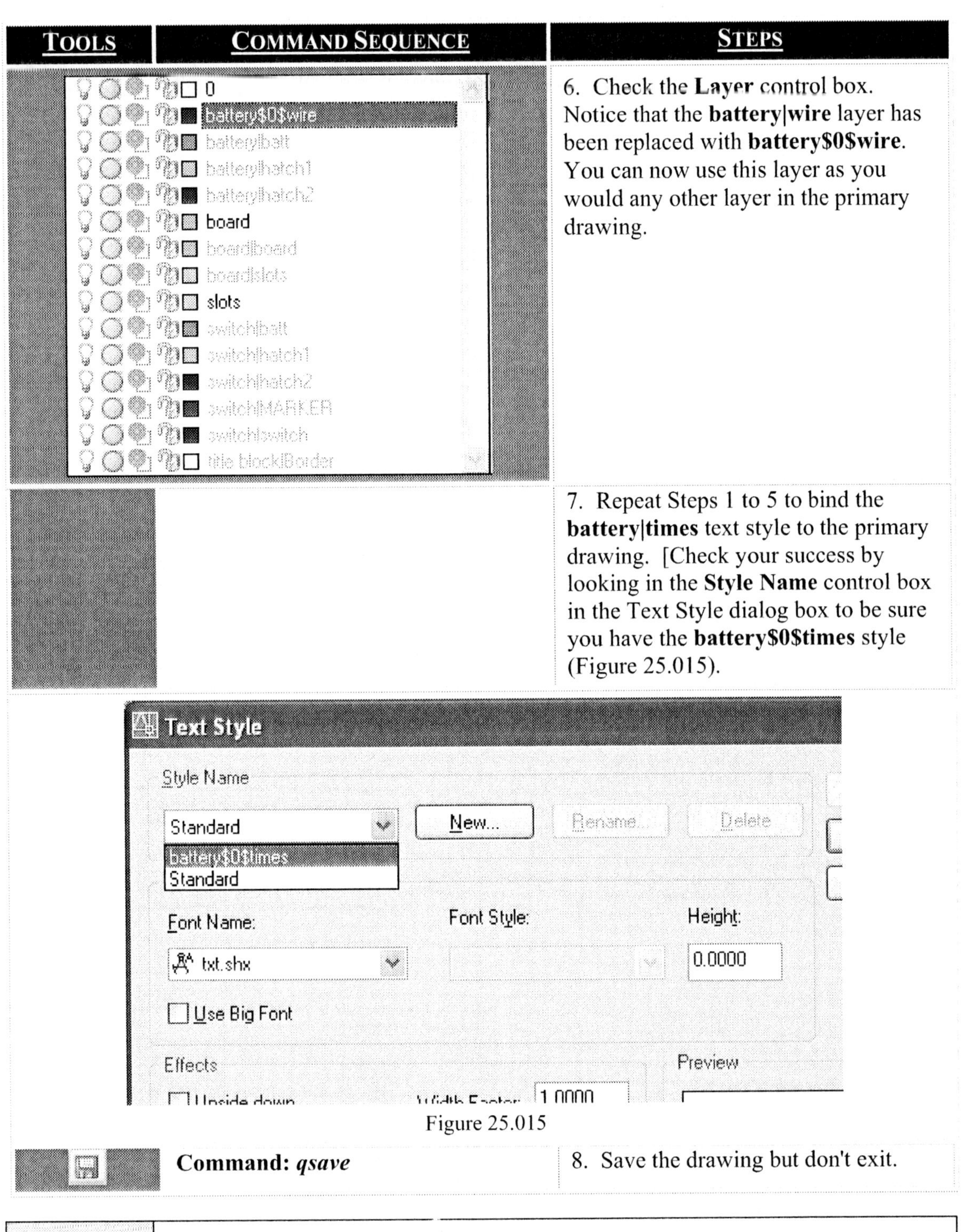

Tools	**Command Sequence**	**Steps**
		6. Check the **Layer** control box. Notice that the **battery|wire** layer has been replaced with **battery0wire**. You can now use this layer as you would any other layer in the primary drawing.
		7. Repeat Steps 1 to 5 to bind the **battery|times** text style to the primary drawing. [Check your success by looking in the **Style Name** control box in the Text Style dialog box to be sure you have the **battery0times** style (Figure 25.015).

Figure 25.015

	Command: ***qsave***	8. Save the drawing but don't exit.

25.1.4 Unloading, Reloading, and Overlaying Xrefs

In Exercise 25.1.2.1, we unloaded the *title block* reference to make our work easier. All we had to do was to select the drawing to unload (*title block*) and then pick the **Unload** button in the Xref Manager. Unloading a reference can speed work by reducing regeneration time. And as we saw, unloading a reference can remove unnecessary, distracting, and even obstructing objects from the display. But eventually, you'll probably have to reload the unloaded reference.

Reloading an unloaded reference is as easy as unloading it. Simply select the drawing to reload and pick the **Reload** button in the Xref Manager. We'll reload the title block in our next exercise.

But first, let's consider the **Attach** versus **Overlay** types of reference. Consider the diagram in Figure 25.016.

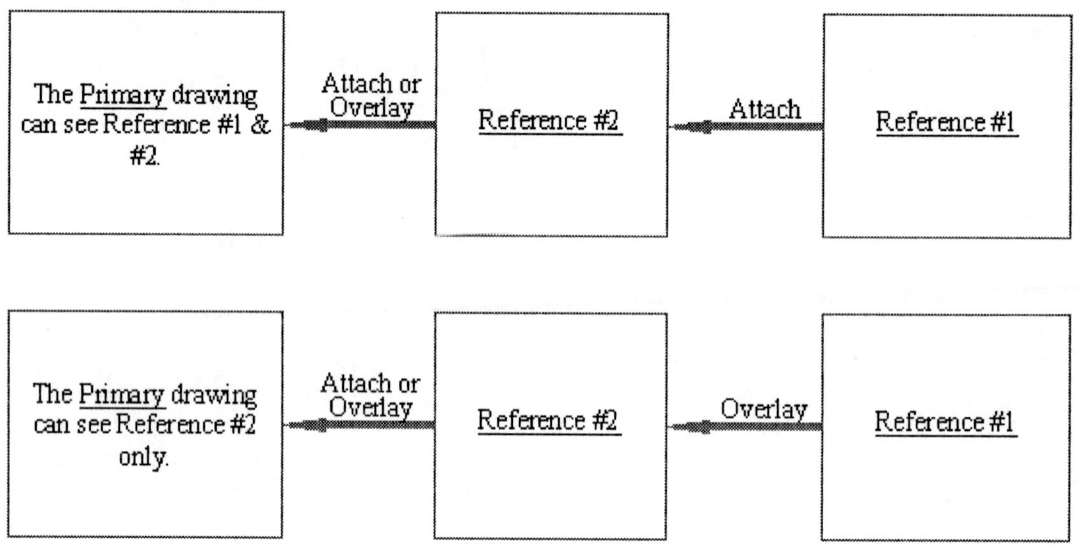

Figure 25.016

As you can see, the **Overlay** type of reference is effective only when used on a nested reference. In other words, overlaying a reference into the primary drawing won't affect the nested reference's visibility. To hide the nested reference, it must be overlaid into the drawing being referenced by the primary drawing. We'll see this in our next exercise.

This is what we'll do: We'll reload our *title block* (which is nested into the *MyBoard* – or *Board* – drawing reference). [*MyBoard* (Reference #2 in the diagram) references *title block* (Reference #1) using the **Attach** type of reference; therefore, we can see it from the primary drawing (*MyCircuit1*).] In our exercise, we'll change the reference type between *MyBoard* and *title block* and see how that affects *MyCircuit1*.

Let's begin.

Do This: 25.1.4.1	Reloading and Overlaying References

I. Be sure you're still in the *MyCircuit1.dwg* file. If not, please open it now.

II. Follow these steps.

TOOLS	COMMAND SEQUENCE	STEPS
[icon]	**Command:** ***xr***	1. Open the Xref Manager.
Reload		2. Select the **title block** reference and then pick the **Reload** button.
OK		3. Complete the procedure. Notice that the title block is again visible. (If necessary, ***zoom*** all to see it.)

Tools	Command Sequence	Steps
	Command: ***qsave***	4. Save the drawing.
	Command: ***xr***	5. Open Xref Manager again.
Open		6. Select the **MyBoard** (or **Board**) reference and pick the **Open** button.
OK		7. Close the Xref Manager. AutoCAD opens the *MyBoard* (*Board*) drawing.
	Command: ***xr***	8. Call the Xref Manager.
Type Overlay		9. Double-click on the word **Attach** in the **Type** column (next to **title block**). Notice that it changes to **Overlay**. (It's just that easy to change the reference type.)
OK		10. Close the Xref Manager.
	Command: ***qsave***	11. Save and close the drawing.
External Reference File Has Changed A reference file has changed and may need reloading: Reload board		12. AutoCAD returns to the *MyCircuit1.dwg* and presents a bubble message telling you that a referenced drawing has changed. Pick on the link (**Reload Board**). AutoCAD reloads the Xref.
		13. Repeats Steps 5 through 15, but this time, set the type of reference to **Attach**.
	Command: ***qsave***	14. Save the drawing but don't exit.

25.2 Editing Xrefs

Although AutoCAD has made it quite simple to edit a referenced drawing, you should do so with caution. Remember that others may have referenced the same drawing and any changes made to it will reflect in their drawings as well.

We've already seen how simple it is to open a referenced drawing for editing. But there's another tool available for this purpose – one of the nicest tools in the AutoCAD command family. It provides the ability for us to edit a referenced drawing (or a block!) without having to leave the primary drawing. Even better is the fact that it's so easy to do.

Three commands make up the reference editing tools.

- ***Refedit*** begins the editing session. It prompts you to select the referenced objects to edit, like this:

  Command: ***refedit***

Select reference: ***[select the referenced drawing]***

[Here, AutoCAD presents the Reference Edit dialog box (Figure 25.017). Complete the options and pick the **OK** ***button to continue. AutoCAD then closes the dialog box and makes the referenced drawing available for editing.]***

Use REFCLOSE or the Refedit toolbar to end reference editing session.
[AutoCAD lets you know how to end the reference editing session.]

- The **Identity Reference** tab of the Reference Edit dialog box (Figure 25.017) provides a list box showing the name of the selected reference and a **Preview** frame where you can see the referenced drawing. It also provides two options:
  - **Automatically select all nested objects** controls whether or not AutoCAD will automatically include nested references in the editing session.
  - A bullet next to **Prompt to select nested objects** lets AutoCAD know that you'd rather individually select nested objects in your editing session.

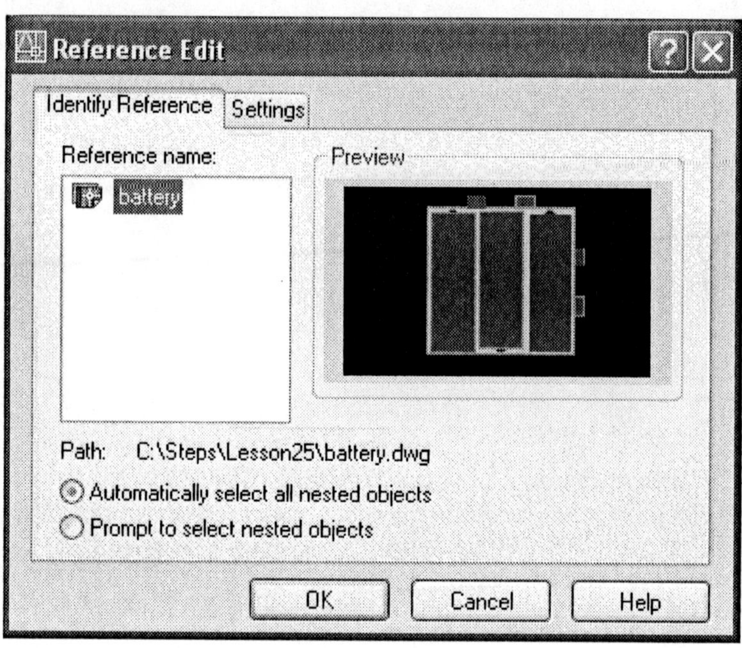

Figure 25.017

- The **Settings** tab of the Reference Edit dialog box (Figure 25.018) provides some options that may make your editing session run more smoothly.
  - A check next to **Create unique layer, style, and block names** tells AutoCAD to use the $#$ procedure for dealing with symbols much as it does when binding an Xref. If unchecked, layer, style, and block names remain the same as in the referenced drawing.
  - Selecting **Display attribute definitions for editing** means that the attribute definitions of blocks within the referenced drawing will be available for your editing.
  - It's best to leave the check next to **Lock objects not in working set**. This prevents you from accidentally editing something in the primary drawing when you're editing your referenced drawing.

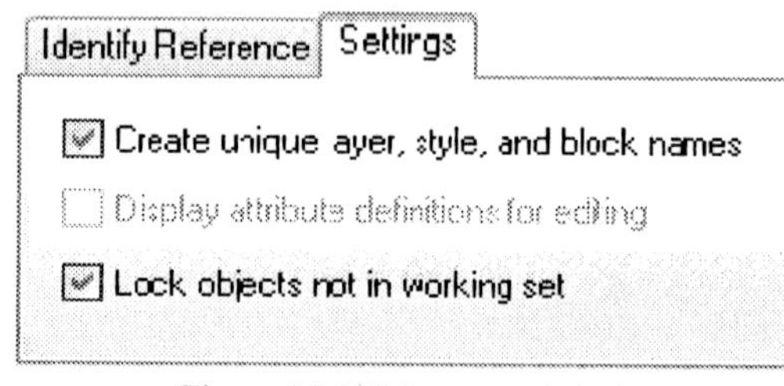

Figure 25.018 (not actual size)

- Use ***Refset*** to add or remove referenced objects from the editing session. It prompts:

  Command: ***refset***

  Transfer objects between the RefEdit working set and host drawing...

Enter an option [Add/Remove] <Add>: ***[enter to add or type R to remove objects from the set]***

Select objects: ***[select the object(s) to add or remove]***

- ***Refclose*** ends the editing session. It prompts

  Command: ***refclose***

  Enter option [Save/Discard reference changes] <Save>: ***[enter to save the changes or type D to discard the changes]***

  AutoCAD presents a warning box (Figure 25.019) telling you what you're about to do. Pick **OK** to continue or **Cancel** to prevent saving.

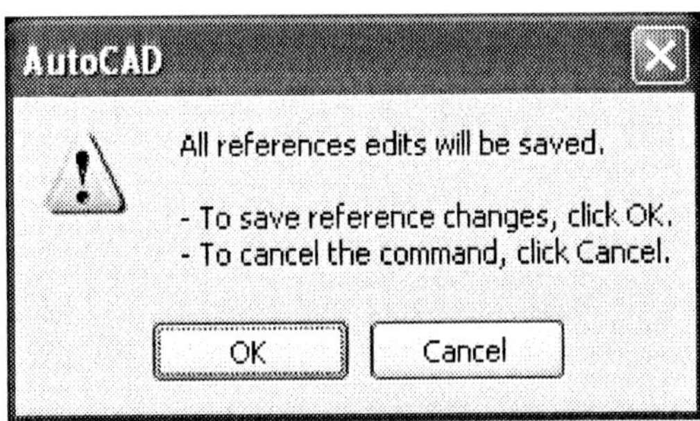

Figure 25.019

AutoCAD also provides buttons on the Refedit toolbar to add or remove objects from the editing session (***Refset***) and to close the session saving or discarding your changes (***Refclose***).

Let's try ***Refedit***.

*Our engineer has determined where the wire connections should be on our battery and switch. We could open those drawings for the changes, but we're in the MyCircuit1.dwg file now and can make the changes here using **Refedit**.*

Do This: 25.2.1	**Editing Referenced Drawings**

I. Be sure you're still in the *MyCircuit1.dwg* file. If not, please open it now.

II. Follow these steps.

TOOLS	COMMAND SEQUENCE	STEPS
	Command: *xc*	1. First, let's remove the clipping planes. Enter the ***XClip*** command.
	Select objects: **Select objects:** ***[enter]***	2. Select the battery and the switch.
ON OFF Clipdepth Delete generate Polyline • New boundary	**Enter clipping option [ON/OFF/Clipdepth/Delete/ generate Polyline/New boundary] <New>:** ***d***	3. Tell AutoCAD you want to **Delete** the clipping plane. AutoCAD presents both references in their entirety.
Edit Reference in Place Button	**Command:** ***refedit***	4. Now we begin the editing session. Enter the ***Refedit*** command at the command prompt. There's no hotkey for this command, but you can pick the **Edit Reference in Place** button on the Refedit toolbar.
	Select reference:	5. Select the battery.

TOOLS	COMMAND SEQUENCE	STEPS
OK		6. AutoCAD presents the Reference Edit dialog box (Figure 25.017). We'll use the default settings, so pick the **OK** button.
	Command: ***e***	7. Enter the ***Erase*** command.
	Select objects: **Select objects:** ***[enter]***	8. Select the wiring connections on the right side of the battery. (There are actually three objects – a hatching and two rectangles.)
Save Reference Edits Button	**Command:** ***refclose***	9. Complete the ***Refedit*** command with the ***Refclose*** command. Hit enter to accept the **Save** option. Alternately, you can pick the **Save Reference Edits** button on the Refedit toolbar.
OK		10. AutoCAD presents a warning box (Figure 27.019). Pick the **OK** button to complete the procedure.
		11. Repeat Steps 4 through 10 to remove the right set of wiring connections on the switch.
	Command: ***qsave***	12. Save and close the drawing.

25.3 Using Our Drawing as a Reference

Now that we've created a drawing with circuit board, battery, and switch, we can begin to create our wiring diagrams. We'll plan on three layouts using the battery and switch in these locations, so we'll use the *MyCircuit1.dwg* file as a reference over which we'll create our layouts.

Let's begin.

Do This: 25.3.1 Using Xrefs to Create Three Wiring Diagrams

I. Start a new drawing using the *Start* template in the C:\Steps\Lesson25 folder. Save the new drawing as *MyCircuit1a.dwg* in the C:\Steps\Lesson25 folder.

II. Follow these steps.

TOOLS	COMMAND SEQUENCE	STEPS
	Command: ***xr***	1. Begin by referencing the *MyCircuit1* drawing. (Follow Steps 1 through 4 of Exercise 25.1.1.1.)

<table>
<tr><th>TOOLS</th><th>COMMAND SEQUENCE</th><th>STEPS</th></tr>
<tr><td></td><td>Command: xb</td><td>2. Xbind the battery|wire layer and the title block|times text style to your new drawing. (Use the procedure detailed in Exercise 25.1.3.1.)</td></tr>
<tr><td></td><td></td><td>3. Rename the new layer to Wire and the new text style to Times.</td></tr>
<tr><td></td><td>Command: qsave</td><td>4. Save the drawing.</td></tr>
<tr><td></td><td>Command: xa</td><td>5. Reference the lamp.dwg file in the C:\Steps\Lesson25 folder and place it at coordinates 6.5,6.</td></tr>
<tr><td></td><td></td><td>6. Using splines, draw the wire shown in Figure 25.020. (Be sure to use the Wire layer.) Add the text on an appropriate layer. (Text size is 3/16" and uses the Times style.)</td></tr>
</table>

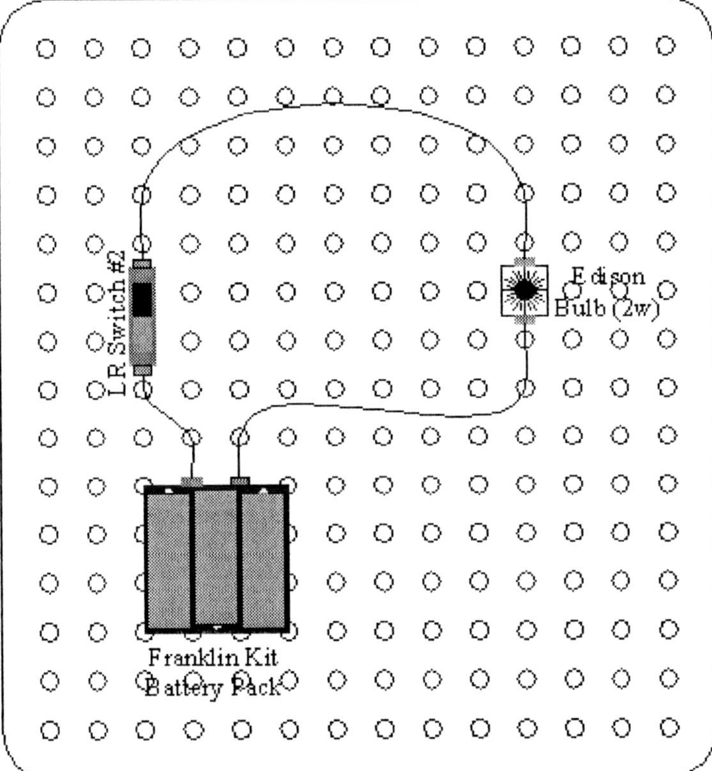

Figure 25.020

<table>
<tr><td></td><td></td><td>7. Insert the block file title info at the lower left corner of the title block (Figure 25.021). (Place it on its own layer, and fill in the data as appropriate for your situation.)</td></tr>
</table>

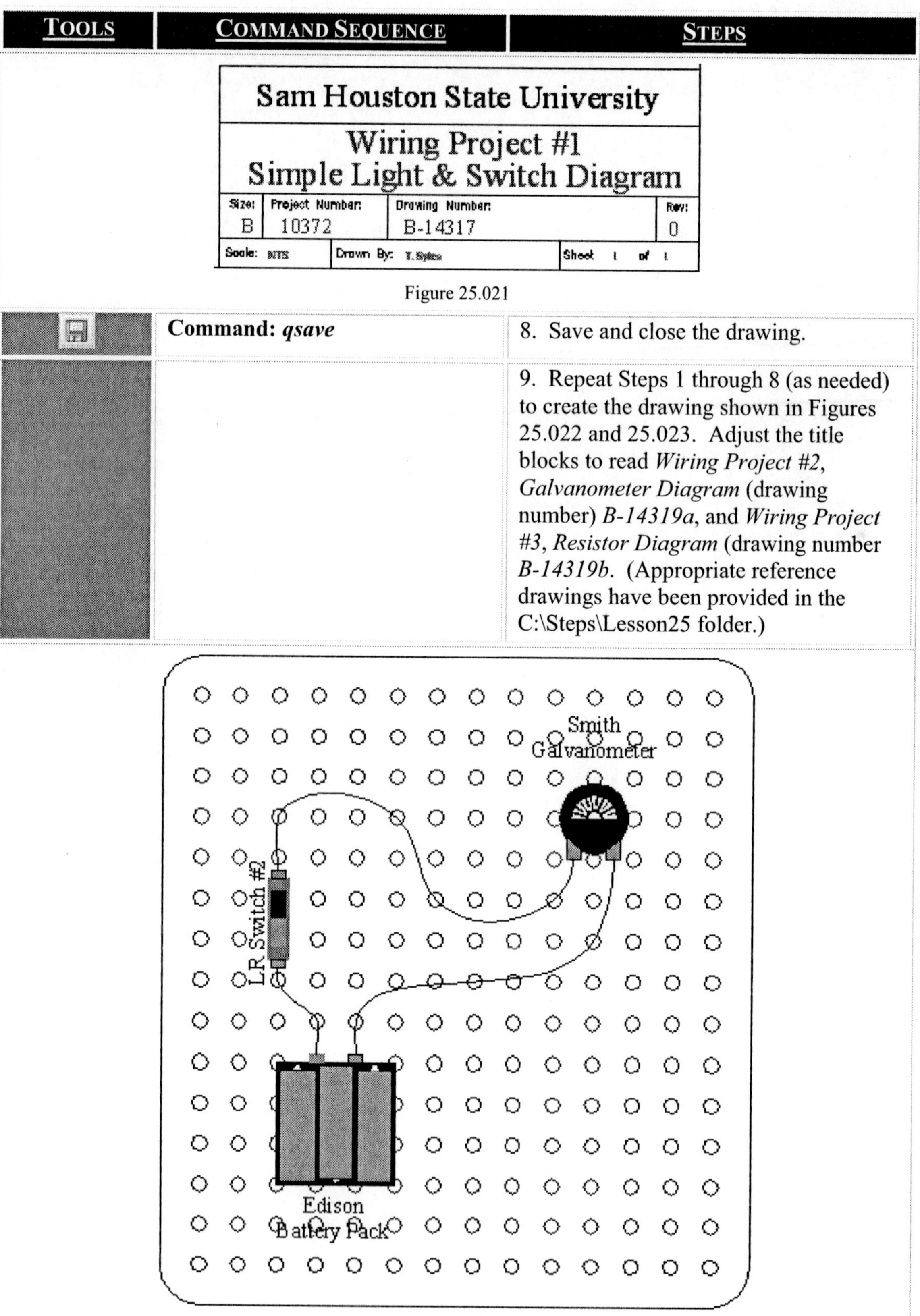

TOOLS	COMMAND SEQUENCE	STEPS
	Command: ***qsave***	8. Save and close the drawing.
		9. Repeat Steps 1 through 8 (as needed) to create the drawing shown in Figures 25.022 and 25.023. Adjust the title blocks to read *Wiring Project #2*, *Galvanometer Diagram* (drawing number) *B-14319a*, and *Wiring Project #3*, *Resistor Diagram* (drawing number *B-14319b*. (Appropriate reference drawings have been provided in the C:\Steps\Lesson25 folder.)

Figure 25.021

Figure 25.022

TOOLS	COMMAND SEQUENCE	STEPS

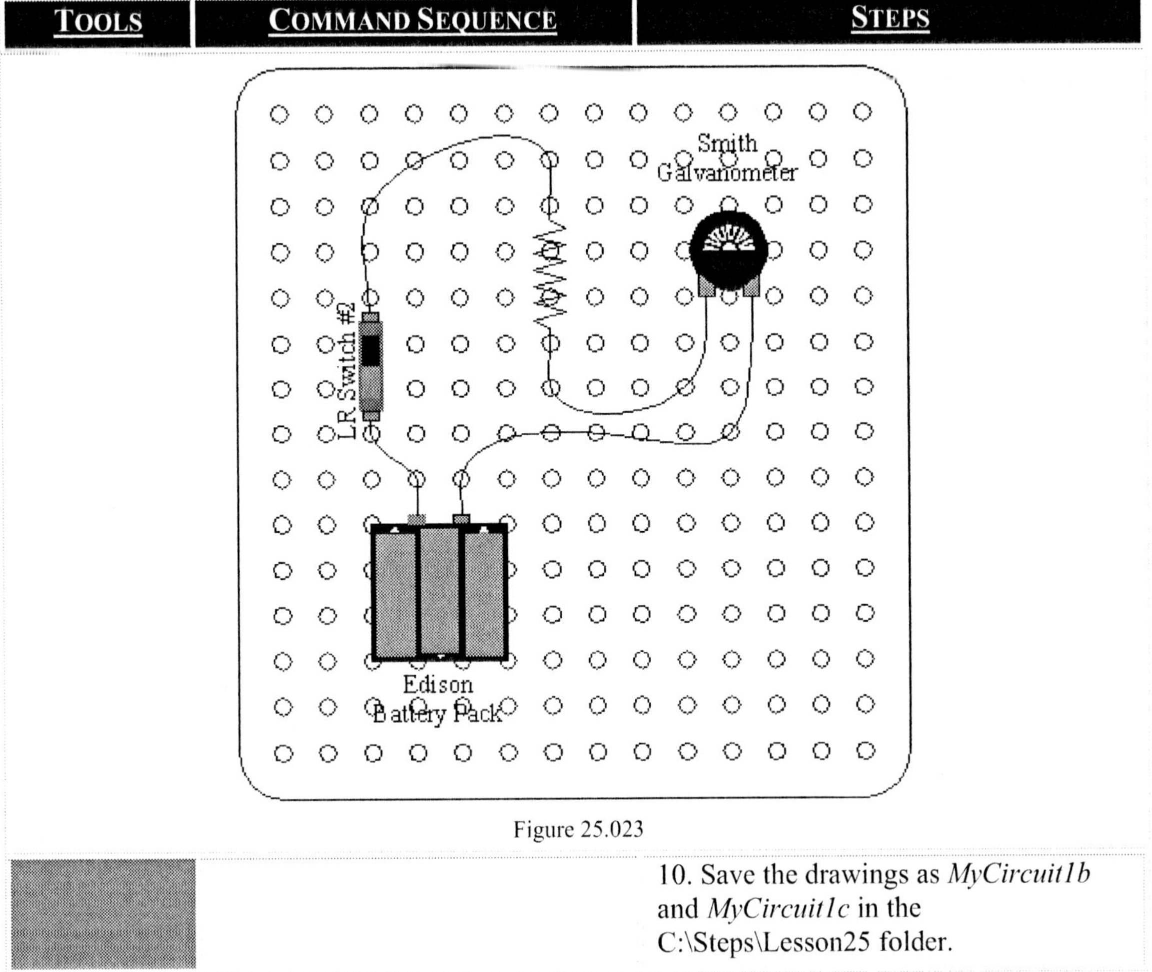

Figure 25.023

		10. Save the drawings as *MyCircuit1b* and *MyCircuit1c* in the C:\Steps\Lesson25 folder.

Congratulations! You've completed three diagrams according to your original job requirements!

You'll have an opportunity to create other diagrams at the end of this lesson. First, however, let's take a look at some special requirements for sending your referenced drawings to your client.

25.4 Binding an Xref to Your Drawing

The biggest problem that arises from the use of Xrefs lies in the location of the referenced file and how AutoCAD keeps track of that location.

By default, AutoCAD will look for referenced files in the **Saved Path** first, and then in folders listed in the **Project Files Search Path**. Again, by default, the **Project Files Search Path** is empty. Therefore, you'll need to add the location (path) of your references to the **Project Files Search Path** or rely on the **Saved Path**. Of course, you could put all the drawings in the same folder, but that's not very organized.

A problem develops, however, when you decide to send your drawing to the client (or somewhere else). First, you must remember to send all the reference files along with the primary file. But even when you do this, the client may not (indeed, probably won't) place the files in a folder with the same name you were using. The result will be that the primary drawing won't be able to locate the references (your client gets frustrated and you look for another job).

You could solve the problem by fully documenting necessary project/folder/path information and sending the documents along with the files (much as eTransmit does). But this means that the client must read instructions about how to view your work – probably not a strong selling point for giving you more business.

You might use the eTransmit tool and/or sheet sets. Indeed, that's probably the best approach, but there is another way. AutoCAD allows you to bind all the references to the primary drawing as blocks. Then you simply send the one file, and the client reads it with any AutoCAD program or viewer.

Binding references, however, dramatically increases the size of the drawing. So you need to wait until the project is complete before doing it. It might even be a good idea to archive the project before binding in case you need to do additional work on the original(s).

As we saw in our study of the Xref Manager (Section 25.1.1), binding isn't difficult. Simply select the references to bind and pick the **Bind** button in the Xref Manager. AutoCAD will ask if you wish to **Bind** or **Insert** (via the Bind Xrefs dialog box (Figure 25.004). (See the discussion of these options in Section 25.1.1.)

Let's see what happens when we bind our references.

Do This: 25.4.1	Binding References

I. Open the *MyCircuit1a.dwg* file in the C:\Steps\Lesson25 folder. (If this file isn't available, you can open *Circuit1a* instead.)

II. Follow these steps.

TOOLS	COMMAND SEQUENCE	STEPS
No Button Available	**Command:** ***dwgprops***	1. Before we bind our references, let's see how large our drawing file is. Enter the ***dwgprops*** command.
Type: AutoCAD Drawing Location: C:\Steps\Lesson25\ Size: 30.60KB (31,373 bytes)		2. AutoCAD presents the [Drawing Name] Properties dialog box. Note the size of the drawing (it's on the **General** tab), and then exit the dialog box.
	Command: ***xr***	3. Open the Xref Manager.
		4. Select the **battery** reference. Notice that the **Bind** button isn't available. The *battery.dwg* file is nested into our primary drawing. (It's there because it was referenced by the *MyCircuit1* drawing which, in turn, was referenced by our primary drawing). To bind a nested reference, bind its primary drawing.
		5. Select the *MyCircuit1* (or *Circuit1*) drawing and then pick the **Bind** button (Figure 25.024).

TOOLS	COMMAND SEQUENCE	STEPS

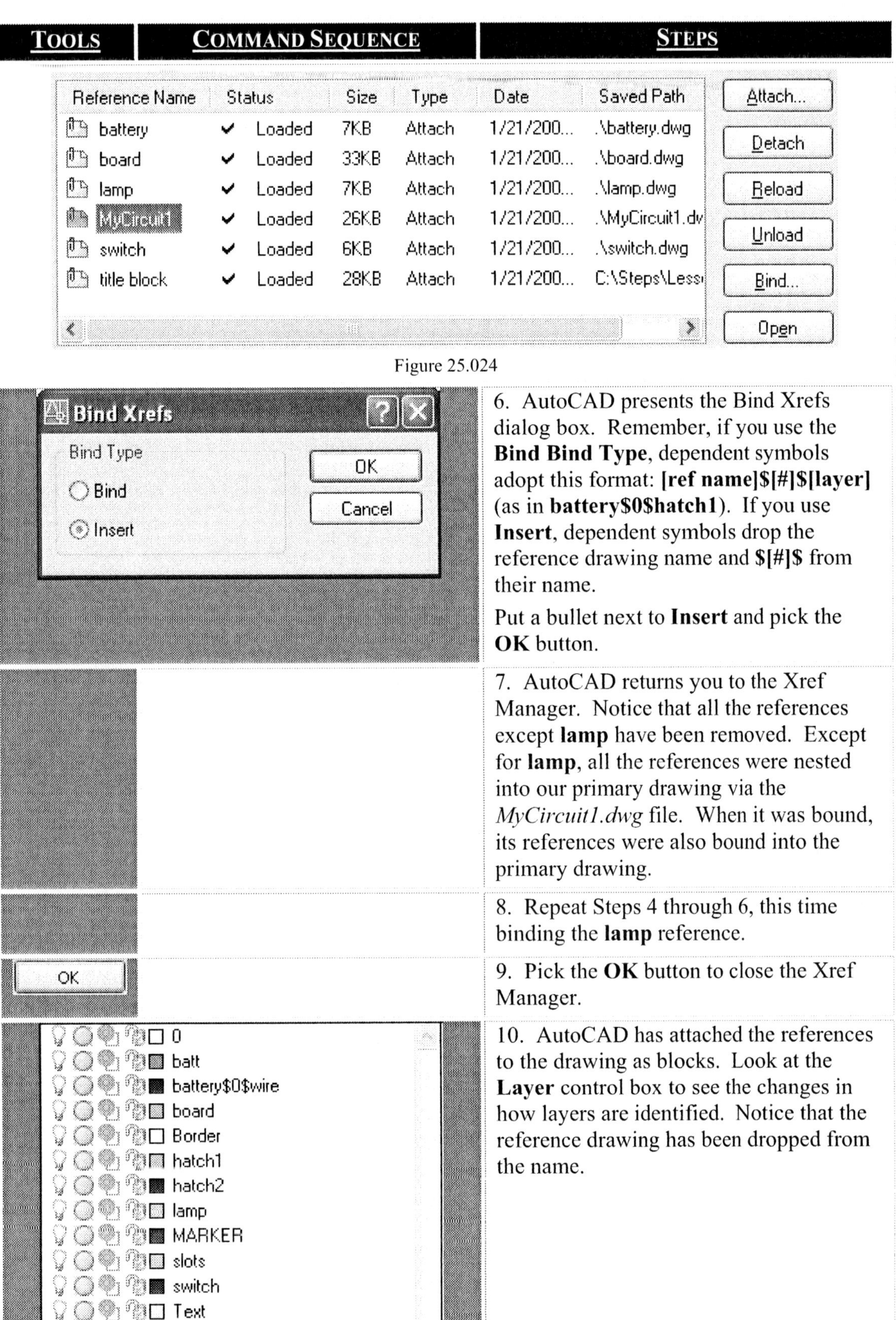

Figure 25.024

6. AutoCAD presents the Bind Xrefs dialog box. Remember, if you use the **Bind Bind Type**, dependent symbols adopt this format: **[ref name]$[#]$[layer]** (as in **battery0hatch1**). If you use **Insert**, dependent symbols drop the reference drawing name and **$[#]$** from their name.

Put a bullet next to **Insert** and pick the **OK** button.

7. AutoCAD returns you to the Xref Manager. Notice that all the references except **lamp** have been removed. Except for **lamp**, all the references were nested into our primary drawing via the *MyCircuit1.dwg* file. When it was bound, its references were also bound into the primary drawing.

8. Repeat Steps 4 through 6, this time binding the **lamp** reference.

9. Pick the **OK** button to close the Xref Manager.

10. AutoCAD has attached the references to the drawing as blocks. Look at the **Layer** control box to see the changes in how layers are identified. Notice that the reference drawing has been dropped from the name.

TOOLS	COMMAND SEQUENCE	STEPS
	Command: ***qsave***	11. Save the drawing but don't exit.
Type: AutoCAD Drawing Location: C:\Steps\Lesson25\ Size: 39.30KB (40,245 bytes)		12. Repeat Steps 1 and 2 and compare the drawing size now with the size before binding the Xrefs. Notice the size increase; this is how much drawing space you saved by using Xrefs! (Imagine how much help they'll be in a 2Mb or 3Mb drawing file!)
	Command: ***x***	13. Now explode all the blocks (except the title block information) and save the drawing. We do this for a comparison of drawing sizes (how large the drawing would have been had we simply drawn each object.)
Type: AutoCAD Drawing Location: C:\Steps\Lesson25\ Size: 53.70KB (54,978 bytes)		14. Repeat Steps 11 and 12. Notice how large the drawing file is now!
	Command: ***close***	15. Close the drawing. (Save the changes.)

You can now send the drawing to your client without fear of losing something in the transmittal!

25.5 Extra Steps

Asking is only half the battle. Listening to the answer reveals the path to success.

Anonymous

So, what do you think of Xrefs? When used properly, they can be tremendous timesavers. But something else is required. Let me tell you a story.

When I was working for one of the big petrochemical companies in Houston a few years ago, a friend of mine (another guru) was assigned to a new project. He was to set up the CAD system for the project.

For some wild reason (wild reasoning isn't uncommon in petrochem), he decided to buck the norm and set up the project the way AutoCAD was designed to work – using things like attributes to track materials and Xrefs to save time. Jim worked diligently for weeks setting up and starting the project.

Then the company fired him. It seemed the project's lead knew nothing about Xrefs and very little about attributes. All he saw was weeks gone with only a few drawings created (remember that proper setup of an AutoCAD project takes time in the beginning but saves time in the end).

The project lead hired a beginning CAD operator, had him teach himself about Xrefs and attributes, and then spent more weeks disassembling, binding, exploding, and so forth all of the drawings and setups which Jim had created.

What is the moral of this story? Jim forgot one crucial fact of CAD operations. That fact involves communication. Many supervisors are simply not aware of AutoCAD's potential or proper use (yet).

Jim didn't explain to the boss what he was doing, nor did the boss bother to learn Jim's "new" system. He replaced it with something he understood (more expensive and time consuming, but also more comfortable for him).

Your Extra Steps exercise is this: Go to your supervisor (or contact a supervisor in the industry in which you hope to work) and set up an interview. Ask if the company uses Xrefs and/or attributes to track materials. Then ask why or why not. If they're using Xrefs, try to convince them to stop (explain that this is an assignment and don't get too combative) and listen closely to their arguments. If they're not using Xrefs, try to convince them to do so. Again, listen closely to their arguments.

25.6 What Have We Learned?

Items covered in this lesson include:

- *The Xref Manager*
- *Dependent Symbols*
- *Manipulating Xrefs – unloading, reloading, overlaying, and binding*
- *Editing Xrefs*
- *Commands:*
    - ***Xref***
    - ***XAttach***
    - ***Xbind***
    - ***XClip***
    - ***Refedit***
    - ***Refclose***
    - ***Refset***
    - ***Dwgprops***

While only a fraction of the people to whom I've spoken about Xrefs actually use them, the number seems to be growing. Xrefs rank well behind blocks in popularity, but they can be almost as useful in their own way. Take some time to get comfortable with them in the exercises at the end of the lesson. Then talk it over with your employer and make an educated decision about how you'll proceed.

The objects of our next lesson – raster images and OLE – closely resemble Xrefs. There we'll discuss referencing other forms of graphics into our drawings. The procedures and dialog boxes resemble those of Xrefs, so the lesson should go fairly smoothly.

But first, let's try a few more Xrefs.

25.7 Exercises

1. Using Xrefs whenever possible, create the drawing in Figure 25.025.
    1.1. Use the following references (included in the C:\Steps\Lesson25 folder):
        1.1.1. *Title block*
        1.1.2. *Battery*
        1.1.3. *Lamp*
        1.1.4. *Galvanometer*
        1.1.5. *MyBoard* (you created this in Exercise 25.1.1.1) or *Board*
        1.1.6. *title info* (insert this as a block to use the attributes)
    1.2. Create layers as needed (you'll need a wire and a text layer)
    1.3. Save the drawing as *MyCircuit1d.dwg* in the C:\Steps\Lesson25 folder.

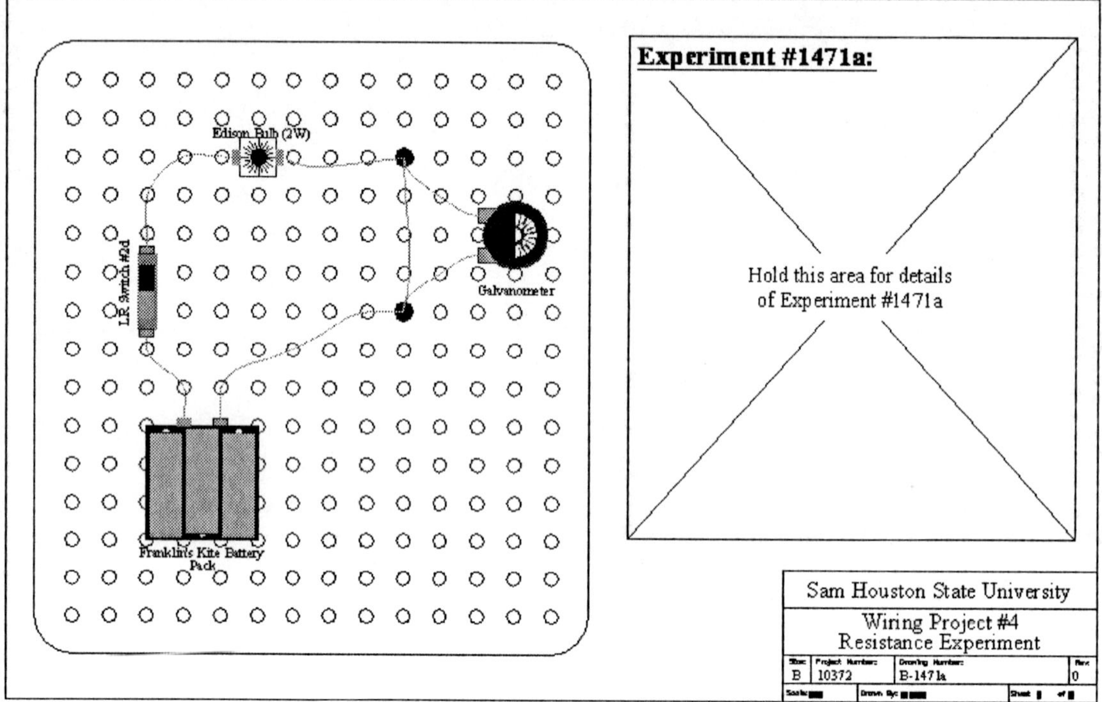

Figure 25.025: *MyCircuit1d.dwg*

2. Create the drawings in Figures 25.026 and 25.027, using Xrefs whenever possible.
    2.1. Use the following references (included in the C:\Steps\Lesson25 folder):
        2.1.1. *Title block-a*
        2.1.2. Other drawings you might wish to create
        2.1.3. *title info* (insert this as a block to use the attributes)
    2.2. Create layers as needed (you'll need a pipe and a text layer)
    2.3. Save the drawings as *Pump Config 1.dwg* and *Pump Config 2.dwg* in the C:\Steps\Lesson25 folder.

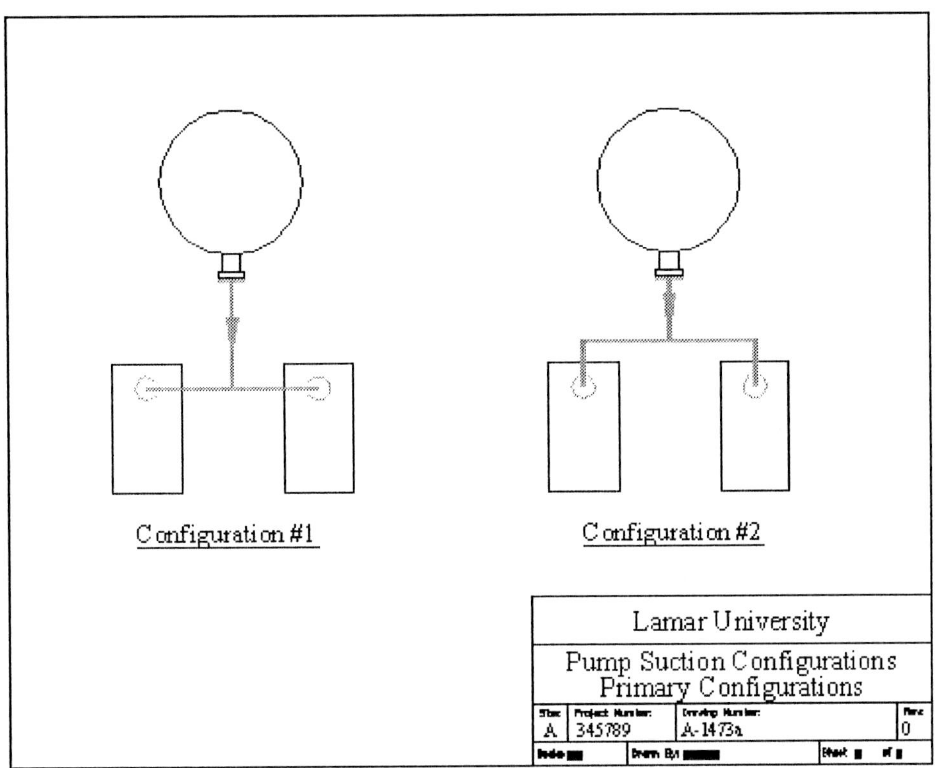

Figure 25.026: *Pump Config 1.dwg*

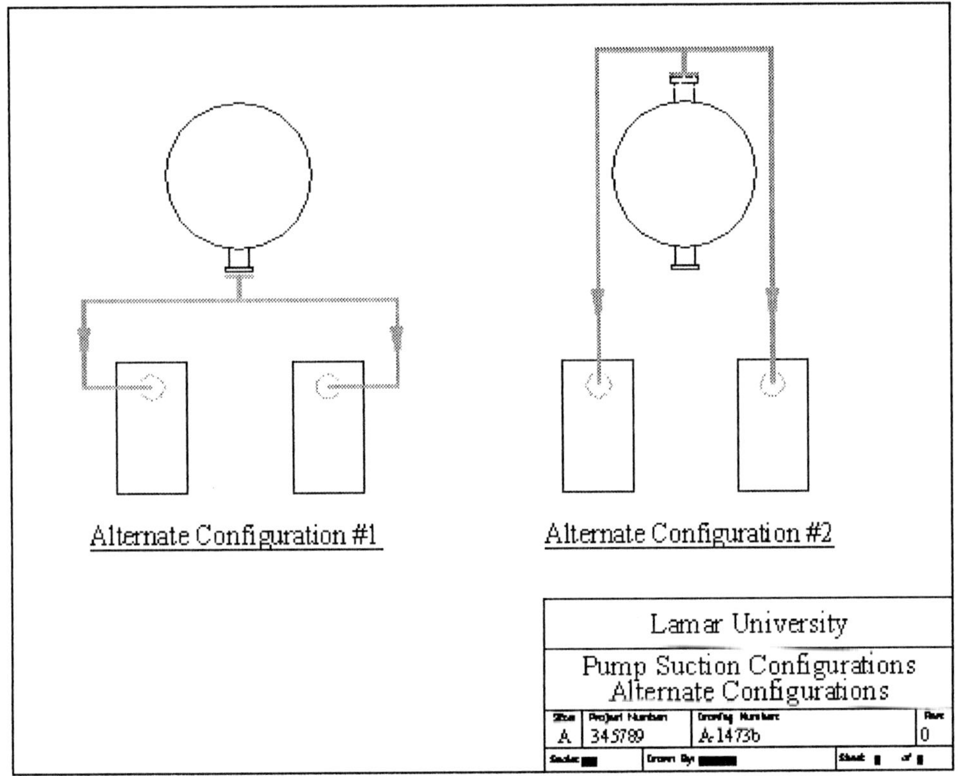

Figure 25.027: *Pump Config 2.dwg*

3. Create the drawings in Figures 25.028 and 25.029, using Xrefs whenever possible.
   3.1. Use the following references (included in the C:\Steps\Lesson25 folder):
      3.1.1. *Title block-a* (you'll need to scale it for ¼"=1'-0" drawing on an 11"x8½" sheet of paper)
      3.1.2. *Desk&chair*
      3.1.3. *Plant*
      3.1.4. *Room*
      3.1.5. *Table&chairs*
      3.1.6. *Vending machine*
      3.1.7. *Wall panel*
      3.1.8. *title info* (Insert this as a block to use the attributes. You'll need to scale it as well.)
   3.2. Create layers as needed
   3.3. Save the drawings as *floor plan layout1.dwg* and *floor plan layout2.dwg* in the C:\Steps\Lesson25 folder.

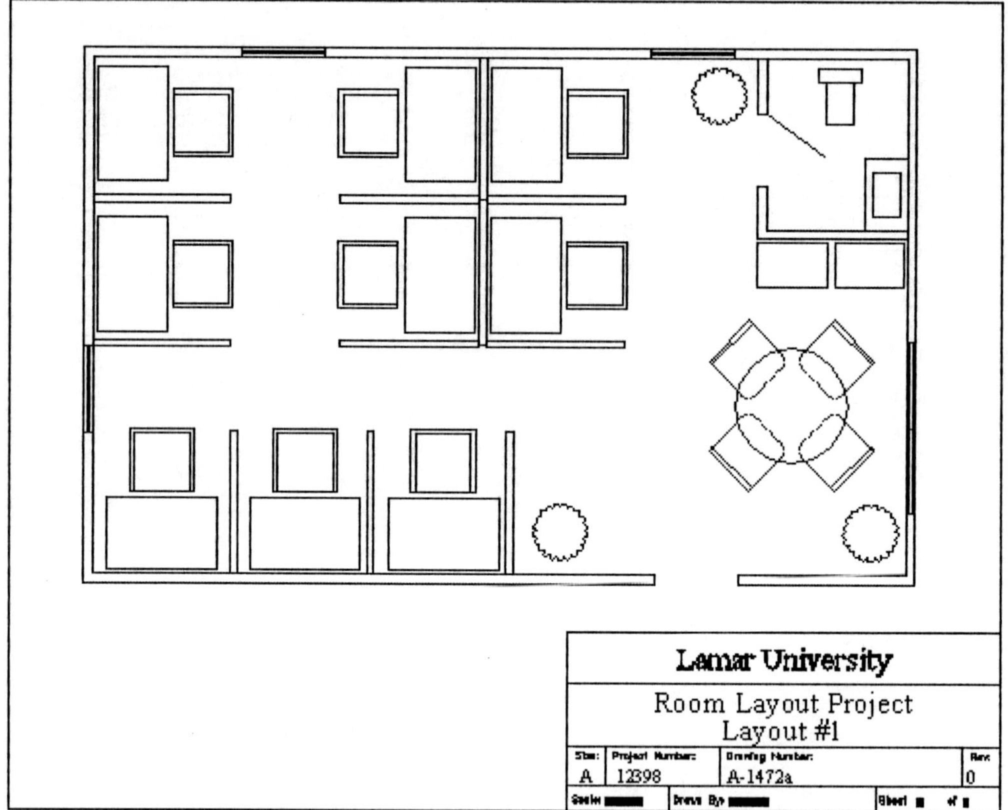

Figure 25.028: Floor Plan Layout1.dwg

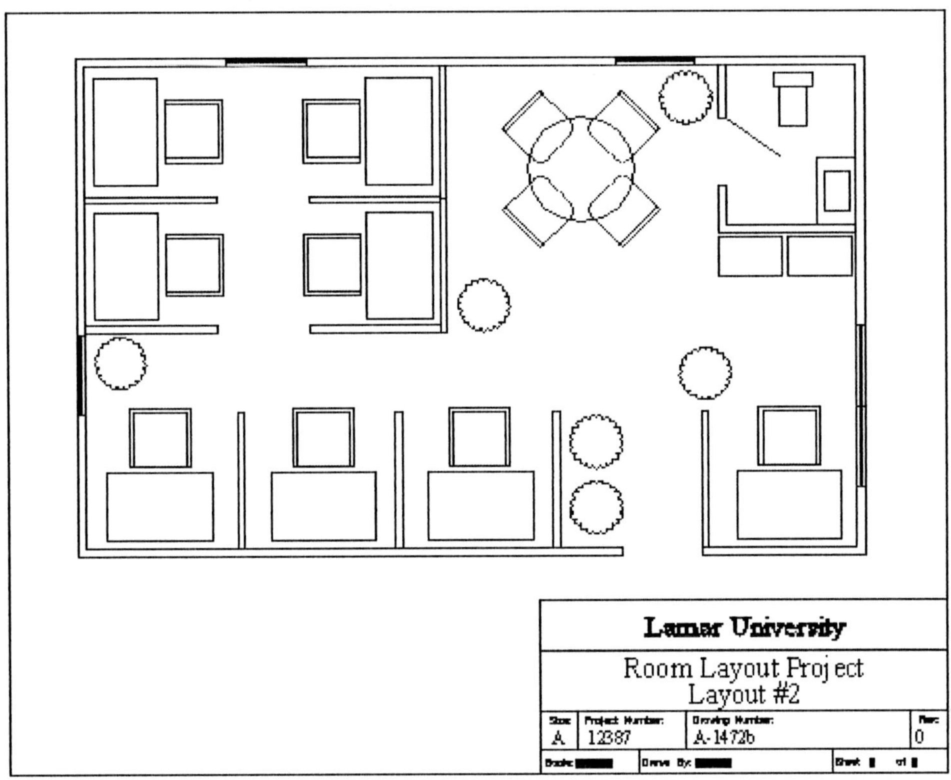

Figure 25.029: *Floor Plan Layout2.dwg*

4. Open the *cutting table.dwg* file in the C:\Steps\Lesson25 folder. Create the 11"x17" layout shown in Figure 25.030.
   4.1. Xref the *ANSI B* title block from AutoCAD's template folder.
   4.2. Create appropriate layers, text styles, linetypes, etc.
   4.3. Use the *title info.dwg* attributed block in the C:\Steps\Lesson25 folder to fill in the title block information.

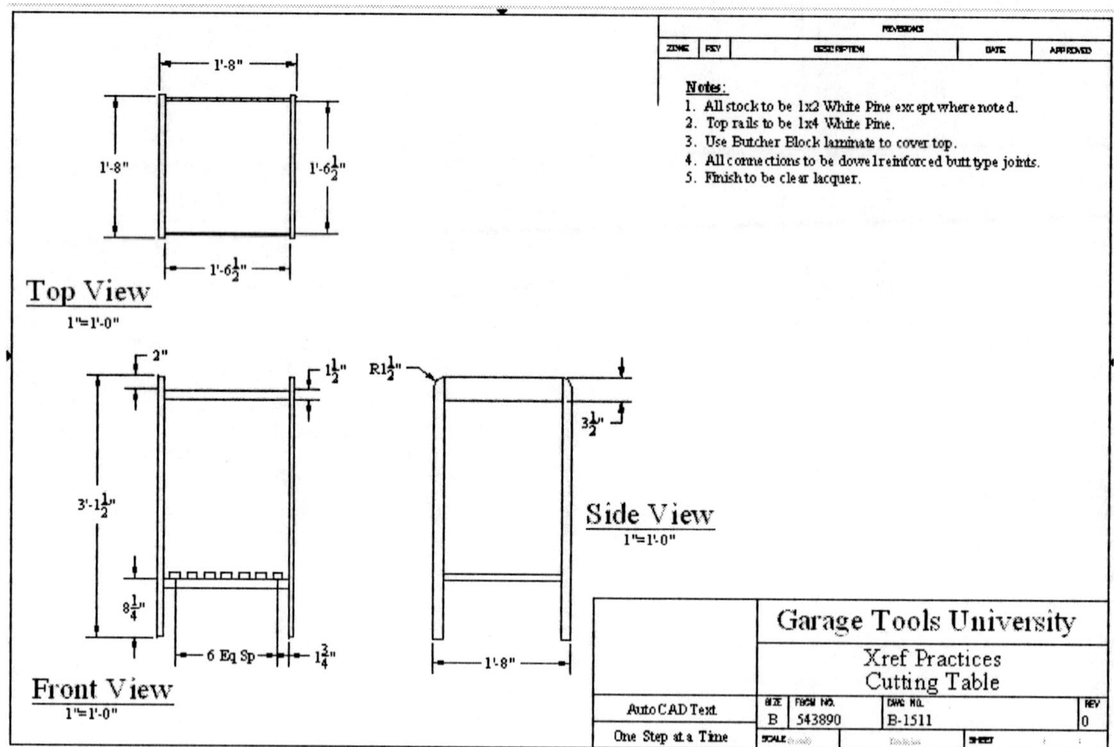

Figure 25.030: Cutting Table

5. Open the *Wheel.dwg* file in the C:\Steps\Lesson25 folder. Create the 8.5"x11" layout shown in Figure 25.031.
    5.1. Xref the *ANSI A* title block from AutoCAD's template folder.
    5.2. Create appropriate layers, text styles, linetypes, etc.
    5.3. Use the *title info.dwg* attributed block in the C:\Steps\Lesson25 folder to fill in the title block information.

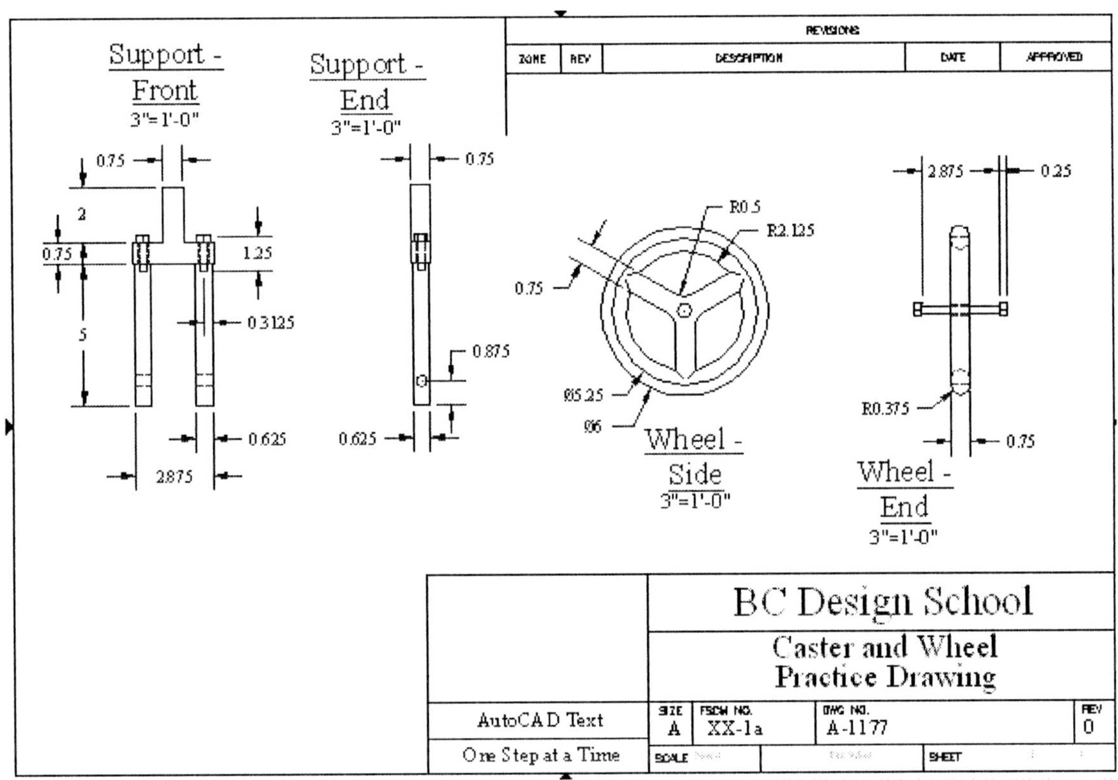

Figure 25.031: Wheel.dwg

6. Open the *table lamp.dwg* file in the C:\Steps\Lesson25 folder. Create the 8.5"x11" layout shown in Figure 25.032.
   6.1. Xref the *ANSI A* title block from AutoCAD's template folder.
   6.2. Create appropriate layers, text styles, linetypes, etc.
   6.3. Use the *title info.dwg* attributed block in the C:\Steps\Lesson25 folder to fill in the title block information.

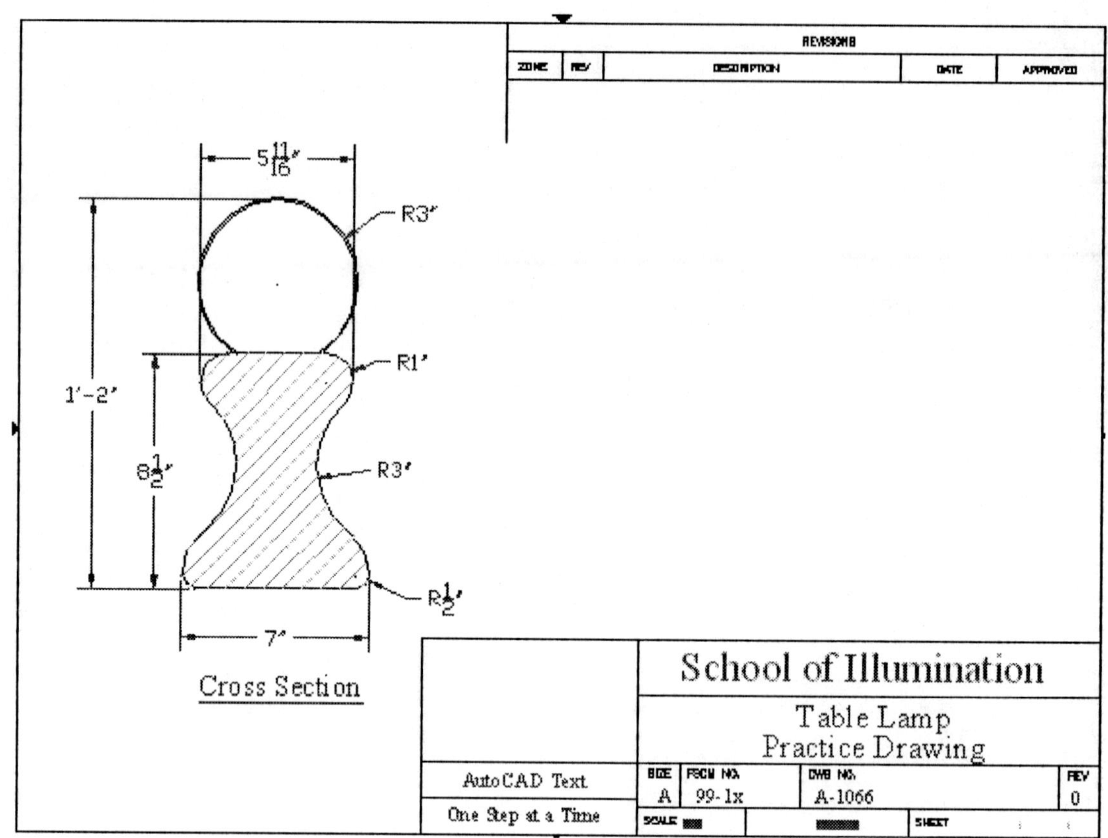

Figure 25.032: Table Lamp

7. Open the *planter.dwg* file in the C:\Steps\Lesson25 folder. Create the 8.5"x11" layout shown in Figure 25.033.
   7.1. Xref the *ANSI A* title block from AutoCAD's template folder.
   7.2. Create appropriate layers, text styles, linetypes, etc.
   7.3. Use the *title info.dwg* attributed block in the C:\Steps\Lesson25 folder to fill in the title block information.

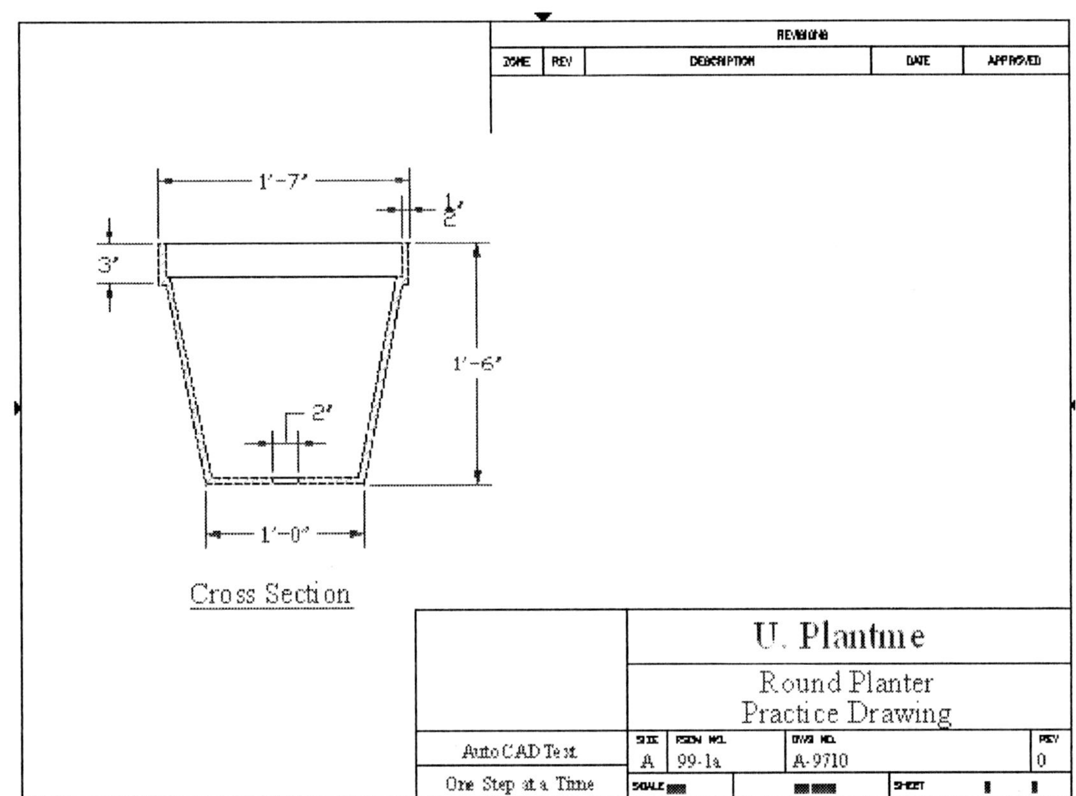

Figure 25.033: Round Planter

8. Open the *patio planter.dwg* file in the C:\Steps\Lesson25 folder. Create the 8.5"x11" layout shown in Figure 25.034.
    8.1. Xref the *ANSI A* title block from AutoCAD's template folder.
    8.2. Create appropriate layers, text styles, linetypes, etc.
    8.3. Use the *title info.dwg* attributed block in the C:\Steps\Lesson25 folder to fill in the title block information.

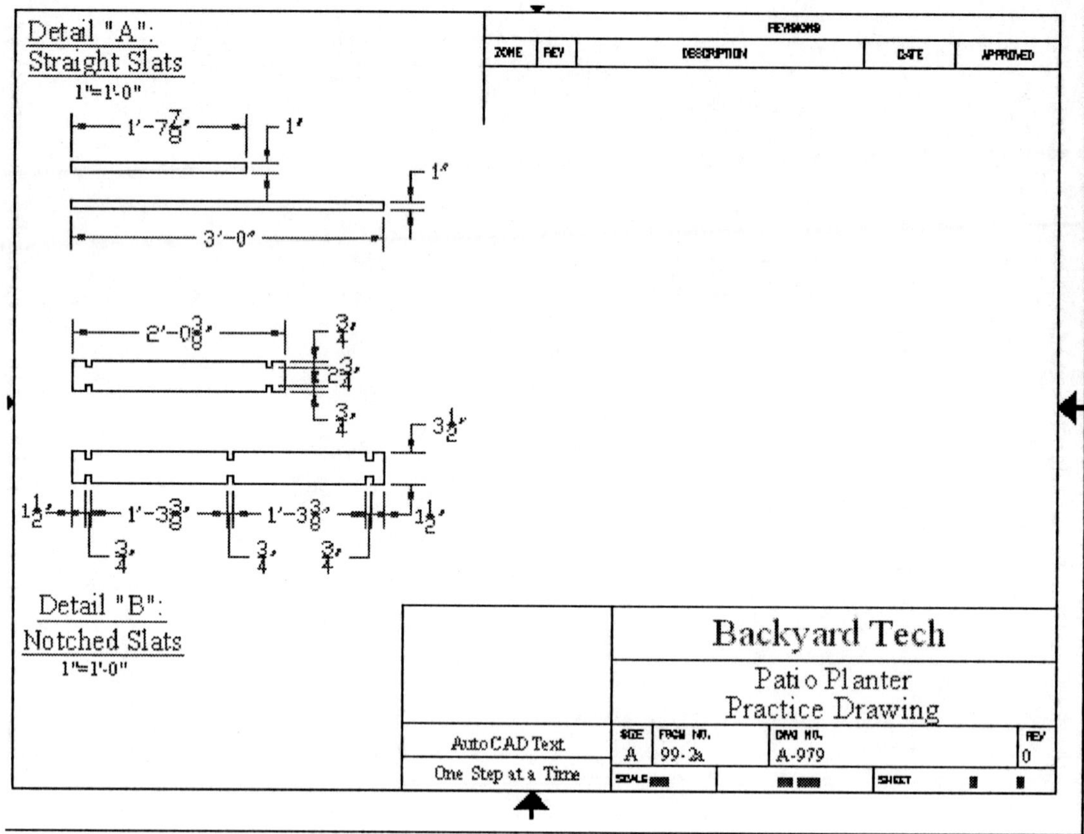

Figure 25.034: Patio Planter

9. Open the *OnArtesia.dwg* file in the C:\Steps\Lesson25 folder. Create the 17"x23" layout shown in Figure 25.036.
    9.1. Xref the *ANSI C* title block from AutoCAD's template folder.
    9.2. Create appropriate layers, text styles, linetypes, etc.
    9.3. Use the *title info.dwg* attributed block in the C:\Steps\Lesson25 folder to fill in the title block information. Use the information in Figure 25.035 to help you.

	www.UNeedCAD.com			
	Artesia House Proposed Retaining Wall			
AutoCAD Text	SIZE C	FSCM NO. 2397	DWG NO. C-2397a	REV 0
One Step at a Time	SCALE NOTED	Tim Sykes	SHEET	

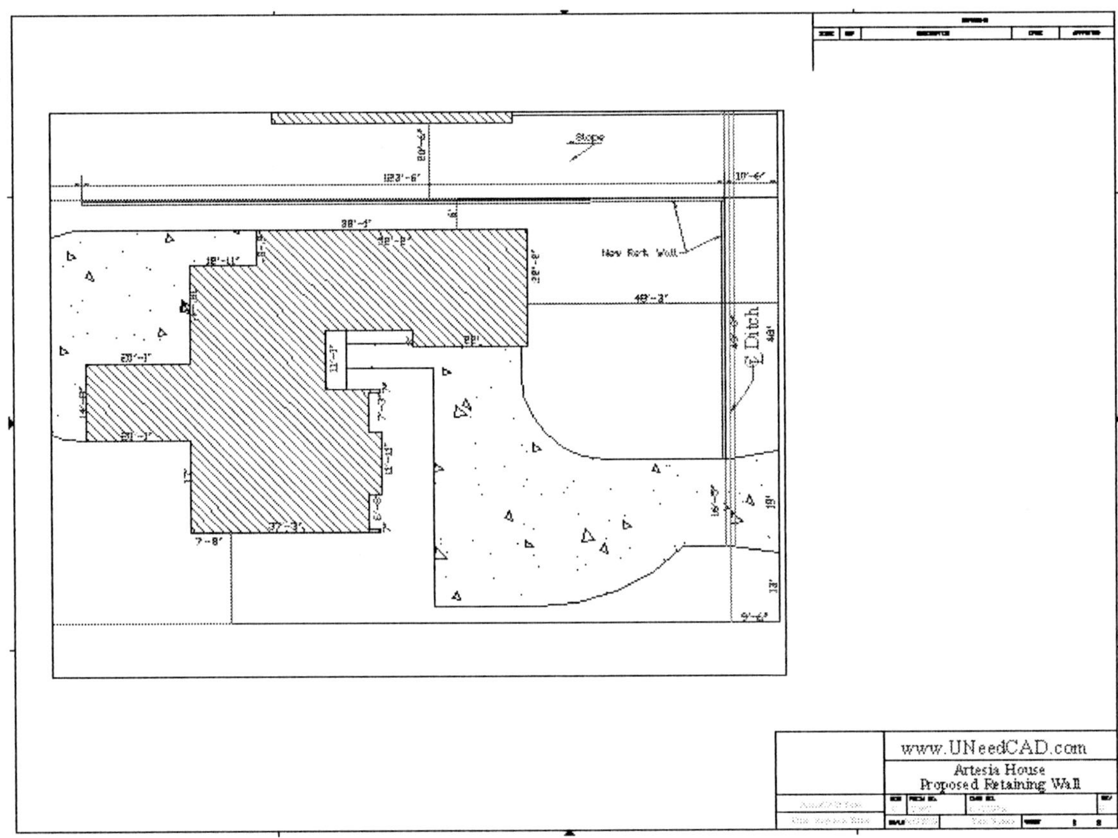

Figure 25.036

25.8	For Web-Based Review Questions, visit: http://www.uneedcad.com/2006/Files/06R25.pdf

Lesson 26

Following this lesson, you will:

- ✓ *Know how to use graphic images from other applications in AutoCAD drawings*
- ✓ *Know how to use AutoCAD drawings in other applications*
- ✓ *Be familiar with raster and vector images*
- ✓ *Know how to use Object Linking and Embedding to share information with other applications*

Other Application Files and AutoCAD

I can think of several reasons why you might want to use other application files in an AutoCAD drawing. How about including a photograph of a completed project on a mechanical drawing? I've used them to show completed pieces of furniture I designed. Or perhaps you might want to include a corporate logo in the title block of your drawing. If you can find a nice, colorful scan of the logo, your employer might be pleased to find it on the design! Architects and plant designers might show an outline of the proposed new building or unit against an aerial photograph of the area.

You can probably think of many uses for other applications' files in your drawings. Thank goodness that the thinkers and doers at AutoCAD also considered the possibilities.

26.1 Two Types of Graphics

Two categories of graphic files are associated with AutoCAD: *Vector Images* and *Raster Images*.

- Vector Images

  By default, AutoCAD creates vector images. In fact, you've been drawing vector images since you began using AutoCAD.

  Vector images locate geometry by definition and coordinate. For example, a line has two defined endpoints. AutoCAD treats it as a single object – a line – by definition.

  Vector images hold their definition regardless of the resolution of the screen or drawing view. Since they only have to define coordinates and objects, their size is quite small compared to a raster image of the same objects.

  Types of files found in this category include:

  - *DWG* – You're already familiar with how AutoCAD shares its drawing files within the AutoCAD program (blocks and Xrefs).
  - *3DS* – This is another Autodesk file. This one works with 3D Studio.
  - *DXF* – ASCII version of the image file.
  - *SAT* – The ACIS file format.
  - *EPS* – Adobe graphic file. Useful for sharing information with Adobe's publishing applications.
  - *WMF* – Windows MetaFiles were created by Microsoft for use in its graphics programs. You can use them to share information with most Microsoft publishing software. (Note: A WMF file actually contains both vector and raster imaging.)

- Raster Images

  Most non-CAD programs use raster images. These images locate geometry by screen pixel coordinate. In other words, objects aren't defined as circles, lines, and so forth, but are the result of the color definition of a series of pixels.

  This method of graphics creation generally requires more memory and tends to lose image quality (sharpness) as the viewer gets close to the image.

  The more popular types of files in this category include:

  - *GIF* – An ideal Internet file because of its small size, the GIF file is no longer supported in AutoCAD drawings.
  - *JPG* – Also good for Internet use, the JPG (pronounced "jay'-peg") file doesn't have the GIF's color limitations, making it perfect for photographs. However, the JPG file can become quite large.
  - *TIF* – Microsoft had a hand in developing this file type, so its acceptability in various graphics programs is almost universal.

- *BMP* – Microsoft's original bitmap, this file type also is almost universal in acceptability. Virtually all IBM-type computers (all those with the Windows operating system) use BMPs in the Windows' Paint program.
- *PCT* – Use this Apple graphics file for easy exchange with the Apple-type computer.

Other and lesser-known file types include *RLE*, *DIB*, *RST*, *GP4*, *MIL*, *CAL*, *CG4*, *FLC*, *FLI*, *BIL*, *IG4*, *IGS*, *PCX*, *PCT*, *PNG*, RLC, AND *TGA*.

Since we're already familiar with the important vector images, let's look at raster images.

26.2 Working with Raster Images: The Image Manager

For working with raster images, AutoCAD provides an Image Manager very similar to the Xref Manager we used in our last lesson. Access it with the ***Image*** command.

Notice the similarities (Figure 26.001). In fact, all of the buttons that you find in the Image Manager work the same way they work in the Xref Manager – with a couple of notable exceptions.

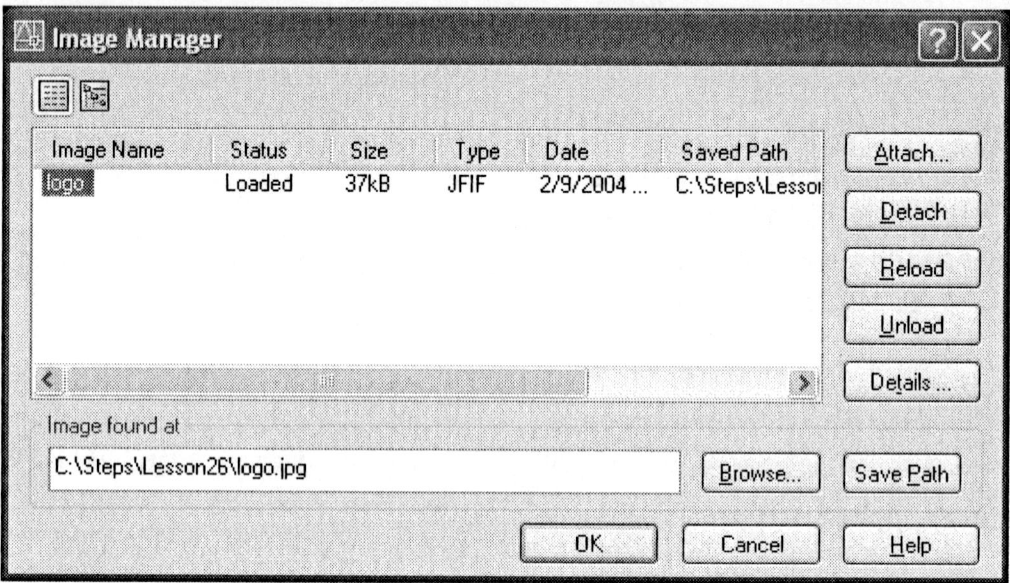

Figure 26.001

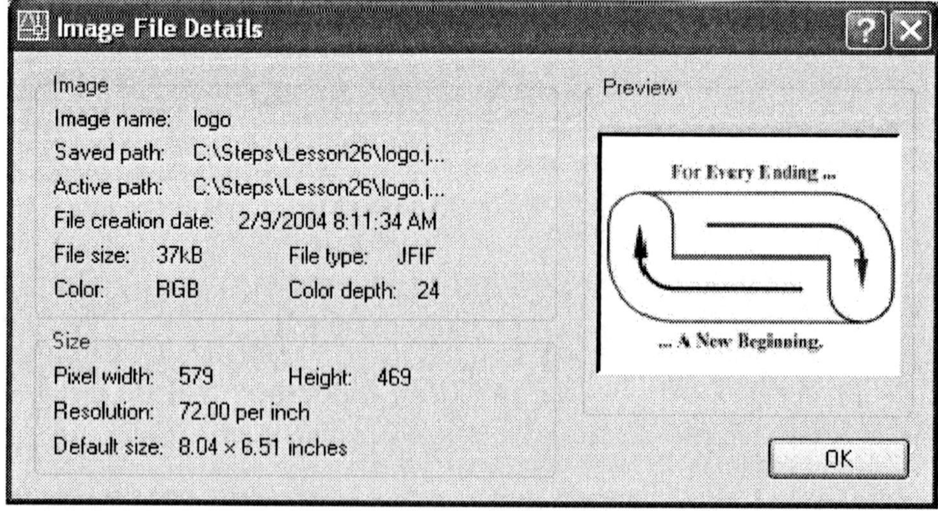

Figure 26.002

First, there's no **Open** button. If you wish to open the graphic for editing, you'll have to do it in an appropriate graphics program.

Then, if you'll notice the fifth button down on the right side of the Image Manager, you'll see that the button reads **Details**. (This button reads **Bind** in the Xref Manager.) The significance of this is really quite important: *You can reference an image file from, but you can't bind an image file to an AutoCAD drawing*. The **Details** button, however, provides some useful information about the highlighted file (Figure 26.002), such as size, location, and type of file providing the image.

> You can also use the ***-Image*** command to access a command line sequence containing the Image dialog box's options. The sequence looks like this:
>
> **Command: *-image***
>
> **Enter image option [?/Detach/Path/Reload/ Unload/Attach] <Attach>:**

26.2.1 Attaching, Detaching, Loading, and Unloading Image Files

As with the Xref Manager, you can use the Image Manager to attach, detach, load, or unload image files (use the ***Image*** command or its hotkey, ***im***). Use the **Image** button on the Image Manager to select an image to load and then proceed to the Image dialog box in Figure 26.003. Notice the similarity between the Image dialog box and the External Reference dialog box we discussed in our last lesson (Figure 25.003). They're almost identical and the function of each button/frame is the same.

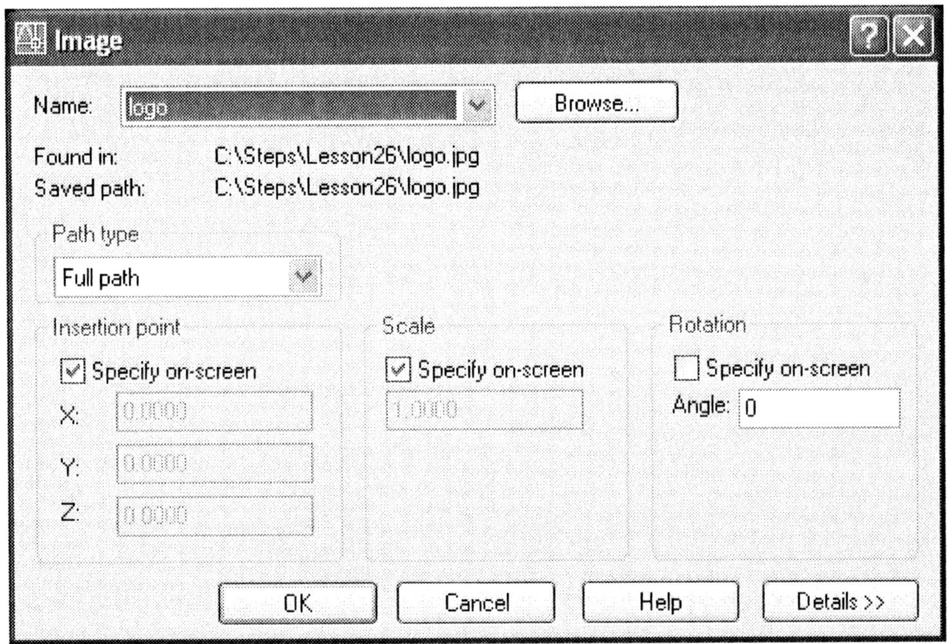

Figure 26.003

There's one notable exception; the **Scale** frame of the Image dialog box has only one text box. The reason for this is simple: while you could scale a reference drawing file along the XYZ axes, a raster image has no XY or Z-axis along which to scale. Therefore, AutoCAD restricts us to a uniform scale for raster images.

Let's reference some images into a file.

Just as Xrefs have a more direct ***XAttach*** command, so images also have an ***ImageAttach*** command. You can enter it at the keyboard or via the Insert pull-down menu. Follow this path:

Insert – Raster Image...

Do This: 26.2.1.1	Working with Images

I. Open the *cutting table26.dwg* file in the C:\Steps\Lesson26 folder. The drawing looks like Figure 26.004.

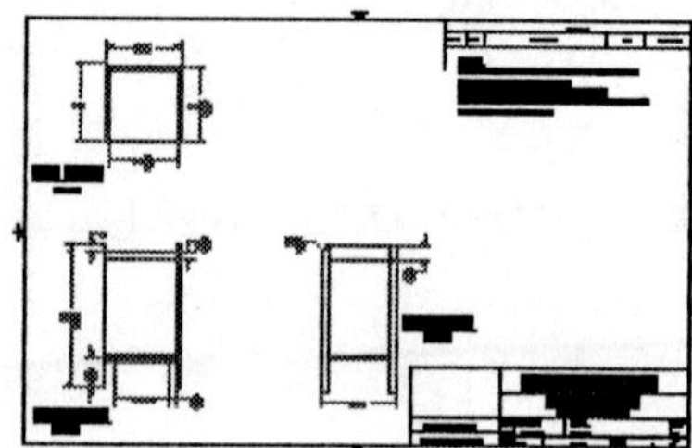

Figure 26.004

II. Thaw the **MARKER** layer.

III. Enter the following command sequence:

Command: *imageframe*

Enter image frame setting [0, 1, 2] <1>: *0*

[We'll discuss image framing after this exercise, but for now, it's best to have it turned off.]

IV. Follow these steps.

TOOLS	COMMAND SEQUENCE	STEPS
Image Manager Button	**Command: *im***	1. Open the Image Manager. Alternately, you can pick the **Image Manager** button on the Reference toolbar.
Attach...		2. AutoCAD presents the Image Manager (Figure 26.001). We'll attach a logo in the title block, so pick the **Attach** button.
Open		3. AutoCAD presents a Windows Select... File dialog box. Select the *logo.jpg* file in the C:\Steps\Lesson26 folder. Pick the **Open** button to continue.
		4. AutoCAD presents the Image dialog box (Figure 26.005). • Be sure there is a check in the **Specify on-screen** check box in the **Insertion point** frame. Clear the check boxes in the other frames. • Enter ***0.2*** into the Scale frame's text box. • Use a **Relative path**. • Pick the **OK** button to continue.

Tools	Command Sequence	Steps

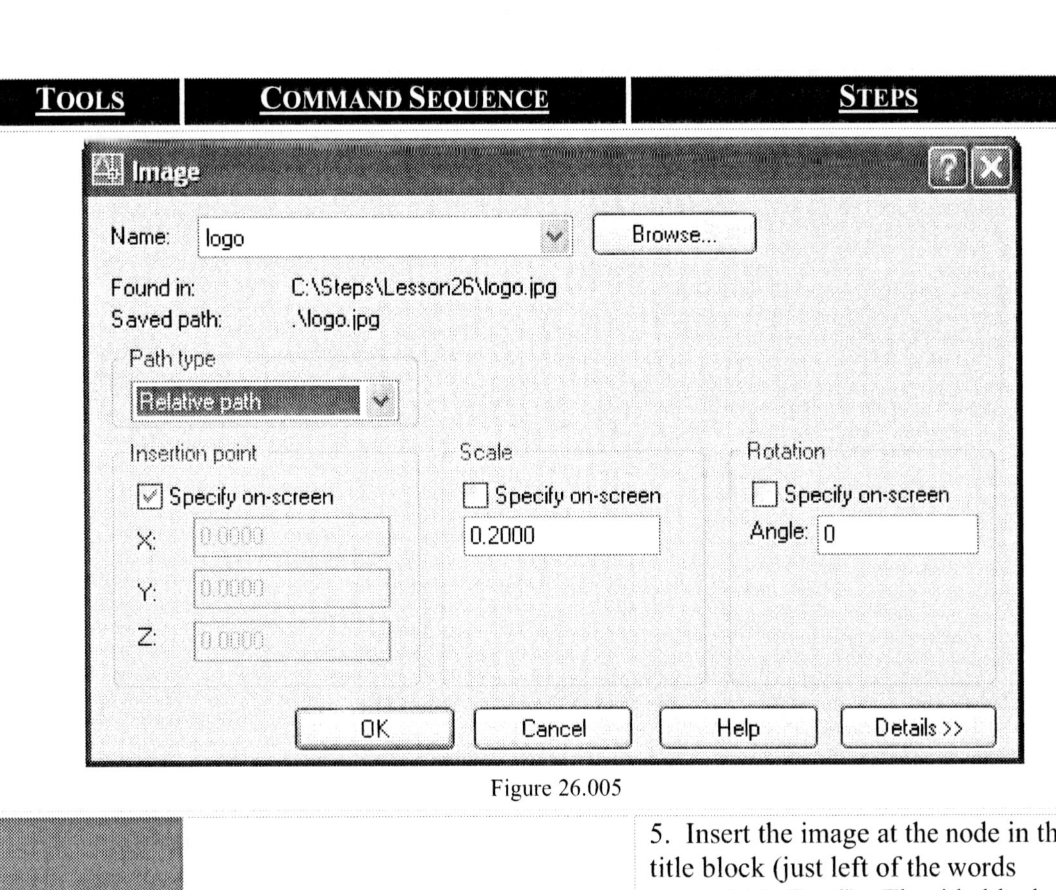

Figure 26.005

Tools	Command Sequence	Steps
		5. Insert the image at the node in the title block (just left of the words "AutoCAD Text"). The title block looks like Figure 26.006.

Figure 26.006

Tools	Command Sequence	Steps
Raster Image Button	**Command:** ***iat***	6. Now let's use the ***ImageAttach*** command to insert a photograph of the cutting table. Enter ***imageattach*** or ***iat*** at the command prompt. Alternately, you can pick the **Raster Image** button on the Reference toolbar.
		7. Repeat Step 3, but select the *cutting table.jpg* file.
		8. This time enter a scale of **.75** (Figure 26.007), and insert the image at the node in the middle of the screen (~6,5). Pick the **OK** button to continue. Your drawing looks like Figure 26.008.

TOOLS	COMMAND SEQUENCE	STEPS

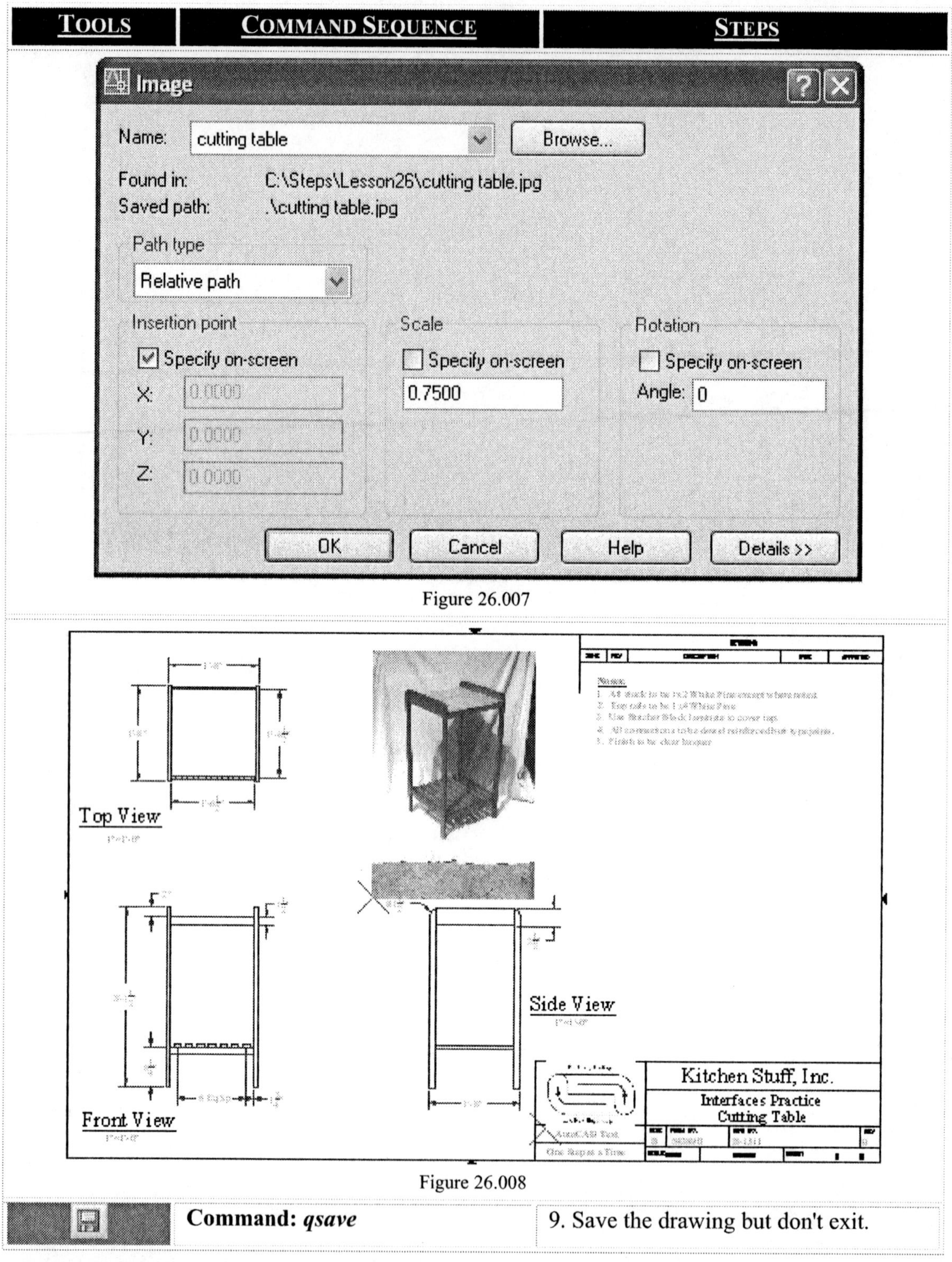

Figure 26.007

Figure 26.008

	Command: ***qsave***	9. Save the drawing but don't exit.

> Note: Images attach on the current layer. You can freeze them, turn them off, lock them, and so forth just like any other object.

Over the course of this exercise, did you try to adjust either of the images we referenced? Did you notice that you couldn't select either one? If not, try to erase one of them now.

Unlike Xrefs, which allow you to use OSNAPs and other modifying tools, images have no vector geometry to select. But AutoCAD doesn't leave you with something you can't modify. It provides a system variable – called **ImageFrame** – that reveals a selectable frame around the image. The command prompts:

Command: ***imageframe***

Enter image frame setting [0, 1, 2] <1>:

When set to **0**, images in the drawing are not selectable; that is, you can't modify them. When set to **1** or **2**, AutoCAD shows a frame around the image. You can select this frame to move, scale, or otherwise modify the image. (When set to **1**, the frame will plot; when set to **2**, it won't.)

In our next exercise, we'll use the frame to adjust our view of the photograph.

> You can also pick the **Frame** button on the Reference toolbar to access the **ImageFrame** system variable. Alternately, you can access the **ImageFrame** system variable via the Modify pull-down menu. Follow this path:
>
> *Modify – Object – Image – Frame*

26.2.2 Clipping Image Files

Clipping an image is no different from clipping an Xref. The command sequence is identical:

Command: ***imageclip*** **(or *icl*)**

Select image to clip: ***[select the image you wish to clip]***

Enter image clipping option [ON/OFF/ Delete/New boundary] <New>: ***[tell AutoCAD what you want to do]***

Enter clipping type [Polygonal/Rectangular] <Rectangular>: ***[tell AutoCAD what type of clipping boundary you wish to use]***

Specify first corner point: Specify opposite corner point: ***[identify the corners of the rectangle or the vertices of the polygon]***

The ***ImageClip*** command automatically activates the **ImageFrame** system variable so that you can select an image.

Let's clip our photograph.

> You can also access the ***ImageClip*** command via the Modify pull-down menu. Follow this path:
>
> *Modify – Clip – Image*

Do This: 26.2.2.1	Clipping Images

I. Be sure you're still in the *cutting table26.dwg* file in the C:\Steps\Lesson26 folder. If not, please open it now.

II. Follow these steps.

TOOLS	COMMAND SEQUENCE	STEPS
Image Button	**Command:** *icl*	1. Enter the ***ImageClip*** command. Alternately, you can pick the **Image** button on the Reference toolbar.

TOOLS	COMMAND SEQUENCE	STEPS
	Select image to clip:	2. (Notice that AutoCAD activates the **ImageFrame** system variable.) Select the frame around the cutting table photograph.
	Enter image clipping option [ON/OFF/ Delete/New boundary] <New>: ***[enter]*** **Enter clipping type [Polygonal/ Rectangular] <Rectangular>:** ***[enter]***	3. Hit ***enter*** twice to accept the **New** and **Rectangular** boundary defaults.
	Specify first corner point: **Specify opposite corner point:**	4. Place a rectangle around the image of the cutting table as shown in Figure 26.009. AutoCAD clips the photograph. The results look like Figure 26.010.
Figure 26.009		Figure 26.010
	Command: ***qsave***	5. Save the drawing but don't exit.

We could do the same thing for the logo, but I want to show you another tool we can use there. Let's continue.

26.2.3 Working with Image Files

AutoCAD provides four tools for use with graphic images that aren't available (nor would they be useful) for Xrefs. These include: ***ImageAdjust***, ***ImageQuality***, ***Transparency***, and ***DrawOrder***.

- The ***ImageAdjust*** command calls the Image Adjust dialog box (Figure 26.011). Here you can adjust the brightness, contrast, or fading effect (how well the image blends with the background color of the drawing) of the image. The dynamic preview image helps you see the results of your modifications before you accept them with the **OK** button.

  Like ***ImageClip***, ***ImageAdjust*** automatically activates the **ImageFrame** system variable.

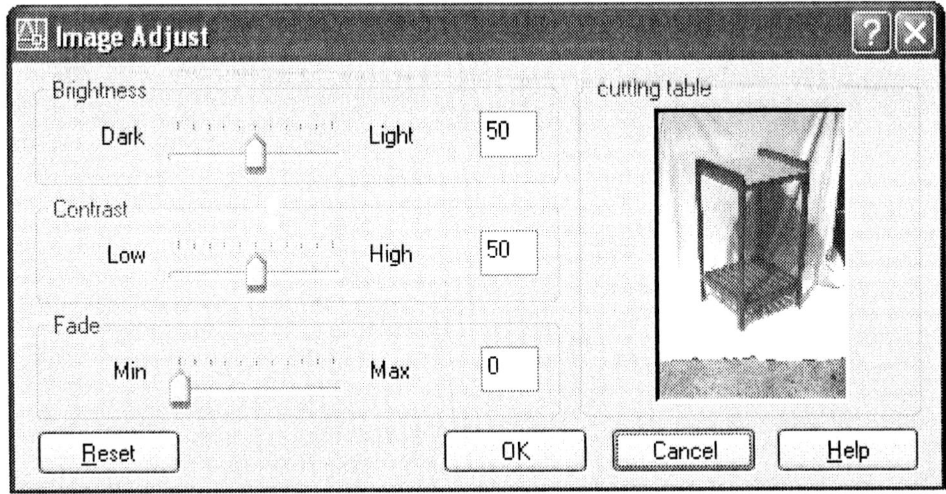

Figure 26.011

- **ImageQuality** is a system variable that affects only the display of your graphic images. It presents the following prompt:

  Command: ***imagequality***

  Enter image quality setting [High/ Draft] <High>:

  High quality presents the best possible image in the display, but it may cause some delay in the initial display or redraw/regen time. Draft quality isn't quite as pretty, but it allows for much faster displays. AutoCAD will always use **High** quality when plotting despite this setting.
- The ***Transparency*** command works only on certain types of graphics that have a transparency property.

  You can set transparency on a per-image basis.
- [We'll discuss ***DrawOrder*** after the next exercise.]

Let's experiment with these commands before looking at our last tool.

> You can also access the ***Transparency***, ***ImageQuality***, and ***ImageAdjust*** commands via the Modify toolbar. Follow this path:
>
> *Modify – Object – Image – [command]*

Do This: 26.2.3.1	**Image Quality**

I. Be sure you're still in the *cutting table26.dwg* file in the C:\Steps\Lesson26 folder. If not, please open it now.

II. Follow these steps.

TOOLS	COMMAND SEQUENCE	STEPS
	Command: *z*	1. We'll begin by adjusting the cutting table photograph. Zoom in a bit closer to it.

Tools	**Command Sequence**	**Steps**
Adjust Button	**Command: *iad***	2. Enter the ***ImageAdjust*** command. Alternately, you can pick the **Adjust** button on the Reference toolbar.
	Select image(s): **Select image(s): *[enter]***	3. Notice that ***ImageAdjust*** activates the **ImageFrame** sysvar. Select the frame around the photograph.
OK		4. AutoCAD presents the Image Adjust dialog box (Figure 26.011). Work with the three settings until you're pleased with the preview image. (Use the **Reset** button in the lower left corner if you need to return to the original settings.) Pick the **OK** button when you're satisfied.
Quality Button	**Command: *imagequality***	5. Now we'll set the ***ImageQuality*** to speed our display time. Enter the command. Alternately, you can pick the **Quality** button on the Reference toolbar.
• High Draft		6. Tell AutoCAD to use a **Draft** quality. Notice the change in the photograph. Remember that the ***ImageQuality*** setting affects only the display.
	Command: *z*	7. Zoom all.
	Command: *qsave*	8. Add the *Product* text, freeze the **MARKER** layer, and save the drawing. It now looks like Figure 26.012.

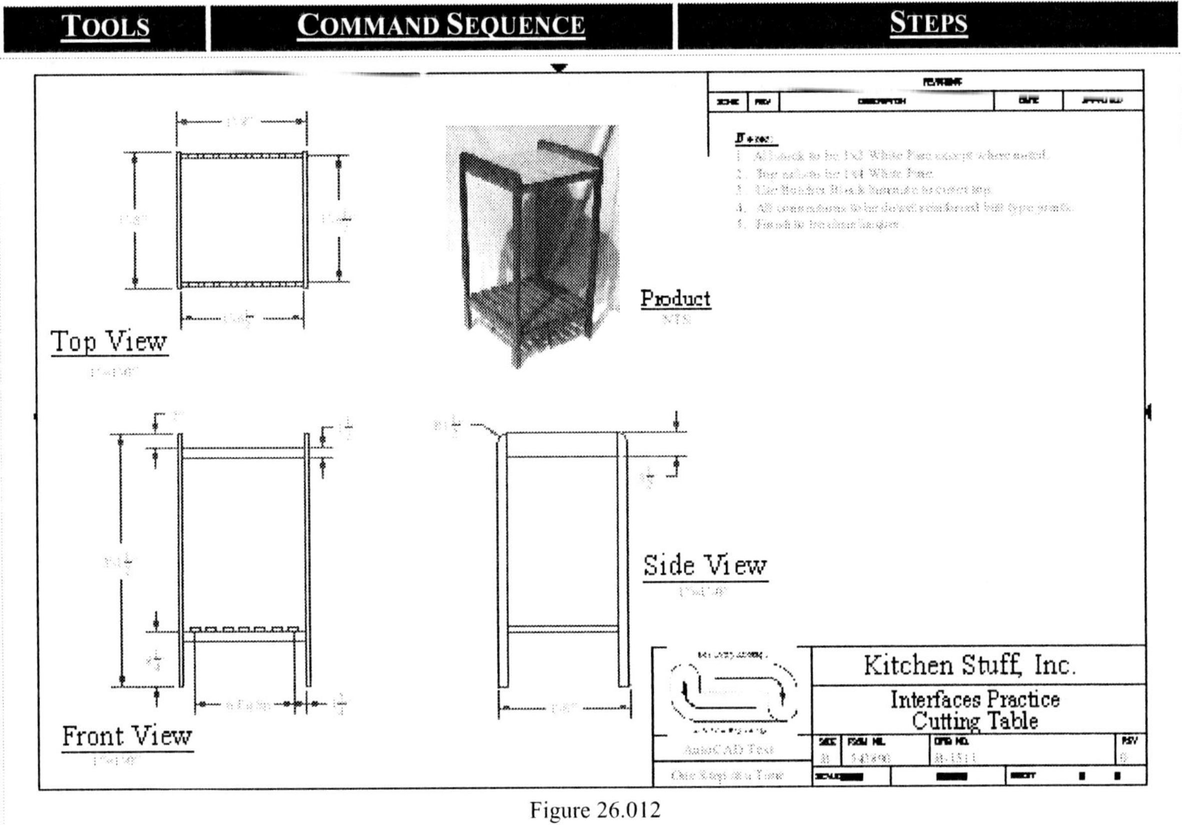

Figure 26.012

- Our last image modification tool is called ***DrawOrder***. By default, AutoCAD displays the last object drawn or inserted atop (or over) previously drawn objects. This may cause certain objects to "hide" behind other objects. ***DrawOrder*** allows you to control the order in which objects are displayed. In other words, use ***DrawOrder*** to control which object appears on top. It presents the following sequence:

  Command: *draworder* (or *dr*)

  Select objects: ***[select an object to modify]***

  Select objects: ***[select more objects or hit enter to confirm the set]***

  Enter object ordering option [Above object/Under object/Front/Back] <Back>: ***tell AutoCAD how to reposition the image/object]***

The options are best explained in an exercise, so let's begin.

> You can also access the various options of the ***DrawOrder*** command via the Tools pull-down menu. Follow this path:
>
> *Tools – Draw Order – [option]*

Do This: 26.2.3.2	Controlling Drawing Order

I. Open the *DrawOrd.dwg* file in the C:\Steps\Lesson26 folder. The drawing looks like Figure 26.013. (The drawing has two polylines and an image.)

II. Follow these steps.

Figure 26.013

TOOLS	COMMAND SEQUENCE	STEPS
Draw Order Button	**Command: *dr***	1. Enter the ***DrawOrder*** command. Alternately, you can pick the **Draw Order** button on the Modify II toolbar.
	Select objects: **Select objects: *[enter]***	2. Select the red horizontal polyline.
Above objects Under objects Front Back	**Enter object ordering option [Above object/Under object/Front/Back] <Back>: *f***	3. Move it to the front. Notice the change in the display (Figure 26.014).

For Every Ending ...

... A New Beginning.

Figure 26.014

I created this file to give you a chance to play with the various options of the ***DrawOrder*** command. Take a few minutes to experiment with each of the options. (Note: You can also use the buttons on the Draw Order toolbar.)

26.3 Exporting Image Files

It seems that there are almost as many ways to export image files as there are types of image files to export. Luckily, AutoCAD has also provided a single command that covers the spectrum. That command is ***Export***, and it works with a Windows standard Save-type dialog box.

The Export Data dialog box works as easily as the Save dialog box. Simply select the type of file you wish in the **Save as type** control box, and then pick the **Save** button.

Let's give it a try.

> You can also access the ***Export*** command via the File pull-down menu. Follow this path:
> *File – Export ...*

Do This: 26.3.1	**Exporting Image Files**

I. Be sure you're still in the *DrawOrd.dwg* file in the C:\Steps\Lesson26 folder. If not, please open it now.

II. Follow these steps.

TOOLS	COMMAND SEQUENCE	STEPS
No Button Available	**Command: *export***	1. Enter the ***Export*** command.
		2. AutoCAD presents the Export Data dialog box. Pick the down arrow next to the Files of type control box, and select **Bitmap (*.bmp)**. (See Figure 26.015.)
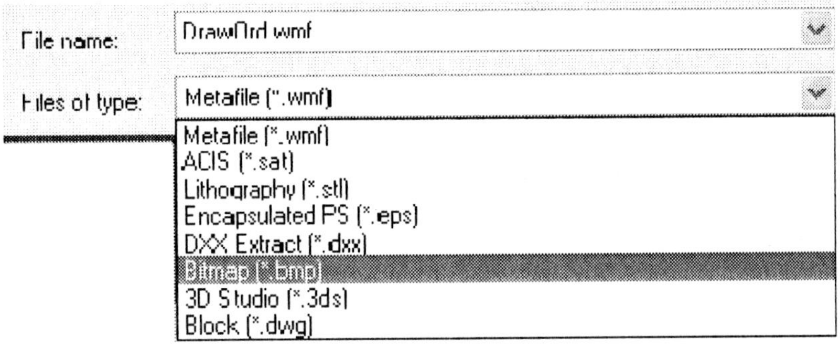 File name: DrawOrd.wmf Files of type: Metafile (*.wmf) Metafile (*.wmf) ACIS (*.sat) Lithography (*.stl) Encapsulated PS (*.eps) DXX Extract (*.dxx) Bitmap (*.bmp) 3D Studio (*.3ds) Block (*.dwg) Figure 26.015		
Save		3. Pick the **Save** button to return to the command line.
	Select objects or <all objects and viewports>: *[enter]*	4. Hit ***enter*** to select all the objects in the drawing.
		5. Use Windows' Paint (or any other graphics program) to view the *DrawOrd.bmp* file you just created in the C:\Steps\Lesson26 folder.

Try repeating the last exercise using the *Cutting table26.dwg* file. Does it work? Now thaw the **VPorts** layer and try it again.

The ***Export*** command usurps several graphics-type-specific commands including the following:

COMMAND	FILE TYPE	COMMAND	FILE TYPE
WMFOut	*WMF*	***ATText***	*DXX*
ACISOut	*SAT*	***BMPOut***	*BMP*
STLOut	*STL*	***3DSOut***	*3DS*
PSOut	*EPS*	***WBlock***	*DWG*
JPGOut	*JPG*		

26.4 Working with Linked Objects – Object Linking and Embedding (OLE)

Let's begin with the obvious: Exactly what is OLE? You've probably heard the term since you began using computers, but what does it mean?

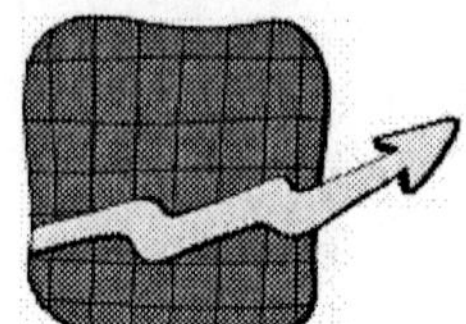

OLE stands for *Object Linking and Embedding*. It refers to the method of creating a compound document – a document that requires more than one application (program) to create. In other words, you might use OLE to show a bill of materials on an AutoCAD drawing by linking directly to the Excel spreadsheet or MS Access database file where the information is stored. (These are Microsoft examples; other programs can be used as well.)

There are actually three *Object* terms. The first – *OLE Object* – I explain below. The second – *OLE Server* – refers to the source program that originated the object. The third – *OLE Container* – refers to the program to which you wish to link or embed the object.

The *Object* part of OLE refers to something that you'll add to your drawing (or other Windows program file). The object is actually a file, part of a file, or graphic image that originated in another program.

The *Linking and Embedding* part of OLE refers to how you wish to attach the OLE Object from the OLE Server to the OLE Container document. A linked document maintains its ties with the server file. Any changes made to it will reflect in the original linked document. An embedded document has no ties with the server file. Changes made to it arc unique within your compound document.

Both linked and embedded documents require the OLE Server application (program) for editing.

26.4.1 Inserting Other Application Data into AutoCAD Drawings

Microsoft and AutoCAD each provide a method for inserting an OLE Object into a document/drawing. The Microsoft method utilizes the clipboard and an AutoCAD dialog box. It gives greater control over exactly what will be inserted but requires that the server file be opened in the server application. The AutoCAD method utilizes two dialog boxes and doesn't require that the server application be opened, but in the past, it didn't offer as much control over what would be inserted.

We'll see each of these methods in our exercise. But first, let's take a look at the AutoCAD dialog boxes.

AutoCAD presents the Insert Object dialog box (Figure 26.016) when you enter the ***InsertObj*** command (or ***io*** hotkey). Here you find two options for creating the image you wish to insert, and a **Display As Icon** check box.

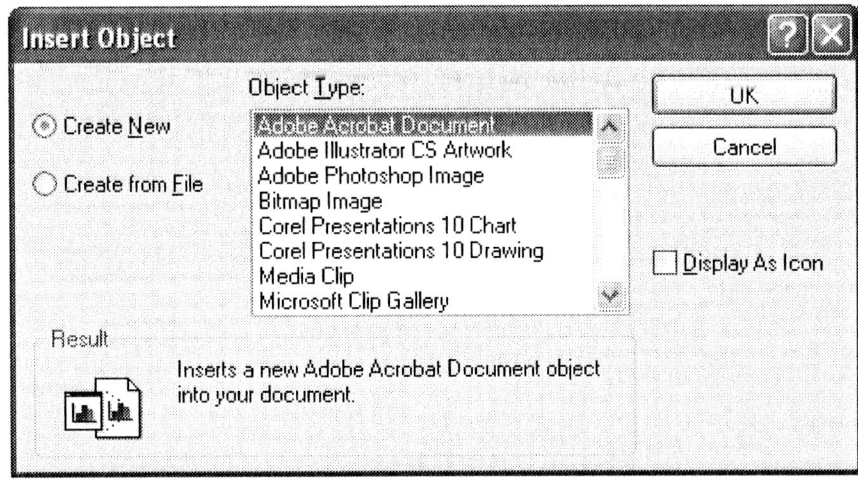

Figure 26.016

- When you place a check in the **Display As Icon** box, AutoCAD displays the server application's icon in the drawing instead of the file itself. Double-clicking on the icon calls the object file for editing. This can speed display time.
- A bullet in the **Create New** option causes the **Object Type** list box to display a list of all the programs on the computer available for OLE communication. Use this approach when an OLE Object doesn't exist and you want to create one. AutoCAD automatically embeds objects created using this method.
- A bullet in the **Create from File** option will cause AutoCAD to switch the **Object Type** list box with the **File** text box, **Browse** button, and **Link** check box shown in Figure 26.017.

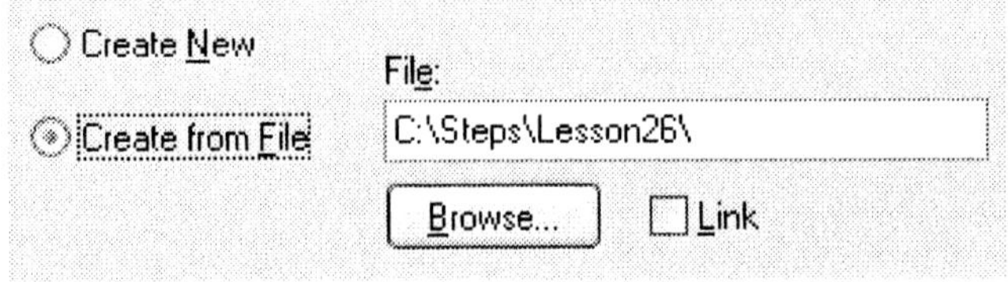

Figure 26.017

  You'll use the **File** text box to enter the name and location of the file you wish to insert. Alternately, you can pick the **Browse** button to use a Windows standard Open File dialog box to select the file you wish to insert.

  A check in the **Link** box will link the object to your drawing rather than embedding it.

Let's insert an Excel spreadsheet into our cutting table drawing. (Note: This exercise requires the use of MS Excel – Office 97 release or better. If you don't have this software on your computer, read through the exercise, but don't try to do it.)

OLE Objects are hidden in a rendered drawing. You can also access the Insert Object dialog box using the **OLE Object** selection on the Insert pull-down menu. Additionally, you can edit OLE properties using the Properties palette.

Do This: 26.4.1.1	**Inserting OLE Objects**

I. Reopen the *cutting table26.dwg* file in the C:\Steps\Lesson26 folder. If you haven't completed work on that drawing, open the *cutting table-done.dwg* file in the same folder.

We'll insert the OLE Object (an Excel spreadsheet) twice to see both methods of insertion and both types of insertion.

- Using the AutoCAD method, we'll embed the object.
- Using the Microsoft method, we'll link the object.

II. Zoom extents.

III. Follow these steps.

TOOLS	COMMAND SEQUENCE	STEPS
OLE Object Button	**Command:** ***io***	1. Enter the ***InsertObj*** command. Alternately, you can pick the **OLE Object** button on the Insert toolbar.
Create from File		2. On the Insert Object dialog box, pick the **Create from File** option. AutoCAD presents the dialog box you saw in Figures 26.016 and 26.017.
Browse...		3. Pick the **Browse** button.
Open		4. AutoCAD presents the Browse dialog box (a Windows Select File dialog box). Select the *Cutting List.xls* file (an Excel spreadsheet) in the C:\Steps\Lesson26 folder. Pick the **Open** button to continue.
Link		5. AutoCAD returns to the Insert Object dialog box. We'll embed the spreadsheet object into our drawing, so be sure the **Link** check box is clear.
OK		6. Pick the **OK** button to complete the command. AutoCAD places the OLE Object in the upper left corner of the screen.
		7. Select the OLE object, and then pick the **Properties** button on the Standard toolbar.
Geometry Position X -0.3139 Position Y 6.7589 Position Z 0.0000 Width 5.5000 Height 3.1213 Scale w... 66.5937 Scale h... 66.3336 Lock as... Yes		8. In the **Geometry** section of the Properties palette, change the width of the object to **5.5**. Close the Properties palette.
	Command: ***m***	9. Move the object to the open area on the right side of the drawing (Figure 26.018).

TOOLS	COMMAND SEQUENCE	STEPS

Product

NTS

Bill of Materials					
Material	Stock	Length	Width	Qty	Part
White Pine	1x2	2'-10"		4	legs
White Pine	1x2	1'-6 1/2"		4	rails
White Pine	1x2	1'-7 1/4"		7	shelf slats
White Pine	1x4	1'-5"		2	shelf sides
Plywood - S2S	3/4"	1'-6 1/2"	1'-6 1/2"	1	shelf
Plywood - S1S	3/4"	1'-6 1/2"	2"	2	shelf supt
Plastic Laminate	BB	1'-6 1/2"	1'-6 1/2"	1	top
Plastic Laminate	BB	1 1/2"	1'-6 1/2"	2	front/back

$3\frac{1}{2}$"

Side View

Figure 26.018

Microsoft Excel (Windows Shortcut)

10. Open the *Cutting List.xls* file in Excel.

11. Return to AutoCAD. (You can pick the **AutoCAD** button on the task bar or hold down the ALT key while tabbing to AutoCAD.)

12. Double-click on the OLE Object to edit it. Notice that the object opens in Excel for editing (Figure 26.019). But notice also that the name of the file being edited is *Worksheet in ... cutting table.dwg*.

Change the value of cell A3 to read ***Red Oak***. (Be sure to hit ***enter*** to finish the procedure.)

Worksheet in C: Steps Lesson26 cutting table-done.dwg

	A	B	C	D	E	F
1	Bill of Materials					
2	Material	Stock	Length	Width	Qty	Part
3	White Pine	1x2	2'-10"		4	legs
4	White Pine	1x2	1'-6 1/2"		4	rails
5	White Pine	1x2	1'-7 1/4"		7	shelf slats
6	White Pine	1x4	1'-5"		2	shelf sides
7	Plywood - S2S	3/4"	1'-6 1/2"	1'-6 1/2"	1	shelf
8	Plywood - S1S	3/4"	1'-6 1/2"	2"	2	shelf supt
9	Plastic Laminate	BB	1'-6 1/2"	1'-6 1/2"	1	top
10	Plastic Laminate	BB	1 1/2"	1'-6 1/2"	2	front/back
11						

Figure 26.019

Tools	Command Sequence	Steps
		13. Repeat Step 11. Notice that the value of the material in the first row has changed (Figure 26.020). (You may need to Regen the drawing to see the change.) This is how you'll edit embedded OLE Objects.

Bill of Materials					
Material	Stock	Length	Width	Qty	Part
Red Oak	1x2	2'-10"		4	legs
White Pine	1x2	1'-6 1/2"		4	rails
White Pine	1x2	1'-7 1/4"		7	shelf slats
White Pine	1x4	1'-5"		2	shelf sides
Plywood - S2S	3/4"	1'-6 1/2"	1'-6 1/2"	1	shelf
Plywood - S1S	3/4"	1'-6 1/2"	2"	2	shelf supt
Plastic Laminate	BB	1'-6 1/2"	1'-6 1/2"	1	top
Plastic Laminate	BB	1 1/2"	1'-6 1/2"	2	front/back

Figure 26.020

Tools	Command Sequence	Steps
		14. Return to Excel and close the *Worksheet in cutting table.dwg* file. Excel then presents the original *Cutting List.xls* file. Notice that it hasn't changed. Remember that the OLE Object was embedded into the OLE Container, not linked to the original file.
	Command: *u*	15. Leave Excel running, but return to AutoCAD and undo all the changes (until the OLE Object is no longer in the file).
		16. Now we'll use the Microsoft method for inserting an OLE Object. Return to the spreadsheet and highlight the data cells (A1:F10) as shown in Figure 26.021.

Cutting List.xls

	A	B	C	D	E	F
1	Bill of Materials					
2	Material	Stock	Length	Width	Qty	Part
3	White Pine	1x2	2'-10"		4	legs
4	White Pine	1x2	1'-6 1/2"		4	rails
5	White Pine	1x2	1'-7 1/4"		7	shelf slats
6	White Pine	1x4	1'-5"		2	shelf sides
7	Plywood - S2S	3/4"	1'-6 1/2"	1'-6 1/2"	1	shelf
8	Plywood - S1S	3/4"	1'-6 1/2"	2"	2	shelf supt
9	Plastic Laminate	BB	1'-6 1/2"	1'-6 1/2"	1	top
10	Plastic Laminate	BB	1 1/2"	1'-6 1/2"	2	front/back

Figure 26.021

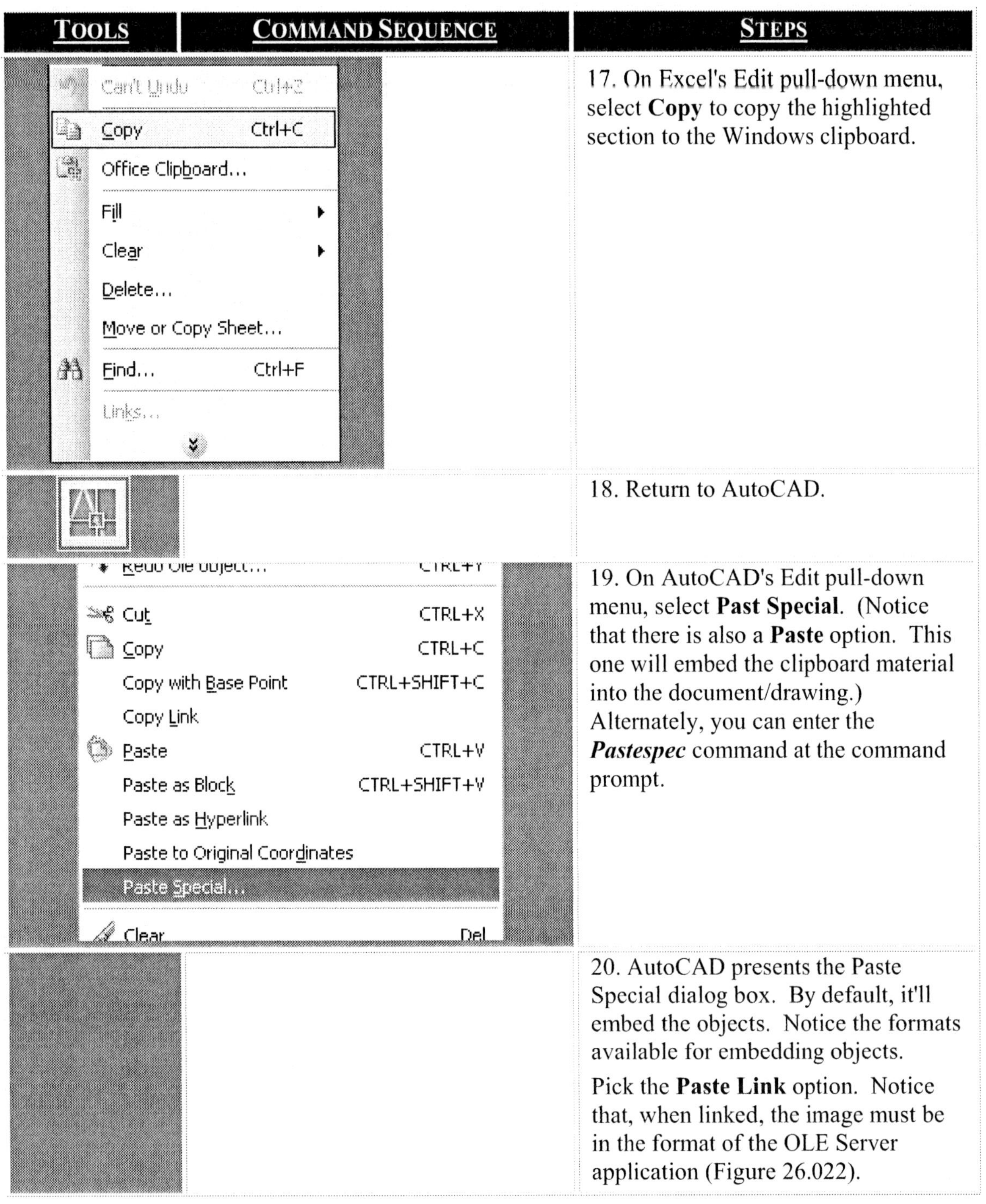

TOOLS	COMMAND SEQUENCE	STEPS
		17. On Excel's Edit pull-down menu, select **Copy** to copy the highlighted section to the Windows clipboard.
		18. Return to AutoCAD.
		19. On AutoCAD's Edit pull-down menu, select **Past Special**. (Notice that there is also a **Paste** option. This one will embed the clipboard material into the document/drawing.) Alternately, you can enter the ***Pastespec*** command at the command prompt.
		20. AutoCAD presents the Paste Special dialog box. By default, it'll embed the objects. Notice the formats available for embedding objects. Pick the **Paste Link** option. Notice that, when linked, the image must be in the format of the OLE Server application (Figure 26.022).

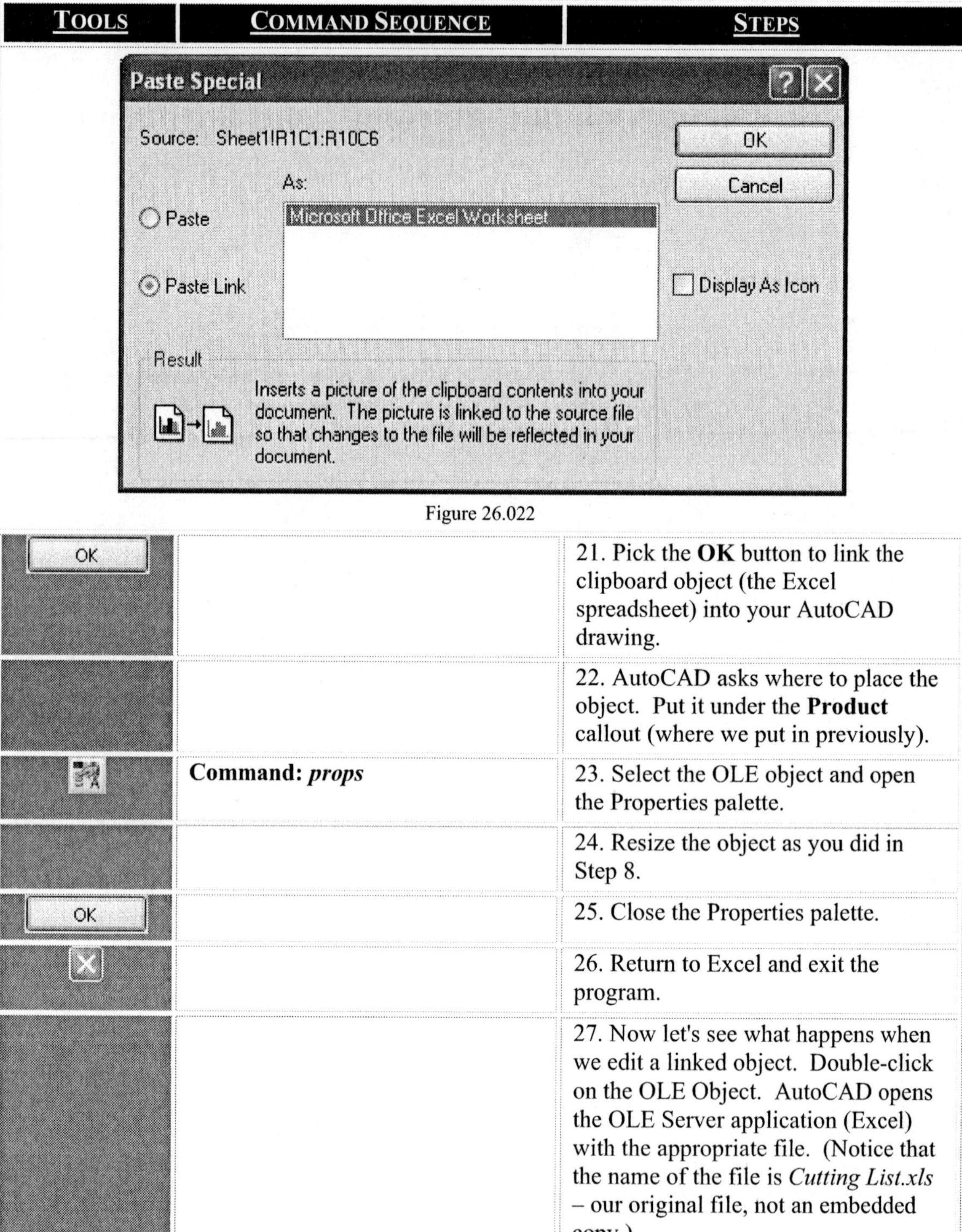

Figure 26.022

TOOLS	COMMAND SEQUENCE	STEPS
OK		21. Pick the **OK** button to link the clipboard object (the Excel spreadsheet) into your AutoCAD drawing.
		22. AutoCAD asks where to place the object. Put it under the **Product** callout (where we put in previously).
	Command: ***props***	23. Select the OLE object and open the Properties palette.
		24. Resize the object as you did in Step 8.
OK		25. Close the Properties palette.
		26. Return to Excel and exit the program.
		27. Now let's see what happens when we edit a linked object. Double-click on the OLE Object. AutoCAD opens the OLE Server application (Excel) with the appropriate file. (Notice that the name of the file is *Cutting List.xls* – our original file, not an embedded copy.)

TOOLS	COMMAND SEQUENCE	STEPS
TechnicLite ABCDEFGHIJ Teen Teen Light Tempus Sans ITC Terminal Times New Roman Times New Roman MT Trebuchet MS Tunga Tw Cen MT Tw Cen MT Condensed Tw Cen MT Condensed Extra		28. To make our OLE Object consistent with our drawing, change the font to **Times New Roman** (in Excel).
		29.Now change the **White Pine** materials to **Ponderosa Pine (**Figure 26.023).

Cutting List.xls

	A	B	C	D	E	F
1			**Bill of Materials**			
2	Material	Stock	Length	Width	Qty	Part
3	Ponderosa Pine	1x2	2'-10"		4	legs
4	Ponderosa Pine	1x2	1'-6 1/2"		4	rails
5	Ponderosa Pine	1x2	1'-7 1/4"		7	shelf slats
6	Ponderosa Pine	1x4	1'-5"		2	shelf sides
7	Plywood - S2S	3/4"	1'-6 1/2"	1'-6 1/2"	1	shelf
8	Plywood - S1S	3/4"	1'-6 1/2"	2"	2	shelf supt
9	Plastic Laminate	BB	1'-6 1/2"	1'-6 1/2"	1	top
10	Plastic Laminate	BB	1 1/2"	1'-6 1/2"	2	front/back

Figure 26.023

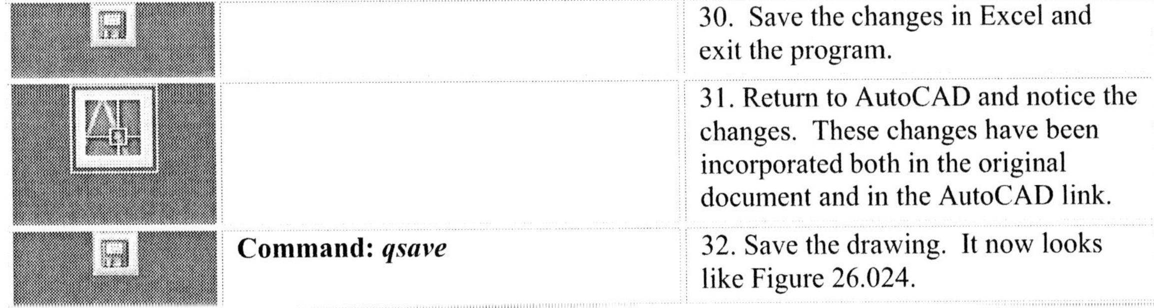

TOOLS	COMMAND SEQUENCE	STEPS
		30. Save the changes in Excel and exit the program.
		31. Return to AutoCAD and notice the changes. These changes have been incorporated both in the original document and in the AutoCAD link.
	Command: ***qsave***	32. Save the drawing. It now looks like Figure 26.024.

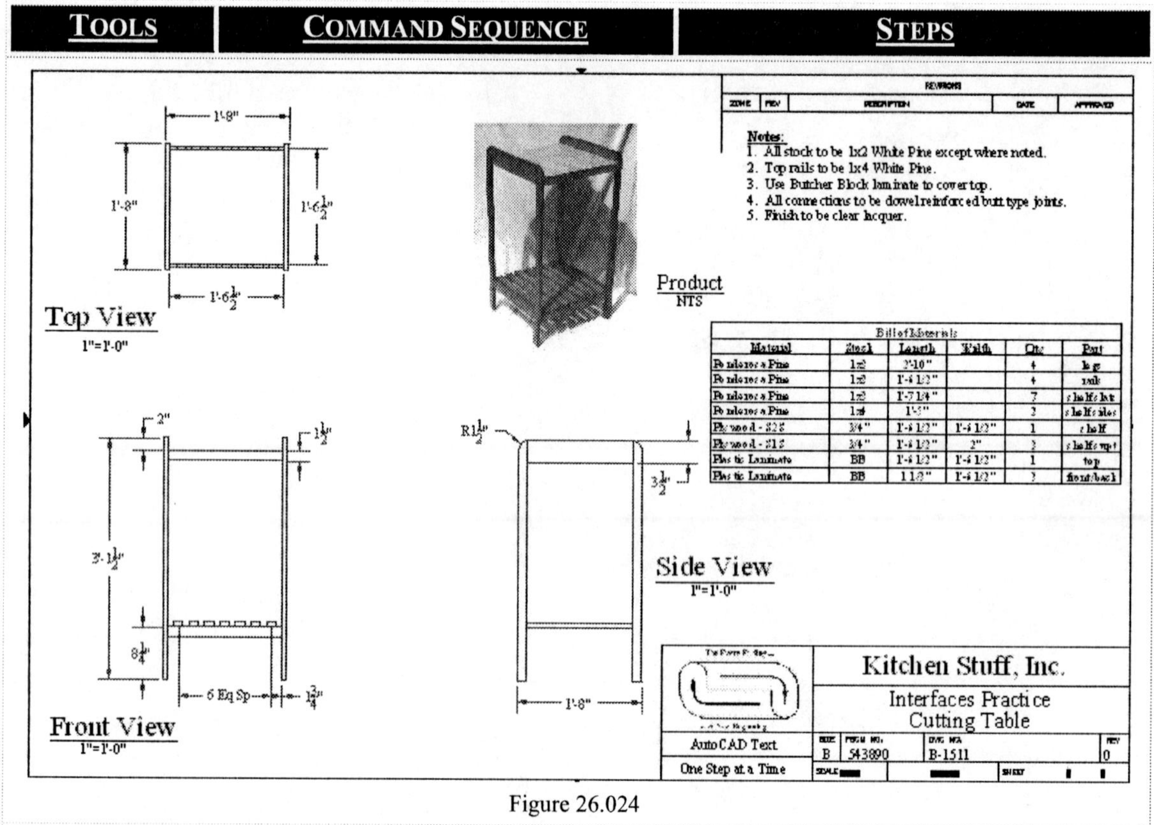

Figure 26.024

You have now practiced inserting OLE Objects. You've seen the difference between embedding and linking, but you haven't seen some of the OLE editing tools AutoCAD provides. Let's take a look at these now.

26.4.2 Modifying OLE Objects

For many reasons, I prefer OLE to imaging via the ***Image*** command. I particularly enjoy the versatility offered by being able to edit an OLE Object using its source application. I'm no longer restricted to AutoCAD's commands and procedures. (Although an impressive program, AutoCAD can't do all things.) But thanks to some brilliant programmers at both Autodesk and Microsoft, I can use all of the programs and applications on my computer in a holistic approach to provide my client with a more complete product.

AutoCAD does, however, provide some additional tools for controlling the OLE image once it becomes part of our drawing. Let's look at these now.

- **Olehide**. You can use any of four settings for the **Olehide** system variable to control the display of an OLE Object both on the screen and when plotting. A setting of
  - **0** (the default) makes all OLE Objects visible and printable.
  - **1** makes only OLE Objects in Paper Space visible and printable.
  - **2** makes only OLE Objects in Model Space visible and printable.
  - **3** hides all OLE Objects and none are printable.
- **Olelinks**. The ***Olelinks*** command presents the Links dialog box (Figure 26.025). Here you find several options.

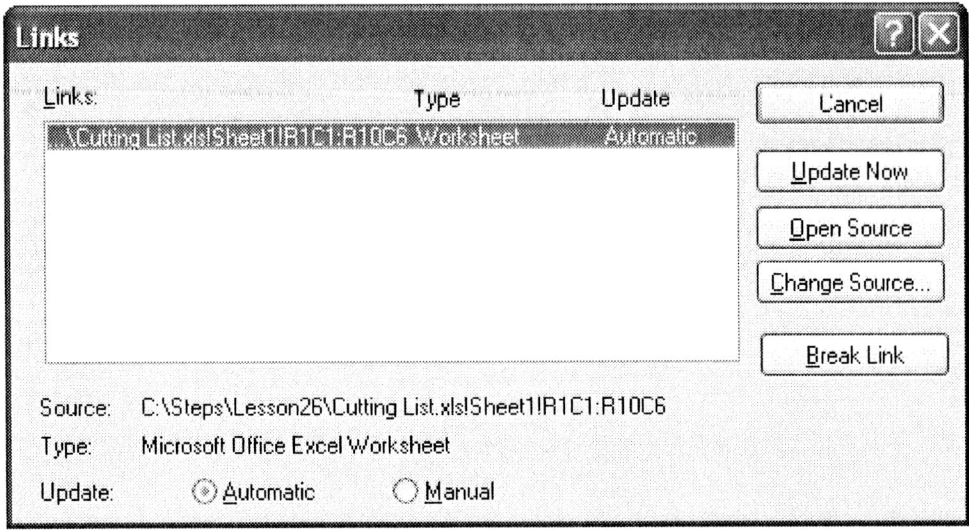

Figure 26.025

- The list box shows all the linked OLE Objects in the drawing. Select the one with which you want to work.
- The **Update Now** button will update the OLE Object by reading the source file and making any necessary adjustments.
- **Open Source** opens the OLE Object in its source application.
- **Change Source** provides an opportunity to change the source of the link.
- **Break Link** converts the selected OLE Object into a picture of the object. Use caution when doing this because you can't modify the picture. It's a handy way, however, to send the drawing to a client who might not have the OLE Server application. Remember: *The OLE Server application must be loaded on the computer for an OLE Object to be visible!*
- At the bottom of the dialog box, you'll find two radio buttons. Selecting **Automatic** means that AutoCAD will update the links as they change. Selecting **Manual** means that you must update the links yourself (using the **Update Now** button) whenever you want them updated.

• **Olescale**. ***Olescale*** calls an OLE Text Size dialog box (Figure 26.026) where you can adjust the size and font of the OLE text. (You have to select an OLE object *before* entering the ***Olescale*** command.)

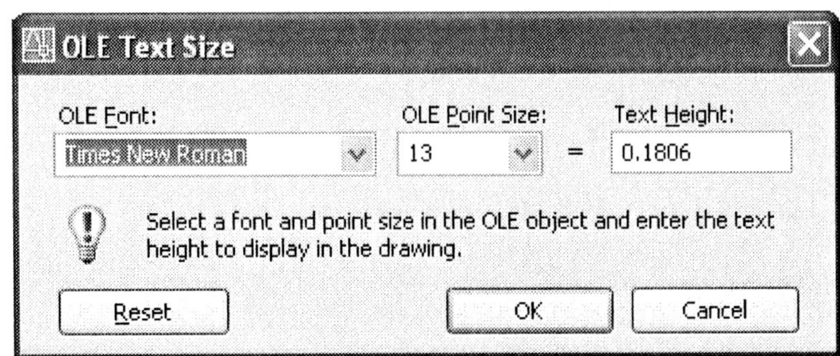

Figure 26.026

• **Olestartup**. This system variable controls whether or not the OLE Server application loads when you plot the drawing. A setting of **0** (the default) won't load the application. A setting of **1** will load the application. Loading the application often improves the quality of a plot.

• **Olequality**. This system variable controls the plot quality of the OLE objects. The possible settings and their meanings follow:

- **0** produces a monochrome plot. This is the lowest quality but is appropriate for embedded spreadsheets.
- **1** (the default) produces low graphics (text) quality. Use this for text documents (like Word or WordPad). (I prefer a setting of **1** for spreadsheets as well, since a spreadsheet is mostly text.)
- **2** produces high graphics quality. It works well for charts, bitmaps, or simple artwork.
- **3** tells AutoCAD to automatically select the quality based on the type of object being plotted.

26.4.3 AutoCAD Data in Other Applications

The methods and procedures for using an AutoCAD drawing in another application (such as Word or Excel) don't differ from what you've already seen. The only limitation involves Paper Space and Model Space views. Remember that you can't select objects in Paper Space if Model Space is active (and vice versa). This presents a problem when copying objects to the clipboard. But let's try an exercise copying our cutting table drawing into a Wordpad document.

Do This: 26.4.3.1 Using AutoCAD Drawings in Other Applications

I. Be sure you're stil in the *cutting table26.dwg* (or *cutting table26 – done.dwg*) file in the C:\Steps\Lesson26 folder. If not, please open it now.

II. Follow these steps.

TOOLS	COMMAND SEQUENCE	STEPS
Model		1. Pick on the **Model** tab.
		2. Without entering a command, select all of the objects on the screen.
	Command: ^*c*	3. Hold down the CTRL key and type ***C***. This places all of the selected objects on the Windows clipboard.
		4. Open WordPad. Follow this path from the **Start** button on Windows' desktop: *Start – All Programs – Accessories – Wordpad*
Undo Ctrl+Z Cut Ctrl+X Copy Ctrl+C Paste Ctrl+V Paste Special... Clear Del Select All Ctrl+A		5. In Wordpad, pick the **Paste Special** option on the Edit pull-down menu.

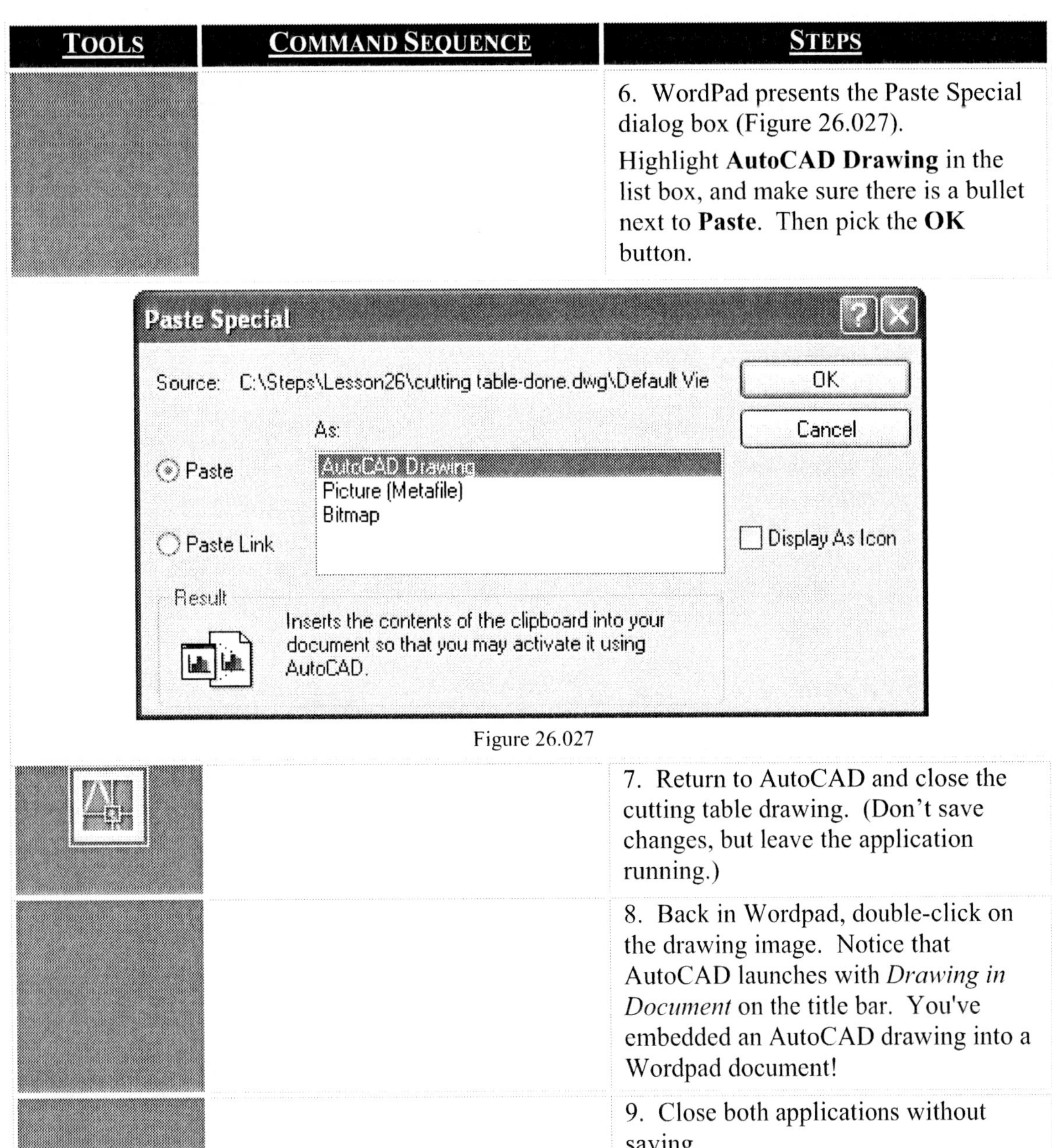

Figure 26.027

TOOLS	COMMAND SEQUENCE	STEPS
		6. WordPad presents the Paste Special dialog box (Figure 26.027). Highlight **AutoCAD Drawing** in the list box, and make sure there is a bullet next to **Paste**. Then pick the **OK** button.
		7. Return to AutoCAD and close the cutting table drawing. (Don't save changes, but leave the application running.)
		8. Back in Wordpad, double-click on the drawing image. Notice that AutoCAD launches with *Drawing in Document* on the title bar. You've embedded an AutoCAD drawing into a Wordpad document!
		9. Close both applications without saving.

Of course, linking an AutoCAD drawing into another application's document is as easy!

26.5 Extra Steps

Return to the *MyCircuit* series of drawings (*1a* through *1d*) you created in Lesson 25. Create a bill of materials in Excel to include all of the block objects in *MyCircuit1a*. Be sure to save the spreadsheet outside of AutoCAD (save as *MyMats.xls* in the C:\Steps\Lesson26 folder). Then insert the spreadsheet into each of the drawings as an OLE Object, changing the list as necessary to reflect the materials in the drawing. Will you embed or link the spreadsheet?*

* You'll need to embed the OLE Object so that your changes are specific to the individual drawings.

26.6 What Have We Learned?

Items covered in this lesson include:

- *Differences between raster and vector imaging*
- *The Image Manager*
- *Exporting image files*
- *Object Linking and Embedding*
- *Using Windows' clipboard in AutoCAD*
- *AutoCAD Commands:*
    - ***Image***
    - ***ImageAttach***
    - ***ImageFrame***
    - ***ImageClip***
    - ***ImageAdjust***
    - ***ImageQuality***
    - ***Transparency***
    - ***DrawOrder***
    - ***Export***
    - ***WMFOut***
    - ***ACISOut***
    - ***STLOut***
    - ***PSOut***
    - ***ATText***
    - ***BMPOut***
    - ***3DSOut***
    - ***InsertObj***
    - ***Olehide***
    - ***Olelinks***
    - ***Olequality***
    - ***Olescale***
    - ***Olestartup***

In this lesson you learned how to use graphic images from several types of applications in your drawing – and even how to use your drawings in other applications! These steps toward publication-quality drawings will serve you well in almost any industry.

26.7 Exercises

1. Open the *Wine Rack.dwg* file in the C:\Steps\Lesson26 folder. Create the layout shown in Figure 26.028. Use the following to guide your setup:
   1.1. Set up to plot on a B-size (17x11) sheet of paper.
   1.2. Use the *ANSI B Title Block.dwg* file in the \Template folder as your border/title block.
   1.3. Use the *title info26.dwg* file to insert data into the title block.
   1.4. The photograph is *winerack.tif* and can be found in the C:\Steps\Lesson26 folder.
   1.5. Embed the BOM using the *Winerack.xls* Excel file.
   1.6. The logo in the title block is *logo.jpg* and can be found in the C:\Steps\Lesson26 folder.
   1.7. Complete the layout and dimension the viewports as indicated.
   1.8. Save the drawing as *MyWineRack.dwg* in the C:\Steps\Lesson26 folder.

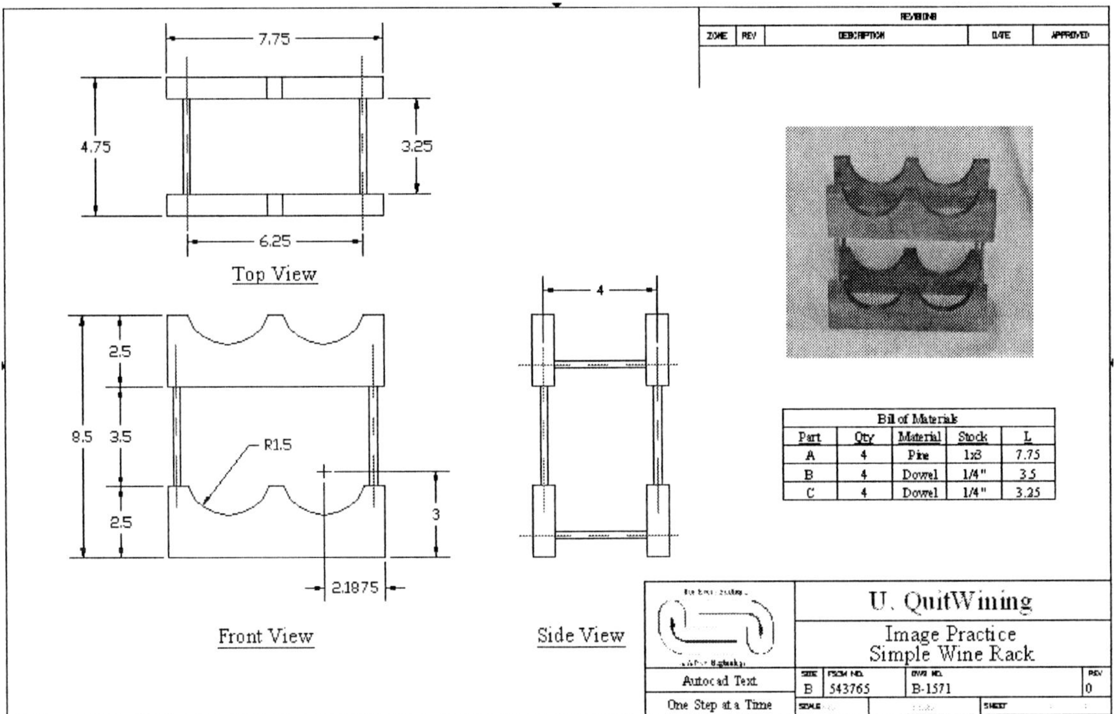

Figure 26.028: Wine Rack

2. Open the *Jewelry Box.dwg* file in the C:\Steps\Lesson26 folder. Create the layout shown in Figure 26.029. Use the following to guide your setup:
   2.1. Set up to plot on a B-size (17x11) sheet of paper.
   2.2. Use the *ANSI B Title Block.dwg* file in the \Template folder as your border/title block.
   2.3. Use the *title info26.dwg* file to insert data into the title block.
   2.4. The photograph is *jewlery box.tif* and can be found in the C:\Steps\Lesson26 folder.
   2.5. Embed the BOM using the *JBox.xls* Excel file.
   2.6. The logo in the title block is *logo-mini.jpg* and can be found in the C:\Steps\Lesson26 folder.
   2.7. Complete the layout and dimension the viewports as indicated.
   2.8. Save the drawing as *MyJewelryBox.dwg* in the C:\Steps\Lesson26 folder.

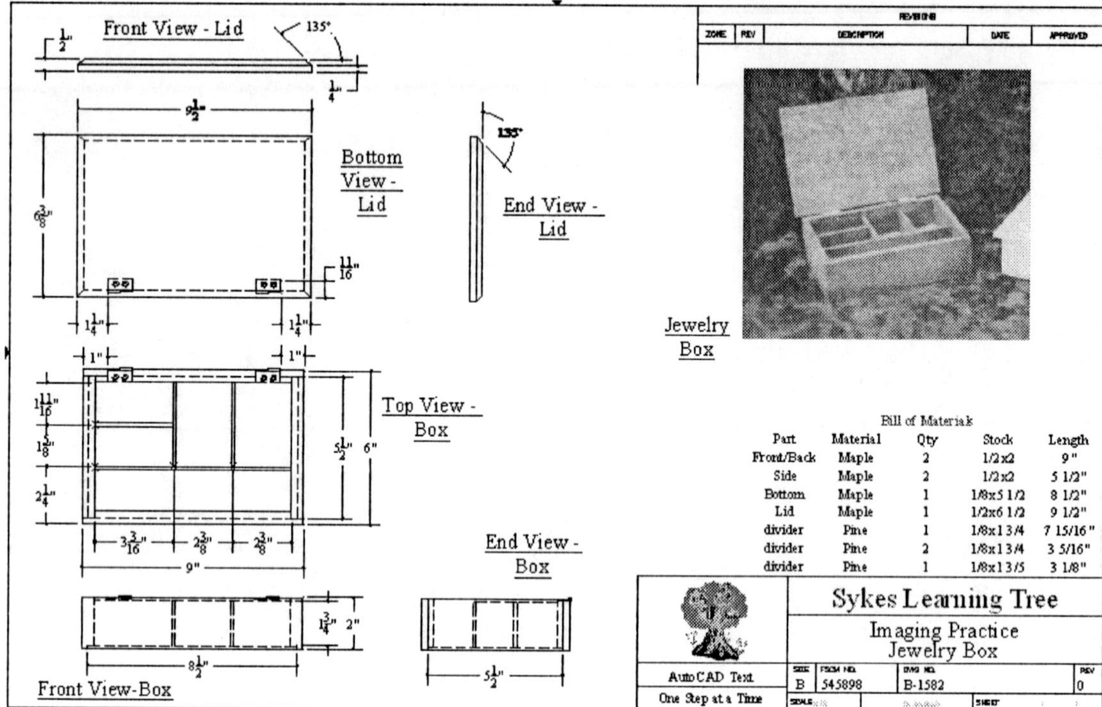

Bill of Materials

Part	Material	Qty	Stock	Length
Front/Back	Maple	2	1/2x2	9"
Side	Maple	2	1/2x2	5 1/2"
Bottom	Maple	1	1/8x5 1/2	8 1/2"
Lid	Maple	1	1/2x6 1/2	9 1/2"
divider	Pine	1	1/8x1 3/4	7 15/16"
divider	Pine	2	1/8x1 3/4	3 5/16"
divider	Pine	1	1/8x1 3/5	3 1/8"

Figure 26.029: Jewelry Box

3. Open the *Chest.dwg* file in the C:\Steps\Lesson26 folder. Create the layout shown in Figure 26.030. Use the following to guide your setup:
   3.1. Set up to plot on a C-size (22x17) sheet of paper.
   3.2. Use the *ANSI C Title Block.dwg* file in the \Template folder as your border/title block.
   3.3. Use the *title info26.dwg* file to insert data into the title block.
   3.4. The photograph is *oak chest.tif* and can be found in the C:\Steps\ Lesson26 folder.
   3.5. The logo in the title block is *logo-mini.jpg* and can be found in the C:\Steps\Lesson26 folder.
   3.6. Complete the layout and dimension the viewports as indicated.
   3.7. Save the drawing as *MyOakChest.dwg* in the C:\Steps\Lesson26 folder.

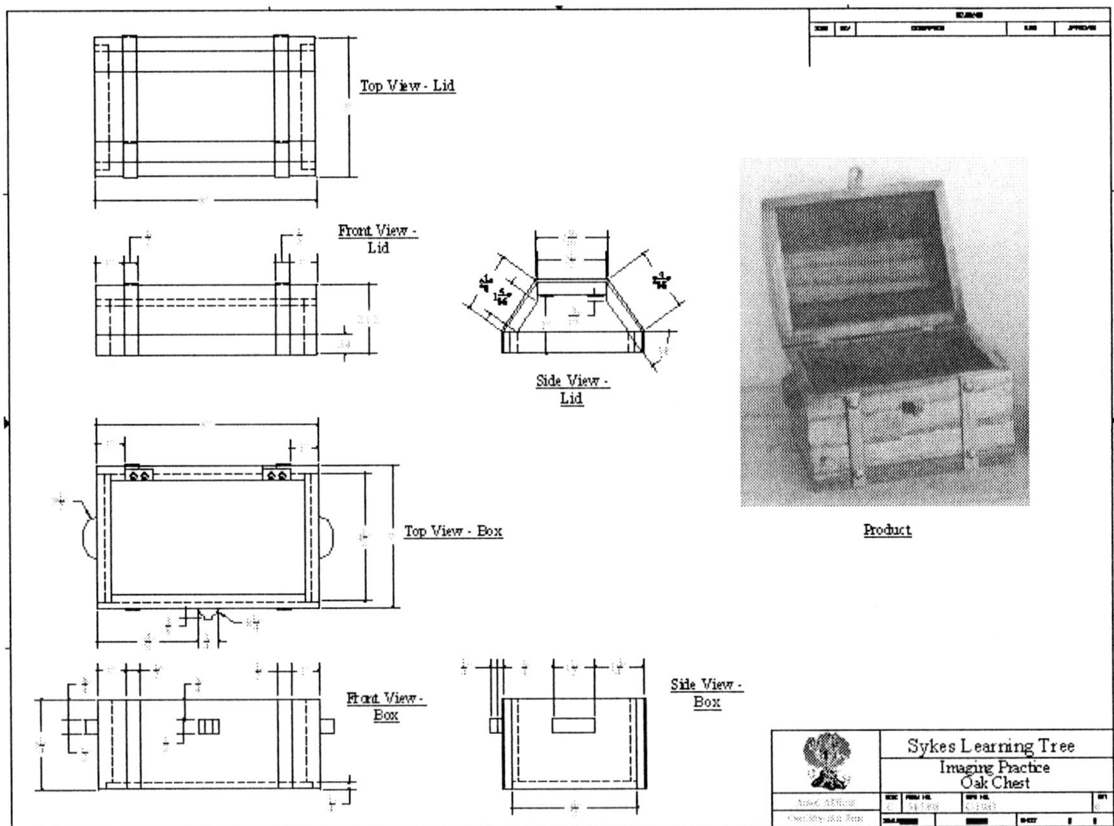

Figure 26.030: Oak Chest

4. Open the *MyPlanter.dwg* file you created in the C:\Steps\Lesson25 folder. (If that drawing isn't available, open the *planter-26.dwg* file found in the C:\Steps\Lesson26 folder.) Add the graphics shown in Figure 26.031. Use the following guidelines:
   4.1. Import the rendered *planter.jpg* image from the C:\Steps\Lesson26 folder and add the text shown.
   4.2. Use the *logo-mini.jpg* file in the title block.
   4.3. Save the drawing as *MyPlanter-26.dwg* in the C:\Steps\Lesson26 folder.

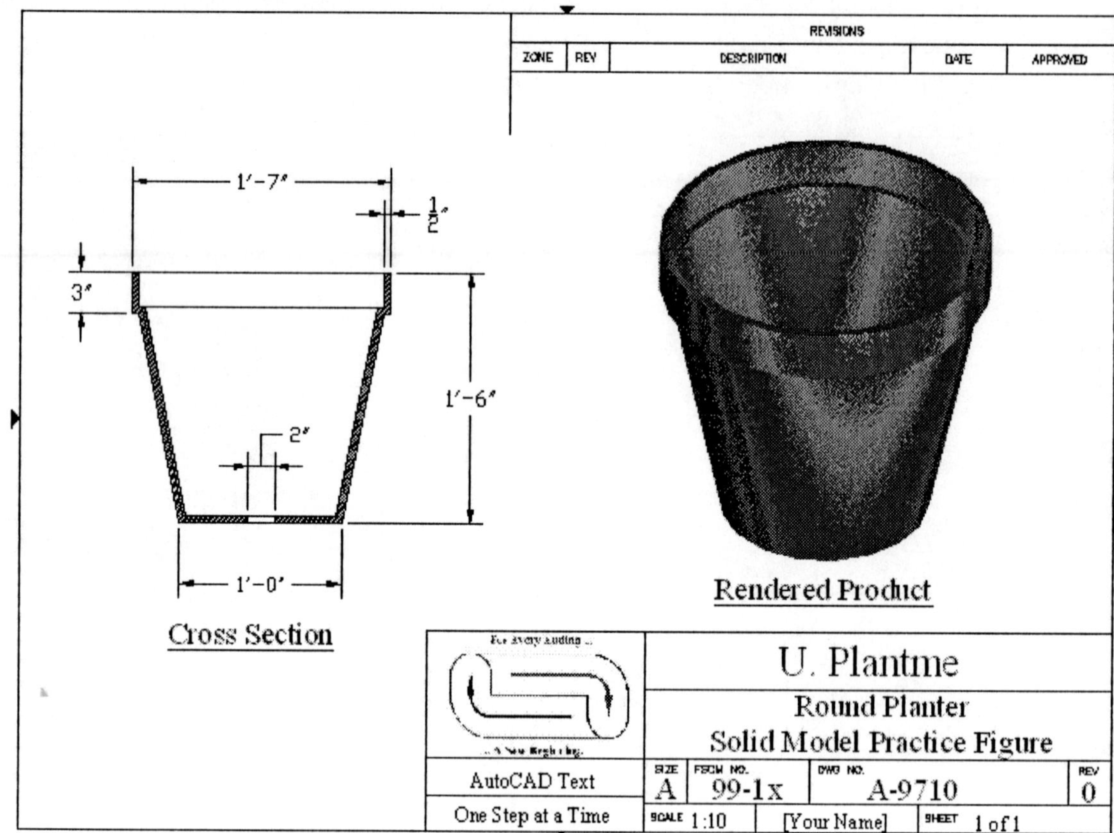

Figure 26.031: Planter

5. Open the *MyPlanterBox.dwg* file you created in the C:\Steps\Lesson25 folder. (If that drawing isn't available, open the *patio planter-26.dwg* file found in the C:\Steps\Lesson26 folder.) Add the graphics shown in Figure 26.032. Use the following guidelines:
   5.1. Resize the existing viewport with the shaded image. Set the **Shademode** in that viewport to ***2D***.
   5.2. Use the *logo.jpg* file in the title block.
   5.3. Save the drawing as *MyPlanterBox-26.dwg* in the C:\Steps\Lesson26 folder.

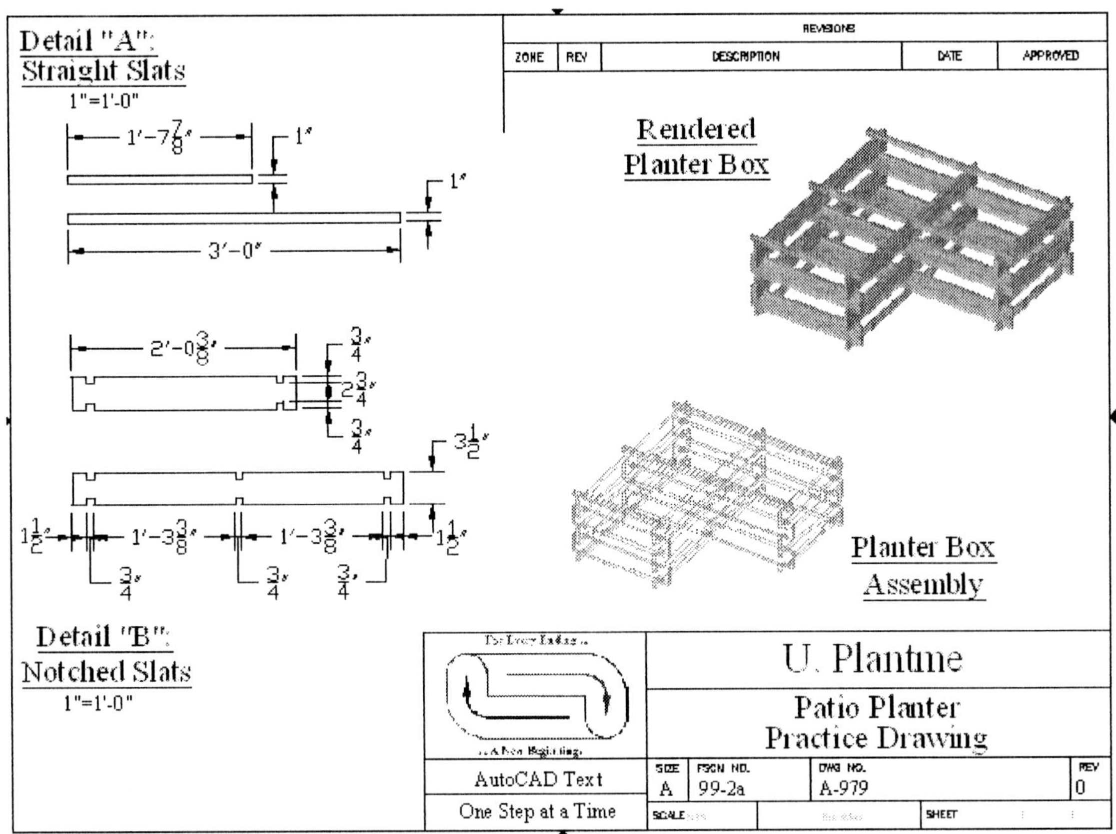

Figure 26.032: PlanterBox

6. Open the *MyTableLamp.dwg* file you created in the C:\Steps\Lesson25 folder. (If that drawing isn't available, open the *TableLamp-26.dwg* file found in the C:\Steps\Lesson26 folder.) Add the graphics shown in Figure 26.033. Use the following guidelines:
   6.1. Use the *logo.jpg* file in the title block.
   6.2. Save the drawing as *MyTableLamp-26.dwg* in the C:\Steps\Lesson26 folder.

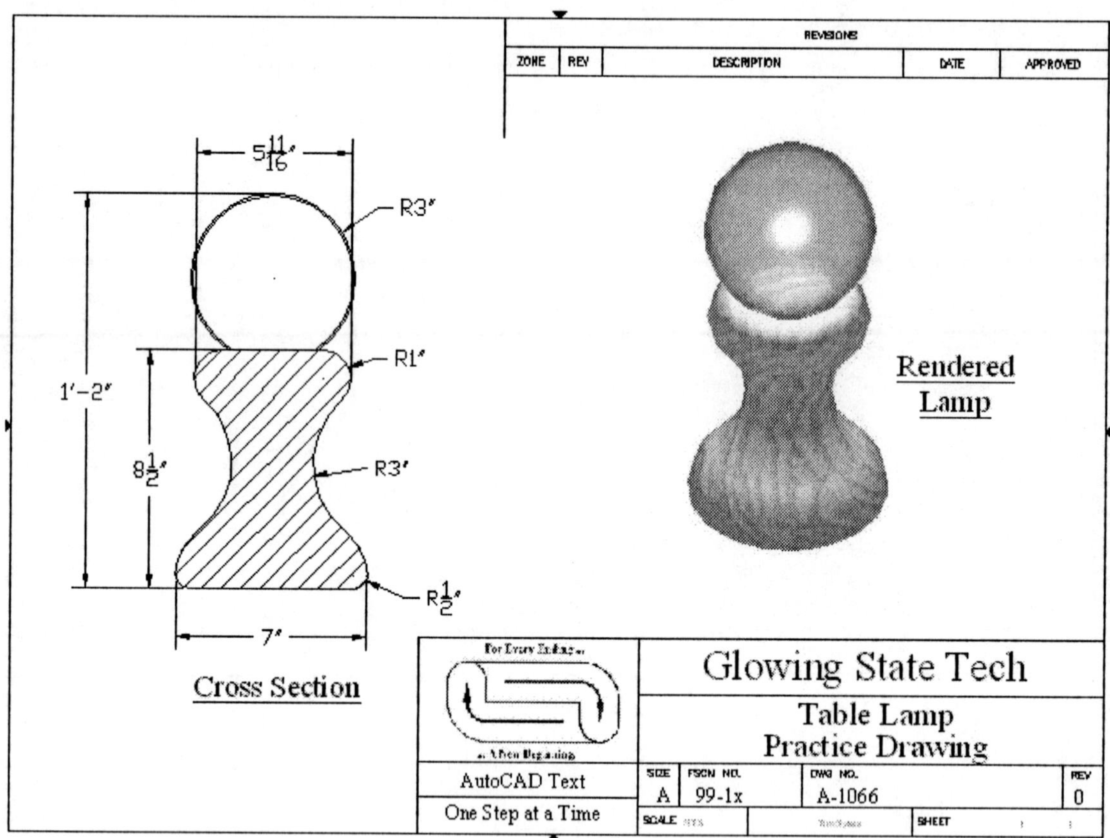

Figure 26.033: Table Lamp

7. Open the *MyWheel.dwg* file you created in the C:\Steps\Lesson25 folder. (If that drawing isn't available, open the *Wheel-26.dwg* file found in the C:\Steps\Lesson26 folder.) Add the graphics shown in Figure 26.034. Use the following guidelines:
   7.1. Use the *Logo-mini.jpg* file in the title block.
   7.2. Save the drawing as *MyWheel-26.dwg* in the C:\Steps\Lesson26 folder.

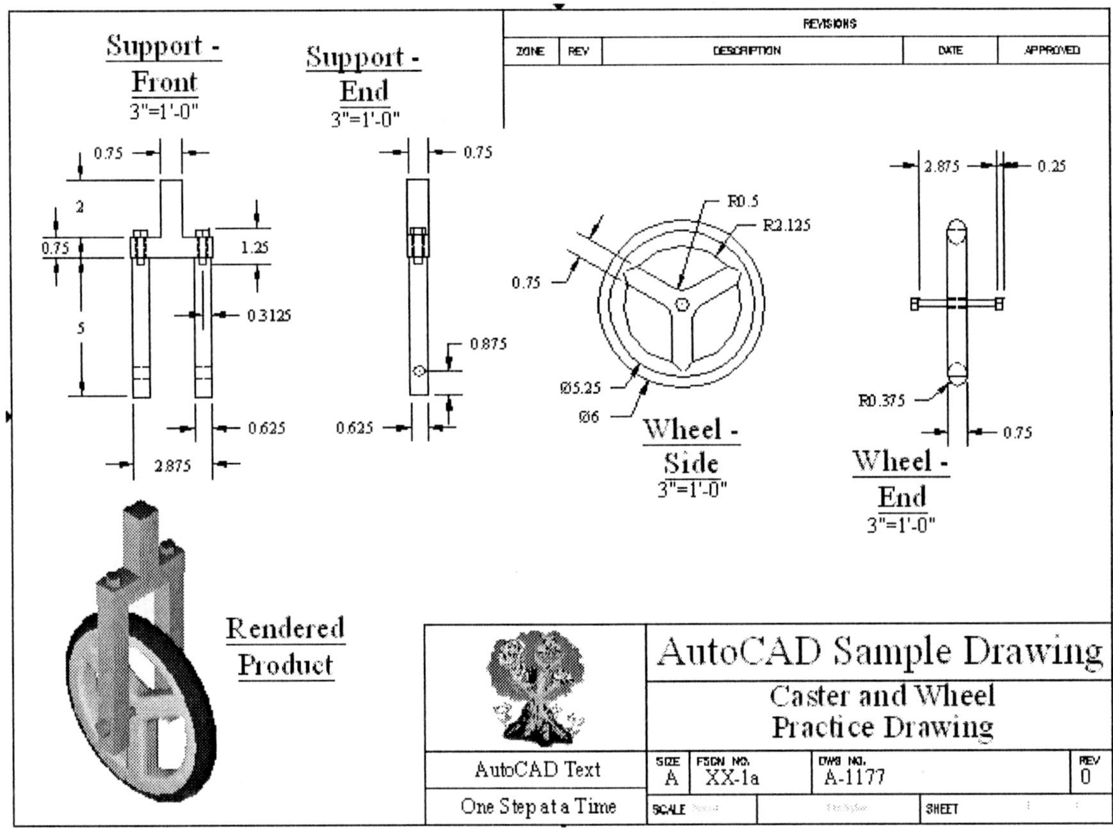

Figure 26.034: Wheel

8. Open the *OnArtesia.dwg* file you created in the C:\Steps\Lesson25 folder. (If that drawing isn't available, open the *OnArtesia-26.dwg* file found in the C:\Steps\Lesson26 folder.) Add the graphics shown in Fig. 26.035. Use the following guidelines:
   8.1. Use the *logo-mini.jpg* file in the title block.
   8.2. Save the drawing as *OnArtesia-26.dwg* in the C:\Steps\Lesson26 folder.

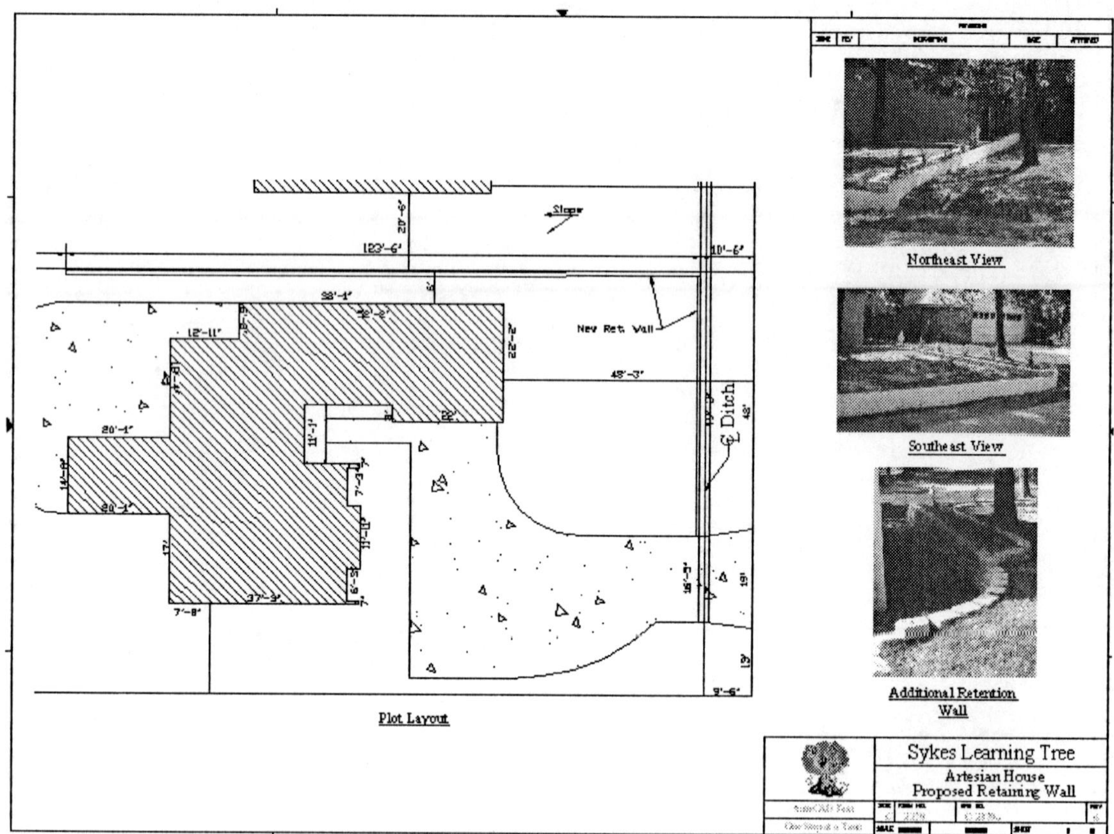

Fig. 26.035: Artesian Home Plan

26.8 For Web-Based Review Questions, visit: http://www.uneedcad.com/2006/Files/06R26.pdf

Lesson 27

Following this lesson, you will:

- ✓ *Know how to set up a data source*
- ✓ *Know how to configure AutoCAD to access a database*
- ✓ *Be familiar with the dbConnect Manager*
- ✓ *Know how to link database records to AutoCAD objects*
- ✓ *Know how to use database records to create AutoCAD callouts*
- ✓ *Know how to query a database for AutoCAD data*

Databases and AutoCAD

Here Be Dragons.

Ancient map designation for unexplored territory.

It's appropriate here in our final lesson that I once again take you to the edge. This edge lies between CAD operation and one of the most powerful computer tools yet developed – databases. As you study, imagine that you're standing on a beach.

Looking outward, you see only the surface of an ocean of possibilities. When the lesson is complete, consider getting your feet wet.

In Lesson 20, we exported block attribute data into an Excel spreadsheet. That spreadsheet served as the base from which the MTO group ordered and tracked project-related materials.

But we had to wait until the project design was completed to send an accurate list of materials to MTO. This invoked groans of impatience because of the time frame between design completion and the beginning of construction – the time needed to actually order, ship, and receive the materials. For special materials, this delay could prove quite costly.

AutoCAD recognized the problem. It created a method for editing a materials database "on the fly." Thus, you can export the block attribute data and create a database (rather than a spreadsheet) much earlier in the project. Then, using dbConnect, you can keep the data current as the design develops. The database remains current because it functions much like a linked OLE object – changes affect both the OLE object in AutoCAD and the original file.

We'll use dbConnect to attach a MS Access database to a drawing and see how useful that connection can be.

While knowledge of databases isn't required for this lesson, I can't overestimate its value. I can't hope to cover all of the ins and outs of database operation in a single lesson, much less how they relate to AutoCAD. (Multi-volume texts are required for proper database training.) However, I will explain some of the basics for database novices.

For a more complete understanding of the application we'll use* (MS Access), I recommend another book from Microsoft Press – *Access Step by Step*.

*You won't need MS Access to complete this lesson

27.1 Databases – A Brief Refresher

A database organizes information (data).

Databases begin their organization by placing information into one or many spreadsheet-like *tables*. For example, a petrochemical plant may have tables for valves, vessels, piping, foundations, and so forth.

We divide data in the tables into categories or criteria called *fields*. Fields appear as columns in the table. Thus, a table of valves in our petrochem plant might include fields such as **Manufacturer**, **Price**, **Rating**, and **Size**.

We call data about a specific item a *record*. Records appear as rows in the table and contain informational entries for some or all of the criterion fields. For example, a specific valve might hold the following data: Ball (in the **Type** field), 2" (in the **Size** field), and Vogt (in the **Manufacturer** field). Databases may contain millions of records.

Rows and columns meet in individual *cells*. A cell contains a single piece of information about the specific record (row). The piece of information falls into the category defined by the field (column).

You can search a database for specific information or cross-referenced information by doing a *query*. This makes databases irreplaceable wherever they're used!

Popular database applications include MS Access, DBase, and FoxPro.

27.2 Configuring Your Operating System to Share the Database

Of course, you can use OLE to include a database in your drawing just as we linked to the Excel spreadsheet in Lesson 26. But using OLE, you can't link each record to a specific AutoCAD object in the drawing. This remarkable procedure helps you keep track of which objects have been listed in the database, which have not, and objects that are listed in the database that are no longer in the drawing. (Reread the last three sentences several times. They're the keys to this entire lesson and the reason why AutoCAD invented ***dbConnect***.)

Unlike OLE, however, you'll soon discover that the application used to create the database *doesn't have to be on the computer*. AutoCAD took a cue from Microsoft applications that connect to databases and include a *jet* – a database engine used to read/modify databases. Let's make that easier to understand: AutoCAD can read a database because it contains some programming (called a jet) that makes it possible.

The jet works on the AutoCAD side of the exchange of information between AutoCAD and the database. The database also contains a jet that works on its side. But you must tell your operating system (in our case, Windows) to allow the jets to share the same controls (to fly together like the Blue Angels). To do that, tell Windows to Open Database Connectivity between them. Use the ODBC Data Source Administrator (Figure 27.001). (Details on how to do this are provided in Exercise 27.2.1.)

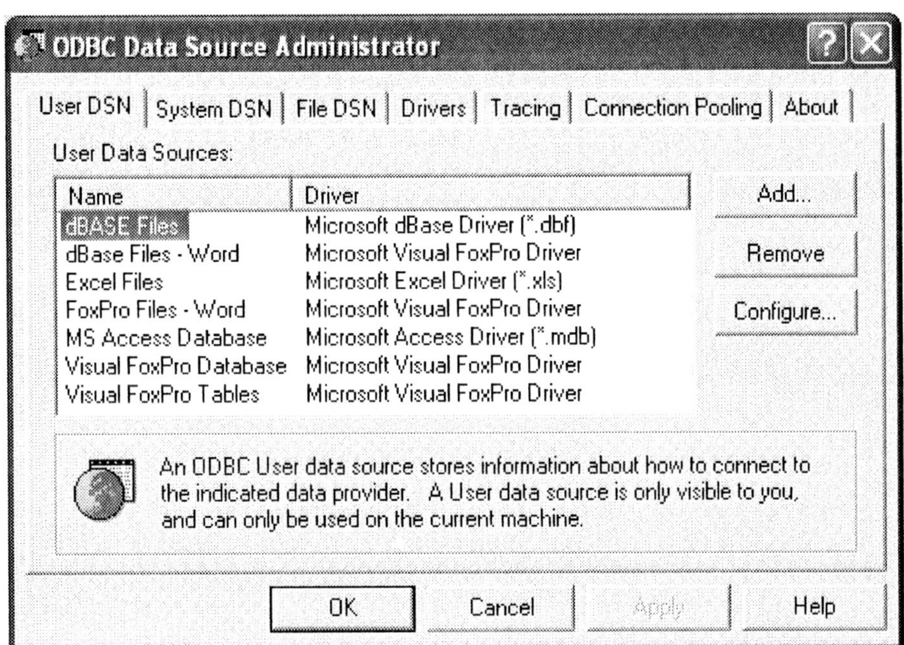

Figure 27.001

Access the ODBC Data Source Administrator via the Windows Control Panel.

Let's walk through the procedure together. For continuity, we'll use the same PID drawing we used earlier and a database that we'll provide.

This is one of the scary parts of being an instructor. I'm about to show you how to change part of the configuration of your computer. Approach this section cautiously and be sure you understand what to do before you do it. *This is a dangerous place to explore or experiment. Please restrict that activity to AutoCAD.*

I'll use the Windows XP Operating System. Your icons and dialog boxes may vary if you use a different version of Windows, although the procedure varies little for Windows 98 and Me.

Do This: 27.2.1	Opening Database Connectivity

I. Completely read through this exercise before beginning.

II. After you've completed Step I above, follow these steps.

Tools	Command Sequence	Steps
	Command: ***exit***	1. Close AutoCAD.
My Computer		2. Double-click on the **My Computer** icon on your desktop. Windows opens the My Computer window.
Control Panel		3. Double-click on the **Control Panel** icon in the My Computer window. Windows opens the Control Panel window.
Administrative Tools		4. Double-click on the **Administrative Tools** icon in the Control Panel window. Windows opens the Administrative Tools window.
Data Sources (ODBC)		5. Double-click on the **Data Sources (ODBC)** icon in the Administrative Tools window. Windows presents the ODBC Data Source Administrator (Figure 27.001).
Add...		6. We must add our database as a data source. Begin by picking the **Add** button.
		7. Windows presents the Create New Data Source dialog box (Figure 27.002). Read through the list of available database drivers. I created our database using MS Access, so select that driver. (This tells Windows how the database file was created.) Pick the **Finish** button to continue.

TOOLS	COMMAND SEQUENCE	STEPS

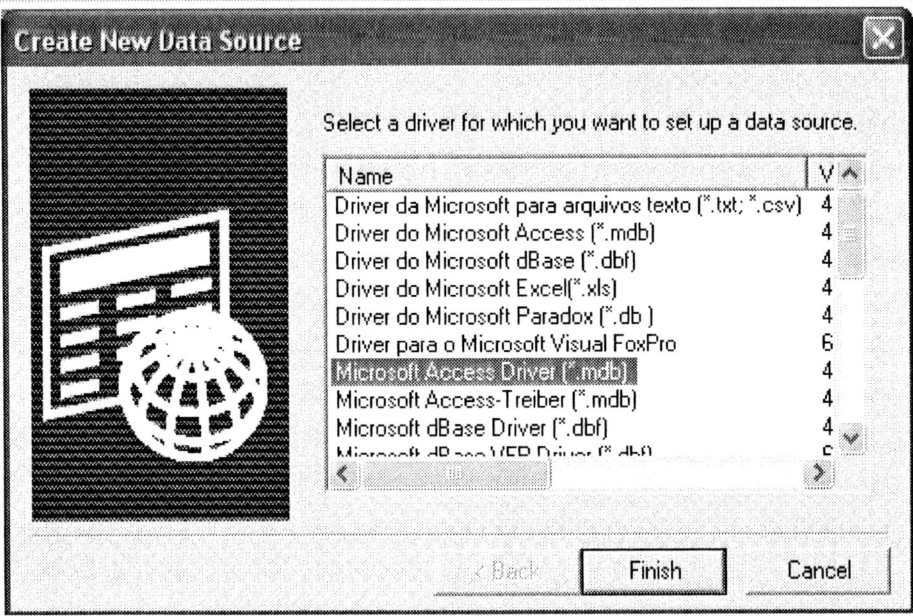

Figure 27.002

		8. Windows presents the ODBC Microsoft Access Setup dialog box (Figure 27.003). Enter the name *My_PID_Database* in the **Data Source Name** text box.

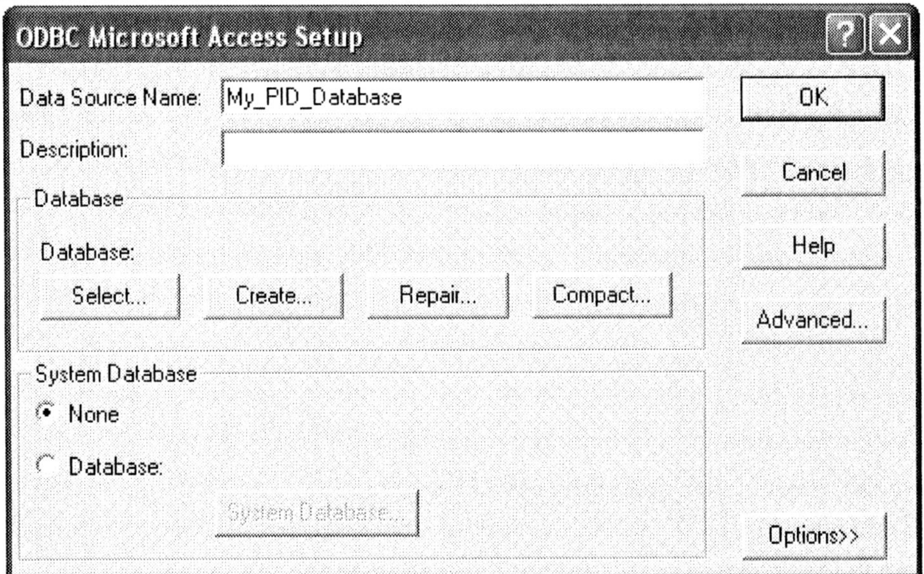

Figure 27.003

		9. Next, we'll specify the actual database that we'll use. Pick the **Select** button in the **Database** frame.

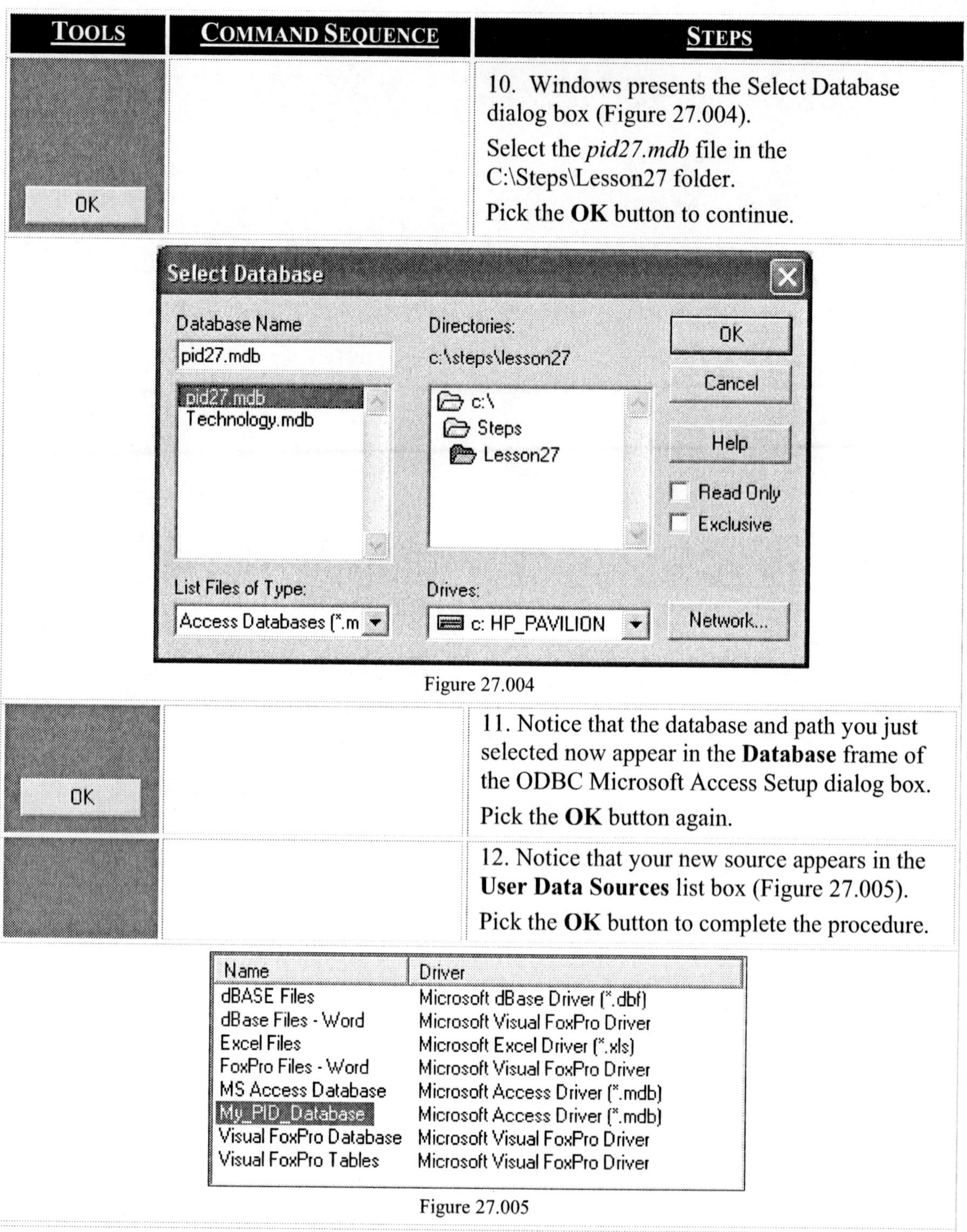

TOOLS	COMMAND SEQUENCE	STEPS
OK		10. Windows presents the Select Database dialog box (Figure 27.004). Select the *pid27.mdb* file in the C:\Steps\Lesson27 folder. Pick the **OK** button to continue.

Figure 27.004

TOOLS	COMMAND SEQUENCE	STEPS
OK		11. Notice that the database and path you just selected now appear in the **Database** frame of the ODBC Microsoft Access Setup dialog box. Pick the **OK** button again.
		12. Notice that your new source appears in the **User Data Sources** list box (Figure 27.005). Pick the **OK** button to complete the procedure.

Figure 27.005

Did you notice that I didn't explain all the tabs on the ODBC Data Source Administrator (and subsequent dialog boxes)? I know you've become accustomed to my explaining everything, but this isn't an AutoCAD dialog box. Simply reloading an application can't repair mistakes here. I must repeat: *This is not an appropriate place for experimentation or exploration.* Leave your computer's operating system to the experts.

Now that I've discouraged your experimentation, let me make a suggestion for those of you who must know more – regardless of the risk. Microsoft offers courses and certifications for all of its Windows products – including its operating systems. Check its web site for more details. Start at *http://www.microsoft.com/learning/default.asp*.

27.3 Linking AutoCAD to the Database – the dbConnect Manager

Now that your database's jet is available for flight (or in more down-to-earth terms, your computer has been set up so that the database can speak to AutoCAD), you must set up AutoCAD's jet so that it can fly with the database. Luckily, AutoCAD has provided the dbConnect Manager to assist you.

I'll introduce you to the dbConnect Manager in our next exercise. But I'll explain most of the details of dbConnect functionality over the course of the next few exercises.

Do This: 27.3.1 Connecting AutoCAD to the Data Source

I. Open the *pid27.dwg* file in the C:\Steps\Lesson27 folder. The drawing looks like Figure 27.006. (The bubbled letters will serve as valve identifiers throughout this lesson.)

II. Follow these steps.

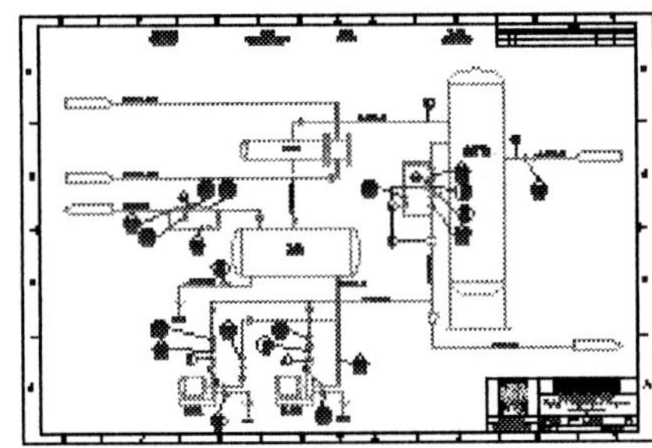

Figure 27.006

TOOLS	COMMAND SEQUENCE	STEPS
No Button Available	**Command:** ***dbc***	1. Open the dbConnect Manager by typing ***dbconnect*** (or ***dbc***) at the command prompt. Alternately, you can select **dbConnect** from the Tools pull down menu.
DBCONNECT M... C:\Steps\Lesson27\pid27.dwg Data Sources jet_dbsamples		2. The dbConnect Manager appears as a tool palette. (The ***dbConnect*** command also produces a dbConnect pull-down menu.) Notice that the dbConnect Manager lists the name and path of the current drawing. Below the drawing, the dbConnect Manager lists **Data Sources** available for use. AutoCAD provides the *dbsamples* database for use with its tutorial. Ignore it for now.
Configure Data Source...		3. We must configure AutoCAD to use *My_PID_Database*. Begin by right-clicking on the **Data Sources** listing. Then pick **Configure Data Source** on the cursor menu

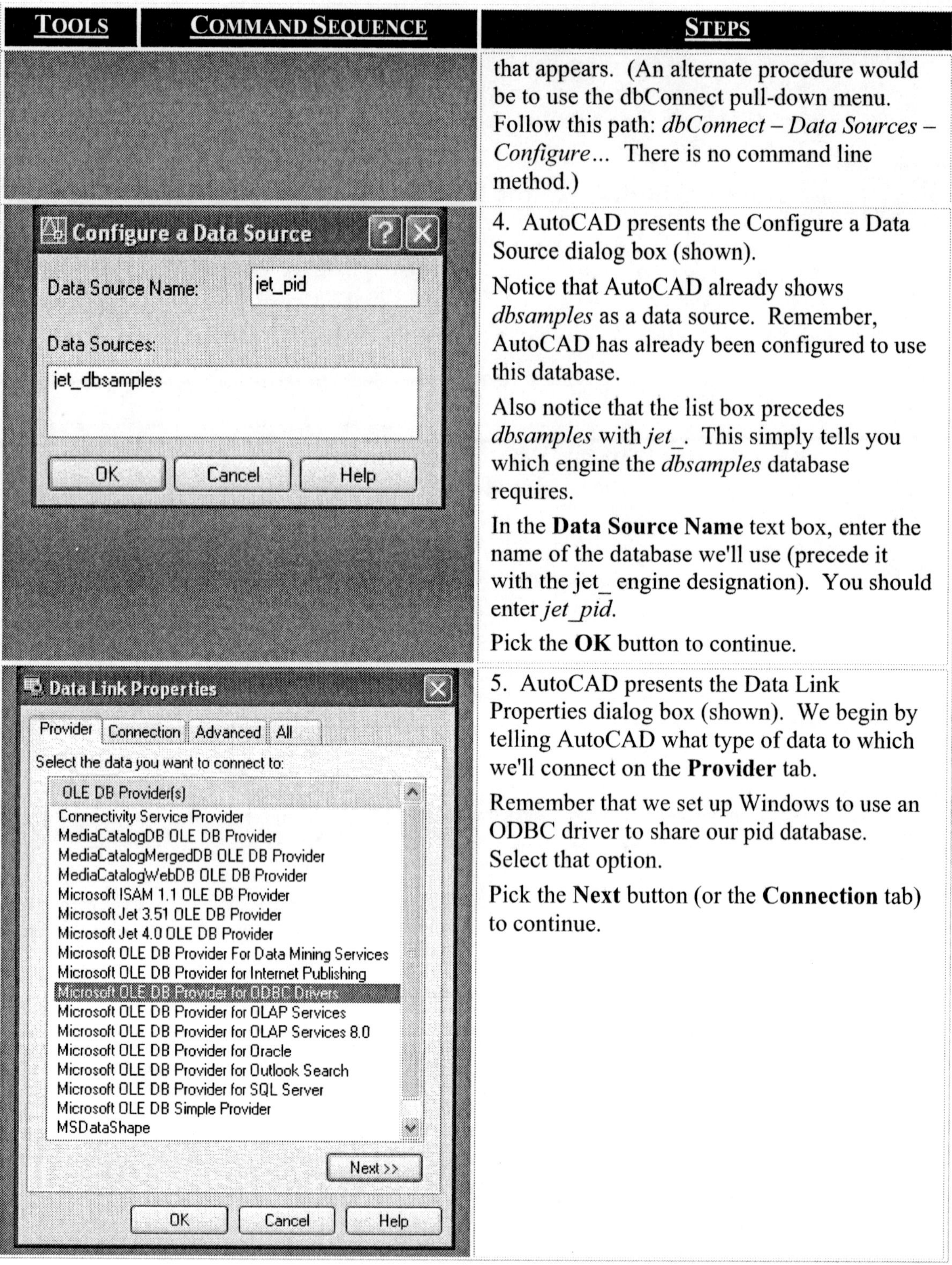

TOOLS	COMMAND SEQUENCE	STEPS
		that appears. (An alternate procedure would be to use the dbConnect pull-down menu. Follow this path: *dbConnect – Data Sources – Configure…* There is no command line method.)
		4. AutoCAD presents the Configure a Data Source dialog box (shown). Notice that AutoCAD already shows *dbsamples* as a data source. Remember, AutoCAD has already been configured to use this database. Also notice that the list box precedes *dbsamples* with *jet_*. This simply tells you which engine the *dbsamples* database requires. In the **Data Source Name** text box, enter the name of the database we'll use (precede it with the jet_ engine designation). You should enter *jet_pid.* Pick the **OK** button to continue.
		5. AutoCAD presents the Data Link Properties dialog box (shown). We begin by telling AutoCAD what type of data to which we'll connect on the **Provider** tab. Remember that we set up Windows to use an ODBC driver to share our pid database. Select that option. Pick the **Next** button (or the **Connection** tab) to continue.

TOOLS	COMMAND SEQUENCE	STEPS
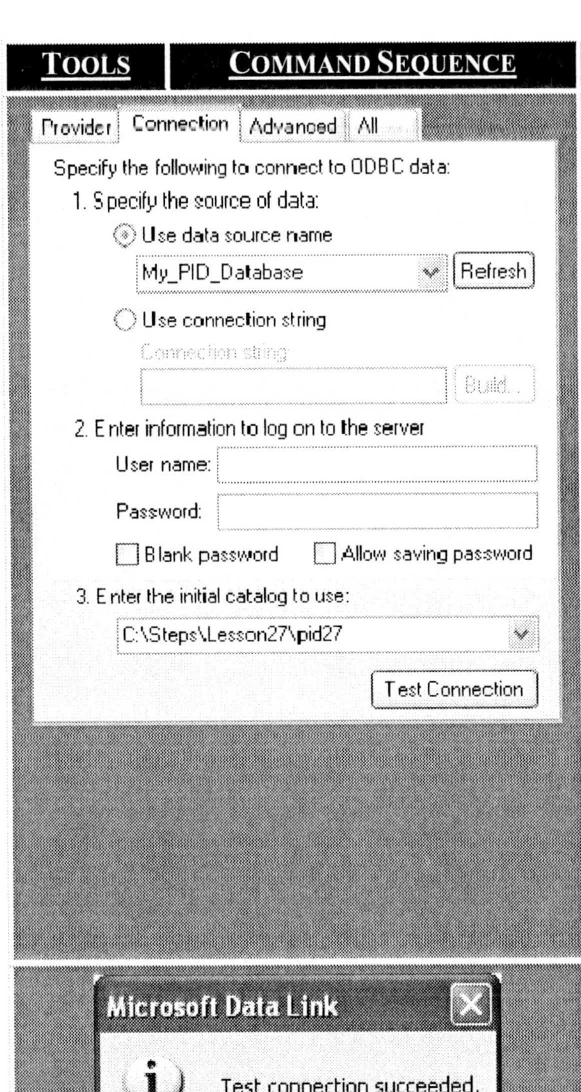		6. On the **Connection** tab, we give AutoCAD the ODBC information it'll need to make the connection. • Begin by selecting the data source name (DSN) we gave Windows in the **Use data source name** control box. (If the *My_PID_Database* DSN doesn't appear in the control box options, pick the **Refresh** button.) (If no DSN has been created, you can select the **Use connection string – Build** button to set it up much as we did in our first exercise in this lesson.) • If the database requires **User name** and **Password** for access, you should place those in the appropriate boxes in Step 2. (Our database doesn't require these so leave these boxes blank.) • You can specify a file to use in Step 3. This isn't required unless the database is located outside the drawing's project search path (**Files** tab of the Options dialog box). We'll use it here to be sure we access the correct file.
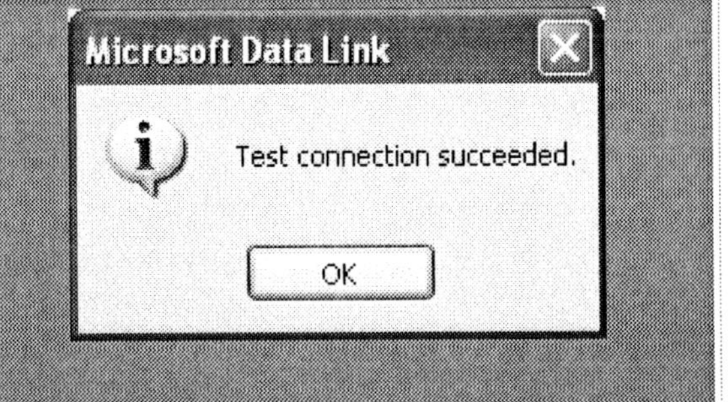		7. Pick the **Test Connection** button to verify that your setup has found the appropriate database. AutoCAD presents the Microsoft Data Link message box indicated. If the test connection doesn't succeed, cancel the process and return to Step 1. If the test connection is successful, pick the **OK** button to close the message box and again to complete the procedure.
		8. The dbConnect Manager now looks like Figure 27.007.

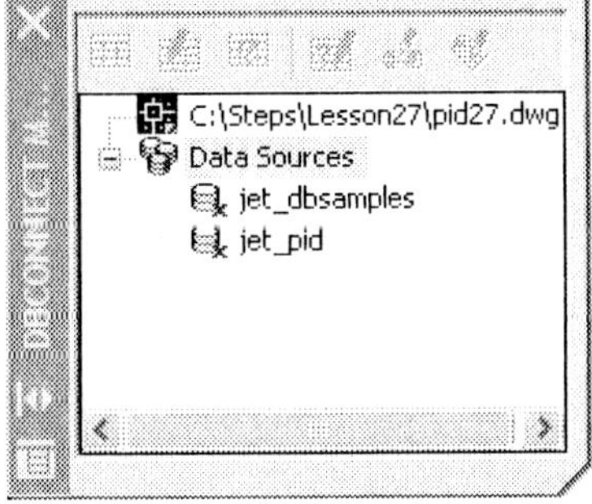

Figure 27.007

Congratulations! You've linked AutoCAD to an MS Access database!

If you don't feel suitably impressed yet, consider that you've just connected your "drafting tool" to one of the most powerful informational tools (a database) ever devised by "mortal man."

Thanks to this ability (together with the ability to tie in to the Internet), you, as the project draftsman/designer, will acquire many new responsibilities (and achieve new status – hopefully with an accompanying raise in salary). You'll now take a greater hand in materials selection and management. In some cases, it even means more control over personnel and equipment assignments (see the exercises at the end of this lesson).

But now that you've tied into a database, what do you do with it? This is the topic of our next section.

27.4 Okay, I'm Attached – Now How Do I Use the Database?

It's all well and good to feel some pride in having attached AutoCAD to a database, but what was the purpose in doing so? Why is this better than simply attaching the database using an OLE connection?

That's a fair question, but the answer requires some additional training before you'll fully understand it. Still, I can give you some hints.

Consider this scenario.

> *You have a rough draft of a P&ID for a new project. The materials people are screaming for work (or they'll start laying off personnel). You don't want to be the cause of fellow employees having weeks of idle time to spend at the beach, so you create a preliminary database of valves for them to begin ordering. But you explain that the list is subject to change.*
>
> *You can (and do) add the valve list to your drawing via OLE linking. You understand that you can easily change the list, and that the changes will show up in the original database for the MTO group to see. But you also understand that, over the course of designing anything, changes are frequent and numerous. This can make your valves list difficult to track properly.*
>
> *So you create a dbConnect link with the database. Through this connection, you link each valve in the database list with the specific valve on the drawing. You try to keep the changes current between the two files, but often lack the time. So once or twice a week, you view the links to be sure you have no listed valves without links, or valves that don't appear in the list. You make corrections as needed. Since you make these corrections to the original database (through your dbConnect link), they appear on the MTO group's computers and, through your OLE connection, on your bill of materials as well.*
>
> *Occasionally, the MTO lead calls to see how many special-order gate valves you anticipate needing for the project. You could ask your summer intern to count them, but he's filling out job applications. So you perform a database query, which gives you the answer in seconds.*

Sound interesting? This scenario requires that you acquire some new skills: linking (and unlinking) database records to AutoCAD objects, and querying a database for specific information. We'll also examine how to use database information to create callouts (labels) on your drawing.

Let's begin with linking objects and records.

27.4.1 Linking AutoCAD Objects to Database Records

Linking AutoCAD objects to database records is as easy as picking a button and selecting an object. You'll follow these steps:

I. **Open the database table** (double-click on the database in the dbConnect Manager and then on the desired table).

II. **Select the Link Template** you wish to use (or create a new one).

III. **Select the record** to link.

IV. **Pick the Link** button.

V. **Select the object**(s) to which you want to link.

- Let's begin with Step I: **Open the database table**.

  To open the database table, double-click on the Data Source (in our case, *jet_pid*). The dbConnect Manager lists the tables available in that source. Double-click on the table you wish to use. AutoCAD presents the Data View window (Figure 27.008). (It also creates a Data View pull-down menu between the dbConnect and Windows menus.) Let's take a look at the Data View window.

Data View - valves (C:\Steps\Lesson27\pid27.dwg)

-- New Link Template -- | -- New La

ID	BlockName	Valve	Size	Rating	Vendor	Price
1	GATE	Gate	4"	300#	Vogt	85
2	GATE	Gate	4"	300#	Vogt	85
3	GLOBE	Globe	3"	300#	Jamesbury	75
4	CONTROLVA	Globe-Control	3"	300#	Jameson	175
5	DRAIN	Gate	3/4"	800#	Vogt	35
6	GATE	Gate	8"	150#	Vogt	385
7	GATE	Gate	6"	150#	Vogt	125
8	GATE	Gate	6"	150#	Vogt	125

Record 1

Figure 27.008

  - The title bar indicates the type of window and the currently opened file.
  - Below the title bar, you'll see the Data View toolbar with several buttons and two control boxes. Let's look at these from left to right.

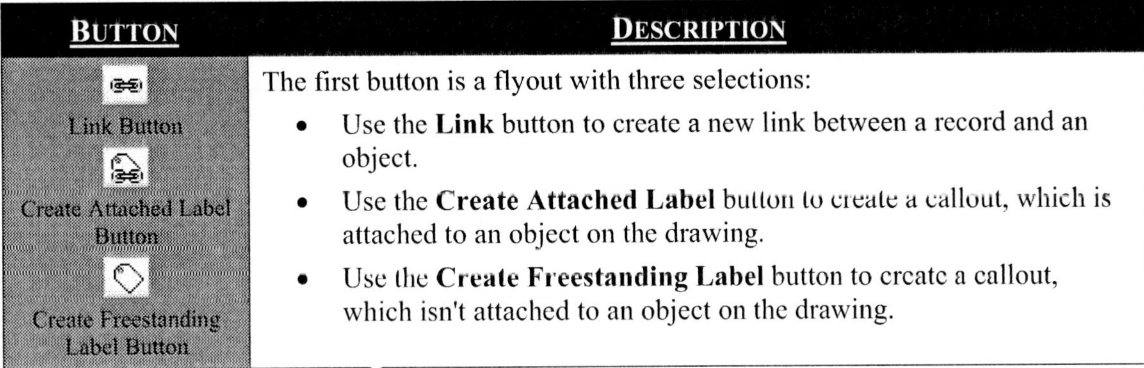

BUTTON	DESCRIPTION
Link Button Create Attached Label Button Create Freestanding Label Button	The first button is a flyout with three selections: • Use the **Link** button to create a new link between a record and an object. • Use the **Create Attached Label** button to create a callout, which is attached to an object on the drawing. • Use the **Create Freestanding Label** button to create a callout, which isn't attached to an object on the drawing.

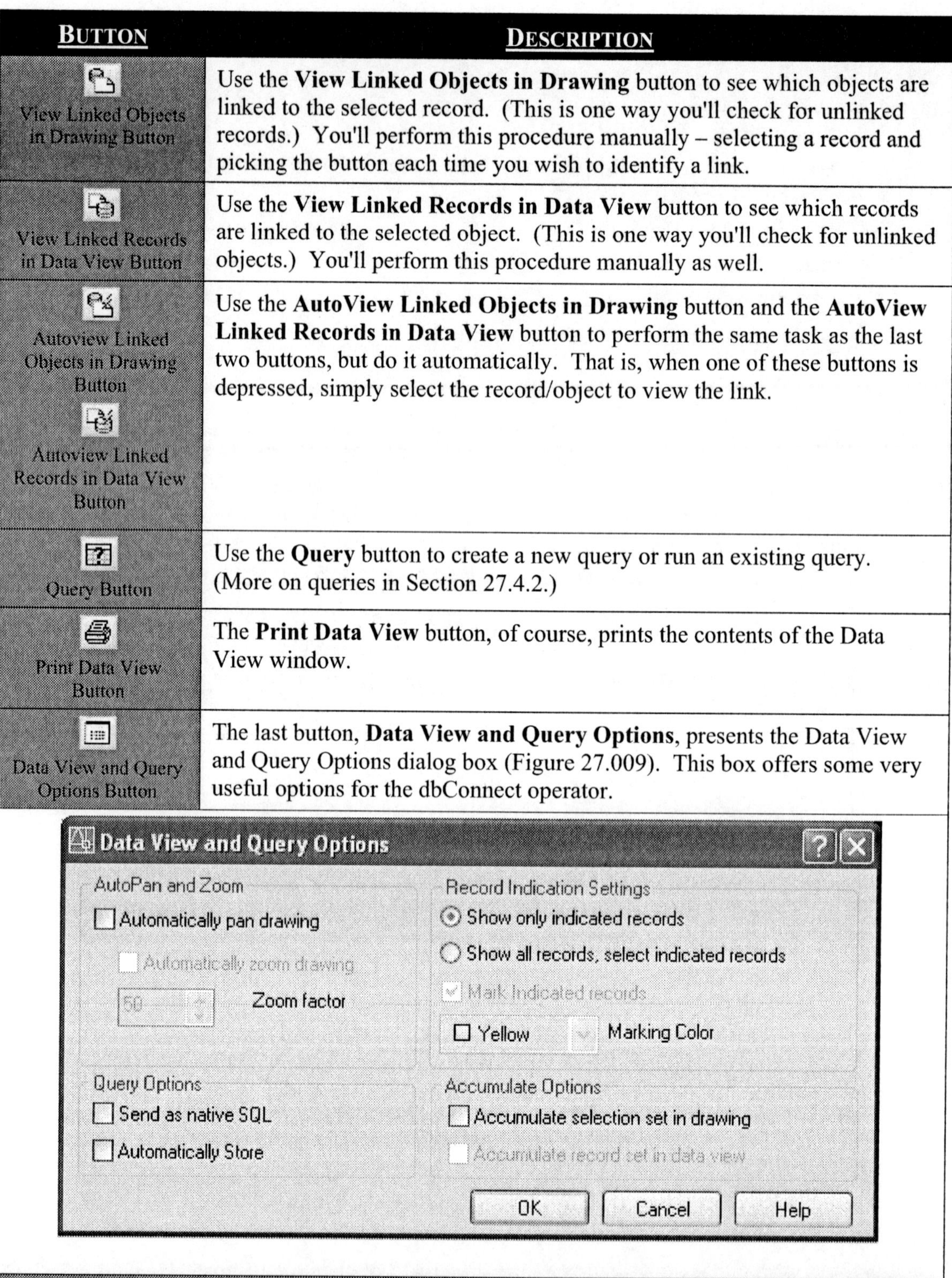

BUTTON	DESCRIPTION
View Linked Objects in Drawing Button	Use the **View Linked Objects in Drawing** button to see which objects are linked to the selected record. (This is one way you'll check for unlinked records.) You'll perform this procedure manually – selecting a record and picking the button each time you wish to identify a link.
View Linked Records in Data View Button	Use the **View Linked Records in Data View** button to see which records are linked to the selected object. (This is one way you'll check for unlinked objects.) You'll perform this procedure manually as well.
Autoview Linked Objects in Drawing Button Autoview Linked Records in Data View Button	Use the **AutoView Linked Objects in Drawing** button and the **AutoView Linked Records in Data View** button to perform the same task as the last two buttons, but do it automatically. That is, when one of these buttons is depressed, simply select the record/object to view the link.
Query Button	Use the **Query** button to create a new query or run an existing query. (More on queries in Section 27.4.2.)
Print Data View Button	The **Print Data View** button, of course, prints the contents of the Data View window.
Data View and Query Options Button	The last button, **Data View and Query Options**, presents the Data View and Query Options dialog box (Figure 27.009). This box offers some very useful options for the dbConnect operator.

- Options in the **AutoPan and Zoom** frame control what happens when you select a record in the Data View window. A check in the **Automatically pan drawing** box causes AutoCAD to pan the drawing so that objects linked to the selected record become visible. A check in the **Automatically zoom drawing** box performs a similar function with the ***Zoom*** command. Set the factor for auto zoom in the

BUTTON	DESCRIPTION
	Zoom factor box. These tools provide enormous assistance in a busy drawing. ▪ The first option in the **Query Options** frame – **Send as native SQL** – involves how a query is handled in programming terms. I strongly suggest leaving this at its default unless you're quite familiar with databases and recognize the need to change it. A check in the **Automatically Store** box causes AutoCAD to automatically store the results of a query in the current drawing. I'd leave this cleared as well. Rerunning a query isn't difficult; storing information that isn't required in a drawing causes its size to increase unnecessarily. ▪ The options in the **Record Indication Settings** frame control which records appear in the Data View. When you put the bullet next to **Show only indicated records** (the default), AutoCAD shows only those records linked to the selected objects in the drawing. If no objects have been selected, all the records appear. This is a handy tool when querying a large database. When you put the bullet next to **Show all records, select indicated records**, the Data View shows all the records. It highlights records linked to selected objects in the color indicated in the **Marking Color** box. This setting works best on small databases. ▪ **Accumulate selection set in drawing**, in the **Accumulate Options** frame, works something like the **Use Shift to Add** selection mode. When cleared (the default), the select set in the drawing changes each time a new set of records is selected in the Data View. When checked, selecting additional records simply adds them to the current selection set.

- o To the right of the **Data View and Query Options** button (back in the Data View window – Figure 27.008), you'll find the **Select a Link Template** control box. This box shows **New Link Template** because we haven't created a link template yet. Once you've created a link template(s), you can select the one you wish to use here.
- o Next to the **Select a Link Template** control box resides the **Select a Label Template** control box. This performs the same function for label templates.

- In Step II: **Select the Link Template**, you'll select an existing link template from the **Select a Link Template** control box mentioned previously. Alternately, you can create a new link template.

  A link template organizes your links into specific categories. It works with the **View Linked Objects in Drawing** and **View Linked Records in Data View** buttons to help identify links.

  A link template categorizes records by data in a specific, user-identified field. Then, when you pick the **View Linked Objects in Drawing** button, AutoCAD identifies the value of that field in the selected record and highlights all the linked objects that contain that value.

  For example, in our *PID* drawing, we'll create a link template using **Valve** as our primary key field. Then while this template is active, we'll select record #1 (a gate valve) and pick the **View Linked Objects in Drawing** button. AutoCAD will then highlight all the gate valves with links in the drawing.

To view single objects or records, you must create a template using a field whose values remain unique. To do this, I suggest using the key field *ID* created by MS Access. MS Access numbers each record as it is entered, so the value will be unique for each record.

(If you try to create a link without creating the template first, AutoCAD will automatically start the **New Link Template** wizard.)

- In Step III: **Select the record** to link, simply select any value in the desired record to identify the record to link.
- In Step IV: **Pick the Link** button, pick the **Link** button in the Data View window.
- In Step V: **Select the object**, you'll select the drawing object to which you want to link the record.

Let's put all of this together in an exercise. We'll use our five-step procedure to link our database records to objects in our drawing.

Do This: 27.4.1.1	Linking Records and Objects

I. Be sure you're still in the *pid27.dwg* file in the C:\Steps\Lesson27 folder. If not, please open it now.

II. Follow these steps.

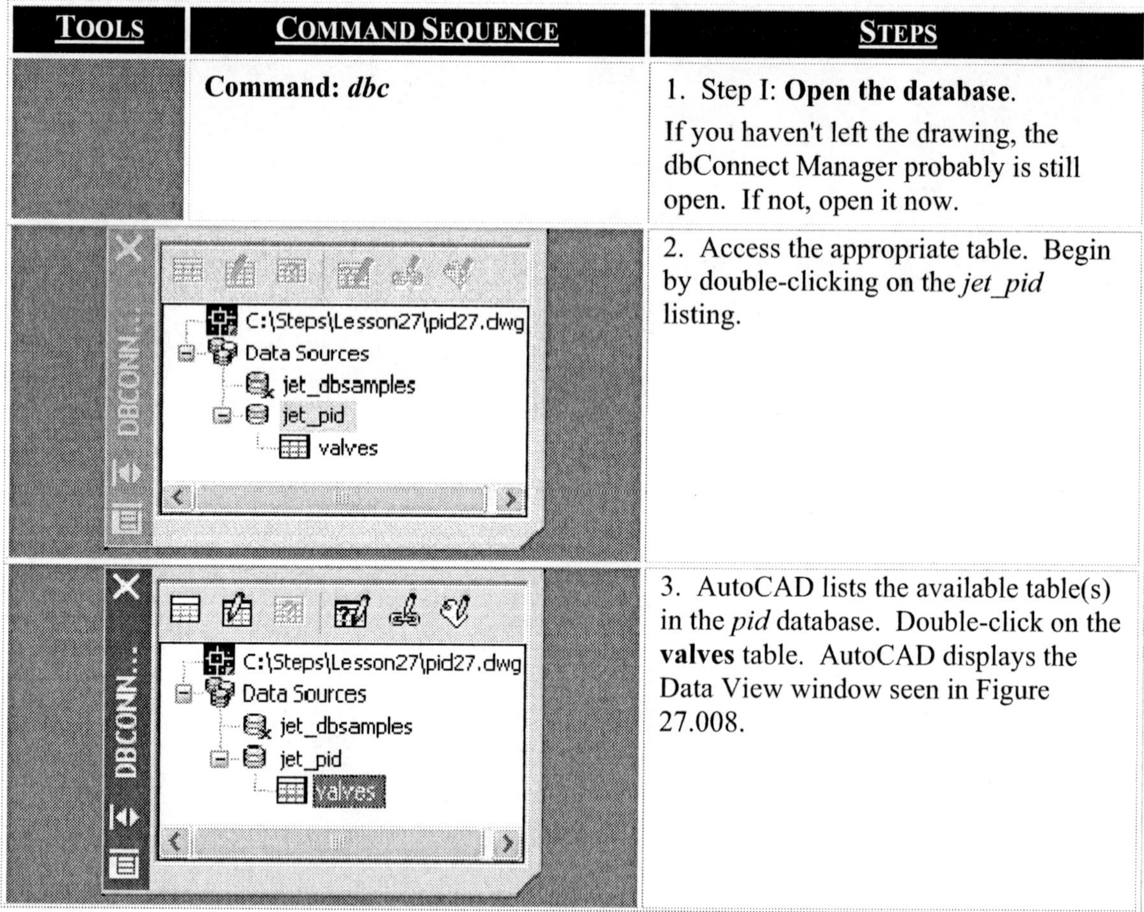

TOOLS	COMMAND SEQUENCE	STEPS
	Command: ***dbc***	1. Step I: **Open the database.** If you haven't left the drawing, the dbConnect Manager probably is still open. If not, open it now.
		2. Access the appropriate table. Begin by double-clicking on the *jet_pid* listing.
		3. AutoCAD lists the available table(s) in the *pid* database. Double-click on the **valves** table. AutoCAD displays the Data View window seen in Figure 27.008.

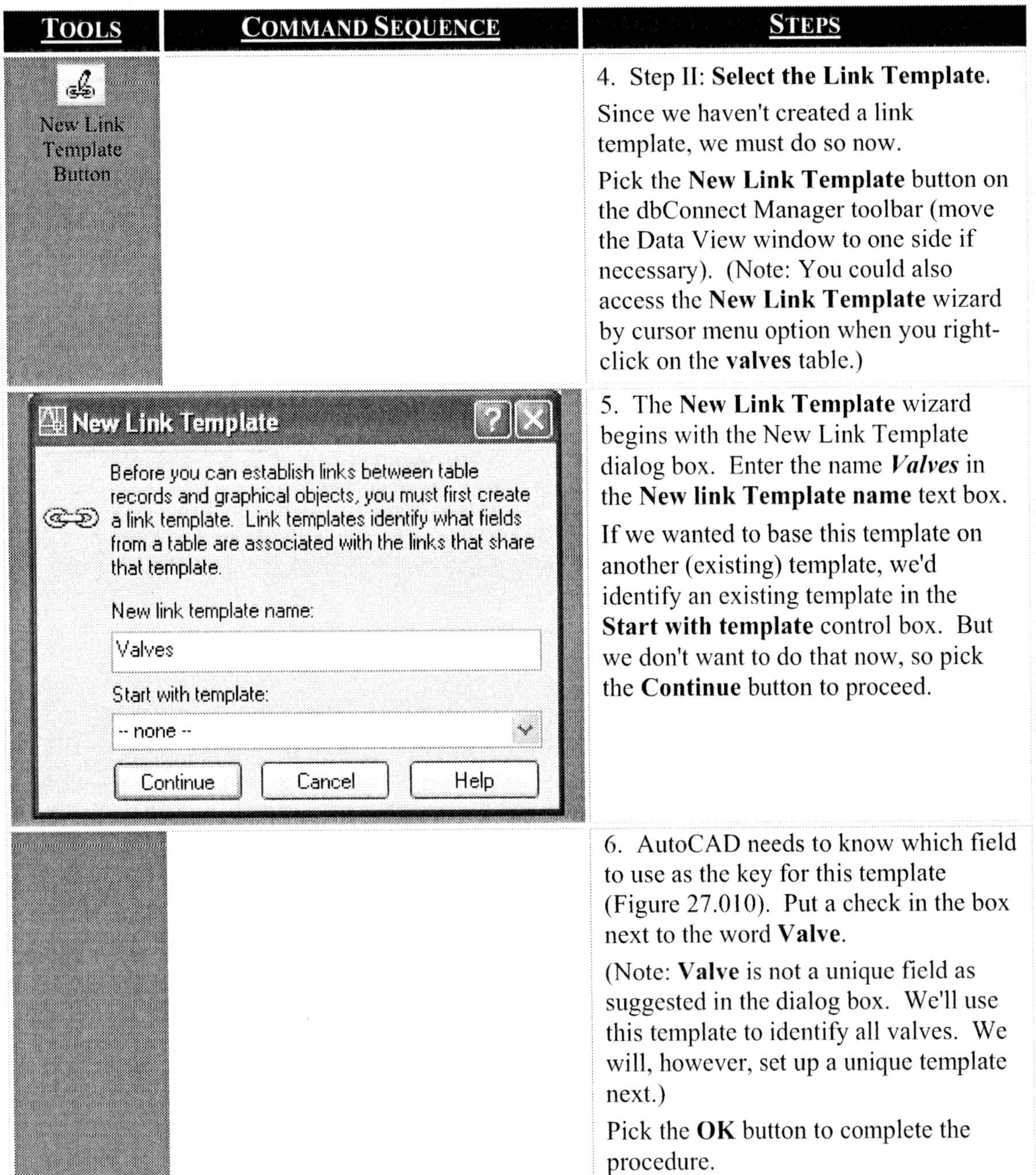

TOOLS	COMMAND SEQUENCE	STEPS
New Link Template Button		4. Step II: **Select the Link Template.** Since we haven't created a link template, we must do so now. Pick the **New Link Template** button on the dbConnect Manager toolbar (move the Data View window to one side if necessary). (Note: You could also access the **New Link Template** wizard by cursor menu option when you right-click on the **valves** table.)
New Link Template Before you can establish links between table records and graphical objects, you must first create a link template. Link templates identify what fields from a table are associated with the links that share that template. New link template name: Valves Start with template: -- none -- Continue Cancel Help		5. The **New Link Template** wizard begins with the New Link Template dialog box. Enter the name ***Valves*** in the **New link Template name** text box. If we wanted to base this template on another (existing) template, we'd identify an existing template in the **Start with template** control box. But we don't want to do that now, so pick the **Continue** button to proceed.
		6. AutoCAD needs to know which field to use as the key for this template (Figure 27.010). Put a check in the box next to the word **Valve**. (Note: **Valve** is not a unique field as suggested in the dialog box. We'll use this template to identify all valves. We will, however, set up a unique template next.) Pick the **OK** button to complete the procedure.

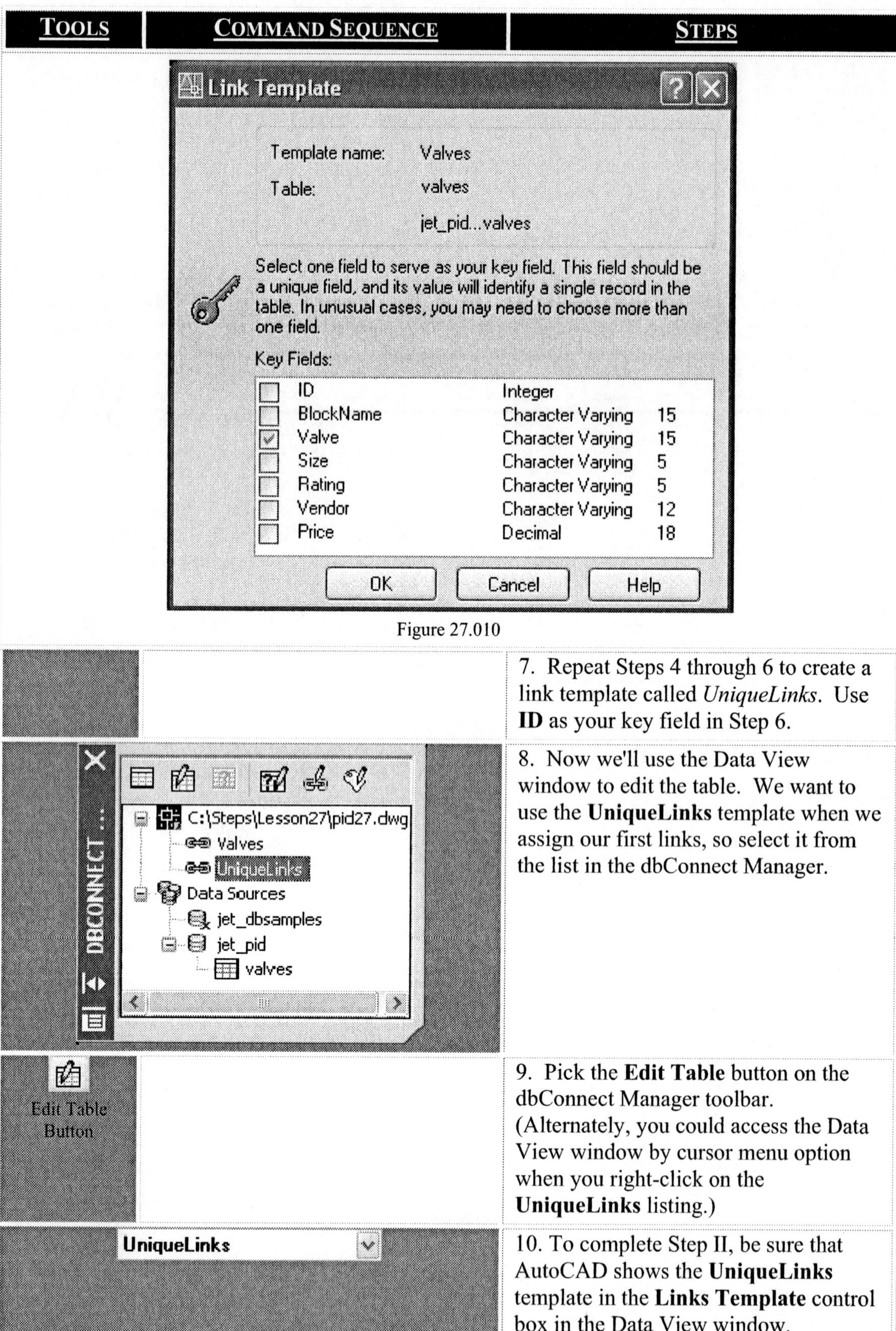

Figure 27.010

TOOLS	COMMAND SEQUENCE	STEPS
		7. Repeat Steps 4 through 6 to create a link template called *UniqueLinks*. Use **ID** as your key field in Step 6.
		8. Now we'll use the Data View window to edit the table. We want to use the **UniqueLinks** template when we assign our first links, so select it from the list in the dbConnect Manager.
Edit Table Button		9. Pick the **Edit Table** button on the dbConnect Manager toolbar. (Alternately, you could access the Data View window by cursor menu option when you right-click on the **UniqueLinks** listing.)
		10. To complete Step II, be sure that AutoCAD shows the **UniqueLinks** template in the **Links Template** control box in the Data View window.

TOOLS	COMMAND SEQUENCE	STEPS
		11. For Step III: **Select the record,** select record 1 in the Data View window (Figure 27.011).

	ID	BlockName	Valve	Size	Rating	
▶	1	GATE	Gate	4"	300#	Vogt
	2	GATE	Gate	4"	300#	Vogt
	3	GLOBE	Globe	3"	300#	Jame
	4	CONTROLVA	Globe-Control	3"	300#	Jame
	5	DRAIN	Gate	3/4"	800#	Vogt
	6	GATE	Gate	8"	150#	Vogt
	7	GATE	Gate	6"	150#	Vogt
	8	GATE	Gate	6"	150#	Vogt

Figure 27.011

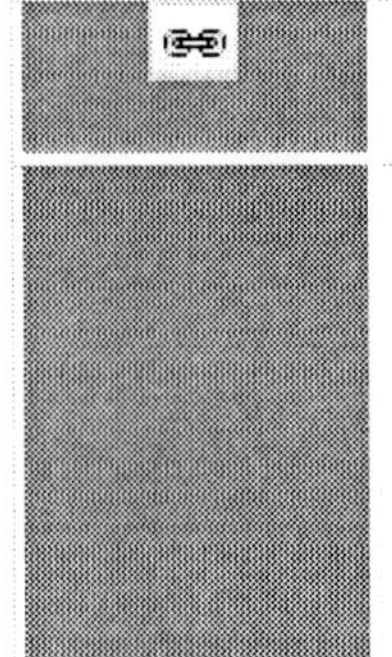

TOOLS	COMMAND SEQUENCE	STEPS
		12. Step IV: **Pick the Link button** in the Data View window.
	Select objects: **Select objects: *[enter]***	13. Step V: **Select the object(s)** to which you want to link. AutoCAD returns to the graphics screen and prompts you to **Select objects** to which you want to link. Select valve **A** (as indicated in Figure 27.012), and then hit ***enter*** to complete the selection.

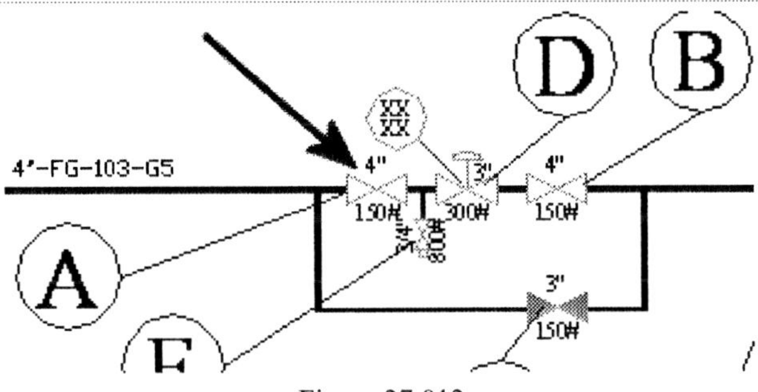

Figure 27.012

To remove a misplaced link,

- Select the drawing object that contains the link.
- Right-click in the drawing.
- Select **Link** from the cursor menu.
- Select **Delete Link** from the flyout menu.

TOOLS	COMMAND SEQUENCE	STEPS
		14. AutoCAD returns to the Data View window and moves to the next record in the list. It marks the first record to show that it has been linked (Figure 27.013). Continue to link the records to the corresponding valve (record 2 to valve B, record 3 to valve C, etc.).

TOOLS	**COMMAND SEQUENCE**	**STEPS**

	ID	BlockName	Valve	Size	Rating	
	1	GATE	Gate	4"	300#	Vogt
▶	2	GATE	Gate	4"	300#	Vogt
	3	GLOBE	Globe	3"	300#	Jame
	4	CONTROLVA	Globe-Control	3"	300#	Jame
	5	DRAIN	Gate	3/4"	800#	Vogt
	6	GATE	Gate	8"	150#	Vogt
	7	GATE	Gate	6"	150#	Vogt
	8	GATE	Gate	6"	150#	Vogt

Figure 27.013

	Command: *qsave*	15. Save your work.
		16. Repeat Steps 10 through 15 using the **Valves** template.

Now that you've created links in two templates, let's take a look at how they'll help you keep track of materials in your drawing.

> To edit a template, use the dbConnect pull-down menu. Follow this path:
>
> *DbConnect – Templates – Edit [type of template] Template...*
>
> (Note: You can't edit a link template if it contains links. You must delete the links it contains before attempting to modify it.)

We'll use the templates and links you created in Exercise 27.4.1.1 to be sure we haven't lost or duplicated any information on our PID design efforts. We'll also use the dbConnect Manager to identify specific valves in our drawing.

Do This: 27.4.1.2	**Reading the Links**

I. Be sure you're still in the *pid27.dwg* file in the C:\Steps\Lesson27 folder. If not, please open it now.

II. Be sure the dbConnect Manager is running and that the Data View window is open.

III. Follow these steps.

TOOLS	**COMMAND SEQUENCE**	**STEPS**
	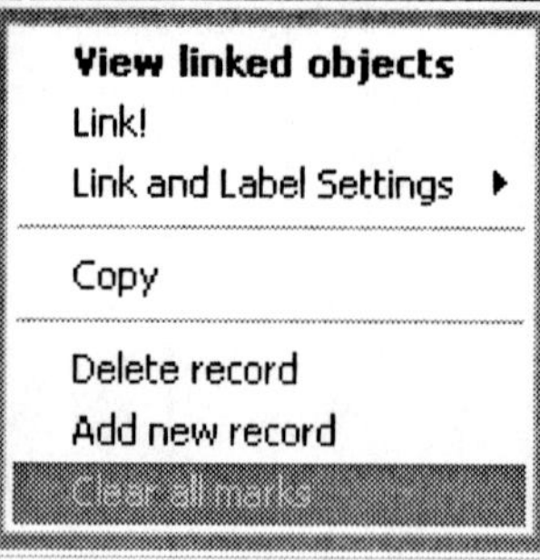 **View linked objects** Link! Link and Label Settings ▸ Copy Delete record Add new record Clear all marks	1. First, let's be sure we have a fresh view in our Data View window. Right-click anywhere in the gray area to the left of any record and select **Clear all marks** from the cursor menu.

TOOLS	COMMAND SEQUENCE	STEPS

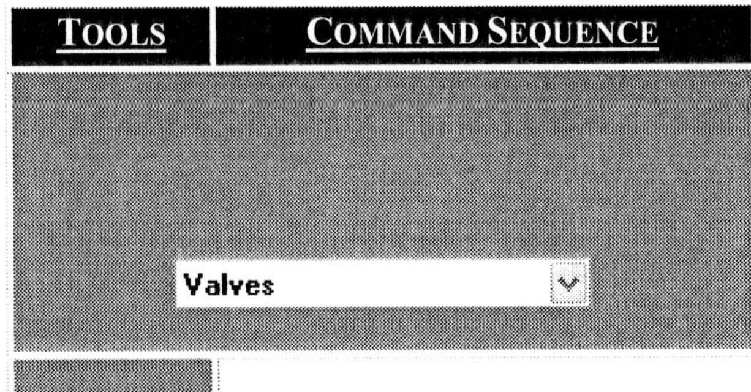

2. The lead engineer has noticed that you have used some globe valves and wants to know where they are. We'll use our links to show him.

Set **Valves** as current in the **Link Template** control box.

3. Select one of the globe valves as shown in Figure 27.014 (I'll use valve 3).

ID	BlockName	Valve	Size	Rating	
1	GATE	Gate	4"	300#	Vogt
2	GATE	Gate	4"	300#	Vogt
3	GLOBE	Globe	3"	300#	Jame
4	CONTROLVA	Globe-Control	3"	300#	Jame
5	DRAIN	Gate	3/4"	800#	Vogt
6	GATE	Gate	8"	150#	Vogt
7	GATE	Gate	6"	150#	Vogt
8	GATE	Gate	6"	150#	Vogt

Figure 27.014

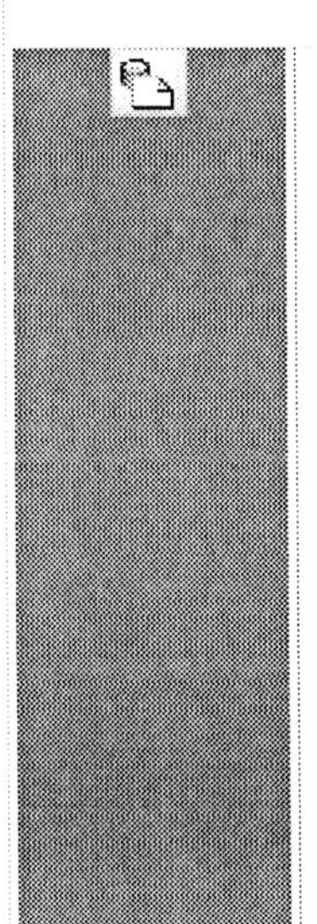

4. Pick the **View Linked Objects in Drawing** button.

- AutoCAD reads the value in the **Valves** field, as we told it to do in Step 6 of our last exercise. (The value in our selected record is **Globe**.)
- It then searches the links for all of the records whose value in the **Valves** field is the same (it looks for all the **Globe** valves).
- Finally, AutoCAD highlights and places grips on the linked objects that match the desired value (it shows you where the globe valves are located in the drawing). See Figure 27.015.

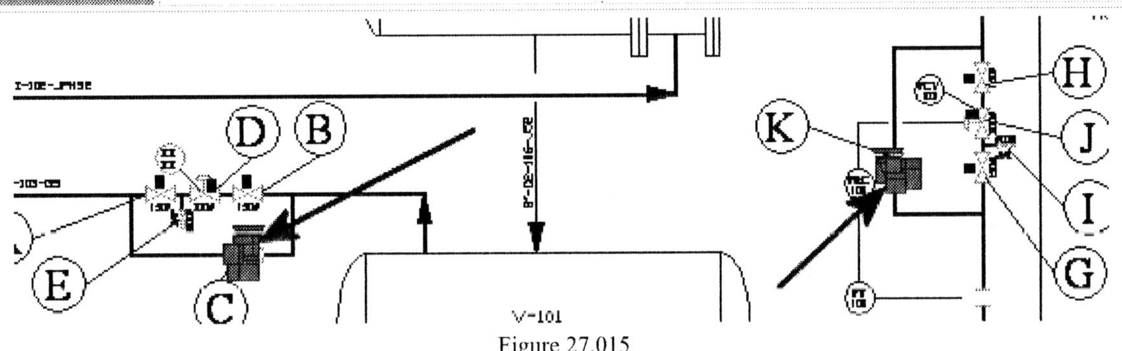

Figure 27.015

5. But suppose you want to find an individual valve. Let's see where the first 10" gate valve in our database is located in

TOOLS	COMMAND SEQUENCE	STEPS
	UniqueLinks	our drawing. (First, clear the grips.) Now set the **UniqueLinks** template current in the **Link Templates** control box.
		6. Now select the valve to locate (valve 15) as shown in Figure 27.016.

	ID	BlockName	Valve	Size	Rating	
	13	GATE	Gate	6"	150#	Vogt
	14	CHECK	Check	6"	150#	Vogt
▶	15	GATE	Gate	10"	150#	Vogt
	16	DRAIN	Gate	3/4"	800#	Vogt
	17	DRAIN	Gate	3/4"	800#	Vogt
	18	GATE	Gate	10"	150#	Vogt
	19	CHECK	Check	6"	150#	Vogt
	20	GATE	Gate	6"	150#	Vogt

Figure 27.016

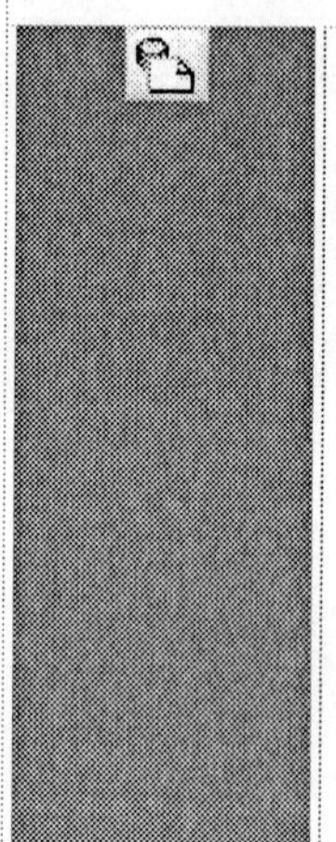

7. Pick the **View Linked Objects in Drawing** button.

- This time, the value in the selected field is unique (remember that we used the **ID** field as the primary key for this template), so AutoCAD will find only the valve we've selected.
- As before, AutoCAD highlights and places grips on the linked object (valve **O**) that matches the selected record (it shows you where the 10" gate valve is located in the drawing). See Figure 27.017.

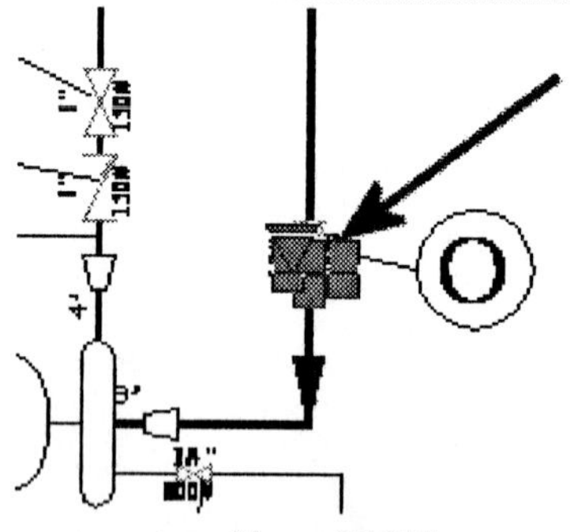

Figure 27.017

AutoView Linked Objects Button	To view valves "on the fly" (as you select the record), depress the **AutoView Linked Objects in Drawing** button on the Data View toolbar. AutoCAD will highlight each object as you select its corresponding record. (Try this now.)

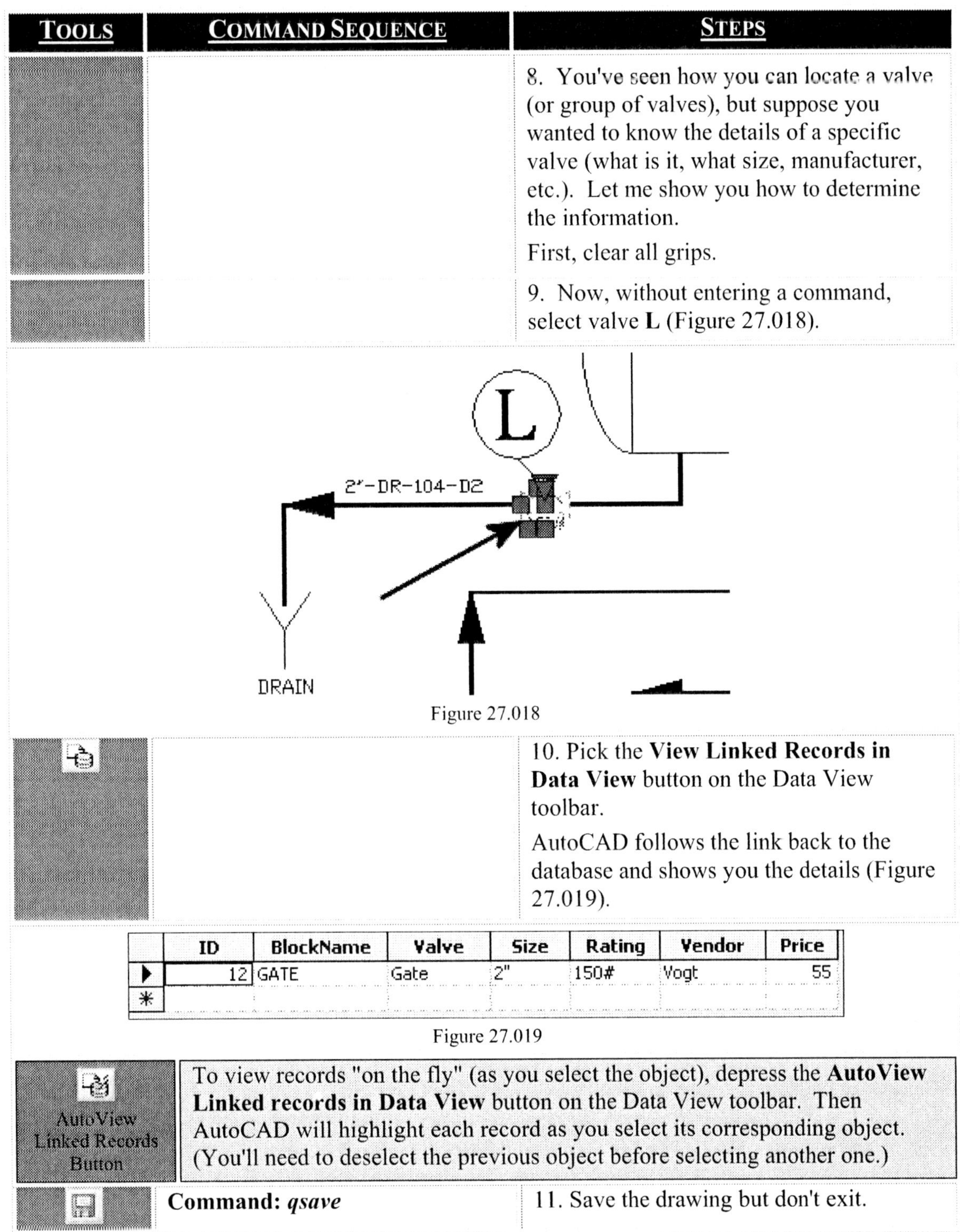

TOOLS	COMMAND SEQUENCE	STEPS
		8. You've seen how you can locate a valve (or group of valves), but suppose you wanted to know the details of a specific valve (what is it, what size, manufacturer, etc.). Let me show you how to determine the information. First, clear all grips.
		9. Now, without entering a command, select valve **L** (Figure 27.018).

Figure 27.018

TOOLS	COMMAND SEQUENCE	STEPS
		10. Pick the **View Linked Records in Data View** button on the Data View toolbar. AutoCAD follows the link back to the database and shows you the details (Figure 27.019).

	ID	BlockName	Valve	Size	Rating	Vendor	Price
▶	12	GATE	Gate	2"	150#	Vogt	55
*							

Figure 27.019

AutoView Linked Records Button	To view records "on the fly" (as you select the object), depress the **AutoView Linked records in Data View** button on the Data View toolbar. Then AutoCAD will highlight each record as you select its corresponding object. (You'll need to deselect the previous object before selecting another one.)

TOOLS	COMMAND SEQUENCE	STEPS
	Command: ***qsave***	11. Save the drawing but don't exit.

What do you suppose would have happened had you followed Steps 8 through 10 of this exercise using the **Valves** links template? Try it and see.*

As you can see, AutoCAD's dbConnect provides much more than a simple OLE link.

* AutoCAD will follow the link back to the database, read the value in the **Valve** field, and reveal all the records that share that value.

But wait; there's more!

27.4.2 Creating and Using Queries

In Lesson 10, we discussed object selection filters. Using them, we created selection sets based on object type, layer, linetype, or other category. This convenient tool helped us when we needed to identify certain objects in our drawing for modification or deletion.

Database queries work in much the same way that object selection filters work. That is, they filter the data to find specific records that adhere to user-specified criteria. (Okay, they help you find just what you want to find.)

Creating a query can be complex, but it doesn't have to be complicated. Follow this procedure:

I. **Select the table** you wish to query.
II. **Pick the New Query** button on the dbConnect Manager toolbar.
III. **Name the Query** using the New Query dialog box (Figure 27.020).
IV. Using the Query Editor dialog box (Figure 27.021), **Tell AutoCAD what filters to use** to locate specific records or objects.
V. **Store &/Or Execute** the query.

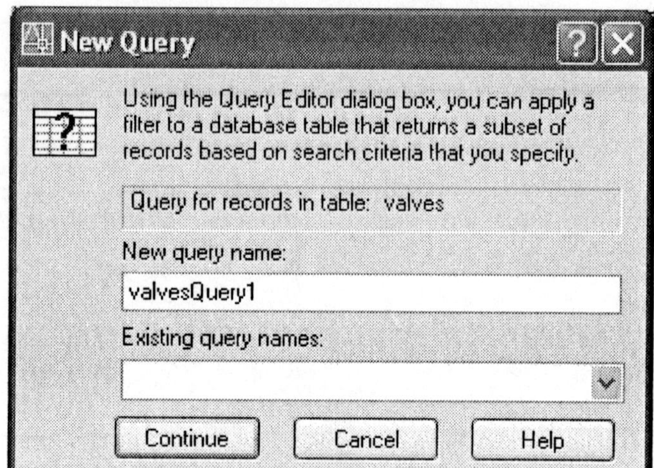

Figure 27.020

AutoCAD provides several methods for identifying filters for the query. Let's take a look at the Query Editor (Step IV).

- The first and easiest method is the **Quick Query**. Follow this procedure:

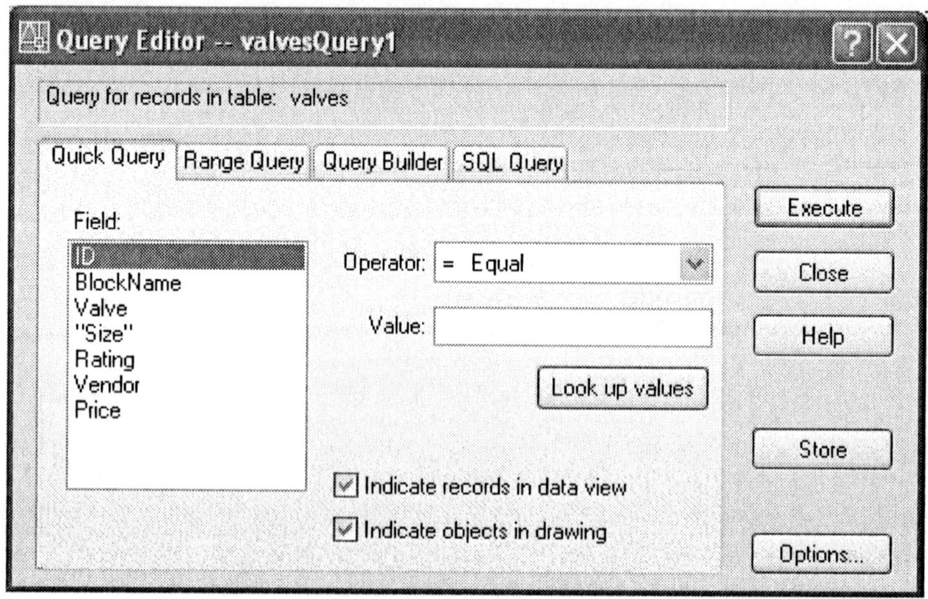

Figure 27.021

  - Pick the **Quick Query** tab.

- Identify the field you'll use for your filter in the **Field** list box.
- Determine the operator you'll use by selecting it in the **Operator** control box. Operators work like their mathematical counterparts.
- Assign a **Value** to the field. (AutoCAD will show you the values used by this field if you pick the **Look up values** button.)

  [You can read the query much as you would a mathematical equation, as in "find all of the *valves* (field) *equal to* (operator) *4"* (value) *in size*."]
- Use the two check boxes – **Indicate records in data view**, and **Indicate objects in drawing** – to tell AutoCAD where you want to see the results of the query.

• Begin the **Range** method for defining a query by selecting the **Range Query** tab (Figure 27.022). The Range method returns a list of records and/or a group of objects that fall within a range of values. For example, I can look up valves that cost between $35 and $125.

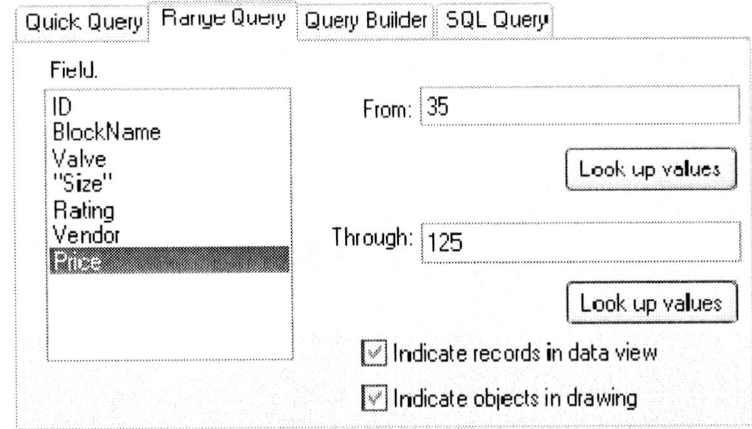

Figure 27.022

- Select the field to search, and then identify the upper and lower limits of the search. [The upper and lower values will be included in the results (in this example, the results would include the **From** and **Through** values – ***35*** and ***125***).]

  You can also use the **Look up values** buttons here as you did on the **Quick Query** tab.

• Whereas the first two queries (Quick and Range) allow you to filter for a single field, the Query Builder allows multiple filters.

The **Query Builder** tab (Figure 27.023) allows you to identify data in two different ways: by filter reference (or cross-reference) in the top half of the dialog box, or by field in the bottom half. (Of course, you can combine the two. For example, you might show just the ratings field of 4" gate valves.)

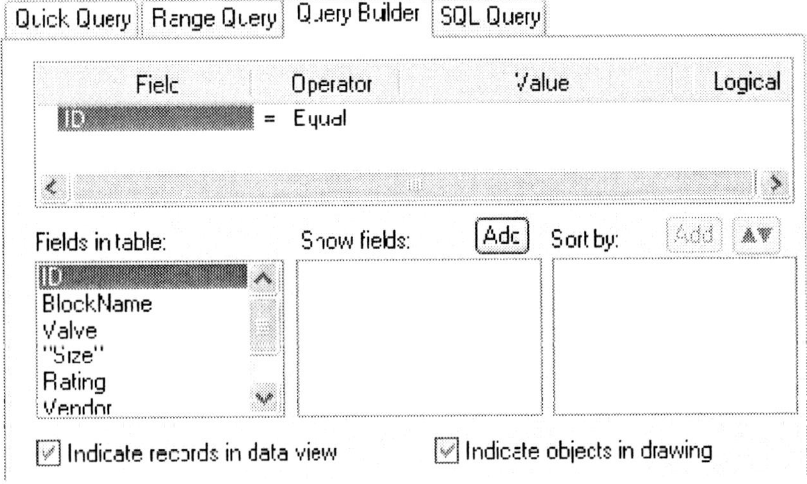

Figure 27.023

- The filters in the top section work just like their counterparts on the other tabs – select a field, identify the operator, and value. However, notice the last field – **Logical**. Use this field to combine sets of filters with either **And** or **Or**. So you might set an initial filter for globe valves and a second filter for 3" valves. Using the logical filter **And**, you can find 3" globe valves. Using the logical filter **Or**, AutoCAD will look for globe valves or 3" valves. The Data View will show both!
- The **Fields** section across the bottom of the tab allows you to show only selected fields of information. For example, I might need to see only the prices of valves used in this drawing. To do that, I would select **Price** in the **Fields in table** list box and add it (using the **Add** button) to the **Show fields** box. I could then sort the list from least to greatest (or vice versa) using the **Sort by** box.

- The **SQL Query** tab (Figure 27.024) works much like a combination of the two sections of the **Query Builder** tab. But here, as you can see, AutoCAD writes out what you're doing in the SQL programming language.

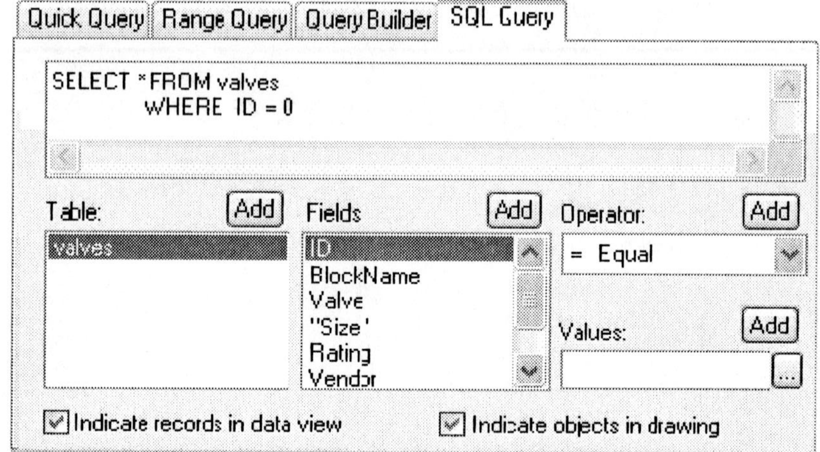

Figure 27.024

Once you've set up the query, you'll use the buttons down the right side of the Query Editor (Figure 27.021) to run it.

- Use the **Store** button to save the query setup. If you wish to save the query, you must do so before executing it.
- Use the **Execute** button to run the query.
- Use the **Close** button to exit the Query Editor without executing the query.
- The **Options** button presents the Data View and Query Options dialog box discussed in Section 27.4.1.
- The handy **Check** button (available only for the SQL Query) has AutoCAD check the program syntax (check the wording of the query) for errors.

Let's create a couple queries to see how they work, and to see how they might be of use to us.

Do This: 27.4.2.1	Creating Queries

I. Be sure you're still in the *pid27.dwg* file in the C:\Steps\Lesson27 folder. If not, please open it now.

II. Be sure the dbConnect Manager is running and that the Data View window is open.

III. Follow these steps.

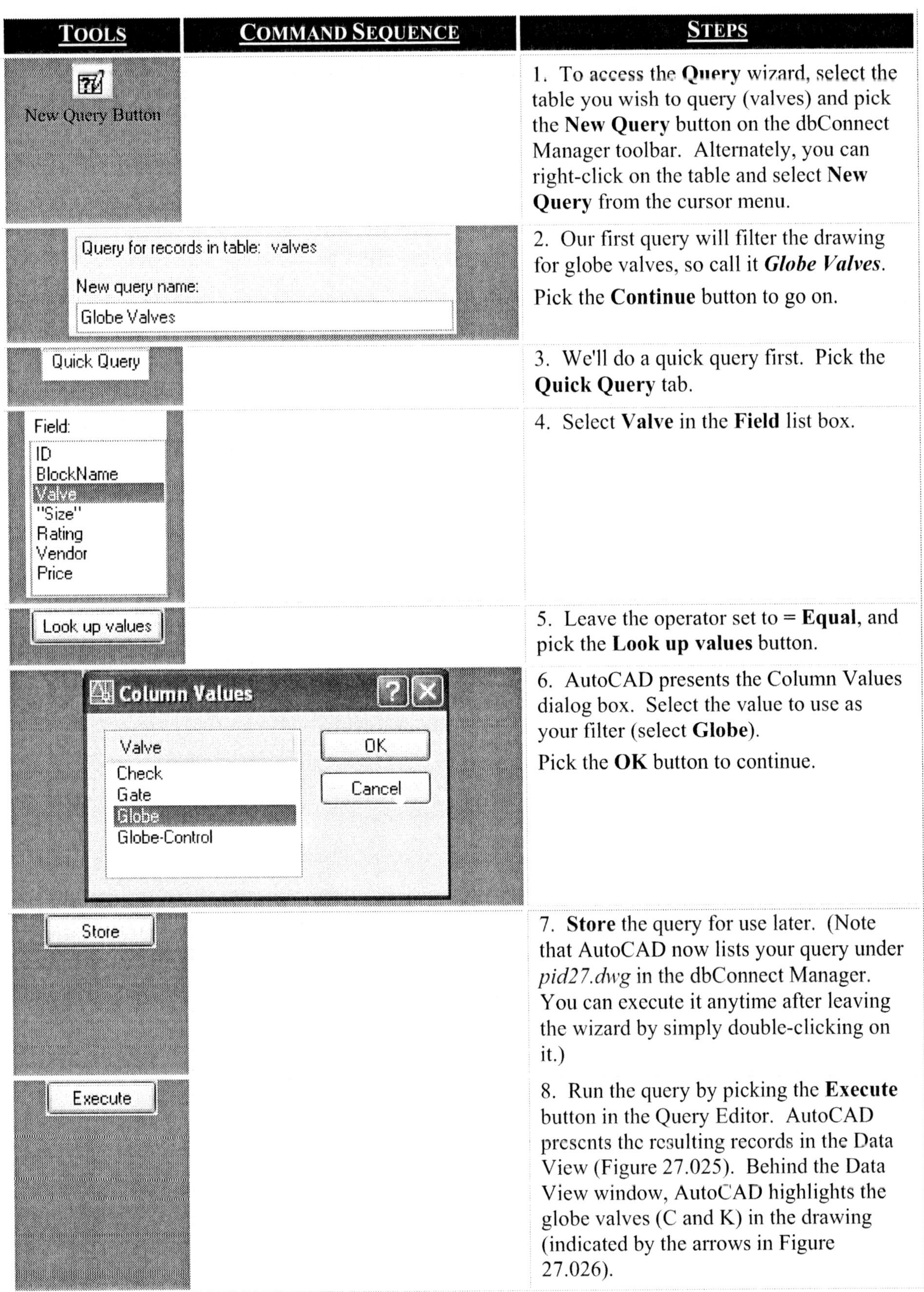

TOOLS	COMMAND SEQUENCE	STEPS
New Query Button		1. To access the **Query** wizard, select the table you wish to query (valves) and pick the **New Query** button on the dbConnect Manager toolbar. Alternately, you can right-click on the table and select **New Query** from the cursor menu.
Query for records in table: valves New query name: Globe Valves		2. Our first query will filter the drawing for globe valves, so call it ***Globe Valves***. Pick the **Continue** button to go on.
Quick Query		3. We'll do a quick query first. Pick the **Quick Query** tab.
Field: ID BlockName Valve "Size" Rating Vendor Price		4. Select **Valve** in the **Field** list box.
Look up values		5. Leave the operator set to = **Equal**, and pick the **Look up values** button.
Column Values Valve Check Gate Globe Globe-Control OK Cancel		6. AutoCAD presents the Column Values dialog box. Select the value to use as your filter (select **Globe**). Pick the **OK** button to continue.
Store		7. **Store** the query for use later. (Note that AutoCAD now lists your query under *pid27.dwg* in the dbConnect Manager. You can execute it anytime after leaving the wizard by simply double-clicking on it.)
Execute		8. Run the query by picking the **Execute** button in the Query Editor. AutoCAD presents the resulting records in the Data View (Figure 27.025). Behind the Data View window, AutoCAD highlights the globe valves (C and K) in the drawing (indicated by the arrows in Figure 27.026).

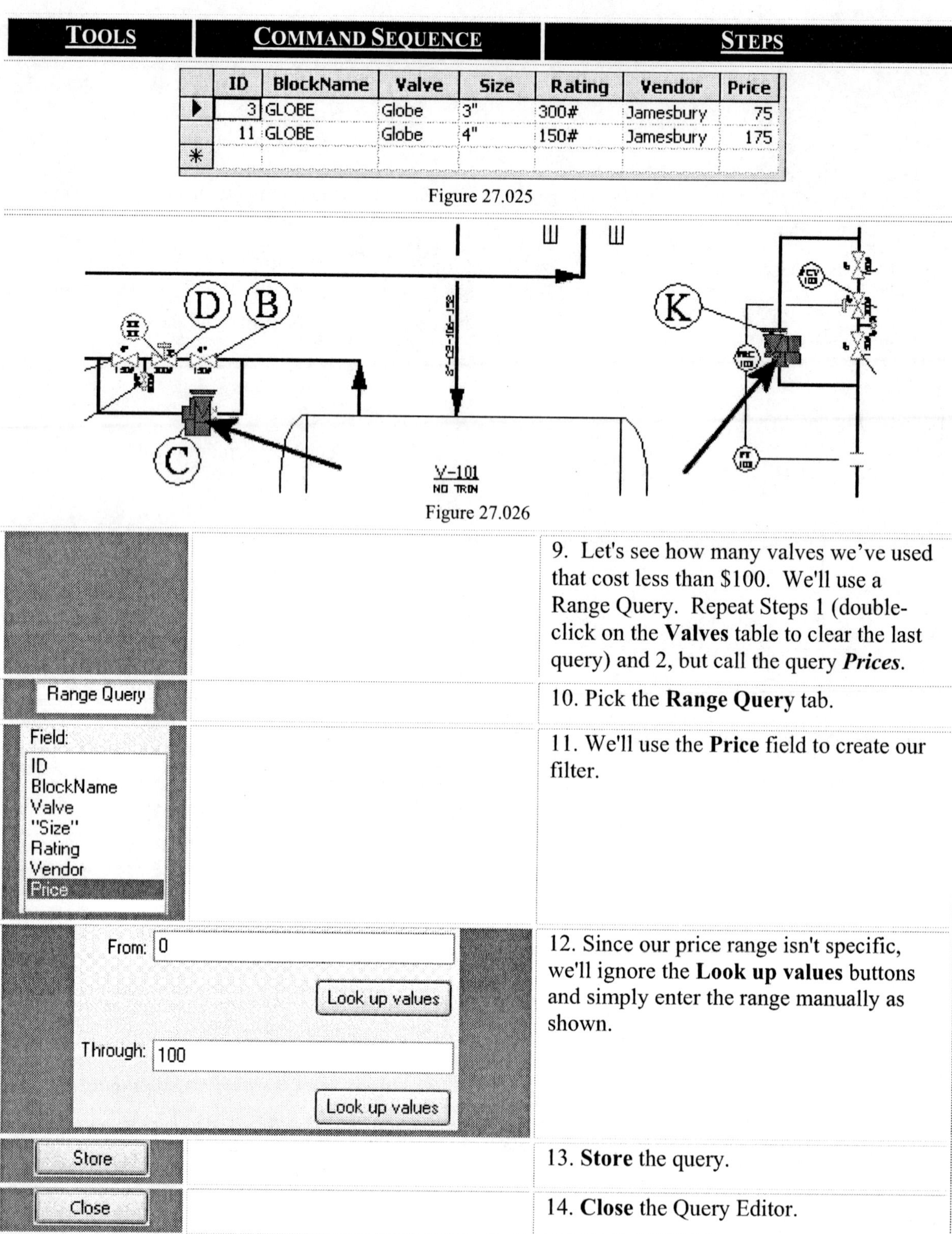

ID	BlockName	Valve	Size	Rating	Vendor	Price
3	GLOBE	Globe	3"	300#	Jamesbury	75
11	GLOBE	Globe	4"	150#	Jamesbury	175

Figure 27.025

Figure 27.026

TOOLS	COMMAND SEQUENCE	STEPS
		9. Let's see how many valves we've used that cost less than $100. We'll use a Range Query. Repeat Steps 1 (double-click on the **Valves** table to clear the last query) and 2, but call the query ***Prices***.
Range Query		10. Pick the **Range Query** tab.
Field: ID BlockName Valve "Size" Rating Vendor Price		11. We'll use the **Price** field to create our filter.
From: 0 Look up values Through: 100 Look up values		12. Since our price range isn't specific, we'll ignore the **Look up values** buttons and simply enter the range manually as shown.
Store		13. **Store** the query.
Close		14. **Close** the Query Editor.

TOOLS	COMMAND SEQUENCE	STEPS

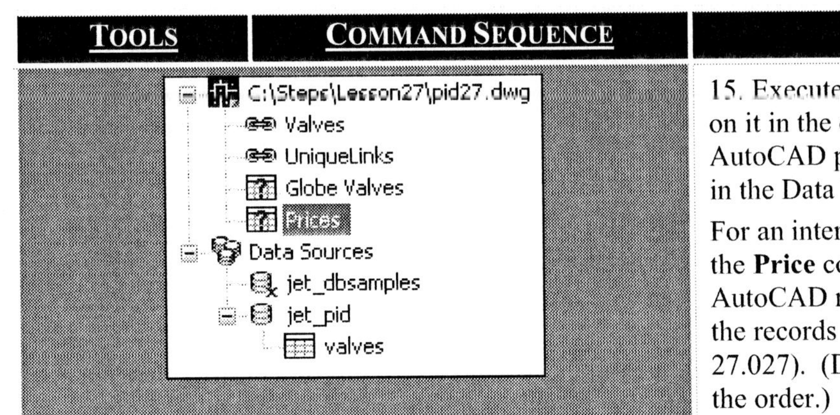

15. Execute the query by double-clicking on it in the dbConnect Manager. AutoCAD presents the resulting records in the Data View.

For an interesting trick, double-click on the **Price** column header. Notice that AutoCAD rearranges the listing to order the records from least to greatest (Figure 27.027). (Double-click again to reverse the order.)

ID	BlockName	Valve	Size	Rating	Vendor	Price
17	DRAIN	Gate	3/4"	800#	Vogt	35
16	DRAIN	Gate	3/4"	800#	Vogt	35
9	DRAIN	Gate	3/4"	800#	Vogt	35
5	DRAIN	Gate	3/4"	800#	Vogt	35
12	GATE	Gate	2"	150#	Vogt	55
3	GLOBE	Globe	3"	300#	Jamesbury	75
2	GATE	Gate	4"	300#	Vogt	85
1	GATE	Gate	4"	300#	Vogt	85

Figure 27.027

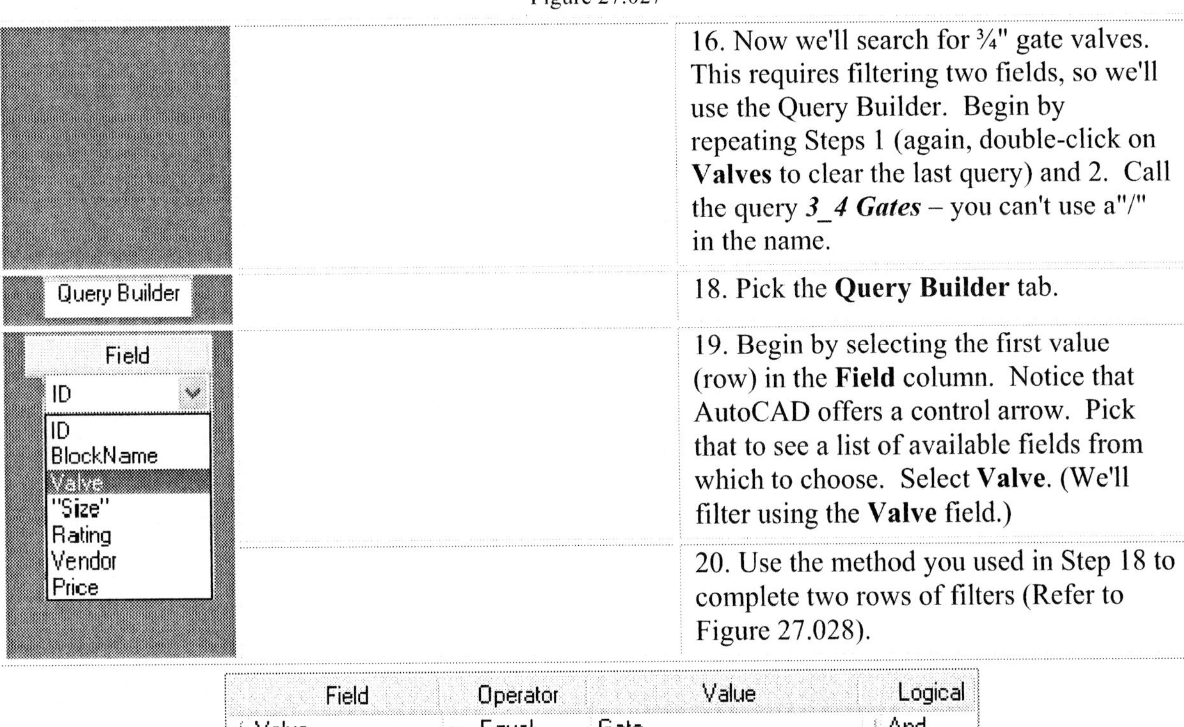

16. Now we'll search for ¾" gate valves. This requires filtering two fields, so we'll use the Query Builder. Begin by repeating Steps 1 (again, double-click on **Valves** to clear the last query) and 2. Call the query ***3_4 Gates*** – you can't use a"/" in the name.

18. Pick the **Query Builder** tab.

19. Begin by selecting the first value (row) in the **Field** column. Notice that AutoCAD offers a control arrow. Pick that to see a list of available fields from which to choose. Select **Valve**. (We'll filter using the **Valve** field.)

20. Use the method you used in Step 18 to complete two rows of filters (Refer to Figure 27.028).

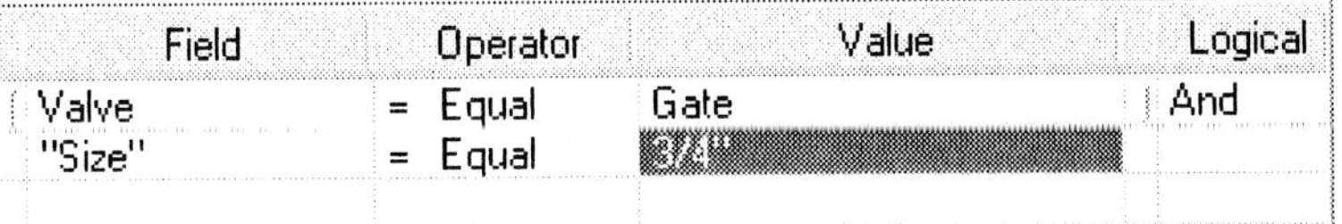

Figure 27.028

21. Store and execute the query. See the results in Figure 27.029.

TOOLS	COMMAND SEQUENCE	STEPS

ID	BlockName	Valve	Size	Rating	Vendor	Price
5	DRAIN	Gate	3/4"	800#	Vogt	35
9	DRAIN	Gate	3/4"	800#	Vogt	35
16	DRAIN	Gate	3/4"	800#	Vogt	35
17	DRAIN	Gate	3/4"	800#	Vogt	35

Figure 27.029

	Command: ***qsave***	22. Save the drawing but don't exit.

So what do you think of queries? Can you think of other uses? Make a list of industries/disciplines that use databases and how they might use queries. Compare and discuss your list with your peers.

Once you've run the query and located a specific record, what do you do next? Let's find out.

27.4.3 Once I've Found the Record, What Do I Do with It? Adding, Deleting, or Modifying Records

If you've ever worked with a spreadsheet (Excel, Lotus, etc.), you can handle a database. Adding or deleting a record is as easy as a mouse-click. Changing data in a specific cell is as easy as selecting the cell and typing the new data.

Let's take a look.

Our engineer has decided that the 2" drain line below the horizontal vessel won't be required. We'll remove it from the drawing and remove its valve from the database. He also wants to resize the 8" line feeding the vertical vessel to 10".

Do This: 27.4.3.1 Modifying Records

I. Be sure you're still in the *pid27.dwg* file in the C:\Steps\Lesson27 folder. If not, please open it now.

II. Be sure the dbConnect Manager is running and that the Data View window is open. (The **UniqueLinks** link template should be current.)

III. Follow these steps.

TOOLS	COMMAND SEQUENCE	STEPS
	Command: ***z***	1. Zoom in below the horizontal vessel. Your drawing will look like Figure 27.030.

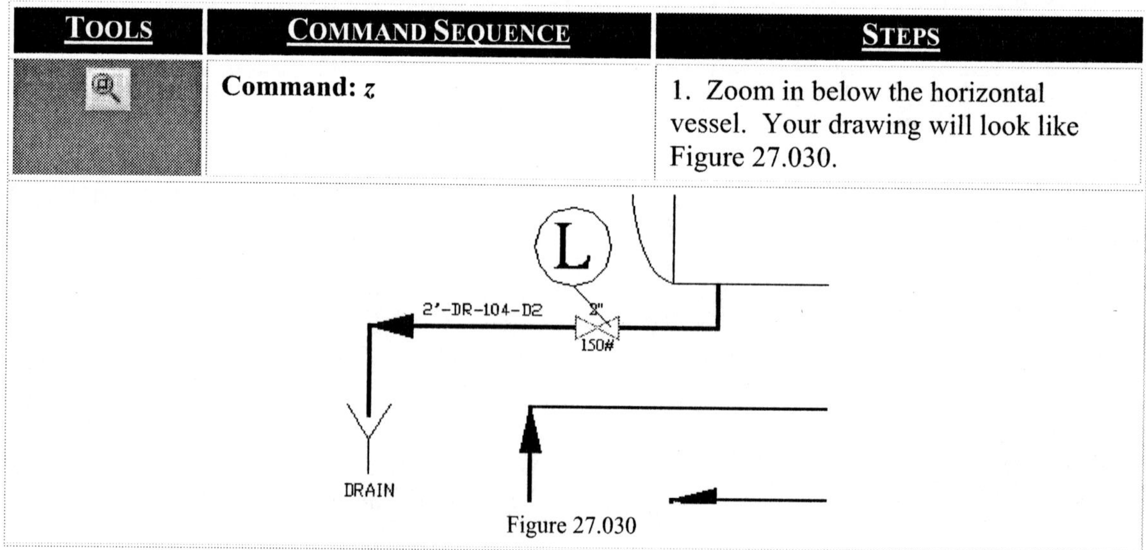

Figure 27.030

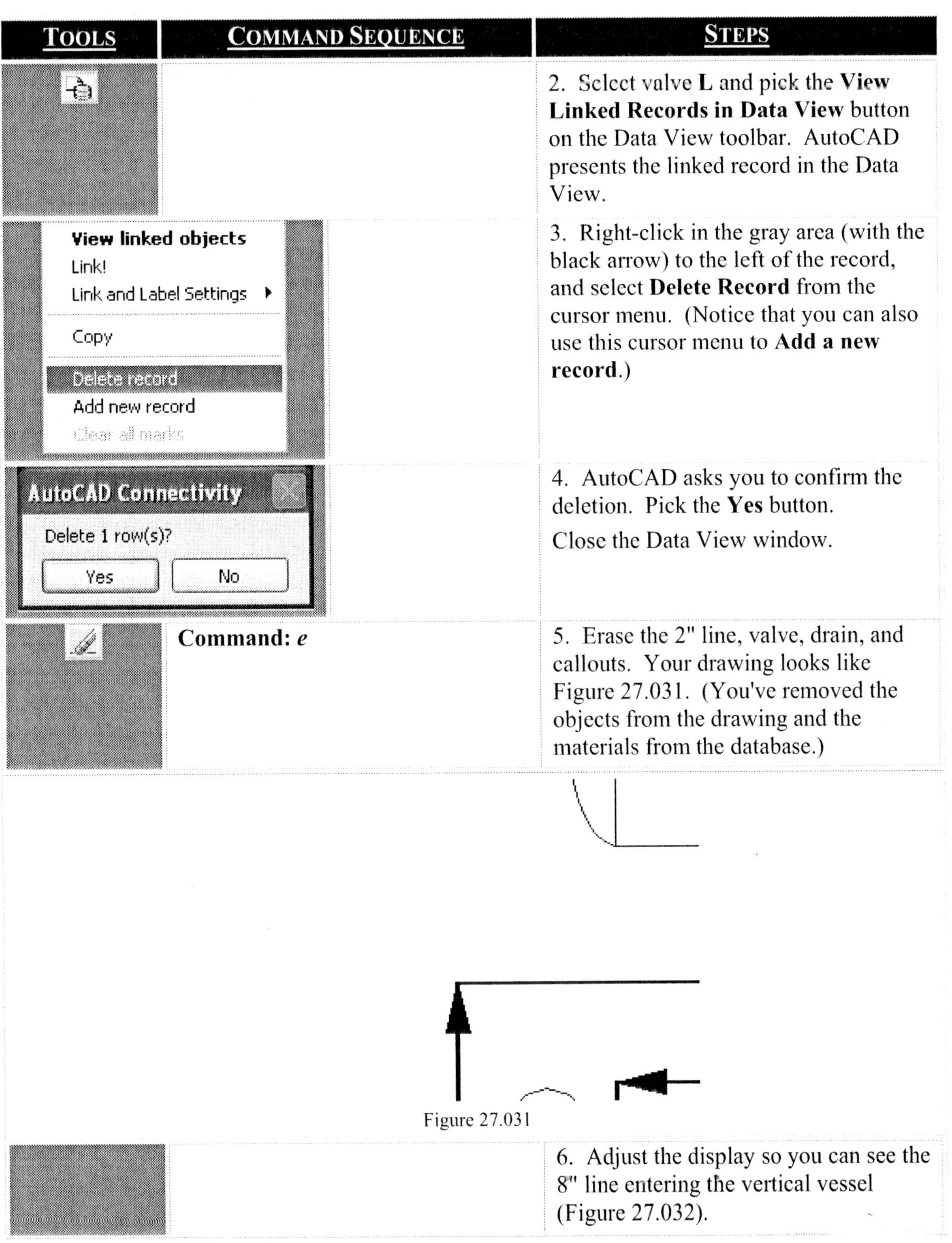

TOOLS	COMMAND SEQUENCE	STEPS
		2. Select valve **L** and pick the **View Linked Records in Data View** button on the Data View toolbar. AutoCAD presents the linked record in the Data View.
View linked objects Link! Link and Label Settings Copy Delete record Add new record Clear all marks		3. Right-click in the gray area (with the black arrow) to the left of the record, and select **Delete Record** from the cursor menu. (Notice that you can also use this cursor menu to **Add a new record**.)
AutoCAD Connectivity Delete 1 row(s)? Yes No		4. AutoCAD asks you to confirm the deletion. Pick the **Yes** button. Close the Data View window.
	Command: ***e***	5. Erase the 2" line, valve, drain, and callouts. Your drawing looks like Figure 27.031. (You've removed the objects from the drawing and the materials from the database.)
	Figure 27.031	
		6. Adjust the display so you can see the 8" line entering the vertical vessel (Figure 27.032).

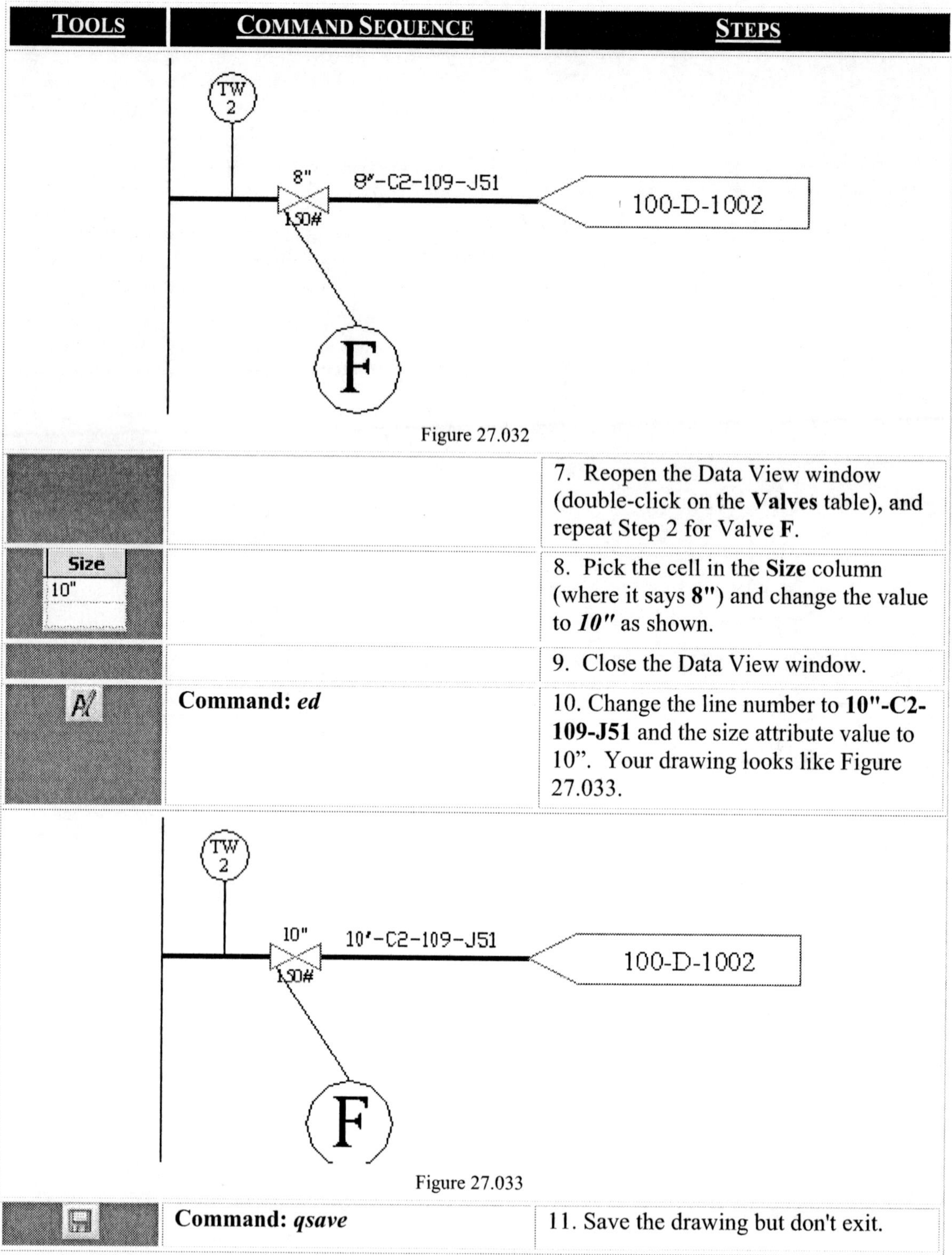

Figure 27.032

TOOLS	COMMAND SEQUENCE	STEPS
		7. Reopen the Data View window (double-click on the **Valves** table), and repeat Step 2 for Valve **F**.
Size 10"		8. Pick the cell in the **Size** column (where it says **8"**) and change the value to ***10"*** as shown.
		9. Close the Data View window.
	Command: ***ed***	10. Change the line number to **10"-C2-109-J51** and the size attribute value to 10". Your drawing looks like Figure 27.033.

Figure 27.033

TOOLS	COMMAND SEQUENCE	STEPS
	Command: ***qsave***	11. Save the drawing but don't exit.

Can you see that queries alone might make the dbConnect tool an invaluable addition to the AutoCAD stable? Remember – the changes you make to the database are visible to the MTO group immediately. But wait! There's another use for dbConnect – creating callouts!

27.4.4 Using Object/Record Links to Create Labels

When we first set up this drawing, we used visible attributes to place specific callouts such as size and rating on our valves. Then we exported data from those attributes (together with the data from some invisible attributes) to create our database. Now I'll show you how to close the circle; that is, I'll show you how to use data in the database to create the callouts (referred to as *labels* by dbConnect).

To make proper use of dbConnect's labels. We'll set ***Attdisp*** to **Off** to hide any visible values.

Here's the procedure for creating labels.

I. **Select the table** you wish to use.

II. **Select the Label Template** you wish to use (or create a new one).

III. In the Data View window, **set AutoCAD to create an attached or freestanding label**.

IV. **Pick the Create... Label** button.

V. **Locate the label**.

- Step I: **Select the table** is simple. Select the table by picking on it (or you can double-click to open the Data View window).
- You'll **Select the Label Template** (Step II) just as you selected a link template – using the **Select a Label Template** control box in the Data View window. However, if a label template hasn't been created, you must create one before labeling anything.

  (If you try to create a label with no template, AutoCAD will automatically launch the **Create Label Template** wizard.)
- To begin the **Create Label Template** wizard, you can pick the **New Label Template** button on the dbConnect Manager toolbar. You can also select **New Label Template** from the cursor menu when you right-click on the table. AutoCAD presents the New Label Template dialog box (Figure 27.034).

  Here you'll name your label template. You can base the creation process on an existing template if you wish by selecting it from the **Start with template** control box.

Figure 27.034

- Once you've named the template, AutoCAD presents the Label Template Editor (Figure 27.035).
  - At the bottom of the dialog box is the status line, which contains useful information for the CAD operator.
    - The left corner of the status line gives a brief description of the currently selected tab.
    - The right corner provides a toggle for the **AutoCAPS** tool. When toggled **On**, **AutoCAPS** will convert any new text (typed or imported) into uppercase letters.

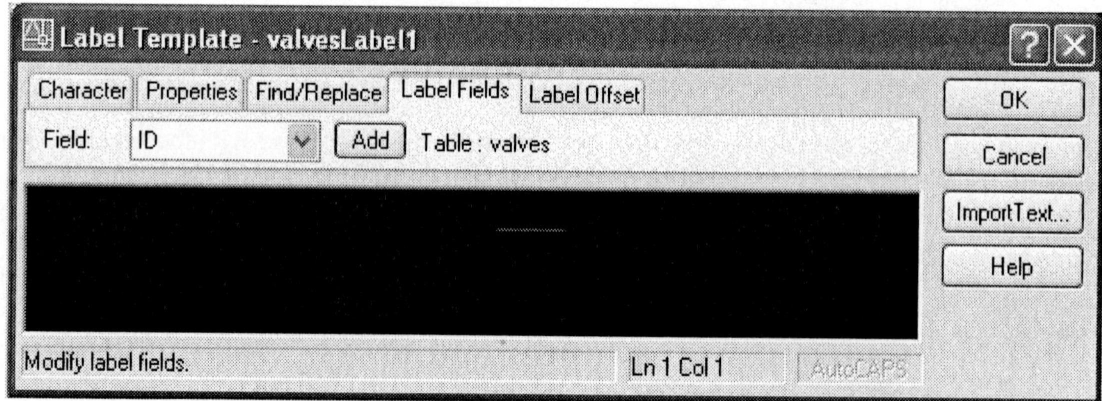

Figure 27.035

- To the left of the **AutoCAPS** toggle is the **Ln/Col** box. This shows the location of the cursor in the text window. **Ln** refers to the number of the line down from the top, and **Col** refers to the number of spaces over from the beginning (left end) of the line.

o The right side of the dialog box has four buttons.

- The top two buttons – **OK** and **Cancel** – are the same buttons standard to most dialog boxes.
- The **Import Text** button presents a Windows Open dialog box. You can insert any text file or file saved in Rich Text Format (.rtf).
- **Help**, of course, calls AutoCAD's Help window.

o Let's look at the tabs.

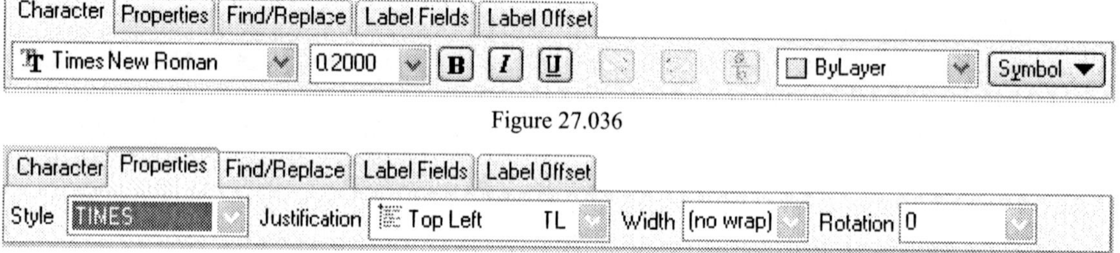

Figure 27.036

Figure 27.037

- The **Character** tab (Figure 27.036) allows you to select a font independently of the current style. In fact, styles can be mixed within the Label Template dialog box allowing you more independence in creating the final appearance of the callout.

  Depending on the font selected, the **Character** tab also gives you access to the more common tools of emphasis in word processors – **Bold**, **Italics**, or **Underlining**. You can even make use of color changes within the text for emphasis.

  Notice the **a/b** button on this tab. Use this to stack your fractions.

  The **Symbol** button will present options (including the Character Map) which we discussed in Lesson 4.

- The **Properties** tab (Figure 27.037) provides the opportunity to set (or reset) the **Style**, **Justification**, or **Rotation** of the callout. You can also adjust the **Width** of the callout.
- On the **Find/Replace** tab (Figure 27.038), you can search the drawing for existing text and replace it if you wish.

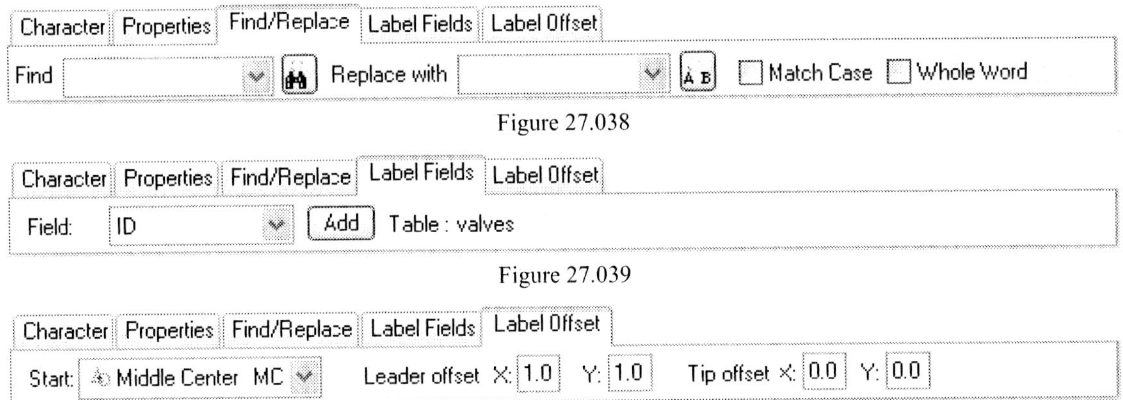

Figure 27.038

Figure 27.039

Figure 27.040

- You'll use the **Label Fields** tab (Figure 27.039) to define your labels by field. Select the field you want to include in the **Field** control box. Then pick the **Add** button to add it to the label definition. It'll appear in the text box as a field definition. Add as many fields as you like. Feel free to add or import additional text you wish to appear in the labels.
- The **Label Offset** tab (Figure 27.040) provides the means for you to define how the label will be inserted.
  - ∴ The setting in the **Start** control box works only on attached labels. Use it to control where the leader begins. It references the object to which the label is attached – so a **Middle Center** setting will cause the leader to begin in the center (vertically) of the middle (horizontally) of the object.
  - ∴ The **Leader offset** setting also works only on attached labels. It locates the text in relation to the end of the leader line.
  - ∴ The **Tip offset** specifies an offset from the insertion point you specify. If you're inserting an attached label, the **Tip offset** works in relation to the **Start** setting.

- Setting **AutoCAD to create an Attached or Freestanding label** (Step III) is quite easy. In the Data View window, pick the down arrow next to the **Link** button and pick an option. AutoCAD provides two methods for creating labels – **Attached** or **Freestanding**.
  - o An **Attached** label is closely linked to the object to which it is attached. Modifications (such as copying, moving, or erasing) will affect the label as well as the object. **Attached** labels use a leader.
  - o **Freestanding** labels exist independently of other objects.
- Once you've set the Attached/Freestanding option, **pick the Create … Label** button (Step IV). The button replaces the **Link** button in the Data View. AutoCAD will prompt you to **Select an object** (for an attached label) or to **Specify point for label** (for a freestanding label).

> A freestanding label can be attached to an object, and an attached label can be freed using the cursor menu. Do this:
>
> 1. Select the label.
> 2. Right-click to acquire the cursor menu.
> 3. Follow this path:
>
> *Label – Detach Label (or Attach to an Object...)*

Whew! That was a lot of information to absorb. Well, wipe your brow and let's create some labels in our *pid* drawing.

Do This: 27.4.4.1	Creating Labels

I. Be sure you're still in the *pid27.dwg* file in the C:\Steps\Lesson27 folder. If not, please open it now.

II. Be sure the dbConnect Manager is running.

III. Set the **TEXT** layer current and the ***AttDisp*** sysvar to **Off**..

IV. Follow these steps.

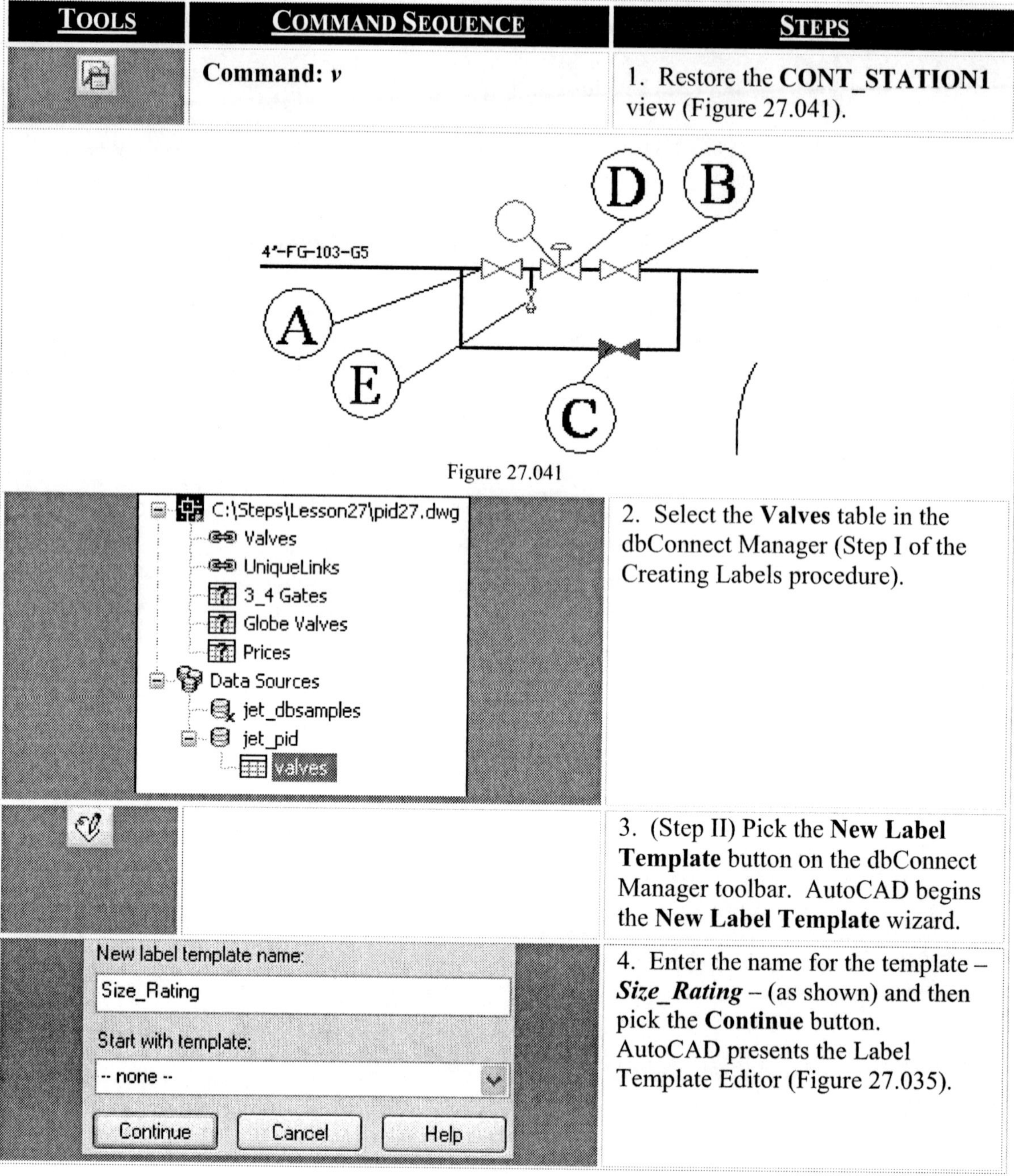

TOOLS	COMMAND SEQUENCE	STEPS
	Command: *v*	1. Restore the **CONT_STATION1** view (Figure 27.041).

Figure 27.041

TOOLS	COMMAND SEQUENCE	STEPS
C:\Steps\Lesson27\pid27.dwg Valves UniqueLinks 3_4 Gates Globe Valves Prices Data Sources jet_dbsamples jet_pid valves		2. Select the **Valves** table in the dbConnect Manager (Step I of the Creating Labels procedure).
		3. (Step II) Pick the **New Label Template** button on the dbConnect Manager toolbar. AutoCAD begins the **New Label Template** wizard.
New label template name: Size_Rating Start with template: -- none -- Continue Cancel Help		4. Enter the name for the template – ***Size_Rating*** – (as shown) and then pick the **Continue** button. AutoCAD presents the Label Template Editor (Figure 27.035).

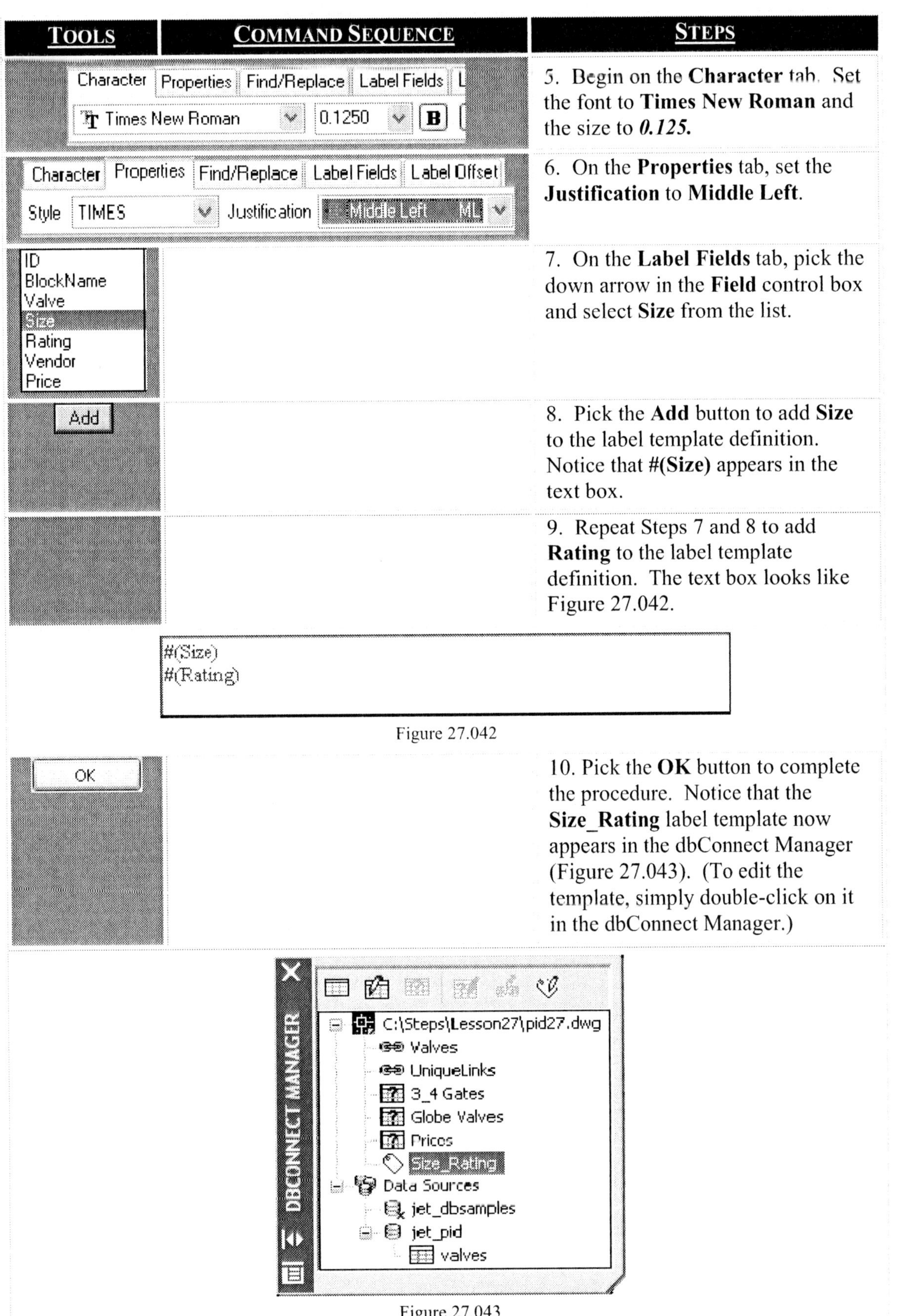

TOOLS	COMMAND SEQUENCE	STEPS
Character / Properties / Find/Replace / Label Fields; Times New Roman; 0.1250; B		5. Begin on the **Character** tab. Set the font to **Times New Roman** and the size to ***0.125.***
Character / Properties / Find/Replace / Label Fields / Label Offset; Style TIMES; Justification Middle Left ML		6. On the **Properties** tab, set the **Justification** to **Middle Left**.
ID, BlockName, Valve, Size, Rating, Vendor, Price		7. On the **Label Fields** tab, pick the down arrow in the **Field** control box and select **Size** from the list.
Add		8. Pick the **Add** button to add **Size** to the label template definition. Notice that **#(Size)** appears in the text box.
		9. Repeat Steps 7 and 8 to add **Rating** to the label template definition. The text box looks like Figure 27.042.

Figure 27.042

TOOLS	COMMAND SEQUENCE	STEPS
OK		10. Pick the **OK** button to complete the procedure. Notice that the **Size_Rating** label template now appears in the dbConnect Manager (Figure 27.043). (To edit the template, simply double-click on it in the dbConnect Manager.)

Figure 27.043

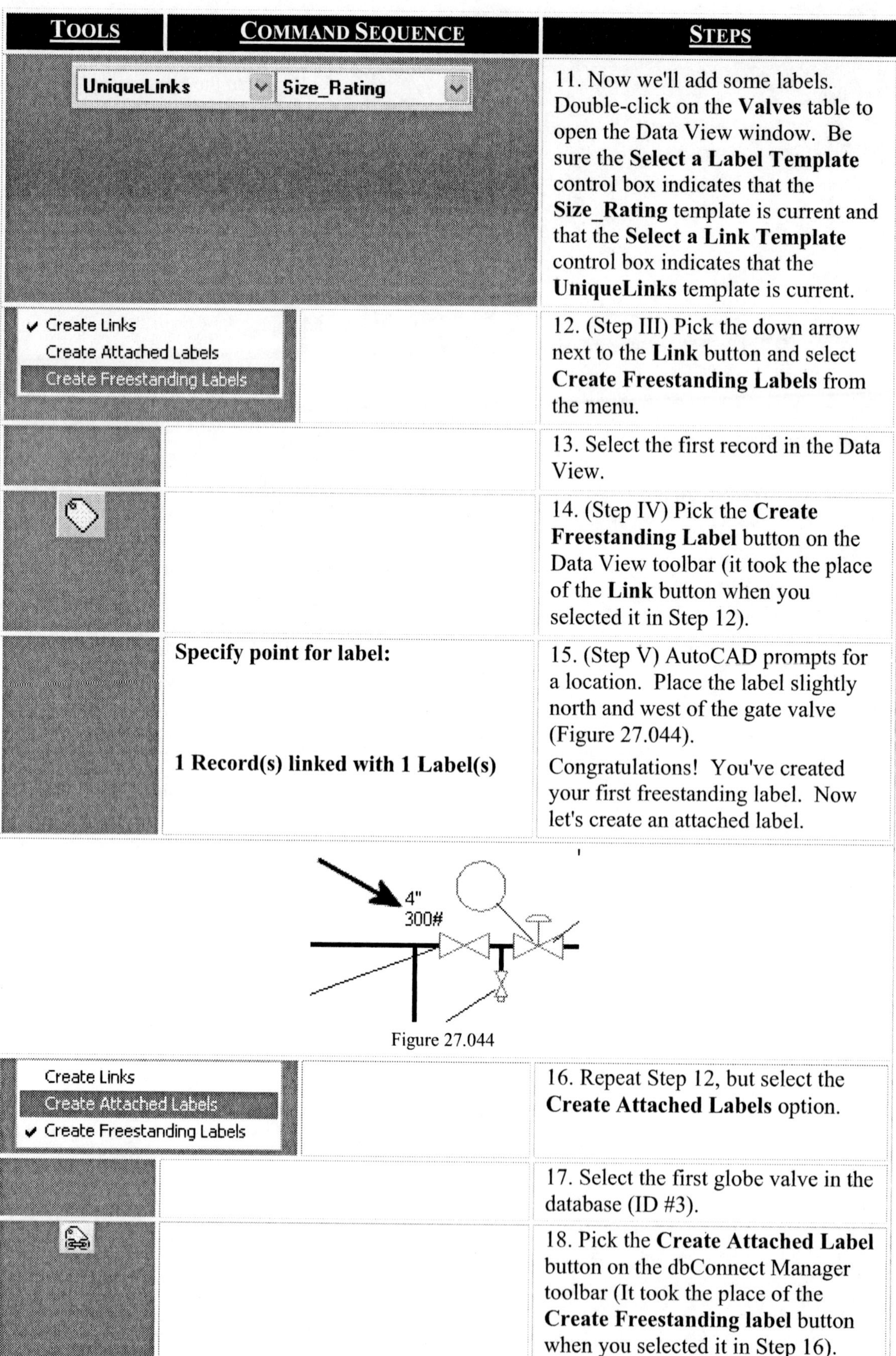

TOOLS	COMMAND SEQUENCE	STEPS
UniqueLinks / Size_Rating		11. Now we'll add some labels. Double-click on the **Valves** table to open the Data View window. Be sure the **Select a Label Template** control box indicates that the **Size_Rating** template is current and that the **Select a Link Template** control box indicates that the **UniqueLinks** template is current.
✔ Create Links Create Attached Labels Create Freestanding Labels		12. (Step III) Pick the down arrow next to the **Link** button and select **Create Freestanding Labels** from the menu.
		13. Select the first record in the Data View.
		14. (Step IV) Pick the **Create Freestanding Label** button on the Data View toolbar (it took the place of the **Link** button when you selected it in Step 12).
	Specify point for label: **1 Record(s) linked with 1 Label(s)**	15. (Step V) AutoCAD prompts for a location. Place the label slightly north and west of the gate valve (Figure 27.044). Congratulations! You've created your first freestanding label. Now let's create an attached label.

Figure 27.044

TOOLS	COMMAND SEQUENCE	STEPS
Create Links Create Attached Labels ✔ Create Freestanding Labels		16. Repeat Step 12, but select the **Create Attached Labels** option.
		17. Select the first globe valve in the database (ID #3).
		18. Pick the **Create Attached Label** button on the dbConnect Manager toolbar (It took the place of the **Create Freestanding label** button when you selected it in Step 16).

TOOLS	COMMAND SEQUENCE	STEPS
	Select objects: **Select objects:** ***[enter]***	19. Select the globe valve on the bypass line (valve "**C**").
	1 Record(s) linked with 1 Object(s)	20. Close the Data View window. Notice where AutoCAD has placed the label (Figure 27.045).

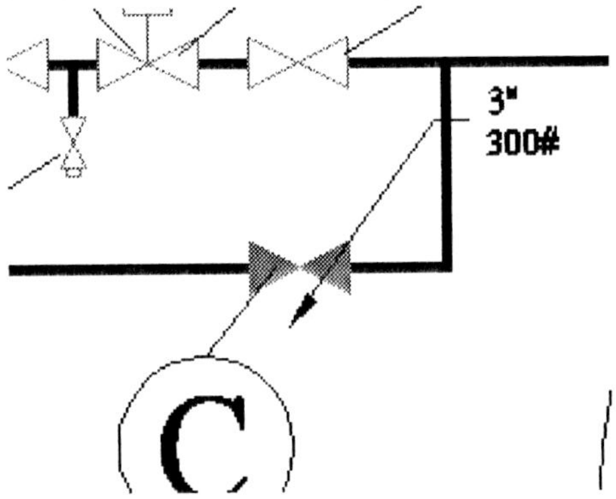

Figure 27.045

TOOLS	COMMAND SEQUENCE	STEPS
		21. Let's change the location of the attached label. Select it (select the label itself, not the leader).
		22. Select the grip and move the label down about 1.5" and west about 0.5". Clear the grip. Notice that the leader adjusts accordingly (Figure 27.046).

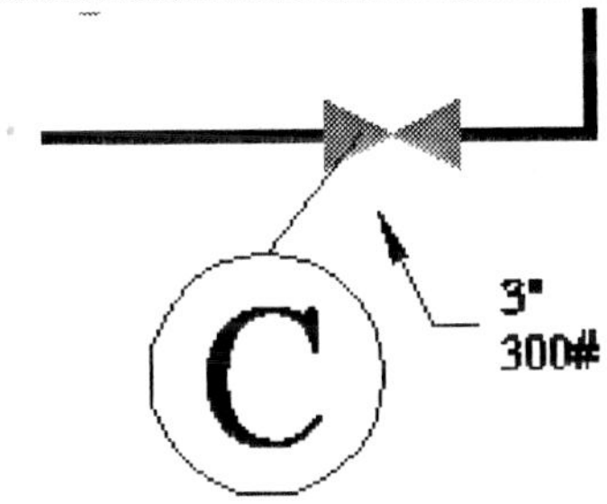

Figure 27.046

TOOLS	COMMAND SEQUENCE	STEPS
	**Command:** ***m***	23. Now let's see how attached versus freestanding labels behave. Move valves A and C to the west about 2". Notice that the attached label moved with the valve, but the freestanding label didn't (Figure 27.047). Can you name some times when you might need attached labels? Freestanding labels?

Tools	Command Sequence	Steps

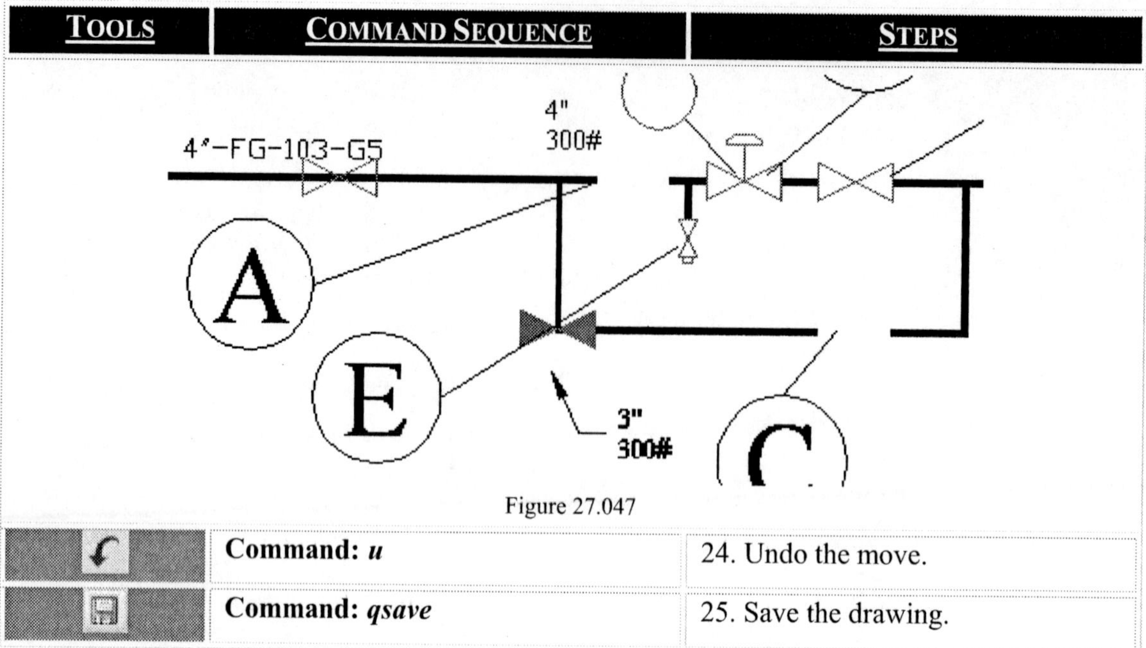

Figure 27.047

Tools	Command Sequence	Steps
	Command: ***u***	24. Undo the move.
	Command: ***qsave***	25. Save the drawing.

Here are some additional notes concerning labels.

- You can hide all labels (just as you did all attributes with the **ATTDisp** system variable) by right-clicking on the template in the dbConnect Manager. Simply select the **Hide Labels** option from the cursor menu. (Show the labels again by repeating the procedure and selecting **Show Labels**.)
- You can delete all labels related to a specific template by following the previous procedure and selecting **Delete Labels** from the cursor menu.
- You can remove a single label using the ***Erase*** command (or selecting the label and hitting the DELETE key on your keyboard.)
- If you change the value of the record on which the label was based, you can automatically update the label by selecting **Reload** from the same cursor menu. However, this method has produced some undesirable effects and isn't always reliable. I suggest watching the labels closely if you use this method. It might be best, however, to simply erase and replace the affected labels.

27.5 Some Final Bits and Pieces about dbConnect

You've seen several ways to access the various dbConnect procedures – the dbConnect Manager, the dbConnect Manager's toolbar, the Data View window, the Data View window's toolbar, various cursor menus, and the dbConnect/Data View pull-down menus. Have you noticed the one AutoCAD tool (the one you've seen throughout this textbook) that you haven't used? You haven't used the command prompt to access a single dbConnect procedure! The reason for this is simple, although you may have trouble understanding it. The reason is that *you haven't been using AutoCAD commands*.

Let me explain.

You've been standing in a corridor (a *virtual* corridor for those of you who like that kinda talk). On one end of the corridor lies AutoCAD with its many capabilities (now familiar to you). On the other end lies a database (in our lesson, we've used an MS Access database). You've been running strings (creating links) from things on one end of the corridor to things on the other, sometimes touching

AutoCAD objects, sometimes touching database records. But you haven't actually been using either application directly.

Living there in the corridor with you has been a quiet tool – a translator of sorts – designed by Microsoft to make running strings between applications. Microsoft called its translator Visual Basic and designed it to be one of the easiest programming languages on the market today. (AutoCAD also makes good use of the C++ and newer C# programming languages.) In fact, you've seen how easily it has integrated itself into AutoCAD and MS Access. It's responsible for many of those buttons and cursor menus you've been using.

Let's look briefly at three simple tools designed to make your corridor visit more comfortable.

- Use the **Synchronize** option to fix problems between the database and AutoCAD. It was designed specifically to deal with problems arising from moving a database from its original location (where it was when you configured AutoCAD to use it). It also works well when the basic structure of the database changes (for example, when you delete a field in the database). When **Synchronize** detects problems, it'll tell you what they are and help you fix them.

  Find the ***Synchronize*** command under the dbConnect pull-down menu or in a Data Source's cursor menu.
- You can import and/or export link templates, label templates, queries, and even links. Access the **Import** or **Export** options on the dbConnect pull-down menu or the cursor menu associated with the drawing name in the dbConnect Manager. These procedures work quite easily using Windows standard dialog boxes with which you are now quite familiar.

27.6 The Final Word

The last thing you'll need to know about dbConnect is how to stop it. That is, how do I remove *pid* (and its associated templates) from the dbConnect Manager (how do I close the corridor)? First, remember two things.

- The corridor doesn't exist within AutoCAD, so you won't close it from there.
- All the strings you've run between AutoCAD objects and database records go through the corridor. They'll be lost when it disappears. (I advise you to export any templates or links that you may need later. Save the exported files in a safe place. If it becomes necessary to reopen the corridor, simply import the strings.)

Considering what it took to configure AutoCAD to use the database, you might expect a procedure to break that connection. It isn't, however, that complicated. To remove a dbConnect configuration, simply erase the associated *.udl* file. Find its location on the **Files** tab of the Options dialog box. Look under **Data Sources Location**. (That was sort of anticlimactic, wasn't it?)

Remove the ODBC data source setup by repeating Steps 1 through 4 of Exercise 27.2.1. Select the *My_PID_Database* data source you created earlier and pick the **Remove** button. It's just that simple.

27.7 Extra Steps

Review anything you can find in the AutoCAD help files related to dbConnect.

(I know, that's not much, but you're at the end of the text, and I thought I'd take it easy on you.)

27.8 What Have We Learned?

Items covered in this lesson include:

- *Setting up a data source through Windows*

- *Configuring AutoCAD to access a database*
- *The dbConnect Manager*
- *Creating link templates*
- *Creating links*
- *Creating label templates*
- *Creating labels*
- *Creating queries*

In your final lesson, I've tried to introduce you to some of the possibilities presented by interfacing (connecting) AutoCAD with a database. We've discovered quite a useful tool as AutoCAD has designed it. You can track materials throughout the design process using dbConnect, thus saving yourself (or your employer) time and money. You've made yourself a more valuable employee by increasing your abilities beyond simple draftsman or CAD operator.

But those of you who recognized the hidden value of the last two instructional sections (27.5 and 27.6) will become the industry leaders of the twenty-first century. I salute each of you. For those of you who don't quite understand, I'll offer a hint in the form of two words – programming languages.

With those words, I'll conclude instruction. The next phase of your education belongs in the three-dimensional world. I've given you a glimpse of the dragons to which that ancient map referred. Only the brave-hearted need continue. (Pick up a copy of *3D AutoCAD 2006: One Step at a Time* if you wish to go on.)

27.9 Exercises

1. Open the *Office.dwg* file in the C:\Steps\Lesson27 folder. Follow these instructions:
   1.1. DbConnect AutoCAD to the *Technology.mdb* database in the C:\Steps\Lesson27 folder. (The database file is an MS Access file.)
   1.2. Create links between the Office Unit (link to the desk) and the Employee (use the Employee table) and between the Office Unit (link to the computer on the desk) and the Computer (use the Computer Equipment table):

OFFICE UNIT	EMPLOYEE	COMPUTER
1	Starbuck	8
2	West	3
3	Brezina	1
4	Miles	4
5	Dominic	6
6	Whitson	9
7	Paul	7
8	Harrington	5
9	Aloysius	2

   1.3. Label each cubicle with the name of its occupant. (Use freestanding labels.) Your drawing looks like Figure 27.048.

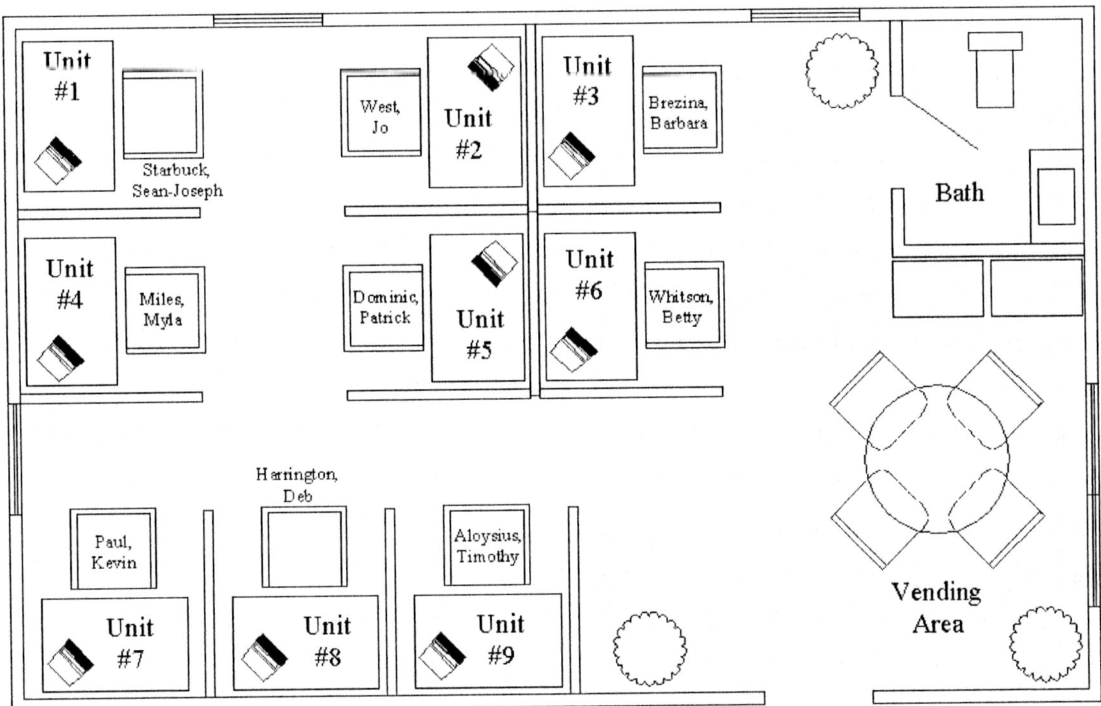

Figure 27.048: Labeled Office Drawing

1.4. Answer the following questions:

- 1.4.1. Where does the Lead Programmer sit?
- 1.4.2. Where does the COO sit?
- 1.4.3. AutoCAD requires a minimum of 32Mb of RAM. Who among the CAD Operators will need an upgrade? (Save the query as *ram_upg*.)
- 1.4.4. Everyone hired before January of 1984 will be receiving a large Christmas bonus. Can you locate the recipients by cubicle for the mailman? (Save the query as *bonus*.)
- 1.4.5. Santa Claus will upgrade all of the Pentium II chips to Pentium IIIs over the holidays. Tell him which cubicles to visit. (Save the query as *santa*.)
- 1.4.6. Everyone with less than 32Mb of RAM and a slower CPU speed than 400MHz will receive a new computer. How many will be needed and where will they go? (Save the Query as *New*.)
- 1.4.7. Which units have computers that use a modem (*-1* indicates a "yes" column)? (Save the Query as *modems*.)
- 1.4.8. What kind of computer does the lead engineer use? How fast is it?

1.5. Export the templates and queries to the C:\Steps\Lesson27 folder.

1.6. Remove the connection between AutoCAD and the *Technology.mdb* database.

1.7. Remove the Data Source you created from the Windows Operating System.

1.8. Save the drawing as *MyOffice.dwg* in the C:\Steps\Lesson27 folder.

27.10 For Web-Based Review Questions, visit: http://www.uneedcad.com/2006/Files/06R27.pdf

To continue, please pick up a copy of *3D AutoCAD 2006: One Step at a Time*.

3D AutoCAD 2006: One Step at a Time

Contents

Appendix – A: Drawing Scales

SCALE (=1')	SCALE FACTOR	DIMENSIONS OF DRAWING WHEN FINAL PLOT SIZE IS: 8½"x11"	11"x17"	17"x22"	22"x34"	24"x36"
1/16"	192	136'x176'	176'x272'	272'x352'	352'x544'	384'x576'
3/32"	128	90'8x117'4	117'4x181'4	181'4x234'8	234'8x362'8	256'x384'
1/8"	96	68'x88'	88'x136'	136'x176'	176'x272'	192'x288'
3/16"	64	45'4x58'8	58'8x90'8	90'8x117'4	117'4x181'4	128'x192'
¼"	48	34'x44'	44'x68'	68'x88'	88'x136'	96'x144'
3/8"	32	22'8x29'4	29'4x45'4	45'4x58'8	58'8x90'8	64'x96'
½"	24	17'x22'	22'x34'	34'x44'	44'x68'	48'x72'
¾"	16	11'4x14'8	14'8x22'8	22'8x29'4	29'4x45'4	32'x48'
1"	12	8'x6'11	11'x17'	17'x22'	22'x34'	24'x36'
1½"	8	5'8x7'4	7'4x11'4	11'4x14'8	14'8x22'8	16'x24'
3"	4	34"x44"	3'8x5'8	8'x6'11	7'4x11'4	8'x12'
(1" =)						
10'	120	85'x110'	110'x170'	170'x220'	220'x340'	240'x360'
20'	240	170'x220'	220'x340'	340'x440'	440'x680'	480'x720'
25'	300	212'6x275'	275'x425'	425'x550'	550'x850'	600'x900'
30'	360	255'x330'	330'x510'	510'x660'	660'x1020'	720'x1080'
40'	480	340'x440'	440'x680'	680'x880'	880'x1360'	960'x1440'
50'	600	425'x550'	550'x850'	850'x1100'	1100'x1700'	1200'x1800'
60'	720	510'x660'	660'x1020'	1020'x1320'	1320'x2040'	1440'x2160'
80'	960	680'x880'	880'x1360'	1360'x1760'	1760'x2720'	1920'x2880'
100'	1200	850'x1100'	1100'x1700'	1700'x2200'	2200'x3400'	2400'x3600'
200'	2400	1700'x2200'	2200'x3400'	3400'x4400'	4400'x6800'	4800'x7200'

Appendix – B: Function Keys and Their Uses

KEY	FUNCTION	KEY	FUNCTION	KEY	FUNCTION
F1	AutoCAD's Help	F5	Isoplane toggle	F9	Snap toggle
F2	Toggle between graphics & text screen	F6	Toggle coordinate indicator on or off	F10	Polar Tracking Toggle
F3	OSNAP settings	F7	Grid toggle	F11	Object Tracking Toggle
F4	Tablet (Digitizer) toggle	F8	Ortho toggle	F12	Dynamic Input Toggle

[Note: Appendix C has been replaced with web addresses for chapter review questions and their answers.]

Appendix – F: Hotkeys

COMMAND	HOTKEY
ADCenter	ADC
Align	AL
Area	AA
Array	AR
Attdisp	ATT
Attedit	ATE
Block	B, -B
Break	BR
Chamfer	CHA
Circle	C
color	COL
Copy	CO, CP
DDEdit	ED
Dimaligned	DAL
Dimangular	DAN
Dimbaseline	DBA
Dimcontinue	DCO
Dimdiameter	DDI
Dimedit	DED
Dimlinear	DLI
Dimordinate	DOR
Dimradius	DRA
Dist	DI
Divide	DIV
Donut	DO
Dsettings	DS
Ellipse	EL
Erase	E
Explode	X
Extend	EX
Fillet	F
Filter	FI
Grid	F7
Grips	GR
Group	G
Hatch	H
HatchEdit	HE
Insert	I
Layer	LA, -LA
Leader	LE
Lengthen	LEN
Line	L
Linetype	LT, -LT

COMMAND	HOTKEY
List	LI
LTScale	LTS
Lweight	LW
MatchProp	MA
Measure	ME
Mirror	MI
MLine	ML
Move	M
MText	MT, T
Offset	O
Open	^O
Ortho	F8
OSNAP	OS, -OS
Pan	P, -P
Pedit	PE
Pline	PL
Point	PO
Polygon	POL
Properties	PROPS
Purge	PU
QSave	^S
Rectangle	REC
Redraw	R
Regen	Re
Rotate	RO
Save	^S
Scale	SC
Snap	SN
Solid	SO
Spell	SP
Spline	SPL
Splinedit	SPE
Stretch	S
Style	ST
Text	DT
Trim	TR
Units	UN
View	V
WBlock	W, -W
Xline	XL
Zoom	Z

Printed in the United States
50340LVS00001B/23-30

9 780976 58885